Lecture Notes in Computer Science 15893

Founding Editors

Gerhard Goos
Juris Hartmanis

Editorial Board Members

Elisa Bertino, *Purdue University, West Lafayette, IN, USA*
Wen Gao, *Peking University, Beijing, China*
Bernhard Steffen ⓘ, *TU Dortmund University, Dortmund, Germany*
Moti Yung ⓘ, *Columbia University, New York, NY, USA*

The series Lecture Notes in Computer Science (LNCS), including its subseries Lecture Notes in Artificial Intelligence (LNAI) and Lecture Notes in Bioinformatics (LNBI), has established itself as a medium for the publication of new developments in computer science and information technology research, teaching, and education.

LNCS enjoys close cooperation with the computer science R & D community, the series counts many renowned academics among its volume editors and paper authors, and collaborates with prestigious societies. Its mission is to serve this international community by providing an invaluable service, mainly focused on the publication of conference and workshop proceedings and postproceedings. LNCS commenced publication in 1973.

Osvaldo Gervasi · Beniamino Murgante ·
Chiara Garau · Yeliz Karaca ·
Maria Noelia Faginas Lago · Francesco Scorza ·
Ana Cristina Braga
Editors

Computational Science and Its Applications – ICCSA 2025 Workshops

Istanbul, Turkey, June 30 – July 3, 2025
Proceedings, Part VIII

Editors
Osvaldo Gervasi
University of Perugia
Perugia, Italy

Beniamino Murgante
University of Basilicata
Potenza, Italy

Chiara Garau
University of Cagliari
Cagliari, Italy

Yeliz Karaca
University of Massachusetts
Worcester, MA, USA

Maria Noelia Faginas Lago
University of Perugia
Perugia, Italy

Francesco Scorza
University of Basilicata
Potenza, Italy

Ana Cristina Braga
University of Minho
Braga, Portugal

ISSN 0302-9743   ISSN 1611-3349 (electronic)
Lecture Notes in Computer Science
ISBN 978-3-031-97644-5   ISBN 978-3-031-97645-2 (eBook)
https://doi.org/10.1007/978-3-031-97645-2

© The Editor(s) (if applicable) and The Author(s), under exclusive license to Springer Nature Switzerland AG 2026

This work is subject to copyright. All rights are solely and exclusively licensed by the Publisher, whether the whole or part of the material is concerned, specifically the rights of translation, reprinting, reuse of illustrations, recitation, broadcasting, reproduction on microfilms or in any other physical way, and transmission or information storage and retrieval, electronic adaptation, computer software, or by similar or dissimilar methodology now known or hereafter developed.
The use of general descriptive names, registered names, trademarks, service marks, etc. in this publication does not imply, even in the absence of a specific statement, that such names are exempt from the relevant protective laws and regulations and therefore free for general use.
The publisher, the authors and the editors are safe to assume that the advice and information in this book are believed to be true and accurate at the date of publication. Neither the publisher nor the authors or the editors give a warranty, expressed or implied, with respect to the material contained herein or for any errors or omissions that may have been made. The publisher remains neutral with regard to jurisdictional claims in published maps and institutional affiliations.

This Springer imprint is published by the registered company Springer Nature Switzerland AG
The registered company address is: Gewerbestrasse 11, 6330 Cham, Switzerland

If disposing of this product, please recycle the paper.

Preface

The compiled 14 volumes (LNCS volumes 15886–15899) consist of the peer-reviewed papers from the 68 Workshops of the 2025 International Conference on Computational Science and Its Applications (ICCSA 2025), which was held between June 30 – July 3, 2025 in Istanbul (Türkiye). The peer-reviewed papers of the main conference tracks are published in a separate set made up of three volumes (LNCS 15648–15650).

The conference was held in a hybrid form, with the large majority of participants in presence, hosted by Galatasaray University, Istanbul, Türkiye. We enabled virtual participation for those who did not attend the event in person due to logistical, political and economic problems, by adopting a technological infrastructure via open-source software (jitsi + riot) and a commercial Cloud infrastructure.

With the 2025 edition, ICCSA celebrated its 25th anniversary, a quarter of a century as a memorable moment that is harmoniously aligned with Istanbul, an extraordinary city located at the crossroads and acting as a bridge connecting Asia and Europe, representing different cultures, beliefs as well as lifestyles, which highlights its intercultural fabric.

ICCSA 2025 marked another fruitful and thought-provoking academic event in the International Conferences on Computational Science and Its Applications (ICCSA) conference series, previously held in Hanoi, Vietnam (2024), Athens, Greece (2023), Málaga, Spain (2022), Cagliari, Italy (hybrid with a few participants in presence in 2021 and completely online in 2020), whilst earlier editions took place in Saint Petersburg, Russia (2019), Melbourne, Australia (2018), Trieste, Italy (2017), Beijing, China (2016), Banff, Canada (2015), Guimaraes, Portugal (2014), Ho Chi Minh City, Vietnam (2013), Salvador, Brazil (2012), Santander, Spain (2011), Fukuoka, Japan (2010), Suwon, South Korea (2009), Perugia, Italy (2008), Kuala Lumpur, Malaysia (2007), Glasgow, UK (2006), Singapore (2005), Assisi, Italy (2004), Montreal, Canada (2003), and (as ICCS) Amsterdam, the Netherlands (2002) and San Francisco, USA (2001).

Computational Science constitutes the main pillar of most present research, industrial and commercial applications, and plays a unique role in exploiting ICT innovative technologies, and the ICCSA conference series has, accordingly, provided ample opportunities to researchers and industry practitioners to discuss new ideas, to share complex problems and their solutions, and to shape new trends in Computational Science. As the conference mirrors society from a scientific point of view, this year's undoubtedly dominant theme was large language models, machine learning and Artificial Intelligence (AI) and their applications in the most diverse technological, economic and industrial fields, amongst the others.

The ICCSA 2025 conference was structured in six general tracks covering the fields of computational science and its applications: Computational Methods, Algorithms and Scientific Applications – High Performance Computing and Networks – Geometric Modeling, Graphics and Visualization – Advanced and Emerging Applications – Information Systems and Technologies – Urban and Regional Planning. In addition, the conference consisted of 68 workshops, focusing on topical issues of utmost importance to science, technology and society: from new computational approaches for earth science, to mathematical methods for image processing, new statistical and optimization methods, several Artificial Intelligence approaches, sustainability issues, smart cities and related technologies, to name some.

In the Workshops' proceedings, we accepted 362 full papers, 37 short papers and 2 Ph.D. Showcase papers from total of 1043 submissions (Acceptance rate 38.4%). In the Main Conference Proceedings, we accepted 71 full papers, 6 short papers and 1 Ph.D. Showcase paper from 269 submissions to the General Tracks of the Conference (with an acceptance rate of 29.9%). We would like to convey our sincere appreciation to the workshops' chairs and co-chairs and program committee members for their diligent work, commitment and dedication.

The success and consistent maintenance of the ICCSA conference series in general, and of ICCSA 2025 in particular, rely upon the support of many people: authors, presenters, participants, keynote speakers, workshop chairs, session chairs, organizing committee members, student volunteers, Program Committee members, Advisory Committee members, International Liaison chairs, reviewers and other individuals in various roles. Thus, we take this opportunity to wholahartedly thank each and everyone.

We additionally wish to thank publisher Springer for their agreement to publish the proceedings, besides sponsoring part of the best papers awards and for their kind assistance and cooperation during the editing process.

We would cordially like to invite you to refer to the ICCSA website https://iccsa.org, where you can find the relevant details regarding this academic endeavor and event of ours.

June 2025

Osvaldo Gervasi
Yeliz Karaca
Beniamino Murgante
Chiara Garau

A Welcome Message from the Organizers

The International Conference on Computational Science and Its Applications (ICCSA) reflects a culmination of meticulous and dedicated efforts and academic endeavors toward the progress of science and technology.

One of the most noteworthy aspects of ICCSA is its fostering of a collective spirit, bringing together a plethora of participants from all over the world. Correspondingly, this merging power manifests itself in the 25th anniversary of ICCSA, which is a quarter of a century, in Istanbul, Türkiye, which connects and acts as a bridge between two continents, namely Asia and Europe. This unique location in the world hosts the 25th year of ICCSA at Galatasaray University, located on Çırağan Avenue by Istanbul's Bosphorus, which is an established international university bestowed with a distinctive past of teaching tradition, research and education exceeding five centuries.

Istanbul, having served as the capital city of four empires, namely the Roman Empire (330–395), the Byzantine Empire (395–1204 and 1261–1453), the Latin Empire (1204–1261) and the Ottoman Empire (1453–1922), is an exceptional city of the Republic of Türkiye founded by Mustafa Kemal Atatürk.

Situated at a strategic location along the historic Silk Road, Istanbul is at the core of extending rail networks which span across Europe and West Asia along with the only sea route between the Black Sea and the Mediterranean.

The cultural, historical and economic pulses of the country are evident in Istanbul whose rooted origins have embraced varying beliefs, lifestyles and populace, which highlights the city's mosaic quality with blended fabric in a constant harmonious flow. This has enabled cultures to grow and be nurtured, which is profoundly rooted in its urban culture.

Computational Science constitutes the main pillar of most present research, industrial and commercial activities besides manifesting a unique role in exploiting and addressing innovative Information and Communication Technologies. Thus, the 25-year-old ICCSA conference series provides remarkable opportunities to get acquainted with leading researchers, scientists, scholars, practitioners and many more while exchanging innovative ideas and initiating new partnerships, associations and bonds.

With the hosting of Galatasaray University, I would personally and on behalf of the Local Organizing Committee, with the members Emre Alptekin, Gülfem Işıklar Alptekin, Cengiz Kahraman, Abdullah Çağrı Tolga and Ayberk Zeytin, like to convey our sincere gratitude and thanks to everyone who exerted their efforts in and contributed to the realization of ICCSA 2025. With these notes and remarks, welcome to Istanbul!

Cordially yours,
On behalf of the Local Organizing Committee.

June 2025   Yeliz Karaca

Organization

Honorary General Chairs

Bernady O. Apduhan	Kyushu Sangyo University, Japan
Kenneth C. J. Tan	Sardina Systems, UK

General Chairs

Yeliz Karaca	University of Massachusetts, USA
Osvaldo Gervasi	University of Perugia, Italy
David Taniar	Monash University, Australia

Program Committee Chairs

Beniamino Murgante	University of Basilicata, Italy
Chiara Garau	University of Cagliari, Italy
Ana Maria A. C. Rocha	University of Minho, Portugal
A. Çağrı Tolga	Galatasaray University, Turkey

International Advisory Committee

Jemal Abawajy	Deakin University, Australia
Dharma P. Agarwal	University of Cincinnati, USA
Rajkumar Buyya	Melbourne University, Australia
Claudia Bauzer Medeiros	University of Campinas, Brazil
Manfred M. Fisher	Vienna University of Economics and Business, Austria
Pierre Frankhauser	University of Franche-Comté/CNRS, France
Marina L. Gavrilova	University of Calgary, Canada
Sumi Helal	University of Florida, USA & Lancaster University, UK
Bin Jiang	University of Gävle, Sweden
Yee Leung	Chinese University of Hong Kong, China

International Liaison Chairs

Ivan Blečić	University of Cagliari, Italy
Giuseppe Borruso	University of Trieste, Italy
Elise De Donker	Western Michigan University, USA
Maria Noelia Faginas Lago	University of Perugia, Italy
Maria Irene Falcão	University of Minho, Portugal
Robert C. H. Hsu	Chung Hua University, Taiwan
Yeliz Karaca	University of Massachusetts Chan Medical School, USA
Tae-Hoon Kim	Zhejiang University of Science and Technology, China
Vladimir Korkhov	Saint Petersburg University, Russia
Takashi Naka	Kyushu Sangyo University, Japan
Rafael D. C. Santos	National Institute for Space Research, Brazil
Maribel Yasmina Santos	University of Minho, Portugal
Anastasia Stratigea	National Technical University of Athens, Greece

Workshop and Session Organizing Chairs

Beniamino Murgante	University of Basilicata, Italy
Chiara Garau	University of Cagliari, Italy

Award Chair

Wenny Rahayu	La Trobe University, Australia

Publicity Committee Chairs

Elmer Dadios	De La Salle University, Philippines
Nataliia Kulabukhova	Saint Petersburg University, Russia
Daisuke Takahashi	Tsukuba University, Japan
Shangwang Wang	Beijing University of Posts and Telecommunications, China

Local Organizing Committee Chairs

Emre Alptekin	Galatasaray University, Turkey
Gülfem Işıklar Alptekin	Galatasaray University, Turkey
Cengiz Kahraman	İstanbul Technical University, Turkey
A. Çağrı Tolga	Galatasaray University, Turkey
Ayberk Zeytin	Galatasaray University, Turkey

Technology Chair

Damiano Perri	University of Perugia, Italy

Program Committee

Vera Afreixo	University of Aveiro, Portugal
Vladimir Alarcon	Northern Gulf Institute, USA
Filipe Alvelos	University of Minho, Portugal
Debora Anelli	Polytechnic University of Bari, Italy
Hartmut Asche	Hasso-Plattner-Institut für Digital Engineering Ggmbh, Germany
Nizamettin Aydın	İstanbul Technical University, Turkey
Ginevra Balletto	University of Cagliari, Italy
Nadia Balucani	University of Perugia, Italy
Socrates Basbas	Aristotle University of Thessaloniki, Greece
David Berti	ART SpA, Italy
Michela Bertolotto	University College Dublin, Ireland
Sandro Bimonte	CEMAGREF, TSCF, France
Ana Cristina Braga	University of Minho, Portugal
Tiziana Campisi	Kore University of Enna, Italy
Yves Caniou	Université Claude Bernard Lyon 1, France
Alessandra Capolupo	Polytechnic University of Bari, Italy
José A. Cardoso e Cunha	Universidade Nova de Lisboa, Portugal
Rui Cardoso	University of Beira Interior, Portugal
Leocadio G. Casado	University of Almería, Spain
Mete Celik	Erciyes University, Turkey
Maria Cerreta	University of Naples Federico II, Italy
Ta Quang Chieu	Thuyloi University, Vietnam
Rachel Chien-Sing Lee	Sunway University, Malaysia
Birol Ciloglugil	Ege University, Turkey
Mauro Coni	University of Cagliari, Italy

Florbela Maria da Cruz Domingues Correia	Polytechnic Institute of Viana do Castelo, Portugal
Alessandro Costantini	INFN, Italy
Roberto De Lotto	University of Pavia, Italy
Luiza De Macedo Mourelle	State University of Rio De Janeiro, Brazil
Marcelo De Paiva Guimaraes	Federal University of Sao Paulo, Brazil
Frank Devai	London South Bank University, UK
Joana Matos Dias	University of Coimbra, Portugal
Aziz Dursun	Virginia Tech University, USA
Laila El Ghandour	Heriot-Watt University, UK
Rafida M. Elobaid	Canadian University Dubai, United Arab Emirates
Maria Irene Falcao	University of Minho, Portugal
Florbela P. Fernandes	Polytechnic Institute of Bragança, Portugal
Paula Odete Fernandes	Polytechnic Institute of Bragança, Portugal
Adelaide de Fátima Baptista Valente Freitas	University of Aveiro, Portugal
Valentina Franzoni	University of Perugia, Italy
Andreas Fricke	University of Potsdam, Germany
Raffaele Garrisi	Centro Operativo per la Sicurezza Cibernetica, Italy
Ivan Gerace	University of Perugia, Italy
Maria Giaoutzi	National Technical University of Athens, Greece
Salvatore Giuffrida	University of Catania, Italy
Teresa Guarda	Universidad Estatal Peninsula de Santa Elena, Ecuador
Sevin Gümgüm	Izmir University of Economics, Turkey
Malgorzata Hanzl	Technical University of Lodz, Poland
Maulana Adhinugraha Kiki	Telkom University, Indonesia
Clement Ho Cheung Leung	Chinese University of Hong Kong, China
Andrea Lombardi	University of Perugia, Italy
Marcos Mandado Alonso	University of Vigo, Spain
Ernesto Marcheggiani	Katholieke Universiteit Leuven, Belgium
Antonino Marvuglia	Luxembourg Institute of Science and Technology, Luxembourg
Michele Mastroianni	University of Salerno, Italy
Hideo Matsufuru	High Energy Accelerator Research Organization, Japan
Fernando Miranda	Universidade do Minho, Portugal
Giuseppe Modica	University of Reggio Calabria, Italy
Majaz Moonis	University of Massachusetts, USA
Nadia Nedjah	State University of Rio de Janeiro, Brazil
Paolo Nesi	University of Florence, Italy

Workshop Program Committee Members

Fabrizio Battisti	University of Florence, Italy
Fabiana Forte	Università della Campania Luigi Vanvitelli, Italy
Orazio Campo	University of Rome "La Sapienza", Italy
Alessio Pino	Kore University of Enna, Italy
Carlo Pisano	University of Florence, Italy
Mariolina Grasso	Università Kore di Enna, Italy

Evaluating Inner Areas Potentials (EIAP 2025)

Workshop Organizers

Diana Rolando	Politecnico di Torino, Italy
Alice Barreca	Politecnico di Torino, Italy
Manuela Rebaudengo	Politecnico di Torino, Italy
Giorgia Malavasi	Politecnico di Torino, Italy

Workshop Program Committee Members

John Accordino	Virginia Commonwealth University, USA
Francesco Bruzzone	Università Iuav di Venezia, Italy
Maria Cerreta	Università degli Studi di Napoli Federico II, Italy
Maddalena Chimisso	Università degli Studi del Molise, Italy
Chiara Chioni	Università degli Studi di Trento, Italy
Annalisa Contato	Università degli Studi di Palermo, Italy
Cristina Coscia	Politecnico di Torino, Italy
Marta Dell'Ovo	Politecnico di Milano, Italy
Benedetta Di Leo	Università Politecnica delle Marche, Italy
Sara Favargiotti	Università degli Studi di Trento, Italy
Maddalena Ferretti	Università Politecnica delle Marche, Italy
Salvo Giuffrida	Università degli Studi di Palermo, Italy
Barbara Lino	Università degli Studi di Palermo, Italy
Umberto Mecca	Politecnico di Torino, Italy
Beatrice Mecca	Politecnico di Torino, Italy
Giuliano Poli	Università degli Studi di Napoli Federico II, Italy
Marco Rossitti	Politecnico di Milano, Italy
Alexandra Stankulova	Politecnico di Torino, Italy
Elena Todella	Politecnico di Torino, Italy
Asja Aulisio	Politecnico di Torino, Italy
Giulia Datola	Politecnico di Milano, Italy

Workshop Program Committee Members

Giuseppe Borruso	University of Trieste, Italy
Beniamino Murgante	University of Basilicata, Italy
Malgorzata Hanzl	Lodz University of Technology, Poland
Anastasia Stratigea	National Technical University of Athens, Greece
Ljiljiana Zivkovic	Republic Geodetic Authority of Serbia, Serbia
Ginevra Balletto	University of Cagliari, Italy
Silvia Battino	University of Sassari, Italy
Mara Ladu	University of Cagliari, Italy
Maria del Mar Munoz Leonisio	University of Cádiz, Spain
Ahinoa Amaro Garcia	University of Las Palmas of Gran Canaria, Spain
Maria Attard	University of Malta, Malta
Enrico D'agostini	World Maritime University, Sweden
Francesca Krasna	University of Trieste, Italy
Brisol Garcia Garcia	Polytechnic University of Quintana Roo, Mexico
Tu Anh Trinh	UEH University, Vietnam
Giovanni Mauro	Università degli Studi della Campania, Italy
Maria Ronza	University of Naples Federico II, Italy
Massimiliano Bencardino	University of Salerno, Italy
Tomasz Bradecki	Silesian University of Technology, Poland
Dorota Kamrowska-Załuska	Gdańsk University of Technology, Poland
Iwona Jażdżewska	University of Lodz, Poland
Yiota Theodora	National Technical University of Athens, Greece
Apostolos Lagarias	University of Thessaly, Greece
George Tsilimigkas	University of the Aegean, Greece
Akrivi Leka	National Technical University of Athens, Greece
Maria Panagiotopoulou	National Technical University of Athens, Greece
Andrea Gallo	Ca' Foscari University of Venice, Italy
Francesca Sinatra	University of Trieste, Italy

Digital Transition: Effects on Housing Mobility, Market, Land Governance (DIGITRANS 2025)

Workshop Organizers

Fabrizio Battisti	University of Florence, Italy
Fabiana Forte	University of Campania, Italy
Orazio Campo	Sapienza University of Rome, Italy
Alessio Pino	Kore University of Enna, Italy
Carlo Pisano	University of Florence, Italy
Mariolina Grasso	Kore University of Enna, Italy

Workshop Program Committee Members

Vadim Lisitsa	Institute of Petroleum Geology and Geophysics SB RAS, Russia
Evgeniy Romenski	Sobolev Institute of Mathematics SB RAS, Russia
Vladimir Cheverda	Sobolev Institute of Mathematics SB RAS, Russia
Tatyana Khachkova	IPGG SB RAS, Russia
Dmitry Prokhorov	IPGG SB RAS, Russia
Mikhail Novikov	Sobolev Institute of Mathematics SB RAS, Russia
Sergey Solovyev	Sobolev Institute of Mathematics SB RAS, Russia
Kirill Gadylshin	LLC RNBashNIPIneft, Russia
Olga Stoyanovskaya	Lavrentev Institute of Hydrodynamics SB RAS, Russia
Yerlan Amanbek	Nazarbaev University, Kazakstan

Workshop on Computational Science and HPC (CSHPC 2025)

Workshop Organizers

Elise de Doncker	Western Michigan University, USA
Hideo Matsufuru	High Energy Accelerator Research Organization, Japan

Workshop Program Committee Members

Elise de Doncker	Western Michigan University, USA
Hideo Matsufuru	High Energy Accelerator Research Organization (KEK), Japan
Fukuko Yuasa	KEK, Japan
Issaku Kanamori	RIKEN, Japan
Hiroshi Daisaka	Hitotsubashi University, Japan
Norikazu Yamada	KEK, Japan
Naohito Nakasato	University of Aizu, Japan
Robert Makin	Western Michigan University, USA

Cities, Technologies and Planning 2025 (CTP 2025)

Workshop Organizers

Giuseppe Borruso	University of Trieste, Italy
Beniamino Murgante	University of Basilicata, Italy
Malgorzata Hanzl	Lodz University of Technology, Poland
Anastasia Stratigea	National Technical University of Athens, Greece
Ljiljana Zivkovic	Republic Geodetic Authority, Serbia
Ginevra Balletto	University of Trieste, Italy

Computational Astrochemistry 2025 (CompAstro 2025)

Workshop Organizers

Marzio Rosi	University of Perugia, Italy
Daniela Ascenzi	University of Trento, Italy
Nadia Balucani	University of Perugia, Italy
Stefano Falcinelli	University of Perugia, Italy

Workshop Program Committee Members

Dario Campisi	Università degli Studi di Perugia, Italy
Giacomo Giorgi	Università degli Studi di Perugia, Italy
Andrea Giustini	Università degli Studi di Perugia, Italy
Luca Mancini	Università degli Studi di Perugia, Italy
Albert Rimola	Universitat Autònoma de Barcelona, Spain
Gianmarco Vanuzzo	Università degli Studi di Perugia, Italy
Dimitrios Skouteris	Master-Tec, Italy
Piero Ugliengo	Università degli Studi di Torino, Italy
Franco Vecchiocattivi	Università degli Sudi di Perugia, Italy
Giacomo Pannacci	Università degli Studi di Perugia, Italy
Costanza Borghesi	Università degli Studi di Perugia, Italy
Marco Parriani	Università degli Studi di Perugia, Italy
Marta Loletti	Università degli Studi di Perugia, Italy
Fernando Pirani	Università degli Studi di Perugia, Italy
Andrea Lombardi	Università degli Studi di Perugia, Italy
Noelia Faginas Lago	Università degli Studi di Perugia, Italy
Paolo Tosi	Università di Trento, Italy
Cecilia Coletti	Università degli Studi Chieti-Pescara, Italy
Nazzareno Re	Università degli Studi Chieti-Pescara, Italy
Linda Podio	Osservatorio Astrofisico di Arcetri INAF, Italy
Claudio Codella	Osservatorio Astrofisico di Arcetri INAF, Italy
Gabriella Di Genova	Università degli Studi di Perugia, Italy

Computational Methods for Porous Geomaterials (CompPor 2025)

Workshop Organizers

Vadim Lisitsa	IPGG SB RAS, Russia
Evgeniy Romenski	IPGG SB RAS, Russia

Computational Optimization and Applications (COA 2025)

Workshop Organizers

Ana Rocha	ALGORITMI Research Centre, LASI, University of Minho, Portugal, Portugal
Humberto Rocha	ALGORITMI Research Centre, LASI, University of Minho, Portugal, Portugal

Workshop Program Committee Members

Florbela Fernandes	Polytechnic Institute of Bragança, Portugal
Clara Vaz	Polytechnic Institute of Bragança, Portugal
Ana Pereira	Polytechnic Institute of Bragança, Portugal
Filipe Alvelos	University of Minho, Portugal
Joana Dias	University of Coimbra, Portugal
Eligius M. T. Hendrix	University of Málaga, Spain
Emerson José de Paiva	Federal University of Itajubá, Brazil
Ana Paula Teixeira	University of Trás-os-Montes and Alto Douro, Portugal
Lino Costa	Universidade do Minho, Portugal

Coastal Cities Versus Inland Areas. Hypotheses for Sustainable Regeneration Through Ecosystem Services of 'Hooking' and Rehabilitation of Brownfield Sites (CoastalCities_VS_InlandAreas 2025)

Workshop Organizers

Celestina Fazia	Università di Enna Kore, Italy
Angrilli Massimo	University of Chieti-Pescara, Italy
Valentina Ciuffreda	University of Chieti-Pescara, Italy
Maurizio Oddo	Università di Enna Kore, Italy
Marcello Sestito	Università di Enna Kore, Italy
Clara Stella Vicari Aversa	University of Reggio Calabria, Italy

Workshop Program Committee Members

Alessandro Camiz	Università d'Annunzio, Italy
Thowayeb Hassan	King Faisal University, Saudi Arabia
Alessandro Barracco	Università Kore di Enna, Italy
Mario Morrica	University of Urbino, Italy
Mariana Ratiu	University of Oradea, Romania
Alanda Akamana	Mohammed VI Polytechnic University, Morocco
Kaoutare Amini Alaoui	Mohammed VI Polytechnic University, Morocco

Computational Methods, Statistics and Industrial Mathematics (CMSIM 2025)

Workshop Organizers

Maria Filomena Teodoro	IST ID, Instituto Superior Técnico, Portugal
Marina Alexandra Pedro Andrade	ISCTE – Lisbon University Institute, Portugal
Paula Simões	University of Lisbon, Portugal
Teresa A. Oliveira	IST ID, Instituto Superior Técnico, Portugal

Workshop Program Committee Members

Amilcar Oliveira	Universidade Aberta and Universidade de Lisboa, Portugal
Victor Lobo	Escola Naval and NOVA IMS Almada, Portugal
António Pacheco	IST Universidade de Lisboa, Portugal
Eliana Costa	Escola Superior de Tecnologia e Gestão IPPorto, Portugal
Aldina Correia	Escola Superior de Tecnologia e Gestão IPPorto, Portugal
Fernando Carapau	University of Évora, Portugal
Ricardo Moura	Portuguese Naval Academy, Portugal
Ana Borges	Escola Superior de Tecnologia e Gestão IPPorto, Portugal
Cristina Lopes	ISCAP IPPorto, Portugal
Fernanda Costa	University of Minho, Portugal
Cabrita Carlos	IPBeja, Portugal
Maria Luísa Morgado	University of Trás os Montes e Alto Douro and University of Lisboa, Portugal
Rosário Ramos	Universidade Aberta, Portugal
Sofia Rézio	Iscal, Instituto Politécnico de Lisboa, Portugal
Matteo Sacchet	University of Turin, Italy
Marina Marchisio Conte	University of Turin, Italy
António Seijas-Macias	University of Coruña, Spain
Luís F. A. Teodoro	University of Glasgow, UK and University of Oslo, Norway
Christos Kitsos	University of West Attica, Greece
M. Filomena Teodoro	Universidade de Lisboa, Portugal
Marina A. P. Andrade	Instituto Universitário de Lisboa, Portugal
Paula Simões	Military Academy and Universidade Nova de Lisboa, Portugal
Teresa Oliveira	Universidade Aberta and Universidade de Lisboa, Portugal

Werner G. Müller	Johannes Kepler University Linz, Austria
Bruna Silva Ramos	University Lusiada de Famalicão, Portugal
Inês Sousa	University of Minho, Portugal
Luís Miguel Rocha Matos	University of Minho, Portugal
Manuel Carlos Figueiredo	University of Minho, Portugal

Cyber Intelligence and Applications (CIA 2025)

Workshop Organizer

Gianni D'Angelo	University of Salerno, Italy

Workshop Program Committee Members

Gianni D'Angelo	University of Salerno, Italy
Francesco Palmieri	University of Salerno, Italy
Massimo Ficco	University of Salerno, Italy
Arcangelo Castiglione	University of Salerno, Italy

Computational Methods for Business Analytics (CMBA 2025)

Workshop Organizers

Cláudio Alves	Universidade do Minho, Portugal
Telmo Pinto	Universidade do Minho, Portugal

Workshop Program Committee Members

Abdulrahim Shamayleh	American University of Sharjah, United Arab Emirates
Ana Rocha	University of Minho, Portugal
Angelo Sifaleras	University of Macedonia, Greece
Cristóvão Silva	University of Coimbra, Portugal
José Valério de Carvalho	University of Minho, Portugal
Miguel Vieira	Universidade Lusófona, Portugal
Rita Macedo	Université de Lille, France
Ana Moura	Universidade de Aveiro, Portugal
Cristina Lopes	ISCAP, Portugal
Eliana Costa e Silva	Instituto Politécnico do Porto, Portugal

Isabel Cacao	University of Aveiro, Portugal
João Morais	Autonomous Technological Institute of Mexico, Mexico
Lidia Aceto	University of Eastern Piedmont, Italy
Luís Ferrás	University of Porto, Portugal
M. Irene Falcão	University of Minho, Portugal
Patrícia Beites	University of Beira Interior, Portugal
Paulo Amorim	FGV EMAp, Brazil
Regina de Almeida	University of Trás-os-Montes e Alto Douro, Portugal
Ricardo Severino	University of Minho, Portugal

Computational and Applied Statistics (CAS 2025)

Workshop Organizer

Ana Cristina Braga	ALGORITMI Research Centre, LASI, University of Minho, Portugal

Workshop Program Committee Members

Adelaide Freitas	University of Aveiro, Portugal
Andreas Futschik	Johannes Kepler University Linz, Austria
Ana Cristina Braga	University of Minho, Portugal
Ângela Silva	University of Minho, Portugal
Arminda Manuela Gonçalves	University of Minho, Portugal
Carina Silva	Polytechnic Intitute of Lisbon, Portugal
Elisete Correia	University of Trás-os-Montes e Alto Douro, Portugal
Frank Westad	Norwegian University of Science and Technology, Norway
Isabel Natario	New University of Lisbon, Portugal
Irene Oliveira	University of Trás-os-Montes e Alto Douro, Portugal
Ivan Rodriguez Conde	University of Vigo, Spain
Joaquim Gonçalves	Instituto Politécnico do Cávado e do Ave, Portugal
Lino Costa	University of Minho, Portugal
Marco Reis	University of Coimbra, Portugal
Maria Filipa Mourão	Polytechnic Institute of Viana do Castelo, Portugal
Maria João Polidoro	Polytechnic Institute of Porto, Portugal
Martin Perez Perez	University of Vigo, Spain
Michal Abrahamowicz	McGill University, Canada
Vera Afreixo	University of Aveiro, Portugal

Advanced Processes of Mathematics and Computing Models in Complex Data-Intensive Computational Systems (AMCM 2025)

Workshop Organizers

Yeliz Karaca	University of Massachusetts Chan Medical School and Massachusetts Institute of Technology, USA
Dumitru Baleanu	Lebanese American University, Lebanon
Osvaldo Gervasi	University of Perugia, Italy
Yudong Zhang	University of Leicester, UK
Majaz Moonis	University of Massachusetts Chan Medical School and Massachusetts Institute of Technology, USA

Workshop Program Committee Members

TaeHoon Kim	Zhejiang University of Science and Technology, China
Martin Bohner	Missouri University of Science and Technology, USA
Shuihua Wang	University of Leicester, UK
Khan Muhammad	Sungkyunkwan University, South Korea
Mahmoud Abdel-Aty	Sohag University, Egypt
Aziz Dursun	Virginia Polytechnic Institute and State University, USA
Kemal Güven Gülen	Namık Kemal University, Turkey
Akif Akgül	Hitit Üniversitesi, Turkey

Advanced Numerical Approaches for Assessment and Design of No-Tension Masonry Structures (ANAMS 2025)

Workshop Organizers

Antonino Iannuzzo	Universitá degli studi del Sannio, Italy
Carlo Olivieri	Universitá Telematica Pegaso, Italy
Andrea Montanino	CIMNE, Spain
Elham Mousavian	University of Edinburgh, UK

Workshop Program Committee Members

Pietro Meriggi	Roma Tre University, Italy
Francesca Perelli	University of Naples Federico II, Italy
Marialuigia Sangirardi	University of Oxford, UK
Sam Cocking	University of Cambridge, UK

Matteo Salvalaggio	University of Minho, Portugal
Vittorio Paris	University of Bergamo, Italy
Luigi Sibille	Norwegian University of Science and Technology, Norway
Natalia Pingaro	Politecnico di Milano, Italy
Martina Buzzetti	Politecnico di Milano, Italy
Generoso Vaiano	Pegaso Telematic University, Italy
Alessandra Capolupo	Politecnico di Bari, Italy
Amal Gerges	Università degli Studi di Cagliari, Italy
Fabian Orozco	National Autonomous University of Mexico, Mexico
Nathanael Savalle	Polytech Clermont and Université Clermont Auvergne, France
Luca Umberto Argiento	University of Naples Federico II, Italy
Bartolomeo Pantó	Durham University, UK

Unveiling the Synergies Between Air Quality and Climate PlAnning (AQCliPA 2025)

Workshop Organizers

Angela Pilogallo	University of L'Aquila, Italy
Luigi Santopietro	University of Basilicata, Italy
Filomena Pietrapertosa	IMAA CNR, Italy
Monica Salvia	IMAA CNR, Italy
Carlo Trozzi	IMAA CNR, Italy
Valeria Scapini	Central University of Chile, Chile

Workshop Program Committee Members

Lucia Saganeiti	IMAA-CNR, Italy
Lorena Fiorini	University of L'Aquila, Italy
Antonio Mazza	IMAA-CNR, Italy
Gabriele Nolè	IMAA-CNR, Italy
Carmen Guida	University of Naples "Federico II", Italy
Floriana Zucaro	University of Naples "Federico II", Italy
Sabrina Lai	University of Cagliari, Italy
Chiara Garau	University of Cagliari, Italy

Advancements in Spatial assessment of Socio-Ecological SystemS (ASSESS 2025)

Workshop Organizers
Daniele Cannatella	TU Delft, The Netherlands
Giuliano Poli	University of Naples Federico II, Italy
Eugenio Muccio	TU Delft, The Netherlands
Claudiu Forgaci	TU Delft, The Netherlands

Workshop Program Committee Members
Daniele Cannatella	TU Delft, The Netherlands
Giuliano Poli	University of Naples Federico II, Italy
Eugenio Muccio	University of Naples Federico II, Italy
Claudiu Forgaci	TU Delft, The Netherlands
Maria Cerreta	University of Naples Federico II, Italy
Maria Somma	University of Naples Federico II, Italy
Laura Di Tommaso	University of Naples Federico II, Italy
Sabrina Sacco	Politecnico di Milano, Italy
Piero Zizzania	University of Naples Federico II, Italy
Gaia Daldanise	CNR IRISS, Italy
Benedetta Grieco	University of Naples Federico II, Italy
Giuseppe Ciciriello	University of Naples Federico II, Italy
Marta Dell'Ovo	Politecnico di Milano, Italy
Francesco Piras	University of Cagliari, Italy
Diana Rolando	Politecnico di Torino, Italy
Stefano Cuntò	University of Naples Federico II, Italy
Ludovica La Rocca	University of Naples Federico II, Italy

Blockchain and Distributed Ledgers: Technologies and Applications (BDLTA 2025)

Workshop Organizers
Vladimir Korkhov	Saint Petersburg State University, Russia
Elena Stankova	Saint Petersburg State University, Russia
Nataliia Kulabukhova	Saint Petersburg State University, Russia

Workshop Program Committee Members
Adam Belloum	University of Amsterdam, the Netherlands
Dmitrii Vasiunin	Deutsche Telekom Cloud Services E.P.E., Greece
Serob Balyan	Osensus Arm LLC, Armenia
Suren Abrahamyan	Osensus Arm LLC, Armenia
Ashot Sergey Gevorkyan	NAS of Armenia, Armenia

Michal Hnatic	Univerzita Pavla Jozefa Šafárika v Košiciach, Slovakia
Michail Panteleyev	Saint Petersburg Electrotecnical University, Russia
Martin Vala	Univerzita Pavla Jozefa Šafárika v Košiciach, Slovakia
Nodir Zaynalov	Tashkent University of Information Technologies named after Muhammad al Khwarizmi, Uzbekistan
Michail Panteleyev	Saint Petersburg Electrotecnical University, Russia
Alexander Degtyarev	Saint Petersburg University, Russia
Alexander Bogdanov	St. Petersburg State University, Russia

Bio and Neuro Inspired Computing and Applications (BIONCA 2025)

Workshop Organizers

Nadia Nedjah	State University of Rio de Janeiro, Brazil
Luiza de Macedo Mourelle	State University of Rio de Janeiro, Brazil

Workshop Program Committee Members

Nadia Nedjha	State University of Rio de Janeiro, Brazil
Luiza de Macedo Mourelle	State University of Rio de Janeiro, Brazil
Luigi Maciel Ribeiro	State University of Rio de Janeiro, Brazil
Joelmir Ramos	Federal University of Rio de Janeiro, Brazil
Rogério Moraes	Brazilian Navy, Brazil
Marcos Santana Farias	Institute of Nuclear Energy, Brazil
Luneque Silva Jr.	Federal University of ABC, Brazil
Alan Oliveira	University of Lisboa, Portugal
Brij Bhooshan Gupta	Asia University, Taiwan

Computational and Applied Mathematics (CAM 2025)

Workshop Organizers

Maria Irene Falcão	University of Minho, Portugal
Fernando Miranda	University of Minho, Portugal

Workshop Program Committee Members

Fernando Miranda	University of Minho, Portugal
Graça Tomaz	Polytechnic of Guarda, Portugal
Helmuth Malonek	University of Aveiro, Portugal

Workshops

Workshop on Advancements in Applied Machine-Learning and Data Analytics (AAMDA 2025)

Workshop Organizers

Alessandro Costantini	INFN, Italy
Daniele Cesini	INFN, Italy
Elisabetta Ronchieri	INFN, Italy
Barbara Martelli	INFN, Italy

Workshop Program Committee Members

Alessandro Costantini	Istituto Nazionale di Fisica Nucleare (INFN), Italy
Daniele Cesini	Istituto Nazionale di Fisica Nucleare (INFN), Italy
Elisabetta Ronchieri	Istituto Nazionale di Fisica Nucleare (INFN), Italy
Barbara Martelli	Istituto Nazionale di Fisica Nucleare (INFN), Italy
Luca Dell'Agnello	Istituto Nazionale di Fisica Nucleare (INFN), Italy

Advanced and Innovative Web Apps 2025 (AIWA 2025)

Workshop Organizers

Damiano Perri	University of Perugia, Italy
Osvaldo Gervasi	University of Perugia, Italy
Stelios Kouzeleas	International Hellenic University, Greece
Sergio Tasso	University of Perugia, Italy

Workshop Program Committee Members

David Berti	ART SpA, Italy
JungYoon Kim	Gachon University, South Korea
TaiHoon Kim	Zhejiang University of Science and Technology, China

Suzan Obaiys	University of Malaya, Malaysia
Marcin Paprzycki	Polish Academy of Sciences, Poland
Eric Pardede	La Trobe University, Australia
Ana Isabel Pereira	Polytechnic Institute of Bragança, Portugal
Damiano Perri	University of Perugia, Italy
Massimiliano Petri	University of Pisa, Italy
Telmo Pinto	University of Coimbra, Portugal
Alessandro Plaisant	University of Sassari, Italy
Maurizio Pollino	ENEA, Italy
Alenka Poplin	Iowa State University, USA
Marcos Quiles	Federal University of São Paulo, Brazil
Nguyen Huu Quynh	Thuyloi University, Vietnam
Albert Rimola	Universitat Autònoma de Barcelona, Spain
Humberto Rocha	University of Coimbra, Portugal
Marzio Rosi	University of Perugia, Italy
Lucia Saganeiti	University of L'Aquila, Italy
Francesco Scorza	University of Basilicata, Italy
Marco Paulo Seabra dos Reis	University of Coimbra, Portugal
Jie Shen	University of Michigan, USA
Francesco Tajani	Sapienza University of Rome, Italy
Rodrigo Tapia Mcclung	Centro de Investigación en Ciencias de Información Geoespacial, Mexico
Eufemia Tarantino	Polytechnic University of Bari, Italy
Sergio Tasso	University of Perugia, Italy
Ana Paula Teixeira	Universidade do Minho, Portugal
Yiota Theodora	National Technical University of Athens, Greece
Giuseppe A. Trunfio	University of Sassari, Italy
Toshihiro Uchibayashi	Kyushu University, Japan
Marco Vizzari	University of Perugia, Italy
Frank Westad	Norwegian University of Science and Technology, Norway
Fukuko Yuasa	High Energy Accelerator Research Organization, Japan
Ljiljana Zivkovic	Republic Geodetic Authority, Serbia

Francesco Calabrò	Università degli Studi Mediterranea di Reggio Calabria, Italy
Valeria Saiu	Università degli Studi di Cagliari, Italy
Maria Rosa Trovato	Università di Catania, Italy

Econometric and Multidimensional Evaluation in Urban Environment (EMEUE 2025)

Workshop Organizers

Maria Cerreta	University of Naples Federico II, Italy
Carmelo Maria Torre	Polytechnic University of Bari, Italy
Pierluigi Morano	Polytechnic University of Bari, Italy
Simona Panaro	University of Naples Federico II, Italy
Felicia Di Liddo	University of Naples Federico II, Italy
Debora Anelli	University of Naples Federico II, Italy

Workshop Program Committee Members

Carmelo Maria Torre	Polytechnic University of Bari, Italy
Maria Cerreta	University of Naples Federico II, Italy
Pierluigi Morano	Polytechnic University of Bari, Italy
Francesco Tajani	Sapienza University of Rome, Italy
Simona Panaro	University of Naples Federico II, Italy
Felicia di Liddo	Polytechnic University of Bari, Italy
Debora Anelli	Sapienza University of Rome, Italy
Giuliano Poli	University of Naples Federico II, Italy
Maria Somma	University of Naples Federico II, Italy
Simona Panaro	University of Campania Luigi Vanvitelli, Italy
Laura Di Tommaso	University of Naples Federico II, Italy
Caterina Loffredo	University of Naples Federico II, Italy
Ludovica La Rocca	University of Naples Federico II, Italy
Sabrina Sacco	Politecnico di Milano, Italy
Piero Zizzania	University of Naples Federico II, Italy
Gaia Daldanise	CNR IRISS, Italy
Benedetta Grieco	University of Naples Federico II, Italy
Giuseppe Ciciriello	University of Naples Federico II, Italy
Marta Dell'Ovo	Politecnico di Milano, Italy
Daniele Cannatella	TU Delft University, The Netherlands
Eugenio Muccio	University of Naples Federico II, Italy
Sveva Ventre	University of Naples Federico II, Italy

Governance of Energy Transition: Environmental, Landscape, Social and Spatial Planning (ENERGY_PLANNING 2025)

Workshop Organizers
Mara Ladu	University of Cagliari, Italy
Ginevra Balletto	University of Cagliari, Italy
Emilio Ghiani	University of Cagliari, Italy
Alessandra Marra	University of Salerno, Italy
Roberto De Lotto	University of Pavia, Italy
Balázs Kulcsár	Chalmers University of Technology, Sweden

Workshop Program Committee Members
Riccardo Trevisan	University of Cagliari, Italy
Marco Naseddu	University of Cagliari, Italy
Giuseppe Borruso	University of Trieste, Italy
Andrea Gallo	University of Trieste, Italy
Francesca Sinatra	University of Trieste, Italy
Maria Attard	University of Malta, Malta
Tu Anh Trinh	UEH University Ho Chi Minh City, Vietnam
Marcello Tadini	University of Eastern Piedmont, Italy
Luigi Mundula	University for Foreigners of Perugia, Italy
Silvia Battino	University of Sassari, Italy
Maria del Mar Munoz Leonisio	University of Cádiz, Spain
Anna Richiedei	University of Brescia, Italy
Michele Pezzagno	University of Brescia, Italy
Federico Mertellozzo	University of Firenze, Italy
Marco Mazzarino	IUAV University Venice, Italy

Ecosystem Services in Spatial Planning for Climate Neutral Urban and Rural Areas (ESSP 2025)

Workshop Organizers
Sabrina Lai	University of Cagliari, Italy
Francesco Scorza	University of Basilicata, Italy
Corrado Zoppi	University of Cagliari, Italy
Beniamino Murgante	University of Basilicata, Italy
Carmela Gargiulo	University of Naples Federico II, Italy
Floriana Zucaro	University of Naples Federico II, Italy

Workshop Program Committee Members

Alfonso Annunziata	University of Basilicata, Italy
Ginevra Balletto	University of Cagliari, Italy
Ivan Blečić	University of Cagliari, Italy
Giuseppe Borruso	University of Trieste, Italy
Barbara Caselli	University of Parma, Italy
Maria Cerreta	University of Naples Federico II, Italy
Chiara Garau	University of Cagliari, Italy
Carmen Guida	University of Naples Federico II, Italy
Federica Isola	University of Cagliari, Italy
Francesca Leccis	University of Cagliari, Italy
Federica Leone	University of Cagliari, Italy
Silvia Rossetti	University of Parma, Italy
Luigi Santopietro	University of Basilicata, Italy
Carmelo Torre	Polytechnic of Bari, Italy

The 15th International Workshop on Future Information System Technologies and Applications (FiSTA 2025)

Workshop Organizers

Bernady O. Apduhan	Kyushu Sangyo University, Japan
Rafael Santos	Brazilian National Institute for Space Research, Brazil

Workshop Program Committee Members

Agustinus Borgy Waluyo	Monash University, Australia
Andre Ricardo Abed Grégio	Federal University of Paraná, Brazil
Eric Pardede	La Trobe University, Australia
Kai Cheng	Kyushu Sangyo University, Japan
Ching-Hsien Hsu	Asia University, Taiwan
Fenghui Yao	Tennessee State University, USA
Yusuke Gotoh	Okayama University, Japan
Alvaro Fazenda	Federal University of São Paulo, Brazil
Kazuaki Tanaka	Kyushu Institute of Technology, Japan
Tengku Adil	MARA Technological University, Malaysia
Toshihiro Yamauchi	Okayama University, Japan
Yasuaki Sumida	Kyushu Sangyo University, Japan
Earl Ryan Aleluya	MSU-Iligan Institute of Technology, Philippines
Cherry Mae G. Villame	MSU-Iligan Institute of Technology, Philippines
Anton Louise De Ocampo	Batangas State University, Philippines
Krishnamoorthy Ranganthan	Chennai Institute of Technology, India

Flow Management in Urban Contexts (FMUC 2025)

Workshop Organizers
Alessio Pino	Kore University of Enna, Italy
Giovanna Acampa	Kore University of Enna, Italy

Workshop Program Committee Members
Giovanna Acampa	University of Florence, Italy
Alessio Pino	Kore University of Enna, Italy
Mariolina Grasso	Università Kore di Enna, Italy
Fabrizio Battisti	University of Florence, Italy
Fabrizio Finucci	Roma Tre University, Italy
Antonella G. Masanotti	Roma Tre University, Italy
Daniele Mazzoni	Roma Tre University, Italy

Geographical Analysis, Urban Modeling, Spatial Statistics 2025 (Geog-And-Mod 2025)

Workshop Organizers
Beniamino Murgante	University of Basilicata, Italy
Giuseppe Borruso	University of Trieste, Italy
Hartmut Asche	University of Potsdam, Germany
Rodrigo Tapia McClung	CentroGeo, Mexico
Andreas Fricke	University of Potsdam, Germany

Workshop Program Committee Members
Giuseppe Borruso	University of Trieste, Italy
Beniamino Murgante	University of Basilicata, Italy
Hartmut Asche	University of Potsdam, Germany
Rodrigo Tapia-McClung	Centro de Investigación en Ciencias de Información Geoespacial (CentroGeo), Mexico
Andreas Fricke	University of Potsdam, Germany
Malgorzata Hanzl	Lodz University of Technology, Poland
Anastasia Stratigea	National Technical University of Athens, Greece
Ljiljiana Zivkovic	Republic Geodetic Authority of Serbia, Serbia
Ginevra Balletto	University of Cagliari, Italy
Silvia Battino	University of Sassari, Italy
Mara Ladu	University of Cagliari, Italy
Maria del Mar Munoz Leonisio	University of Cádiz, Spain
Ahinoa Amaro Garcia	University of Las Palmas of Gran Canaria, Spain
Maria Attard	University of Malta, Malta

Enrico D'agostini	World Maritime University, Sweden
Francesca Krasna	University of Trieste, Italy
Brisol García García	Polytechnic University of Quintana Roo, Mexico
Tu Anh Trinh	UEH University, Vietnam
Giovanni Mauro	Università degli Studi della Campania, Italy
Maria Ronza	University of Naples Federico II, Italy
Massimiliano Bencardino	University of Salerno, Italy
Andrea Gallo	Ca' Foscari University of Venice, Italy
Francesca Sinatra	University of Trieste, Italy
Salvatore Dore	University of Trieste, Italy

Geogames for Sustainable Development (Geogames 2025)

Workshop Organizer

Alenka Poplin	Iowa State University, USA

Workshop Program Committee Members

Alenka Poplin	Iowa State University, USA
Bruno Amaral de Andrade	Portucalense University, Portugal
Brian Tomaszewski	Rochester Institute of Technology, USA
Deepak Marhatta	Tribhuvan University, Nepal
Alessandro Plaisant	University of Sassari, Italy
David Schwartz	Rochester Institute of Technology, USA
Silvia Rossetti	University of Parma, Italy
Floriana Zucaro	University of Naples Federico II, Italy
Alfonso Annunziata	University of Basilicata, Italy
Reza Askarizad	University of Cagliari, Italy
Chiara Garau	University of Cagliari, Italy
Tanja Congiu	University of Sassari, Italy

Geomatics for Resource Monitoring and Management (GRMM 2025)

Workshop Organizers

Alberico Sonnessa	Politecnico di Bari, Italy
Eufemia Tarantino	Politecnico di Bari, Italy
Alessandra Capolupo	Politecnico di Bari, Italy

Workshop Program Committee Members

Umberto Fratino	Politecnico di Bari, Italy
Valeria Monno	Politecnico di Bari, Italy

Antonino Maltese	Università degli studi di Palermo, Italy
Athos Agapiou	Cyprus University of Technology, Cyprus
Michele Mangiameli	Università di Catania, Italy
Angela Gorgoglione	Universidad de la República de Uruguay, Uruguay
Roberta Ravanelli	University of Liège, Belgium
Ester Scotto di Perta	Università degli studi di Napoli Federico II, Italy
Giacomo Caporusso	CNR, Italy
Andrea Montanino	International Centre for Numerical Methods in Engineering of Barcelona, Spain
Antonino Iannuzzo	Università degli studi del Sannio, Italy
Alessandro Pagano	Politecnico di Bari, Italy
Francesco Di Capua	Università degli Studi della Basilicata, Italy
Albertini Cinzia	CNR-IREA, Italy
Alessandra Saponieri	Università degli studi del Salento, Italy
PierFrancesco Recchi	Università degli studi di Napoli Federico II, Italy
Vincenzo Totaro	Politecnico di Bari, Italy
Stefania Santoro	CNR Water Research Institute, Italy
Francesco Bimbo	University of Foggia, Italy
Cristina Proietti	Istituto Nazionale di Geofisica e Vulcanologia, Italy
Carla Cavallo	University of Salerno, Italy
Gaetano Falcone	Università degli Studi di Napoli Federico II, Italy
Valeria Belloni	Sapienza University of Rome, Italy
Alessandra Mascitelli	University of Chieti-Pescara, Italy

HERitage and CLIMAte neutrality. Resilient approach for nature centered/based sustainable cities (HERCLIMA 2025)

Workshop Organizers

Celestina Fazia	Università di Enna Kore, Italy
Angrilli Massimo	University of Chieti-Pescara, Italy
Clara Stella Vicari Aversa	University of Reggio Calabria, Italy
Dorina Camelia Ilies	University of Oradea, Romania
Mariana Ratiu	University of Oradea, Romania

Workshop Program Committee Members

Alessandro Camiz	Università d'Annunzio, Italy
Mario Morrica	University of Urbino, Italy
Thowayeb Hassan	King Faisal University, Saudi Arabia
Alessandro Barracco	Università Kore di Enna, Italy
Kaoutare Amini Alaoui	Mohammed VI Polytechnic University (UM6P), Morocco

Mariana Ratiu — University of Oradea, Romania
Valentina Ciuffreda — Università Chieti-Pescara, Italy

International Workshop on Information and Knowledge in the Internet of Things (IKIT 2025)

Workshop Organizers

Teresa Guarda	Universidad Estatal Península de Santa Elena, Ecuador
Luis Enrique Chuquimarca Jimenez	Universidad Estatal Península de Santa Elena, Ecuador
Gustavo Gatica	Universidad Andrés Bello, Chile
Filipe Mota Pinto	Polytechnic Institute of Leiria, Portugal
Arnulfo Alanis	Instituto Tecnológico de Tijuana, Mexico
Luis Mazon	Universidad Estatal Península de Santa Elena, Spain

Workshop Program Committee Members

Arnulfo Alanis	Instituto Tecnológico de Tijuana, Mexico
Bruno Sousa	University of Coimbra, Portugal
Carlos Balsa	Instituto Politécnico de Bragança, Portugal
Filipe Mota Pinto	Instituto Politécnico de Leiria, Portugal
Gustavo Gatica	Universidad Andrés Bello, Chile
Isabel Lopes	Instituto Politécnico de Bragança, Portugal
José-María Díaz-Nafría	Universidad a Distancia, Spain
Maria Fernanda Augusto	BiTrum Research Group, Spain
Maria Isabel Ribeiro	Instituto Politécnico Bragança, Portugal
Modestos Stavrakis	University of the Aegean, Greece
Simone Belli	Universidad Complutense de Madrid, Spain
Walter Lopes Neto	Instituto Federal de Educação, Brazil

International Workshop on territorial Planning to integrate Risk prevention and urban Ontologies (IWPRO 2025)

Workshop Organizers

Beniamino Murgante	University of Basilicata, Italy
Roberto De Lotto	University of Pavia, Italy
Elisabetta Maria Venco	University of Pavia, Italy
Caterina Pietra	University of Pavia, Italy

Workshop Program Committee Members

Stefano Borgo	Consiglio Nazionale delle Ricerche ISTC, Italy
Valentina Costa	Università di Genova, Italy
Hamid Danesh Pajouh	Middle East Technical University, Turkey
Ilaria Delponte	Università di Genova, Italy
Lorena Fiorini	Università de L'Aquila, Italy
Veronica Gazzola	Politecnico di Milano, Italy
Ghazaleh Goodarzi	Islamic Azad University, Iran
Michele Grimaldi	Università degli Studi di Salerno, Italy
Alessandra Marra	Università degli Studi di Salerno, Italy
Naghmeh Mohammadpourlima	Åbo Akademi University, Finland
Francesca Pirlone	Università di Genova, Italy
Silvia Rossetti	Università di Parma, Italy
Bahareh Shahsavari	University of Minnesota, USA
Ilenia Spadaro	Università di Genova, Italy
Maria Rosaria Stufano Melone	Politecnico di Bari, Italy

Regional Connectivity, Spatial Accessibility and MaaS for Social Inclusion (MaaS 2025)

Workshop Organizers

Mara Ladu	University of Cagliari, Italy
Ginevra Balletto	University of Cagliari, Italy
Gianfranco Fancello	University of Cagliari, Italy
Tanja Congiu	University of Sassari, Italy
Patrizia Serra	University of Cagliari, Italy
Francesco Piras	University of Cagliari, Italy

Workshop Program Committee Members

Marco Naseddu	University of Cagliari, Italy
Italo Meloni	University of Cagliari, Italy
Giuseppe Borruso	University of Trieste, Italy
Andrea Gallo	University of Trieste, Italy
Francesca Sinatra	University of Trieste, Italy
Maria Attard	University of Malta, Malta
Tu Anh Trinh	UEH University, Vietnam
Marcello Tadini	University of Eastern Piedmont, Italy
Luigi Mundula	University for Foreigners of Perugia, Italy
Silvia Battino	University of Sassari, Italy
Brunella Brundu	University of Sassari, Italy
Veronica Camerada	University of Sassari, Italy

Maria del Mar Munoz Leonisio	University of Cádiz, Spain
Anna Richiedei	University of Brescia, Italy
Michele Pezzagno	University of Brescia, Italy
Marco Mazzarino	IUAV University Venice, Italy

The Development of Urban Mobility Management, Road Safety and Risk Assessment (MANTAIN 2025)

Workshop Organizers

Antonio Russo	Università degli Studi di Enna, Italy
Corrado Rindone	University of Reggio Calabria, Italy
Antonio Polimeni	University of Messina, Italy
Florin Rusca	Politehnica University of Bucharest, Romania
Grigorios Fountas	Aristotle University of Thessaloniki, Greece
Antonio Comi	University of Rome Tor Vergata, Italy

Workshop Program Committee Members

Massimo Di Gangi	University of Messina, Italy
Orlando Marco Belcore	University of Messina, Italy
Antonio Polimeni	University of Messina, Italy
Socrates Basbas	Aristotle University of Thessaloniki, Greece
Claudia Caballini	Polytechnic of Torino, Italy
Efstathios Bouhouras	Aristotle University of Thessaloniki, Greece
Stefano Ricci	Sapienza University of Rome, Italy
Marina Zanne	University of Lubljana, Slovenia
Kh Md Nahiduzzaman	Mohammed VI Polytechnic University, Morocco
Alexsandra Deluka Tibljaš	University of Rijeka, Croatia
Guilhermina Torrao	Aston University, UK

Multidimensional Evolutionary Evaluations for Transformative Approaches (MEETA 2025)

Workshop Organizers

Maria Cerreta	University of Naples Federico II, Italy
Giuliano Poli	University of Naples Federico II, Italy
Maria Somma	University of Naples Federico II, Italy
Gaia Daldanise	CNR IRISS, Italy
Ludovica La Rocca	University of Naples Federico II, Italy

Workshop Program Committee Members

Maria Cerreta	University of Naples Federico II, Italy
Giuliano Poli	University of Naples Federico II, Italy
Maria Somma	University of Naples Federico II, Italy
Laura Di Tommaso	University of Naples Federico II, Italy
Sabrina Sacco	Politecnico di Milano, Italy
Piero Zizzania	University of Naples Federico II, Italy
Gaia Daldanise	CNR IRISS, Italy
Benedetta Grieco	University of Naples Federico II, Italy
Giuseppe Ciciriello	University of Naples Federico II, Italy
Marta Dell'Ovo	Politecnico di Milano, Italy
Daniele Cannatella	TU Delft, The Netherlands
Eugenio Muccio	University of Naples Federico II, Italy
Francesco Piras	University of Cagliari, Italy
Diana Rolando	Politecnico di Torino, Italy
Sveva Ventre	University of Naples Federico II, Italy
Caterina Loffredo	University of Naples Federico II, Italy
Ludovica La Rocca	University of Naples Federico II, Italy
Simona Panaro	University of Campania Luigi Vanvitelli, Italy

Building Multi-dimensional Models for Assessing Complex Environmental Systems (MES 2025)

Workshop Organizers

Vanessa Assumma	University of Bologna, Italy
Caterina Caprioli	Politecnico di Torino, Italy
Giulia Datola	Politecnico di Milano, Italy
Federico Dell'Anna	University of Bologna, Italy
Marta Dell'Ovo	Politecnico di Milano, Italy
Marco Rossitti	Politecnico di Milano, Italy

Workshop Program Committee Members

Vanessa Assumma	Università di Bologna, Bologna
Caterina Caprioli	Politecnico di Torino, Italy
Giulia Datola	DAStU Politecnico di Milano, Italy
Federico Dell'Anna	Politecnico di Torino, Italy
Marta Dell'Ovo	Politecnico di Milano, Italy
Marco Rossitti	Politecnico di Milano, Italy
Francesca Torrieri	Politecnico di Milano, Italy
Mariarosaria Angrisano	Università Telematica Pegaso, Italy
Maksims Feofilovs	Riga Technical University, Latvia

Danny Caprini	Politecnico di Milano, Italy
Giulio Cavana	Politecnico di Torino, Italy
Sebastiano Barbieri	Politecnico di Torino, Italy
Marta Bottero	Politecnico di Torino, Italy
Francesco Cosentino	Politecnico di Milano, Italy
Silvia Ronchi	Politecnico di Milano, Italy
Chiara Mazzarella	TU Delft, Netherlands
Marco Volpatti	Politecnico di Torino, Italy
Chiara D'Alpaos	Università degli Studi di Padova, Italy
Alessandra Oppio	Politecnico di Milano, Italy
Alessia Crisopulli	Politecnico di Milano, Italy
Domenico D'Uva	Politecnico di Milano, Italy
Giorgia Malavasi	Politecnico di Torino, Italy
Rubina Canesi	Università degli Studi di Padova, Italy
Elena Todella	Politecnico di Torino, Italy
Beatrice Mecca	Politecnico di Torino, Italy
Giulia Marzani	University of Bologna, Italy
Isabella Giovanetti	University of Bologna, Italy
Lucia Petronio	University of Bologna, Italy
Franco Corti	University of Padova, Italy
Salvatore De Pascalis	Politecnico di Milano, Italy
Valeria Vitulano	Politecnico di Torino, Italy
Lorenzo Diana	Università degli studi di Napoli Federico II, Italy
Maksims Feofilovs	Riga Technical University, Latvia
Marco De Luca	Politecnico di Torino, Italy
Ilaria Cazzola	Politecnico di Torino, Italy
Andrea De Toni	Politecnico di Milano, Italy
Eugenio Muccio	University of Naples Federico II, Italy
Giuliano Poli	University of Naples Federico II, Italy
Francesco Sica	University "La Sapienza" of Rome, Italy
Elena Di Pirro	Università degli Studi del Molise, Italy
Riccardo Alba	Università di Torino, Italy
Irene Regaiolo	Università di Torino, Italy
Francesca Cochis	Università di Torino, Italy

Modelling Liveable Cities: Techniques, Methods, Challenges, and Perspectives Behind the 'X-Minute' City (MLC 2025)

Workshop Organizers

Federico Mara	University of Pisa, Italy
Valerio Cutini	University of Pisa, Italy
Alessandro Araldi	Université Côte d'Azur, France

Flávia Lopes — Chalmers University of Technology, Sweden
Giovanni Fusco — Université Côte d'Azur, France

Workshop Program Committee Members

Simone Rusci	University of Pisa, Italy
Lorena Fiorini	University of L'Aquila, Italy
Chiara Di Dato	University of L'Aquila, Italy
Francesco Zullo	University of L'Aquila, Italy
Alfonso Annunziata	University of Basilicata, Italy
Beniamino Murgante	University of Basilicata, Italy
Alessandro Araldi	Universitè Côte d'Azur, France
Chiara Garau	University of Cagliari, Italy
Giampiero Lombardini	Università di Genova, Italy
Flavia Lopes	Chalmers University of Technology, Sweden
Giovanni Fusco	Universitè Côte d'Azur, France

Mathematical Methods for Image Processing and Understanding 2025 (MMIPU 2025)

Workshop Organizers

Ivan Gerace	Università degli Studi di Perugia, Italy
Gianluca Vinti	Università degli Studi di Perugia, Italy
Arianna Travaglini	Università degli Studi della Basilicata, Italy

Workshop Program Committee Members

Ivan Gerace	University of Perugia, Italy
Gianluca Vinti	University of Perugia, Italy
Arianna Travaglini	University of Basilicata, Italy
Marco Baioletti	University of Perugia, Italy
Marco Donatelli	University of Insubria, Italy
Anna Tonazzini	C.N.R. Pisa, Italy
Muhammad Hanif	Ghulam Ishaq Khan Institute of Engineering Sciences and Technology, Pakistan
Francesco Marchetti	University of Padua, Italy
Wolfgang Erb	University of Padua, Italy
Danilo Costarelli	University of Perugia, Italy
Francesco Santini	University of Perugia, Italy
Valentina Giorgetti	University of Perugia, Italy

Mobility Opportunities Bridging Inequalities: Social Inclusion and Gender Equity Initiatives Strategies Against Fragmentation and Complexity of Mobility (MOBIL-EGI 2025)

Workshop Organizers

Tiziana Campisi	University of Enna Kore, Italy
Guilhermina Torrao	Aston University, UK
Socrates Basbas	Aristotle University of Thessaloniki, Greece
Tanja Congiu	University of Sassari, Italy
Stefanos Tsigdinos	National Technical University of Athens, Greece
Florin Nemtanu	Politehnica University of Bucharest, Romania

Workshop Program Committee Members

Massimo Di Gangi	University of Messina, Italy
Orlando Marco Belcore	University of Messina, Italy
Francesco Russo	Mediterranean University of Reggio Calabria, Italy
Alexandros Nikitas	University of Huddersfield, UK
Marilisa Nigro	Rome Tre University, Italy
Kh Md Nahiduzzaman	Mohammed VI Polytechnic University, Morocco
Efstathios Bouhouras	Aristotle University of Thessaloniki, Greece
Antonio Comi	University of Rome Tor Vergata, Italy
Edouard Ivanjko	University of Zagreb, Slovenia
Osvaldo Gervasi	University of Perugia, Italy
Beniamino Murgante	University of Basilicata, Italy
Chiara Garau	University of Cagliari, Italy

MOdels and indicators for assessing and measuring the urban settlement deVElopment in the view of NET ZERO by 2050 (MOVEto0 2025)

Workshop Organizers

Lorena Fiorini	University of L'Aquila, Italy
Lucia Saganeiti	CNR-IMAA, Italy
Angela Pilogallo	CNR-IMAA, Italy
Alessandro Marucci	University of L'Aquila, Italy
Francesco Zullo	University of L'Aquila, Italy

Workshop Program Committee Members

Ginevra Balletto	University of Cagliari, Italy
Giuseppe Borruso	University of Trieste, Italy
Chiara Garau	University of Cagliari, Italy

Beniamino Murgante	University of Basilicata, Italy
Giulia Desogus	University of Cagliari, Italy
Ljiljana Zivkovic	Republic Geodetic Authority, Serbia
Luigi Santopietro	University of Basilicata, Italy
Ilaria Delponte	University of Genoa, Italy
Carmen Guida	University of Naples Federico II, Italy
Chiara Di Dato	University of L'Aquila, Italy

5th Workshop on Privacy in the Cloud/Edge/IoT World (PCEIoT 2025)

Workshop Organizers

Lelio Campanile	Università degli Studi della Campania Luigi Vanvitelli, Italy
Mauro Iacono	Università degli Studi della Campania Luigi Vanvitelli, Italy
Michele Mastroianni	Università degli Studi di Foggia, Italy

Workshop Program Committee Members

Arcangelo Castiglione	Università degli Studi di Salerno, Italy
Maria Ganzha	Warsaw University of Technology, Poland
Daniel Grzonka	Cracow University of Technology, Poland
Antonio Iannuzzi	Università degli Studi Roma Tre, Italy
Armando Tacchella	Università degli Studi di Genova, Italy
Biagio Boi	University of Salerno, Italy
Marco De Santis	University of Salerno, Italy
Fiammetta Marulli	Università degli Studi della Campania "L. Vanvitelli", Italy
Christian Riccio	Università degli Studi della Campania "L. Vanvitelli", Italy
Luigi Piero Di Bonito	Università degli Studi di Napoli Federico II, Italy

Preserving Our Past: Spatial and Remote Sensing Technologies for Cultural Heritage in a Changing Climate (POP 2025)

Workshop Organizers

Maria Danese	CNR-ISPC, Italy
Nicola Masini	CNR-ISPC, Italy
Rosa Lasaponara	CNR-IMAA, Italy

Workshop Program Committee Members

Maria Danese	CNR-ISPC, Italy
Nicola Masini	CNR-ISPC, Italy
Rosa Lasaponara	CNR-IMAA, Italy
Dario Gioia	CNR-ISPC, Italy
Giuseppe Corrado	Università degli Studi della Basilicata, Italy
Canio Sabia	CNR-ISPC, Italy

Processes, methods and tools towards RESilient cities and cultural and historic sites prone to SOD and ROD disasters (RES 2025)

Workshop Organizers

Elena Cantatore	Polytechnic University of Bari, Italy
Dario Esposito	Polytechnic University of Bari, Italy
Alberico Sonnessa	Polytechnic University of Bari, Italy

Workshop Program Committee Members

Elena Cantatore	Politecnico di Bari, Italy
Dario Esposito	Politecnico di Bari, Italy
Alberico Sonnessa	Politecnico di Bari, Italy
Valeria Belloni	Sapienza University of Rome, Italy
Michela Ravanelli	Sapienza University of Rome, Italy
Silvano Dal Sasso	University of Basilicata, Italy
Francesco Chiaravalloti	CNR - IRPI, Italy
Roberta Ravanelli	University of Liège, Belgium
Alessandra Mascitelli	University of Chieti-Pescara, Italy
Francesco Di Capua	University of Basilicata, Italy
Gabriele Bernardini	Università Politecnica delle Marche, Italy
Vito Domenico Porcari	University of Basilicata, Italy
Carmen Rosa Fattore	University of Basilicata, Italy
Stefania Santoro	Water Research Institute, Italy

Scientific Computing Infrastructure (SCI 2025)

Workshop Organizers

Vladimir Korkhov	Saint Petersburg State University, Russia
Elena Stankova	Saint Petersburg State University, Russia
Nataliia Kulabukhova	Saint Petersburg State University, Russia

Workshop Program Committee Members

Adam Belloum	University of Amsterdam, the Netherlands
Dmitrii Vasiunin	Deutsche Telekom Cloud Services E.P.E., Greece
Serob Balyan	Osensus Arm LLC, Armenia
Suren Abrahamyan	Osensus Arm LLC, Armenia
Ashot Sergey Gevorkyan	NAS of Armenia, Armenia
Michal Hnatic	Univerzita Pavla Jozefa Šafárika v Košiciach, Slovakia
Michail Panteleyev	Saint Petersburg Electrotecnical University, Russia
Martin Vala	Univerzita Pavla Jozefa Šafárika v Košiciach, Slovakia
Nodir Zaynalov	Tashkent University of Information Technologies named after Muhammad al Khwarizmi, Uzbekistan
Michail Panteleyev	Saint Petersburg Electrotecnical University, Russia
Alexander Degtyarev	Saint Petersburg University, Russia
Alexander Bogdanov	St. Petersburg State University, Russia

Ports and Logistics of the Future - Smartness and Sustainability (SmartPorts 2025)

Workshop Organizers

Andrea Gallo	Università degli Studi di Trieste, Italy
Gianfranco Fancello	University of Cagliari, Italy
Giuseppe Borruso	Università degli Studi di Trieste, Italy
Enrico D'agostini	World Maritime University, Sweden
Silvia Battino	Università degli Studi di Sassari, Italy
Veronica Camerada	Università degli Studi di Sassari, Italy

Workshop Program Committee Members

Giuseppe Borruso	University of Trieste, Italy
Beniamino Murgante	University of Basilicata, Italy
Ginevra Balletto	University of Cagliari, Italy
Silvia Battino	University of Sassari, Italy
Mara Ladu	University of Cagliari, Italy
Maria del Mar Munoz Leonisio	University of Cádiz, Spain
Ahinoa Amaro Garcia	University of Las Palmas of Gran Canaria, Spain
Maria Attard	University of Malta, Malta
Enrico D'agostini	World Maritime University, Sweden
Francesca Krasna	University of Trieste, Italy

Tu Anh Trinh	UEH University - Ho Chi Minh City, Vietnam
Giovanni Mauro	Università degli Studi della Campania, Italy
Maria Ronza	University of Naples Federico II, Italy
Massimiliano Bencardino	University of Salerno, Italy
Andrea Gallo	Ca' Foscari University of Venice, Italy
Francesca Sinatra	University of Trieste, Italy
Salvatore Dore	University of Trieste, Italy
Veronica Camerada	University of Sassari, Italy
Brunella Brundu	University of Sassari, Italy
Gianfranco Fancello	University of Cagliari, Italy
Marcello Tadini	University of Eastern Piedmont, Italy
Marco Mazzarino	IUAV University Venice
José Ángel Hernández Luis	University of Las Palmas de Gran Canaria, Spain
Marco Naseddu	University of Cagliari, Italy
Maurizio Cociancich	Adriafer, Italy
Giovanni Longo	University of Trieste, Italy
Luca Toneatti	University of Trieste, Italy
Martina Sinatra	University of Cagliari, Italy
Enrico Vanino	University of Sheffield, UK
Patrizia Serra	University of Cagliari, Italy
Agostino Bruzzone	University of Genoa, Italy
Marco Petrelli	University of Roma 3, Italy

Smart Transport and Logistics - Smart Supply Chains (SmarTransLog 2025)

Workshop Organizers

Francesca Sinatra	University of Trieste, Italy
Maria del Mar Munoz	Universidad de Cádiz, Spain
Brunella Brundu	University of Sassari, Italy
Patrizia Serra	University of Cagliari, Italy
Salvatore Dore	University of Trieste, Italy
Marco Naseddu	University of Cagliari, Italy

Workshop Program Committee Members

Giuseppe Borruso	University of Trieste, Italy
Beniamino Murgante	University of Basilicata, Italy
Ginevra Balletto	University of Cagliari, Italy
Silvia Battino	University of Sassari, Italy
Mara Ladu	University of Cagliari, Italy
Maria del Mar Munoz Leonisio	University of Cádiz, Spain
Ahinoa Amaro Garcia	University of Las Palmas of Gran Canaria, Spain

Maria Attard	University of Malta, Malta
Enrico D'agostini	World Maritime University, Sweden
Francesca Krasna	University of Trieste, Italy
Tu Anh Trinh	UEH University, Vietnam
Giovanni Mauro	Università degli Studi della Campania, Italy
Maria Ronza	University of Naples Federico II, Italy
Massimiliano Bencardino	University of Salerno, Italy
Andrea Gallo	Ca' Foscari University of Venice, Italy
Francesca Sinatra	University of Trieste, Italy
Salvatore Dore	University of Trieste, Italy
Veronica Camerada	University of Sassari, Italy
Brunella Brundu	University of Sassari, Italy
Gianfranco Fancello	University of Cagliari, Italy
Marcello Tadini	University of Eastern Piedmont, Italy
Marco Mazzarino	IUAV University Venice
José Ángel Hernández Luis	University of Las Palmas de Gran Canaria, Spain
Marco Naseddu	University of Cagliari, Italy
Maurizio Cociancich	Adriafer, Italy
Giovanni Longo	University of Trieste, Italy
Luca Toneatti	University of Trieste, Italy
Martina Sinatra	University of Cagliari, Italy
Enrico Vanino	University of Sheffield, UK
Patrizia Serra	University of Cagliari, Italy
Agostino Bruzzone	University of Genoa, Italy
Marco Petrelli	University of Roma 3, Italy

Smart Tourism (SmartTourism 2025)

Workshop Organizers

Silvia Battino	University of Sassari, Italy
Francesca Krasna	University of Trieste, Italy
Ainhoa Amaro	University of Las Palmas de Gran Canaria, Spain
Maria del Mar Munoz	University of Cádiz, Spain
Brisol García García	Polytechnic University of Quintana Roo, Mexico
Marta Meleddu	University of Sassari, Italy

Workshop Program Committee Members

Giuseppe Borruso	University of Trieste, Italy
Beniamino Murgante	University of Basilicata, Italy
Gianfranco Fancello	University of Cagliari, Italy
Mara Ladu	University of Cagliari, Italy

Martina Sinatra	University of Cagliari, Italy
Salvatore Dore	University of Trieste, Italy
Marco Mazzarino	IUAV University Venice, Italy
Veronica Camerada	University of Sassari, Italy
Brunella Brundu	University of Sassari, Italy
Maria Attard	University of Malta, Malta
Ginevra Balletto	University of Cagliari, Italy
Giovanni Mauro	University degli Studi della Campania, Italy
Salvatore Lampreu	University of Sassari, Italy
Maria Ronza	University of Naples, Italy
Massimiliano Bencardino	University of Salerno, Italy

Sustainable evolution of long-Distance frEight and paSsenger Transport (SOLIDEST 2025)

Workshop Organizers

Francesco Russo	University of Reggio Calabria, Italy
Andreas Nikiforiadis	Democritus University of Thrace, Greece
Orlando Marco Belcore	University of Messina, Italy
Antonio Comi	University of Rome Tor Vergata, Italy
Tiziana Campisi	Kore University of Enna, Italy
Aura Rusca	Politehnica University of Bucharest, Romania

Workshop Program Committee Members

Massimo Di Gangi	University of Messina, Italy
Orlando Marco Belcore	University of Messina, Italy
Antonio Polimeni	University of Messina, Italy
Socrates Basbas	Aristotle University of Thessaloniki, Greece
Efstathios Bouhouras	Aristotle University of Thessaloniki, Greece
Marina Zanne	University of Lubljana, Slovenia
Marilisa Nigro	Rome Tre University, Italy
Edoardo Marcucci	Molde University College, Norway
Eugen Rosca	Polytechnic University of Bucharest, Romania
Kh Md Nahiduzzaman	Mohammed VI Polytechnic University, Morocco
Beniamino Murgante	University of Basilicata, Italy
Chiara Garau	University of Cagliari, Italy

Sustainability Performance Assessment: Models, Approaches, and Applications Toward Interdisciplinary and Integrated Solutions (SPA 2025)

Workshop Organizers

Francesco Scorza	University of Basilicata, Italy
Sabrina Lai	University of Cagliari, Italy
Francesco Rotondo	Università Politecnica delle Marche, Italy
Jolanta Dvarioniene	Kaunas University of Technology, Lithuania
Michele Campagna	University of Cagliari, Italy
Corrado Zoppi	University of Cagliari, Italy

Workshop Program Committee Members

Federico Amato	University of Lausanne, Switzerland
Ferdinando Di Carlo	University of Basilicata, Italy
Maddalena Floris	University of Cagliari, Italy
Federica Isola	University of Cagliari, Italy
Giuseppe Las Casas	University of Basilicata, Italy
Federica Leone	University of Cagliari, Italy
Giampiero Lombardini	University of Genoa, Italy
Federico Martellozzo	University of Florence, Italy
Alessandro Marucci	University of L'Aquila, Italy
Ana Clara Moura	Universidade Federal de Minas Gerais, Brazil
Beniamino Murgante	University of Basilicata, Italy
Silviu Nate	Lucian Blaga University of Sibiu, Romania
Anastasia Stratigea	National Technical University of Athens, Greece
Francesco Zullo	University of L'Aquila, Italy
Luigi Santopietro	University of Basilicata, Italy
Benedetto Manganelli	University of Basilicata, Italy

Specifics of Smart Cities Development in Europe (SPEED 2025)

Workshop Organizers

Chiara Garau	University of Cagliari, Italy
Katarína Vitálišová	Matej Bel University, Slovak Republic
Marco Fanfani	University of Florence, Italy
Anna Vaňová	Matej Bel University, Slovak Republic
Kamila Borsekova	Matej Bel University, Slovak Republic
Paola Zamperlin	University of Florence, Italy

Workshop Program Committee Members

Claudia Loggia	University of KwaZulu-Natal, South Africa
Francesca Maltinti	University of Cagliari, Italy
Alessandro Plaisant	University of Sassari, Italy
Alenka Poplin	Iowa State University, USA
Silvia Rossetti	University of Parma, Italy
Gerardo Carpentieri	University of Naples Federico II, Italy
Carmen Guida	University of Naples Federico II, Italy
Floriana Zucaro	University of Naples Federico II, Italy
Anastasia Stratigea	National Technical University of Athens, Greece
Yiota Theodora	National Technical University of Athens, Greece
Giovanna Concu	University of Cagliari, Italy
Paolo Nesi	University of Florence, Italy
Emanuele Bellini	University of Roma Tre, Italy
Mana Dastoum	Polytechnic University of Madrid, Spain
Barbara Caselli	University of Parma, Italy
Martina Carra	University of Brescia, Italy
Alfonso Annunziata	University of Basilicata, Italy
Elisabetta Venco	University of Pavia, Italy
Caterina Pietra	University of Pavia, Italy
Enrico Collini	University of Florence, Italy
Luciano Alessandro Ipsaro Palesi	University of Florence, Italy

Smart, Safe, and Healthy Cities (SSHC 2025)

Workshop Organizers

Chiara Garau	University of Cagliari, Italy
Gerardo Carpentieri	University of Naples Federico II, Italy
Carmen Guida	University of Naples Federico II, Italy
Tanja Congiu	University of Sassari, Italy
Martina Carra	University of Brescia, Italy
Alenka Poplin	Iowa State University, USA

Workshop Program Committee Members

Rosaria Battarra	Istituto di Studi sul Mediterraneo, Italy
Barbara Caselli	University of Parma, Italy
Francesca Maltinti	University of Cagliari, Italy
Romano Fistola	Università degli Studi di Napoli Federico II, Italy
Alessandro Plaisant	University of Sassari, Italy
Silvia Rossetti	University of Parma, Italy
Marco Fanfani	University of Florence, Italy
Reza Askarizad	University of Cagliari, Italy

Floriana Zucaro   University of Naples Federico II, Italy
Anastasia Stratigea   National Technical University of Athens, Greece
Yiota Theodora   National Technical University of Athens, Greece
Giovanna Concu   University of Cagliari, Italy
Francesco Zullo   University of L'Aquila, Italy
Paola Zamperlin   University of Florence, Italy
Vincenza Torrisi   University of Catania, Italy
Tiziana Campisi   University of Enna Kore, Italy
Katarína Vitálišová   Matej Bel University, Slovakia
Tazyeen Alam   University of Cagliari, Italy
Mana Dastoum   Polytechnic University of Madrid, Spain
Martina Carra   University of Brescia, Italy
Alfonso Annunziata   University of Basilicata, Italy
Elisabetta Venco   University of Pavia, Italy
Caterina Pietra   University of Pavia, Italy

Smart and Sustainable Island Communities (SSIC 2025)

Workshop Organizers
Chiara Garau   University of Cagliari, Italy
Anastasia Stratigea   National Technical University of Athens, Greece
Yiota Theodora   National Technical University of Athens, Greece
Giovanna Concu   University of Cagliari, Italy

Workshop Program Committee Members
Milena Metalkova-Markova   University of Portsmouth, UK
Tarek Teba   University of Portsmouth, UK
Alenka Poplin   Iowa State University, USA
Gerardo Carpentieri   University of Naples Federico II, Italy
Carmen Guida   University of Naples Federico II, Italy
Floriana Zucaro   University of Naples Federico II, Italy
Silvia Rossetti   University of Parma, Italy
Barbara Caselli   University of Parma, Italy
Martina Carra   University of Brescia, Italy
Alfonso Annunziata   University of Basilicata, Italy
Maria Panagiotopoulou   National Technical University of Athens, Greece
Apostolos Lagarias   University of Thessaly, Greece
Paola Zamperlin   University of Florence, Italy
Vincenza Torrisi   University of Catania, Italy
Giuseppina Vacca   University of Cagliari, Italy
Roberto Minunno   Curtin University, Australia
Marco Zucca   University of Cagliari, Italy

Elisabetta Venco	University of Pavia, Italy
Caterina Pietra	University of Pavia, Italy
Pietro Crespi	Politecnico di Milano, Italy

From STreet Experiments to Planned Solutions (STEPS 2025)

Workshop Organizers

Silvia Rossetti	Università degli Studi di Parma, Italy
Angela Ricciardello	Kore University of Enna, Italy
Francesco Pinna	Università degli Studi di Cagliari, Italy
Chiara Garau	Università degli Studi di Cagliari, Italy
Tiziana Campisi	Kore University of Enna, Italy
Vincenza Torrisi	University of Catania, Italy

Workshop Program Committee Members

Martina Carra	University of Brescia, Italy
Barbara Caselli	University of Parma, Italy
Tanja Congiu	University of Sassari, Italy
Gabriele D'Orso	University of Palermo, Italy
Matteo Ignaccolo	University of Catania, Italy
Md Kh Nahiduzzaman	Mohammed VI Polytechnic University, Morocco
Muhammad Ahmad Al-Rashid	University of Malaya, Malaysia
Alessandro Plaisant	University of Sassari, Italy
Marianna Ruggieri	University of Enna Kore, Italy
Michele Zazzi	University of Parma, Italy

Sustainable Tourism Evaluations: approaches, methods and indicators (STEva 2025)

Workshop Organizers

Mariolina Grasso	Università Kore di Enna, Italy
Fabrizio Finucci	Roma Tre University, Italy
Daniele Mazzoni	Roma Tre University, Italy
Antonella G. Masanotti	Roma Tre University, Italy
Giovanna Acampa	University of Florence, Italy

Workshop Program Committee Members

Giovanna Acampa	University of Florence, Italy
Fabrizio Finucci	Roma Tre University, Italy
Mariolina Grasso	"Kore" University of Enna, Italy

Alberto Marzo	Ministero della Cultura, Italy
Antonella G. Masanotti	Roma Tre University, Italy
Daniele Mazzoni	Roma Tre University, Italy
Rocco Murro	Sapienza University of Rome, Italy
Claudio Piferi	University of Florence, Italy
Alessio Pino	"Kore" University of Enna, Italy
Nicoletta Setola	University of Florence, Italy
Laura Calcagnini	Roma Tre University, Italy
Antonio Magarò	Roma Tre University, Italy
Janos Ghyerghyak	University of Pécs, Hungary
Ágnes Borsos	University of Pécs, Hungary
Fabrizio Battisti	University of Florence, Italy

Sustainable Development of Ports (SUSTAINABLEPORTS 2025)

Workshop Organizers

Tiziana Campisi	University of Enna KORE, Italy
Giuseppe Musolino	University of Reggio Calabria, Italy
Efstathios Bouhouras	Aristotle University of Thessaloniki, Greece
Elen Twrdy	University of Ljubljana, Slovenia
Elena Cocuzza	University of Catania, Italy
Aura Rusca	Politehnica University of Bucharest, Romania

Workshop Program Committee Members

Massimo Di Gangi	University of Messina, Italy
Orlando Marco Belcore	University of Messina, Italy
Antonio Polimeni	University of Messina, Italy
Claudia Caballini	Polytechnic of Torino, Italy
Gianfranco Fancello	University of Cagliari, Italy
Marina Zanne	University of Lubljana, Slovenia
Stefano Ricci	Sapienza University of Rome, Italy
Beniamino Murgante	University of Basilicata, Italy
Chiara Garau	University of Cagliari, Italy

Theoretical and Computational Chemistry and Its Applications (TCCMA 2025)

Workshop Organizers

Noelia Faginas Lago	Università di Perugia, Italy
Andrea Lombardi	Università di Perugia, Italy
Marcos Mandado Alonso	University of Vigo, Spain

Workshop Program Committee Members

Noelia Faginas-Lago	University of Perugia, Italy
Andrea Lombardi	University of Perugia, Italy
Marcos Mandado	University of Vigo, Spain
Angeles Peña	University of Vigo, Spain
Luca Mancini	Universiy of Perugia, Italy
Massimiliano Bartolomei	CSIC, Spain
Cecilia Coletti	University of Chieti-Pescara, Italy
Iñaki Tuñón	Universidad de Valencia, Spain
Albert Rimola Gilbert	Universitat Autònoma de Barcelona, Spain
Stefano Falcinelli	University of Perugia, Italy
Dario Campisi	University of Perugia, Italy
Ernesto García Para	University of the Basque Country, Spain
Giacomo Giorgi	University of Perugia, Italy
Tomás González Lezana	IFF CSIC, Spain
Enrique M. Cabaleiro Lago	Universidade de Santiago de Compostela, Spain
Aurora Costales	Universidad de Oviedo, Spain
Angel Martin	Universidad de Oviedo, Spain
Jose Manuel	University of Vigo, Spain
Annarita Laricchiuta	CNR ISTP Bari, Italy
Fernando Pirani	University of Perugia, Italy

Transport Infrastructures for Smart Cities (TISC 2025)

Workshop Organizers

Francesca Maltinti	University of Cagliari, Italy
Mauro Coni	University of Cagliari, Italy
Benedetto Barabino	University of Brescia, Italy
Nicoletta Rassu	University of Cagliari, Italy
James Rombi	University of Cagliari, Italy

Workshop Program Committee Members

Francesco Pinna	University of Cagliari, Italy
Chiara Garau	University of Cagliari, Italy
Mauro D'Apuzzo	University of Cassino, Italy
Roberto Minunno	Curtin University, Australia
Tiziana Campisi	University of Enna Kore, Italy
Roberto Ventura	University of Brescia, Italy
Alessandro Plaisant	University of Sassari, Italy
Massimo Di Francesco	University of Cagliari, Italy

Vincenza Torrisi University of Catania, Italy
Paola Zamperlin University of Florence, Italy

Transforming Urban Analytics: The Impact of Crowdsourced Mapping and Advanced AI Techniques on Future Cities (Tr-UrbAna 2025)

Workshop Organizers
Ayse Giz Gulnerman Gengec Ankara Hacı Bayram Veli University, Turkey
Müslüm Hacar Tildiz Technical University, Turkey
Himmet Karaman Istanbul Technical University, Turkey

Workshop Program Committee Members
Beniamino Murgante University of Basilicata, Italy
Abdulkadir Memduhoğlu Harran University, Turkey
Zeynel Abidin Polat İzmir Katip Çelebi University, Turkey
Güzide Miray Perihanoğlu Van Yüzüncü Yıl University, Turkey
Tugba Memisoglu Baykal Ankara Hacı Bayram Veli University, Turkey

From structural to TRAnsformative-change of City Environment: challenges and solutions and perspectives (TRACE 2025)

Workshop Organizers
Pierluigi Morano Polytechnic University of Bari, Italy
Maria Rosaria Guarini Sapienza University of Rome, Italy
Francesco Sica Sapienza University of Rome, Italy
Francesco Tajani Sapienza University of Rome, Italy
Marco Locurcio Polytechnic University of Bari, Italy
Debora Anelli Polytechnic University of Bari, Italy

Workshop Program Committee Members
Felicia di Liddo Politecnico di Bari, Italia
Valeria Saiu Università di Cagliari, Italia
Emma Sabatelli Sapienza Università di Roma, Italia
Antonella Roma Sapienza Università di Roma, Italia
Giuseppe Cerullo Sapienza Università di Roma, Italia
Lucia della Spina Università di Reggio Calabria, Italia
Alejandro Segura de la Cal Politecnico di Madrid, Spain
Yilsy Nuñez Politecnico di Madrid, Spain
Gabriella Maselli Università di Salerno, Italy
Maria Rosa Trovato Università di Catania, Italy

Manuela Rebaudengo	Politecnico di Torino, Italy
Pierfrancesco De Paola	Università di Napoli Federico II, Italy
Daniela Tavano	Università della Calabria, Italy
Maria Saez	University of Granada, Spain
Paola Amoruso	LUM "Giuseppe Degennaro" University, Italy

Temporary Real Estate management: Approaches and methods for Time-integrated impact assessments and evaluations (TREAT 2025)

Workshop Organizers

Chiara Mazzarella	TUDelft, The Netherlands
Hilde Remoy	TUDelft, The Netherlands
Maria Cerreta	University of Naples Federico II, Italy

Workshop Program Committee Members

Chiara Mazzarella	TU Delft, The Netherlands
Hilde Remoy	TU Delft, The Netherlands
Maria Cerreta	University of Naples Federico II, Italy
Maria Somma	University of Naples Federico II, Italy
Simona Panaro	University of Campania Luigi Vanvitelli, Italy
Laura Di Tommaso	University of Naples Federico II, Italy
Caterina Loffredo	University of Naples Federico II, Italy
Ludovica La Rocca	University of Naples Federico II, Italy
Sabrina Sacco	Politecnico di Milano, Italy
Piero Zizzania	University of Naples Federico II, Italy
Gaia Daldanise	CNR IRISS, Italy
Benedetta Grieco	University of Naples Federico II, Italy
Giuseppe Ciciriello	University of Naples Federico II, Italy
Marta Dell'Ovo	Politecnico di Milano, Italy
Daniele Cannatella	TU Delft, The Netherlands
Eugenio Muccio	University of Naples Federico II, Italy
Sveva Ventre	University of Naples Federico II, Italy

Supporting the Transition to Ecological Economy in Cities Regeneration: Circular Model Tools for Reusing Architecture and Infrastructures (TReE 2025)

Workshop Organizers

Mariarosaria Angrisano	Pegaso University, Italy
Giulio Cavana	Politecnico di Torino, Italy
Francesca Buglione	CNR-ISPC, Italy

Antonia Gravagnuolo	CNR-ISPC, Italy
Piera Della Morte	Pegaso University, Italy

Workshop Program Committee Members

Giulia Datola	Politecnico di Milano, Italy
Vanessa Assumma	University of Bologna, Italy
Marco Volpatti	Politecnico di Torino, Italy
Sebastiano Barbieri	Politecnico di Torino, Italy
Caterina Caprioli	Politecnico di Torino, Italy
Marta Dell'Ovo	Politecnico di Milano, Italy
Federico Dell'Anna	Politecnico di Torino, Italy
Elena Todella	Politecnico di Torino, Italy
Danny Casprini	Politecnico di Milano, Italy
Grazia Neglia	Università Telematica Pegaso, Italy
Francesca Nocca	Università degli Studi di Napoli Federico II, Italy
Giulio Cavana	Politecnico di Torino, Italy
Francesca Buglione	CNR-IPSC, Italy
Marco Rossitti	Politecnico di Milano, Italy
Jhon Escorcia	Politecnico di Torino, Italy
Beatrice Mecca	Politecnico di Torino, Italy
Sara Biancifiori	Politecnico di Torino, Italy

Urban Digital Twins and Data Spaces: Shaping the Future of Sustainable Cities (TwinAbleCities 2025)

Workshop Organizers

Dessislava Petrova Antonova	Sofia University, GATE Institute, Bulgaria
Beniamino Murgante	University of Basilicata, Italy
Senthil Rajendran	RMSI, Bahrain
Tiziana Campisi	Kore University of Enna, Italy
Mila Koeva	University of Twente, The Netherlands

Workshop Program Committee Members

Dessislava Petrova-Antonova	Sofia University, Bulgaria
Mila Koeva	The University of Twente, The Netherlands
Beniamino Murgante	University of Basilicata, Italy
Senthil Rajendran	RMSI, Bahrain
Tiziana Campisi	Kore University of Enna, Italy

Urban Regeneration: Innovative Tools and Evaluation Model (URITEM 2025)

Workshop Organizers

Fabrizio Battisti	University of Florence, Italy
Giovanna Acampa	University of Florence, Italy
Orazio Campo	Sapienza University of Rome, Italy
Melania Perdonò	University of Florence, Italy

Workshop Program Committee Members

Fabrizio Battisti	University of Florence, Italy
Giovanna Acampa	University of Florence, Italy
Orazio Campo	University of Rome "La Sapienza", Italy
Melania Perdonò	Università degli Studi di Firenze, Italy

Urban Space Accessibility and Mobilities (USAM 2025)

Workshop Organizers

Chiara Garau	DICAAR, University of Cagliari, Italy
Alessandro Plaisant	University of Sassari, Italy
Barbara Caselli	University of Parma, Italy
Mauro D'Apuzzo	University of Cassino and Southern Lazio, Italy
Gabriele D'Orso	University of Palermo, Italy
Matteo Ignaccolo	University of Catania, Italy

Workshop Program Committee Members

Mauro Coni	University of Cagliari, Italy
Martina Carra	University of Brescia, Italy
Tiziana Campisi	University of Enna Kore, Italy
Tanja Congiu	University of Sassari, Italy
Francesca Maltinti	University of Cagliari, Italy
Silvia Rossetti	University of Parma, Italy
Barbara Caselli	University of Parma, Italy
Angela Pilogallo	University of L'Aquila, Italy
Lorena Fiorini	University of L'Aquila, Italy
Reza Askarizad	University of Cagliari, Italy
Francesco Pinna	University of Cagliari, Italy
Aime Tsinda	University of Rwanda, Rwanda
Youssef El Ganadi	International University of Rabat, Morocco
Marco Migliore	University of Palermo, Italy
Alessio Salvatore	Italian National Research Council, Italy
Giuseppe Stecca	Italian National Research Council, Italy

Paola Zamperlin	University of Florence, Italy
Vincenza Torrisi	University of Catania, Italy
Gerardo Carpentieri	University of Naples Federico II, Italy
Carmen Guida	University of Naples Federico II, Italy
Floriana Zucaro	University of Naples Federico II, Italy
Alfonso Annunziata	University of Basilicata, Italy
Elisabetta Venco	University of Pavia, Italy
Caterina Pietra	University of Pavia, Italy
Tazyeen Alam	University of Cagliari, Italy
Valerio Cutini	University of Pisa, Italy

UX Mobility 2025: Placing User Experience at the Center of Urban Mobility: Methods and Frameworks (UXM 2025)

Workshop Organizers

Carmen Guida	Università degli Studi di Napoli Federico II, Italy
Gerardo Carpentieri	Università degli Studi di Napoli Federico II, Italy
Federico Messa	Systematica srl, Italy
Lamia Abdelfattah	Systematica srl, Italy

Workshop Program Committee Members

Rosaria Battarra	Istituto di Studi sul Mediterraneo CNR, Italy
Romano Fistola	Università degli Studi di Napoli Federico II, Italy
Lucia Saganeiti	IMAA-CNR, Italy

Virtual Reality and Augmented reality and applications (VRA 2025)

Workshop Organizers

Damiano Perri	University of Perugia, Italy
Osvaldo Gervasi	University of Perugia, Italy
Chau Ma Thi	University of Engineering and Technology, Vietnam National University, Hanoi, Vietnam
Paolo Nesi	University of Florence, Italy
Pierfrancesco Bellini	University of Florence, Italy

Workshop Program Committee Members

David Berti	ART SpA, Italy
JungYoon Kim	Gachon University, South Korea

TaiHoon Kim	Zhejiang University of Science and Technology, China
Marcelo de Paiva Guimares	Federal University of São Paulo, Brazil
Sergio Tasso	University of Perugia, Italy

Workshop on Advanced and Computational Methods for Earth Science Applications (WACM4ES 2025)

Workshop Organizers

Luca Piroddi	University of Cagliari, Italy
Patrizia Capizzi	University of Palermo, Italy
Marilena Cozzolino	University of Molise, Italy
Sebastiano D'Amico	University of Malta, Malta
Chiara Garau	University of Cagliari, Italy
Giuseppina Vacca	University of Cagliari, Italy

Workshop Program Committee Members

Andrea Angelini	CNR ISPC, Italy
Ilaria Barone	Università degli Studi di Padova, Italy
Patrizia Capizzi	University of Palermo, Italy
Luigi Capozzoli	CNR, Italy
Alberto Carletti	University of Cagliari, Italy
Emanuele Colica	University of Malta, Malta
Marilena Cozzolino	Università del Molise, Italy
Sebastiano D'Amico	University of Malta, Malta
Chiara Garau	University of Cagliari, Italy
Luciano Galone	University of Malta, Malta
Peter Iregbeyen	University of Malta, Malta
Mariano Lisi	Basilicata Aerospace Cluster CLAS, Italy
Raffaele Martorana	Università di Palermo, Italy
Paolo Mauriello	Università del Molise, Italy
Veronica Pazzi	University of Florence, Italy
Raffaele Persico	Università della Calabria, Italy
Luca Piroddi	University of Cagliari, Italy
Sina Saneiyan	Binghamton University, USA
Mercedes Solla	Universidade de Vigo, Spain
Deodato Tapete	ASI, Italy
Giuseppina Vacca	University of Cagliari, Italy
Enrica Vecchi	University of Cagliari, Italy

Sponsoring Organizations

ICCSA 2025 would not have been possible without the tremendous support of many organizations and institutions, for which all organizers and participants of ICCSA 2025 express their sincere gratitude:

Galatasaray University, Istanbul, Türkiye
(https://gsu.edu.tr/en)

African Mathematical Union
(https://www.africanmathunion.org/)

Springer Nature Switzerland AG, Switzerland
(https://www.springer.com)

The University of Massachusetts, USA
(https://www.umass.edu/)

University of Perugia, Italy
(https://www.unipg.it)

University of Basilicata, Italy
(http://www.unibas.it)

Monash University, Australia
(https://www.monash.edu/)

Kyushu Sangyo University, Japan
(https://www.kyusan-u.ac.jp/)

University of Minho, Portugal
(https://www.uminho.pt/)
Venue
ICCSA 2025 took place in: **Galatasaray University, Istanbul, Türkiye**

Additional Reviewers

Reviewers
The review tasks for each workshop have been carried out by the workshop Organizers and the members of the workshop Program Committee.

Plenary Lectures

Sky Safe with GAI and Post-quantum Computing

Elizabeth Chang

Professor of Cyber Security and Head of Discipline, University of the Sunshine Coast, Australia

Abstract. Professor Chang's talk in this presentation has two distinct parts. To start, she will introduce the landscape of cybersecurity development, attacks, threats, and vulnerabilities, as well as state-of-the-art cyber protection, cyber defence, and cyber incident prevention. This is followed by a discussion of the impact of Generative AI (GAI) and quantum-safe cryptographic computing, highlighting the major issues and challenges in research, education, and training. In conclusion, she will present a vision for Sky Safe solutions, aiming to achieve cyber resilience that supports business and economic stability, enhances human capabilities, and promotes environmental sustainability.

Disaster Preparedness and Risk Profiling in the Digital Era from Earth Observation Lens

Jagannath Aryal

Department of Infrastructure Engineering, University of Melbourne, Australia

Abstract. Natural hazards which turn into disasters result in severe losses of lives, infrastructure, and property. Disasters such as earthquakes and landslides and their impacts on transportation safety, infrastructure resilience, and displacement of people to new places are challenges. To address such challenges, earth observation data and intelligent methods can provide potential solutions in developing decision support systems. This talk will present the state of the art in Earth observation for disaster resilience using intelligent methods. In the Earth observation space, digitalisation has revolutionised the way we map, monitor, and develop decision support systems. Global case study examples covering earthquake-induced landslides from the Himalayan region will cover the digital capabilities. The digital capabilities will embrace object recognition, interpretation, and their accurate and precise capture to integrate into digital models. The developed digital models from representative case studies can be leveraged in other jurisdictions in profiling risks to protect lives and infrastructure and creating disaster preparedness in the era of digital age and digital economy.

Intelligent Image Enhancement for Real-World Applications in Adverse Atmospheric Conditions

Khan Muhammad

Department of Global Convergence, Sungkyunkwan University, South Korea

Abstract. The adverse impacts of atmospheric conditions such as haze, fog, and low-light environments pose significant challenges for real-world applications reliant on computer vision, including autonomous driving, surveillance, and remote sensing. This keynote explores cutting-edge advancements in intelligent image enhancement, drawing insights from two pivotal studies. The first introduces HazeSpace2M, a comprehensive dataset and novel classification-guided dehazing framework that improves image clarity across diverse atmospheric conditions, addressing the gap between synthetic and real-world dehazing performance. The second focuses on LoLI-Street, a benchmark for low-light image enhancement tailored to urban environments, extending beyond enhancement to enable robust object detection and scene understanding. Taken together, these contributions demonstrate how integrating domain-specific datasets, advanced algorithms, and performance benchmarks can significantly elevate the reliability of computer vision systems under challenging weather and lighting conditions. Attendees will gain valuable insights into the methodologies, datasets, and practical applications driving innovation in this field, with implications for research and industry alike.

In Memory of Carmelo Torre

Unfortunately, Professor Carmelo Torre, one of the cornerstones of the ICCSA Conference, passed away last December, leaving everyone stunned and deeply saddened. His loss has created a profound void within our academic community. Carmelo was not only a respected scholar and dedicated contributor to the success and growth of ICCSA, but also a generous colleague, mentor, and friend to many. His intellectual rigor, warm personality, and unwavering commitment to advancing research will be remembered with great admiration. As we continue the work he helped shape, we honor his legacy and the indelible mark he left on all of us. Carmelo Torre graduated in engineering at the Polytechnic of Bari with a thesis on urban planning under Dino Borri's guidance. He began his research career by collaborating with Franco Selicato. During his PhD at the University of Naples Federico II under Luigi Fusco Girard, he specialized in real estate market analysis and multi-criteria evaluation methods. He explored the social impacts of urban transformations with his lifelong friend Maria Cerreta. His first ICCSA participation was in Perugia in 2008, in the session Geographical Analysis, Urban Modeling, Spatial Statistics. Instantly captivated by the conference, his charisma enabled him to involve various Italian scientific communities, including those in real estate and statistics. ICCSA became a yearly commitment for him, where he valued the high editorial quality of the proceedings and the dynamic post-presentation discussions and debates he passionately and expertly enriched. In 2012, alongside Maria Cerreta and Paola Perchinunno, he organized the workshop Econometrics and Multidimensional Evaluation in the Urban Environment (EMEUE), fostering dialogue on critical topics. His influence steadily grew, drawing numerous research groups to ICCSA and establishing real estate and assessment as one of the conference's leading fields. A pillar of ICCSA, he was involved across all facets of the event. Torre's contributions to academic discourse were marked by intellectual rigor and innovative thinking. His conference interventions consistently challenged conventional wisdom, offering insights transcending disciplinary boundaries. Beyond the conference, he passionately advocated for equity and social justice. His left-leaning ideology, though firm, earned respect from those with differing views, thanks to his sincerity and loyalty. He was creative, generous, and always willing to help, even at a personal cost. Despite battling illness, he maintained his characteristic optimism, warmth, cheerfulness, and commitment, supported by his partner, Caterina Rinaldo. His legacy lives on in his ideas, dedication, and unmatched generosity.

Contents – Part VIII

Building Multi-dimensional Models for Assessing Complex Environmental Systems (MES 2025)

Transforming Urban Spaces Through Sustainable Agriculture: An Integrated Analysis and Design Perspective 3
   Sofia Bonini, Alberto Cozzi, Marco De Luca, Marta Lamanna, Shizuka Sasaki, and Alice Zorzan

A Multi-Criteria Rating Model for Evaluating the Attractiveness of Medium-Sized Italian Cities 21
   Francesco Cosentino, Federico Dell'Anna, and Marta Dell'Ovo

Assessing the Tourist Carrying Capacity of a UNESCO World Heritage proposed site 38
   Sebastiano Barbieri, Caterina Caprioli, Barbara Baronetto, Marta Bottero, and Marco Valle

Unlocking Energy Efficiency in the Italian Public Housing Legacy: A Typological Blueprint for Cost-Effective Retrofitting 55
   Rubina Canesi, Chiara D'Alpaos, Giuliano Marella, Diletta Romagnolo, and Umberto Turrini

Spatial Multicriteria Decision Aiding for Regional Energy Planning and Assessment. The Case Study of Gotland, Sweden 73
   Lucia Petronio, Vanessa Assumma, Johanna Liljenfeldt, and Angela Santangelo

Public-Private Partnership for the Valorization of Cultural Heritage: Evidence from Case Studies 89
   Francesca Torrieri and Alessia Crisopulli

The Circular Adaptive Reuse Project of Cultural Heritage Buildings in Salerno (Italy): from Abandoned Assets to nZEB Buildings 102
   Angrisano Mariarosaria, Gravagnuolo Antonia, Gianluca Cavalaglio, Grazia Neglia, and Francesco Fabbrocino

An Integrated MCA–GIS Framework for Ground Mounted Solar Photovoltaic (GMPV) Site Selection: Methodological Proposal for the Italian Context 120
   Caterina Caprioli, Federico Dell'Anna, and Francesco Fiermonte

Integrated Strategic Approach for Sustainable Urban Planning Applied
to the Milan Rogoredo Case Study 137
    Giulia Buongiovanni, Marianna Camerota, Valentina Giustinelli,
    Francesco Pittau, and Giorgia Sugoni

Development of a District Heating Resilience Index: A Multi-criteria
Assessment Approach Based on Latvian Case Studies 154
    Maksims Feofilovs, Renate Lakste, and Francesco Romagnoli

Sustainable Event Management: A Comparative Analysis of Protocols
and Music Festivals 166
    Agnese Baldoni, Laura Calisi, Salvatore De Pascalis,
    Francesca Falconi, Matteo Napodano, and Giacomo Seratoni Gualdoni

Investigating the Factors that Influence the Allocation of Nature-Based
Solutions in Italy 181
    Francesco Sica, Maria Rosaria Guarini, Francesco Tajani,
    and Pierluigi Morano

Introducing Indicators for Assessing the Readiness of Buildings
for Greening Interventions 194
    Lorenzo Diana, Federica Melotta, Francesca Pia Pondo,
    Roberto Castelluccio, and Francesco Polverino

Towards a Methodological Framework for Evaluating Urban Resilience:
Spatial Indicators for Addressing Complex Urban Systems 207
    Ilaria Cazzola, Benedetta Giudice, Manuela Rebaudengo,
    and Valeria Vitulano

Green Gentrification: A Literature Review of Trends, Challenges,
and Research Opportunities 222
    Marta Dell'Ovo, Giulia Datola, Daniela Maiullari, Alessandra Oppio,
    and Martina Schretzenmayr

Mapping Real Estate Values: A Semi-systematic Literature Review
of Spatial Evaluation Methods and Approaches 234
    Eugenio Muccio and Daniele Cannatella

Measuring Settlement Efficiency. Application to an Urban Regeneration 249
    Federica Cicalese, Michele Grimaldi, and Isidoro Fasolino

5th Workshop on Privacy in the Cloud/Edge/IoT World (PCEIoT 2025)

Invisible Threats: Rethinking Privacy in Digital Healthcare 267
   Parinaz Tabari, Mattia De Rosa, Gennaro Costagliola,
   and Vittorio Fuccella

Privacy Risks in Connected Vehicles: Profiling Threats and Mitigation
Strategies 285
   Marco De Santis, Christian Esposito, and Michele Mastroianni

A TOPSIS-Based Approach to Evaluate Alternative Solutions
for GDPR-Compliant Smart-City Services Implementation 303
   Lelio Campanile, Mauro Iacono, Michele Mastroianni,
   Christian Riccio, and Bruna Viscardi

Toward Privacy-Aware Environmental Monitoring of CO_2 and Air
Pollutants in Southern Italy 317
   Lelio Campanile, Luigi Piero Di Bonito, Fiammetta Marulli,
   Antonio Balzanella, and Rosanna Verde

Multidimensional Evolutionary Evaluations for Transformative Approaches (MEETA 2025)

Exploring Spatial Distribution and Interactions Toward SDG 11 Indicators
at the Neighborhood Level: An Experimental Analysis 337
   Francesco Piras and Valeria Saiu

Energy Performance Certificates and Housing Transaction Prices:
Empirical Evidence from Market Data Analysis 350
   Alice Barreca, Elena Fregonara, Giorgia Malavasi, and Diana Rolando

Contextualising Indicators for SDG 11: The GLOSSA Approach to Impact
Assessment of Local Plans 370
   Marco Ederle, Giuliano Poli, and Stefano Cuntò

EURECA: Exploring Urban touRist Environment Through Child-Based
Activities 389
   Laura Di Tommaso, Caterina Loffredo, Ludovica La Rocca,
   Simona Panaro, and Maria Cerreta

Ex-Post Evaluation Framework for Intersectional Bottom-Up Regeneration
Process of Public Spaces: Learning from a Youth Empowerment Experience ... 406
   Renata Boeri, Piero Zizzania, and Maria Cerreta

Music Meets Sustainability
: First Steps Toward a Framework for Greener Festivals 423
   Agnese Baldoni, Laura Calisi, Salvatore De Pascalis,
   Francesca Falconi, Matteo Napodano, and Giacomo Seratoni Gualdoni

Author Index 439

Building Multi-dimensional Models for Assessing Complex Environmental Systems (MES 2025)

Transforming Urban Spaces Through Sustainable Agriculture: An Integrated Analysis and Design Perspective

Sofia Bonini[1], Alberto Cozzi[1], Marco De Luca[2(✉)], Marta Lamanna[1], Shizuka Sasaki[1], and Alice Zorzan[2]

[1] Politecnico di Milano, 20133 Milan, MI, Italy
{sofia.bonini,alberto.cozzi,marta.lamanna,shizuka.sasaki}@asp-poli.it
[2] Politecnico di Torino, 10129 Torino, TO, Italy
{marco.deluca,alice.zorzan}@asp-poli.it

Abstract. The increasing urbanization projected to reach 60% of the global population by 2030 needs innovative approaches to urban sustainability challenges. This study investigates the potential of vertical farming as a nature-based solution for urban regeneration in underutilized spaces, with a specific focus on the Magazzini Raccordati of Milano Centrale railway station. The research employs a multi-method qualitative approach integrating three complementary analytical frameworks: SWOT analysis to evaluate internal and external factors affecting implementation feasibility, stakeholder analysis utilizing a Power-Interest Matrix to identify key stakeholders and their relationships, and Ecosystem Services Evaluation to assess environmental and social benefits. Following a systematic assessment of four potential locations in Milan, the Magazzini Raccordati site was selected for its strategic position, accessibility, and potential for social and environmental impact. Three development scenarios were formulated and evaluated: (1) local production with educational programs focusing on community engagement and food security; (2) restaurant-based culinary education emphasizing gastronomic awareness and circular food systems; and (3) research and innovation hub advancing urban farming technologies through academic partnerships. Results demonstrate distinct trade-offs among scenarios: scenario 1 maximizes provisioning and cultural services, scenario 2 enhances cultural services while maintaining strong provisioning benefits, and scenario 3 optimizes supporting and regulating services. The study concludes that an integrated approach combining elements from all scenarios would best leverage the site's potential while addressing urban regeneration needs. Future research would benefit from quantitative assessment methods such as Multi-Criteria Analysis or Cost-Benefit Analysis to further validate these findings.

Keywords: Urban Farming · Ecosystem Services Evaluation · Nature-Based Solutions

1 Introduction

By 2030, almost 60% of the global population will live in cities [1], causing severe implications for food security, social cohesion and environmental sustainability [2]. This demographic shift will transform traditional food systems into long and complex supply chains vulnerable to climate change and economic disruptions [3]. The United Nations' Sustainable Development Goal 2 (SDG 2) highlights the urgent need to address urban food security by promoting sustainable agriculture and ensuring equitable access to nutritious food [4]. Achieving this goal requires a systemic transformation of urban food systems, integrating sustainability from production to consumption while fostering social cohesion and civic engagement [5].

Even if urban agriculture initiatives have been implemented globally, existing literature lacks methodological frameworks that integrate multi-dimensional analysis for developing urban farming models. Current approaches often focus on either social, environmental, or economic aspects separately instead of adopting a combination of analytical tools. This research aims to develop and apply an integrated methodological framework combining SWOT Analysis, Stakeholder Analysis, and Ecosystem Services (ES) Evaluation to assess the viability of vertical farming projects. This step is followed by the evaluation of three different scenarios for the area of interest Magazzini Raccordati, establishing a replicable model for urban regeneration through agriculture that balances social inclusion, economic sustainability, and environmental benefits.

The present work explores the potential of the FARMER project, which seeks to enhance food security in Milan by repurposing abandoned spaces for agricultural purposes and developing a sustainable urban farm network. The innovation of the proposed approach lies in three key aspects: (1) the integration of multidisciplinary analytical tools as both assessment and design instruments; (2) a comparative analysis that enables strategic scenario development and evaluation; and (3) a specific focus on the integration of vertical farming within dense urban environments as a catalyst for urban regeneration, aligning with the most recent and current paradigm of the New European Bauhaus initiative [6], which promotes an integrated approach to implement the sustainable development pillars in urban transformations.

The FARMER project, developed within the Alta Scuola Politecnica program, held by Politecnico di Milano and Politecnico di Torino, aligns with broader research initiatives like STRutture Agricole MEtropolitane (STRAME), which aims to redefine urban farming concepts [7]. The project's contribution extends this work by creating a urban agriculture model that simultaneously revitalizes abandoned urban areas, empowers communities, and promotes environmental sustainability [8].

The paper is structured as follows: Sect. 2 analyzes best practices related to urban farming, Sect. 3 outlines the methodology used (SWOT, stakeholder and ES analyses), Sect. 4 applies this framework to the Magazzini Raccordati area of Milano Centrale station and Sect. 5 concludes with key findings, limitations, and future perspectives.

2 Urban Farming Best Practice Analysis

Among the innovative practices that have emerged in recent years, community gardens and vertical farming stand out as effective Nature-Based Solution (NBS) that offer multiple benefits for social revitalization, community engagement and sustainable food production [8]. These models, representing different approaches to urban agriculture, serve as reference points for defining the project objectives and implementation strategies [9].

2.1 Community Gardens

Community gardens have proliferated globally due to their proven ability to foster social cohesion, revitalize abandoned areas, and promote environmental awareness through local food production. These initiatives typically reflect their local socio-economic contexts and cultural traditions, resulting in diverse implementation models across different regions and communities.

A comprehensive review of exemplary cases reveals several notable initiatives:

- LUNGS [10] in New York City established a network of over 50 green spaces through strategic coordination and advocacy;
- Allmende-Kontor [11] in Berlin transformed a former Nazi airport runway into a 6,000 m² community space;
- The Homeless Garden Project [12] in Santa Cruz provides transitional employment through sustainable agriculture;
- Detroit Black Community Food Security Network (DBCFSN) [13] addresses food justice and racial equity through urban farming;
- Power Plant Farm and Newmarket Farm at Boston Medical Center [14] integrate agriculture with healthcare services.

LUNGS [10] particularly exemplifies effective network governance in urban agriculture. Formed in 2011, this initiative united numerous volunteer organizations across multiple neighborhoods while preserving each garden's autonomy and unique character. Through coordinated advocacy and educational programming, LUNGS promotes intergenerational knowledge transfer and community support systems that enhance neighborhood resilience.

Similarly, Allmende-Kontor [11], established in 2010 by activist researchers, demonstrates how urban agriculture can reclaim historically significant spaces and transform them into centers for social innovation. Beyond food production, the project hosts educational workshops on beekeeping, gardening, and sustainable practices, creating a multifunctional community space that connects environmental awareness with social engagement [11].

These case studies illustrate how community gardens function as more than food production sites—they serve as platforms for addressing complex urban challenges, from social isolation to environmental degradation, while building community capacity and resilience. The success factors identified across these initiatives—inclusive governance, multifunctionality, educational programming, and community ownership—provide valuable insights for the project design.

2.2 Vertical Farming Projects

Vertical farming represents an advanced and innovative approach to urban agriculture to optimize space use and resource needs. Thanks to controlled environment technology, this method allows continuous production, independent of climate conditions and season, making it particularly suitable for dense urban environments.

The performed analysis of leading vertical farming initiatives includes: Nature Urbaine (NU) [15] in Paris, which produces 200 kg of fresh produce daily on a rooftop farm while hosting educational events; Vertical Harvest [16] in Jackson, USA, which uses hydroponic farming to prioritize employment opportunities for individuals with disabilities; Sky Greens [17] in Singapore, focused on using rotating cultivation systems to maximize sunlight exposure and minimize energy use; and Plenty [18], a technology-driven initiative that uses LED lighting to achieve high indoor production.

Nature Urbaine (NU) [15], established in 2020, aims to produce food in a responsible way, establishing circular economy to local agriculture. Combining innovation and sustainability, NU Paris reuses what the city offers to agriculture, such as vacant spaces, organic waste, waste heat, turning them into valuable resources for food production. Its diversified economic model includes rental cultivation spaces, educational programming and event hosting, demonstrating how vertical farming can integrate multiple revenue streams to achieve financial sustainability [19].

Vertical Harvest [16], founded in 2016, illustrates the social impact of urban agriculture through inclusive employment models. The farm provides customized job roles to foster professional development, personal discovery and community impact, prioritizing both social impact and profitability. It engages the community through educational programs, public events, and partnerships that support food security and social inclusion [20].

From the analysis of these case studies, several key findings emerge. First, successful projects integrate multiple functions beyond food production, including education, research, and community engagement, as described for LUNGS and Allmende-Kontor. Circular economy approaches, similar to Nature Urbaine (NU) model, enhance sustainability and reduce operational costs; while partnerships with different stakeholders strengthen project resilience. Lastly, technological innovation must be balanced with social inclusion to maximize community benefits, as the Vertical Harvest project shows.

These findings directly serve as a basis for the project's scenario development for the Magazzini Raccordati site, particularly in how each scenario integrates technological solutions with social objectives to create multifunctional urban spaces.

3 Methodology for Scenarios Implementation

A qualitative multi-method approach has been proposed and adopted [21] to assess, design, and evaluate different scenarios for urban regeneration. This approach integrates complementary analytical frameworks that examine the intervention from different perspectives, ensuring comprehensive consideration of socio-economic, environmental, and governance factors.

The methodological framework builds upon the work of Bottero and colleagues [5], which emphasizes the value of integrating qualitative approaches to understand complex urban systems.

This research proposes an integrated multimethod approach based on the integration of SWOT Analysis, Stakeholders Analysis and ES Analysis. Their combination is effective according to their complementarity and ability in addressing different dimensions of urban agriculture implementation and to create multidimensional framework stand out for understanding both the current conditions and potential futures of the site.

The project's methodology was implemented in three phases: (1) preliminary assessment of four potential locations in Milan, including site visits, mapping, interviews, and initial analyses; (2) detailed analysis of the selected site (Magazzini Raccordati) using the core analytical tools; and (3) scenario development and evaluation based on the analytical findings.

3.1 SWOT Analysis

The SWOT analysis [22] is a planning tool that helps to assess both internal and external factors influencing a project by identifying the strengths (S), the weaknesses (W), the opportunities (O) and the threats (T). Organized as a four-quadrant matrix, this method facilitates classification of factors into two categories: endogenous factors (strengths and weaknesses) and possible exogenous factors that could occur in the future (opportunities and threats) [5].

Unlike conventional SWOT analyses that often remain descriptive, the proposed approach links identified factors to decision-making by evaluating how certain interventions can leverage strengths and opportunities while mitigating weaknesses and threats. This approach transforms SWOT from a purely analytical tool into an instrument that actively informs design choices and strategic priorities [23].

In the present study, SWOT analysis was applied to assess the feasibility of urban farming in the Magazzini Raccordati site, identifying potential collaboration with local stakeholders, highlighting the constraints and delving into the opportunities linked to urban regeneration. The results of this analysis validate the selection of scenarios that empower the strengths of the project while mitigating weaknesses and threats.

3.2 Stakeholder Analysis

Stakeholder Analysis [24] plays a useful role in urban transformation and planning, first by identifying all the actors involved and interested in the process under analysis and, consequently, by highlighting their capacity to affect the diffusion or inhibition of strategies. To develop this strategy, the initial step is related to the identification of each actor and its characteristics, such as the level of intervention, their corresponding roles, needs and expectations [5].

This study takes into consideration the Power-Interest Matrix method, which graphically represents the power and interest of each stakeholder in the specific project. This helps distinguish between different types of stakeholders and clearly identify the needs that should be prioritized and the expectations that should be considered first. It allows drawing a structured approach to stakeholder engagement, improving the process of decision-making and the relative effectiveness [5,23,25].

In the proposed project, the Stakeholder Analysis reinforced the decision to focus on the Magazzini Raccordati area, as it better aligned with the interests and influence of key stakeholders. Furthermore, it also gives further details and information for the scenario-building process, ensuring that the design and interventions of the project are aligned with stakeholders' priorities and needs [26].

3.3 ES Analysis

ES Analysis provides a framework for evaluating how urban interventions affect the benefits that natural systems, as green spaces, water bodies and cultivated land, provide to human beings. These services can be classified into four main categories [27]:

1. provisioning services, that include material products extracted directly from nature, such as food and raw materials;
2. regulating services, involving key natural processes that moderate natural phenomena, such as flood control, carbon storage and air purification;
3. cultural services, providing non-material benefits related to education and well-being;
4. supporting services, including fundamental processes that sustain life on Earth, such as nutrient cycling and soil formation.

Urban agriculture represents a NBS that can enhance multiple ES simultaneously. For instance, local food production through urban gardens reduces transportation emissions while improving nutritional access [28]. Urban vegetation improves air quality by filtering pollutants, with studies showing filtration rates of up to 85% in parks and 70% along tree-lined streets [28]. Green spaces strengthen cultural ES by providing spaces for education and community building. Case studies like the LUNGS gardens [10] and Nature Urbaine in Paris [15] show how these projects offer all these benefits to the urban community.

In the context of this project, the assessment of ES serves as an fundamental tool to evaluate the social benefits of the urban farming initiative. For each scenario, the evaluation was carried out through a qualitative assessment, which categorizes the ecological functions and benefits into three levels (low, medium and high), depending on the impact and contribution provided by the intervention on that service. This comparison revealed trade-offs between different intervention types and defined a more balanced approach that maximizes multiple ES.

4 Application

4.1 Case Study

The main objective of the project is to use urban agriculture as a strategy to regenerate degraded or underutilized urban areas, with dutiful and realistic attention to dimensions related to social, environmental and economic sustainability.

Four areas were initially identified for the study, each representing a significant urban void within the fabric of Milan, yet holding considerable social potential. The areas initially identified for the study were four, all representing important urban voids in Milan fabric but with high social potential: Magazzini Raccordati of Milano Centrale, Via Cogne, East Beltway, and Via Medici del Vascello. These areas, characterized by different sizes and locations, share the need for regeneration and strengthening of the weak and fragmented social network. Each site was systematically evaluated through site visits, stakeholder interviews, and preliminary analyses to understand their physical characteristics, socio-economic contexts, and regeneration potential. For the current phase of the project, one of these four areas, The Magazzini Raccordati of Milano Centrale was selected as the pilot site based on the outcomes of the subsequent analytical process. The long-term objective is to progressively expand the project's scope and management strategies, thereby embracing a broader urban perspective in future implementation stages.

The Magazzini Raccordati of Milano Centrale (Fig. 2a) represents a strategic node within Milan's urban fabric due to its central location, transportation connectivity, and historical significance. This area, consisting of underutilized warehouse spaces, suffers from fragmentation and disconnection between surrounding urban functions despite its high accessibility.

Via Cogne (Fig. 2d) ion the other hand, is in a residential neighborhood characterized by high housing density in which it is possible to find small shops, such as bakeries, fruit sellers and mini-markets and just a few bigger supermarkets.

The East Beltway site (Fig. 2c) represents an infrastructure area that currently serves as a physical barrier between different parts of the city. In particular, the affected area appears to be a series of now unusable underground parking lots that could provide an interesting area for indoor agriculture.

Via Medici del Vascello (Fig. 2b) is characterized by the presence of a preexisting community garden, which foster green activity involvement from the community. Its proximity to extensive green areas enhances exposure to nature among residents, promoting individual health and local biodiversity (Fig. 1).

4.2 Preliminary Analysis

To guarantee the FARMER project's success, several preliminary analyses were conducted to understand the particulars of the four regions that were proposed and to ascertain the opportunities and difficulties associated with the implementation of urban agriculture in those areas. A socioeconomic analysis, a general SWOT analysis for every site, and an evaluation of ES were all part of this phase.

Fig. 1. Areas Overview and Urban context. Data source: https://www.citypopulation.de/

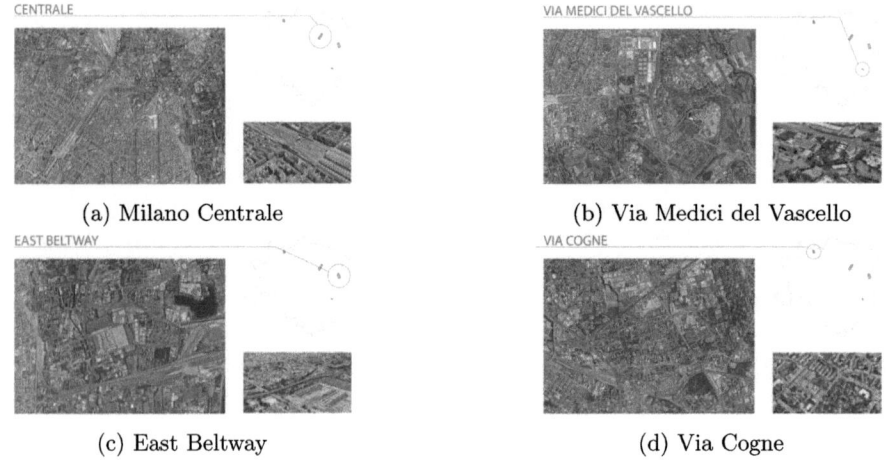

Fig. 2. Orthophoto and location of the four case studies

Socioeconomic analysis revealed significant demographic and economic variations between sites. Milano Centrale is distinguished by a multicultural populace that includes commuters, tourists and local residents across socioeconomic strata, though the area suffers from inadequate green infrastructure and limited public space accessibility. Demographic data indicates that the population in this district has a higher proportion of foreign-born residents (23.4%) compared to the city average (19.2%), reflecting its role as a transportation hub and transition zone [29].

On the other hand, most of the residents of Via Cogne are middle-class or lower-class, and they have a strong need for communal spaces for social interaction and education.

The East Beltway area's proximity to educational institutions and recreational facilities attracts diverse user groups. However, infrastructure barriers and perceived safety issues currently limit full utilization of this space.

Via Medici del Vascello benefits from existing green infrastructure and community networks but faces significant challenges from railway barriers that fragment the area physically and socially.

One of the main focuses of the analyses was to reach a better understanding of the urban farming current development in Milan urban fabric to consider the power of each area to integrate in the network. The existence of Urban farming initiatives and farms active in the city of Milan, which can serve as strategic partners for project implementation, is highlighted on the map of active local realities (Fig. 3).

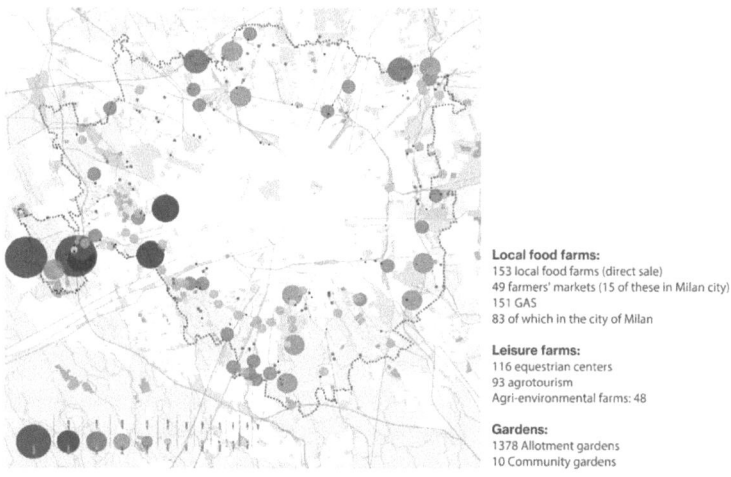

Fig. 3. Urban Agriculture Types [27]

4.3 Identification of Project Area: Magazzini Raccordati of Milano Centrale

Based on the comprehensive preliminary assessment, the Magazzini Raccordati at Milano Centrale station was selected as the primary intervention site due to several strategic advantages. The choice emerged from systematic evaluation of each site's transformation potential, stakeholder dynamics, accessibility, and alignment with project objectives.

The context of the warehouses offers the opportunity to collaborate with a diverse and at the same time problematic social reality by restoring space for sociality and sharing. With approximately 40,000 square meters of covered space across 100 warehouse units, the site provides sufficient scale for meaningful intervention while allowing phased implementation [30]. The modular structure enables diverse programming that can evolve over time in response to community needs and operational feedback.

The site's strategic position within Milan's urban fabric represents a significant advantage. Located between Milano Centrale station and the Martesana canal, the area functions as a potential connector between major urban nodes that are currently disconnected. This position enables the project to serve both local residents and visitors, maximizing its reach and potential impact on urban connectivity.

The area's demographic complexity presents both challenges and opportunities for social intervention. While the district experiences social issues typical of transit hubs, including transient populations and safety concerns, it also hosts numerous community organizations and cultural initiatives that could serve as implementation partners. The proximity to the Sammartini Centre, which provides social services to marginalized populations, offers particular potential for workforce development and social inclusion programming through the agricultural initiative.

Transportation accessibility represents another key advantage, with the site directly connected to Milan's subway system, regional trains, and bicycle infrastructure. This connectivity facilitates stakeholder engagement, product distribution, and visitor access—essential factors for operational viability and community integration.

Despite these advantages, the site presents implementation challenges that require strategic approaches. The private ownership by RFI (Italian Railway Network) necessitates complex partnership arrangements, while the aging infrastructure requires substantial renovation to meet modern operational standards. Safety concerns and negative perceptions of the area must also be addressed through integrated design that enhances visibility, activity, and community presence.

The selection of Magazzini Raccordati represents a strategic choice to maximize project impact by positioning urban agriculture as a catalyst for broader urban regeneration. This site enables the project to simultaneously address food security, social inclusion, and urban connectivity while leveraging existing infrastructure and institutional networks.

Spatial SWOT Analysis. The SWOT analysis of the Milano Centrale area provides a structured assessment of factors affecting implementation viability (Fig. 4). This analysis explicitly connects site characteristics to strategic decisions, informing scenario development and implementation approaches.

Among the advantages, the site's strategic position stands out: it is in a reachable urban area and well connected to the public transport system. Furthermore, the area is important for Milan's urban system since it directly connects Milano Centrale, one of the city's most vital infrastructure nodes, with the Martesana canal, a very interesting destination for young people and communities. This spatial configuration has the potential to develop a sustainable mobility system that promotes urban continuity and environmental sustainability, encouraging the use of bicycle and pedestrian paths and reducing dependence on motorized traffic.

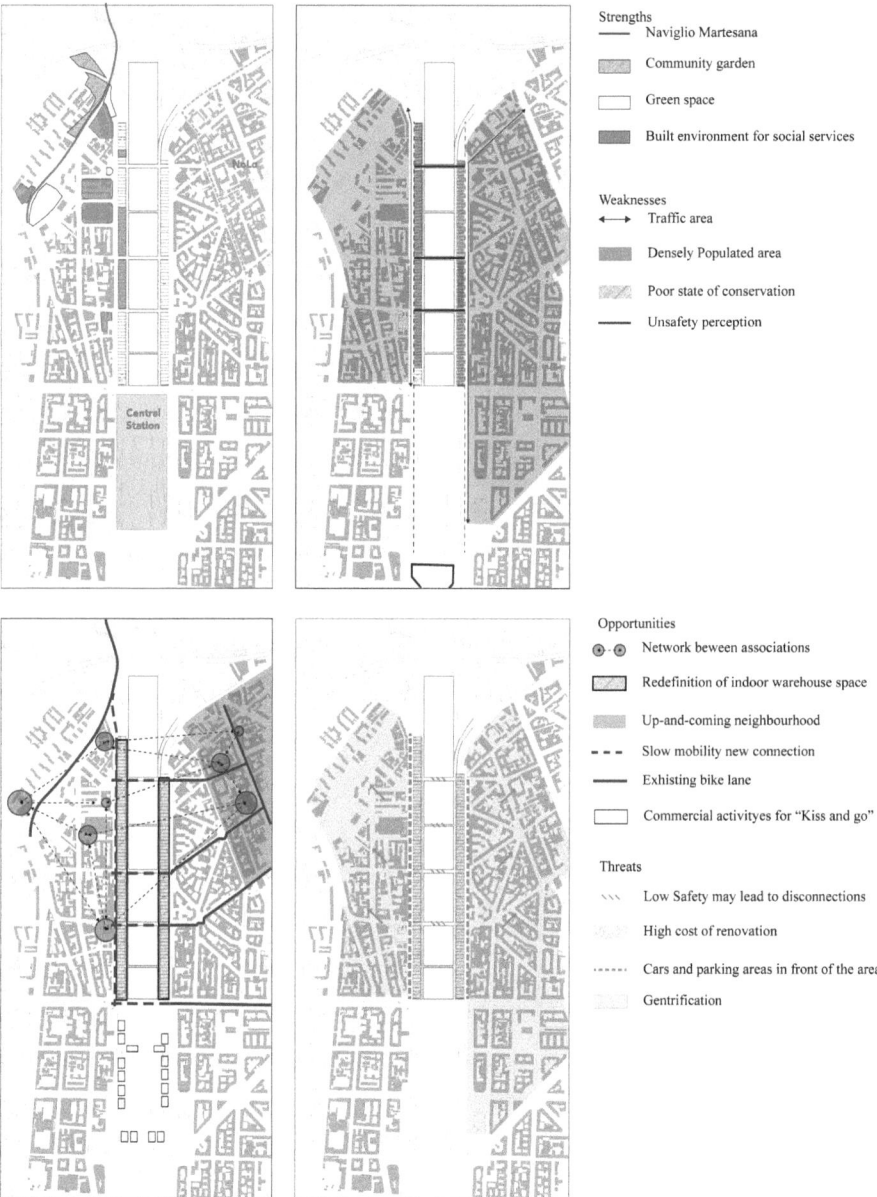

Fig. 4. Graphical SWOT analysis of Magazzini Raccordati of Milano Centrale Area

Covered areas of the old warehouses provide perfect conditions for activities needing microclimatic control and access management. Furthermore, the surrounding environment produces an optimal ecosystem because of the closeness of schools, social care centers and green areas, all of which may encourage projects of educational and social inclusion. Particularly, the closeness to the Sammartini Centre, which provides social and health services to those in marginal circumstances, offers a chance to support training and social reintegration initiatives by assisting with urban agriculture projects and educational seminars. The area also has several active associations that could be strategic partners for territorial regeneration projects including those connected to the "Cassina de' Pomm" Community Garden and urban renewal efforts.

The social balance of the area could be compromised by the danger connected to gentrification and the high expenses connected to upgrading, therefore reducing the access of the new functions to the most vulnerable population group. Ultimately, the use of space may be discouraged by the sense of insecurity and urban decay, which call for an integrated approach comprising security measures, social inclusion, and community involvement to guarantee sustainable and resilient regeneration.

Stakeholders Analysis. According to the above-mentioned objectives, different stakeholders have been for the area of Milan Central Station. In this context, the Power-Interest Matrix, a tool used to categorize stakeholders based on two key dimensions, power and interest, was applied to map the stakeholders.

Power is defined as the stakeholder's ability to accomplish desired results using their influence. On the other hand, interest characterizes the worries regarding the problem to be addressed and the issue that needs to be solved. This matrix allows for the identification of key players, keep informed, and strategic positioning, as illustrated in (Fig. 5).

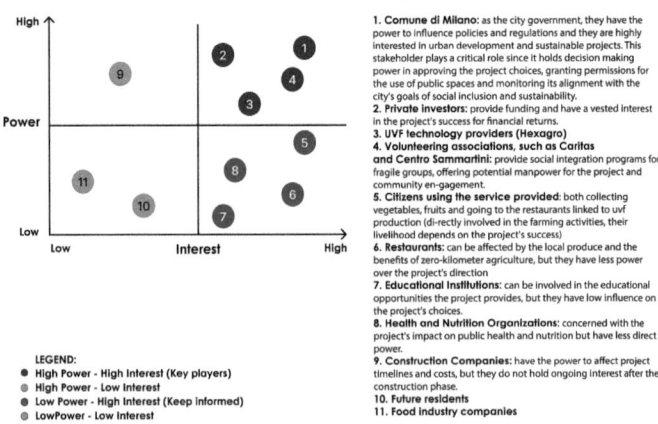

Fig. 5. Power interest matrix for the stakeholders involved

Among the high power and high interest stakeholders (key-player), the Milano municipality has been identified, since, as the city government, they have the power to influence policies and regulations and are highly interested in urban development and sustainability projects. On the same quadrant of the matrix, it is essential to cite the UVF technology providers, in this case the HEXAGRO start-up: they have a high interest in its successful implementation and a high power to drive decisions during the project development.

In the High interest - Low power quadrant, the stakeholders involved are the main clients and customers of the project, such as private citizens and families, interested in local food security and in the community aspects, and restaurants, interested in local and fresh produce sales. Similarly, the educational institutions and health and nutrition organizations have comparable levels of power and interest, due to their limited direct influence on the project and their significant engagement with educational opportunities and health impact.

4.4 Strategic Scenarios Design

Based on the preliminary analyses, several development scenarios have been found that each tackle particular urban issues and optimise the possibilities of urban vertical farming, market integration, and educational and research centres. These scenarios seek to create a sustainable and multifunctional urban ecosystem supporting social reintegration, economic viability, and environmental resilience.

The formulation of the three strategic scenarios was guided by the results of preliminary site analyses, including site visits, stakeholder interviews, and spatial assessments. Criteria used for scenario differentiation included: (1) level of community engagement required, (2) spatial adaptability for indoor agriculture, (3) potential for economic sustainability, and (4) alignment with stakeholder interests and institutional partnerships. These criteria were evaluated through a SWOT analysis and ecosystem service potential, allowing the design team to explore diverse yet context-sensitive alternatives. The scenarios were then constructed to emphasize different strategic priorities: social reintegration (Scenario 1), circular economy and food culture (Scenario 2), and research and innovation (Scenario 3).

Scenario 1: UVF Production, Market, and Educational Labs. In the present context, warehouses in the Milano Centrale district will be transformed into Urban Vertical Farms (UVFs) that will be operated by personnel from the nearby support facilities. The program will enhance social reintegration through the provision of basic competencies in hydroponic and aeroponic cultivation. This framework not only backs social empowerment but also helps add to local food security via the provision of fresh, zero-kilometer, organic products. The cultivation process will emphasize efficiency in resource utilization, namely in optimizing water and energy utilization, and minimizing land dependence and environmental impact.

A committed urban market will be created to manage the distribution of the produce grown. The market will serve the local population and restaurants that prefer sustainable sourcing. By promoting direct exchange between producers and consumers, this activity champions short supply chains, economic resilience, and lowered carbon emissions that typically accompany traditional food distribution channels. Moreover, the market should act as a hub of community activity, thereby strengthening neighborhood identity and facilitating environmentally friendly consumption habits.

A further dimension of this scenario involves the integration of educational laboratories that will function as centers for skill development and community outreach. These spaces will provide structured training programs, particularly for marginalized individuals, in the principles of urban farming. In collaboration with local schools such as Scuola Primaria Galvani and Istituto Comprensivo Statale "Teodoro Ciresola", the labs will also offer educational workshops aimed at fostering environmental awareness among younger generations. Through hands-on learning experiences, students will gain insight into sustainable agricultural practices, nutritional awareness, and urban ecology.

Scenario 2: Urban Vertical Farming, Restaurant, and Culinary Workshops. This scenario expands upon the previous model by integrating a restaurant and culinary laboratory within the intervention area, thereby establishing a circular food system where fresh produce is cultivated, prepared, and consumed within the same urban setting. The direct linkage between UVF production and food services ensures the highest quality of ingredients and minimizes waste and energy use.

The restaurant will function as both a dining venue and an experimental kitchen, where chefs and researchers collaborate to explore innovative plant-based cuisine and food sustainability solutions. This setting also provides a training ground for individuals undergoing professional reintegration, equipping them with culinary and hospitality skills that can enhance their employment prospects. The culinary workshops will serve as an extension of this initiative, engaging the wider public in interactive cooking sessions focused on sustainable gastronomy.

In addition to fostering economic sustainability, this scenario incorporates a specialized food market offering prepared meals and artisanal products derived from UVF ingredients. The project expands its economic reach, ensuring financial viability while reinforcing the principles of local and sustainable food systems. The combined effect of these interventions is the creation of a dynamic urban space where social inclusion, economic regeneration, and environmental sustainability converge in a cohesive and replicable model.

Scenario 3: Research and Innovation Hub for Sustainable Urban Farming. A third possible development focuses on transforming the area into a research and innovation hub dedicated to agronomy studies, food engineering and related academic activity. This scenario investigates scientific exploration, aiming to optimize urban agricultural practices through empirical research and technological innovation.

The research hub, developed in collaboration with Politecnico di Milano, will investigate crop optimization, examining the suitability of various plant species for controlled indoor environments. Researchers will assess sustainable technologies such as precision irrigation systems, energy-efficient lighting solutions, and automated climate control mechanisms to enhance the ecological footprint of vertical farming operations.

The hub will also serve as a knowledge-sharing platform, facilitating collaborations with universities, policymakers, and private sector stakeholders. By promoting interdisciplinary research and technological advancements, this scenario contributes to the broader discourse on urban food security and climate adaptation strategies.

ES Evaluation of Strategic Scenarios. The evaluation of ES provides a key framework to compare the three proposed strategic scenarios for the Milano Centrale site. By analyzing the impact of each scenario on provisioning, regulating, cultural, and supporting services, this assessment highlights which interventions generate the most significant environmental and social benefits.

The integration of agriculture in an urban context presents multiple advantages to enhance sustainability and promote community well-being. However, these benefits vary depending on how the intervention is designed and implemented. Below, each scenario is assessed through the ES.

The first scenario enhances provisioning services, as it promotes the local food production and sales through the related market that offers fresh produce to the community of the area. Secondly, the educational labs integration strengthens cultural services, fostering community engagement and awareness, focusing on activities for children and teenagers of the neighborhood. However, its regulating and supporting services are limited.

The second scenario stands out for the cultural services, focusing more on promoting food awareness through culinary workshops and through the presence of gastronomy and restaurants with local fresh products. At the same time, provisioning services are also addressed, however, it lacks on providing regulation and supporting benefits, as indoor farming and food preparation have a minimal effect on these aspects.

Lastly, the third option is the most effective in supporting and regulating services, as it emphasizes technological advancements, sustainable research and university collaborations. The research of innovative farming techniques can contribute to the improvement and development of new urban sustainable solutions. However, this scenario has less direct impact on fostering community engagement and social inclusion, that represent two of the main objectives of the FARMER project (Table 1).

Table 1. ES Scenario Evaluation. ∗: Low. ∗∗: Medium. ∗ ∗ ∗: High.

ES	Scenario 1	Scenario 2	Scenario 3
Provisioning services	∗ ∗ ∗	∗ ∗ ∗	∗∗
Regulating services	∗	∗	∗∗
Cultural services	∗ ∗ ∗	∗∗	∗
Supporting services	∗∗	∗	∗ ∗ ∗

5 Conclusion

This research aims at reflecting on how a multidisciplinary approach can address the complex challenges of urban regeneration and networking, with specific reference to urban farming. The use of complementary analysis tools, SWOT, Stakeholder and ES Evaluation, has allowed for valuable qualitative insights into the dynamics of the context, guiding both the strategic selection of Milano Centrale as the intervention area and the development of potential scenarios.

While the proposed analysis highlights the opportunity to combine several elements from different scenarios, it is important to acknowledge the significant limitations of the predominantly qualitative methodology. The qualitative nature of the evaluation represents one of the main constraints due to the lack of precision, which is instead a value of quantitative methodologies. The absence of quantitative metrics and measurable outcomes restricts the ability to make precise comparisons between scenarios or predict their specific impacts with confidence.

Future studies will allow to progress in the analysis by integrating systematic evaluation techniques closer to the concept proposed in Multi-Criteria Analysis (MCA), Cost-Benefit Analysis (CBA), or Community Impact Evaluation (CIE). These approaches would lead to a more precise and quantitative definition of the project's impacts and enhance the ability to assess economic, social and environmental benefits across different scenarios.

The transition from a qualitative to a quantitative analysis represents an important evolution of this research, allowing a precise definition of impacts and supporting the development of more effective urban farming models [31–34].

Acknowledgments. This research is part of the work of the FARMER (Fostering Agriculture to Regenerate Milan Environments and neighbouRhoods) project, which is inserted in the context of Alta Scuola Politecnica.

Disclosure of Interests. The authors have no competing interests to declare that are relevant to the content of this article.

References

1. Oppio, A., Dell'Ovo, M., Caprioli, C., Bottero, M.: A proposal to assess the benefits of urban ecosystem services. In: Calabrò, F., Della Spina, L., Piñeira Mantiñán, M.J. (eds.) New Metropolitan Perspectives: Post COVID Dynamics: Green and Digital Transition, Between Metropolitan and Return to Villages Perspectives, pp. 1947–1955. Springer, Cham (2023). https://doi.org/10.1007/978-3-031-06825-6_187
2. United Nations Department of Economic and Social Affairs: World Urbanization Prospects: The 2018 Revision (2019). https://doi.org/10.18356/b9e995fe-en, sT/ESA/SER.A/420
3. de Pee, S., Taren, D., Bloem, M.W. (eds.): Nutrition and Health in a Developing World. NH, Springer, Cham (2017). https://doi.org/10.1007/978-3-319-43739-2
4. United Nations: Food security and nutrition and sustainable agriculture. https://sdgs.un.org/topics/food-security-and-nutrition-and-sustainable-agriculture
5. Bottero, M., Datola, G.: Addressing social sustainability in urban regeneration processes. an application of the social multi-criteria evaluation. Sustainability **12**(18), 7579 (2020). https://doi.org/10.3390/su12187579
6. European Union Commition: New European Bauhaus initiative (2021). https://new-european-bauhaus.europa.eu/index_en. Accessed 18 Mar 2025
7. Paganin, G., Orsini, F., Migliore, M., Venis, K., Poli, M.: Metropolitan farms: long term agri-food systems for sustainable urban landscapes. In: Technological Imagination in the Green and Digital Transition, pp. 649–657. Springer (2023). https://doi.org/10.1007/978-3-031-29515-7_58
8. Oppio, A., Datola, G., Oksuz, T., Ozgur, D., Sdino, L.: Innovating urban systems through nature-based solution for a circular economy enhancement: a general framework. In: Gervasi, O., Murgante, B., Garau, C., Taniar, D., Rocha, A.M.A.C., Lago, M.N.F. (eds.) Computational Science and Its Applications - ICCSA 2024 Workshops. LNCS, vol. 14821, pp. 176–188. Springer (2024). https://doi.org/10.1007/978-3-031-65308-7_13
9. Green.org: Vertical farming and community gardens (2024). https://green.org/2024/01/30/vertical-farming-and-community-gardens/
10. LUNGS - Loisaida United Neighborhood Gardens: About lungs (2024). https://lungsnyc.org/about/
11. Green Service: Allmende kontor è l'orto urbano che ha trasformato berlino (2016). https://www.greenservice.it/blog/2016/02/11/allmende-kontor-orto-berlino/
12. Homeless Garden Project: Homeless garden project (2025). https://homelessgardenproject.org/
13. Detroit Black Community Food Sovereignty Network: Dbcfsn (2025). https://www.dbcfsn.org/
14. BostonMedicalCenter: Community rooftop farm (2025). https://www.bmc.org/
15. Viparis: Nature urbaine (2022). https://www.viparis.com/en/news-events/news/nature-urbaine-2
16. Vertical Harvest Farms: Vertical harvest farms (2025). https://verticalharvestfarms.com/
17. Sky Greens: Sky greens (2025). https://www.skygreens.com/
18. Plenty Unlimited Inc.: Plenty (2025). https://www.plenty.ag/
19. Agripolis and Cultures en Ville: Nature urbaine (2025). https://www.nu-paris.com/

20. Mainwaring, S.: Vertical harvest: cultivating food, futures, & social impact (2023). https://www.forbes.com/sites/simonmainwaring/2023/07/31/vertical-harvest-cultivating-food-futures--social-impact/
21. Bottero, M., Assumma, V., Caprioli, C., Dell'Ovo, M.: Decision making in urban development: the application of a hybrid evaluation method for a critical area in the city of Turin (Italy). Sustain. Urban Areas **72**, 103028 (2021). https://doi.org/10.1016/j.scs.2021.103028
22. Gürel, E.: SWOT analysis: a theoretical review. J. Int. Soc. Res. **10**(51), 994–1006 (2017). https://doi.org/10.17719/jisr.2017.1832
23. Caruso, N., Datola, G.: Temporary housing in Turin: the Ma.Ri. house case study. Valori e Valutazioni **32**, 107–119 (2023). https://doi.org/10.48264/VVSIEV-20233209
24. Freeman, R., McVea, J.: A stakeholder approach to strategic management. SSRN Electron. J. (2001). https://doi.org/10.2139/ssrn.263511
25. Yang, R.J.: An investigation of stakeholder analysis in urban development projects: empirical or rationalistic perspectives. Int. J. Project Manage. **32**(5), 838–849 (2014). https://doi.org/10.1016/j.ijproman.2013.10.011
26. Dente, B.: Understanding Policy Decisions. Springer (2014). https://doi.org/10.1007/978-3-319-02520-9
27. Bolund, P., Hunhammar, S.: Ecosystem services in urban areas. Ecol. Econ. **29**(2), 293–301 (1999). https://doi.org/10.1016/S0921-8009(99)00013-0
28. Evans, D.L., et al.: Ecosystem service delivery by urban agriculture and green infrastructure - a systematic review. Ecosyst. Serv. **54**, 101405 (2022). https://doi.org/10.1016/j.ecoser.2022.101405
29. Tuttitalia.it: Cittadini stranieri Milano 2023 (2023). https://www.tuttitalia.it/lombardia/18-milano/statistiche/cittadini-stranieri-2023/. Accessed 20 Mar 2025
30. Fondo Ambiente Italiano: Magazzini raccordati della stazione centrale di milano (2025). https://fondoambiente.it/luoghi/magazzini-raccordati-della-stazione-centrale-di-milano?ldc
31. Abastante, F., Caprioli, C., Gaballo, M.: The economic evaluation of projects as a structuring discipline of learning processes to support decision-making in sustainable urban transformations. Int. J. Sustain. Dev. Plann. **17**(4), 1297–1307 (2022). https://doi.org/10.18280/ijsdp.170427
32. Bottero, M., Caprioli, C., Datola, G., Caruso, N.: Assessing the impacts of a social housing project through the community impact evaluation (CIE) methodology. In: Sustainable Urban Development and Planning, pp. 183–194. Springer (2022). https://doi.org/10.1007/978-3-031-10542-5_13
33. Caprioli, C.: The integration of multi-agent system and multicriteria analysis for developing participatory planning alternatives in urban contexts. Environ. Impact Assess. Rev. **113**, 107855 (2025). https://doi.org/10.1016/j.eiar.2025.107855
34. Bottero, M., Caprioli, C., Datola, G., Oppio, A., Torrieri, F.: Regeneration of Rogoredo railway: a combined approach using multi-criteria and financial analysis [un approccio integrato per la rigenerazione dello scalo ferroviario di rogoredo]. Valori e Valutazioni **31**, 89–102 (2023). https://doi.org/10.48264/VVSIEV-20223107

A Multi-Criteria Rating Model for Evaluating the Attractiveness of Medium-Sized Italian Cities

Francesco Cosentino[1], Federico Dell'Anna[2(✉)], and Marta Dell'Ovo[3]

[1] Politecnico di Milano, Piazza Leonardo da Vinci 32, 20133 Milan, MI, Italy
[2] Interuniversity Department of Regional and Urban Studies and Planning (DIST), Politecnico di Torino, Viale Mattioli 39, 10125 Turin, (TO), Italy
federico.dellanna@polito.it
[3] Department of Architecture and Urban Studies (DASTU), Politecnico di Milano, via Bonardi 3, 20133 Milan, MI, Italy

Abstract. Medium-sized cities in Italy are becoming more attractive to private investors. This is due to their stable economic growth, less saturated markets, and improving infrastructure. However, to understand their real investment potential, a structured method is needed, one that considers economic, social, and governance aspects together.

Most existing urban rankings are not designed for investors. They often do not include flexible weighting systems or clear criteria that reflect investment needs. In addition, they rarely offer a multi-criteria approach that allows a fair comparison between different cities.

This study presents a Multi-Criteria Rating Model based on the Multi-Attribute Value Theory (MAVT), developed to evaluate the attractiveness of medium-sized Italian cities for private investors. The method follows a structured process that considers different points of view, including economic performance, infrastructure, education, welfare, demography, real estate, and tourism. These aspects are measured with indicators and weighted using expert opinions to reflect investor preferences. The data is then normalized through value functions to allow comparisons between cities. Finally, a City Attractiveness Index (CAI) is calculated by combining the weighted scores.

By including several important issues related to attractiveness in one transparent framework, this tool helps investors compare cities and make better decisions based on their investment goals.

Keywords: Urban attractiveness · Multi-Criteria Decision Making (MCDM) · Investment potential

1 Introduction

Cities have historically driven the development of surrounding territories and countries by bringing economic and strategic leadership, fostering the development of transport and communication infrastructures, and facilitating major innovation processes through the agglomeration of knowledge and entrepreneurial skills [1]. In the contemporary era, the competitive positioning of urban areas has become increasingly contingent upon their capacity to implement sustainable development paradigms [2, 3]. This creates competition between cities to maintain or improve their regional and global position [4].

Within the Italian urban hierarchy, medium-sized cities, generally defined as urban centers with populations between 50,000 and 250,000 inhabitants, occupy a distinctive structural position. Exemplars such as Bologna, Brescia, Modena, Reggio Calabria, and Perugia typically function as provincial capitals or significant regional hubs, characterized by their economic specialization, cultural heritage, and administrative functions that serve surrounding territories. While they lack the global prominence of metropolises like Milan, Rome, or Naples, they often maintain strong local identities and economic specializations that shape their development trajectories. Recent scholarship has highlighted the strategic relevance of these intermediate urban systems within what has been termed the "in-between Italy", *l'Italia di mezzo*, a vast and diverse set of territories that are neither fully urban nor rural, yet home to over half of the Italian population and land surface [46, 47]. Despite their demographic and economic weight, these territories often suffer from limited political attention and planning tools that fail to capture their complexity. Many face persistent challenges: demographic stagnation, brain drain, aging infrastructure, and struggles to maintain competitiveness in an increasingly globalized and polarized economy. The COVID-19 pandemic has further exacerbated these vulnerabilities, creating a landscape where structural weaknesses and development opportunities coexist.

Assessing their attractiveness requires a structured approach that integrates financial, infrastructural, social, cultural, and governance factors [5]. In recent years, the evaluation of urban attractiveness has increasingly required tools that go beyond traditional rankings, which often fail to incorporate criteria tailored to the needs of private investors. The complexity of investment decisions, particularly in urban contexts, demands analytical frameworks capable of capturing the multidimensional nature of cities, encompassing economic vitality, infrastructural assets, institutional quality, and social conditions [7]. In this regard, multi-criteria evaluation methods represent a promising approach, as they allow for the integration of heterogeneous indicators within a coherent framework. While the literature on urban competitiveness has expanded, there remains a notable gap in the application of structured evaluation models in the Italian context, especially when it comes to supporting investment strategies. Given that urban competitiveness is the result of several interacting factors, a composite index becomes a valuable instrument to synthesize diverse urban attributes into a single interpretable outcome. This study presents a Multi-Criteria Rating Model grounded in the Multi-Attribute Value Theory (MAVT), developed to evaluate the investment attractiveness of medium-sized Italian cities. The model assesses urban performance through six interrelated dimensions: economic development, infrastructure quality, governance efficiency, social well-being, education, tourism, and real estate dynamics. Each dimension employs context-sensitive indicators, calibrated to reflect these cities' unique intermediacy. Through normalized aggregation, the City Attractiveness Index (CAI) enables systematic comparisons, supporting investment and policy decisions with a nuanced diagnostic tool that acknowledges these cities' specific opportunities and constraints within national and regional development contexts.

The chapter is divided into five sections. After an introduction outlining the research question, the second section presents the existing urban attractiveness assessment in Italy and justifies the new and enhanced methodology. Section 3 introduces the methodological proposal based on MAVT, which includes a normalization process using value functions, weighting, and aggregation, ensuring a transparent and replicable evaluation process. Sections 4 and 5 are devoted to discussing the results and the conclusions. The results aim to discuss possible future applications of the model as a decision-support tool for investors and policymakers and enable a systematic comparison of cities based on their investment potential.

2 Research Background

2.1 Existing Urban Attractiveness Index

Over the last twenty-five years [8], broadening investors' sphere of interest has made urban attractiveness progressively more complex. Suppose international investors and administrations need information on a specific location to assess investment opportunities and policy scope. In that case, the approach must be open to the economic phenomenon of modern globalization and its multidimensionality.

The assessment of territorial attractiveness involves quantitative and qualitative interpretations [9], given its multidimensional nature, which spans economics, geographic, and social dimensions.

Real estate companies and multinational consultancies carefully observe foreign investment trends as a reliable thermometer capable of measuring the health of the attractiveness of a specific real estate market [10]. This awareness has driven the need to develop investment strategies and forecasting tools that support real estate planning.

Investment decisions are influenced by two key factors: knowledge or risk. Investors seek accurate information to reduce uncertainty and mitigate risks associated with their objectives. There is an inverse relationship between knowledge and risk: as knowledge about an area increases, the perceived risk decreases. By using attractiveness assessment methodologies, investors can better orient themselves in an increasingly competitive and dynamic market, improving their ability to plan long-term strategies.

Various national reports assess Italian cities' competitiveness but are not explicitly designed for investment decision-making. One of the most prominent tools in Italy is the 'Italy2Invest' (I2I) index, developed by Nomisma in 2017 [11], to support real estate developers in benchmarking municipalities and identifying profitable and low-risk investments. This attractiveness of Italian territories is measured through an integrated scoring system developed on 8 thematic domains and 125 indicators on population, environment, economy and society, business, real estate, infrastructure and services, public administration, and tourism. The indicators belonging to each domain were summarised in scores between 0.00 (absolute absence of attractiveness) and 100.00 (maximum level of attractiveness). The scores for each thematic area flow, in turn, into a general I2I score, which summarizes the attractiveness of a municipality or territory in a single value (also between 0 and 100). I2I is the only data intelligence and communication platform available in Italy for investors, offering customized reports and snapshots on specific municipalities.

However, apart from Italy2Invest, there are no comprehensive indices in Italy specifically designed to measure and compare the competitiveness of cities. The lack of complex tools to measure competitiveness represents a key barrier to accurately measuring a city's competitive potential and elaborating effective strategies to increase competitiveness. Since urban attractiveness is dynamic and interdisciplinary, the need for more structured methodologies remains crucial for future regional and urban planning strategies.

2.2 Research Gaps

Historically, Italy has been characterized by a complex and heterogeneous urban structure [3]. Due to the high number and diversity of cities across the country, Italy has often been called the 'country of 100 cities' [12].

Recent dossiers [13–15] are offering a representation of Italian medium-sized cities, on which administrative functions, production specializations, services, and strategic infrastructures gravitate, to propose coherent institutional and governance solutions for a real improvement in the governance of our cities: economic potential, identity vocations, production specializations, business concentration, added value and excellence in terms of projects and strategies.

Although several studies of urban economics prefer to focus mainly on more extensive, international cities, even for medium-sized Italian cities, the factors that implement their attractiveness are multiple and not necessarily related to urban size [16];

Italy has a long-standing tradition of territorial policy analysis, which primarily focuses on regional dynamics, often overlooking the specificity and multidimensional nature of urban problems. The debate on the development potential of medium-sized cities is a topic that is not yet known enough but has been showing newfound and dynamic attention in several academic and institutional studies and publications over the last fifteen years.

As a result, a stronger focus on medium-sized cities could be strategically advantageous and economically beneficial for the national economy. Specifically, this approach may be helpful in the Italian territory to reduce the push towards excessively concentrated development, which has a negative impact on overall competitiveness, and to exploit more deeply the necessarily dispersed territorial capital as well as the specific excellences of individual cities [17].

Several important points have become clear. First, there are very few indicators that show how well Italian cities support private investment. Second, there is a clear need to focus more on medium-sized cities [18]. Third, investors increasingly need tools to evaluate cities and data that can help them make better decisions.

In recent years, the use of multi-criteria and spatial assessment tools to better understand urban systems has grown significantly, and this trend is likely to continue. As cities and governance are under more pressure to prove themselves competitive and flexible, it is natural to anticipate that an increasing number of cities may experiment with new indices or modify existing ones to implement new keys to comparative analysis. With a predictable race to interpret more refined and numerous data and indicators, the latest cycle of urban studies promises to be more topical than ever.

3 Methodology Proposal

3.1 Conceptual Framework of the Rating Model

The proposed methodology is organized into three main phases, Intelligence, Design, and Review (Fig. 1), each contributing to the assessment of the investment potential of medium-sized cities.

The Intelligence phase sets the analytical foundation by selecting a set of indicators that reflect investor preferences and capture key aspects of urban development. These indicators, chosen for their relevance in urban analysis, define the scope of the model and shape its overall structure. To identify the most appropriate indicators, a variety of sources were consulted, including reports, assessment protocols, and academic literature. This preliminary review ensured that the selected criteria were both theoretically sound and aligned with current investment and planning practices.

In the Design phase, the conceptual configuration is translated into a decision-support tool through Multi-Criteria Decision Analysis (MCDA). A panel of experts from academia and the real estate sector supported the refinement of evaluation criteria to ensure both methodological soundness and practical relevance. The model uses Multi-Attribute Value Theory (MAVT) to manage the multiplicity of the indicators. During this phase, the model undergoes three essential operations. Indicators data are normalized between 0 and 1 using value functions, which transform raw measurements into standardized scores reflecting their relative desirability [48]. This enables meaningful comparisons across different urban contexts. Then, weights are assigned to the indicators based on expert input reflecting investors' priotities [19]. Finally, the weighted values are aggregated into a single measure, named City Attractiveness Index (CAI), which summarizes a city's investment appeal on a scale from 0.00 to 1.00. To aid interpretation, the CAI is divided into five categories, with higher scores indicating stronger attractiveness.

The Review phase is dedicated to validating the results and assessing the robustness of the model. This step helps identify possible adjustments and ensures that the methodology remains responsive to real-world decision-making. It also enables a critical reflection on the results, offering valuable insights for both policy and investment strategies. Through this validation, the model becomes a useful tool to support informed choices by public and private stakeholders [20].

While the Review phase is an integral component of the methodology, this contribution focuses primarily on the development and implementation of the evaluation model.

3.2 Selection of Criteria and Indicators

The need to account for the diverse priorities of stakeholders and the inherent complexity of urban systems highlights the importance of a comprehensive evaluation framework.

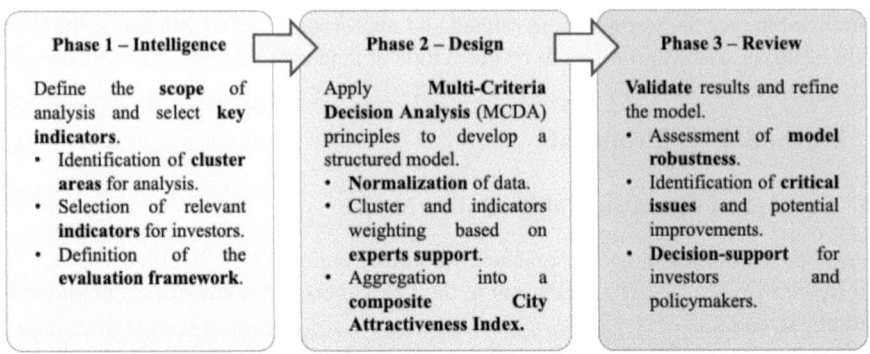

Fig. 1. Methodological framework.

Cities function as dynamic entities where economic, social, infrastructural, and environmental dimensions interact, requiring an approach that can effectively integrate multiple criteria and indicators into an assessment model.

An in-depth analysis of existing attractiveness indices and evaluation models was conducted to ensure methodological rigor. The review examined academic articles identified through a keyword search on Scopus, industry reports published by real estate firms and consulting companies, and research papers presented by institutes and financial media experts [11]. From this extensive analysis, 256 indicators were identified, covering seven key thematic dimensions: Accessibility and Infrastructure, Welfare and Well-being, Demography, Economy and Employment, Education, Research and Development, Real Estate Market, and Tourism.

Given the many indicators, a selection process was implemented to refine the dataset. A comparative matrix was developed to cross-reference the indicators with the existing literature, prioritizing those with the highest recurrence and relevance. The primary criterion for selection was redundancy, ensuring that indicators frequently referenced in the state-of-the-art analysis were retained. As a result, 75 indicators emerged as the most significant, while the others were excluded.

The selection of indicators was carried out in collaboration with multidisciplinary experts, including urban planners, economists, and investment professionals. Particular attention was paid to avoiding redundancies and minimizing correlation among indicators, to ensure their independence, a key requirement for the proper application of the MAVT model [19]. Their input was crucial in validating the final set of indicators, ensuring their practical relevance for investment decision-making. Each expert assessed the indicators within their area of expertise, focusing on their significance, reliability, and applicability to private investors. Indicators deemed redundant or of limited importance were removed.

Following this expert validation [19], the final framework is constituted of 28 indicators grouped into seven thematic clusters, as detailed in Table 1. This selection process ensured that the key factors influencing urban attractiveness were effectively captured, balancing academic rigor with real-world applicability.

Table 1. Thematic clusters, indicators, definitions, and data sources.

Cluster	Indicators	Definition	Source and year
Economy and employment	Innovative startup density	Number of innovative startups per 1,000 corporations	InfoCamere, 2024 [21]
	Unemployment rate	Percentage of the labor force without employment	ISTAT, 2023 [22]
	High-revenue companies	Number of companies with a turnover above €500 million among the top 30 by revenue (province-level data)	Registro Aziende, 2023 [23]
	Income per capita	Average income per person (€/inhabitant)	Ministry of Economy and Finance, 2022 [24]
	NRRP investment per capita	Ratio of NRRP project investments to resident population (€/inhabitant)	Italia Domani, 2024 [25]
	Youth entrepreneurship	Number of companies with an owner under 35 per 100 registered companies	InfoCamere, 2023 [21]
Accessibility and infrastructure	High-Speed railway	Presence of High-Speed railway stations within 30 km from the town centre (Yes/No)	Trenitalia e Italo NTV, 2024 [26, 27]
	Digitalisation of Public Administration	Average Cityrank FPA score on digital governance	FPA, 2024 [28]
	Hospital facilities	Number of hospital beds per 1,000 inhabitants	Ministry of Health, 2024 [29]
	International airports	Presence of international airports within 50 km from the town centre (Yes/No)	ENAV, 2024 [30]

(*continued*)

Table 1. (*continued*)

Cluster	Indicators	Definition	Source and year
	Public transport	Number of local public transport buses per 100,000 inhabitants	ISTAT, 2022 [31]
Education, research and development	Graduates	Percentage of graduates in the total resident population (%)	ISTAT, 2022 [22]
	University quality	Average ranking of Italian universities in the CENSIS report	CENSIS, 2024 [32]
	Non-resident students	Percentage of students studying away from their home province	Ministry of University and Research, 2024 [33]
	Italian superior graduate schools	Number of superior graduate schools	Ministry of University and Research, 2024 [33]
Welfare and well-being	Air quality	Number of days exceeding the PM10 pollution	ISTAT, 2022 [31]
	Socio-educational services for infancy day-care	Approved nurseries per 100 children aged 0–2 (%)	ISTAT, 2022 [34]
	Crime incidence	Number of reported crimes (with identified suspect) per 100,000 inhabitants (%)	Ministry of Intern, 2022 [35]
Demography	Residential Attractiveness index	Ratio of cumulative household migration balances (2004–2023) to total residents in 2003	ISTAT, 2023 [36]
	Foreign population	Percentage of foreign residents in total population	ISTAT, 2023 [36]
	Age dependency ratio	Ratio of non-working-age to working-age population	ISTAT, 2023 [36]

(*continued*)

Table 1. (*continued*)

Cluster	Indicators	Definition	Source and year
Real Estate Market	Average residential rents	Average rent for stately and civilian dwellings in the city center (€/sqm/year)	Nomisma, 2024 [11]
	Normalized Number of Transactions	Number of housing purchases and sales	Agenzia delle Entrate, 2023 [37]
	Average sales times	Average time required to sell a residential property (months)	Immobiliare.it, 2024 [38]
	Unoccupied conventional dwellings	Percentage of houses not permanently occupied	ISTAT, 2021 [22]
Tourism	Average stay duration	Average number of nights per tourism trip	ISTAT, 2021 [39]
	Luxury hotel bed capacity	Percentage of luxury hotel rooms (4 and 5 stars) out of total hotel capacity	ISTAT, 2023 [39]
	Foreign tourist arrivals	Percentage of foreign tourists among total arrivals	ISTAT, 2022 [39]

3.3 Normalization Through Value Functions

Using value functions enables the normalization of indicators, ensuring comparability and consistency across all criteria. These functions act as mathematical models of human judgment, systematically converting raw indicator values into a standard evaluation scale [40]. This transformation ensures comparability across all criteria since indicators are often expressed in different units, such as percentages, monetary values, or absolute counts. Bringing all indicators onto a uniform scale ensures that each criterion contributes proportionally to the overall assessment without being influenced by differences in measurement units.

Each value function was designed based on the nature of the data it represents. Indicators with continuous numerical values were normalized using MinMax scaling, mapping their original range onto a 0.00 to 1.00 scale.

A stepwise or piecewise function was applied for categorical indicators, assigning discrete scores instead of interpolating between values. The selection of thresholds and scoring logic depended on the distribution and interpretability of the data, ensuring that each function accurately captured the impact of the indicator on urban attractiveness.

3.4 Weighting Process

A central challenge in the Design phase was determining whether all dimensions of urban attractiveness should contribute equally to investment potential. To address this, we implemented a weighting system to define each component's role in the overall assessment [19].

The weighting process relied on the direct assignment method [49], conducted through expert consultation. This method, grounded in multi-criteria decision theory, makes it possible to explicitly capture the value judgments of stakeholders, ensuring that the relative importance of each criterion reflects both theoretical priorities and practical relevance [19]. These weights were then validated by the same experts to ensure their relevance and consistency with real-world investment priorities. This iterative process ensured that the assigned weights accurately reflected the experts' views and investment considerations.

To maintain consistency and comparability, a normalization process was applied. Within each thematic cluster, the total weight of the indicators was set to 1.00, ensuring that the importance of each indicator was assessed relative to others in the same category. This approach prevented clusters with more indicators from disproportionately influencing the final score. Additionally, the sum of the weights across all seven clusters was normalized to 1.00, preserving balance in the evaluation framework.

The final weightings assigned to each category and indicator are presented in Table 2, offering a view of how different aspects of urban attractiveness contribute to the overall assessment. Experts emphasized that economic factors, infrastructure, and education are decisive in shaping investment choices. These dimensions also indirectly influence real estate market trends, demographic patterns, and tourism potential. The Welfare and Well-being cluster was assigned an intermediate weight, recognizing its significance while ensuring it did not overshadow the more investment-driven dimensions.

3.5 Aggregation Process

The overall evaluation of an option was obtained through a weighted sum of normalized performances, where each criterion contributes to the final score based on its assigned weight. This aggregated score, which ranges from 0.00 to 1.00, reflects the city's overall appeal as perceived by decision-makers and is given by Eq. 1:

$$I_{attr}(a) = \sum_{i=1}^{n} w_{cli} \cdot w_i \cdot v_i(a) \quad (1)$$

where $I_{attr}(a)$ is the final attractiveness score (City Attractiveness Index, CAI) for city a, w_{cli} is the weight assigned to each thematic cluster, w_i represents the importance of each indicator, $v_i(a)$ is the normalized value for the indicator i.

Table 2. Weightings associated with the clusters and indicators.

Cluster	Clusterweight (w_{cli})	Indicators	Indicators weight (w_i)
Economy and labour	0.250	Innovative startup density	0.167
		Unemployment rate	0.167
		High-revenue companies	0.167
		Income per capita	0.167
		NRPP investment per capita	0.167
		Youth entrepreneurship	0.167
Accessibility andinfrastructure	0.22	High-Speed railway	0.300
		Digitalization of Public Administration	0.300
		Hospital facilities	0.250
		International airports	0.100
		Public transport	0.050
Education, research and development	0.200	Graduates	0.400
		University quality	0.300
		Non-resident students	0.200
		Italian superior graduate schools	0.100
Welfare and well-being	0.150	Air quality	0.450
		Socio-educational services for infancy day-care	0.350
		Crime incidence	0.200
Demography	0.100	Residential attractiveness index	0.450
		Foreign population	0.350
		Age dependency ratio	0.200

(*continued*)

Table 2. (*continued*)

Cluster	Clusterweight (w_{cli})	Indicators	Indicators weight (w_i)
Real Estate market	0.060	Average residential rents	0.400
		Normalized Number of Transactions	0.300
		Average sales times	0.200
		Unoccupied conventional dwellings	0.100
Tourism	0.020	Average stay duration	0.450
		Luxury hotel bed capacity	0.350
		Foreign arrivals	0.200

While the overall score provides a useful composite measure, more detailed insights can be gained by examining results at the cluster level. Analyzing the evaluation across distinct thematic dimensions allows for a better understanding of how specific factors contribute to a city's appeal. For example, a city may perform well economically but struggle with infrastructure or transportation accessibility, highlighting areas for strategic improvement.

To facilitate interpretation of the CAI, it has been classified into five levels, with higher values indicating greater attractiveness. A score between 0.00 and 0.20 indicates a lack of attractiveness, reflecting cities facing significant challenges in terms of infrastructure, economy and investment potential. A score between 0.21 and 0.40 indicates low attractiveness, meaning that these cities show some development potential, but with some shortcomings in key urban dimensions. Cities with a score between 0.41 and 0.60 are classified as mid-level attractive, as they offer stable conditions but may require improvements to increase their competitiveness. A score between 0.61 and 0.80 represents high attractiveness, indicating cities that perform well in multiple dimensions and offer strong foundations for investment. Finally, a score between 0.81 and 1.00 reflects excellent attractiveness, representing cities with excellent performance.

4 Discussion of Findings

4.1 Interpretation of the City Attractiveness Index

The rating model provides a quantitative comparison of cities for investors. The configuration of the model and its outputs made it possible to identify the strengths and weaknesses of cities to guide them in territorial development.

The research enabled the acquisition of information related to attractiveness and multicriteria methodologies. Although there is no unambiguous definition in the literature, attractiveness can be defined as the ability of an area to attract users, services, tourists, new residents, and investment [41], which represent the key elements underlying the development of territories [42–44].

The model highlights which criteria drive attractiveness and how different cities perform across dimensions. Each cluster was assigned a set of indicators based on raw data, which were then transformed into normalized scores through the MAVT methodology, thus ensuring an objective and comparable assessment.

The indicators and clusters considered have included multidisciplinary issues such as economic growth, employment conditions, accessibility to transportation and broader infrastructure, demographic development, availability of high human capital, quality of life, tourism, university and vocational training, and residential real estate market trends.

The application of the model made it possible to analyze the configuration of medium-sized cities and their development in response to the challenges of the last decade. Interpreting the indicators and scores assigned in the different clusters showed in which dimensions of attractiveness some cities perform better than others, providing several insights.

The cities with the highest performance will have more concrete opportunities to witness new development possibilities in the long term that will generate important impacts: stakeholders will see in the most virtuous performance the conditions necessary to launch new investment initiatives. For these cities, the watchword is 'concentration'; e.g., the concentration of services, innovative businesses, young entrepreneurs, connections, universities and centers of high education, welfare services, quality accommodations, dynamic real estate market, and jobs.

On the other hand, one can find contexts with greater difficulty that have lost ground in competition with other cities and are experiencing negative demographic and economic trends. Urban centers that face the most extreme consequences will enter a vicious cycle of impoverishment and demographic aging, both residents' quantitative presence and the quality of life in general, translated into less provision of a good network of territorial public services [10].

4.2 Implications for Investors and Policymakers

The development of this rating model reflects the growing reliance on aggregate indices in urban analysis. Understanding both the overall scores and the detailed contributions of individual thematic clusters is critical for guiding policymakers and investors toward informed, multidimensional decision-making [21]. For instance, studies have highlighted how urban competitiveness can drive economic growth, while more recent research emphasizes the importance of targeted interventions to enhance investment potential.

These insights provide opportunities for local governments to increase urban competitiveness and improve investment conditions by better responding to the needs of foreign investors and aligning development strategies with global market trends. Ultimately, the goal is to create urban environments in which investment thrives, thereby supporting local economies and communities.

For investors, the model provides a dynamic framework adaptable across key sectors including logistics, technology, and real estate. In inherently uncertain urban investment environments, the systematic evaluation of city performance across multiple indicators serves to reduce information asymmetries and reveal strategic opportunities. The comprehensive assessment of urban assets and liabilities allows investors to mitigate risks while identifying competitive advantages that might otherwise remain obscured in conventional analyses.

From a policymaking perspective, the model offers an evidence-based foundation for territorial development strategies. By diagnosing relative strengths and weaknesses across thematic clusters, municipal and regional governments can design targeted interventions to enhance competitiveness while promoting spatial equity. This governance function proves particularly crucial for medium-sized cities, which often face the dual challenge of competing with larger metropolitan areas while addressing internal disparities.

Beyond working as a decision-support tool, the model also informs investment strategies by shaping the narrative behind investment choices. The selected indicators not only assess feasibility but also highlight strengths and pinpoint weaknesses, ensuring a coherent and forward-looking planning process. Continuous monitoring and regular review are essential to adapt to changing urban dynamics and maintain competitiveness [19, 45].

By integrating these perspectives, the rating model offers a robust framework for both public and private stakeholders, supporting strategic, data-driven decisions that can lead to improved urban environments and sustainable economic development.

5 Conclusions and Future Perspectives

This research proposes an alternative to existing city rankings by introducing a MAVT-based evaluation model grounded in academic principles rather than corporate metrics. By integrating established theories on decision-making with practical insights from the investment world, the model offers a more refined perspective on what makes a city attractive today.

Our model provides a detailed view of a city by exploring seven key dimensions: economy and employment, accessibility and infrastructure, education, research and development, welfare and well-being, demography, the real estate market, and tourism. This structure allows for a deeper understanding of urban dynamics revealing strengths and weaknesses across different areas, particularly useful for decision-makers: public authorities can use the results to support planning choices and allocate resources more effectively, while investors gain access to a framework that reduces uncertainty and supports informed decisions.

A key strength of this work lies in the interdisciplinary contribution of professionals from urban planning, economics, and investment. Their collaboration ensured that the selection of indicators was both theoretically robust and practically grounded.

However, several challenges and opportunities accompany the implementation of such a model. One limitation lies in the availability of data across cities, which may affect comparability. Additionally, the model's effectiveness depends on the relevance and timeliness of the indicators used, an area that may require ongoing revision as urban dynamics evolve. There is also a risk of oversimplification when complex qualitative dimensions are translated into quantitative scores, potentially limiting the model's sensitivity to context-specific factors.

Adaptation efforts will be necessary to tailor the model to different national or regional contexts, including the integration of local priorities and stakeholder inputs. Transparent communication of the model's assumptions and limitations will also be crucial to ensure its credibility and usability among diverse audiences.

Looking forward, the Review phase should include a pilot application to two medium-sized Italian cities with contrasting socio-economic and urban characteristics. This would allow for a practical test of the model's capacity to reflect investor expectations in varied contexts. Continuing the validation process through real-world applications and dialogue with stakeholders will be essential to improve the model further and ensure its long-term utility.

References

1. Jacobs, J.: The Economy of Cities, 1st edn. Edward Arnold, London (1969)
2. Zajczyk, F.: Presentazione. Quad. Sociol. **52**, 3–12 (2010). https://doi.org/10.4000/qds.715
3. Balducci, A.: L'agenda urbana ragioni e contesto. In: Calafati, G.A. (ed.) Città tra Sviluppo e Declino: Un'agenda Urbana Per l'Italia, p. 446. Donzelli Editore, Rome (2014)
4. EUROCITIES Homepage. https://eurocities.eu/. Accessed 10 Jan 2025
5. Musolino, D., Volget, S.: Towards a multinational approach to the study of territorial attractiveness, Working Papers (2020). https://hal.science/hal-02501582
6. Kresl, P.K.: Competitiveness and the urban economy: twenty-four large US metropolitan areas. Urban Stud. **36**(5–6), 1017–1027 (1999). https://doi.org/10.1080/0042098993330
7. Begg, I.: Cities and competitiveness. Urban Stud. **36**(5–6), 795–809 (1999). https://doi.org/10.1080/0042098993222
8. Godin, B.: Innovation contested: the idea of innovation over the centuries. 1st edn. Routledge, New York (2015). https://doi.org/10.4324/9781315855608
9. Janssen, O.: Job Demands, perceptions of effort-reward fairness and innovative work behaviour. J. Occup. Organ. Psychol. **73**, 287–302 (2000). https://doi.org/10.1348/096317900167038
10. Buciuni, G.: Periferie competitive: lo sviluppo dei territori nell'economia della conoscenza, 1st edn. Il Mulino, Bologna (2023)
11. NOMISMA Homepage. https://www.nomisma.it/. Accessed 02 Mar 2025
12. Cicalese, M.L., Musi, A.: L'Italia delle cento città, 1st edn. FrancoAngeli, Milan (2005)
13. IFEL Fondazione ANCI: Il Potenziale delle Città Medie nel Sistema Italia. 1st edn. ANCI Città Medie, Rome (2019). https://www.fondazioneifel.it/documenti-e-pubblicazioni/item/download/2956_066dc223d81ecb6ad9fe896fbcc3e0bf
14. Gori, G.: Le città medie protagoniste della rinascita del Paese. In: ALI, Consiglio Nazionale ALI, Naples (2021). https://aliautonomie.it/wp-content/uploads/2021/07/RElazione-CITTA-MEDIE-Ali-23.07.2021-1.pdf
15. Decaro, A.: Presentazione. In: Mecenate 90 Association L'Italia Policentrica. Il fermento delle città intermedie, pp. 11–14. FrancoAngeli, Milan (2020)
16. Camagni, R., Capello, R., Caragliu, A.: The rise of second-rank cities: what role for agglomaration economies? Eur. Plan. Stud. **23**, 1069–1089 (2014)

17. Micelli, E., Righetto, E.: The great concentration. demography, economy, real estate values and development of Italian metropolitan cities. In: Giuffrida, S., Trovato, M.R., Rosato, P., Fattinnanzi, E., Oppio, A., Chiodo, S. (eds.) Science of Valuations Green Energy and Technology, pp. 133–148. Springer, Cham (2024). https://doi.org/10.1007/978-3-031-53709-7_10
18. Longo, A., Cicirello, L.: Città Metropolitane e pianificazione di area vasta. Prospettive di governo territoriale per la gestione delle metamorfosi urbane. 1st edn. FrancoAngeli, Milan (2016)
19. Centis, L., Micelli, E.: Regenerating places outside the metropolis. a reading of three global art-related processes and development trajectories. Sustainbility 13(22), 12359 (2021). https://doi.org/10.3390/su132212359
20. Roy, B., Słowiński, R.: Questions guiding the choice of a multicriteria decision aiding method. EURO J. Decis. Process. 1(1–2), 69–67 (2013). https://doi.org/10.1007/s40070-013-0004-7
21. INFOCAMERE Homepage. https://www.infocamere.it/. Accessed 02 Mar 2025
22. ISTAT Permanent Census Data Warehouse. http://dati-censimentipermanenti.istat.it/. Accessed 02 Mar 2025
23. Registro Aziende Homepage. https://registroaziende.it/. Accessed 02 Mar 2025
24. Ministry of economy and finance dipartimento delle finanze, dipartimento delle finanze statistiche sulle dichiarazioni. Accessed 02 Mar 2025
25. Italia Domani Hompage. https://www.italiadomani.gov.it/content/sogei-ng/it/it/home.html. Accessed 02 Mar 2025
26. Trenitalia Homepage. https://www.trenitalia.com/it.html. Accessed 02 Mar 2025
27. Italo NTV Homepage. https://www.italotreno.com/it. Accessed 02 Mar 2025
28. FPA ICity Rank. https://www.forumpa.it/icity-rank/. Accessed 02 Mar 2025
29. Ministry of Health Open Data Homepage. https://www.salute.gov.it/portale/documentazione/p6_2_8.jsp?lingua=italiano. Accessed 02 Mar 2025
30. ENAV Homepage. https://www.enav.it/. Accessed 02 Mar 2025
31. ISTAT "Ambiente Urbano". https://www.istat.it/comunicato-stampa/ambiente-urbano-anno-2022-2/. Accessed 02 Mar 2025
32. CENSIS University Ranking Homepage. https://www.censis.it/formazione/la-classifica-censis-delle-universit%C3%A0-italiane-edizione-20242025. Accessed 02 Mar 2025
33. Ministry of University and Research Open Data Homepage. https://dati-ustat.mur.gov.it/. Accessed 02 Mar 2025
34. ISTAT Data by Theme Social Security and Welfare. http://dati.istat.it/Index.aspx?QueryId=23231. Accessed 02 Mar 2025
35. Ministry of Intern Data and Statistics Homepage. https://www.interno.gov.it/it/stampa-e-comunicazione/dati-e-statistiche. Accessed 02 Mar 2025
36. ISTAT Demo Main structural characteristics of the population. https://demo.istat.it/?l=en#sezione1. Accessed 02 Mar 2025
37. Agenzia delle Entrate Homepage OMI Homepage. https://www.agenziaentrate.gov.it/portale/web/guest/schede/fabbricatiterreni/omi/forniture-dati-omi. Accessed 02 Mar 2025
38. Immobiliare.it Homepage. https://www.immobiliare.it/. Accessed 02 Mar 2025
39. ISTAT Data by Theme Services Tourism. http://dati.istat.it/Index.aspx?lang=en&SubSessionId=3be5238a-f7e4-41e6-9c3d-27bf8807f833. Accessed 02 Mar 2025
40. Torrieri, F., Oppio, A., Rossitti, M.: Cultural heritage social value and community mapping. In: Bevilacqua, C., Calabrò, F., Della Spina, L. (eds.) New Metropolitan Perspectives. NMP 2020. Smart Innovation, Systems and Technologies, vol. 178, pp. 1778–1795. Springer, Cham (2021). https://doi.org/10.1007/978-3-030-48279-4_169
41. Servillo, L., Van Den Broeck, P.: The social construction of planning systems: a strategic-relational institutionalist approach. Plan. Pract. Res. 27(1), 41–61 (2012). https://doi.org/10.1080/02697459.2012.661179

42. Rossitti, M., Oppio, A., Torrieri, F., Dell'Ovo, M.: Tactical urbanism interventions for the urban environment: which economic impacts? Land **12**(7), 1457 (2023). https://doi.org/10.3390/land12071457
43. Della Spina, L., Assumma, V.: Development strategies for the mediterranean coastal landscape: adaptive decision-making processes for implementing the circular economy in the redevelopment of the reggio calabria waterfront. Land **14**(2), 301 (2025). https://doi.org/10.3390/land14020301
44. Datola, G., Bottero, M., de Angelis, E.: Enhancing urban resilience capacities: an analytic network process-based application. Environ. Clim. Technol. **25**(1), 1270–1283. Riga Technical University (2021). https://doi.org/10.2478/rtuect-2021-0096
45. Cerreta, M., Daldanise, G., Sposito, S.: Culture-led regeneration for urban spaces: monitoring complex values networks in action. Urbani Izziv **29**, 9–28 (2018). https://doi.org/10.5379/urbani-izziv-en-2018-29-supplement-001
46. Mattioli, F.: La via di mezzo. In: Lanzani, A. (ed.) Italia di mezzo. Sguardi, politiche, immaginari, pp. 39–49. Donzelli Editore, Rome (2024)
47. Curci, F., Ricchiuto, M.: Politiche urbane tra logiche locali e traiettorie sovralocali. In: Lanzani, A. (ed.) Italia di Mezzo. Sguardi, Politiche, Immaginari, pp. 107–116. Donzelli Editore, Rome (2024)
48. Beinat, E.: Multiattribute value function theory. In: Value Functions for Environmental Management, pp. 21–45. Environment & Management **7** Springer, Dordrecht (1997). https://doi.org/10.1007/978-94-015-8885-0_2
49. Bottomley, P.A., Doyle, J.R., Green, R.H.: Testing the reliability of weight elicitation methods: direct rating versus point allocation. J. Mark. Res. **37**(4), 508–513 (2000). https://doi.org/10.1509/jmkr.37.4.508.18794(Originalworkpublished2000)

Assessing the Tourist Carrying Capacity of a UNESCO World Heritage proposed site

Sebastiano Barbieri[1](✉), Caterina Caprioli[1], Barbara Baronetto[2], Marta Bottero[1], and Marco Valle[2]

[1] Dipartimento Interateneo di Scienze, Progetto e Politiche del Territorio (DIST), Politecnico di Torino, Viale Mattioli, 39, 10125 Torino, TO, Italy
{sebastiano.barbieri,caterina.caprioli,marta.bottero}@polito.it
[2] Links Foundation, Via Pier Carlo Boggio, 61, 10138 Torino, TO, Italy
{barbara.baronetto,marco.valle}@linksfoundation.com

Abstract. In destinations where tourism represents a significant economic and cultural development source, it is crucial to address and mitigate the associated threats and challenges. In this regard, the present study aims to analyze the concept of sustainable tourism. This concept promotes tourism development while protecting environmental resources and preserving local cultural identities. The tool employed for this analysis is the Tourism Carrying Capacity (TCC), a methodology that was initially developed to define the maximum number of visitors a destination can handle without compromising its sustainability. The paper explores the evolution of this concept from both a theoretical and practical point of view, applying the most recent approach. The integrated methodology employed in this study aims to evaluate this concept to propose management guidelines for the management of cultural heritage sites. This paper will apply the methodology to the real-case study of the Sacra di San Michele. This abbey is a site of significant cultural, historical and spiritual value to the region of Piedmont and is currently listed as a tentative World Heritage Site. The results highlight the need to redesign the direct access to Sacra, with a better management of public transport and interchanges between public and private transport. In addition to setting the basis for a balanced management of the site while preserving the environmental and cultural values, this paper aims to demonstrate the importance of adopting integrated methodologies for decision support in complex contexts such as the cultural heritage sites.

Keywords: Tourist Carrying Capacity · Sustainable Tourism · Indicator system · UNESCO · Management Plan

1 Sustainable Tourism

In the contemporary context, tourism has emerged as a significant catalyst for economic and cultural development. Nevertheless, it is imperative to address and mitigate the challenges associated with this phenomenon [1]. Tourism exerts a considerable influence on various components of the territory, including the environment, the local economy, and the social dimension [2, 3]. The World Tourism Organization (WTO) asserts that ensuring the long-term sustainability of tourism requires a balance between the environmental, economic, and socio-cultural dimensions that are inextricably linked to the tourism sector. In accordance with this perspective, sustainable tourism should (a) make optimal use of environmental resources; (b) respect the socio-cultural authenticity of host communities; and (c) ensure profitable and long-term economic operations that distribute benefits equally. Moreover, the development of sustainable tourism needs informed engagement of all relevant stakeholders [4–6]. This is true for all tourist locations, but it is especially important for UNESCO sites and places of cultural significance. These sites have to combine the socioeconomic development of the territory with resource protection and enhancement [5, 7]. In particular, the inscription of a site in the World Heritage List (WHL) generally produces certain benefits in terms of safeguarding cultural assets, but it can also exert negative repercussions on the territory if management practices are not balanced with the principles of sustainability. One of the most evident impacts is overtourism. For WHS, the risk associated with this phenomenon is even more relevant, as they are globally recognized and subject to significant tourist flows, especially at certain times of the year. This phenomenon has been widely studied in the literature, taking into account different types of tourism and different contexts around the world [8–11].

Within this context, the necessity of tools to support tourism management decisions is becoming increasingly evident. To manage tourism in a sustainable manner, national and local governments have increasingly available technics that support decision-making processes, often in conjunction with one another [12, 13]. In particular, decision-making approaches have evolved to encompass systemic, nonlinear, and integrated perspectives to support a development that has become increasingly complex [14]. This approach consists of the synergistic use of aspects from different disciplines and proves to be fundamental in contexts such as tourism, in which the problems to be addressed are complex in nature, characterized by uncertainties and interdependencies [15]. Among the various decision-support approaches, Tourism Carrying Capacity (TCC) is particularly useful for quantifying the optimal number of tourists that a given destination can accommodate. Generally, the concept of carrying capacity is predicated on the measurement of the sustainable utilization of a given resource [7, 16]. When applied to the evaluation of tourism phenomena, the application of this approach becomes complex due to the numerous environmental and socioeconomic factors that interact with the tourist destination [7, 17]. Many of these factors also depend on the subjective perception of tourists and the host community [7]. According to the official definition proposed by the WTO, the carrying capacity of a tourist location consists of the maximum number of people who visit that place in the same period, without compromising its environmental, physical, economic and sociocultural characteristics and without reducing tourist satisfaction [18]. However, various definitions of TCC and supporting methodologies exist. The paper will explore them in detail in Sect. 2. This intense debate about TCC highlights the pivotal role in pursuing sustainable tourism. Indeed, the calculation of TCC facilitates the establishment of practical and feasible limits, thereby contributing to the development of sustainable tourism practices.

In this paper, the TCC is considered both as a statical indicator of sustainability and dynamic and informative tool, as the recent definition proposed by the SITi research institute (now named LINKS Foundation and hereafter simply mentioned as LINKS) of Politecnico di Torino in 2017 [19]. Specifically, the calculation method proposed by LINKS is applied in this work to a WHL proposed, namely an abbey in the municipality of Turin (Italy) called the Sacra di San Michele. The site is a relevant and prestigious example of cultural, historical, and spiritual value, considered as the symbol of the Piedmont region. The calculation of the TCC provides the foundation for the formulation of guidelines for this site to enhance the future management of the UNESCO property, with the objective of safeguarding its natural and cultural values in accordance with the principles of conservation and protection.

After this introduction, the paper is structured as follows. Section 2.1 presents the different definitions of TCC and methodologies for its calculation. Based on this, the methodology chosen is presented in Sect. 2.2. Section 3 describes the case study of the Sacra di San Michele with an in-depth on the main strengths, weaknesses, opportunities and threats, useful for the TCC calculation. Section 4 details the application of TCC to the case study, while the results are highlighted in Sect. 5. Conclusive remarks are finally provided in Sect. 6.

2 Tourist Carrying Capacity

2.1 Definitions of TCC

The concept of carrying capacity is derived from civil engineering, where it indicates the maximum load a structure can support before failure. Subsequently, this concept was integrated into the tourism sector. However, various definitions of tourist carrying capacity can be found in literature. The term has evolved over time and across different disciplines, emerging as a multidisciplinary concept that supports decision-making processes.

Initially, the TCC was associated with environmental sustainability, specifically as the physical limit an area could withstand without compromising the integrity of the local ecosystem. This initial concept is elucidated by the definitions proposed by Mathieson & Wall (1982) and Canestrelli & Costa (1991) [21, 22]. Mathieson & Wall (1982) [22] defined TCC as the unacceptable alteration of the physical environment resulting from unsustainable tourism, while Canestrelli & Costa (1991) emphasized the ecological dimension of tourist destinations, identifying the maximum level of environmental stress beyond which tourism causes substantial damage [21].

Subsequently, the growing recognition of the links between the environment, culture and economy expanded the idea of TCC to include a wider range of factors, such as social, economic and cultural aspects. This is evidenced by the definition of the World Tourism Organization (WTO) in 2000, which defined TCC as " the maximum number of people that may visit a tourist destination at the same time, without causing destruction of the physical, economic and socio-cultural environment and an unacceptable decrease in the quality of the visitors" [18].

A more recent conceptualization of TCC was proposed between 2010 and 2020 by LINKS. The latter institute proposed a definition of TCC that not only considers the maximum number of tourists as a location can accommodate without suffering damage, but also as a dynamic tool, updatable over time and oriented to an analysis of the current situation of the site under study, its state of conservation and possible management problems [23]. Therefore, the TCC becomes an instrument to direct tourism strategies according to the specific location under analysis and by facilitating its decision-making processes related to tourism management.

As was the case with the definition of TCC, the scientific community does not hold a consensus on the identification of the dimensions affected by over tourism. Fisher & Krutilla (1972) [24] adopts the ecological and economic dimension of TCC. In 2004, WTO introduced other three dimensions, i.e. cultural, social and psychological, and infrastructural. LINKS in 2017, identified six components of the TCC:

- TCC Theoretical: maximum number of tourists based on the surface of the good;
- TCC Physical/Functional: equal to the TCC Theoretical to which (qualitative or quantitative) adjustments are applied according to physical limits (such as safety conditions of the property, the presence of any architectural barriers, etc.);
- TCC Social: residents' perception of the tourism phenomenon, both in terms of quantity and quality. This assessment includes for example the level of seasonalization of flows, the attitude of tourists, and the number of visitors;
- TCC Psychological: tourists' perceptions of the property they are visiting and the level of satisfaction at the end of the visit; it derives mainly from evaluations related to the presence of tourist services, the efficiency of reception policies, the existence of adequate signage etc.;
- TCC Infrastructural/Territorial: consider aspects related to a broader scale, including infrastructure conditions and adequacy of mobility policies, the number of available parking spaces (compared to a surrounding area), and factors related to the specific conditions of the area, such as its ability to accommodate, absorb and manage the flow of tourists;
- TCC Management: cross-cutting and concluding element that guides all other indicators, to respond to the system's weaknesses.

Given the plurality of definitions and the variety of dimensions associated with the concept of TCC, as evidenced by the extant literature, it is evident that the methodologies employed for its calculation also vary. For a complete review of the existing methodologies, it is possible to refer to Cimnaghi et al. (2017) [19]. Among them, the present work adopts the integrated method proposed by Cimnaghi et al. (2017) [19], detailed in Sect. 2.2.

2.2 Links Foundation Methodology

The methodology proposed by LINKS derives from a research project developed in collaboration with the Italian Ministry of Cultural Heritage, Activities and Tourism in 2007. The objective of the work of Cimnaghi et al. (2017) [19] was to define a framework capable of taking into account the critical aspects that characterize cultural heritage in the tourism phenomenon. To this end, the evolution of the TCC concept and the application purposes proposed by different authors have been examined in the literature. The main issues included are the accessibility of the site, the ability to communicate its value to the population, the existence of infrastructural limitations, but especially the preservation of the exceptional value of these sites. In this sense, the TCC aims to be a dynamic tool capable of reconciling the conservation of the property with the maximization of the quality of the tourist experience. The original method, tested on simple case studies (such as museums and enclosed sites), was subsequently updated by the LINKS itself, which applied it to the World Heritage sites of the Lombardy region in Italy, experimenting with more complex and wider contexts.

The method consists of three main phases (Fig. 1): (1) the phase of recognition and identification of the dynamics affecting the site, along with the compilation of the preliminary Carrying Capacity form; (2) the core phase of the methodology, in which the Table of Indicators is developed; and (3) the compilation of the results sheet with the consequent drafting of management guidelines.

The first stage is to complete the preliminary carrying capacity form, which collects the main information on the intrinsic characteristics of the property. This is followed by information on the management and conservation of the site in terms of its degree of usability. Finally, it is possible to implement the required information, giving space to the state of conservation of the property in order to highlight possible criticalities.

The second phase is to define the indicators that can be used to describe the current state of the site from different perspectives. In particular, the table of indicators can be divided into the 5 themes previously analyzed, giving for each indicator the name, a brief description, the level of comparison used (insert explanatory note) and the value measured in relation to the data collected or found *in situ*. For the value of the theoretical TCC, the calculation used is taken directly from the formula of Cifuentes (1992) [25]. A comparison level is defined for each indicator. This level indicates whether (a) the target value is provided by law or if it is a quantifiable factor; (b) the target value is derived from a reference in the literature or from a best practice; (c) the target value needs to be defined *in situ* with the site managers; (d) no target value is defined, so the qualitative indication needs to be defined by experts and site managers [19].

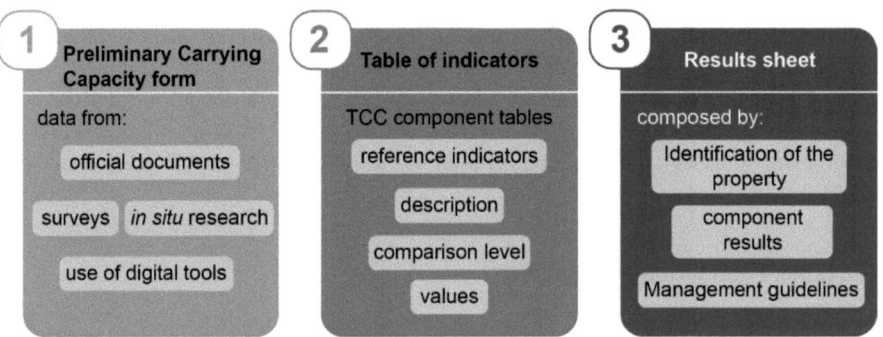

Fig. 1. Methodological diagram and results

In the final stage, the findings obtained are collected and summarized in the 'results sheet'. This includes a first section summarizing information about the site, including maps and figures where appropriate. This is followed by considerations for each of the components of the TCC. Firstly, the theoretical TCC is calculated, which should be compared with flows observed in previous periods to highlight any conditions of overuse and overtourism. After an evaluation of the other components, the form ends with a section dedicated to management guidelines, in which strategic indications are given for the cultural property analyzed.

3 Case Study

The case study investigates a historical and religious building called the Sacra di San Michele located in the Northwest Italy, and more precisely close to the city of Turin, in the municipality of Sant'Ambrogio di Torino (TO) in the Piedmont Region (Fig. 2).

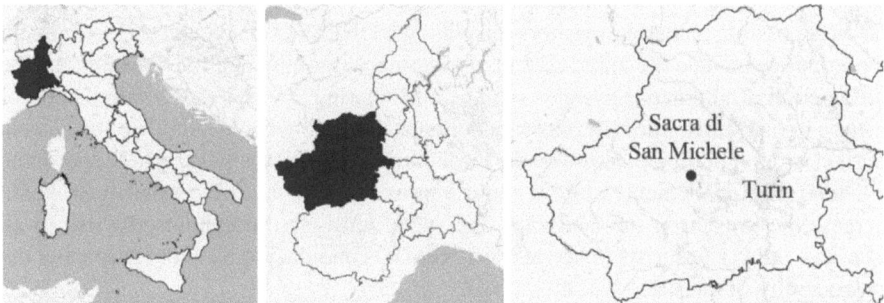

Fig. 2. Location of Piedmont Region (left), Metropolitan City of Turin (center) and Sacra di San Michele (right).

The building is an abbey on the top of a rocky promontory called Mount Pirchiriano at an altitude of 962 m [26]. The founding year of the abbey remains undocumented and unconfirmed. However, recent historical studies suggest that its construction occurred between 983 and 987, marking an expansion of an earlier chapel dedicated to the Archangel St. Michael [27]. The Sacra di San Michele has historically functioned as a prominent landmark in the region, serving as a point of cultural and aesthetic significance for the local community. In recognition of its historical and visual importance, it was designated as a Monument Symbol of Piedmont in 1994. Moreover, from a national perspective, the Sacra di San Michele represents one of the most important centers of Benedictine spirituality. In 2016, the Sacra di San Michele complex has been included in the Italian "Tentative List" as a serial site, with the ambition of entering the UNESCO World Heritage List. The Abbey is also located along the "Via Francigena," and it is the initial stop on Italian territory. Furthermore, it is an integral component of the "St. Michael Line," a geographically aligned succession of seven shrines erected for St. Michael that goes from Ireland to Israel.

The designation of the Abbey as a UNESCO heritage site necessitates a meticulous analysis of all the aspects in play, as required in the formulation of a management plan [28]. Among the required tools, SWOT analysis [29] was conducted to highlight strengths, weaknesses, opportunities and threats of the site and area where it is located. Several strengths are identified, including good accessibility, guaranteed by efficient infrastructures such as the Turin-Bardonecchia highway and the Turin-Susa railway line, which offers an integrated ticket to facilitate public transport. The landscape and cultural value of the area is high, thanks to the presence of landscape protection laws that preserve the integrity of Mount Pirchiriano and numerous historical elements such as churches, chapels and ancient communication routes. Tourist activity is already well established, both because of the importance of the site and the presence of the Avigliana Lakes, which attract active daily tourism. However, direct access to the Sacra di San Michele is limited to scenic routes with no direct connection to Sant'Ambrogio, the nearest town. Parking lots near the site are also inadequate and expensive, while the shuttle service operates only at weekends with vehicles of limited capacity. In addition, the visual impact of the Turin-Bardonecchia highway and the railway trails reduces the environmental quality. The current touristic pressure highlights some shortcomings in accommodation facilities, especially in Avigliana and Sant'Ambrogio, which may not be sufficient to handle a possible increase in visitors linked to the UNESCO candidature. Development opportunities include the improvement of sustainable mobility, public transport and the introduction of alternative systems such as bike-sharing, as well as the valorization of historic hiking trails. The redevelopment of unused housing could stimulate sustainable tourism without putting pressure on the local fabric. The new Lyon-Turin high speed line is a controversial element: while it could improve international accessibility, it would increase the impact on the landscape and social tensions. In addition, the risk of an excessive influx of tourists linked to the UNESCO candidacy raises concerns about the sustainability of the site.

In this context, the candidacy necessitates an in-depth examination of the potential tourism impact that might result from the inclusion of the site in the UNESCO list. For doing that, the implementation of a TCC is instrumental in identifying the potential tourism scenarios for the Sacra di San Michele in the event of its inclusion on the WHL.

4 Application

4.1 Carrying Capacity Preliminary Form

Information derived from preliminary analyses on the Sacra di San Michele Site was included in the Carrying Capacity Preliminary form (Table 1). According to the methodology, this is the first step with the aim of creating a site profile. It is important to highlight that in the sheet only the information available is reported, but it can be updated as soon as new information related to the site is available.

Table 1. Carrying Capacity preliminary form

CARRYING CAPACITY PRELIMINARY FORM	
TYPE OF SITE: Abbey	**ID:** 001
	DATE: 30 September 2024
	COMPILER: Sebastiano Barbieri
NAME: Sacra di San Michele della Chiusa	
TYPOLOGY: Monument, place of worship, tomb, bell tower, door, engravings, mosaic, fresco, complex, area intended for worship, settlement.	
ADDRESS: via alla Sacra 14, 10057 Sant'Ambrogio di Torino (TO), Italy	
LOCATION:　　　　　historic center　　　　　periphery　　　　　extra urban	
ENVIRONMENT **Geomorphology:**　　seaside　　mountain　　hill　　plain **Seismic risk**: Seismic zone 3S (according to the 2019 regional classification) **Hydrogeological risk**: geology of the area: metamorphic, volcanic and plutonic rocks. Area subject to the Hydrogeological Constraint. Area bound ope legis pursuant to art. 142 of the Code of Cultural Heritage and Landscape (Legislative Decree 42/2004). **Rainfall**: average rainfall 782 mm per year	
DISTANCE TO MAIN PUBLIC TRANSPORT: 　airport: 49 km (Turin) 　train station: 14 km (Avigliana) 　bus station: 800 m (Piazzale Croce Nera)	
LEGAL STATUS: Ente religioso Sacra di San Michele, state-owned complex since 1866	
MANAGEMENT BODY: Ente religioso Sacra di San Michele	
PROTECTION MEASURES: Law No. 1089/39, Artt. 10-12 Leg. Decree No. 42/2004, Regional Law No. 68/1994	
TIMEFRAME: X - XI century	
BEGINNING OF ACTIVITY (YEAR): X century	
STATUTE AND PLANNING: Ente religioso Sacra di San Michele's statute	
AREA*: 　total (parcel): 26,630.82 m² 　total (building): 2,290.60 m²	
ARCHAEOLOGICAL ACTIVITIES:　　in progress　　previous　　none	
NUMBER OF VISITORS (per year): 1.385.457 (2023)	
DISABLED ACCESSIBILITY:　　　　none　　　　partial　　　　total	
PRESENCE OF A TOURISTIC TERRITORIAL PLAN: Regional Law No. 14/2016	
NUMBER OF OPENING DAYS (per year): 348 days (2024)	
PRICES AND DISCOUNTS: 　Ticket: 8,00 € - Reduced price ticket: 6,00 €	

* Area calculation made in QGIS with data provided from Piedmont Regional Geoportal

4.2 Review of Indicators for the Case Study

To select the most appropriate indicators for the application of the TCC to the Sacra di San Michele, it is essential to consider past experiences in which the method developed by the LINKS has been successfully applied. In particular, the two case studies of the Cinque Terre (Italy) and the Venetian Fortress of Bergamo (Italy) offer a useful reference framework for understanding which indicators have been used in contexts with different territorial, cultural and management characteristics. Through this analysis, it will be possible to assess the transferability of certain indicators and adapt them to the case of the Sacra di San Michele, identifying the most effective metrics to measure the tourist sustainability of the site with a solid, empirical evidence-based approach.

The application of the methodology to the Fortified City of Bergamo, included in the world heritage site of the "Venetian Works of Defence between the 16th and 17th Centuries" employed a very diversified set of indicators, covering all the thematic components investigated by the TCC [30]. For this site, a tentative calculation of the theoretical TCC has been made, adapting from the formula devised by Cifuentes (1992):

$$TCC = S/Su * V \tag{1}$$

where S is the site's accessible surface, Su is the area required for one visitor (m^2/person), V is the number of shifts or daily changes.

Some of the indicators used to analyze these phenomena include: for the social TCC, the level of satisfaction of tourists and the quality of life of residents; for the psychological TCC, the perception of the tourist experience after the visit and the presence of services to support the visit; for the infrastructural/territorial TCC, the efficiency of public transport (both ordinary and dedicated), the availability of parking, the quality of signs inside and outside the site and the availably for accommodation. The functional TCC analyzed the ratio of tourists to the visitable area, the capacity of the main access infrastructure, specifically the funicular railway, to transport visitors, and the presence of architectural barriers. The indicators identified a number of critical issues, including congestion, low awareness of the reason for the UNESCO candidacy, inefficient distribution of tourist flows and limited synergy with other UNESCO sites in Lombardy.

Similarly, the application of the methodology to the World Heritage Site "Portovenere, Cinque Terre, and the Islands (Palmaria, Tino and Tinetto)" employed a set of indicators similar to that of "The Venetian Fortress of Bergamo", with some differences reported below. In this case, no theoretical TCC was calculated because of the vastness of the Cinque Terre territory. In addition to the indicators already mentioned for the previous case study, the social TCC examines residents' perception of living in a World Heritage Site, employment levels, and the number of commercial activities. The psychological TCC assesses the adequacy of the cultural offer, critical issues reported by visitors, tourists' awareness of being in a World Heritage Site, and the seasonality of tourist flows. The infrastructural/territorial TCC considers the availability of services for tourists near the site, such as accommodation and restaurants. Finally, the functional TCC relies on indicators to evaluate tourism management, including the presence of projects and programs for sustainable flow management, awareness-raising campaigns for tourists and residents, and measures to regulate and distribute visitor numbers throughout the year.

Thanks to these indicators, critical issues concerning the state of tourist use of the site have been highlighted. Some of them are: excessive exploitation and environmental degradation, strong seasonality of flows, especially in villages overlooking the sea, high tourist pressure (30% by 2021 and rising), an explosion of second homes, traffic congestion and lack of parking spaces, a lack of tourist information and suboptimal waste management [31].

5 Results

5.1 Table of Indicators

The analysis of similar cases allowed for the identification of indicators relevant to study the context of the Sacra di San Michele, with particular focus on the tourism aspect. Although the indicators chosen mainly refer to those used in the two LINKS case studies, the table of indicators was further enriched with additional indicators tailored to site-specific characteristics that need to be thoroughly investigated.

For the assignment of value to the indicators, the color rating scale from red (Poor value) to green (Excellent value) was taken into account (Table 2).

Table 2. Values for the assessment

	Excellent
	Good
	Sufficient
	Not sufficient
	Poor

For the quantitative indicators, target values (i.e. the best performing value for the indicator) were established and associated with Excellent value. The other values are assigned proportionally according to target value. The dichotomous indicators, which indicate the existence or absence of a particular element, were classified into the two extreme values of the scale (Excellent and Poor). Finally, the qualitative indicators were evaluated and compared to similar cases analyzed with the support of LINKS experts.

5.2 Management Guidelines

In view of the issues that have emerged from the evaluation of the indicators, the management of the Sacra di San Michele must take into account several fundamental aspects in order to ensure the optimal use of the site, improving accessibility, tourist services and the influx of visitors.

In terms of accessibility, the three lifts leading up to the church provide access for the disabled. Additional assistant devices could further improve this aspect. The narrow passages in some places could restrict the flow of tourists at peak times, so better management of the paths in and out of the church or access regulation systems are suggested. From a mobility point of view, the distance from the main public transport hubs implies the need for more appropriate solutions, such as the introduction of shuttle services during periods of high tourist activity. The scarcity of parking lots in Piazzale della Croce Nera is another obstacle, which underlines the need to increase the availability of parking lots or to promote the use of public transport and hiking trails to reach the Sacra di San Michele. The implementation of the public transport system could also be a solution to this problem, reducing the number of parking spaces in the close area of the site and proposing alternative means of transport at the Avigliana and Sant'Ambrogio di Torino interchanges.

The Sacra's opening hours vary according to the season, with planned closures in January and extended opening hours during the summer months. The influx of tourists peaks in April, when the number of visitors is 4 times higher than in February. To compensate for this seasonal variation, more diversification of the tourist offer in the less crowded months could be considered, through cultural events, targeted promotions or exceptional openings of areas normally closed to the public. The Sacra di San Michele offers a range of services to enhance the tourist experience. Guided tours are available on weekends and, in a special form, once a month, with access to areas that are normally closed. To encourage participation in these experiences and maximize access, promotion through digital channels should be increased and the availability of guided tours should be extended. The site's lighting system and video surveillance are very good, but constant maintenance is required to ensure maximum security and respect for the site.

Finally, effective management of the Sacra di San Michele must be based on a balance between heritage conservation, improved accessibility, optimization of tourist services and sustainable management of visitor influx.

6 Conclusions

The paper explored the concept of TCC both in theoretical and practical terms. Starting from an analysis of the term in the literature, the work proposed the use of the recent approach to the calculation of TCC, proposed by LINKS in 2017. In particular, the paper applied the methodology to the Sacra di San Michele, an abbey in the metropolitan city of Turin, proposed to the WHL. The application of the TCC calculation to a real-world case study highlighted the dynamic ability of the approach that can be updated over time and is aimed at providing information on the current situation of the site under study, its state of conservation and any management issues. In this way, it serves as the basis for developing guidelines for this site that will improve the UNESCO property's future management with the aim of preserving its natural and cultural values in line with conservation and protection principles.

A future phase of the research will explore the possibility of assigning values to indicators included in Table 3 that currently lack data due to the unavailability of supporting information. This limitation should be addressed in the future steps of the research through on-site visits, to gather information on tangible items in place, but also through interviews and surveys of local population and tourists to gather perceptions and satisfaction.

Table 3. Table of indicators for the TCC components

Indicator	Description	Theoretical TCC level	Value	Notes
No. of tourists compared to the total area of the site	Tourists are calculated according to the TCC formula (TCC = S/Su * V)	a	TCC = 2.290/4*2= 1.145 persons ([1])	S = site's accessible surface Su = 4 m²/person V= 2 rounds
Physical/functional TCC				
Maximum crowding	Existence of safety rules	d	Excellent	
Physical accessibility	Presence of architectural barriers, difficult or tiring routes	a	Good	The building is equipped with three elevators. (the construction of a fourth lift is being evaluated)
Opening hours		a	348 days per year (2024)	Winter (November-February) Mon-Sat: 9.30am - 4.30pm, Sun: 10.45am – 4.30pm Summer (March-October) Mon-Sat: 9.30am – 5.30pm, Sun: 10.45am – 5.30pm
Lighting	Degree of illumination of the Site internally and externally	c	Existence of indoor and outdoor lighting system	
Safety of the Site	Existence of a plan for the security of the Site	d	Existence	Presence of surveillance cameras
Visitors' safety	Existence of a risk prevention plan	d	Existence	
Microclimate	Existence of an air conditioning system	d	Existence	

Management guidelines: Improving the accessibility of the Abbey for people with motor disabilities, while respecting the historical architectural structure.

Indicator	Description	Psychological TCC level	Value	Notes
Satisfaction levels of tourists (accessibility, comprehension of the value, fruition)	Surveys	c	ND	
Percentage of tourists believing that the site is too crowded	Surveys	c	ND	
Existence of policies to		d	Existence	The basic ticket can also be purchased

(*continued*)

Table 3. (*continued*)

reduce Crowding				online, while the ticket with the guided tour must be purchased online.
Adequacy of the cultural offer	Field observation	c	Excellent	Brochures are available at the ticket office in 12 different languages. Along the path there are QR codes that allow you to access explanatory videos in Italian, English, French on YouTube.
Communication and promotion	Interviews with selected stakeholders	b	Good	High level of use of the official website and social media such as Instagram and Facebook.
Presence of services	Field observation and interviews with selected stakeholders	c	Sufficient	The library, the noble floor and the museum areas of the old monastery are open to the public only on the first Saturday and Sunday of the month. A bar was built in the entrance of the Abbey complex.

Management guidelines: allow access to the library, the main floor and the museum areas of the old monastery, also on Saturdays and Sundays following the beginning of the month, and if possible, even weekly. Expand guided tours even during the week (compatibly with an adequate number of admissions with guided tours)

Social TCC				
Perception of the touristic flow (in terms of quantity of tourists)	Interviews with selected stakeholders	c	ND	
Perception of the touristic flow (in terms of behavior)	Interviews with selected stakeholders	c	Good	The behavior of tourists is quite respectful since they are in a place of worship.
Seasonality	Number of tourists during the most and the less visited	c	Not sufficient	Seasonality index equal to 4.06 (source: Osservatorio culturale Piemonte, 2023)

(*continued*)

Table 3. (*continued*)

Resident/tourist ratio	Ratio between the no. of residents and the no. of tourists within a significant area	b	(1,511+4,509)/15,653 = 0.38 residents/tourists (^{2})	Considering both residents of Chiusa San Michele and Sant'Ambrogio di Torino
Accidents, vandalism acts, thefts	Number of problems	a	ND	Existing video surveillance cameras help avoid these kinds of problems.

Management guidelines: improve the management of seasonal peaks through better organisation of events and links with the Sacra di San Michele during periods of lower tourist influx. Since the number of tourists is greater than the number of inhabitants in the neighbouring municipalities, a sharing of common spaces and services must be guaranteed, without the population perceiving discomfort or harm.

Infrastructural/territorial TCC				
Efficiency of public transport	Number of dedicated transport to reach the Abbey	a	Not sufficient	
Efficiency of signs			Good	
Presence of proper accommodation structures		a	Sufficient	The number of structures in close proximity to the site is not high but is compensated by the high presence in the Susa valley.
Efficiency of Ordinary parking lots		a	Poor	
Number of dedicated parking lots	Field observation and interviews with the management body	a	Poor	
Number of trash bins	Field observation		ND	

Management guidelines: increase the availability of parking spaces. In the event that this is not possible due to the morphological characteristics of the area, the request for parking at the base of the mountain could be met and a bus service leading to the square of the Black Cross could be guaranteed with optimized frequency.

(^{1}) The indicator value is considered good, as the average daily number of tourists is always below the calculated threshold. In the busiest months (such as April and August), the number of tourists may approach the threshold on weekdays with religious celebrations.
(^{2}) In this case, the proportion of 1 tourist 1 resident was considered as excellent value, which is why the value of 0.38 is considered not sufficient.

Another exploration could regard the calculation of a synthetic index to express the overall performance of all indicators. This could provide information for comparison of alternative solutions, as well as between different WHSs.

The ultimate purpose of the paper is to demonstrate the ability to support decision makers in the management of the territory, considering the physical component, but also the economic, social and cultural one. In the complex relationship between sustainable tourism and the economic needs of territories characterized by the presence of WHSs, TCC seeks to support the achievement of a balance. Often, the economic fragilities of the area drive local governments to focus exclusively on tourism to improve their situation, without regard to the social and natural dimensions that are being impacted. TCC is configured as a strategic planning tool to make sure that tourism has economic spin-offs in the area, sometimes identifying unexploited potential, but maintaining respect for the limits of social, cultural and environmental sustainability. One approach coherent with these purposes is sustainable marketing [32], which promotes tourism products and services capable of creating economic value while protecting natural and cultural capital. An application of this approach was used by Eiseman (2018) [33] in his study of the Amsterdam canal tour.

The application of the proposed methodology shows the possibility of integrating the opinions of the various stakeholders and it develops shared strategies capable of systemizing the different needs, according to the diverse constituent elements of the TCC as well as the possible weights to be assigned. In this sense, TCC can function as a valuable source of decision-support within the domain of cultural heritage management. Moreover, its integration with other assessment methods could provide a valuable opportunity to study these phenomena holistically. Future perspectives aim to limit this gap by integrating methods such as Multi-Criteria Decision Analysis (MCDA), which enables the simultaneous integration of multiple criteria, even in the presence of conflicts or trade-offs between dimensions, by explicitly assigning weights to each criterion based on management priorities or stakeholder preferences. Finally, a combination among multiple methods would also facilitate the identification of specific actions that should be prioritized when determining the allocation of funds from public and private sources.

Acknowledgments. This publication is part of the project PNRR-NGEU which has received funding from the MUR – DM 117/2023. Special thanks to Chiara Rondana, whose thesis on Tourist Carrying Capacity served as the starting point for this research, and to Roberta De Bonis Patrignani as the LINKS Foundation's expert on Tourist Carrying Capacity.

References

1. Assumma, V., Barbieri, S., Bottero, M., Caprioli, C.: Supporting the planning management of UNESCO sites: a literature review between urban showcase and gentrification. In: Computational Science and Its Applications ICCSA 2024 Workshops. ICCSA 2024. Lecture Notes in Computer Science, pp 147–162. Springer, Cham (2024)
2. Della Lucia, M., Franch, M.: The effects of local context on world heritage site management: the dolomites natural world heritage site, Italy. J. Sustain. Tour. **25**, 1756–1775 (2017). https://doi.org/10.1080/09669582.2017.1316727
3. Assumma, V., Datola, G., Mondini, G.: New cohesion policy 2021–2027: the role of indicators in the assessment of the SDGs targets performance. In: International Conference on Computational Science and its Applications, pp 614–625 (2021)

4. Assumma, V, Bottero, M, Cassatella, C, Cotella, G.: Planning sustainable tourism in UNESCO wine regions: the case of the Langhe-Roero and Monferrato area. Eur. Spat. Res. Policy **29**, 93–113 (2022). https://doi.org/10.18778/1231-1952.29.2.06
5. Barbieri, S., Bottero, M., Caprioli, C., Mondini, G.: Supporting the management plan of a world heritage site nomination through a multi-step evaluation approach. In: International Conference on Computational Science and Its Applications, pp 498–511 (2023)
6. Conradin, K., Engesser, M., Wiesmann, U.: Four decades of world natural heritage how changing protected area values influence the UNESCO label. Erde **146**, 34–46 (2015). https://doi.org/10.12854/erde-146-4
7. LINKS Foundation: Valutazione dell'attrattività culturale e turistica dei Siti UNESCO della Lombardia. Report (2020)
8. Gotham, K.F.: Tourism gentrification: the case of new orleans' vieux carre (french quarter). Urban Stud. **42**, 1099–1121 (2005). https://doi.org/10.1080/00420980500120881
9. Cocola-Gant, A.: Tourism gentrification. In: Handbook of Gentrification Studies. Edward Elgar Publishing (2018)
10. Cáceres-Seguel, C.: Valparaíso: touristification and displacement in a UNESCO city. J. Urban Aff. **1–13**,(2023). https://doi.org/10.1080/07352166.2023.2203400
11. González-Pérez, J.M., Novo-Malvárez, M.: Ibiza (Spain) world heritage site: socio-urban processes in a touristified space. Sustainability **14**, 9554 (2022). https://doi.org/10.3390/su14159554
12. Fregonara, E.: Valutazioni per strategie di sviluppo turistico sostenibile dell'iglesiente. Territorio **123–133**,(2014). https://doi.org/10.3280/TR2014-069018
13. Colucci, E., Matrone, F., Noardo, F., et al.: Documenting cultural heritage in an INSPIRE-based 3D GIS for risk and vulnerability analysis. J. Cult. Heritage Manage. Sustain. Dev. **14**, 205–234 (2024). https://doi.org/10.1108/JCHMSD-04-2021-0068
14. Dell'Ovo, M., Dezio, C., Mottadelli, M., Oppio, A.: How to support cultural heritage-led development in Italian inner areas: a multi-methodological evaluation approach. Eur. Plan. Stud. **31**, 1799–1822 (2023). https://doi.org/10.1080/09654313.2022.2135367
15. Amer, M., Daim, T.U., Jetter, A.: A review of scenario planning. Futures **46**, 23–40 (2013). https://doi.org/10.1016/j.futures.2012.10.003
16. Caro-Carretero, R., Monroy-Rodríguez, S.: Residents' perceptions of tourism and sustainable tourism management: planning to prevent future problems in destination management the case of Cáceres. Spain. Cogent Soc. Sci. **11**,(2025). https://doi.org/10.1080/23311886.2024.2447398
17. Bottero, M., Dell'Anna, F., Nappo, M.: Evaluating tangible and intangible aspects of cultural heritage: an application of the promethee method for the reuse project of the ceva–ormea railway. In: Integrated Evaluation for the Management of Contemporary Cities: Results of SIEV 2016, pp 285–295 (2018)
18. World Tourism Organization: Sustainable development of tourism a compilation of good practices (2000)
19. Cimnaghi, E., Valle, M., Mondini, G.: La capacità di carico turistica. Uno strumento per la gestione del patrimonio culturale. Roma (2017)
20. Mathieson, A., Wall, G.: Tourism: economic, physical, and social impacts. Longman Pub Group (1982)
21. Canestrelli, E., Costa, P.: Tourist carrying capacity: a fuzzy approach. Ann. Tourism Res. **18**(2), 295–311 (1991).https://doi.org/10.1016/0160-7383(91)90010-9
22. Mathieson, A., Wall, G.: Tourism: economic, physical, and social impacts. Longman Pub (1982)
23. Bottero, M., Devoti, C.: Il valore del patrimonio. studi per giulio mondini. All'Insegna del Giglio (2022)

24. Fisher, A.C., Krutilla, J.V.: Determination of optimal capacity of resource-based recreation facilities. Nat. Resour. J. **12**, 417–444 (1972)
25. Cifuentes, M.: Determinación de la capacidad de carga turística de áreas protegidas (1992)
26. Tosco, C.: La sacra di san michele come monumento europeo: l'architettura dei secoli X-XIII. In: Il Valore del Patrimonio. Studi per Giulio Mondini. Edizioni All'Insegna del Giglio s.a.s., Sesto Fiorentino, pp 43–53 (2022)
27. Calosso, F.: La sacra di san michele simbolo del piemonte (2020)
28. Ministero per i Beni e le Attività Culturali: ll modello del Piano di Gestione dei Beni Culturali iscritti alla lista del Patrimonio dell'Umanità Linee Guida (2004)
29. Humphrey, A.S.: Getting management commitment to planning—a new approach. Long Range Plann. **7**, 45–51 (1974). https://doi.org/10.1016/0024-6301(74)90078-8
30. LINKS Foundation: Valutazione dell'attrattività culturale e turistica dei Siti UNESCO della Lombardia. Allegato 1 Elaborazioni in termini di CCT. Opere di difesa Veneziana tra XVI e XVII Secolo: Stato da Terra-Stato da Mar occidentale: CIttà fortificata di Bergamo (2020)
31. LINKS Foundation: Studio della Capacità di Carico Turistica del sito UNESCO Portovenere, Cinque Terre e Isole (Palmaria, Tino e Tinetto) 2022 (2023)
32. Martin, D., Schouten, J.: Sustainable marketing, 1st ed. pearson (2012)
33. Eiseman, D.: Marketing sustainable tourism: principles and practice. In: Tourism Planning and Destination Marketing. Emerald Publishing Limited, pp 121–140 (2018)

Unlocking Energy Efficiency in the Italian Public Housing Legacy: A Typological Blueprint for Cost-Effective Retrofitting

Rubina Canesi[(✉)], Chiara D'Alpaos, Giuliano Marella, Diletta Romagnolo, and Umberto Turrini

Department of Civil, Environmental and Architectural Engineering (ICEA), University of Padova, Padova, PD, Italy
rubina.canesi@unipd.it

Abstract. Improving the energy efficiency of existing buildings through retrofitting interventions is essential to reduce energy consumption and mitigate climate change impacts. However, implementing effective retrofit strategies requires a deep and comprehensive analysis of the existing residential building stock. Our research work focuses on the Italian Public Residential Building stock (PRB) built between 1950 and 1980. During this historical period, attention to energy performance was not a priority, resulting in low thermal efficiency. Building on previous efforts such as the TABULA and EPISCOPE projects, which provided a taxonomy of harmonized European residential typologies, this study aims to develop a detailed and refined typological analysis specific to the public residential building sector in Italy. The methodology involves an extensive literature review to create a comprehensive database incorporating parameters such as building geometry, construction materials, energy systems and climate conditions. This database allows the identification and definition of distinct PRB typologies based on planimetric configurations, volumetric characteristics and aggregation patterns. This typological taxonomy will serve as a basis for the future implementation of a "retrofit intervention matrix" to assess the cost-effectiveness of various retrofit strategies in different typologies.

Keywords: Building Typology · Energy Retrofit · Public Residential Building stock · TABULA

1 Introduction

The building sector accounts for a significant portion of global energy consumption and greenhouse gas emissions. In the European Union, buildings are responsible for approximately 40% of energy consumption and 36% of CO_2 emissions [1]. Improving the energy efficiency of existing buildings through retrofitting is critical for lowering energy consumption, combating climate change [2–4]. But implementing effective retrofit strategies calls for a comprehensive knowledge of the building's features, energy performance, and related expenses. Underfunded by the Intelligent Energy Europe Program from 2009–2012, the TABULA (Typology Approach for BUiLding stock energy Assessment) project sought to create a harmonized framework for European residential building typologies to support energy performance calculations and retrofit strategies. Comprising building typology data for 13 European nations categorized based on age, size, and construction type, the TABULA project developed a web tool. This gave a structure for assessing possible energy-saving retrofit strategies and approximating the energy performance of several kinds of residential buildings [5, 6]. Building upon TABULA, the subsequent EPISCOPE (Energy Performance Indicator tracking Schemes for the Continuous Optimization of refurbishment Processes in European housing stocks) project from 2013–2016, also funded by Intelligent Energy Europe, further developed and expanded this harmonized typology approach. EPISCOPE aimed to monitor building stock energy performance and refurbishment rates, as well as optimize renovation processes across European housing sectors [7, 8]. EPISCOPE initially used the TABULA typologies but improved and integrated them with additional parameters such as energy vectors and systems to better represent the variety of architectural features influencing energy use [9]. To more accurately estimate energy performance and evaluate renovation measures for particular building typologies, these two complementary projects offered a thorough and crucial framework for classifying residential buildings according to their size, age, construction type, energy systems, and other important parameters.

However, while TABULA and EPISCOPE have laid the general foundations for the analysis of residential building typology, there is a need for more detailed and specific investigations, especially for the public residential sector. Public residential buildings (PRBs) play an important and primary role in the Italian national context in addressing housing needs in situations of economic hardship. Many PRBs in Italy were in fact built between the 1950s and 1980s, before the introduction of national energy regulations (e.g., Law 373/1976), a period in which energy efficiency was not a primary concern, resulting in poor thermal performance and high energy consumption [10–15]. Building upon the foundations established by the TABULA and EPISCOPE projects, this contribution is part of a multi-phase project aimed at analyzing the costs of energy retrofit interventions applied to Italian PRBs constructed between 1950 and 1980. In this contribution, we will present Phase I of the project, which focuses on i) analyzing the existing PRB stock, and ii) defining a reference database that includes 2,115 PRBs models. A detailed database and analysis of retrofit costs will be beneficial to policymakers, building owners and all parties involved in planning and implementing energy-efficient retrofits for PRBs [16–18]. These findings will be particularly crucial given the recent implementation of incentive policies in Italy aimed at improving building energy efficiency [19–22], supporting the design of customized incentive schemes and policies that address the unique challenges of low-income households living in energy-inefficient PRBs.

2 PRB Stock: The Italian Case

Following World War II, Italy faced a severe housing shortage, with many urban areas devastated and a rapidly growing population. To address this crisis, in 1949, the Italian government launched the INA-Casa (Istituto Nazionale delle Assicurazioni) program. This was an ambitious public housing initiative aimed at stimulating construction, providing employment, and developing affordable housing for low-income families [23]. The INA-Casa program was structured into two seven-year phases spanning from 1949 to 1963. During this period, numerous public housing projects were constructed across Italy following architectural and urban planning guidelines, compiled in four booklets [24]. These series of "Suggestions, norms, and schemes" for building and urban planning proved useful both in the initial phase of competitions for selecting designers to be included in the INA-Casa lists and in the subsequent project drafting phase. Although intended as "recommendations", these guideline booklets effectively functioned as actual norms [25]. The first two booklets were published in 1949 and 1950, aiming to provide designers with schemes, illustrated examples, advice, and warnings. These documents were later updated and republished in 1956 in anticipation of the INA-Casa Plan extension. The first booklet summarizes the Plan's fundamental principles. The suggestions mainly concerned the approach to being taken on projects from an economic perspective and the need to achieve a balance between various requirements. These included avoiding any superfluous expenses by studying room dimensions and space utilization to achieve perfect functionality. As well as the need to conceptualize the project to obtain adequate building exploitation, good living conditions, and a high level of formal quality [24]. Furthermore, there was a desire for the Plan's housing to be "psychological housing," aimed at creating the best environmental conditions for workers' lives, both in neighborhood creation and housing realization. It was thus prescribed that projects should thoroughly study technical and architectural details from constructive, economic, and human perspectives. These guidelines also introduced the concept of "building types" (detached houses, terraced houses, blocks, etc.). Building types were used to schematically define shapes along with housing capacity (1, 2, or 3 bedrooms) and living habits (about the kitchen-living room-dining room relationship). The identified building types were: i) Continuous multi-story building with 2 apartments per floor-staircase; ii) Isolated multi-unit building with two apartments per floor; iii) Single-story row house; iv) Two-story row house. Interestingly, the described "building types" are actually very generic, allowing great freedom for designers. There is no characterization of buildings in terms of plan-volumetric configuration, dimensions relative to the total number of apartments, etc. It is not specified what is meant by "continuous multi-story building" or "isolated multi-unit building." The Booklets, therefore, deal with "building types" with the aim of giving recognizable characteristics to INA-Casa buildings and somehow guaranteeing certain building standards, as well as urban planning standards. The system adopted by INA-Casa, of entrusting the conception of neighborhoods and buildings to freelance professionals, was designed to give the complex of constructions a unitary imprint, in urban, technical, economic, and social terms. However, while providing essential accommodation, numerous of these buildings were constructed with minimal attention to thermal efficiency, resulting in substandard thermal performance and elevated energy ingestion [26, 27]. Today, the aging RPSs stock represents a major challenge regarding energetic deprivation. People living in government apartments are at high risk because these buildings usually have poor insulation, old heating equipment, and other energy waste issues [28–32].

3 Materials and Method

This contribution concerns the first Phase of larger and extensive research which is divided into three sequential Phases, as illustrated in Fig. 1

I. Literature analysis of the public residential heritage and its classification, followed by direct analysis of the same and the creation of a reference database.
II. The identification, definition and application of a matrix of energy requalification strategies/scenarios (ERS) to the typological case studies identified in Phase I. This phase includes Energy Performance and Class assessments for each typology.
III. The assessment of the costs of such ERS, to be related to the energy class leap obtained.

As mentioned, this contribution presents the results obtained at the end of Phase I of the research. Extensive bibliographic research and integrative analyses were developed to catalogue the buildings according to a series of parameters, including first the construction period, the building typology, the planimetric configuration, building geometry, the construction materials, energy systems, climatic conditions, etc. Following this subphase, the generation of a Database consultable via pivot tables for the facilitated extrapolation of data was created. Through this approach, in Phase I, the research aims were to achieve the following two objectives:

1. Develop a comprehensive and structured database of Italian PRBs constructed between 1950 and 1980, incorporating detailed information of 2,115 buildings.
2. Refine the building typology classification by identifying and defining specific and unique features across the sample.

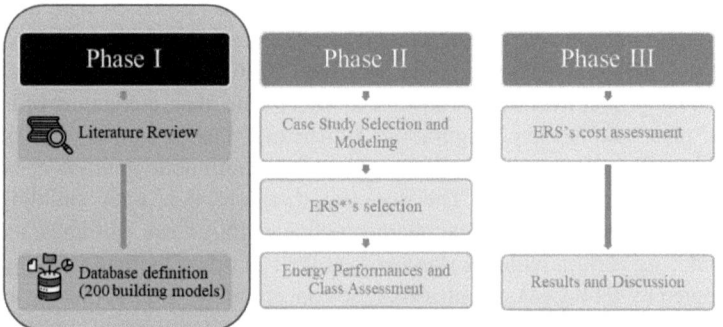

Fig. 1. Research Phases

Literature review, which included bibliographic sources, supplemented by archival sources and freely accessible online databases, revealed a lack of systematic and functional organization of information/data. Various texts collect data in a mostly descriptive manner, with tabular information primarily focusing on the number of housing units built in different provinces and years, and macro-scale costs incurred by INA-Casa over various seven-year periods. However, there's a notable absence of summarized geometric, typological, and constructive data, resulting in a lack of detailed and specific insights into the constructed properties. Instead, greater emphasis is placed on constructions as "Neighborhoods" with certain urban parameters and planned community services.

The research aimed to systematize data, extracting crucial information to create a comprehensive and updatable knowledge framework of ERP (Public Residential Housing). These considerations led to the development of an expandable DATABASE that collects, integrates, and processes data on ERP built in Italy between 1950 and 1980. The 2,115 buildings, included in our database, were identified by cross-referencing data from INA-CASA reports and MEF (Ministero dell'Economia e delle Finanze) databases [33]. The analysis focused on this timeframe as it represents the period of greatest ERP construction, coinciding with the development of the INA-Casa plan.

As mentioned, the parameters that define the PRB Database have been identified to describe in depth the geometric-constructive aspects of the buildings under analysis. In particular, two objectives guided the generation of this dataset:

1) to catalog the PRB heritage at a typological level,
2) to collect information to conduct energy analyses on these buildings and characterize the properties based on energy consumption.

For these reasons, the parameters used are summarized in Table 1, and fully described in detail in Table A1, reported in the appendix. The selected parameters are divided into five macro areas: Anagraphic, Geometric, Typological, Structural, and Climatic. The Anagraphic section includes identifiers, location details, and construction period information. The Geometric area covers building dimensions info, including e.g. volume, number of stories and number of units. The Typological section focuses on building shapes, aggregation schemes, typologies, and subtypologies. The Structural portion lists parameters related to the physical structure, such as building components and materials. Finally, the Climatic area includes the climate zone and orientation details relevant to the building's environmental context.

The Access database, containing information on 2,115 buildings, was initially populated using INA-CASA reports and other bibliographic sources to enhance and support our database compilation [24, 25, 33]. These sources included existing databases, reports, academic papers and researches, and archival sources [9, 24, 34–39], providing additional information such as location details, construction periods, and architectural drawings. For data not available in these reports (e.g., dimensions, number of floors, building structure, etc.), we conducted desk research, cross-referencing cadastral information with photogrammetry data from Google Earth Pro. This tool was also used for surface area calculations and visual inspections to complement the collected information.

In the following Section, we present some results obtained from the analysis of this collected data, which provided an overview of the Italian PRB stock. Finally, a comparison was made with the database previously proposed by TABULA.

Table 1. Parameters detected for each ERP building analyzed

	DATA									
Anagraphic		**Geometric**		**Typological**		**Structural**		**Climatic**		
Building	ID#	Dimension		Stairwell Position		Building Structure		Cliamte Zone	CZ	
District Name	DN#	District Covered Area	DCA	Number of Ramps	Nr	Vertical	Vbs	Orientation	O	
Location		Building Covered Area	BCA	Units per Ramp	Ur	Slab type	St			
Location	IDl	Unit Covered Area	UCA	Plan Shape	PS	Roof type	Rt			
City	IDc	Gross Leasable Area	GLA	Aggregation scheme		Roof finishing	Rf			
Address	IDa	Building Perimeter	P	Building typology	BT	Windows and Doors				
Construction Period		Dispersing surface	DS	Building sub typology	BsT	W&D Type	WDt			
Start	Ys	Surface/Volume	SV	Basic Module Number	BM	W&D Blinds	WDb			
End	Ye	Stories								
Period	Yp	Number of stories	NS							
Building Use	BU	Residential stories	RS							
		Volume								
		District Volume	DV							
		Building Volume	BV							
		Number of Units								
		Number of Units per District	NuB							
		Number of Units per Building	NuBldg							
		Number of Units per Floor	NuF							

4 Results and Discussion

4.1 Data Distribution

The 2,115 analyzed buildings are distributed throughout Italy, with a predominance in the north, as shown in the graph in Fig. 2 and Fig. 3a.

As mentioned earlier, the buildings analyzed were constructed between 1950 and 1980. The graph in Fig. 3b demonstrates that the period of greatest development was between the 1950s and 1960s, coinciding with the First Seven-Year Period of the INA-Casa Plan. Between the 1960s and 1970s, during the final part of the Second Seven-Year Period, fewer buildings were developed compared to the previous period. The

Fig. 2. PRBs distribution on a National Scale

subsequent period, between the 1970s and 1980s, was undoubtedly the one with the least development.

According to the D.P.R. 26 August 1993 n.412 (Table A in Annex A, updated on 24.10.2018), Italy is divided into 6 climatic zones/exposure classes based on degree-day (DD) clusters. As shown in Fig. 3c, the majority of the analyzed buildings are located in zone E.

4.2 Typological Results

A significant part of the research work involved defining the typological analysis on the PRBs sample. As previously mentioned, the study aims to determine the actual outcomes of the design process carried out during the INA-Casa Plan years, following the generic guidelines regarding "building typologies" provided by the Agency in its publications. The inclusion of buildings in the Database and their categorization according to their plan-volumetric configuration resulted in the identification of 5 building typologies that encompass the PRB stock: Terraced house (Th), Detached house (Dh), Townhouse (T), High-Rise building (HRb), and Block building (Bb).

The following table (Table 2) provides a concise description and the typical graphical configurations of the identified Building Typologies (BT), in relation to the average data of other parameters (surface area, number of floors, number of units, etc.) derived from the analysis.

The graph in Fig. 3d shows that the most prevalent building typology is the Terraced house (Th), representing 50% of the properties. This is followed by the Townhouse (T), Detached house (Dh), High-Rise building (HRb), and finally the Block building (Bb) at only 2%. For each building typology, except for the HRb, "sub-typologies"

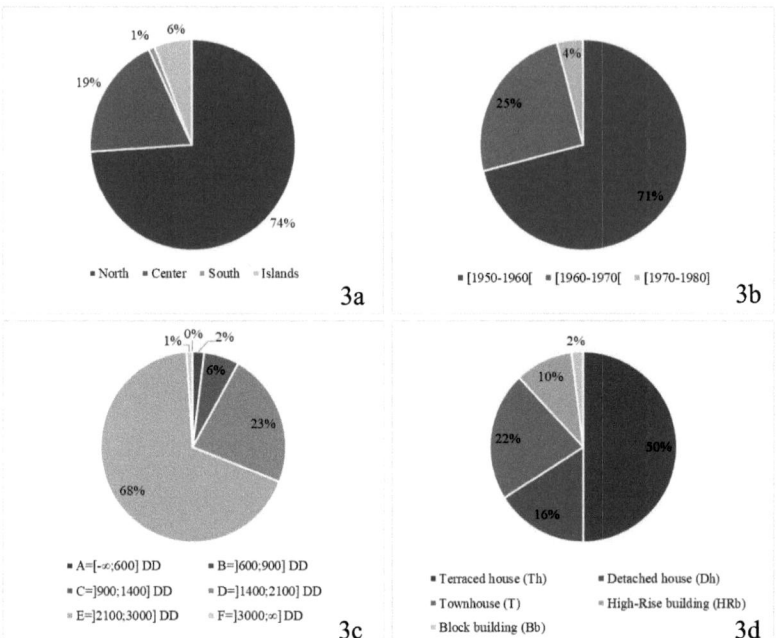

Fig. 3. Percentage distribution of the analyzed PRBs: 3a-Location; 3b-Construction period; 3c-Climatic Zone; 3d-Building Typology

were also identified (Table 3). A brief description and schematic representation of these sub-typologies are provided, along with their average data derived.

Figure 4 illustrates the percentage distribution of sub typologies for each building typology. For the Th typology, the linear configuration Th1 is predominant (68.18%). Among Dh buildings, the multi-family Dh1 is most common (81.74%), while for T buildings, the staggered single-family units T2 are prevalent (95.50%). The HRb typology, having no subcategory, naturally represents 100%. Lastly, among Bb typology, the linear configuration Bb1 is most common (60.78%).

Figure 5a shows the percentage distribution by typology of vertical structure (Vbs) across the entire sample of analyzed buildings, which reveals that 50.93% of the buildings under analysis have a Reinforced Concrete frame structure Vbs(RC).

This is followed by Load-bearing Masonry, Vbs(M), with 26.70%, and Prefabricated Concrete Vbs(PC) and Mixed structured Vbs(MA) with a percentage respectively around 12.19% and 10.17%. Figure 5b presents the percentage distribution of Vbs according to building typology. The typology "Terraced house (Th)", "High-Rise building (HRb)" and "Block building (Bb)" are predominantly built with Vbs(RC).

The Detached house (Dh) and Townhouse (T) typology, on the other hand, are mostly built with Vbs(M). These results are reliable, as Th, HRb and Bb buildings are generally much larger in size and higher compared to T and Dh and therefore require a structure with greater load-bearing capacity for vertical development. Conversely, T and Dh typologies have lower average heights, and thus load-bearing masonry is sufficient.

Table 2. Buildings'typology description (BT)

BT		DESCRIPTION	AXONOMETRIC REPRESENTATION
Th	Terraced house	Repetition (n-times) of a basic module, usually rectangular shape. The most common configuration is the "rectilinear" or in which the basic unit is arranged in succession, maintaining li ear and uniform elevations. On average, the building is compos of 4 basic units, total surface area of 1,120 m², 5 floors, volur of 21,140 m³.	
Dh	Detached house	Basic module, usually rectangular in shape, isolated from su rounding buildings. The multi-family typology is widespread, building with multiple floors, each with two residential units p floor. On average, the building has a total surface area of 230 n 2 floors, and a volume of 1,520 m³.	
T	Townhouse	It is composed of a basic unit, single-family, usually rectangul in shape, repeated n-times. Often in rectilinear succession. Ge erally, it is distributed on two levels. On average, the building made up of 5 basic units, total surface area of 450 m², has 2 floo and a volume of 2,970 m³.	
HRb	High-Rise building	It consists of a basic module, usually square in shape, isolat from the surrounding buildings. It is characterized by a notab height. On average, it is made up of 9 floors, total surface area 800 m², volume of 27,790 m³, 4 housing units per floor.	
Bb	Block building	It is characterized by the repetition (n-times) of a basic modu usually rectangular in shape. The basic unit is not placed in rec linear succession, but is repeated by configuring C-shapes, courtyard, Greek, or in general creating asymmetric configu tions. On average, the building is made up of 9 basic units, tot surface area of 2,700 m², 4 floors, volume of 38,880 m³.	

Table 3. PRBs' Sub-Typology (BsT) description and configuration

BT	BsT	Definition	Description	Plan
Th	Th1	In line	Repetition (n-times) of a basic module, usually rectangular in shape. It is arranged in succession, maintaining linear and uniform elevations.	
	Th2	Comb-shaped	The basic module, usually with a shape like Th2a or like Th2b, is arranged in succession, giving movement to the building's elevation by alternating full and empty spaces.	(Th2a) (Th2b)
	Th3	Multiple wings	The shape of the basic module is generally rectangular or square, with the exception of the connections. It can be "star" (Th3a), "T", "mirrored T" (Th3b), etc.	(Th3a) (Th3b)
	Th4	Angled wing	The basic module, usually rectangular, is multiplied n-times and arranged in succession by varying its planimetric inclination, which can be slight (Th4a), or greater up to 90°, leading to an "L" configuration of the building (Th4a).	(Th4a) (Th4b)

(*continued*)

Table 3. (*continued*)

	Th5	Staggered blocks	The basic module, usually rectangular, is multiplied n-times and arranged in staggered succession, interrupting the linearity of the elevation. The units can be arranged with the same pattern (Th5a) or varying it (Th5a).
	Th6	Inner courtyard	This typology of building is characterized by the central presence, in the basic module, of an empty space (e.g. patio or courtyard). The basic module can have a variety of shapes, usually square or rectangular.
	Th7	Balcony access	This typology of building is characterized by the presence of external balconies for access to the housing units, located on the facade. The basic module can have a variety of shapes, usually square or rectangular.
Dh	Dh1	Multi-family	The isolated building is composed of a basic module, usually rectangular in shape, isolated from the surrounding buildings. It is a multi-story building, each with two residential units per floor.
	Dh2	Two-family	The basic module is generally rectangular in shape. Usually, the two residential units are distributed over two floors.
	Dh3	Single-family	The basic module is generally square or rectangular in shape. The residential unit can be distributed over one floor (Dh3a), or over two (Dh3b).
	Dh4	Multi-family Patio	The isolated "patio" building is characterized by the arrangement of the basic modules, generally rectangular or "L" shaped, so as to form a central patio.
T	T1	In line Single-family	The terraced building is composed of a basic unit, single-family, usually rectangular in shape, repeated n times. The unit is placed in succession in a rectilinear way, generally the housing unit is placed on two floors
	T2	Staggered Single-family	The basic unit, single-family, rectangular, repeated n times, is placed in succession in a staggered way. Generally, the housing unit is designed on two floors.
HRb	HRb1	High-Rise building	A basic module, isolated from the surrounding buildings, is repeated vertically. Usually, the footprint is square in shape (RHb1a), but it can also take on a "star" configuration (RHb1b).
Bb	Bb1	Linear	The generic block building is characterized by the repetition (n-times) of a basic module, usually rectangular in shape. The basic unit is repeated creating non-symmetrical configurations (e.g. Bb1a, Bb1b).

(*continued*)

Table 3. (*continued*)

Bb2	Obtuse angles	The basic module, usually rectangular, is multiplied n-times and arranged in succession by varying its planimetric inclination and creating complex configurations.	
Bb3	Single court	The basic module, usually rectangular, is multiplied n-times and arranged in succession creating a central courtyard.	
Bb4	Linear court	The basic module, usually square, has a central courtyard. It is then arranged in linear succession.	
Bb5	Double court	The basic module, usually square, has a central empty space. Together with another unit, which can be of various shapes (square, rectangular, Z-shaped, L-shaped, etc.) it forms another courtyard with a larger size.	

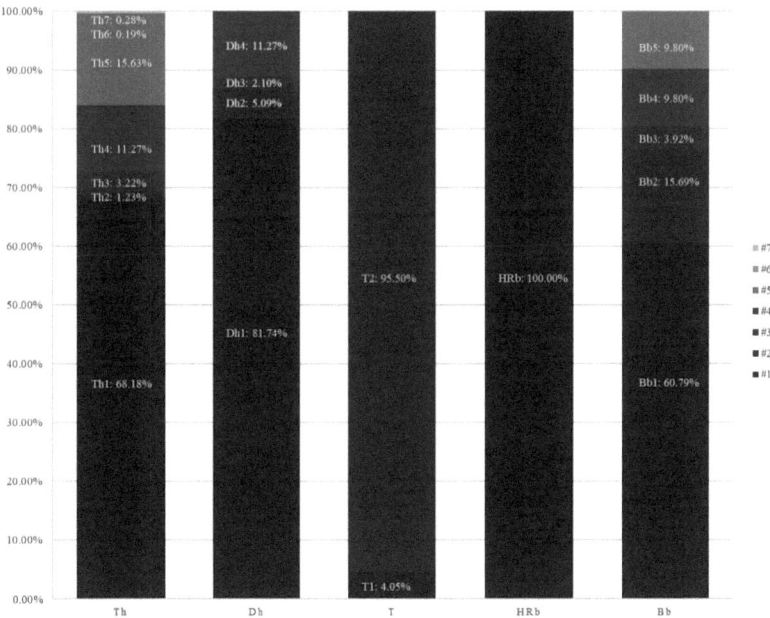

Fig. 4. Percentage distribution of the analyzed PRBs' Sub-Typology (BsT).

4.3 Structural Results

Regarding the Slab type (St), and particularly the Roof Type (Rt), four main categories have been identified (See Table A1), among which the reinforced Concrete and masonry structure prevails with 94.14% for the former category, as well as Concrete and masonry Roof (RtSM) at 64.71% and only 11.34% in wooden roofing (RtW) for the latter. As for the Roof finishing (Rf), four types have been identified (see table A1 in Annex), the prevalent ones are, with 60%, those in Clay Tiles (RfCT) and, unfortunately, there

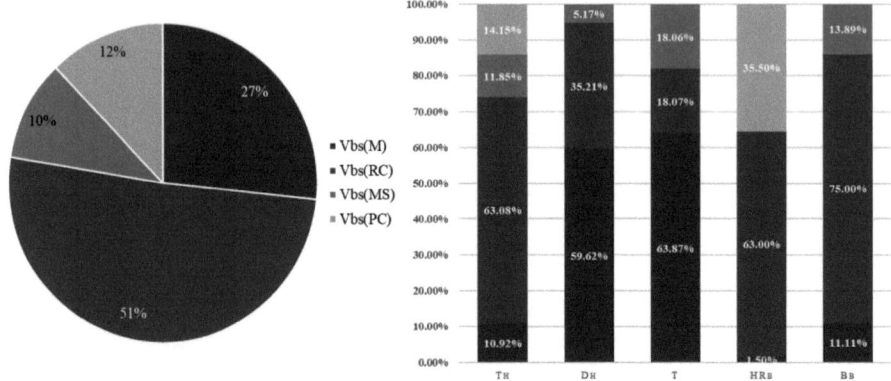

Fig. 5. Percentage distribution of the analyzed PRBs: 5a Vertical Building Structure (Vbs); 5b-Vbs by Typology.

are still many buildings (27.71%) that have asbestos as roof finishing (RfE). Regarding the windows and doors, information was obtained on material type (Wdt) and Shading Type (WDb). It emerges that the most used material for the frame of windows and doors is wood (59.81%), followed by aluminum (25.16%). As for Blinds, the most common types are wooden roller blinds (46.23%) and wooden shutters (34.68%).

4.4 TABULA Comparison

Finally, the last aim of Phase I of this research was to delve deeper into what was carried out by the "TABULA" project [9] regarding the classification of buildings according to their "Building Typology". As we previously mentioned, TABULA is a European project, which had the general objective of making energy renovation processes in the European housing sector transparent and effective, in line with energy policies. TABULA uses "MACRO-typologies", identified within a building stock as a starting point to evaluate energy renovation processes in order to guide stakeholders in their energy requalification projects, in terms of costs and effective energy savings. Compared to the TABULA project, this study focused solely on public residential stock and expanded the number of identified typologies (BT) from four to five. Climate zones (CZ) were considered without aggregation. Building Data (Bd) was collected through desk research, georeferencing, and estimated geometric data, either measured or provided by cadastral surveys, increasing from one variable in TABULA to 20 in this project. The concept of "Building Typology" from TABULA has been expanded, resulting in a more detailed classification. The Building Typologies (BT) identified here are primarily based on the typological layout and the building's planimetric-volumetric configuration, considering factors such as surface area, height, surface-to-volume ratio, shape, aggregation methods, and more. These typologies enable the assessment of how the aggregation of individual residential units influences the building's energy performance. Further investigations were conducted on various parameters described by TABULA, including climatic, dimensional, and constructional data. To complete the study, it was deemed necessary to associate each building with its construction typology, including building materials, in relation to the building type, based on geographical area and data available in literature. Regarding the construction period, as previously mentioned, this study focused on a narrow range between the 1950s and 1980s, which represents the period of greatest development in public residential construction in Italy. Table 4 provides additional details concerning the differences between the two projects. This approach allows for a more comprehensive analysis of the building stock, taking into account the complex interplay between building typology, construction methods, and geographical context.

Table 4. Comparison between TABLUA's and the Current Stud's Variables

TABULA	OUR STUDY
Residential Buildings	Public Residential Buildings
Building Typology (BT)	
4: Single-family; Townhouse; Multifamily; Block building	5: TH; DH; T; HRb; Bb
Building Sub-Typology (BsT)	
No	Yes (total 19 Sub-Typologies)
Climatic Zone (CZ)	
3: E; F; and A-B-C-D	6: A; B; C; D; E; F
Building Data (Bd)	
1: Number of Units	20: LCA; BCA; ACA; P; DS; NS; NhS; BV; BldgV; NuB; NuBldg; NuF; Nr; Ur; Vbs; St; Rt; Rf; WDt; WDb
Building Structure Vertical Categories (Vbs)	
3: Masonry; Reinforced concrete; Other	4: Masonry (subcat. 1-8); Reinforced concrete (subcat. 1-10); Mixed structure (subcat. 1-4); Prefabricated Concrete (subcat. 1-5)
Construction Period (Yp)	
8 Classes: between 1900 and 2005 (20 yrs gap between the classes)	3 Classes: between 1950-1980 (10 yrs gap between the classes)

Extending the TABULA methodology, this study provided a deeper understanding of the physical, spatial and dimensional characteristics of PRBs in Italy, providing a starting Atlas to develop more targeted and effective energy efficiency retrofit strategies.

5 Conclusions

This research has made significant strides in classifying and analyzing the Italian PRB stock constructed between 1950–1980 during the INA-Casa program era. Through an extensive literature review and data collection process, a comprehensive database was created containing detailed information on 2,115 public residential buildings across Italy. The analysis identified five distinct building typologies terraced houses, detached houses, townhouses, high-rise buildings, and block buildings along with 19 sub-typologies based on their planimetric configurations and volumetric characteristics. Key parameters such as geometry, construction materials, energy systems, and climate zones were cataloged for each typology.

This refined typological classification advances previous efforts like TABULA by providing a more granular understanding tailored specifically to Italy's public housing sector. While Phase I has successfully established this detailed database, it is limited by its focus on classification without yet addressing energy performance or retrofit strategies. The database serves as a robust foundation for the subsequent phases of this research. Phase II will build upon this typological framework by evaluating the energy performance of representative buildings from each identified typology. This will involve energy simulations and analyses to quantify current consumption patterns and identify areas for improvement. Phase III will then focus on developing and assessing cost-effective energy retrofit strategies tailored to each typology, considering technical, economic, and environmental factors.

Ultimately, the outcomes of this multi-phase project have the potential to inform policymakers in developing targeted incentive programs and policies to improve energy efficiency, mitigate climate change impacts, and alleviate energy poverty afflicting low-income households residing in these aging, energy-inefficient public residential buildings. By bridging the gap between generic classifications and the realities of Italy-'s public housing stock, this research represents a crucial step towards achieving national and international sustainability goals while enhancing the living conditions and well-being of vulnerable populations.

Funding. This study was funded by the European Union NextGenerationEU, Mission 4, Component 2, in the framework of the GRINS Growing Resilient, INclusive and Sustainable project (GRINS PE00000018 – CUP C93C22005270001). The views and opinions expressed are solely those of the authors and do not necessarily reflect those of the European Union, nor can the European Union be held responsible for them.

Disclosure of Interests. The authors have no competing interests to declare that are relevant to the content of this article.

APPENDIX

Table A1. Database variables acronym, description and unit of measure (*$NC = Nominal\ Categorical$, $Co = Continuous$, $Du = Dummy$, $Di = Discrete$)

PARAMETERS	Description	Data type *	Unit of measurement
ID#	Building ID Number	Di	Progressive Number
DN#	District Name	NC	Name (Text)
Location			
IDl	Italian Geographical Area	NC	North (IDl1); Center (IDl2); South (IDl3); Islands (IDl4)
IDc	City	NC	Name (Text)
IDa	Building Address	Di	GCS
Construction Period			
Ys	Year of construction start	Di	Year
Ye	Year of construction end	Di	Year
Yp	Building construction period	Di	[1950-1960[; [1960-1970[; [1970-1980]
BU	Type of residential building	Du	Public (1); Private (0)
Dimension			
DCA	Gross covered area of the entire INA-Casa district	Co	m2
BCA	Gross covered area of the building	Co	m2
UCA	Gross covered area of the single unit	Co	m2
GLA	Total gross area of the single unit	Co	m2
P	Building Perimeter	Co	m
DS	Building dispersing surface. Sum of the surface of the external facades, the lower floor and the roof	Co	m2
SV	Dispersing Surface/Building Volume Ratio	Co	m2/m3
Stories			
NS	Number of floors above ground. Basement and semi-basement floors are excluded. The height above ground of the latter is considered in the volume calculation	Di	Number
RS	Number of residential units floors. Useful for identifying the presence of commercial floors or garages on the lower floors of the building	Di	Number
Volume			
DV	Gross volume of the entire INA-Casa district. Obtained by adding the BVs with the same DN#	Co	m3
BV	Gross Building Volume. Obtained by multiplying BCA by RS	Co	m3
Number of Units			
NuB	Total number of units in the entire INA-Casa district	Di	Number
NuBldg	Total number of units in the building, multiplying NuF by RS	Di	Number
NuF	Number of units per floor of the building	Di	Number
Typological			

(*continued*)

Table A1. (*continued*)

PS	The shape of the floor plan of the basic module of the building (if single-family) or of the building itself (if multifamily)	NC	Square (1); Rectangle (2); L-shape (3); T-shape (4); Clover (5); H/butterfly (6); Star (7); Hexagon (8); Z-shape (9); Cross (10)
Aggregation scheme			
BT	Spatial shape of the building. It derives from geometric considerations (e.g. surface/volume ratio, planimetric development, etc.) and aggregation (isolated or composed of multiple repeated basic units or modules)	NC	Th; Dh; T; RHb; Bb
BsT	Subcategory for each Building Typology (BT). Defined based on particular shapes of single or aggregate modules, such as the direction of aggregation and its angle	NC	Th1; Th2; Th3; Th4; Th5; Th6; Th7; Dh1; Dh2; Dh; Dh4; T1; T2; HRb1; Bb1; Bb2; Bb3; Bb4); Bb5
Stairwell Position			
Nr	Number of ramps that make up the access staircase to the building	Di	Number
Ur	Number of dwellings served by a single stairwell in the building	Di	Number
BM	Number of "basic units/modules" in the building	Di	Number
Building Structure			
Vbs	Type of structure of vertical load-bearing walls	NC	Masonry -Vbs(M); Reinforced concrete - Vbs(RC); Mixed structure - Vbs(MS); Prefabricated Concrete - Vbs(PC)
St	Type of structure of intermediate floors	NC	Concrete and masonry (StCM); Varese type (StV); Hollow-core concrete (StC); Other (StO)
Rt	Type of structure of the roof slab	NC	Wood (RtW); Concrete and masonry (RtSM); Other (RtO)
Rf	Finishing material of the building roof	NC	Clay Tiles (RfCT); Marseille Tiles (RfMT); Eternit (RfE); Concrete Squares (RfCS)
Windows and Doors			
WDt	Window frame material	NC	Wood (WDtW); Aluminum (WDtA); PVC (WDtP); Iron (WDtI); Generic Metal (WDtM); Steel (WDtS)
WDb	Window shading type	NC	Wooden roller shutters (WDbW); Roman shutters (WDbR); Plastic shutters (WDbP); Wooden board shutters (WDbWB); Generic roller shutters (WDbG); brise-soleil (WDbS)
Climatic			
CZ	Climate zone in which the building is located, according to Presidential Decree 26 August 1993 n.412 (Table A in Annex A, updated on 24.10.2018)	NC	A=[-∞;600]; B=]600;900]; C=]900;1400]; D=]1400;2100]; E=]2100;3000]
O	Orientation of the largest facade	NC	North-South (O1); Ovest-East (O2); NO-SE (O3); NE-SO (O4)

References

1. European commission energy performance of buildings directive. https://energy.ec.europa.eu/topics/energy-efficiency/energy-efficient-buildings/energy-performance-buildings-directive_en?etransnolive=1. Accessed 4 Feb 2025
2. Canesi, R., Marella, G.: Towards European transitions: indicators for the development of marginal urban regions. Land (Basel) **12**, 27 (2023). https://doi.org/10.3390/land12010027
3. Russo, F.; Maselli, G.; Nesticò, A.: Life cycle costing and BIM: an integrated approach for a sustainable construction sector. In: Proceedings of the Lecture Notes in Networks and Systems, vol. 1186, pp. 490–500. LNNS (2024)
4. Panza Uguzzoni, A.M.; Fregonara, E.; Ferrando, D.G.; Anglani, G.; Antonaci, P.; Tulliani, J.M.: Concrete self-healing for sustainable buildings: a focus on the economic evaluation from a life-cycle perspective. Sustainability (Switzerland) **15** (2023). https://doi.org/10.3390/su151813637

5. TABULA project team typology approach for building stock energy assessment. main results of the TABULA project: final project report. https://episcope.eu/building-typology/. Accessed 10 Feb. 2025
6. Canesi, R.: A multicriteria approach to prioritize urban sustainable development projects | un approccio multicriteri per Il ranking di progetti urbani sostenibili. Valori e Valutazioni **2023**, 117–132 (2023). https://doi.org/10.48264/vvsiev-20233309
7. Loga, T., Stein, B., Diefenbach, N.: TABULA building typologies in 20 European countries—making energy-related features of residential building stocks comparable. Energy Build. **132**, 4–12 (2016). https://doi.org/10.1016/j.enbuild.2016.06.094
8. Florio, P., Teissier, O.: Estimation of the energy performance certificate of a housing stock characterised via qualitative variables through a typology-based approach model: a fuel poverty evaluation tool. Energy Build. **89**, 39–48 (2015). https://doi.org/10.1016/j.enbuild.2014.12.024
9. Corrado, V.; Ballarini, I.; Corgnati, S.P.; Talà, N.: Building typology brochure--Italy. Il progetto TABULA (Typology approach for building stock energy assessment, 2009–2012). Episcope, Ed. ISBN 9788882020651 (2014)
10. Fabbri, K.: Energy poverty and poor buildings: a brief literature review to promote new topics for future studies. Sustainability **16** (2024)
11. Aristondo, O., Onaindia, E.: Inequality of energy poverty between groups in Spain. Energy **153**, 431–442 (2018)
12. Bouzarovski, S., Petrova, S.: A global perspective on domestic energy deprivation: overcoming the energy poverty-fuel poverty binary. Energy Res. Soc. Sci. **10**, 31–40 (2015)
13. Canesi, R., Gallo, B.: Risk assessment in sustainable infrastructure development projects: a tool for mitigating cost overruns. Land (Basel) **13**, 41 (2023). https://doi.org/10.3390/land13010041
14. Maselli, G.; Ascione, F.; Nesticò, A.: Life cycle costing for structural analysis and design. In: Proceedings of the Procedia Structural Integrity, vol. 64, pp. 1743–1751. (2024)
15. D'Alpaos, C., Bragolusi, P.: Energy retrofitting in public housing and fuel poverty reduction: cost–benefit trade-offs. In: Bisello, A., Vettorato, D., Haarstad, H., Borsboom-van Beurden, J. (eds.) Smart and Sustainable Planning for Cities and Regions. SSPCR 2019. Green Energy and Technology, pp. 539–554. Springer, Cham (2021). ISBN 978–3–030–57332–4. https://doi.org/10.1007/978-3-030-57332-4_38
16. Canesi, R.; D'Alpaos, C.; Marella, G.: Forced sale values vs. market values in Italy. J. Real Estate Lit. **24**, 377–401 (2016). https://doi.org/10.1080/10835547.2016.12090434
17. Canesi, R., Antoniucci, V., Marella, G.: Impact of socio-economic variables on property construction cost: evidence from Italy. Int. J. Appl. Bus. Econ. Res. **14**, 9407–9420 (2016)
18. Canesi, R., D'Alpaos, C., Marella, G.: Foreclosed homes market in Italy: bases of value. Int. J. Hous. Sci. Appl. **40**, 201–209 (2016)
19. Mecca, U.; Mecca, B.: Surfacing values created by incentive policies in support of sustainable urban development: a theoretical evaluation framework. Land (Basel) **12** (2023)
20. Rebaudengo, M.; Mecca, U.; Gotta, A.: "Fit to 55": financial impacts of italian incentive measures for the efficiency of the building stock and the revitalization of fragile areas BT new metropolitan perspectives. In: Calabrò, F., Della Spina, L., Piñeira Mantiñán, M.J. (eds.) Proceedings of the International Symposium: New Metropolitan Perspectives, pp. 201–210. Springer International Publishing: Cham (2022)
21. Papi, L.L.: Riqualificazione del patrimonio edilizio: un bilancio delle recenti misure di incentivazione. Moneta e Credito **75**, 491–509 (2022)
22. Shazmin, S.A.A., Sipan, I., Sapri, M., Ali, H.M., Raji, F.: Property tax assessment incentive for green building: energy saving based-model. Energy **122**, 329–339 (2017). https://doi.org/10.1016/j.energy.2016.12.078

23. La Camera dei deputati ed il Senato della Repubblica Provvedimenti per Incrementare l'occupazione Operaia, Agevolando La Costruzione Di Case per Lavoratori; Italy (1949)
24. Anguissola, L.B.: I 14 Anni Del Piano INAcasa; Staderini, Ed.; Roma, Italy. ISBN SBL0134260 (1963)
25. Vittorini, R.: Reconstructing housing and communities: the INA-casa plan. Docomomo J. 50–55 (2021). https://doi.org/10.52200/65.A.UM4KVUFJ
26. D'Alpaos, C., Bragolusi, P.: Buildings energy retrofit valuation approaches: state of the art and future perspectives. Valori e Valutazioni (2018)
27. Mortarotti, G., Morganti, M., Cecere, C.: Thermal analysis and energy-efficient solutions to preserve listed building façades: the INA-casa building heritage. Buildings **7** (2017)
28. D'Alpaos, C., Canesi, R.: Risks assessment in real estate investments in times of global crisis. WSEAS Trans. Bus. Econ. **11**, 369–379 (2014)
29. De Paola, P., Ferraro, M., Manganelli, B., Tajani, F., Del Giudice, F.P.: A model to define a real estate investment risk index for the administrative municipalities of Naples. Procedia Struct. Integrity **64**, 1696–1703 (2024)
30. Mondini, G., Assumma, V., Bottero, M., Caprioli, C., Datola, G., Dell'Anna, F.: Planning sustainable and resilient cities: the role of strategic environmental assessment (SEA). In: Giuffrida, S., Trovato, M.R., Rosato, P., Fattinnanzi, E., Oppio, A., Chiodo, S. (eds.) Science of Valuations. Green Energy and Technology, vol. Part F2560, pp. 199–212. Springer, Cham (2024). https://doi.org/10.1007/978-3-031-53709-7_14
31. Oppio, A.; Caprioli, C.; Dell'Ovo, M.; Bottero, M.: Assessing ecosystem services through a multimethodological approach based on multicriteria analysis and cost-benefits analysis: a case study in Turin (Italy). J. Clean Prod. **472** (2024). https://doi.org/10.1016/j.jclepro.2024.143472
32. Napoli, G., Giuffrida, S., Trovato, M.R.: Efficiency versus fairness in the management of public housing assets in Palermo (Italy). Sustainability (Switzerland) **11**, 1–21 (2019). https://doi.org/10.3390/su11041199
33. INA CASA L'INA-CASA al IV Congresso Nazionale Di Urbanistica; INA Istituto Nazionale delle Assicurazioni Gestione INA-Casa: Roma, Italy (1952)
34. Griffini, E.A.: Nuovi sistemi costruttivi, nuovi materiali, opere di finitura; U. Hoepli: Milano (1948)
35. Griffini, E.A.; Griffini, E.A.: Costruzione razionale della casa: I nuovi materiali: orientamenti attuali nella costruzione, la distribuzione, la organizzazione della casa. U. Hoepli (1932)
36. Neufert, E., Piardi, S., Baglioni, A., Lenzi, L.: Enciclopedia pratica per progettare e costruire: manuale ad uso di architetti, ingegneri, periti edili e costruttori, docenti e discenti: norme e prescrizioni per progettare, costruire, dimensionare, distribuire; U. Hoepli (1988)
37. Capomolla, R., Vittorini, R.: L'architettura INA casa (1949–1963): aspetti e problemi di conservazione e recupero; gangemi. Roma, Italy (2003)
38. Magliulo, N.L.: La grande dimensione nell'edilizia residenziale pubblica dal 1956 al 1982. Riqualificare o demolire? phd thesis, università degli studi di napoli federico ii, supervisor: prof. sergio stenti **194** (2013)
39. Maniero, A.: Phd thesis, università degli studi di padova, supervisor: prof. umberto turrini, p. 433 (2022)

Spatial Multicriteria Decision Aiding for Regional Energy Planning and Assessment. The Case Study of Gotland, Sweden

Lucia Petronio[1], Vanessa Assumma[1(✉)], Johanna Liljenfeldt[2], and Angela Santangelo[1]

[1] Department of Architecture, University of Bologna, 40136 Bologna, Italy
lucia.petronio@studenti.unibo.it, {vanessa.assumma, angela.santangelo}@unibo.it
[2] Department of Earth Sciences; Wind Energy, Uppsala Universitet, 621 67 Visby, Sweden
johanna.liljenfeldt@geo.uu.se

Abstract. The transition to renewable energy requires regional planning approaches that integrate spatial, environmental, and social dimensions. This study develops a Multi-Criteria Spatial Decision-Support System (MC-SDSS) to support regional energy planning by combining geospatial data analysis, future scenario development, and multi-criteria evaluation techniques. The methodology is structured into four phases - contextual analysis, energy potential mapping and future scenarios, integrated evaluation and decision support, and implementation and monitoring. The approach is applied to Gotland, Sweden, a region with ambitious decarbonization goals and unique geographic characteristics. Renewable energy potential is assessed through thematic mapping using Geographic Information Systems (GIS) tools, focusing on wind, solar, and biomass resources. In the evaluation phase, a Spatial Multi-Criteria Analysis (SMCA) is conducted to assess and compare the scenarios. Five main criteria are identified Society and Culture, Technology and Infrastructure, Economy, Land-use, Environment each associated with specific measurable spatial indicators. Criteria weights are derived using the Simple Multi-Attribute Rating Technique Exploiting Ranks (SMARTER) method with the purpose of weighting the indicators maps and then aggregating them into suitability maps for Renewable Energy Sources (RES) power plants installation. By embedding the decision-support system within a spatial planning perspective, this study promotes a transparent, replicable, and stakeholder-sensitive approach to regional energy planning. The proposed framework supports the identification of hybrid scenarios and fosters alignment between energy objectives, territorial characteristics, and community needs—contributing to more resilient and place-based energy transitions.

Keywords: Spatial Multi-Criteria Analysis · Regional Energy Planning · Decision-Support System

1 Introduction

Energy planning has become increasingly crucial across Europe, as the sector contributes about 73% of the EU's greenhouse gas emissions [1]. Achieving climate neutrality by 2050, as outlined in the European Green Deal and then the Climate Law [2, 3], requires energy policies across all governance levels, with regional planning playing a key role. Spatial planning links energy infrastructure to land use and environmental considerations, promoting holistic and sustainable approaches. However, integrating energy and spatial planning requires decision-support tools that can tackle multidimensional problems and conflicting objectives. The regional spatial planning level is suitable to reflect local consumption, environmental, and socio-economic conditions, requiring context-specific approaches [4]. Spatial Multi-Criteria Analysis (SMCA), combining GIS and multicriteria hierarchical approach, enables the assessment of renewable energy scenarios while managing land-use trade-offs.

This study proposes an integrated methodology to support the assessment and the localisation of Renewable Energy Sources (RES) to bridge the current gap of standardized methodologies in regional energy planning. The main research question explores how spatial and decision-making tools can aid regional integration of renewables. This can be unpackaged into three sub-questions, each one linked to definite phases of the proposed methodology (Fig. 1). In detail: (1) literature and case study review, (2) development of a framework combining SMCA, scenario building, and Geographic Information Systems (GIS) into a unique framework, and (3) application of the methodology to Gotland.

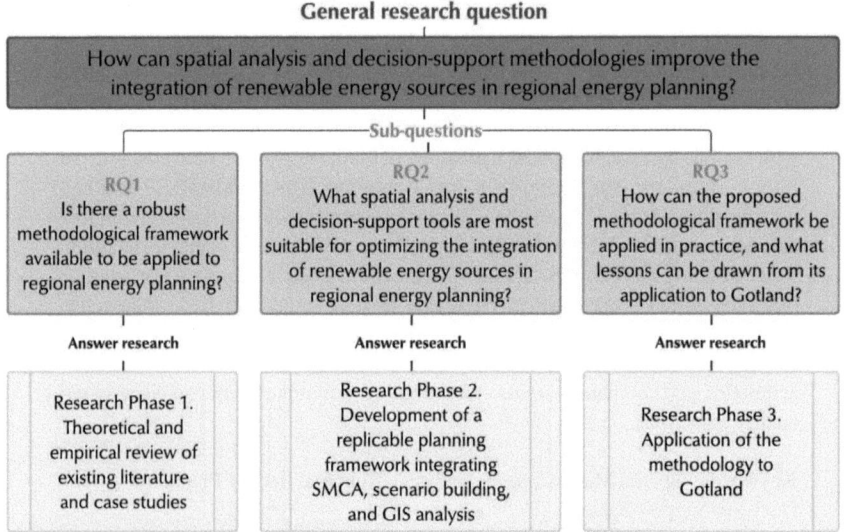

Fig. 1. Research questions and methodology.

The study is organized accordingly, concluding with a discussion on findings, replicability, and limitations. The Gotland case demonstrates the method's flexibility and stresses the relevance of data and stakeholder input.

2 Setting the Framework for Regional Energy Planning

The Brundtland Commission (1987) defined Sustainable Development (SD) as meeting present needs without compromising future generations [5]. This powerful concept continues to address global challenges today (e.g. climate change, resource depletion, or social justice). Over time, the concept has evolved from mere conservation efforts to include resilience—the ability of systems to adapt to disruptions [6, 7]. This vision shapes global agendas like the UN's Agenda 2030 and the Paris Agreement [8, 9], with the Sustainable Development Goals (SDGs) replacing the Millennium Development Goals in 2015. Yet, global crises such as COVID-19, conflicts, and climate emergencies continue to slow progress [10].

Renewable Energy Sources (RES)— i.e. wind, solar, bioenergy, hydropower, ocean, and geothermal—play a key role in sustainable development, offering an alternative to fossil fuels, which are the primary contributors to Greenhouse Gas (GHG) emissions and air pollution. As a matter of fact, the energy sector might be one of the engines for sustainability, but it accounts for approximately 73% of GHG emissions [11]. Despite their high potential, RES technologies can carry pressures on people's health and the Environment, but also noise pollution, visual disturbance, and land-use/land-cover issues [12]. For this reason, the 7th SDG, "Affordable and Clean Energy", highlights the sector's foundational role in achieving broader sustainability [13], since RES efficiency could be capable of cutting 94% of energy-related CO_2 emissions by 2050 [14].

For this reason, a multidisciplinary approach is essential to align energy development with long-term sustainability, especially as energy demand grows and fossil fuels decline [15, 16].

At the European level, policies such as the European Green Deal, Fit for 55 package, or the Energy Union Strategy aim to reach climate neutrality by 2050 or even the Renewable Energy Directive (RED), the Energy Efficiency Directive (EED), and the Energy Performance of Buildings Directive (EPBD) [17–19] guide EU countries members in adopting sustainable practices across sectors. Complementary instruments such as the Hydrogen Package and REPower EU aim to accelerate the deployment of clean energy technologies and reduce reliance on fossil fuel imports, by considering geopolitical disruptions [20, 21]. EU states have developed National Energy and Climate Plans (NECPs), to align with EU-wide targets (i.e. security, integration, efficiency, decarbonization, and innovation). For example, Sweden and Italy follow different energy scenarios—Sweden aims for 100% renewable electricity by 2040, whereas Italy includes a potential nuclear role [22, 23]. However, some knots must still be solved. If revised NECPs are expected to increase ambition, their success closely depends on more effective coordination, investment, and stakeholder engagement [24, 25]. In the Swedish government system, the Covenant of Mayors supports municipalities in adopting Sustainable Energy and Climate Action Plans (SECAPs), targeting emissions, climate resilience, and energy poverty [21, 26–28]. Yet regional authorities often lack resources or legal authority due to centralized governance traditions, particularly in Eastern and Scandinavian countries [29]. Closing these gaps demands better policy alignment, inclusive governance, and capacity-building at the regional level [26, 30].

3 A Spatial Planning Approach to Regional Energy Planning

Spatial planning is crucial in managing human activities and mitigating their impact on ecosystems. Evolving from urban planning, it now integrates environmental, social, and economic factors across all governance levels: international, national, regional, and local. The European Spatial Development Perspective (ESPD), adopted in 1999, helped promote this approach, encouraging cross-border cooperation and subsidiarity [31].

The regional level emerges as a strategic scale for addressing cross-sectoral challenges such as energy, biodiversity, and infrastructure. Regions act as intermediaries, tailoring national strategies to local contexts and supporting participatory governance [32]. Sectoral planning, including energy, water and transport, benefits from integration into regional frameworks, improving policy coherence. For instance, coordinating regional energy infrastructure with land use supports sustainable renewable energy deployment [33, 34].

Energy planning itself has transitioned from a purely technical domain to a multifaceted discipline that integrates environmental and social objectives. Energy planning has shifted from a technical field to a multidimensional discipline that includes environmental and social goals. Regional energy planning can address local resource variations and encourage stakeholder involvement. Integrated Spatial and Energy Planning (ISEP) offers a holistic model linking land use with energy supply and demand [35]. As the energy transition advances, spatial planning helps manage decentralization, infrastructure upgrades, and public acceptance by aligning renewable energy development with ecological and cultural concerns [36, 37].

Community participation is vital for effective spatial and energy planning. It builds trust, improves acceptance, and ensures that local needs are reflected [38]. While resource and methodological challenges remain, participatory tools like workshops and digital platforms can help bridge technical planning with community priorities [39, 40].

In this context, participatory planning is essential for a fair and sustainable regional energy transition. Even if economic and/or social resources are not always available to open participation process to a wider pool of stakeholders and community (e.g. workshops, or digital platforms) these can make the difference in fostering sustainable inclusive development in REP scenarios [40].

4 Decision-Support Toolbox for Regional Energy Planning

Regional energy planning needs for addressing sustainability challenges by enabling strategies tailored to local environmental, socio-economic, and infrastructure conditions. Unlike top-down national policies, it offers a more detailed, place-based approach. REP can integrate a diverse set of decision-support tools, ranging from spatial analysis like GIS, strategic analysis tools as SWOT Analysis, scenario-building, or participatory analysis, and decision-aiding techniques like Multi-Criteria Decision Analysis (MCDA).

These aid Decision and Policy Makers in providing data-driven, inclusive, and spatially grounded planning for renewable energy deployment.

This paper lays the groundwork for developing a methodological framework capable of generating spatial energy scenarios aligned with regional needs and guiding decision-making processes.

4.1 Spatial and Strategic Analysis Tools

Geographic Information Systems (GIS) have evolved from logic mapping systems to sophisticated and interoperable platforms for aiding public bodies and urban planners freelancers, and other specialists to take decisions [41–43]. Despite their potential, GIS applications in energy planning remain limitedly widespread due to technical, financial, and institutional barriers [44]. Similarly, SWOT (Strengths, Weaknesses, Opportunities and Threats) Analysis—while often criticized for its subjectivity— remains the most common used method in strategic planning [45, 46] since its added value significantly increase when combined with other analysis and evaluation methods [47].

4.2 Decision-Making Tools

Given the multidimensional nature of energy planning, structured decision-aiding tools are essential. Drawing on foundations in operational research and decision theory [48–50] these tools support structured evaluations and take long-term decisions.

Multi-Criteria Decision Analysis (MCDA) is used to compare and prioritize alternatives based on multiple criteria, providing a robust framework for integrating environmental, technical, economic, and social factors into planning processes [51–53]. Within the MCDA family, several specific methods are particularly relevant in regional energy planning.

The Analytic Hierarchy Process (AHP) can assess the impact of renovation measures addressing consumer behavior in different scenarios or rather aiding the definition and implementation of policy decisions for energy saving in buildings [28]. Therefore, preferences elicited from stakeholder input are crucial. SMARTER [54, 55], on the other hand, has recently been considered more expedient than AHP for weights elicitation, since facilitate experts in the ranking of elements, often in contexts where time or data availability are limited [56]. SMCA extends the traditional MCDA approach by integrating spatial data and criteria within GIS environments, making it particularly valuable for territorial energy planning where location-based trade-offs are essential [57].

Therefore, MCDA can support in structuring fostering transparency, especially when combined with participatory inputs and spatial analysis.

4.3 Stakeholder and Participation Tools

Stakeholder analysis ensures that diverse interests are acknowledged and balanced using tools such as social network analysis or power-interest grids [58, 59].

Participation methods are analyzed through democratic, social learning, and policy-driven lenses. Arnstein's ladder illustrates power dynamics in participation, while authors like Rowe and Frewer [60] and Palm & Thoresson [61] highlight practical shortcomings. Participatory tools such as ESTEEM, MCDA, and participatory GIS enhance inclusiveness, yet challenges such as cost, time, and unequal power relations often limit their effectiveness [38, 40].

4.4 Scenario Building

Scenario building, whether qualitative or quantitative, helps explore plausible energy futures, often including baseline, trend, and policy-driven trajectories [61–63]. When integrated with GIS and MCDA, scenario methods become powerful tools for testing the implications of planning decisions under uncertainty.

4.5 Insights from Regional Energy Plans and Research Case Studies

The literature review on regional energy planning included both real-world planning documents and academic case studies, each offering different contributions to the development of the proposed framework. This review focused on frameworks from the Central-Western Europe government systems such as the *Schéma Régional Climat Air Energie* (SRCAE) *de la Corse* (France) and the *Integriertes Energie und Klimaschutzkonzept* (IEKK) of Baden-Württemberg (Germany).

The review of actual plans focused on understanding the practical structure, content, and outputs of existing strategies—generally aligned with national and EU directives, but often lacking in the use of MCDA techniques, with limited GIS application and varying levels of community participation.

By contrast, academic case studies reflected evolving research trends, highlighting integrated methods (e.g., MCDA with GIS), participatory approaches, and scenario modeling. The findings can bridge the gap between practical issues (e.g. how to engage stakeholders more effectively) and methodological innovation in regulatory frameworks.

5 A Decision-Support Framework for Regional Energy Planning

A flexible four-phase framework for regional energy planning is proposed (Fig. 2), integrating spatial analysis, decision-support tools, and participatory processes to create tailored, evidence-based strategies. Each phase targets specific components of the energy planning process, from baseline assessments to strategic recommendations and performance tracking.

The first phase, Contextual analysis, assesses geographic, climatic, socio-economic, and energy system features. GIS is employed to analyze topography, climate, land use, and demographic patterns, whereas a spatial SWOT analysis summarizes strengths, weaknesses, opportunities, and threats. An organigraph is suggested to map governance structures, clarifying institutional roles and responsibilities. This phase identifies initial renewable energy opportunities [64].

In the second phase, Energy potential mapping and future scenarios, RES are evaluated through GIS and scientific datasets. Areas with development constraints are spatially excluded to produce maximized energy scenarios. These conceptual maps serve

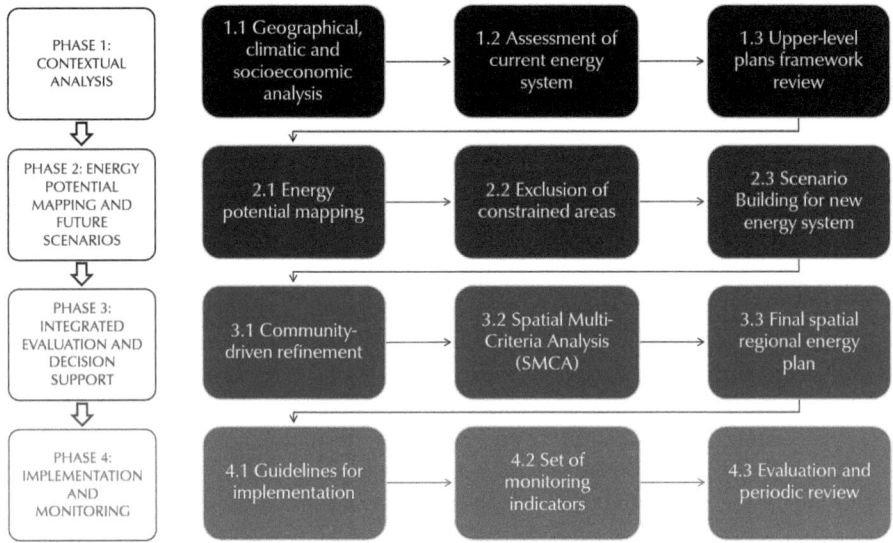

Fig. 2. Methodological workflow

as discussion tools to gather stakeholders and community feedback. This process favors negotiation between technical assessments and local perceptions, involving a diverse range of stakeholders—such as regional and municipal authorities, energy providers, environmental organizations, local businesses, and citizen associations—each bringing specific knowledge, interests, and priorities. Negotiation gaps can be mitigated through transparent communication, early involvement, and simple elicitation techniques such as surveys or facilitated workshops. In this phase, scenario building is supported by storytelling techniques, which help communicate alternative development paths during the ongoing evaluation phase.

The third phase, Integrated evaluation and decision support, applies SMCA with weighted criteria via the SMARTER method [54, 55], incorporating community input to generate suitability maps and prioritize interventions. A sensitivity analysis tests the robustness of the outcomes by adjusting criterion weights, while comparative surface analysis supports the identification of priority intervention zones and informs policy directions.

In the fourth phase, Implementation and monitoring, guidelines are defined for action prioritization, financial planning, and institutional responsibilities. A set of quali-quantitative indicators monitor and review performance and adaptability to new data, technologies, and policy shifts.

To ensure an active participation, it is important to involve a diverse range of stakeholders—including regional and municipal authorities, energy providers, environmental organizations, local businesses, and citizen associations—each bringing specific knowledge, interests, and expectations. Differences in influence and technical understanding may lead to negotiation gaps, which can be mitigated through transparent communication, early involvement, and simple elicitation techniques such as surveys or facilitated workshops. In this phase, scenario building through storytelling can help actors in better communicating alternative development paths during the ongoing evaluation process.

6 Application to the Case Study of Gotland

6.1 Introduction and Contextual Analysis

Gotland, Sweden's largest island, is both a municipality and a region, making it a unique setting for testing regional energy planning. Its governance reflects the Scandinavian model of local autonomy and state coordination. Gotland's energy ambitions, as a pioneer in renewables, are guided by national and regional strategies aimed at sustainability and decarbonization. The contextual analysis shows strong potential for wind, solar, and biomass energy on the island, while other RES are constrained by natural limitations. The island's context—defined by dispersed rural settlements, an aging population, and an economy rooted in tourism and clean energy—highlights both the challenges and opportunities of sustainable development in insular regions.

6.2 Energy Potential Mapping and Scenario Building

The second phase mapped energy potential using spatial data from authoritative sources: Global Wind Atlas, Global Solar Atlas, and Swedish Forest Agency. The final energy potential maps, rasterized into five levels of potential, are shown in Fig. 3. Exclusion layers—military zones, protected areas, and 1 km building buffers—were overlaid to create optimized development scenarios for each energy source (Fig. 4). The intention was to use the outcomes of this hypothetical consultation as one of the criteria in the subsequent phase, serving as a spatial indicator for the socio-cultural criterion. However, due to time and resource limitations, this was not possible, and alternative approximations were considered for this evaluation.

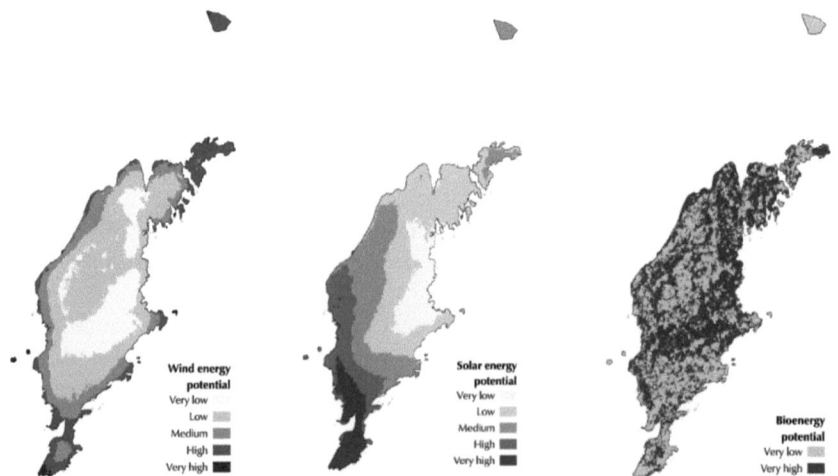

Fig. 3. Energy potential maps: wind (left), solar (middle), biomass (right)

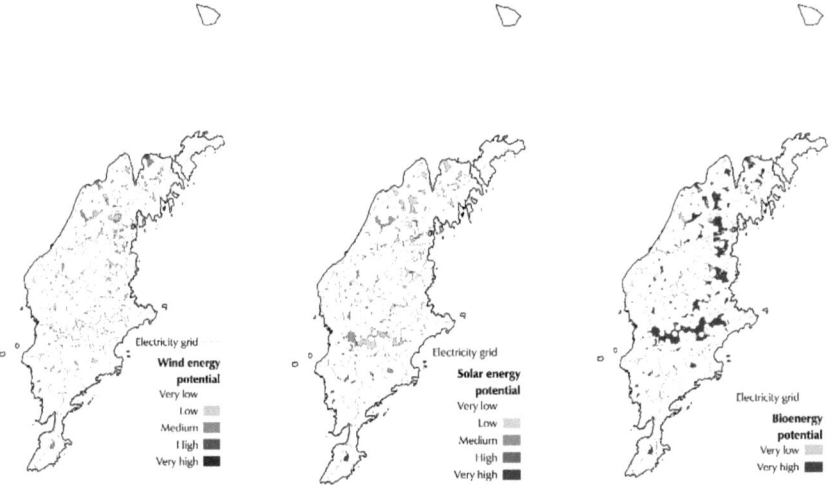

Fig. 4. Maximized development scenarios for wind (left), solar (middle), bioenergy (right)

6.3 Integrated Evaluation and Spatial Decision Support

The third phase implemented a SMCA to integrate qualitative and quantitative factors using the SMARTER method, including technical-infrastructural, environmental, economic, social-cultural, and land-use conflict dimensions, each further broken down into measurable sub-criteria (Fig. 5).

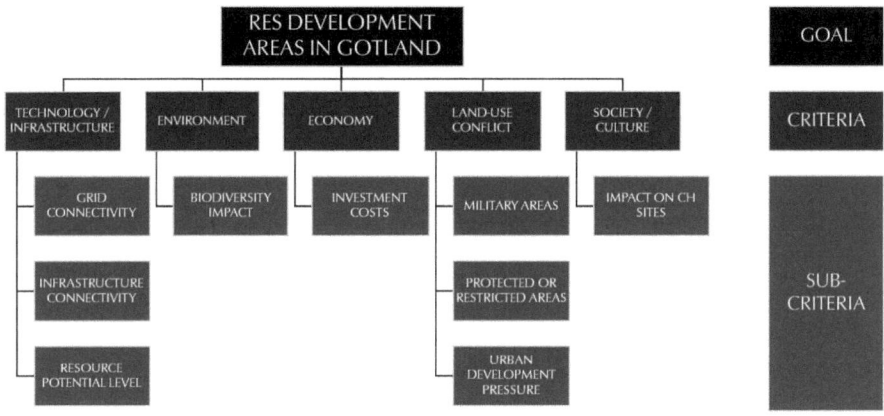

Fig. 5. Decision tree

These sub-criteria were translated into spatial indicators, represented as score maps, each displaying performance values from 1 to 5 across the regional territory from the perspective of that specific sub-criterion. Figure 6 provides examples of these maps, where darker shades consistently indicate higher scores, representing areas most suitable for RES development according to that criterion.

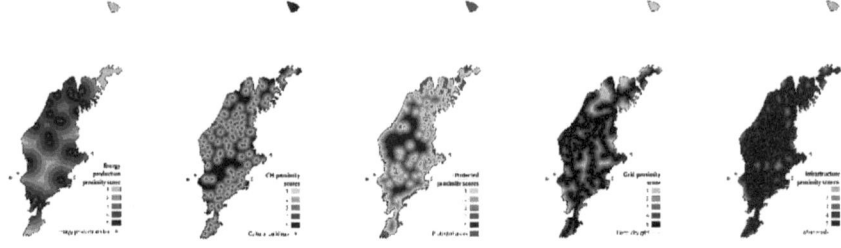

Fig. 6. Score map examples

Next, a qualitative ranking of the five main criteria was established in consultation with local university experts (see Table 1). A similar ranking process was applied at the sub-criteria level when a criterion included multiple sub-criteria. A linear weighted sum was then used to aggregate the scores into calibrated suitability maps, providing overall suitability values from 1 to 5. These values accounted for all criteria, each weighted according to the ranking-based weights derived from the SMARTER method.

The weights, which range from 0 and 1 and sum to 1 by convention, can be calculated using the following formula:

$$w_k = \left(\frac{1}{K}\right) \sum_{i=k}^{K} \left(\frac{1}{i}\right) \tag{1}$$

where K represents the total number of attributes, and w_k is the weight assigned to the kth attribute.

These weights were then used in the final aggregated utility calculation, following the additive model proposed by Barron and Barrett [50]:

$$U_h = \sum_{k=1}^{K} w_k u_h(x_{hk}) \tag{2}$$

where U_h is the total utility score for each evaluation unit h (in this case, a 50 × 50 m pixel of the regional territory). The term $u_h(X_{hk})$ represents the single-dimensional utility scores for each criterion, while w_k denotes the weights assigned to each criterion or value dimension.

Table 1. Criteria ranking using the Rank Order Centroids by SMARTER.

Rank	Criterion	ROC weight
1	Economy	0,4567
2	Land-use	0,2567
3	Environment	0,1567
4	Society and culture	0,0900
5	Technology and infrastructure	0,0400
	Total	1,0000

Despite limited stakeholder involvement, expert input from Campus Gotland guided the weighting process. The analysis produced four suitability maps—general and source-specific—identifying optimal areas for RES development (Fig. 7). Results indicated that central Gotland is the most suitable area for renewable energy development, while coastal and protected zones were deprioritized due to land-use and regulatory constraints. The contrast between energy potential maps and overall suitability maps underscores how contextual factors like infrastructure and land-use outweigh raw resource availability, validating the robustness of the adopted criteria hierarchy.

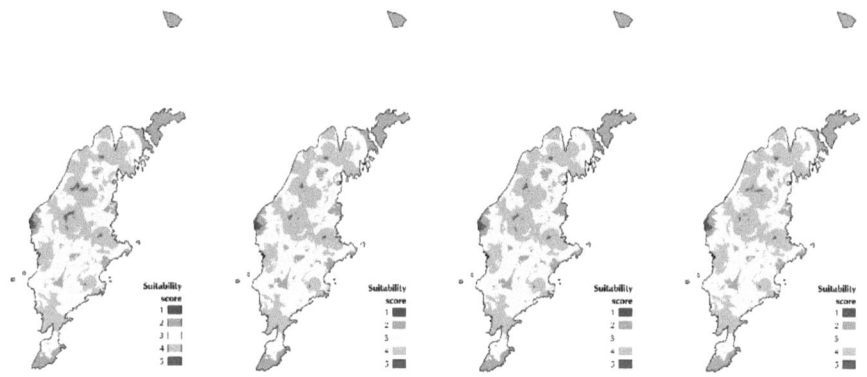

Fig. 7. Suitability maps

6.4 Sensitivity Analysis and Final Reflections

The final phase tested the model's resilience through sensitivity analysis, revealing how prioritizing individual criteria—such as technical and infrastructural factors—expanded high-suitability zones, particularly for wind energy. However, this often came at the expense of environmental and land-use considerations, reinforcing the need for a balanced, multi-criteria approach. While infrastructure and resource availability shape feasibility, long-term planning must also account for biodiversity, cultural heritage, and social acceptance. The study concludes that Gotland's conditions support diversified renewable energy development, and the methodology is broadly replicable, with adjustments for governance, geography, and data availability.

7 Discussion of Results

The proposed methodological framework for regional energy planning demonstrates the capacity to combine and integrate spatial analysis, scenario building, and participatory processes into a structured, adaptable planning method aligned with national and EU sustainability goals.

Applied to Gotland, the framework successfully identified renewable energy potentials, mapped spatial constraints, and generated plausible future development scenarios.

As previously presented, the final suitability maps revealed that central areas of the island are the most promising zones for renewable energy deployment. Conversely, coastal and environmentally protected areas, although rich in physical energy potential, were deprioritized due to regulatory or land-use constraints.

The comparison between source-specific and aggregated suitability maps showed that, in this case, the low weight assigned to the technological and infrastructural criterion—including source-specific energy potential—resulted in minimal differences among the RES options, with development priorities shaped primarily by socio-environmental constraints. However, in other regional contexts, differing priorities or needs may elevate the influence of specific criteria, making one energy source consistently more favorable than others. These specific spatial findings confirm that the methodology is capable of translating complex trade-offs into clear, actionable outputs—an essential condition for effective planning.

The study confirms the framework's replicability, with adjustments for regional governance, data access, and technical capacity. Gotland's streamlined governance and strong renewable resources eased implementation, but challenges such as data requirements and stakeholder engagement remain. Overall, the framework's strength lies in generating context-sensitive strategies through spatial data, local insights, and a transparent, replicable workflow using GIS and SMCA.

8 Conclusions and Future Perspectives

This study proposed a robust and flexible methodological framework for regional energy planning that integrates GIS, scenario modeling, multi-criteria assessment, and participatory tools. Developed to address fragmented governance and implementation gaps, the framework aligns with EU and national sustainability goals and is adaptable to various territorial contexts.

The application to the case study of Gotland demonstrated its effectiveness in identifying renewable energy potential, managing spatial constraints, and structuring development scenarios. While the island's simplicity and resource availability aided implementation, limitations in data resolution and stakeholder engagement pointed to areas for refinement. The results help answer the core research question on how spatial and decision-support tools can strengthen regional planning, along with sub-questions on tool selection, coherence, and applicability.

To support broader adoption, the framework could be embedded within the Strategic Environmental Assessment (SEA) process, as required by Directive 2001/42/EC. The procedural compatibility between SEA and the framework—across phases such as scoping, environmental reporting, and stakeholder consultation—offers opportunities to strengthen the spatial and participatory dimensions of energy planning. A comparison with both the Italian *Valutazione Strategica Ambientale e Territoriale* (VALSAT) and the Regional Energy Plan of Emilia-Romagna confirms the frameworks feasibility for institutional integration. However, effective implementation will require improved data infrastructures, technical training, and long-term political commitment.

Looking forward, further research should focus on enhancing participatory components, increasing the resolution and reliability of spatial data, and applying the framework in more complex regional contexts. Integrating emerging technologies—such as artificial intelligence and dynamic geospatial platforms—may further increase planning responsiveness and support evidence-based decision-making. As energy transition accelerates, structured yet adaptable tools such as the one developed in this study will be crucial to support inclusive, data-informed, and spatially grounded regional energy strategies.

Disclosure of Interests. The authors declare they have no competing interests.

References

1. European Commission: Renewable energy targets (2023). https://en-ergy.ec.europa.eu/. Accessed May 2025
2. European Commission: The European green deal (2019). https://commission.europa.eu/strategy-and-policy/priorities-2019-2024/european-green-deal_en. Accessed May 2025
3. European Commission: The climate law (2021). https://eur-lex.eu-ropa.eu/legal-content/EN/TXT/?uri=CELEX:32021R1119. Accessed May 2025
4. Domac, J., Segon, V., Przulj, I., Rajic, K.: Regional energy planning methodology, drivers and implementation karlovac County case study. Biomass Bioenergy **35**(11), 4504–4510 (2011). https://doi.org/10.1016/j.biombioe.2011.07.018
5. Brundtland Commission. Report our common future (1987). https://sustainabledevelopment.un.org/content/documents/5987our-common-fu-ture.pdf. Accessed May 2025
6. Holling, C.S.: Resilience and stability of ecological systems. Annu. Rev. Ecol. Syst. **4** (1973). https://www.jstor.org/stable/2096802. Accessed May 2025
7. Walker, B.H.: Resilience: what it is and is not. Ecol. Soc. **25**(2), 1–3 (2020). https://doi.org/10.5751/ES-11647-250211
8. United Nations: Transforming our world: the 2030 agenda for sustainable development (2015). https://sdgs.un.org/2030agenda. Accessed May 2025
9. UNFCCC: The paris agreement. https://unfccc.int/sites/de-fault/files/english_paris_agreement.pdf. Accessed May 2025
10. United Nations: The sustainable development goals report 2024 (2024). https://unstats.un.org/sdgs/report/2024/. Accessed May 2025
11. Ritchie, A., Roser, M., Rosado, P.: Renewable energy. ourworldindata.org (2020). https://ourworldindata.org/renewable-energy. Accessed May 2025
12. Knopper, L.D., Ollson, C.A.: Health effects and wind turbines: a review of the literature. Environ. Health **10**(1) (2011). https://doi.org/10.1186/1476-069X-10-78
13. United Nations: Affordable and clean energy (2015). https://www.un.org/sustainabledevelopment/energy/. Accessed May 2025
14. Gielen, D., Boshell, F., Saygin, D., Bazilian, M.D., Wagner, N., Gorini, R.: The role of renewable energy in the global energy transformation. Energy Strateg. Rev. **24**, 38–50 (2019). https://doi.org/10.1016/j.esr.2019.01.006
15. UNESCO: Impacts of wind energy projects and their assessment. https://whc.unesco.org/en/wind-energy/impacts. Accessed May 2025
16. Höök, M., Tang, X.: Depletion of fossil fuels and anthropogenic climate change – a review. Energy Policy **52**, 797–809 (2013). https://doi.org/10.1016/j.enpol.2012.10.046
17. European Commission: Renewable energy directive (2024). https://energy.ec.europa.eu/. Accessed May 2025
18. European Commission: State of the union: commission raises climate ambition and proposes 55% cut in emissions by 2030 (2020). https://ec.eu-ropa.eu/commission/presscorner/detail/en/ip_20_1599. Accessed May 2025

19. European Commission: Hydrogen and decarbonised gas market (2024). https://en-ergy.ec.europa.eu/
20. European Commission: RePowerEU at a glance (2022). https://commission.eu-ropa.eu/. Accessed May 2025
21. IEA: Sweden 2024 (2024). https://www.iea.org/reports/sweden-2024. Accessed May 2025
22. Ministero dell'Ambiente e della Sicurezza Energetica: Piano Nazionale Integrato per l'Energia e il Clima (2024). https://www.mase.gov.it (Last access May 2025)
23. CAN Europe: My country is breaking EU law Demand accountability now! (2024) https://climateplans.caneurope.org/#about. Accessed May 2025
24. Economidou, M., et al.: National energy and climate plans for 2021–2030 under the EU energy union: assessment of the energy efficiency dimension (2020). https://doi.org/10.2760/678371
25. Climate ADAPT: Covenant of mayors (2024). https://climate-adapt.eea.eu-ropa.eu/en/eu-adaptation-policy/covenant-of-mayors. Accessed May 2025
26. Rossitti, M., Torrieri, F.: How to manage conflicting values in minor Is-lands: a MCDA methodology towards alternative energy solutions assessment. In: Gervasi, O., et al. Computational Science and Its Applications ICCSA 2021. ICCSA 2021. Lecture Notes in Computer Science(), vol. 12955. Springer, Cham (2021). https://doi.org/10.1007/978-3-030-87007-2_42
27. Santangelo, A.: Energy behaviour-driven strategies for urban regeneration. Edifir Edizioni Firenze srl (2023). ISBN 978–88–9280–150–9. https://hdl.handle.net/11585/913465
28. Newman, P., Thornley, A.: Urban Planning in Europe: International Competition. National Systems and Planning Projects. Routledge, London (1996)
29. Camelo Vega, A.M.: Financing pathways for the energy transition: a regional approach. New York: Columbia center on sustainable investment (CCSI) (2024). https://ccsi.columbia.edu/sites/ccsi.columbia.edu/files/con-tent/docs/publications/ccsi-financing-pathways-energy-transition.pdf. Accessed May 2025
30. European Commission: ESDP European spatial development perspective (1999). http://europa.eu.int. Accessed May 2025
31. Johnson, C., VanDeveer, S.D.: Energy regionalisms in theory and practice. Rev. Policy Res. **41**(2), 290–309 (2024). https://doi.org/10.1111/ropr.12422
32. Folmer, H., McMillan, D.P., Yeung, H.: SpringerBriefs in regional science series editors. ISSN 2192–0435 (2016)
33. UN-Habitat: Our city plans (2024). https://ourcityplans.org/. Accessed May 2025
34. Stoeglehner, G.: Integrated spatial and energy planning: a means to reach sustainable development goals. Evol. Inst. Econ. Rev. **17**(2), 473–486 (2020). https://doi.org/10.1007/s40844-020-00160-7
35. Manolan Kandy, D., et al.: Spatial multicriteria framework for sustainable wind-farm planning accounting for conflicts. Renew. Sustain. Energy Rev. **189** (2024). https://doi.org/10.1016/j.rser.2023.113856
36. Terrados, J., Almonacid, G., Pérez-Higueras, P.: Proposal for a combined methodology for renewable energy planning. Renew. Sustain. Energy Rev. **13**(8), 2022–2030 (2009). https://doi.org/10.1016/j.rser.2009.01.025
37. Irvin, R.A., Stansbury, J.: Citizen participation in decision making: is it worth the effort? Public Adm. Rev. **64**(1), 55–65 (2004). https://doi.org/10.1111/j.1540-6210.2004.00346.x
38. Buono, F., Pediaditi, K., Carsjens, G.J.: Local community participation in italian national parks management: theory versus practice. J. Environ. Policy Plan. **14**(2), 189–208 (2012). https://doi.org/10.1080/1523908X.2012.683537
39. Stober, D., et al.: What is the quality of participatory renewable energy planning in Europe?. Energy Res. Soc. Sci. **71** (2021). https://doi.org/10.1016/j.erss.2020.101804

40. Colucci, E., et al.: Documenting cultural heritage in an INSPIRE-based 3D GIS for risk and vulnerability analysis. J. Cult. Heritage Manage. Sustain. Dev. **14**(2), 205–234 (2024). https://doi.org/10.1108/JCHMSD-04-2021-0068
41. Wegener, M.: GIS and spatial planning. Environ. Plann. B: Plann. Des. **25**(7) (1998). https://doi.org/10.1177/239980839802500
42. Steiniz, C.: A framework for geo-design: changing geography by design. Esri press. ISBN 9781589483330
43. Caprioli, C., Dell'Anna, F., Fiermonte, F.: Renewable energy sources and ecosystem services: measuring the impacts of ground-mounted photovoltaic panels. In: Gervasi, O., et al. Computational Science and Its Applications ICCSA 2023 Workshops. ICCSA 2023. Lecture Notes in Computer Science, vol. 14108. Springer, Cham (2023). https://doi.org/10.1007/978-3-031-37117-2_29
44. Benzaghta, M.A., Elwalda, A., Mousa, M., Erkan, I., Rahman, M.: SWOT analysis applications: an integrative literature review. J. Glob. Bus. Insights **6**(1), 55–73 (2021). https://doi.org/10.5038/2640-6489.6.1.1148
45. Gürel, E., Tat, M.: Swot analysis: a theoretical review. J. Int. Soc. Res. **10**(51), 994–1006 (2017). https://doi.org/10.17719/jisr.2017.1832
46. Treves, A., Terenziani, A., Angst, C., Comino, E.: Predicting habitat suitability for castor fiber reintroduction: maxEnt vs SWOT-Spatial multicriteria approach. Ecol. Inform. **72** (2022). https://doi.org/10.1016/j.ecoinf.2022.101895
47. Tsoukiàs, A.: From decision theory to decision aiding methodology. Eur. J. Oper. Res. **187**(1), 138–161 (2008). https://doi.org/10.1016/j.ejor.2007.02.039
48. Bouyssou, D., Marchant, T., Pirlot, M., Tsoukiàs, A., Vincke, P.: Aiding to decide: concepts and issues. In: Evaluation and Decision Models with Multiple Criteria: Case Studies, pp. 16–34. Springer, Berlin Heidelberg (2015). https://doi.org/10.1007/978-3-662-46816-6_2
49. Cinelli, M., Kadziński, M., Gonzales, M., Słowiński, R.: How to support the application of multiple criteria decision analysis? let us start with a comprehensive taxonomy. Omega **96**, 102261 (2020). https://doi.org/10.1016/j.omega.2020.102261
50. Ferretti, V., Bottero, M., Mondini, G.: From Indicators to composite indexes: an application of the multi-attribute value theory for assessing sustainability. Adv. Eng. Forum **11**, 536–541 (2014). https://doi.org/10.4028/www.scientific.net/aef.11.536
51. Datola, G., Bottero, M., de Angelis, E.: Enhancing Urban Resilience Capacities: An Analytic Network Process-based Application. Environ. Clim. Technol. **25**(1), 1270–1283. Riga Technical University (2021). https://doi.org/10.2478/rtuect-2021-0096
52. Oppio, A., Caprioli, C., Dell'Ovo, M., Bottero, M.: Assessing ecosystem services through a multimethodological approach based on multicriteria analysis and cost-benefits analysis: a case study in Turin (Italy) J. Cleaner Prod. **472**, 143472 (2024). https://doi.org/10.1016/j.jclepro.2024.143472
53. Edwards, W., Barron, F.H.: Smarts and smarter: improved simple methods for multiattribute utility measurement. Organ. Behav. Hum. Decis. Process. **60**, 306–325 (1994). https://doi.org/10.1006/obhd.1994.1087
54. Barron, F.H., Barrett, B.E.: The efficacy of SMARTER-simple multi-attribute rating technique extended to ranking. Acta Psychol. **93** (1996)
55. Assumma V., Bottero, M., De Angelis, E., Lourenço, J.M., Monaco, R., Soares, A.J.: A decision support system for territorial resilience assessment and planning: an application to the Douro Valley (Portugal). Sci. Total Environ. **756**, 143806 (2021). https://doi.org/10.1016/j.scitotenv.2020.143806
56. Malczewski, J.: GIS-based multicriteria decision analysis: a survey of the literature. Int. J. Geog. Inf. Sci. **20**(7), 703–726 (2006). https://doi.org/10.1080/13658810600661508
57. Bourne, L., Walker, D.H.T.: Visualising and mapping stakeholder influence. Manag. Decis. **43**(5), 649–660 (2005). https://doi.org/10.1108/00251740510597680

58. World Health Organization: Stakeholder network analysis tool to support collabora-tion for better health: Stakeholder.Net (2024). https://iris.who.int/bit-stream/handle/10665/379376/WHO-EURO-2024-10830-50602-76523-eng.pdf?sequence=1
59. Rowe, G., Frewer, L.J.: Public participation methods: a framework for evaluation. Sci. Technol. Hum. Values. **25**(1) (2000) https://doi.org/10.1177/016224390002500101
60. Palm, J., Thoresson, J.: Strategies and implications for network participation in regional climate and energy planning. J. Environ. Policy Plan. **16**(1), 3–19 (2014). https://doi.org/10.1080/1523908X.2013.807212
61. Amer, M., Daim, T.U., Jetter, A.: A review of scenario planning. Futures **46**, 23–40 (2013). https://doi.org/10.1016/j.futures.2012.10.003
62. Durrant, L.J., Vadher, A.N., Sarač, M., Başoğlu, D., Teller, J.: Using organigraphs to map disaster risk management governance in the field of cultural heritage. Sustainability **14**(2), 1–12 (2022). https://doi.org/10.3390/su14021002
63. Lobo, G., Costa, S., Nogueira, R., Antunes, P., Brito, A.: A scenario building methodology to support the definition of sustainable development strategies: the case of the Azores region. In: 11th International Sustainable Development Research. Helsinki, Finland (2005). https://repositorium.sdum.umi-nho.pt/bitstream/1822/3692/1/Lobo_Helsinki2%5B1%5D.pdf. Accesseed May 2025

Public-Private Partnership for the Valorization of Cultural Heritage: Evidence from Case Studies

Francesca Torrieri and Alessia Crisopulli(✉)

dABC, Politecnico di Milano, Via Ponzio 31, 20133 Milano, (MI), Italy
{francesca.torrieri,alessia.crisopulli}@polimi.it

Abstract. This paper investigates the role of Public-Private Partnerships (PPPs) in valorizing cultural heritage buildings as a strategic approach aligned with the principles of sustainable development. It explores how PPP models can effectively integrate economic viability with cultural preservation, generating shared value for society while addressing administrative and financial constraints. These partnerships balance public interests with private sector efficiency, enabling adaptive reuse and sustainable management of heritage assets. PPPs provide financial resources and ensure that cultural heritage retains its intrinsic values through shared responsibilities between stakeholders. Through analyzing case studies and regulatory frameworks from diverse regions, this study aims to provide insights into the successful implementation of PPPs for cultural heritage projects, ensuring long-term benefits for present and future generations.

Keywords: Public-Private Partnership · Cultural Heritage · Valorisation · Economic viability

1 Introduction

The 2030 Agenda for Sustainable Development, adopted by the United Nations General Assembly in 2015, underscores the strategic role of cultural heritage conservation as both a driver and enabler of development and people-centered societies (Goal 11, Target 11.4). Similarly, the New European Agenda for Culture highlights the potential of restoring and enhancing cultural and natural heritage to foster economic growth and sustainability.

A key priority in this framework is the implementation of cross-cutting policies that reinforce the intrinsic value of cultural heritage. These policies must establish the necessary conditions for cultural heritage to contribute effectively to sustainable development. To achieve this, objectives must be set across multiple policy domains, including smart, sustainable, and inclusive growth, as well as the promotion of architectural policies [1].

Today, heritage conservation is increasingly integrated into a broader sustainability paradigm, where culture plays a vital role in fostering sustainable and inclusive development alongside economic, social, and environmental objectives, particularly in urban contexts [2]. This approach implies that cultural heritage enhancement processes are guided not only by the preservation of the assets' cultural value but also by integration with economic and social components to meet sustainability goals [3]. Therefore, innovation and creativity become essential components of cultural heritage management. By embracing this recognition, innovative financial tools to preserve and enhance cultural heritage are being experimented [4]. Among them, Public-Private Partnerships (PPPs), in the most recent forms, are proving to be effective mechanisms as they can cope with limited public resources and budgetary constraints.

By leveraging the strengths of the public and private sectors, PPPs enable the sustainable management of heritage assets while promoting the social and cultural economic development of the context in which they are embedded [5].

Italy, with its extensive cultural heritage, can represent a relevant case to critically reflect on these tools. A substantial part of the cultural heritage is in public ownership, which is responsible for its conservation. Furthermore, the cultural heritage sector has faced significant disruptions since the beginning of the 21st century, including the 2007–2008 financial crisis, which severely constrained funding for cultural initiatives. More recently, the COVID-19 pandemic in 2020 further impacted the sector. Although a recovery phase is underway in both Italy and the EU, cultural spending remains lower than in the late 2010s, despite signs of improvement. According to 2023 data, major Italian monuments, archaeological sites, and museums are benefiting from the resurgence of tourism, particularly from international visitors, which is aiding the sector's recovery.

Despite this recovery, however, the scarcity of public resources makes it hard for many public administrations to fulfill their responsibilities. Such a struggle mainly depends on the widespread distribution of heritage sites across the country, the shortage of specialized resources, the complexity of regulatory frameworks, and the existence of different regional policies. Nevertheless, the primary challenge stems from dealing with a condition of financial constraint [6].

To address this issue, governments have increasingly sought partnerships with private entities, thus introducing the need for clear legislation and well-structured regulations to effectively manage such collaborations. Developing a clear legal and operational framework for PPPs, indeed, is essential to ensure the long-term preservation and enhancement of cultural heritage while aligning with broader sustainability goals.

In this context, the paper aims to analyze the application of PPPs in cultural heritage enhancement projects within the Italian legal framework. By examining case studies and regulatory frameworks from various regions, the study seeks to identify the main factors contributing to the success or failure of PPP initiatives in this sector. The paper is structured as follows: the first part presents the regulatory framework currently governing PPPs, with particular attention to the Italian legislation. It delves into the various forms of PPP models applied to cultural heritage conservation in Italy with a focus on Special Public-Private Partnerships (SP3s). In the second part, it analyzes a series of case studies to highlight the strengths and weaknesses of different PPP models applied to cultural heritage conservation projects. The conclusions critically discuss the results and potential research development in this field.

2 PPPs Definition and Normative Framework

PPPs are an innovative mechanism for collaboration between the public and private sectors. These partnerships are introduced to facilitate the financing, development, and management of public assets and services while leveraging private expertise and resources. The European Commission Regulation No. 549/2013 (SEC 2010) defines a PPPs as a "complex long-term contract between two entities, typically involving a company (or a consortium of public or private companies) and a public administration". This definition underscores three fundamental aspects: the long-term nature of the agreement, the interdependence of the two sectors, and the multidisciplinary expertise required for implementation. Similarly, the Green Paper of the European Commission (2004) conceptualizes PPPs as cooperative arrangements between public authorities and private enterprises, aimed at securing the funding, construction, renovation, management, or maintenance of infrastructure and services.

In the Italian legal framework, Article 174 of the Legislative Decree 36/2023 further refines the definition of PPPs. It describes them as "economic operations" based on a long-term contractual relationship between a public granting entity and one or more private operators, to achieve an outcome of public interest.

PPPs are distinguished by several features:

- A long-term contractual framework, ensuring sustained cooperation between public and private entities across different project phases.
- A co-financing model, where private capital is complemented by public funding mechanisms.
- Active involvement of the private sector in multiple stages, from design and financing to construction, operation, and maintenance.
- A clearly defined public role, focused on setting strategic objectives, ensuring service quality, and enforcing regulatory compliance.
- Risk-sharing mechanisms, distributing financial and operational risks between the partners to enhance project sustainability [7].

Traditionally, PPPs have been widely applied in different sectors of public interest, such as healthcare, transportation, and infrastructure development [8]. However, their implementation in the heritage conservation and management field represents something relatively recent and constantly evolving.

The application of PPPs in the Italian cultural heritage sector, indeed, has undergone significant transformations over the past three decades, reflecting a progressive interest towards private sector involvement while maintaining stringent public control.

The Ronchey Law (1993) paved the to mixed public-private models in the heritage field by first enabling the delegation of services, such as ticketing, security, and visitor assistance, to private operators. A few years later, the Consolidated Act on Cultural Heritage (1999), allowed the outsourcing of cultural assistance services, thus fostering deeper collaboration between public institutions and private stakeholders.

In 2004, the Cultural Heritage Code formally recognized the role of private entities in valorizing cultural assets. This period also led to the introduction a horizontal subsidiarity principle, thus advocating for cooperation between public institutions and private actors in conserving and promoting heritage resources. Between 2002 and 2011, PPPs gained increasing traction in both infrastructure and cultural heritage sectors, supported by the Public Contracts Code (Legislative Decree 163/2006). In the next years, additional legislative measures tried to facilitate private sector involvement: The Cresci Italia Decree (2012) introduced the "availability contract," a legal tool aimed at integrating private capital into cultural projects. The Art Bonus (Law 106/2014) provided tax incentives for private donations to cultural heritage preservation, thus encouraging private investment in the sector. The 2016 Public Contracts Code (Legislative Decree 50/2016) introduced Special Public-Private Partnerships (SP3s) for a more financially flexible management of immovable cultural assets. More recently, the Public Contracts Code of 2023 (Legislative Decree 36/2023) further refined the regulatory framework for PPPs, analyzing the various existing contractual forms, improving transparency and accountability, and establishing monitoring mechanisms.

Despite the growing role of PPPs in cultural property management, Italian law still imposes stringent regulatory constraints to ensure public ownership control over cultural property. Article 54 of the Cultural Heritage Code explicitly denies the sale or transfer of public cultural property, except for extraordinary circumstances. Articles 10 and 12 further reinforce this protection by automatically subjecting all publicly owned assets older than 70 years to preservation regulations, thus preventing any form of alienation. Article 115 of the Cultural Heritage Code states that private management of cultural assets is only admitted through concessions and agreements, without any implications for ownership transfer. Article 174 allows PPPs exclusively for service or works concessions, explicitly excluding models such as Build, Operate, Transfer (BOT) and Build, Own, Operate, Transfer (BOOT), which would entail a transfer of ownership. Article 180 mandates that, even under the adoption of project financing mechanisms, public authorities must retain control to ensure alignment with conservation and valorization objectives. Article 183 further specifies that even in cases where private entities are entrusted with public works, ownership must remain within the public administration. At the regional level, Italian legislation aligns closely with national principles, reinforcing public oversight while enabling controlled private sector participation. The Lombardy Regional Law No. 25/2016 exemplifies this approach. The Ministry of Culture's Guidelines on PPPs for Cultural Heritage (Ministerial Decree 19.02.2018) reaffirm these principles. According to it, private sector involvement is restricted to management, maintenance, valorization, or digitalization, and the ownership must remain public. Regular monitoring and inspections are mandated to ensure compliance with preservation and valorization objectives.

A noteworthy innovation, in recent years, is represented by the introduction of SP3s, first formalized under the Legislative Decree 50/2016, and further refined by Legislative Decree 36/2023. SP3s have been increasingly applied in cultural heritage management due to their unique contractual structure, which allows for no-cost collaborations, thus providing private entities with the opportunity to contribute without direct financial compensation to ensuring public access to cultural assets and their safeguarding under the State's oversight [8]. The increasing use of SP3s and other tailored PPP models highlights a growing recognition of the private sector's role and potential in the heritage conservation and valorization challenges. The following section will explore the most widely adopted partnership models in cultural heritage valorization today.

3 PPP Typologies for Cultural Heritage Conservation in the Italian Context

The introduction of partnership-based management models between public and private entities in cultural heritage valorization remains limited. There are still few cases that can be considered successful, even though the introduction of the SP3s is experiencing significant attempts at application. In general, the different types of PPPs applicable to the cultural sector can be identified, as outlined in the study "The Forms of PPP and the Fund for Cultural Project Development" by Fondazione ANCI and Federculture (2013), as:

- The Concession for Valorization. It is the oldest and most used PPP form, which can be applied to all partnership operations lacking additional specifications. It is a contract for pecuniary interest, whereby one or more public entities entrust a private economic operator (the concessionaire) with the execution of works or the provision and/or management of services. A key characteristic of the concession is that the remuneration consists of the right to manage the works or services covered by the contract, together with any direct payment for the services provided. One of the main challenges in awarding a concession is ensuring that, throughout the entire duration of the contractual relationship, both economic and financial balance are maintained for both the public and private entities. An essential element of the concession is the transfer of operational risk to the concessionaire, as established by Article 177 of Directive 2014/23/EU, which includes both the demand-side risk and the supply-side risk. The former risk (demand-side) is associated with the actual demand for the works or services covered by the contract. The latter one (supply-side) can be identified in the risk that the service's provisions do not meet the qualitative and quantitative standards stipulated in the contract due to circumstances beyond the operator's control.
- Sponsorships. This PPP model is based on the private entity's provision of financial support to cultural institutions, theaters, or opera foundations. This type of contribution is often linked to specific events, valorization projects, or restoration interventions. However, sponsorships merely provide financial resources without the contractual complexity or risk-sharing typically associated with PPPs. The benefits for the private, thus, are mainly related to a reputational return.
- The Leasing Contract: A leasing contract involves a private entity constructing and managing an asset, which is then made available to the public administration as a public service. In return, the public administration compensates the private entity through periodic payments. Under this model, the private partner assumes the investment and operational risks in exchange for agreed payments. On the other side, the public administration benefits from the continuous availability and maintenance of the asset without the need for immediate capital expenditure. At the end of the contract, the public administration may acquire ownership of the asset by paying an

additional residual amount, calculated based on prior payments and the remaining market value of the asset. This type of partnership is rare in the Italian cultural heritage sector compared to other contractual models. Most of the cultural buildings are state-owned, and in most cases, private entities are unwilling to sell such properties. Consequently, leasing contracts are difficult to apply in this sector.

- The *Atipico* (Atypical) Contract, first introduced in 2023 with the adoption of the new Public Contracts Code, is specifically designed for the provision of services within the PPPs framework.
- SP3s are defined by Article 151 of the Public Contracts Code (Legislative Decree No. 50/2016) as "special forms of partnership" that the Ministry of Cultural Heritage and Tourism can establish with public and private entities for recovery, restoration, planned maintenance, management, public accessibility, and enhancement of cultural heritage assets. Initially, only the Ministry of Culture was authorized to activate such partnerships for State-owned cultural heritage. However, following amendments to Article 151, Regions and other local authorities are now also permitted to initiate SP3 agreements. SP3s constitute a collaborative agreement between a public entity and another entity—either public or private—entrusted with overseeing the enhancement process. This model transcends the traditional division between public administration and private interest, embodying the principle of "Shared Administration." SP3s fall within the discretionary actions of public authorities and are governed solely by the principles outlined in Article 30 of the Public Contracts Code. Their contractual scope is not predetermined but rather defined through an ongoing collaborative process, ensuring operational flexibility and co-design between stakeholders. The primary objective of SP3s is to ensure public access to cultural heritage and promote scientific research applied to its preservation. Unlike traditional PPPs, SP3s prioritize social and cultural value over economic returns. These agreements rely on trust-based collaboration and an orientation toward the public interest, fostering the involvement of third-sector entities, such as foundations and nonprofit organizations, that share the mission of cultural heritage enhancement for the benefit of the community.

  The private partner responsible for the enhancement process assumes exclusive responsibility for the operational management but does not receive exclusive economic exploitation rights over the asset. Instead, the partner is required to reinvest profits and revenues into strengthening and sustaining the enhancement process. The adoption of the SP3 model significantly simplifies administrative procedures, particularly in the selection of private partners, which occurs through non-competitive and simplified procedures based on the partner's reputation and professional track record. Additionally, SP3 contracts offer greater flexibility compared to traditional public contracts, allowing interventions to be tailored to the specific needs of the cultural asset [9].

  SP3s represent a strategic opportunity for revitalizing Italy's cultural heritage, promoting a more inclusive, flexible, and effective governance model. However, to fully unlock their potential, stronger regulatory and training efforts are needed to consolidate their implementation and ensure long-term, sustainable outcomes [10].
- An evolution of traditional PPP models is also represented by the Public-Private-People Partnership (P4) [11]. This model includes active participation by civil society and local communities in cultural heritage management. The goal of P4 partnerships

is to establish proactive and participatory approaches not only in the initial stages of urban development (planning and design) but also in the construction, management, and operational phases. Financing and management tools used in P4 projects are based on citizen involvement and may include civic crowdfunding, online petitions, and financial contributions from foundations. P4 models are particularly relevant for cultural heritage assets, which do not attract widespread interest or attention, unlike high-profile monuments, thus requiring more resilient and locally focused strategies for resource mobilization. In these cases, the engagement of local stakeholders becomes essential.

The following section will present some cases of PPPs developed in the Italian context, highlighting the models adopted and the main results achieved.

4 Case Studies in Italy

4.1 Identification of the Significant PPP Practice in Italy

To better evaluate the evolution of PPPs in Italy over the past decades, a systematic review of PPP case studies has been conducted. Such a review aims to identify significant Italian PPP practices and, through their examination alongside the legislative framework outlined in the previous chapter, determine common patterns that highlight both positive and negative trends in the national context. Additionally, this study aims to provide a preliminary critical reflection on the consequences of PPP implementation on local development from a cultural, social, and economic perspective.

The literature review was carried out in three phases. The first phase involved identifying relevant case studies using two types of sources. Data was gathered through academic databases such as SCOPUS and Google Scholar, as well as web-based sources, including articles, magazines, and institutional websites. Keywords used in the search process included combinations of "cultural heritage," "PPP," "public-private partnership," "Italy," "valorization," "management," and specific PPP typologies. Based on initial results, the search was refined using city names, PPP types, and involved partners. The SCOPUS search yielded fifteen sources, most of which examined PPPs from a theoretical perspective, but six offered in-depth analysis of case studies and valuable insights. The same methodology applied to Google Scholar identified twelve relevant papers, with six providing relevant information on practical implementations.

Web-based research further expanded the dataset by increasing the number of identified partnerships and additional information on existing PPPs. In the second phase, a screening process was conducted to remove duplicate records and assess the eligibility of cases for inclusion in the final report. Several partnerships were excluded due to various reasons: some of them were public-public partnerships, others did not progress beyond the planning phase, and some were still under negotiation.

The final research dataset comprises 55 Italian PPP initiatives spanning approximately 25 years, from the landmark Baratti and Populonia case in 1998 to partnerships recorded up until 2023. This preliminary result is affected by the lack of mandatory contract publication before 2023, which posed a challenge in retrieving official information on earlier partnerships. Additionally, obtaining detailed financial data, particularly regarding private sector returns, proved difficult. For projects involving small firms and third-sector entities, only initial costs and investments were typically documented, whereas profit or loss figures were either unavailable or required extensive research. Published data mainly covered concession costs, foundation donations, and investments made by private partners. Larger corporations, on the other hand, provide financial reports, but specific details on individual PPPs are often aggregated within broader cultural operations, making it challenging to isolate data on a single initiative.

The literature process is described in Fig. 1

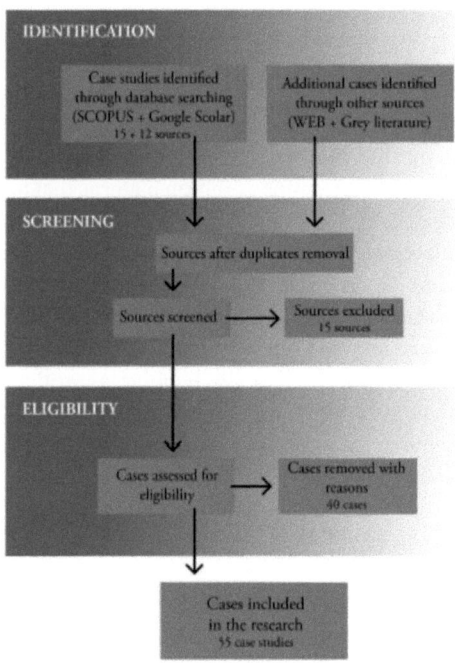

Fig. 1. Literature review process

4.2 A Preliminary Analysis of PPP Models in Italy

The analysis of PPP models in Italy reveals a significant increase in their adoption over time. During the early 2000s, only a few projects were initiated each year, with a notable peak in 2013, when five cultural heritage sites underwent restoration, compared to a maximum of two per year in the previous period. A major turning point came with the introduction of the new Public Contracts Code in 2016, further reinforced by its 2023 revision, which introduced more favorable conditions for PPPs in the cultural sector. Consequently, the number of active partnerships doubled between 2011 and 2020 compared to the previous decade. This trend has accelerated even further in recent years (2021–2023), with the number of new projects surpassing the total for 2001–2010 and reaching half of the 2011–2020 total, hinting at a growing "investment" in PPPs for cultural heritage preservation and valorization.

This upward trend has been strengthened by the widespread adoption of SP3s, which, along with sponsorship models, currently represent the most adopted partnership model in Italy. The case study analysis categorized projects into four distinct groups. While numerous contractual forms exist, this study focuses on concessions, pure and technical sponsorships, and SP3s. This limitation is due to two primary reasons: atypical contracts were only introduced in 2023, and financial lease agreements remain largely absent in Italy.

Notably, SP3s have replaced Project Financing as a contractual category following its formal abolition in 2023. Given their similarities, operations previously categorized under Project Financing have been grouped under SP3s for analytical consistency (Figs. 2 and 3).

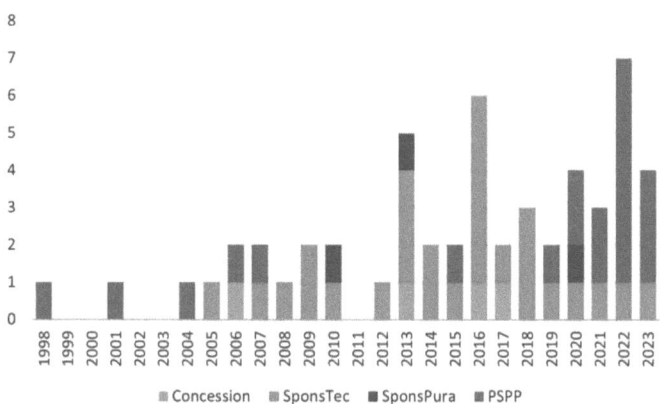

Fig. 2. Evolution of PPPs Over Time

Going into the details of the research's findings, it identifies 55 PPP operations, with the majority classified as sponsorships and SP3s. Since 1998, a total of 30 major sponsorship contracts have been signed in Italy, of which 27 are categorized as technical sponsorships and 3 as pure sponsorships. Additionally, 20 SP3s cases and 5 concession contracts are recorded, contributing to the total.

A piece of noteworthy information is related to the geographical diffusion of partnerships. It is possible to note three main locations that concentrate most of these operations: Rome, Milan, and Naples alone count for 67% of the total investigated Italian PPPs.

Especially in Rome and Milan, almost all these collaborations took the shape of technical sponsorships, thus revealing that half of the implemented operations in Italy were driven by visibility and/or economic reasons. Since heritage assets have an equal

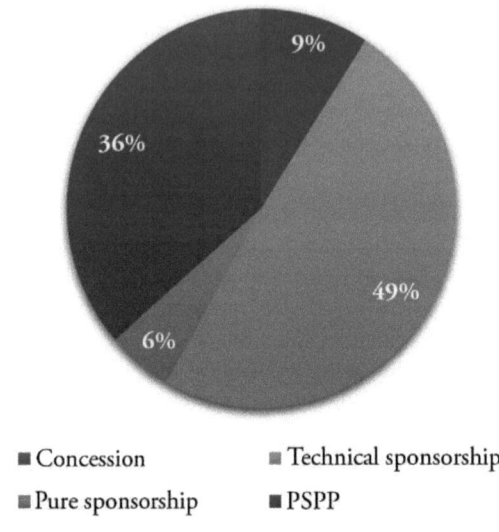

Fig. 3. Percentage per Typology of PPP

geographical distribution across the country, this information further reveals that there was a tendency to operate in places with a more prosperous economic situation.

The development of the SP3s practices has slightly modified this tendency. Following the positive example of the Rione Sanità and Parco Archeologico of Campi Flegrei, special partnerships have started to be used to catalyze local development all around the country.

A common characteristic of PPPs in the last decade is that they have primarily been driven by financial motivations, providing economic benefits and increased visibility for private firms involved in these projects. However, a noteworthy trend has emerged in recent years. Since 2020, the number of SP3s has increased significantly, likely due to legislative enhancements since 2016 that have bolstered their role in the Italian context. Until the late 2010s, cultural heritage preservation was largely dominated by sponsorships, primarily carried out by a single firm, Urban Vision. While its contributions were valuable, the firm's operations remained relatively limited, with an annual average of just 1.1 partnerships. The introduction of SP3s represents a promising advancement, offering a more scalable and sustainable approach to heritage conservation. Even Urban Vision has begun engaging in SP3s, as evidenced by its projects in Rome, such as the "Viscontino" and "Cadlolo" school initiatives, further highlighting the growing potential of this model.

The long-term perspective is crucial in evaluating the impact of PPP initiatives. Unfortunately, many ongoing projects remain in their early phases, making it difficult to conduct comprehensive assessments. While some initial indicators may suggest potential outcomes, definitive conclusions remain speculative. Nonetheless, the rapid increase in these partnerships is a positive sign of their potential effectiveness (Fig. 4).

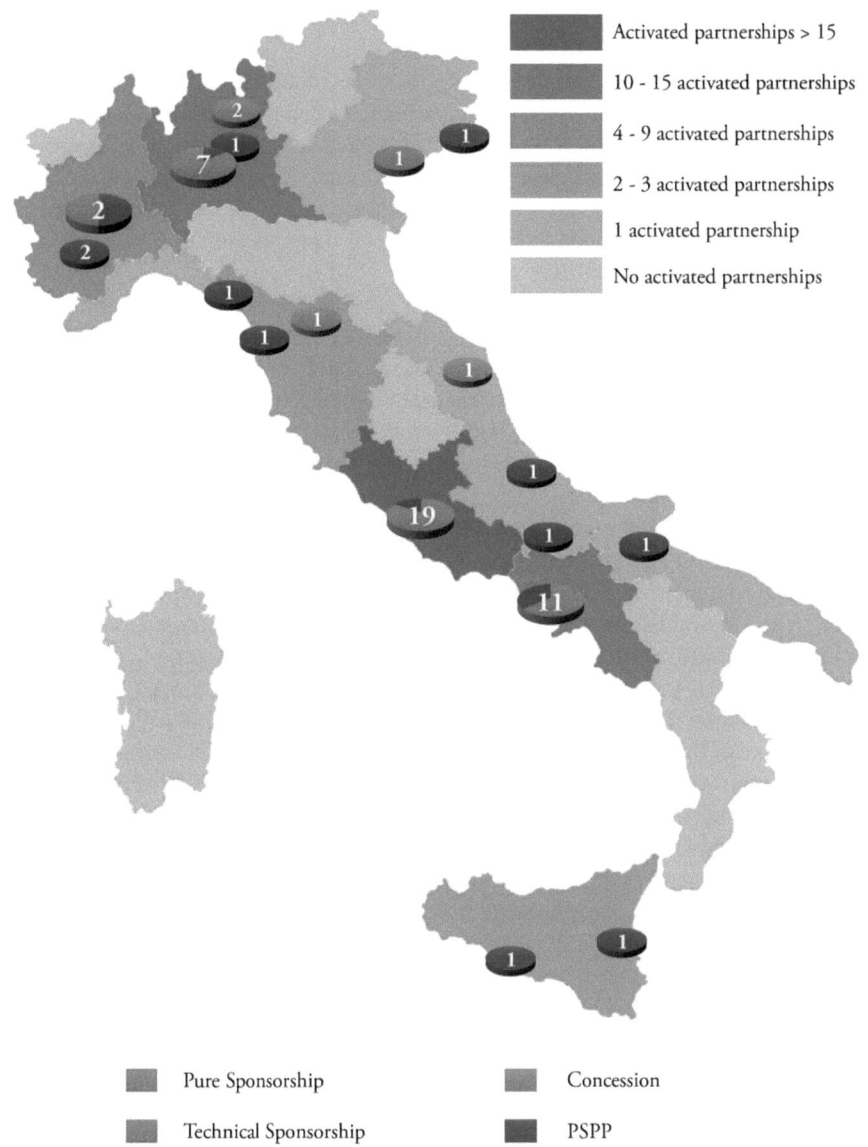

Fig. 4. Geographical distribution of different Typology of PPPs

5 Conclusion

In the context of increasing budgetary constraints in the public sector, investments in cultural heritage face significant challenges despite their undeniable economic, social, and identity-related value. PPPs have emerged as an effective tool to address these challenges, offering innovative solutions that integrate economic sustainability with cultural conservation objectives. By leveraging private sector resources and expertise, PPPs facilitate the adaptive reuse and long-term maintenance of cultural assets while ensuring public accessibility and heritage protection [12].

The Italian experience highlights the progressive evolution of regulatory frameworks, which have strengthened public oversight and safeguarded the intrinsic value of cultural heritage. The introduction of SP3s has further enhanced collaboration by minimizing direct public expenditure and ensuring continued state supervision. However, despite their advantages, PPPs in the cultural sector face several obstacles, including complex contractual structures, the need to balance financial interests among stakeholders, and stringent legislative requirements.

To maximize the effectiveness of PPPs in cultural heritage valorization, it is crucial to develop innovative contractual models that equitably distribute risks and benefits between the public and private sectors. Additionally, strengthening monitoring and transparency mechanisms is essential to ensure compliance with conservation objectives.

Increased uptake of SP3s and other PPP models can be promoted through tax incentives and awareness-raising initiatives, which can help set sustainable models for the management of heritage assets.

The assessment of the feasibility of initiatives, not only considering economic-financial aspects but also indirect costs and benefits, such as the environmental, social, cultural, and economic impacts of the initiatives, becomes a crucial aspect. Indeed, when dealing with cultural heritage projects, indirect effects, such as increased tourism flows, employment growth, increased property values, improved infrastructure, and increased cultural awareness, must be considered in the decision-making process.

In this context, there is a need for an evaluation framework that follows the entire decision process from the initial stages to the restoration works and operational stages, thus providing a holistic understanding of the long-term impact of PPPs. Although further research and empirical studies are needed to refine these models, the potential of PPPs to generate sustainable and shared value is recognized. The success of these partnerships will ultimately depend on their ability to adapt to local specificities while maintaining the fundamental goal of preserving culture and the environment for future generations.

References

1. Diana, L., D'Auria, S., Acampa, G., Marino, G.: Assessment of disused public buildings: strategies and tools for reuse of healthcare structures. Sustainability (Switzerland) **14**(4), 2361 (2022). https://doi.org/10.3390/su14042361
2. Rossitti, M., Torrieri, F.: Circular economy as 'catalyst' for resilience in inner areas. Sustain. Mediterr. Constr. (Print) Land Cult. Res. Technol. **5**, 64–67 (2021)
3. Throsby, D.: Sustainability and culture some theoretical issues. Int. J. Cult. Policy **4**(1), 7–19 (1997). https://doi.org/10.1080/10286639709358060
4. Ost, C., Innovative financial approaches for culture in urban development, in Culture Urban Future, Global Report on Urban Sustainable Development, UNESCO, Paris, (2016)
5. Consiglio S., D'Isanto M., Pagano F.: Partneriato Pubblico Privato e organizzazioni ibride di comunità per la gestione del partimonio culturale. Il capitale culturale, pp. 357–353 (2020)
6. Rossitti, M., Oppio, A., Torrieri, F.: The financial sustainability of cultural heritage reuse project: an integrated approach for the historical rural landscape. Sustainability (Switzerland) **13**(23), 13130 (2021). https://doi.org/10.3390/su132313130

7. Del Giudice, V., Passeri, A., De Paola, Pf., Torrieri, F.: Estimation of risk-return for real estate investments by applying Ellwood's model and real options analysis: an application to the residential real estate market of Naples. Appl. Mech. Mater. **651–653**, 1570–1575 (2014). https://doi.org/10.4028/www.scientific.net/AMM.651-653.1570
8. Del Giudice, V., Torrieri, F., De Paola, Pf.: Risk analysis within feasibility studies: an application to cost-benefit analysis for the construction of a new road. Appl. Mech. Mater. **651–653**, 1249–1254 (2014). https://doi.org/10.4028/www.scientific.net/AMM.651-653.1249
9. Consiglio, S., D'Isanto, M., Pagano, F.: Il Partneriato Pubblico Privato come obiettivo strategico: il caso del Parco Archeologico dei Campi Flegrei, 15° Rapporto Federculture, Cangemi editori, Roma (2019)
10. Boniotti, C.: The public–private–people partnership (P4) for cultural heritage management purposes. J. Cult. Heritage Manag. Sustain. Dev. **13**(1), 1–14 (2023). https://doi.org/10.1108/JCHMSD-12-2020-0186
11. Rossitti, M., Torrieri, F.: Action research for the conservation of architectural heritage in marginal areas: the role of evaluation. Valori e Valutazioni **30**, 3–42 (2022). https://doi.org/10.48264/VVSIEV-20223002
12. Torrieri, F., Crisopulli, A., Rossitti, M.: Assessing the feasibility of PPPs for cultural heritage enhancement in UNESCO sites: the case of Matera (Italy). Land **14**(4), 898 (2025). https://doi.org/10.3390/land14040898

The Circular Adaptive Reuse Project of Cultural Heritage Buildings in Salerno (Italy): from Abandoned Assets to nZEB Buildings

Angrisano Mariarosaria[1](✉) ⓘ, Gravagnuolo Antonia[2] ⓘ, Gianluca Cavalaglio[1] ⓘ, Grazia Neglia[1] ⓘ, and Francesco Fabbrocino[1] ⓘ

[1] Department of Engineering, Pegaso Telematic University, 80143 Naples, Italy
*mariarosaria.angrisano@unipegaso.it
[2] Institute of Heritage Science, National Research Council (CNR-ISPC), 80134 Naples, Italy

Abstract. The construction sector has a significant impact on urban pollution, causing an important amount of CO_2 emissions. However, existing building reuse, with a circular economy perspective, can play a crucial role in the energy transition, thanks to the adoption of energy-efficient projects. This paper investigates how innovative technologies and bio-based materials in building reuse can reduce operational CO_2 emissions, while highlighting their potential for long-term energy savings and operational costs reductions. In this perspective, is presented the adaptive reuse project of the historic Monastery of San Pietro a Maiella and San Giacomo in Salerno, in Italy. The study employs a mixed-method approach, combining Energy Performance Analysis, Material Innovation Assessment and Cost-Benefit Evaluation to assess the potential benefits of a circular adaptive reuse of the historic building.

Keywords: Reuse of cultural heritage · Circular economy · Biomaterials · nZEB buildings (Nearly Zero-Energy Buildings)

1 Introduction

The built environment is recognized as one of the sectors that contribute to urban pollution due to the use of materials, energy, and manufacturing technologies. On average, the building stock, throughout its lifecycle construction, operation, and demolition produces 36% of annual CO_2 emissions, 40% of energy consumption, and 50% of raw material extraction in Europe [1, 2].

However, the reuse of the built environment, according to the circular economy perspective, has the potential to contribute to the energy transition through the implementation of energy-efficient building projects that combine the use of renewable energy technologies as well as innovative materials such as nanomaterials and biomaterials [3, 4].

In particular, cultural heritage adaptive reuse contributes to the recovery of existing buildings by minimizing raw materials extraction and soil consumption; but, as cultural resources, the regeneration of cultural values represents an additional and relevant benefit in a broader circularity perspective. In general, adaptive reuse of cultural heritage, within the context of the circular economy, aims to achieve different objectives, including the preservation of cultural significance, economic feasibility, environmental regeneration, social cohesion, community welfare, and local economic growth [5].

The objective of this paper is to present the adaptive reuse project of the former Convent of San Pietro a Maiella and San Giacomo in Salerno (Italy), which was carried out in the city of Salerno, Italy. Specific green technologies and materials were used for the design project. The primary aim is to understand how these materials can contribute to a significant reduction of CO_2 emissions in the environment, but more importantly, how the building's operational costs can decrease over time.

The CNR, in collaboration with the Municipality of Salerno, the EBRIS Foundation, and the Pegaso Telematic University, presented this reuse project called "Hub di innovazione città circolare della salute" within the context of the "Expression of interest Ecosystems of innovation in Southern Italy - Interventions for the redevelopment and re-functionalisation of sites for the creation of ecosystems of innovation in Southern Italy" as part of the PNRR call for projects (National Recovery Funds).

2 New Materials and Technologies for the Adaptive Reuse of Historic Buildings

In this paragraph, an overview of new materials and technologies currently used for the adaptive reuse of historic buildings is presented, based on recent studies and reports, including relevant case studies.

To achieve the status of "Nearly Zero-Energy Buildings" (nZEB), nanomaterials and biomaterials can be effectively used [1]. Moreover, innovative technologies for cultural heritage circular reuse and renovation can be applied, including the so-called "Nature Based Solutions" (NBS).

Sustainable and circular projects for the reuse of historic buildings can provide an important boost to cities' ecological transition. It is important that these projects adhere to the principles of circular design, where the use of biomaterials and new technologies plays a key role in the development of nZEB.

By 2030, the European Commission has recommended that buildings move from the current nearly zero-energy buildings to zero-emission buildings [6].

NZEB buildings are designed and built to minimize energy consumption by employing renewable sources for energy production, high-performance materials, and innovative technological solutions [7, 8].

In this perspective, nanomaterials (ENM), such as aerogel, cellulose nanofibers, carbon nanotubes, insulating panels based on nano-composites, etc., are among the most widely used new and innovative materials in the construction sector to realize nZEB buildings. These materials are often used to improve the property of many building materials, including concrete, plaster, glass, tiles, insulating metals, paints, and more. The European Commission defines nanomaterials as natural substances or products comprising particles in a dispersed condition, either as aggregates or agglomerates [9].

Nanomaterials are characterized by small dimensions and differ in physical and chemical properties from traditional materials [10]. Their installation is quick, resulting in a substantial reduction in thermal bridging and the prevention of fungal growth, mould, and moisture. Furthermore, they have excellent resistance to corrosion and fire [10, 11].

Among the innovative materials, biomaterials contribute to developing nZEB buildings. Nowadays, various architectural elements are created using materials such as hemp, cork, wood wool fibres, cellulose, sugarcane, sunflower, peanut, seeds, stalks and leaves, flax, potato, rice, wheat, pineapple, and so on.

These biomaterials are characterized by low thermal conductivity in both hot and cold conditions. They are ideal for extremely humid environments. When compared to other insulation materials, they offer the advantage of absorbing and releasing moisture over time.

In this regard, several studies have investigated the huge potential of these materials [10]. For example, Arup conducts studies on the production of building materials from organic waste processing (from the production of urban bio-waste) [12], which includes microalgae, mushrooms (to realize new bricks), flax, hemp and jute, corn cobs, cellulose, sugarcane, sunflowers, peanut, seeds, stalks and leaves, flax, potatoes, rice, wheat, and pineapple. These materials can be used to produce panels with a variety of shapes and properties by adding water, heat, pressure, and no additives, as needed.

In a report by Interreg Central Europe it is affirmed that the use of new technologies for mapping and monitoring existing buildings, such as recording methods, 3D scanning, electronic tachometry, digital photogrammetry, drone photography, laser scanning, degree photography, visualization techniques 3D, GIS, diagnostic methods, thermography, damage inspection, nuclear magnetic resonance, thermal analysis, etc., is becoming more frequent to realize nZEB buildings [13].

Moreover, photovoltaic systems are among the innovative technologies for renovating existing buildings, used to create nZEB buildings. Photovoltaic glass, for example, is incorporated in fixtures and absorbs solar radiation to generate electricity while maintaining the building's visual look thanks to a transparent gel containing amorphous silicon. These glasses might be transparent, semi-transparent, or coloured to match the architectural environment. Photovoltaic tiles are also very popular since their colour looks similar to that of terracotta tiles, which facilitates aesthetic and architectural integration in existing buildings.

Finally, Nature-Based Solutions (NBS) are commonly employed on flat roofs and external walls of buildings [14]. This technology consists of low-maintenance sedum-like vegetation. It entails planting essences that can survive in harsh drought conditions and have an elevated rate of regeneration and self-propagation. This technological finish offers several advantages to buildings, including waterproofing protection and microclimate regulation through lower air temperature. In addition, to enhance energy savings, green roofs are often coated with an insulating layer.

3 The Reuse/Reuse Project of the Former Convent of San Pietro a Maiella and San Giacomo in Salerno (Italy)

The reuse project of the former Convent of San Pietro a Maiella and San Giacomo in Salerno (Italy) is part of the "Edifici Mondo" complex in Salerno (Italy). The CNR, in collaboration with the Municipality of Salerno, the EBRIS Foundation, and the Pegaso Telematic University, presented this reuse project called "Hub di innovazione città circolare della salute" within the context of the "Manifestazione di interesse Ecosistemi dell'innovazione nel Mezzogiorno - Interventions for the redevelopment and re-functionalisation of sites for the creation of ecosystems of innovation in Southern Italy" as part of the PNRR call for projects (National Recovery Funds).

Salerno is an Italian municipality with around 130,000 inhabitants in the south of Italy. It is the second largest municipality in the Campania region by population [15].

The "Edifici Mondo" is a complex of four large abandoned historic buildings in Salerno's historic city centre: The San Massimo Palace, the former Convent of San Francesco, the former Convent of San Pietro a Maiella and San Giacomo, and the former Convent of Santa Maria of the Consolazione, which altogether approximately include 20,000 square meters. Despite their size and strategic location in the city centre, they are in dire need of restoration [15].

The regeneration project of "Edifici Mondo" (developed within the Horizon 2020 CLIC project "Circular models Leveraging Investments in Cultural heritage adaptive reuse") aimed to design the redevelopment of these historic buildings in order to revitalise the surrounding urban context. It was proposed to connect the buildings with green pathways and to restore the pedestrian ramps previously used by Benedictine monks. Two of the buildings, in fact, are former convents (Convent of San Francesco and Convent of San Pietro a Maiella and San Giacomo). One of the buildings is the Palazzo San Massimo, a noble building of high prestige with elegant decorations, monumental staircases, and frescoed ceilings.

A participatory design approach was employed to identify the new functions to be assigned to the buildings, which include a research centre, cultural activity spaces, applied research laboratories, coworking spaces, craft workshops, and offices for spin-offs and start-ups. The laboratories and equipment set up in the buildings should be used to foster collaborations among private enterprises, research institutes, and universities, as well as the project's partner promoters, to support the development, experimentation, and implementation of innovative products and services in the medical-pharmaceutical sector and the circular economy. Finally, large areas are reserved for advanced training activities, which are an important component of the Hub's activities related to the development and attraction of human capital, as well as conferences/cultural events capable of engaging the local context and projecting it into an international entrepreneurial and innovation ecosystem [15].

The focus of this paper is on the adaptive reuse project of the San Pietro a Maiella and San Giacomo complex (Fig. 1).

After many inspections, the primary faults with the building have been identified. Specifically, the roofs and floors appear to be severely damaged, with obvious evidence of wear. Furthermore, the facades display signs of water runoff stains and exfoliation phenomena, indicating that the external surfaces have degraded. Partial or complete

Fig. 1. San Pietro a Maiella and San Giacomo complex

plaster detachments have also been discovered, compromising the wall's integrity. The thresholds are frequently missing or damaged, and colour changes and efflorescence are visible, indicating a humid environment conducive to the formation of moulds, mosses, and lichens. The building's windows are in dire condition, with several glass components damaged or missing. Furthermore, condensation stains have been discovered on the upper levels' ceilings, most likely due to an inadequate or complete absence of waterproofing on the roof terrace. The internal walls also show signs of condensation and humidity, indicating infiltrations into the internal spaces. Another issue discovered is the humidity in the shafts, which is caused by infiltrations from existing downspout damage. Finally, the presence of rising damp was discovered, which exacerbates the building's decay.

3.1 Materials and Innovative Solutions Used in the Project

Before moving on to the description of the reuse project, it is necessary to point out that each design choice was influenced both by the need to meet the requirements of the Italian Superintendence for Historic Buildings and by the necessity to use solutions compatible with cultural heritage values conservation, as well as the surrounding historic city context. The choice of specific materials and technologies was carefully conducted, taking into account the compatibility of each single intervention.

The intervention's design was orientated towards defining processes dedicated to optimising energy, plant, and architectural quality and thus towards defining design choices aimed at improving the healthiness and well-being of the occupants, which are currently completely absent due to the level and severity of the degradation observed.

The design, therefore, was developed pursuing the eco-efficiency of the building envelope, optimising, among other things, energy consumption and environmental impact, while also being dedicated to improving the architectural quality of the building, paying particular attention to the maintenance and management aspects of the properties, with the aim of increasing the useful life of the works and individual components. Within the building project, high-performance materials related to the geometries and functionality of the existing envelope were identified, thereby maximising the concept of adaptable and flexible space through the pursuit of eco-systemic quality, resulting in the buildings receiving the nZEB classification.

The individual assumptions and design decisions targeted at improving the building envelope's energy efficiency have been investigated, as well as technological compatibility and implementation and maintenance costs.

Every design choice was also influenced by the necessity to meet the requirements of the Italian Superintendence for historical buildings.

In particular, for opaque vertical partitions, the intervention was chosen not only to maximise thermal performance and thus achieve perfect insulation by addressing the identified issues but also to restore the architectural value of the buildings in question.

Regarding the opaque vertical envelope, the chosen technological solution consists of the use of nanotechnological plasters with very low thermal conductivity (k = 0.06 W/mK), capable of ensuring, with extremely thin layers (on the order of mm), performance comparable to that derived from the application of traditional insulating material panels.

In more detail, nanotechnological plasters are a unique combination of highly insulating and thermo-reflecting materials. The combination of the reflecting power of cellular glass microspheres and "coccio pesto" results in a mass with a high concentration of air cells with strong insulating and reflective properties, capable of retaining the mass's breathability.

However, the aforementioned nanotechnological plasters are only suitable for walls that are accessible from the outside. It was assumed to use, whenever possible, nanotechnological plasters with a thickness of 1.5 cm.

No intervention has been planned on the areas of the walls that are inaccessible due to Heritage authority limits to protect the existing internal architectural components. However, on some portions of walls that are not accessible from the outside and where the aforementioned limits do not apply, it was decided to install insulation from the inside using natural hemp fibre panels (k = 0.038 W/mK) with a thickness of 10 cm. These panels work well in both cold and hot conditions, thanks to their low thermal conductivity and high specific heat, which causes the heat within the material to evaporate quickly. These panels are ideal for extremely humid conditions. In fact, unlike other insulators, hemp absorbs moisture and releases it over time. Its permeable properties prevent the formation of interstitial condensation, resulting in healthy living spaces devoid of bacteria, mould, and microorganisms. Furthermore, hemp fibres are characterised by numerous other environmental benefits, including: 1) they produce oxygen and absorb large amounts of CO_2 from the atmosphere; 2) they are a completely renewable natural fibre; 3) they are a low-energy input crop; 4) they are an environmentally advantageous material, as considering the CO_2 absorbed by the plant during cultivation, their carbon footprint is close to zero (0.138 kg of CO_2-eq); 5) the production of the insulating panel requires modest energy consumption compared to mineral fibre insulators and does not require the use of water and chemical products.

So-called "green roofs" were planned on flat roofs. It is an alternative to existing technologies that involves greening the exterior of the roof slab. A green roof fits all of the structural, mechanical, and thermal requirements of any covering while also providing agronomic and drainage capabilities. It is usually a system that is thin and light enough to be used on roofs and requires minimal upkeep because it includes sedum species that must be able to survive in harsh drought conditions while also having high regeneration and self-propagation capabilities. It is a technological finish that provides several benefits to the building, including waterproofing protection, microclimate regulation due to lower air temperature in urban environments, combating the heat island effect, reducing the presence of fine dust, creating new habitats for wildlife, and having a lower environmental and aesthetic impact. Furthermore, in line with the green roofs, an insulating material layer has been planned to maximise energy savings. Even in this case, the panels are composed of hemp fibres, which have already been mentioned for their potential. The thickness of the previously indicated covering panels is considered to be 12 cm.

Furthermore, insulation using the same hemp panels was planned for the sloped roofs to be repaired in order to minimise thermal dispersions as much as possible while completely respecting the limits to which the buildings in question are subjected.

Insulating the floors lying on the rock wall or embankments is intended to boost the envelope's thermal performance even further. This intervention provides an efficient barrier against moisture rising from the ground's capillarity, so improving the health of the building and its interior environs. Even in this case, the insulation is made of 10 cm thick hemp fibre panels.

In accordance with the current shapes and colours, thermal break wood-aluminium frames for the fixtures were planned for the transparent vertical components.

Thermal break doors, characterised by very low thermal transmittance values, should be installed for the building's access doors without altering the aesthetic aspect of the existing doors.

To complete the intervention, the use of photocatalytic paints should be applied on all buildings' external perimeter walls. Photocatalytic paints can clean the air of pollutants, which is why they are often called "smog-eating paints". Utilising the photocatalytic process of titanium dioxide nanoparticles (a light-sensitive catalyst), these are capable of acting on nitrogen oxides, the protagonists of the chemical reactions in the atmosphere that produce ozone, and converting them into nitric acid, which is more easily handled. The use of photocatalytic paints contributes to the reduction of air pollution generated by automobile emissions, factories, and domestic heating. In addition, photocatalytic paints not only break down organic and inorganic pollutants that settle on surfaces, but they also function as bactericides and fungicides.

3.2 Plant Interventions and the Use of the Latest Technologies

The project includes a variety of system changes designed to maximise energy and economic savings while minimising environmental effect.

To advance with the size of the plant systems, the thermal characteristics of the building were assessed using a series of simulations to determine the building's thermal demand and, as a result, proceed with the sizing of all the plant systems.

A preliminary design solution was proposed for systems that recover white, grey, and black water.

In terms of water recovery, rainwater collection and reuse are expected to reduce energy consumption and environmental effects while increasing economic convenience. Rainwater is a continuous source that requires simple and cost-effective treatments to be reused for non-potable purposes. Rainwater recovery systems reuse water collected from building downspouts, creating an appropriate reserve for irrigation or service water outflow. These systems allow for the development of rainwater recovery opportunities, which, rather than being squandered, can be profitably employed for the aforementioned reasons. The proposed system ensures that the rainwater collected from the roof flows into the gutter and is sent to the storage tank after proper filtration (primary filter). Following that, the filtered and collected rainwater in the tank is sent to the utilities via a specific suction machine. The recovered water is used to irrigate green roofs and gardens, as well as to flush toilets and wash machines (where present), and for all other non-potable uses.

It is additionally planned to recover grey water, which refers to water used for personal hygiene. The grey water recovery and reuse technology enables significant reductions in drinking water consumption. In fact, the approved system returns grey water to a hygienic state through the designated system.

Finally, each building will have a system in place to recover black water. An activated sludge plant serves as the foundation of the black water recovery and treatment system. First and foremost, a primary treatment step is required, which involves primary sedimentation in a tank. Next, the pre-treated effluents are biologically oxidised using an activated sludge system, followed by secondary sedimentation downstream of the oxidation system. The treated waters are also planned to be used for filling toilet cisterns, irrigating green areas, cleaning buildings.

The second proposed design solution is for the installation of a ground/water geothermal heat pump, which requires the excavation of a geothermal field through which the system's pipes will pass for thermal exchange with the ground.

The intervention is expected to lower electricity consumption by more than half when compared to typical asynchronous motors.

To complete the plant interventions, an automated system for optimal control and regulation of the building's heat generation system was considered. The system includes external and internal temperature sensors, immersion probes in the pipes, occupancy sensors, twilight sensors, and anemometers in order to measure all the thermodynamic features that contribute to determining thermal and cooling energy requirements. Such sensors can interact with each other thanks to proximity and functionality logics, and they are all linked to a central gateway. The latter, in turn, based on the data measured by the sensors, having memory of similar past situations, sends commands to the actuators in order to minimise not only the energy needs due to the system but also the discomfort of the occupants, thereby maximising the thermo-hygrometric well-being conditions within each building.

3.3 Renewable Sources and Photovoltaic Systems

In terms of the photovoltaic systems that will be built, a novel technique that is not architecturally obtrusive was designed: photovoltaic tiles on sloped roofs.

This technology allows the most efficient use of renewable sources while preserving the aesthetic appearance of buildings. As a result, according to the authors, its usage is permissible even in the presence of Heritage protection regulations limitations, provided that the restrictions for the buildings in question in this paper are strictly followed.

To properly design each of the plants, the design principle employed is to maximise the capture of the available annual solar radiation.

The proposed modules operate on the premise of low molecular density. Each module is made of a non-toxic, recyclable polymer compound that can absorb photons. The module has standard monocrystalline silicon cells with an efficiency of roughly 12%. The surface seems opaque, but it is transparent to sun rays, allowing solar energy to power the cells.

The photovoltaic tiles have no impact on the artistic and architectural value of the buildings on which they are installed. As a result, the building's sloped roofs will be completely refurbished with such solar tiles. Furthermore, the planned photovoltaic tiles, like the paints for the facade, have a photocatalytic effect, which considerably improves the overall air quality.

4 Results Obtained in Terms of Improving the Energy Performance of the Building Through the Use of Photovoltaic Technologies

To evaluate the building's energy performance (also in terms of costs), the study employed an integrated approach combining Building Information Modeling (BIM) (used for the entire architectural design) with Termus software (Acca Software) for dynamic thermal-energy simulations. This methodology enabled systematic analysis of the monastery's energy behavior, based on the proposed design solutions. This allowed to estimate operational energy consumption and costs for different design options, supporting the adaptive reuse design team in the choice of the most satisfactory solutions in terms of environmental performances, as well as heritage values conservation. The integration of innovative materials and technologies with cultural heritage was one of the key aspects considered for the choice of the final solution.

In terms of energy performance, the proposed interventions for reusing the historic buildings of San Pietro a Maiella and San Giacomo allow for significant energy savings. Furthermore, due to compliance with the minimal coverage from renewable sources, the building has achieved the nZEB classification, fully respecting the Italian Superintendence's requirements.

The key findings in terms of renewable energy coverage are presented below.

The adaptive reuse project of the convent of San Pietro a Maiella and San Giacomo first demonstrates how a planned photovoltaic system partially meets the requirement for electrical energy for heating services (see. Fig. 2). As expected, in the months of December and January, when thermal demand is particularly high and the photovoltaic system's productivity is lower due to reduced solar irradiation, the amount of electricity drawn from the national grid is significantly higher than that produced by the system and self-consumed. In the months of November and February, when external climatic conditions are generally less harsh and there is more intense irradiation, the difference between the electricity produced and self-consumed for heating purposes and that obtained from the grid for the same service is lower. Finally, during the month of March, usually with milder external temperatures, the electricity produced and self-consumed for heating is even higher than that supplied by the electrical grid.

Regarding the cooling service, in Fig. 2 it is possible to observe how this service is primarily provided by the electrical energy generated by the photovoltaic system planned for the roof. This is made possible by the significant solar radiation values that characterise the months when refrigeration energy for the cooling service is higher in demand, as well as the planned photovoltaic system's peak size. More specifically, the solar system provides the majority of the cooling service between the months of April and August. In the month of September, however, there is a significant need for electricity from the national power system. Finally, throughout the month of October and, therefore, in the lead-up to the start of the heating season, demand is fulfilled mostly through grid electricity, with the photovoltaic system supplying the remainder. This is explained by the fact that, as previously observed, during the months of the heating season, the intensity of solar radiation is lower, and as a result, the productivity of the photovoltaic system is lower.

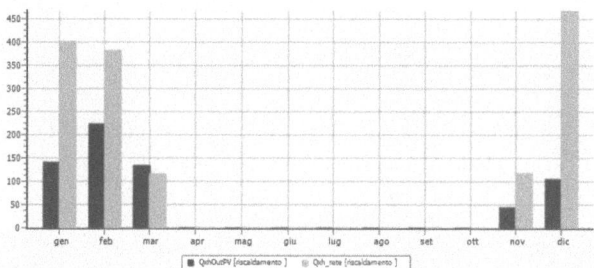

Fig. 2. Monthly self-consumed energy or obtained from the grid for heating service according to the radiation expected per month

Regarding the service of producing hot water for sanitary use DHW (Domestic Hot Water), the situation is roughly similar to that of the heating and cooling services (see Figs. 3, 4). In detail, during the colder months, the electricity produced and self-consumed to meet this service is less than that obtained from the electrical grid; however, during the warmer months, the same service is predominantly met through the electricity generated by the photovoltaic system. The only exception is the months of September and October. In fact, during the first month, significant integration from the national electricity grid is required, as the photovoltaic system's electricity cannot cover the complete requirement for DHW production. In contrast, during the second month, the share obtained from the electrical grid is more than that produced by the photovoltaic system (see Figs. 3, 4).

Overall, renewable sources account for 80.3% of heating, cooling, and residential hot water generation.

Figures 5 and 6 show that during the warm months, from April to September, the lighting service and the movement of people and goods are almost entirely satisfied by the electricity produced by the photovoltaic system, whereas during the cold months, from October to February, the electricity obtained from the grid accounts for a greater share than that produced on-site. The sole exception is the month of March. In March, the self-consumption and grid withdrawal components were similar, with the former somewhat greater than the latter.

Figure 7 depicts the monthly renewable energy coverage for all of the services described above. In detail, renewable energy sources provide for more than 70% of heating service, peaking at 80% in March. The cooling service coverage varies greatly

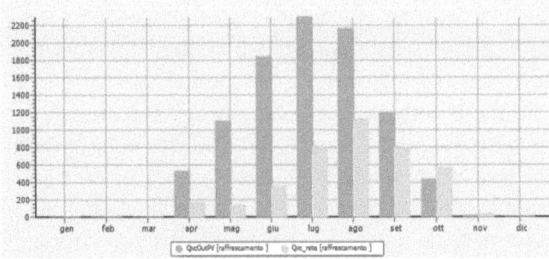

Fig. 3. Monthly self-consumed energy or obtained from the grid for cooling service

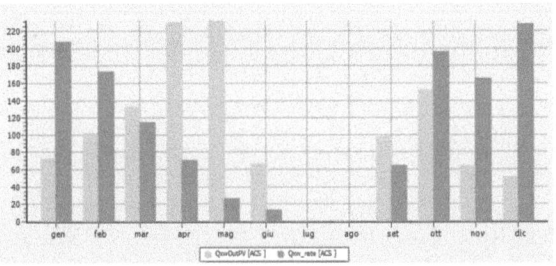

Fig. 4. Monthly self-consumed energy or obtained from the grid for DHW service

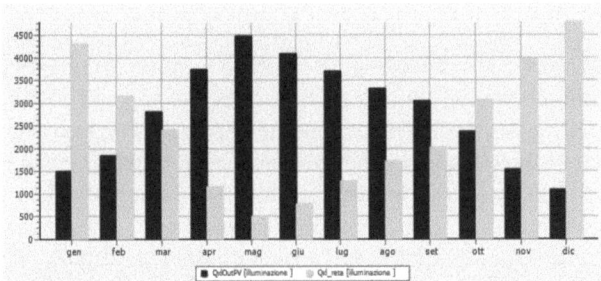

Fig. 5. Monthly self-consumed energy or obtained from the grid for lighting service

throughout the year, ranging from 30% in the cooler months to peaks just above 80% (May). In terms of DHW production, renewable sources meet more than 80% of the whole requirement throughout the year, with peaks near 100% between May and August. Regarding lighting and the movement of people and goods, it is possible to observe that renewable sources are largely covered during the warmer months, when incident solar radiation is stronger, while only marginally during the colder months. Specifically, the coverage ranges from around 30% of the demand during the months of January and December to slightly more than 80% in May.

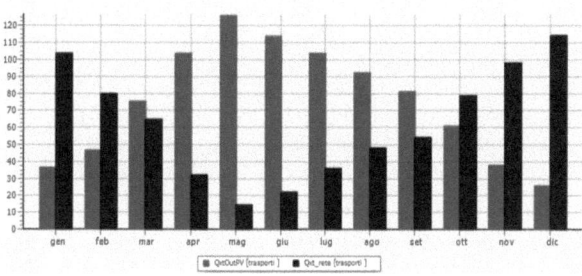

Fig. 6. Monthly self-consumed energy or obtained from the grid for movement of people and goods service

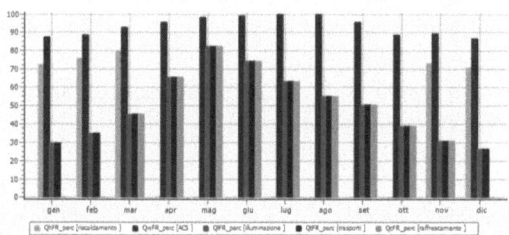

Fig. 7. Monthly renewable sources coverage for all services

4.1 Analysis of Avoided Costs and CO_2 Reduction in the Environment Due to the Use of Photovoltaic Technology Sample

After conducting a thorough cost analysis of each intervention for the reuse project of the former Convent of San Pietro a Maiella and San Giacomo (using Termus and Primus software of Acca Software), the total cost amounts to €5,490,265.60 (the water-sanitary system cost €332,537.58, the thermal system cost €1,052,994.19, the electrical system cost €2,402,787.01, and the thermal insulation required an investment of €1,523,064.60).

After moving beyond this purely economic analysis, the focus shifted to understanding how the use of innovative technologies and specific green materials can produce remarkable results in terms of energy savings (reduced CO_2 emissions) and operational costs associated with the building's functioning.

In particular, the transition to photovoltaic technology resulted in a 30% reduction in building heating operational costs. In reality, without the contribution of photovoltaics, the operating cost for heating would have been approximately €533.60 (per year), however with the use of solar energy, the actual cost has decreased to €371.22, resulting in an economic saving of €162.38 (Table 1). This saving demonstrates how photovoltaics can reduce the cost impact of a fundamental utility, such as heating.

Regarding the production of domestic hot water (DHW), photovoltaics had an even more significant impact. If the cost of producing domestic hot water (DHW) without photovoltaics have been €614.28 (per year), the adoption of solar technology has lowered the cost to €314.73, with a savings of €299.54, or nearly 49% of the original costs (Table 1). This finding validates photovoltaics' effectiveness in boosting energy efficiency in household hot water production.

Instead, photovoltaics have significantly reduced the cost of cooling the structure by 71%. Prior to the implementation of photovoltaics, the cost for cooling was €3,379.92 (per year), but thanks to the energy produced by the panels, it was reduced to €987.98, resulting in a savings of €2,391.95. This finding indicates photovoltaics' high efficiency in environments with high energy demand (see Table 1).

Even for lighting, photovoltaics have had a significant impact, lowering costs by over 50%. Without solar energy, the cost for lighting would have been €15,685.79 (per year), but with the adoption of photovoltaics, it has decreased to €7,301.65, resulting in an economic saving of €8,384.14 (see Table 1). In this case, photovoltaics had the greatest economic impact, demonstrating its ability to significantly reduce costs.

Overall, the use of photovoltaic technologies has resulted in a total economic savings of €11,464.17, reducing overall costs from €20,626.40 to €9,162.23, with a cost reduction of 55% for each calendar year.

Besides the economic benefits, the adoption of photovoltaic panels has also had a positive impact on CO_2 emissions reduction.

In particular, CO_2 emissions from the facility's heating operations, were reduced from 1,511.15 kg to 1,051.30 kg (per year), a decrease of 459.85 kg. Although the economic savings from avoided emissions were minor (€36.79), the photovoltaic system still contributed to improve the system's energy efficiency (Table 2).

In the case of the production of domestic hot water (DHW), CO_2 emissions have significantly decreased from 1,739.63 kg to 891.32 kg (per year), with a reduction of 848.30 kg, thus generating an economic saving of €67.86 (Table XX). This reduction in emissions confirms the efficiency of photovoltaics in this area, where significant economic savings have been achieved.

Cooling had the greatest reduction in CO_2 emissions, dropping from 9,571.94 kg to 2,797.95 kg, representing a reduction of 6,773.99 kg, or almost 71%. This resulted in an economic saving of € 541.92, highlighting the importance of photovoltaics in high-energy-consuming applications such as summer cooling (Table 2).

CO_2 emissions from lighting have drastically decreased from 44,422.14 kg to 20,678.26 kg (per year), a reduction of 23,743.88 kg (Table 2). This led to a €1,899.51 cost savings, demonstrating the efficacy of photovoltaics in this area and significant economic benefits.

4.2 Analysis of the Results of the Entire Adaptive Reuse Project of the Former Convent of San Pietro a Maiella and San Giacomo

The reuse project of the former convent of San Pietro a Maiella and San Giacomo, according to the principles of the circular economy, yielded very significant results, both environmentally and socio-economically, demonstrating the efficacy of an intervention aimed at combining heritage preservation with technological innovation. One of the most notable outcomes has been an improvement in air quality and living comfort for future building users as well as residents living near the historic building. The building will benefit from optimised ventilation management while reducing thermal fluctuations within the spaces as a result of the adoption of advanced energy solutions, such as thermal

Table 1. Costs avoided by using photovoltaics for building operation

CONVENT OF SAN PIETRO A MAIELLA AND SAN GIACOMO						
Service	Total electricity demand [kWh]	Electricity from the grid [kWh]	Electricity produced by photovoltaic [kWh]	Operating cost (in absence of PV)	Actual operating cost (with PV)	Cost savings guaranteed by PV
Heating	2.134,39	1.484,88	649,51	€ 533,60	€ 371,22	€ 162,38
DHW	2.457,10	1.258,93	1.198,17	€ 614,28	€ 314,73	€ 299,54
Cooling	13.519,69	3.951,91	9.567,78	€ 3.379,92	€ 987,98	€ 2.391,95
Lighting	62.743,14	29.206,58	33.536,56	€15.685,79	€ 7.301,65	€ 8.384,14
Transport	1.651,26	746,62	904,64	€ 412,82	€ 186,66	€ 226,16
TOT	82.505,58	36.648,92	45.856,66	€ 20.626,40	€ 9.162,23	€ 11.464,17

Table 2. CO_2 emissions reduction due to energy use

CONVENT OF SAN PIETRO A MAIELLA AND SAN GIACOMO						
Service	CO_2-eq emissions (in the absence of PV) [kg]	Actual CO_2-eq emissions (with PV) [kg]	CO_2 emissions avoided thanks to PV [kg]	Cost of CO_2 emissions (in the absence of PV)	Cost of actual CO_2 emissions (with PV)	Savings due to avoided CO_2 emissions thanks to PV
Heating	1.511,15	1.051,30	459,85	€ 120,89	€ 84,10	€ 36,79
DHW	1.739,63	891,32	848,30	€ 139,17	€ 71,31	€ 67,86
Cooling	9.571,94	2.797,95	6.773,99	€ 765,76	€ 223,84	€ 541,92
Lighting	44.422,14	20.678,26	23.743,88	€ 3.553,77	€ 1.654,26	€ 1.899,51
Transport	1.169,09	528,61	640,49	€ 93,53	€ 42,29	€ 51,24
TOT	58.413,95	25.947,44	32.466,52	€ 4.673,12	€ 2.075,79	€ 2.597,32

and acoustic insulation, via specific biomaterials and nanomaterials analysed in paragraph 3.1, 3.2, 3.3. This will contribute to a healthier and more habitable environment, increasing the well-being of future users.

Moreover, future users will see clear economic benefits, including a significant reduction in energy bills. The integration of photovoltaic panels and the overall efficiency improvement of the building (see paragraph 3.3) will greatly reduce the energy consumption obtained from the grid, resulting in huge cost savings.

Furthermore, the convent's reuse project will have a good impact on the urban setting in which it is located, as it will boost the beauty of the neighbourhood while also contributing to the development of the microclimate.

The reuse of the historic building has the potential to reignite interest in the neighbourhood, drawing visitors and opening up new prospects for local investment. The integration of sustainable solutions, in terms of technologies and new materials, as well as the focus on preserving the architectural heritage, will make the neighbourhood more interesting and vibrant, fostering urban renewal that will also benefit the local economy.

In parallel, since the phase of defining the new functions to be attributed to the building was shared with the community, a process of raising awareness among the interested stakeholders has been observed in terms of increasing their awareness of the importance of reuse and energy efficiency of historic buildings, emphasising how it is possible to preserve cultural heritage without compromising sustainability and residential comfort. This has stimulated a broader discussion on the necessity of sustainable practices in historic building management, both locally and among professionals.

Finally, one of the most significant objectives of the project was to transform the historic building into zero-energy building. It will be able to reduce energy consumption and corresponding CO_2 emissions by implementing technologies such as photovoltaics, enhanced thermal insulation, and high-efficiency heating and cooling systems, attaining a high level of energy self-sufficiency. This has been a significant step not only towards environmental sustainability but also towards fulfilling global emission reduction targets and transitioning to a low-carbon future.

5 Conclusions

The pressing environmental and social issues of our day necessitate novel methods. This also concerns the cultural heritage sector, to exploit its potential as an engine of sustainable growth and long-term prosperity for people, the planet, and places [16].

The building sector, responsible for a large amount of CO_2 emissions, is critical in fighting climate change. Reusing historic buildings in accordance with circular economy principles represents a solution capable of contributing to urban ecological transition. The adaptive reuse project of the former Convent of San Pietro a Maiella and San Giacomo in Salerno has demonstrated how integrating innovative technologies and eco-sustainable materials can drastically cut CO_2 emissions and long-term operational costs.

The use of photovoltaic panels, in particular, proved to be critical in improving the building's energy efficiency, resulting in considerable economic savings and emissions reductions across all operational aspects, including heating, sanitary hot water generation, cooling, and lighting.

Furthermore, the experience of the adaptive reuse project for the Convent of San Pietro a Maiella is a virtuous example of how technological innovation can potentially coexist with historical heritage, offering a replicable model for other building realities while adhering to correct heritage conservation criteria.

The adaptive reuse project has the potential to regenerate an entire historic district of the city of Salerno by defining new functions that have significant economic and social benefits, in line with urban regeneration aims. Urban regeneration initiatives can include micro, meso, and macro-level interventions, such as revitalising entire neighbourhoods, derelict historical sites, abandoned industrial zones, and other spaces. The purpose of urban regeneration is to revitalise underutilised areas, redistribute opportunities, and ultimately boost urban prosperity and overall quality [17].

This study presents limitations concerning the assessment of environmental and economic impacts, which could be addressed by using more complete assessment tools such as Life Cycle Costing (LCC) and Life Cycle Assessment (LCA). The adoption of these methods would in fact allow the environmental and economic costs to be analysed not only during the building's operation phase, but also during the project's realisation and until the disposal phase [2]. The use of these tools will also make it possible to carry out a comparative analysis of different project scenarios, offering more precise benchmarks and testing opportunities for the proposed solutions.

However, in the preliminary phase, the assessment conducted did provide useful insights for the development of the subsequent phases of the study.

Finally, it is worth to note that environmental performances are not the only criteria for a circular adaptive reuse of cultural heritage, as previous studies demonstrate [18, 19]. In fact, compatibility between historic/cultural values preservation, environmental performances and social value should be realized. Thus, "circular" adaptive reuse projects could be conducted engaging communities and stakeholders in co-design exercises since the early stages of ideation, putting in synergy expert and non-expert knowledge, also considering that actual performances are clearly influenced by users' behaviour. This would ensure that communities are aware of environmental impacts of different options for buildings reuse. Furthermore, early stage co-design would allow that the selected solutions are in line with the community's needs and wishes, as well as with the most advanced technological and cultural preservation criteria.

Author Contributions. Conceptualization, M.A., F.F., and A.G.; methodology, M.A., F.F. and G.C.; formal analysis, M.A., F.F., and A.G, investigation G.N., G.C. M.A., F.F., and A.G.; data curation, G.N., M.A., F.F., A.G., G.C.; writing—original draft preparation, M.A., writing, review and editing, M.A., G.N., G.C., and. A.G.; supervision, M.A., F.F. and A. G. All authors have read and agreed to the published version of the manuscript.

Funding. Research Grant PRIN 2020 No. 2020EBLPLS on "Opportunities and challenges of nanotechnology in advanced and green construction materials". Italian Ministry of University and Research (MUR).

PRA project Pegaso Telematic University. "BIOMAPS- Sviluppo di materiali, tecniche e tecnologie innovative e processi sostenibili per l'ottenimento di bio-prodotti in ambito industriale, civile e medicale", CUP PRA2024008.

References

1. Angrisano, M., Bosone, M., Martone, A., Gravagnuolo, A.: Adapting historic cities towards the circular economy: technologies and materials for circular adaptive reuse of historic buildings. In: The Future of Liveable Cities, Springer Book (2024)
2. Gravagnuolo, A., Angrisano, M., Nativo, M.: Evaluation of environmental impacts of historic buildings conservation through Life Cycle Assessment in a circular economy perspective. *AESTIMUM* 2020 Special Issue: 241–272 (2020).

3. Attia, S., Santos, M.C., Al-Obaidy, M., Baskar, M.: Leadership of EU member States in building carbon footprint regulations and their role in promoting circular building design. IOP Conf. Ser. Earth Environ. Sci. **855**(1), 012023 (2021). https://doi.org/10.1088/1755-1315/855/1/012023
4. Nocca, F., Angrisano, M.: The multidimensional evaluation of cultural heritage regeneration projects: a proposal for integrating level(s) tool—the case study of Villa Vannucchi in San Giorgio a Cremano (Italy). Land **11**(9), 1568 (2022). https://doi.org/10.3390/land11091568
5. Gravagnuolo, A., Bosone, M., Fusco Girard, L., De Toro, P., Iodice, S., Micheletti, S., Buglione, F., Aliona, L.: Methodologies for Impact Assessment of Cultural Heritage Adaptive Reuse; Deliverable D2.5; 2021. Available online: https://www.clicproject.eu/wp-content/uploads/2022/01/D2.5-Methodologies-for-impact-assessment-of-cultural-heritage-adaptive-reuse.pdf. Accessed 19 March 2022
6. European Commission.: Progress of the Member States in implementing the Energy Performance of Building Directive (2021). https://doi.org/10.2760/914310 (online)
7. Attia, S.: Net Zero Energy Buildings (nZEB): concepts, frameworks and roadmap for project analysis and implementation. In Net Zero Energy Buildings (nZEB): Concepts, Frameworks and Roadmap for Project Analysis and Implementation (2018a). https://doi.org/10.1016/C2016-0-03166-2
8. ICLEI Europe.: *Edifici nZEB: una guida per le Pubbliche Amministrazioni al fine di sviluppare competenze.* Progetto nZEB Ready (2024).
9. European Commission.: The Future for religious heritage. European cultural heritage strategy for 21th century. www.coe.int/strategy21 (2021)
10. Amendola, A., Fabbrocino, F., Feo, L., Fraternali, F.: Dependence of the mechanical properties of pentamode materials on the lattice microstructure. In: Proceedings of the ECCOMAS Congress 2016-The 7th European Congress on Computational Methods in Applied Sciences and Engineering; 2016 June 5; Crete Island, Greece. Barcelona: ECCOMAS
11. Amendola, A., Fabbrocino, F., Feo, L., Fraternali, F.: Dependence of the mechanical properties of pentamode materials on the lattice microstructure. In: Proceedings of the ECCOMAS Congres 2016-The 7th European Congress on Computational Methods in Applied Sciences and Engineering; 2016 June 5; Crete Island, Greece. Barcelona: ECCOMAS
12. Arup.: Report: The urban bio-loop growing, making and regenerating (2017)
13. Interreg Central Europe: Report assessing innovative restoration techniques, technologies and materials used in conservation. Deliverable D. **T1**(3), 1 (2018)
14. Netti A.M., Abdelwahab, O.M.M., Datola, G., Ricci, G.F., Damiani, P., Oppio, A., Gentile, F.: Assessment of nature-based solutions for water resource management in agricultural environments: a stakeholders' perspective in Southern Italy. Sci. Rep. **14**, 1 (2024)
15. Gravagnuolo, A., Angrisano, M., Bosone, M., Buglione, F., De Toro, P., Fusco Girard, L.: Participatory evaluation of cultural heritage adaptive reuse interventions in the circular economy perspective: A case study of historic buildings in Salerno (Italy). In: Journal of Urban Management – Elsevier, pp. 1–33 (2024)
16. Fusco Girard, L.: The circular "human-centred" adaptive reuse of cultural heritage: theoretical foundations. In: Fusco Girard, L., Gravagnuolo, A (Eds.), Adaptive Reuse of Cultural Heritage: Circular Business, Financial and Governance Models. Springer Book (2024).
17. Colucci, E., Martine, F., Noardo, F., Assumma, V., Datola, G., Appiotti, F., Bottero, M., Chiabrando, F., Lombardi, P., Migliorini, M., Rinaldi, E., Spanò, A.: Documenting cultural heritage in an INSPIRE-based 3D GIS for risk and vulnerability analysis. J. Cult. Heritage Manag. Sustain. Dev. **14** (2022).
18. Fusco Girard, L., Gravagnuolo, A.: Adaptive reuse of cultural heritage. Circular Business, Financial and Governance Models. Springer Book (2024).

19. Buglione, F., Gravagnuolo, A., Angrisano, M., Iodice, S., Bosone, M., De Toro, P., Fusco Girard, L.: Understanding best practices of cultural heritage adaptive reuse in the perspective of the circular economy: in-depth assessment of case studies. In: Adaptive Reuse of Cultural Heritage. Circular Business, Financial and Governance Models. Springer Book (2024).

An Integrated MCA–GIS Framework for Ground Mounted Solar Photovoltaic (GMPV) Site Selection: Methodological Proposal for the Italian Context

Caterina Caprioli[✉][iD], Federico Dell'Anna[iD], and Francesco Fiermonte[iD]

Interuniversity Department of Regional and Urban Studies and Planning (DIST), Politecnico di Torino, Viale Mattioli, 39, 10125 Turin, TO, Italy
{caterina.caprioli,federico.dellanna,
francesco.fiermonte}@polito.it

Abstract. The increasing demand for renewable energy has led to a growing interest in ground-mounted photovoltaic (GMPV) installations. However, the selection of suitable locations for these installations requires a multi-dimensional evaluation that integrates regulatory, environmental, and technical constraints. This study addresses the challenge of locating suitable land for GMPV systems in Italy. We develop a spatial decision support model that integrates Multi-Criteria Analysis (MCA) with Geographic Information Systems (GIS) to incorporate multiple factors, including regulatory requirements, hydrogeological and geotechnical hazards, land use attributes, solar irradiation potential, proximity to infrastructures, and terrain morphology. Each criterion is assigned a weighted value reflecting its relative significance, and the combined analysis yields a priority index that supports decision-makers in identifying optimal sites for photovoltaic deployment. The methodology aims to reconcile the need for increased renewable energy production with broader environmental, social, and economic objectives, ensuring minimal conflicts with other land uses. By systematically evaluating risks such as flood vulnerability and slope instability, the framework facilitates the avoidance of high-risk zones. Furthermore, by considering variables like irradiation levels, land productivity, and ease of grid connection, it maximizes energy yields while limiting environmental impacts and infrastructural costs. This structured and transparent approach can guide regional authorities, urban planners, and private investors in implementing sustainable energy projects. The stakeholder perspective is integral to building consensus, facilitating more inclusive decision-making, and ensuring long-term acceptance and viability at the local level. This ultimately fosters more collaborative planning, aligning energy goals with societal and environmental demands.

Keywords: Sustainable Land Use · Multi-Criteria Spatial Decision Support System (MC-SDSS) · solar farm

1 Introduction

The transition from non-renewable energy sources to renewable ones is an increasingly relevant issue, worldwide [1]. The deployment of renewable energy sources (RESs) supports the acceleration of the green transition and the achievement of greater energy autonomy [2]. Within this framework, the aim of the European Union to reduce greenhouse gas (GHG) emissions and to achieve climate neutrality is dependent on a significant expansion of renewable energies [3]. Among the different RESs, the growth of solar photovoltaic installations is crucial to the global energy transition. In particular, ground-mounted photovoltaic panels (GMPV) have become pervasive in Europe, driven by the deployment of large-scale solar power plants [2].

The large-scale and the dependence of energy production on solar features make GMPV location a relevant issue. Additionally, their installation requires high construction costs and the consideration of long lifetimes with various benefits and impacts [4]. Therefore, selecting suitable sites for GMPV must consider multiple aspects, spanning regulatory, economic, environmental, social and technical constraints. Site selection of GMPV is thus a complex problem, where different aspects are in play and multiple stakeholders take part in the discussion and choice. The evaluation procedure must therefore be able to include these different aspects, often conflicting, and include the opinions and preferences of the stakeholders in a comprehensive framework. At the same time, strong locational dependence requires the integration of the spatial dimension into the evaluation procedure.

Multicriteria Analysis (MCA) is particularly suitable for synthetizing the full range of aspects involved, taking into account the stakeholders' perspectives. However, to include the spatial heterogeneity of impacts and aspects in the evaluation procedure, the integration of Geographic Information Systems (GIS) into MCA is fundamental. Recent literature trends show the adoption of S-MCA in different contexts and for different decision-making processes, spanning from allocation of infrastructures and services, site selection problems, ecosystem services distribution, mitigation of natural risks, and enhancement strategies for cultural built heritage [5]. Furthermore, S-MCA has recently become widely applied in GMPV site selection, considering regulatory requirements, hydrogeological and geotechnical hazards, land use attributes, solar irradiation potential, proximity to infrastructures, and terrain morphology, among others.

Within this context, this study addresses the challenge of locating suitable land for GMPV systems in Italy, proposing a common framework to be applied in different contexts. Italy, in particular, has to manage a critical issue related to the lack of alignment between geographic information (cartographic data) and existing regulations, despite the fact that legislative frameworks often reference spatial data. This misalignment creates barriers to efficient planning and implementation. Nationally and globally, GMPV mapping mostly relies on data from measurement campaigns, existing standardized databases, or crowdsourcing projects like OpenStreetMap [6]. As a result, the mapping data's coverage, quality, and currency vary greatly, relying mostly on the work of each community and must be confirmed and validated by knowledgeable users [6].

This contribution tries therefore to answer the following research questions: is it possible to define a common national framework for GMPV site selection? Which MCA method is most appropriate for this purpose? Is it possible to address the lack of alignment between regulatory frameworks and spatial evaluation?

After this introduction, the remaining paper is structured as follows. Section 2 contains the research background, which explores the literature regarding the use of S-MCA for GMPV site selection. Additionally, this section describes the regulatory framework in Italy for this technology. Section 3 is devoted to the illustration of the methodological proposal, which combines MCA and GIS potential. Section 4 presents the list of criteria and indicators selected according to the specific problem under analysis, its context, and the methodological proposal. Finally, Sect. 5 contains the concluding remarks and implications of the research undertaken.

2 Research Background

2.1 Multi-criteria Techniques for GMPV Site Selection

The integration of GIS and MCA methodologies has become a cornerstone in GMPV site selection, leveraging spatial analysis alongside structured decision-making frameworks. GIS facilitates the incorporation of diverse environmental, infrastructural, and regulatory datasets, while MCA methods systematically evaluate competing criteria, ensuring that site selection processes are both rigorous and transparent. The studies analyzed can be categorized into two main groups: those employing a single MCA method with GIS and those utilizing comparative or hybrid approaches to enhance decision reliability. A systematic literature search was conducted using the Scopus database to identify peer-reviewed journal articles related to photovoltaic site selection. The search criteria focused on studies incorporating both GIS and MCA methodologies, using keywords such as "Photovoltaic site selection," "PV site suitability," "Ground-mounted photovoltaic," and "Solar farms," combined with "MCA", "MCDA," "MCDM," "GIS," "Multi-Criteria Analysis," and "Spatial Decision Support." This query yielded a total of 96 relevant publications.

Among the most used multicriteria methods[1], the Analytic Hierarchy Process (AHP) has been widely applied in combination with GIS due to its effectiveness in structuring complex decisions through hierarchical decomposition and expert-driven weight assignment. Giamalaki and Tsoutsos (2019) employed AHP to identify optimal solar farm locations in Crete, Greece, incorporating techno-economic and socio-environmental criteria [7]. Their findings underscored AHP transparency in decision-making, particularly in engaging stakeholders, though its reliance on expert judgment introduced subjectivity, potentially biasing the weight assignments. Finn and McKenzie (2020) applied a similar AHP approach in Northern Ireland, integrating a weighted sum overlay with pairwise comparisons [8]. Their study demonstrated the advantages of high-resolution spatial data in improving site selection accuracy but highlighted limitations in adaptability due to the exclusion of dynamic variables such as real-time solar irradiation. Guaita-Pradas et al. (2019) also utilized AHP in Valencia, Spain, to assess PV potential based on solar radiation, land use, and environmental constraints [9]. Their research emphasized

---
[1] To further expand knowledge on the differences between MCA techniques, please refer to Greco et al., 2016 [48].

the benefits of GIS visualization for stakeholder communication. These applications illustrate the strengths of AHP in structuring decision problems and improving spatial accuracy, but they also reveal challenges related to subjectivity in weight assignments.

TOPSIS (Technique for Order Preference by Similarity to Ideal Solution) has also been frequently integrated with GIS to enhance PV site selection, ranking alternatives based on their relative proximity to an ideal solution. Asrami et al. (2023) applied TOPSIS in a regional suitability study, emphasizing economic constraints and filtering unsuitable areas before ranking potential sites [10]. Vagiona et al. (2022) extended the use of TOPSIS to offshore solar PV selection in the Aegean Sea, incorporating marine spatial constraints [11].

Although PROMETHEE has been used less frequently as a standalone method, it remains a valuable tool in decision-making for PV site selection. Ayough et al. (2022) integrated PROMETHEE with GIS to assess solar power deployment, emphasizing its ability to handle conflicting criteria effectively [4]. While the method provided structured rankings, defining preference functions proved to be a challenge, potentially affecting decision robustness.

Other studies adopted a comparative or hybrid approach to improve decision reliability. Sánchez-Lozano et al. (2016) systematically compared AHP, TOPSIS, and ELECTRE TRI in a GIS framework for solar farm site selection in Murcia, Spain, revealing inconsistencies in rankings between methods and reinforcing the necessity of sensitivity analysis in GIS-based MCA applications [12]. Vagiona (2021) compared AHP, TOPSIS, and PROMETHEE for solar farm site selection in Greece, demonstrating that different MCA techniques yield varying rankings [13]. PROMETHEE was found to offer a more detailed evaluation due to its use of preference functions, but it was also sensitive to weight assignments, a limitation shared with AHP and TOPSIS. Nagababu et al. (2022) implemented a two-stage MCA approach, using GIS to filter potential sites before applying AHP and TOPSIS for final ranking based on technical, environmental, and economic trade-offs [14]. This structured methodology improved computational efficiency and ensured that only relevant sites were included in the MCA analysis. These findings reinforce the importance of integrating validation mechanisms, as the combination of multiple MCA methods can mitigate individual weaknesses and increase decision-making robustness.

The widespread integration of GIS with MCA methods in PV site selection underscores several key advantages. GIS efficiently processes spatial data, enabling the visualization and exclusion of unsuitable areas based on environmental and infrastructural constraints. Meanwhile, MCA techniques such as AHP, TOPSIS, ELECTRE, and PROMETHEE provide a structured framework for weighing and ranking site suitability criteria, ensuring transparency and replicability, stakeholder participation, and the ability to communicate results visually. These methodologies also allow for application across multiple scales. Moreover, these techniques employing sensitivity analyses help to assess the impact of uncertainty. However, challenges persist in the subjectivity of weight assignments and the computational complexity of some MCA techniques, which future research should aim to refine.

Despite the extensive use of GIS-MCA integration in PV site selection, no applications of Multi-Attribute Value Theory (MAVT) were identified in the reviewed studies.

This omission is notable given MAVT advantages over other MCA methods. Unlike AHP, TOPSIS, PROMETHEE or ELECTRE, MAVT explicitly constructs value functions that model decision-makers' preferences, ensuring consistent and compensatory trade-offs between criteria. This structured approach enhances transparency, robustness, and interpretability, making MAVT particularly suited for complex, large-scale energy planning scenarios that require balancing environmental, economic, social, and technical factors. Furthermore, MAVT allows for systematic stakeholder preference integration and advanced sensitivity analysis, making it a powerful tool for supporting well-informed decisions. Given its strengths, this research explores MAVT application in ground mounted solar PV site selection to support decision-making providing a systematic approach for integrating stakeholder preferences, allowing decision-makers to reflect diverse perspectives while maintaining methodological consistency.

2.2 Regulatory and Policy Framework in Italy

In the selection of suitable sites for GMPV systems in Italy, regulatory and policy considerations are as essential as technical, environmental, and economic factors. National regulations provide the general framework, starting with the Legislative Decree 199/2021 (implementing the EU Directive 2018/2001/UE - RED II), which defines "suitable areas" for renewable energy development and streamlines authorization procedures. The Legislative Decree 190/2024 further facilitates the installation process for projects located in industrial, commercial, and degraded areas, while ensuring compliance with environmental requirements. Additionally, the Decree-Law 63/2024 introduces restrictions on the use of agricultural land for PV systems, allowing exceptions only for projects aligned with renewable energy community initiatives or the objectives of the National Recovery and Resilience Plan (PNRR).

Beyond national legislation, regional and local authorities hold significant responsibilities in implementing these directives. Regions can establish additional zoning regulations and environmental protection measures tailored to their specific territorial needs, while municipalities regulate land-use planning and issue building permits, often imposing stricter conditions in areas subject to landscape or cultural heritage protection. This multi-level governance structure requires that any suitability framework incorporate both national directives and local regulatory contexts.

Considering these regulatory dimensions within the suitability framework is fundamental to ensuring that selected sites meet both technical requirements and legal compliance. Integrating national, regional, and municipal regulations into the decision-making process allows for the identification of locations where PV development is not only feasible but also aligned with broader environmental, social, and policy objectives. This approach strengthens the framework's relevance in supporting sustainable energy strategies and facilitating the implementation of projects in accordance with Italy's regulatory landscape.

3 Methodology Proposal

The implementation of integrated evaluation methodologies proves particularly beneficial in supporting decision-makers (DMs) [15]. They address the complexity of urban issues, equipping DMs with the necessary tools to formulate comprehensive responses to the diverse challenges faced by cities and territories [16–18]. Specifically, S-MCA assists DMs in the generation of geographical alternatives, integrating geographic data (i.e. criteria maps) with stakeholders' preferences and uncertainties (i.e. value judgements) [19, 20]. This process also fosters stakeholder dialogue and mitigates conflicts by providing a clear and accessible representation of suitable and unsuitable areas in the resulting maps [21].

On the one hand, MCA facilitates the management of the full range of aspects, both quantitative and qualitative, involved in the transformation [22, 23]. On the other hand, GIS have the capacity to collect, store, retrieve, transform and display spatial data [24]. Specifically for urban and territorial decision problems, GIS makes it possible to conduct spatial analyses, providing integrated knowledge about territory and explicitly considering the spatial dimension of the decision-making problem [25–27].

S-MCA considers the contribution and reinforcement of the two methodologies along the entire evaluation process. In particular, the flow of activities (Fig. 1) starts with the classical MCA phase called problem definition (phase 1), where the evaluation objectives are clearly defined, as well as the stakeholders involved. Subsequently, the analysis is devoted to the identification of the criteria and the most suitable MCA technique (phase 2). After the criteria identification, spatial data are collected, processed and analyzed in GIS environment (phase 3). In phase 4, MCA contributes with weighting and standardized procedures, in order to assign different importance to the set of criteria and make them comparable. Finally, it is possible to aggregate all maps with the set of weights in GIS, in order to obtain the final maps of suitability (phase 5). Additionally, sensitivity analysis (phase 6) could be conducted in the last phase of the analysis to verify the robustness of the evaluation performed.

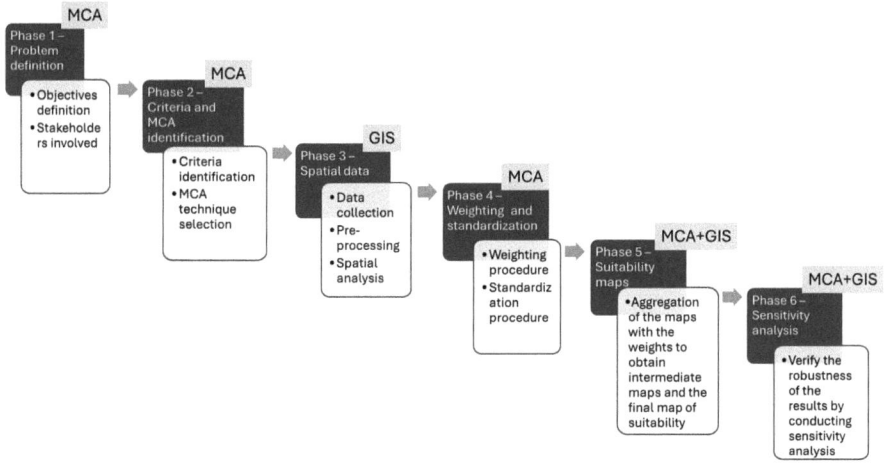

Fig. 1. S-MCA flow of activities

3.1 Problem Definition - MCA

The first step is constituted by problem definition. This phase is devoted to identifying the aim of the MCA, as well as DMs, key actors and stakeholders [28, 29]. Although this phase might seem trivial, a clear definition of the objective of the MCA helps to establish the tasks and steps of the evaluation and to maintain transparency in the entire evaluation process [30, 31]. For the purpose of our contribution, the aim of the evaluation should be expressed as the need to "find the most suitable location of GMPV in Italy".

This step also highlights the stakeholders involved or affected by the decision problem. Their different viewpoints and needs are fundamental and must be included, as much as possible, since the first step of the evaluation process, to avoid conflicts and oppositions in the subsequent phases. According to our evaluation aim, the main stakeholders involved are: landowners and land users, local and national authorities, electricity providers, investors and possible lenders, local communities, environmental organizations, construction companies/suppliers, planners and operators/maintainers, and eventually research bodies or universities.

3.2 Criteria Identification and MCA Technique Selection - MCA

The second phase is devoted to the identification of the criteria. Criteria and sub-criteria are the performance measures through which evaluate alternatives [32]. Therefore, the definition of the set of criteria for evaluation is a key phase for the proper development of MCA, since the criteria are the basis for evaluation [30]. Their identification must consider, at the same time, technical aspects related to the objective of the evaluation, the specific context in which the analysis is conducted, and the different points of view of the main stakeholders involved. For their proper selection, it could be necessary to examine the regulatory and legislative framework, to conduct a literature review and interviews with specific interest groups.

In S-MCA, this phase requires particular attention in the consideration of the spatial component embedded in the evaluation by the integration of GIS. Therefore, the set of criteria must respect completeness, operativity, dimension and multiple time effects and avoid redundancy, as in all MCA, but also the ability to explain the spatial heterogeneity of phenomena and aspects [27].

Based on the GMPV location, the selection of the criteria started with an in-depth literature review (see Sect. 4.1). The results of this analysis highlighted multiple aspects in play, spanning technical, environmental, social and economic once (e.g., solar irradiation, land use constraints, proximity to infrastructure, landslide risks).

According to the problem definition (step 1) and the set of criteria selected, this phase must also identify the most appropriate MCA technique to be used. There are different MCA techniques used to solve different site selection problems, such as PROMETHEE, ELECTRE, TOPSIS or AHP (see for references [33]). Also in GMPV locational problems, different techniques are applied, as explained in detail in Sect. 2.1. In our proposal, the use of MAVT is proposed on the basis of its capacity to explicitly construct value functions that model DMs' preferences [34], thereby ensuring consistent and compensatory trade-offs between criteria.

3.3 Data Collection, Processing and Spatial Analysis - GIS

After the criteria identification, it is necessary to source useful data and information in order to create a map for each criterion. Existing open data is the easiest way to create maps of each criterion. Governmental agencies, municipal and regional databases, but also crowdsourcing projects provide a useful starting point for data collection [5]. The data required can include geospatial layers for land use, topography, irradiation, infrastructural network, hydrogeological risks, among others. The data collection requires a strong effort by the analyst, who should be able to create a database of spatial data as up-to-date and complete as possible with respect to the elements to be considered in the evaluation process.

This phase also requires pre-processing work in a GIS environment to make all the data in the same coordinate system. In some cases, it could be also useful to execute some initial spatial operations, such as overlay analysis, clipping, buffering and reclassification, to make the data usable in the following steps. These analyses can be performed using QGIS, a free software, or ArcGIS Pro, a software licensed by ESRI.

On the resulting georeferenced maps, different spatial analyses have to be conducted in order to make the maps operational with respect to the purpose of the evaluation. Generally, two main spatial calculations are used in urban and territorial evaluation problems, i.e., Kernel Density and Euclidean Distance. Kernel Density creates a density map, calculated based on the number of points in a location [35]. Larger numbers of clustered points result in larger values [35]. Euclidean Distance calculates the distance between two points, namely the measure of the segment having as extremes the two points. Both Kernel Density and Euclidean distance require the definition of a specific radius and distance, that require the consultation of references and validation by experts. This consultation of references and experts is generally conducted during the definition of the standardization function, as detailed in Sect. 3.4.

3.4 Weights and Standardization Procedure - MCA

The spatial analysis in GIS produces a number of maps, one for each criterion considered. These maps are characterized by different units of measurement, but they have the same importance with respect to the achievement of the evaluation objective. This fourth step is therefore devoted to making all maps on the same scale (e.g., from 0 to 1) and assigning their different importance [36, 37]. According to the MCA technique chosen (Sect. 3.2), specific standardization and weighted procedures have to be implemented. As anticipated, MAVT was suggested as the most appropriate for the purpose of our work. According to this technique, the analyst develops specific value functions that could be used in GIS for map standardization [38]. The definition of the value functions could incorporate experts' and stakeholders' feedbacks, in order to ensure reliability. Additionally, experts and stakeholders could be engaged in workshops, focus groups or surveys to assign weights to the different criteria (and maps). In MAVT, the following weighting techniques are generally used [29, 32]: swing-weights, rating, pairwise comparison, trade-off, and qualitative translation. Among these approaches, our methodological proposal suggests a swing-weights procedure. The main advantage of the Swing method is that weight assignment is independent of value function shape, requiring only knowledge of attribute ranges [29].

3.5 Composite Index and Suitability Mapping – MCA + GIS

The fifth step of the proposal considers the integration of MCA and GIS. In particular, once all maps are standardized and the set of weights is defined according to MCA, it is possible to aggregate them in GIS. The easiest way to combine the single maps, considering the set of weights assigned by experts and stakeholders, is through a weighting sum [39], expressed as follows:

$$S_j = \sum W_i X_i$$

where S_j is the suitability for pixel j, W_i the weight of factor i, and X_i the standardized criterion score of factor i.

This aggregation results in a composite index, which is visualized through a map of suitability. In particular, the composite index expresses the degree of suitability of each cell of the area under analysis, with respect to all the criteria considered. The index of suitability varies from 0 to 1, where values close to 0 mean low suitability, while values close to 1 show high suitability. The resulting map graphically expresses these variations of suitability on the territory, using a colored scale from red (low suitability) to green (high suitability). The representation through maps facilitates the debate among the various stakeholders that take part in the process. In particular, they can observe the entire process of analysis, which starts from the single maps and ends with the final map of suitability which also includes the weights (i.e., the different opinions) of the experts and stakeholders involved.

3.6 Validation and Sensitivity Analysis – MCA + GIS

An additional phase regards the validation of the model performed. This phase is devoted to checking if the results obtained are reliable or if uncertainty was accumulated during the process [20]. In particular, the weighting phase is influenced by the subjective judgements of the stakeholders involved. To verify the robustness of the model with respect to the weighting system, sensitivity analysis is conducted. Sensitivity analysis conducted on the weights is developed by implementing and comparing different scenarios where weights are varied. One of the most applied approaches to sensitivity analysis is the One-At-Time method, which, as the name suggests, varies weights one after the other [40]. According to this approach, the results of the evaluation are compared with a balanced scenario (i.e., where the same weight is assigned to all criteria) and a number of other scenarios to give priority to one criterion at time.

Sensitivity analysis is particularly relevant in site selection to present to all parties involved the results obtained through the different sensitivity scenarios. The ability of the model to maintain stable results simplifies and supports public debate, avoiding oppositions [5].

4 Results

From literature reviews, because this study aims to develop a model adapted to the Italian context, only studies conducted in the European Union were selected. This is because the specific environmental conditions and regulatory constraints of the European energy sector can significantly influence the installation of GMPV systems. Understanding the approaches and methodologies used in other European countries can provide a basis for developing a context-specific model that addresses Italy's unique challenges and opportunities. Then, the dataset was filtered to select appropriate indicators, only studies focused on European regions, resulting in a total of 22 articles.

4.1 Criteria and Indicators Definition

Selecting suitable sites for renewable energy projects is rarely straightforward, it is a multifaceted process shaped by diverse criteria that consistently align across eight key domains: technical, economic, environmental, social, physical-geographical, cultural, natural hazard, and legal considerations.

When it comes to technical factors, the literature consistently highlights the importance of access to strong solar radiation, favorable topographical conditions, and proximity to infrastructure like power grids, substations, and transportation networks. These elements are essential for maximizing energy generation and ensuring ease of operation [11, 41, 42].

In terms of economic feasibility, studies frequently emphasize the weight of financial factors such as initial capital costs, operational expenses, and financial indicators like net present value (NPV), discount rates, and payback periods [9]. Market conditions, project efficiency, and expected returns also emerge as recurring themes, underlining the importance of a solid financial foundation for project viability.

Environmental sustainability is often at the forefront of research, with numerous studies assessing issues like land-use conflicts, biodiversity conservation, and soil conditions, including fertility and erosion risks. Additionally, the proximity of potential sites to protected areas and wildlife habitats is frequently analyzed to minimize ecological disruption [43, 44].

Physical and geographical features also play a critical role. Factors such as slope, elevation, proximity to water bodies, and distance from coastlines can significantly influence both technical performance and environmental impact [7, 45]. At the same time, natural hazards like floods, landslides, and extreme weather events are increasingly seen as vital considerations that could affect infrastructure resilience and long-term sustainability [9, 46].

Though sometimes overlooked, cultural and heritage factors carry significant weight, especially for sites near archaeological or historically important locations. Respecting these areas not only meets legal requirements but also helps foster positive relationships with local communities and increases project acceptance [13, 43].

The role of social acceptance is equally pivotal. Public perception, landscape impacts, and potential job creation are often highlighted as influential factors, particularly in areas where community engagement and rural development are key to gaining local support [47].

From a legal and regulatory standpoint, adherence to zoning laws, spatial restrictions, and renewable energy policies is non-negotiable. Additionally, the ease of obtaining permits and access to government incentives can often make or break a project's success [12].

Table 1. Review of indicators for GMPV site delection in European studies.

Domain	Indicator	Unit of Measure	Source
Technical	Battery efficiency / Number of cycles	Percentage (%) / Number of Cycles	[41]
	Distance from electrical grid / Ease of connection	Kilometers (km) / Qualitative Index	[11, 13, 41]
	Distance from power lines / Power network	Kilometers (km)	[12, 42, 43, 45]
	Distance from cities / urban areas / residential areas / buildings	Kilometers (km)	[12, 42, 43, 45]
	Distance to electrical substations	Kilometers (km)	[12, 43]
	Distance to roads / main roads / road network accessibility	Kilometers (km)	[12, 42, 43, 45, 47]
	Energy yield	kWh/year	[41]
	Features of land	Qualitative Index	[41]
	Global solar radiation levels	kWh/m^2/day	[42]
	Pv efficiency / Efficiency after 25 years	Percentage (%)	[41]
	Presence of obtrusive objects causing shading	Presence/Absence	[41]
	Self-consumption fraction	Percentage (%)	[41]
	Serving population	Population Size	[11]

(*continued*)

Table 1. (*continued*)

Domain	Indicator	Unit of Measure	Source
Economic	Discount rates	Percentage (%)	[9]
	Initial capital cost	Currency (e.g., Euro)	[9]
	Lifetime of the project	Years	[9]
	Net present value (npv)	Currency (e.g., Euro)	[41]
	Payback period	Years	[41]
	Project efficiency	Efficiency Index	[9]
	Land rent price	Currency (e.g., Euro)	[9]
Environmental	Absolute humidity	Grams per cubic meter (g/m^3)	[47]
	Annual sunshine hours	Hours per year	[47]
	Distance from protected areas	Kilometers (km)	[11, 13]
	Ground concurrency	Presence/Absence	[41]
	Habitat loss	Presence/Absence	[41]
	Installation site area limitations	Square Kilometers (km^2)	[11, 13]
	Land cover	Category	[13]
	Landscape and visual impacts	Visual Impact Index	[41]
	Life cycle carbon emission reduction	Tonnes CO_2e/year	[41]
	Life cycle environmental impact	Environmental Impact Score	[41]
	Solar irradiation	kWh/m^2/year	[44, 45]
	Temperature	Degrees Celsius (°C)	[47]
	Trade-offs between renewable energy sources and agricultural productivity	Trade-off Score	[43]

(*continued*)

Table 1. (*continued*)

Domain	Indicator	Unit of Measure	Source
	Water use	Cubic Meters (m³)	[41]
Social	Landscape visual impact	Visual Impact Index	[43]
	Potential demand	Electricity Demand Index	[47]
	Social acceptance of renewable energy projects	Social Acceptance Scale	[43]
Physical-Geographical	Aspect / Orientation	Degrees (°)/Classes	[7, 12, 45]
	Altitude / Elevation	Meters (m)	[7, 13]
Cultural	Distance from archaeological areas	Kilometers (km)	[13]
	Cultural heritage proximity	Kilometers (km)	[43]
Natural Hazard	Flood hazard zones / wind risk	Categorical/Index	[46]
	Landslide risk	Risk Index	[9]
	Natural deposits	Category or index	[46]
Legal	Aquaculture zones	Presence/Absence	[11]
	Areas licensed for exploration and exploitation of hydrocarbons	Presence/Absence	[11]
	Areas with existing or planned offshore renewable energy projects	Presence/Absence	[11]
	Agricultural areas with high-value food production (DOP, IGP, DOCG)	Protected Area Classification	[43]
	Military exercise areas	Presence/Absence	[11]
	Ports and shipping routes (for offshore plants)	Kilometers (km)	[11]

(*continued*)

Table 1. (*continued*)

Domain	Indicator	Unit of Measure	Source
	Renewable energy policy constraints	Policy Constraint Index	[43]
	Distance from airports	Kilometers (km)	[13]

Notably, the results from the literature review are consistent with Italian regulatory constraints, particularly those defined in the Legislative Decree 199/2021 and Decree-Law 63/2024, which emphasize environmental protection, land-use regulations, and restrictions on agricultural land for renewable energy development. The alignment between the literature and the Italian regulatory framework reinforces the relevance of the selected indicators and validates their applicability within the Italian context.

5 Conclusions and Future Perspectives

The paper presented a methodological proposal that supports the identification of suitable locations for GMPV in Italy. The proposal took into account both the regulatory framework of GMPV installations and the multiple aspects in play. In particular, a spatial decision support model was proposed, that integrated MCA and GIS. This integration allow to consider the spatial heterogeneity of technical, regulatory, environmental, and social aspects. At the same time, it made it possible to include experts' and stakeholders' opinions with respect to the proper site selection of these technologies.

The proposed framework could potentially inform various land use policies and energy strategies, not only identifying suitable locations of GMPV, but also suggesting priority interventions, guiding investment decisions, preventing conflicts with existing land uses, and aligning with environmental and landscape goals. Additionally, it could be applied in different contexts, by selecting the most appropriate set of criteria, according to the area under investigation, as well as the set of weights assigned by stakeholders and DMs.

Future perspectives of this work will regard the application of the proposed framework to a real-world case study, in the Piedmont region (Italy). This application could highlight the pros and cons regarding the methodology proposed, the availability of the data, and the multi-scalarity of the problem under investigation.

References

1. Batz Liñeiro, T., Müsgens, F.: Pay-back time: increasing electricity prices and decreasing costs make renewable energy competitive. Energy Policy **199**, 114523 (2025). https://doi.org/10.1016/j.enpol.2025.114523

2. Caprioli, C., Dell'Anna, F., Fiermonte, F.: Renewable energy sources and ecosystem services: measuring the impacts of ground-mounted photovoltaic panels. In: Gervasi, O., et al. (eds.) Computational Science and Its Applications – ICCSA 2023 Workshops. ICCSA 2023. Lecture Notes in Computer Science, vol. 14108. Springer, Cham (2023). https://doi.org/10.1007/978-3-031-37117-2_29
3. Sponagel, C., Weik, J., Feuerbacher, A., Bahrs, E.: Exploring the climate change mitigation potential and regional distribution of agrivoltaics with geodata-based farm economic modelling and life cycle assessment. J. Environ. Manag. **359**, 121021 (2024). https://doi.org/10.1016/j.jenvman.2024.121021
4. Ayough, A., Boshruei, S., Khorshidvand, B.: A new interactive method based on multi-criteria preference degree functions for solar power plant site selection. Renew. Energy **195**, 1165–1173 (2022). https://doi.org/10.1016/j.renene.2022.06.087
5. Caprioli, C., Bottero, M.: Addressing complex challenges in transformations and planning: a fuzzy spatial multicriteria analysis for identifying suitable locations for urban infrastructures. Land Use Policy **102**, 105147 (2021). https://doi.org/10.1016/j.landusepol.2020.105147
6. Ronchetti, G., Aiello, M., Maldarella, A.: Leveraging semantic segmentation for photovoltaic plants mapping in optimized energy planning. Remote Sens. (Basel) **17**, 483 (2025). https://doi.org/10.3390/rs17030483
7. Giamalaki, M., Tsoutsos, T.: Sustainable siting of solar power installations in Mediterranean using a GIS/AHP approach. Renew. Energy **141**, 64–75 (2019). https://doi.org/10.1016/j.renene.2019.03.100
8. Finn, T., McKenzie, P.: A high-resolution suitability index for solar farm location in complex landscapes. Renew. Energy **158**, 520–533 (2020). https://doi.org/10.1016/j.renene.2020.05.121
9. Guaita-Pradas, I., Marques-Perez, I., Gallego, A., Segura, B.: Analyzing territory for the sustainable development of solar photovoltaic power using GIS databases. Environ. Monit. Assess. (2019). https://doi.org/10.1007/s10661-019-7871-8
10. Asrami, R.F., Sohani, A., Sayyaadi, H., Moradi, M.H.: Geographical information system as an approach for PV power plants allocation with 3E criteria. Sol. Energy (2023). https://doi.org/10.1016/j.solener.2023.111966
11. Vagiona, D.G., Tzekakis, G., Loukogeorgaki, E., Karanikolas, N.: Site selection of offshore solar farm deployment in the Aegean Sea, Greece. J. Mar. Sci. Eng. (2022). https://doi.org/10.3390/jmse10020224
12. Sánchez-Lozano, J.M., García-Cascales, M.S., Lamata, M.T.: Comparative TOPSIS-ELECTRE TRI methods for optimal sites for photovoltaic solar farms. Case study in Spain. J. Clean. Prod. **127**, 387–398 (2016). https://doi.org/10.1016/j.jclepro.2016.04.005
13. Vagiona, D.G.: Comparative multicriteria analysis methods for ranking sites for solar farm deployment: a case study in Greece. Energies (Basel) (2021). https://doi.org/10.3390/en14248371
14. Nagababu, G., Puppala, H., Pritam, K., Kantipudi, M.P.: Two-stage GIS-MCDM based algorithm to identify plausible regions at micro level to install wind farms: a case study of India. Energy (2022). https://doi.org/10.1016/j.energy.2022.123594
15. Oppio, A., Caprioli, C., Dell'Ovo, M., Bottero, M.: Assessing ecosystem services through a multimethodological approach based on multicriteria analysis and cost-benefits analysis: a case study in Turin (Italy). J. Clean. Prod. **472**, 143472 (2024). https://doi.org/10.1016/j.jclepro.2024.143472
16. Bottero, M., Caprioli, C., Datola, G., Oppio, A., Torrieri, F.: Regeneration of Rogoredo railway: a combined approach using multi-criteria and financial analysis [Un approccio integrato per la rigenerazione dello scalo ferroviario di Rogoredo]. Valori e Valutazioni. **31**, 89–102 (2023). https://doi.org/10.48264/VVSIEV-20223107

17. Assumma, V., Bottero, M., Pontiglione, I.: A spatial multicriteria analysis for exploring territorial scenarios of economic attractiveness. In: Proceedings of the Energy for Sustainability International Conference (2019)
18. Bottero, M., Caprioli, C., Berta, M.: Urban problems and patterns of change: the analysis of a downgraded industrial area in Turin. In: Mondini, G., Oppio, A., Stanghellini, S., Bottero, M., Abastante, F. (eds.) Values and Functions for Future Cities. Green Energy and Technology. Springer, Cham (2020). https://doi.org/10.1007/978-3-030-23786-8_22
19. Jelokhani-Niaraki, M., Malczewski, J.: Decision complexity and consensus in Web-based spatial decision making: a case study of site selection problem using GIS and multicriteria analysis. Cities **45**, 60–70 (2015). https://doi.org/10.1016/j.cities.2015.03.007
20. Comino, E., Bottero, M., Pomarico, S., Rosso, M.: Exploring the environmental value of ecosystem services for a river basin through a spatial multicriteria analysis. Land Use Policy **36**, 381–395 (2014). https://doi.org/10.1016/j.landusepol.2013.09.006
21. Rossitti, M., Torrieri, F.: How to manage conflicting values in minor Islands: a MCDA methodology towards alternative energy solutions assessment. Presented at the (2021). https://doi.org/10.1007/978-3-030-87007-2_42
22. Cinelli, M., Coles, S.R., Kirwan, K.: Analysis of the potentials of multi criteria decision analysis methods to conduct sustainability assessment. Ecol. Indic. **46**, 138–148 (2014). https://doi.org/10.1016/j.ecolind.2014.06.011
23. Roy, B.: Multicriteria methodology for decision analysis. Kluwer Academic Publishers (1985)
24. Burrough, P., McDonnell, R.: Principles of geographical information systems for land resources assessment. (1986)
25. Malczewski, J.: GIS and Multicriteria Decision Analysis. John Wiley & Sons (1999)
26. Malczewski, J.: Spatial Multicriteria Decision Making and Analysis: A Geographic Information System Science Approach. Ashgate Publishing Company, Hants, England (1997)
27. Malczewski, J.: GIS-based land-use suitability analysis: A critical overview. Prog. Plann. **62**, 3–65 (2004). https://doi.org/10.1016/j.progress.2003.09.002
28. Keeney, R.L.: Value-Focused Thinking: A Path to Creative. Harvard University Press (1996)
29. Ferretti, V., Bottero, M., Mondini, G.: Decision making and cultural heritage: An application of the multi-attribute value theory for the reuse of historical buildings. J. Cult. Herit. **15**, 644–655 (2014). https://doi.org/10.1016/j.culher.2013.12.007
30. Department for Communities and Local Government: Multicriteria Analysis: A manual, London (2009)
31. Oppio, A., Dell'Ovo, M.: Cultural heritage preservation and territorial attractiveness: a spatial multidimensional evaluation approach. In: Pileri, P., Moscarelli, R. (eds.) Cycling & Walking for Regional Development. Research for Development. Springer, Cham (2021). https://doi.org/10.1007/978-3-030-44003-9_9
32. Beinat, E.: Value functions for environmental management. In: Value Functions for Environmental Management, pp. 77–106. Springer Netherlands, Dordrecht (1997). https://doi.org/10.1007/978-94-015-8885-0_4
33. Vahidnia, M.H., Alesheikh, A.A., Alimohammadi, A.: Hospital site selection using fuzzy AHP and its derivatives. J. Environ. Manag. **90**, 3048–3056 (2009). https://doi.org/10.1016/j.jenvman.2009.04.010
34. Cristina, B., Lorenzo, B., Marta, B., Giulio, C., Giovanna, F., Alessandro, S.: Renewable energy communities: an urban capability-based approach to evaluate differential participation in cities. In: Gervasi, O., Murgante, B., Garau, C., Taniar, D., Rocha, A.M.A.C., Faginas Lago, M.N. (eds.) Computational Science and Its Applications – ICCSA 2024 Workshops. ICCSA 2024. Lecture Notes in Computer Science, vol. 14821. Springer, Cham (2024). https://doi.org/10.1007/978-3-031-65308-7_15
35. QGIS: 24.1.6. Interpolation, https://docs.qgis.org/3.40/en/docs/user_manual/processing_algs/qgis/interpolation.html, last accessed 2025/03/21

36. Ferretti, V., Pomarico, S.: Integrated sustainability assessments: a spatial multicriteria evaluation for siting a waste incinerator plant in the Province of Torino (Italy). Environ. Dev. Sustain. **14**, 843–867 (2012). https://doi.org/10.1007/s10668-012-9354-8
37. Oppio, A., Bottero, M., Arcidiacono, A.: Assessing urban quality: a proposal for a MCDA evaluation framework. Ann. Oper. Res. **312**, 1427–1444 (2022). https://doi.org/10.1007/s10479-017-2738-2
38. Keeney, R.L., Raiffa, H.: Decisions with multiple objectives: preferences and value trade-offs. (1993)
39. Bottero, M., Comino, E., Duriavig, M., Ferretti, V., Pomarico, S.: The application of a multicriteria spatial decision support system (MCSDSS) for the assessment of biodiversity conservation in the Province of Varese (Italy). Land Use Policy **30**, 730–738 (2013). https://doi.org/10.1016/j.landusepol.2012.05.015
40. Chen, Y., Yu, J., Khan, S.: Spatial sensitivity analysis of multi-criteria weights in GIS-based land suitability evaluation. Environ Model Softw. **25**, 1582–1591 (2010). https://doi.org/10.1016/j.envsoft.2010.06.001
41. Bandaru, S.H., Becerra, V., Khanna, S., Espargilliere, H., Torres Sevilla, L., Radulovic, J., Hutchinson, D., Khusainov, R.: A general framework for multi-criteria based feasibility studies for solar energy projects: application to a real-world solar farm. Energies (Basel). (2021). https://doi.org/10.3390/en14082204
42. Rodrigues, S., Coelho, M.B., Cabral, P.: Suitability analysis of solar photovoltaic farms: a Portuguese case study. Int. J. Renew. Energy Res. **7**, 244–254 (2017)
43. Zardo, L., Granceri Bradaschia, M., Musco, F., Maragno, D.: Promoting an integrated planning for a sustainable upscale of renewable energy. A regional GIS-based comparison between ecosystem services tradeoff and policy constraints. Renew. Energy (2023). https://doi.org/10.1016/j.renene.2023.119131
44. Sánchez-Lozano, J.M., Teruel-Solano, J., Soto-Elvira, P.L., Socorro García-Cascales, M.: Geographical information systems (GIS) and multi-criteria decision making (MCDM) methods for the evaluation of solar farms locations: case study in south-eastern Spain. Renew. Sustain. Energy Rev. **24**, 544–556 (2013). https://doi.org/10.1016/j.rser.2013.03.019
45. Adjiski, V., Serafimovski, D.: GIS-and AHP-based decision systems for evaluating optimal locations of photovoltaic power plants: case study of Republic of North Macedonia. Geomatics Environ. Eng. **18**, 51–82 (2024). https://doi.org/10.7494/geom.2024.18.1.51
46. Bobrowski, J., Łaska, G.: Using spatial elimination and ranking methods in the renewable energy investment parcel search process. Energy (2023). https://doi.org/10.1016/j.energy.2023.129517
47. Hosouli, S., Hassani, R.A.: Application of multi-criteria decision making (MCDM) model for solar plant location selection. Results Eng. (2024). https://doi.org/10.1016/j.rineng.2024.103162
48. Greco, S., Ehrgott, M., Figueira, J.R.: Multiple Criteria Decision Analysis. State of the Art Surveys. Springer, New York, NY (2016)

Integrated Strategic Approach for Sustainable Urban Planning Applied to the Milan Rogoredo Case Study

Giulia Buongiovanni[1], Marianna Camerota[1], Valentina Giustinelli[1], Francesco Pittau[2(✉)], and Giorgia Sugoni[3,4]

[1] School of Architecture Urban Planning and Construction Engineering (AUIC), Politecnico di Milano, Via Ampere 2, 20133 Milan, Italy
{giulia.buongiovanni,marianna.camerota,
valentina.giustinelli}@mail.polimi.it
[2] Department of Architecture, Built Environmental and Construction Engineering (DABC), Politecnico di Milano, Via Ponzio 31, 20133 Milan, Italy
francesco.pittau@polimi.it
[3] Department of Architecture and Urban Studies (DAStU), Politecnico di Milano, Via Bonardi 3, 20133 Milan, Italy
giorgia.sugoni@polimi.it
[4] Links Foundation, Via Pier Carlo Boggio, 61, 10138 Turin, Italy

Abstract. This study presents an integrated methodological approach for sustainable urban planning applied to the case study of Milan Rogoredo, a peripheral district of Milan characterized by complex social and environmental challenges. The applied methodology combines conventional analysis tools, such as SWOT+STEEP analysis, with mixed techniques such as Stakeholder analysis (Power Interest and Social Network Analysis) and Multi-Criteria Analysis, with particular emphasis to the Analytic Hierarchy Process (AHP). The main objective is the identification of the most advantageous solution in terms of district regeneration, considering a broad spectrum of interconnected factors, including environmental, social, and economic aspects. SWOT+STEEP analysis has allowed to investigate the current state of the site, identifying strengths, weaknesses, opportunities, and threats, laying the foundation for the subsequent phases of analysis. Stakeholder analysis has highlighted the levels of power and interest of the actors involved, while Multi-Criteria Analysis has allowed the evaluation of three alternative development scenarios. The results of the study demonstrate that the strategic scenario, which emphasizes social inclusion and environmental sustainability, is the most advantageous solution for achieving an urban transformation of Milan Rogoredo. This transformation is aimed at positioning the district as a pole of attraction and social well-being for the entire community. This multi-level methodological approach provides an effective model for urban planning in complex peripheral contexts, promoting decisions oriented towards sustainability and circular regeneration.

Keywords: Social and Environmental Sustainability · Multilevel Urban regeneration · Stakeholder analysis · Alternative development scenarios · Analytic Hierarchy Process (AHP)

1 Introduction

Urbanization, a global phenomenon, triggers a series of transformations that shape our environment, society, and economy. The expansion of urban areas leads to increased land consumption, resulting in loss of biodiversity and increased pollution. Cities have become centers of energy consumption and waste production, exacerbating climate change issues [1]. From a social perspective, urbanization can deepen inequalities, creating pockets of poverty and marginalization. Housing density and competition for resources can generate social tensions and security problems [2]. However, cities are also engines of economic development, offering job and growth opportunities.

To manage these complex dynamics, spatial planning uses analysis tools that allow us to assess the impact of urban choices and define sustainable development strategies. SWOT analysis identifies the strengths and weaknesses of a territory, as well as external opportunities and threats [3]. Its extension, SWOT+STEEP, also considers social, technological, economic, environmental, and political factors, providing a broader view of the urban context [4]. Stakeholder analysis allows for the involvement of different social actors in the decision-making process, while scenario building helps to imagine possible futures and assess the impact of urban policies [5]. Finally, multi-criteria analysis enables the comparison of different intervention options based on economic, social, and environmental criteria. The integration of these tools, along with geographic information systems and urban simulation models, is essential for effective spatial planning and sustainable urban design.

In the following article, the application of these principles will be presented in the case study of Milan Rogoredo, highlighting how these planning tools are particularly effective for the territorial regeneration of urban contexts facing environmental and social challenges.

2 Integrated Multi-level Methodology

2.1 Framing of the Problem

The entire analysis process was previously illustrated and applied in the case study under analysis (see Fig. 1).

Following the definition of the problem related to the case study and the context under examination, a stakeholder analysis is conducted as a first decision-making method in order to understand all the actors involved and their engagement in the applied strategies, ensuring their effectiveness.

Stakeholder analysis is necessary to highlight potential conflicts of interest from the early stages and to avoid negative effects in subsequent phases. Given the difficulties that can be encountered in the study of Milan Rogoredo due to the critical issues that characterize it, it is necessary to address different interests among stakeholders. The development phases must be designed in such a way as to classify the various parties involved in order to address social challenges in the most complete way possible.

Among the various approaches to develop a Stakeholder Analysis, the combination of the following methodologies has been proposed: the Power-Interest Matrix, the Circle Methodology, and the Social Network Analysis.

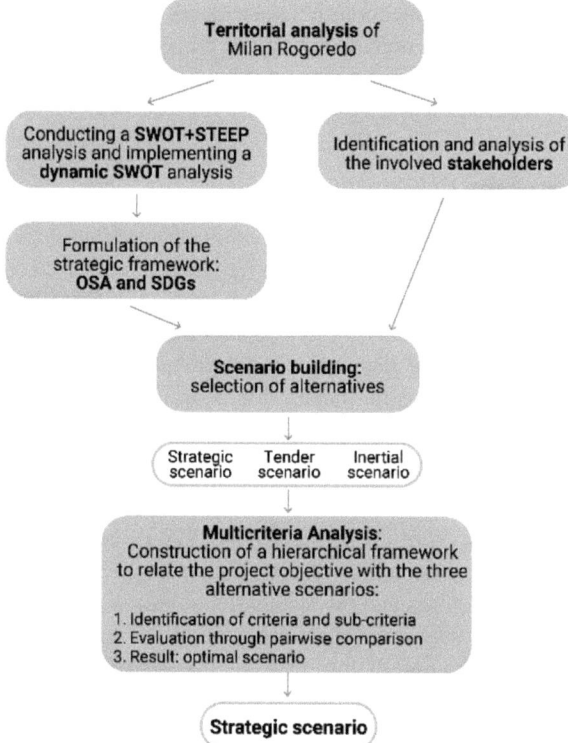

Fig. 1. Methodological synthesis of the process.

Their combination arises from the need to integrate the potential of these approaches: the Power-Interest Matrix and the Circle Methodology, which allow us to understand the influence and power that individual actors have in the individual phases of the process, and the Social Network Analysis, which identifies the relationships between stakeholders [6].

Power/Interest Matrix. This is an evaluation tool that visualizes the levels of power and interest of each stakeholder. The rationale behind the power/interest matrix is that stakeholders possess different levels of power to influence the implementation of construction projects and express different degrees of interest in project decisions. This highlights the priorities of the individual actors involved and ensures effective management during the project life cycle [7].

Circle Methodology. It is an innovative approach to identify and analyze the stakeholders that are involved in the design phase. Unlike the power/interest matrix, it is a practical and visual tool as it guarantees an immediate visualization of the influence of the actors involved. This allows us to implement strategic communication and to increase the probability of success in the organization of projects [8].

Social Network Analysis. It is a method to collect and analyze the communication networks that are established between stakeholders during the process phases. It uses specific tools to measure the connections between actors within the network, identifying the most influential actors and understanding the relationships that can influence the decision-making process [9]. It is possible to visualize the size and shape of the network through a visual representation and a qualitative analysis [10].

2.2 Alternative Scenario Construction

In recent decades, the popularity of strategic planning through scenarios has grown significantly. In the latter decades of the last century, there has been an effort to enhance the synergy between future vision and strategy, which has materialized through a planning process using scenarios. The objective of this approach is to propose strategic guidelines and measures based on scenarios that replicate the global context [11].

Today, it is crucial that decision-makers focus on researching new tools that can ensure more efficient management of sustainable development in urban contexts, successfully overcoming and avoiding those risks that often arise from complex and unstable environmental situations [12].

SWOT+STEEP Analysis. Starting in the 1980s, SWOT began to be used to analyze alternative development scenarios in the public sector. Today, this technique has expanded to territorial diagnoses and the evaluation of regional programs.

Among the strategic management tools provided by the academic world to support planners, SWOT analysis is one of the most widely used in territorial planning. Its frequent application by professionals testifies to its practical effectiveness, surpassing the use of other similar tools [13].

The objective of SWOT analysis is to identify the Strengths (S), Weaknesses (W), Opportunities (O), and Threats (T) of a specific territory, project, or program. Strengths and Weaknesses represent endogenous factors, inherent to the context of analysis, modified through the proposed interventions, while Opportunities and Threats are exogenous factors as they derive from the external context and are difficult to modify.

Often, this tool is combined with other complementary tools to achieve more effective results.

STEEP Analysis is integrated with SWOT Analysis (STEEP+SWOT). This is a more recent tool used in decision-making and the analysis of complex dynamics to better examine the characteristic factors of a specific territory, project, or program for the formulation of objectives and actions related to transformation scenarios.

STEEP (Societal, Technological, Economic, Environmental, and Political) analysis therefore utilizes established methodologies to evaluate the importance of technological research topics related to scenarios defined by a selection of global trends [14].

Dynamic SWOT. SWOT analysis has an evident weakness related to the fact that the four groups of elements it is composed of are not correlated with each other. This makes it difficult to understand whether they produce a favorable or unfavorable scenario for the implementation of the plan or program, and where it is possible to intervene to improve any critical issues [15]. To solve this problem, attempts have been made to transform SWOT into a dynamic tool by establishing relationships between all its elements.

The "Dynamic" (or Relational) SWOT is an intuitive tool that allows for binary comparison between the elements to establish the relationships of influence that exist between them, regardless of the category they belong to. Crucially, it acknowledges that the influence exerted by one element on another is not necessarily reciprocal, allowing for the identification of asymmetric dynamics within the evolving strategic environment. [15].

Scenario Building. The construction of scenarios empowers decision-makers to visualize alternative futures, thus advancing a better quality of life and the protection of the environment [16]. The tool plays a very important role in supporting decision-makers in strategic planning and policy decisions, as well as guiding private sector organizations in selecting key variables for competitive decisions.

A scenario illustrates visions of a possible future or aspects of it. In this way, it is possible to analyze the different cases to highlight discontinuities in the present and to reveal the available choices and their potential consequences.

2.3 Problem Evaluation

Multi-Criteria Analysis (MCA) is an evaluation process that verifies the stability and robustness of alternatives, previously generated, through the simulation of hypothetical scenarios [17].

It can consider a wide range of factors, both economic and non-economic, and analysis of how the needs and opinions of various stakeholders influence each other during the decision-making process [18].

The Analytic Hierarchy Process (AHP), a decision-making method developed by Saaty, is a key tool in MCA for addressing complex decisions and estimations. It hierarchizes objectives and criteria, assigns priority weights to alternatives, and is based on measurement using a ratio scale [19].

The versatility of multi-criteria methods allows them to be used in synergy with existing evaluation tools, enabling a comprehensive analysis of economic, environmental, energy, and social sustainability, as well as the aesthetic and performance quality of projects [20].

These methods are particularly effective in structuring complex problems, supporting both the initial and comparative phases of decision-making processes. They facilitate the identification of conflicts and the pursuit of shared solutions, also allowing for the aggregation and comparison of parameters with different units of measurement, through a weighting system [20].

Within Multi-Criteria Analysis, AHP is a suitable approach for dealing with complex non-linear problems. It structures the examined variables hierarchically, from which it is possible to produce qualitative and quantitative evaluations. AHP is a method that can be applied to establish outcomes in both the physical and social domains [21].

Outcomes are formulated according to preference, through pairwise comparisons between criteria concerning a specific project objective. The method unfolds through three successive operational phases:

- Decomposition of the problem data into their fundamental components (based on the principle of decomposition). This step consists of identifying a series of criteria, possible sub-criteria, and alternatives, structured hierarchically.

- By pairwise comparison, to obtain, at each level of decomposition, a scale of priorities between them through the principle of comparative judgments, according to which a positive real number is assigned to each binary relation (based on Saaty's "fundamental scale") that corresponds to a judgment of value.
- Calculation of priority rankings (based on the principle of priority synthesis). Priority scales or weights are produced, up to the final ranking of preference for the options [20]

The fundamental steps of an AHP-based investigation are:

- Identification of alternatives.
- Identification of evaluation criteria (e.g., cost, environmental impacts, employment repercussions, etc.).
- Estimation of weights to be assigned to the criteria.
- Measurement of the characteristics of each alternative with each criterion (e.g., cost of each alternative, environmental impacts of each alternative, etc.).
- Normalization of measures according to a comparable scale.
- Calculation of synthetic values [22].

3 Application

3.1 Case Study; Milano Rogoredo

The Rogoredo district is in Municipality 4 in the suburban part located southeast of the City of Milan. The case study is in the provincial capital of Lombardy, one of the regions of Italy (see Fig. 2).

The district borders the districts of Nosedo to the northwest, Morsecchio to the northeast, and the Municipality of San Donato Milanese to the southeast.

It is an important transportation hub of the city. There are two stations on the M3 line of the Milan metro, Rogoredo and San Donato. Various bus lines, operated by ATM, connect Rogoredo to the neighboring districts and the center of Milan.

Rogoredo is also served by the homonymous station, which is located at the junction between the railway link, the Milan-Bologna railway and the Milan-Genoa railway. The station is served by suburban and regional trains, becoming in recent years also an interchange station for high-speed lines.

The location is an area in continuous transformation, becoming a new attractive pole, with a combination of residential, commercial and industrial buildings. It is located near the developing area of the Santa Giulia district, which is undergoing an important phase of urban redevelopment due to the upcoming Milan-Cortina 2026 Winter Olympics.

The area under examination was involved in the International Design Competition "Il Bosco della Musica" which involves the construction of a new campus of the "G. Verdi" Conservatory of Milan in the former industrial part of the district. The intervention includes the construction of a multifunctional structure equipped with classrooms, laboratories, auditorium, student residences, refreshment areas and the redevelopment of the "Ex Chimici" building of the former Redaelli steelworks. The competition was won by the Settanta7 Studio, and the works are currently underway.

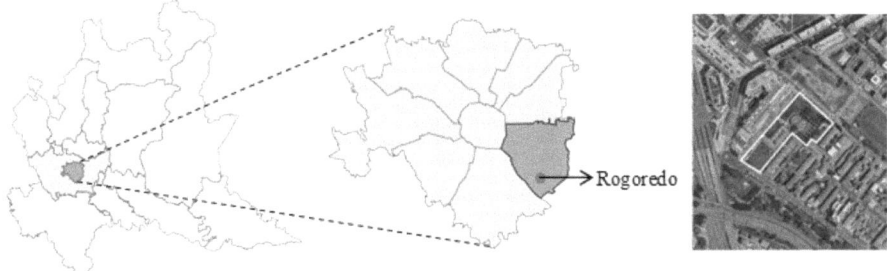

Fig. 2. Lombardy Region+Municipality 4+Milano Rogoredo, project area.

3.2 Stakeholders Analysis

Following the identification of the project phases represented namely: initial phase, design phase, implementation phase, closure phase, and monitoring phase, the relevant stakeholders during the process are determined (see Fig. 3). Subsequently, they are categorized using the Power/Interest Matrix Method (see Fig. 4), based on their level of influence. Furthermore, the relationships between the actors involved were analyzed through a Social Network Analysis.

As mentioned earlier, the area was the subject of the international competition notice "Il Bosco Della Musica" because the Municipality of Milan deliberately chose the Rogoredo district so that this project could become an active part of the urban regeneration process, also addressing a series of social issues and criticalities.

Initially, using a matrix, it was possible to identify the various actors present in the design phase and highlight the stakeholders directly involved, and then highlight their presence in the different steps.

Subsequently, they were categorized according to their level and type of membership. This is an important process as it monitors the influence that individual actors have in the various phases of the process.

The involvement of stakeholders in the decision-making process plays a fundamental role, as it allows for the consideration of different perspectives and ensures greater transparency. However, the level of participation may vary depending on the role, interests, and influence of each stakeholder, determining different degrees of involvement in decisions.

Implementing these strategies is positive because it allows for the clear identification of the different groups involved, a better understanding of their needs and priorities, and more effective management of communication and involvement. Furthermore, it helps to establish targeted strategies to involve each category based on the level of influence and interest, thereby improving the decision-making process and fostering greater collaboration and transparency.

144   G. Buongiovanni et al.

ACTORS - LEVELS - **TYPOLOGY**

● National ● Regional ● Local   ● Political ● Bureaucratic ● Special interests ● General interests ● Experts

	INITIAL PHASE	DESIGN PHASE	IMPLEMENTATION PHASE	CLOSURE PHASE	MONITORING PHASE
MINISTRIES	●	●		●	
LOMBARDY REGION	●	●		●	
MUNICIPALITY OF MILAN	●	●	●	●	●
COMPETITION TEAM: • Engineers • Architects and landscape architects • Consultants • Investors, contractors, jury...	● ●	● ●	● ●	● ●	● ●
ARPA - REGIONAL AGENCY FOR ENVIRONMENTAL PROTECTION AND METROPOLITAN CITY	●	●	●		
PROJECT MANAGEMENT COMPANIES	●	●	●	●	
COMMUNICATION AND MARKETING COMPANIES	●	●	●	●	
CONSTRUCTION COMPANY: • Carpenters and workers • Installers...		●	●		
SUPPLIERS (MANUFACTURERS AND RESELLERS)		●	●		
TRANSPORTERS		●	●		
TESTERS				●	
CONTROL BODIES: • VVF • Superintendency • UE(SAL) • ASL		●	●	●	●
USERS					●

Fig. 3. Stakeholders and Actors, classified according to Dende's criteria (2014).

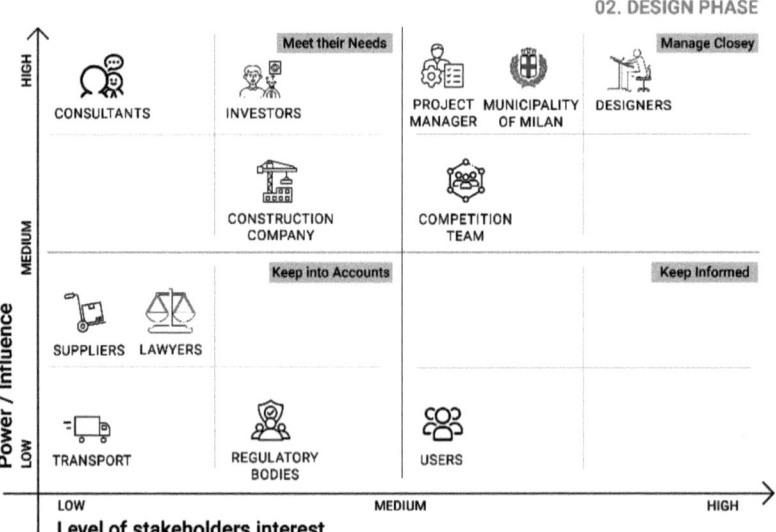

Fig. 4. Output of the Stakeholders Power/Interest analysis.

3.3 SWOT+STEEP Analysis

The SWOT analysis integrated with the STEEP analysis is a decision support tool used to identify the strengths, weaknesses, opportunities, and threats of a specific territory, allowing the determination of its main characteristics (see Table 1).

Regarding the strengths, the presence of strategic connections through public transportation (buses, railways, trams, metro) and main roads well-connected to the highway network emerged. However, these elements have also been identified as weaknesses because they cause noise pollution. Other weaknesses include the presence of the railway that divides the neighborhood into two distinct parts, the absence of public green spaces and a well-organized slow mobility network. The main opportunity factor, on the other hand, relates to the project for the regeneration of the Santa Giulia district in the Milano Rogoredo area, while the risks are particularly linked to the possible formation of gentrification phenomena caused by these redevelopment processes, which could lead to sociocultural changes.

Following the identification of the area's main characteristics, it was possible to proceed with the development of the dynamic SWOT, which allowed a binary comparison between all the SWOT elements previously identified based on the positive or negative synergy between them. The comparison is made by assigning a rating from $+2$ to -2 (see Table 2).

Finally, the SWOT elements, identified with a code, were divided based on the STEEP analysis into different categories: mobility, economy, environment, technology, and society.

3.4 Strategic Framework: Objectives, Strategies and Actions (OSA) and Sustainable Development Goals

Starting from the SWOT+STEEP analysis, it was possible to work on defining the strategic scenario. This consists of Objectives, Strategies, and Actions (OSA) whose purpose is to guide the design in a more precise and targeted way in order to achieve results as consistent as possible with the territorial needs emerging from previous analyses.

The area under study has evident critical issues from the point of view of integration with the rest of the territory, both in terms of mobility infrastructure and accessibility. These factors inevitably have repercussions on the spheres of environmental sustainability and the socio-economic well-being of the community. The identification of these problems was the starting point for defining the objectives of the design action:

- **Environmental sustainability**: for the realization of this objective of sustainable urban regeneration, the main strategies introduced concern ecological design, the integration of green spaces, the protection of biodiversity through the creation of ecological spaces and the redevelopment of degraded habitats, and strong community awareness through educational programs and participatory initiatives, trying to respond to SDGs 3, 6, 7, 13, 15.
- **Social inclusion**: in this case, the proposed strategies aim at the involvement of the entire neighborhood through social inclusion policies, designed to strengthen the sense of belonging and combat marginalization, educational and cultural support programs without forgetting the promotion of professional training programs to support

Table 1. Output of the SWOT+STEEP Analysis.

	Strength	Weaknesses	Opportunities	Threats
Mobility	**SM1**: Presence of Level I interchange hubs (high-speed rail), specifically Milano Rogoredo station **SM2**: Strategic public transport & distributed stops **SM3**: Highway-connected main roads (A1) **SM4**: Rogoredo: city & national rail connections	**WM1**: Absence of a well-organized slow mobility system **WM2**: Railway separates residential/commercial from South Milan Agricultural Park	**OM1**: Via Toledo road redevelopment project **OM2**: "Diagonal" infrastructure tender (Santa Giulia) **OM3**: Introduction of bike sharing, car sharing systems, and cycle paths	
Economics	**SEC1**: Presence of urban renewal areas (Via Medici, Ponte Lambro…)	**WEC1**: Lack of leisure/multi-purpose facilities	**OEC1**: Spark District: commercial, office, residential development **OEC2**: Soul project: new urban retail destination **OEC3**: Linfa: green residential complexes **OEC4**: Eventim Arena project **OEC5**: Social Housing (ERS) complex construction	**TEC1**: Possible increase in average rental rates due to area regeneration projects
Environment	**SEN1**: Presence of urban green spaces (Trapezio Park, South Milan Agricultural Park)	**WEN1**: Absence of a well-connected and integrated public green system with the built environment	**OEN1**: Planning of the new Santa Giulia Park	**TEN1**: Possible area pollution and lack of remediation (presence of abandoned industries and degraded areas on the territory)
Society	**SS1**: Strongly multi-ethnic population (sociocultural mix) **SS2**: Presence of sports complexes ("Rogoredo 84")." **SS3**: Increased residential development (Milan) **SS4**: Redevelopment of housing and public services near the project site	**WS1**: Limited presence of squares and communal spaces available for public use **WS2**: Poorly lit, abandoned areas between neighborhood and station cause insecurity **WS3**: Presence of unemployment rate within the territory	**OS1**: Construction of a children's science museum	**TS1**: Rising gentrification from urban redevelopment **TS2**: Potential for increased crime (lack of control) **TS3**: Illicit activity & petty crime (social tension)
Technology		**WT1**: Degraded area within the project site, currently used as a parking lot	**OT1**: Redevelopment of the former railway yard area of Milano Rogoredo station	

Table 2. Dynamic SWOT Comparison.

		INFLUENCING ELEMENTS																	
		STRENGHTS										WEAKNESSES							
		SM1	SM2	SM3	SM4	SS4	SS3	SEC1	SEN1	SS2	SS1	WT2	WS2	WM2	WM1	WS1	WEC1	WEN1	WT1	WS3
INFLUENCED ELEMENTS / STRENGHTS	SM1		2	0	2	0	0	1	0	0	0	2	0	2	0	0	-1	-1	0	0
	SM2	2		0	2	1	1	1	0	1	0	2	1	0	-2	2	-1	-1	0	0
	SM3	0	0		0	0	0	0	0	0	0	0	0	0	0	0	0	0	0	0
	SM4	2	0	0		0	0	0	0	0	0	-1	-2	0	0	0	0	0	0	0
	SS4	0	1	0	0		2	2	2	2	1	-1	-2	-1	0	-2	-2	-1	-1	0

(*continued*)

Table 2. (*continued*)

		SM1	SM2	SM3	SM4	SS4	SS3	SEC1	SEN1	SS2	SS1	WT2	WS2	WM2	WM1	WS1	WEC1	WEN1	WT1	WS3
INFLUENCED ELEMENTS / STRENGHTS	SS3	2	2	2	2	2		2	1	1	1	-1	-2	-1	0	-1	-2	-1	-1	-2
	SEC1	0	2	0	0	0	1		1	1	1	-1	-2	0	-1	-1	-2	-1	-1	0
	SEN1	0	0	0	0	2	2	2		1	0	0	-1	-1	0	-1	-1	-2	-1	0
	SS2	0	0	0	0	2	2	2	1		0	0	-1	0	-2	0	-2	0	0	0
	SS1	0	0	0	0	1	1	1	0	0		0	-1	0	0	0	0	0	0	0

+2 The element in the row significantly increases its effects thanks to the synergy created with the element in the column.

+1 The element in the row increases its effects thanks to the synergy created with the element in the column.

0 The elements in the row and column are independent.

-1 The element in the row is hindered by the element in the column, but it still manages to develop its effects in a reduced form.

-2 The element in the row is strongly hindered, or even canceled out, by the element in the column.

the community that can be supported by collaboration with local associations. The SDGs that are sought to be satisfied are 1, 3, 4, 5, 8, 11, 17.

- **Integration with the urban context and accessibility**: to respond to this objective, it is intended to guarantee the strengthening of slow mobility infrastructures, such as safe and well-connected cycle paths and pedestrian routes, but above all the implementation of sustainable transport methods, ranging from incentivizing low-emission local public transport to the spread of electric and shared micromobility, simultaneously ensuring physical accessibility for all citizens, regardless of their abilities or conditions, through the universal design of infrastructures and services that eliminate architectural and sensory barriers. In this case, attention is focused on SDGs 8, 9, 10, 11.

To these first three objectives, a fourth is added, more closely linked to the role that the architectural project will play for the territory of Milan Rogoredo:

- **Educational and cultural innovation**: In response to SDGs 3, 4, 17, this objective is achieved through the implementation of strategies that favor the design of innovative spaces and multidisciplinary approaches to music education. Specifically, this translates into the creation of stimulating and flexible learning environments that integrate cutting-edge technologies and interactive teaching methodologies to foster an engaging and personalized musical experience.

Once the objectives, strategies and consequent actions have been identified, it was possible to proceed with the identification of possible future scenarios and the criteria that will characterize the subsequent Multi-Criteria Analysis.

3.5 Scenario Development

Based on the STEEP+SWOT analysis and with the objectives defined in the OSA in the previous section, several alternatives were defined evaluating future scenarios (see Fig. 5).

Fig. 5. Narrative supporting scenario development.

To achieve the set objectives, actions were proposed, including the creation of large public and service spaces, such as parking for bicycles, scooters and other electric vehicles, as well as initiatives to engage the neighborhood.

Furthermore, urban implementation of renewable energy production plants and the design of large green spaces are also useful for raising awareness and educating the population.

In all this, the social needs of the community are not forgotten by introducing collaborations with public bodies for professional internships, for psychological support and for support towards fragility. Finally, the design of multifunctional and adaptable classrooms and the promotion of collaboration with other disciplines is foreseen.

3.6 Multi-criteria Analysis

The starting point for conducting the Multi-Criteria Analysis is the construction of a hierarchical scheme that can relate the objective of the design activity with the three alternative scenarios identified previously:

- Strategic Scenario (scenario resulting from the implementation of the design actions)
- Tender Scenario (scenario foreseen if what is envisaged by the winning project of the tender is realized)
- Inertial Scenario (an alternative that foresees the total absence of a design action)

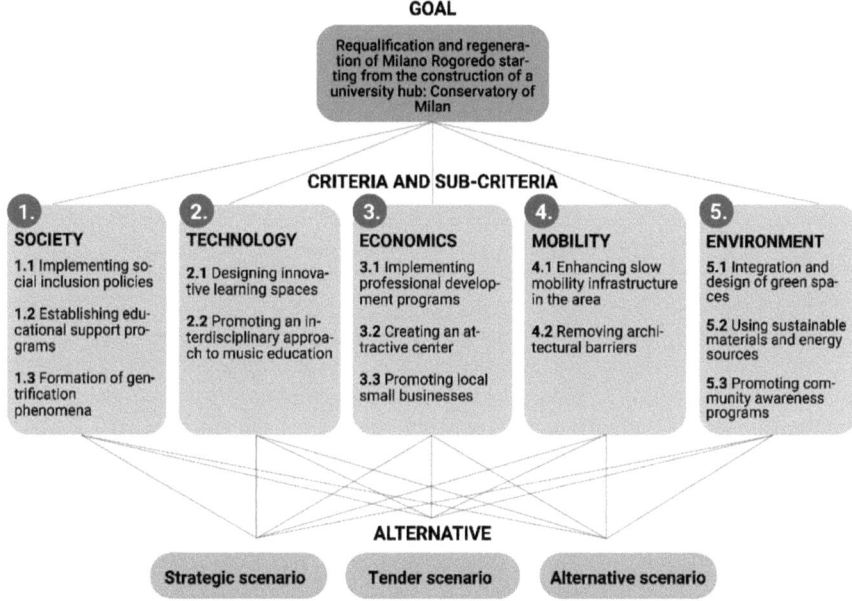

Fig. 6. Analytic Hierarchy Process (AHP) Diagram.

The correlation between the objective and the alternatives is established through the formulation of a set of criteria and sub-criteria, identified starting from the results of the SWOT+STEEP analysis and the consequent OSA. These are fundamental for evaluating the three envisaged scenarios (see Fig. 6).

Once the hierarchical structure was defined, the pairwise comparison phase began using comparison matrices. The process started from the comparison of all the criteria with each other, the sub-criteria of a criterion and the sub-criteria in the alternatives (see Table 3). The use of comparison matrices made it possible to quantify subjective judgments by assigning a value between 1 and 9, always paying considerable attention to maintaining the level of inconsistency between the matrices below an accepted tolerance of 10%. Each matrix exhibited a distinct inconsistency index. Consequently, by computing the arithmetic mean of these indices, a value of 0,053 was derived.

All the analyses conducted were performed using the software "SuperDecisions".

Table 3. Example of pairwise comparison criteria, sub-criteria, and alternatives.

COMPARISON OF SUB-CRITERIA ACROSS ALTERNATIVES

Green space integration and planning

Strategic scenario	≥9.5	9	8	**7**	6	5	4	3	2	1	2	3	4	5	6	7	8	9	≥9.5	Inertial scenario
Strategic scenario	≥9.5	9	8	7	6	5	4	3	**2**	1	2	3	4	5	6	7	8	9	≥9.5	Tender scenario
Inertial scenario	≥9.5	9	8	7	6	5	4	3	2	1	2	3	4	5	6	**7**	8	9	≥9.5	Tender scenario

Promoting community awareness programs

Strategic scenario	≥9.5	9	**8**	7	6	5	4	3	2	1	2	3	4	5	6	7	8	9	≥9.5	Inertial scenario
Strategic scenario	≥9.5	9	8	7	6	5	**4**	3	2	1	2	3	4	5	6	7	8	9	≥9.5	Tender scenario
Inertial scenario	≥9.5	9	8	7	6	5	4	3	2	1	2	**3**	4	5	6	7	8	9	≥9.5	Tender scenario

Through this methodology, it was determined that the strategic scenario, characterized by its comprehensive social inclusion and environmental sustainability initiatives, offered greater overall benefits compared to the other scenarios (see Fig. 7).

4 Discussion and Conclusion

This research presents an integrated methodological approach to the territorial analysis and urban planning of Milan Rogoredo, considering a wide range of interconnected factors, including the environment, economy, society, and culture. This study process is based on the implementation of conventional evaluation tools, such as SWOT analysis and scenario building, with mixed techniques, such as stakeholder analysis (Power Interest and Social Network Analysis) and Multi-Criteria Analysis. It serves as an effective guide for sustainability-oriented decisions, aiming for a regenerative circular economy in the urban context.

Starting from the SWOT+STEEP analysis, a deeper understanding of the territory was achieved, identifying its potential and fragilities. This laid the foundations for further investigations, which are strictly dependent on these initial findings. This process

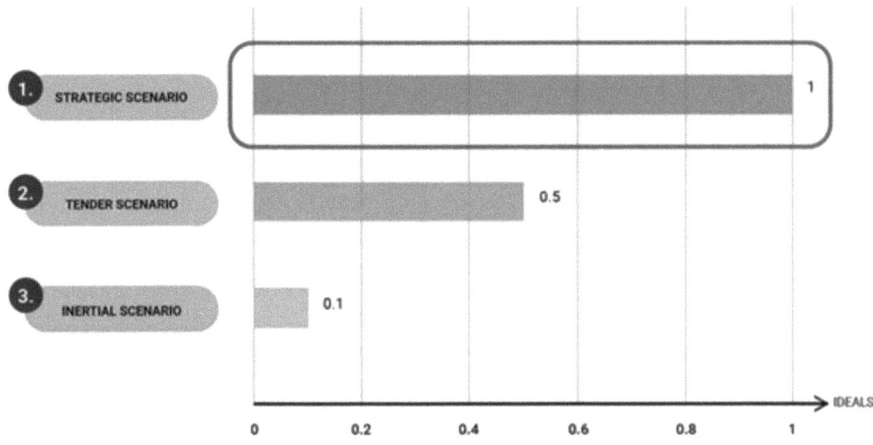

Fig. 7. Conclusion AHP.

highlights the interconnections between the different phases of a sustainability project, demonstrating how the initial SWOT analysis feeds the subsequent systemic evaluation.

The application of this methodology to the case study allowed the evaluation of a wide range of criteria and sub-criteria, weighting them according to their relative importance within three alternative scenarios, formulated during the Scenario Building phase. For the evaluation of the variants, the Analytic Hierarchy Process (AHP) was applied, allowing for pairwise comparison of all the criteria and sub-criteria in relation to the project objective across the three scenarios.

In peripheral urban contexts such as Milan Rogoredo, characterized by significant social and spatial criticalities, dependent on frequent transformation interventions, not always attentive to territorial needs, multi-level strategic planning stands as a key solution to delineate future development scenarios.

The objective of the study focused on identifying the most advantageous option for the redevelopment and revitalization of the neighborhood, aiming to transform it into a new pole of attractiveness and social well-being for the city and its inhabitants.

The design of a complete neighborhood tailored to the community and founded on the principles of sustainability and circularity is therefore evaluated. This would create a thriving and resilient urban environment that guarantees all the necessary services for the citizens.

The application of this methodology highlighted the strategic scenario which, compared to the tender scenario, places a stronger emphasis on promoting social inclusion and environmental sustainability. Through a wide selection of concrete actions declined in the strategic framework; this scenario emerges as the most advantageous solution.

Given the multifaceted nature of urban regeneration, future studies could delve deeper into the interplay between infrastructural development, social inclusion, and economic revitalization at the Milan Rogoredo site by employing alternative analysis methodologies. For example, Multi-Criteria Analysis can be implemented by integrating other analytical approaches, such as sensitivity analysis, to enhance the robustness and reliability of the decision-making process.

Furthermore, it is possible to explore these themes by conducting comparisons with the city of Milan as a whole or with other neighborhoods.

Acknowledgments. The work was developed within the teaching course "Strumenti per la Valutazione della Sostenibilità Ambientale", Academic Year 2023–24, of the Master Degree Program in Architectural Engineering of Politecnico of Milano.

Disclosure of Interests. The authors have no competing interests to declare that are relevant to the content of this article.

References

1. Haase, D., Güneralp, B., Dahiya, B., Bai, X., Elmqvist, T.: Global urbanization. In: Urban Planet, pp. 19–44. Cambridge University Press (2018). https://doi.org/10.1017/9781316647554.003
2. Liddle, B.: Urbanization and inequality/poverty. Urban Sci. **1**, 35 (2017). https://doi.org/10.3390/urbansci1040035
3. Comino, E., Ferretti, V.: Indicators-based spatial SWOT analysis: supporting the strategic planning and management of complex territorial systems. Ecol. Indic. **60**, 1104–1117 (2016). https://doi.org/10.1016/j.ecolind.2015.09.003
4. Cairns, G., Goodwin, P., Wright, G.: A decision-analysis-based framework for analysing stakeholder behaviour in scenario planning. Eur. J. Oper. Res. **249**, 1050–1062 (2016). https://doi.org/10.1016/j.ejor.2015.07.033
5. Dean, M.: A Practical Guide to Multi-Criteria Analysis. https://doi.org/10.13140/RG.2.2.15007.02722
6. Bottero, M., Assumma, V., Caprioli, C., Dell'Ovo, M.: Decision making in urban development: the application of a hybrid evaluation method for a critical area in the city of Turin (Italy). Sustain. Cities Soc. (2021). https://doi.org/10.1016/j.scs.2021.103028
7. Ginige, K., Amaratunga, D., Haigh, R.: Mapping stakeholders associated with societal challenges: a methodological framework. In: Procedia Engineering, pp. 1195–1202. Elsevier Ltd (2018). https://doi.org/10.1016/j.proeng.2018.01.154
8. Raeis Abdollahi, H., Mojtaba Hosseini, S., Alimohammadzadeh, K.: Stakeholder analysis using the matrix of interest-power in insurance industry: case study of Hafez Atiehzasan insurance. Manag. Appl. Sci. Technol. **10**, 1906–9642 (2019). https://doi.org/10.14456/ITJEMAST.2019.89
9. Zhu, Q., Xi, J., Hu, X., Chong, H.-Y., Zhou, Y., Lyu, S.: Stakeholder mapping and analysis of off-site construction projects: utilizing a power-interest matrix and the fuzzy logic theory. Buildings **14**, 2865 (2024). https://doi.org/10.3390/buildings14092865
10. Prell, C., Hubacek, K., Reed, M.: Stakeholder analysis and social network analysis in natural resource management. Soc. Nat. Resour. **22**, 501–518 (2009). https://doi.org/10.1080/08941920802199202
11. Godet, M.: The Art of Scenarios and Strategic Planning: Tools and Pitfalls. (2000)
12. Szpilko, D., Glińska, E., Szydło, J., Glińska, E., Szpilko, D., Szydło, J.: STEEPVL and Structural Analysis as a Tools Supporting Identification of the Driving Forces of City Development. (2020)
13. King, T., Freyn, S., Morrison, J.: SWOT analysis problems and solutions: Practitioners' feedback into the ongoing academic debate. (2023)

14. Szigeti, H., Majumdar, A., Eynard, B., Messaadia, M.: STEEP analysis as a tool for building technology roadmaps _CLEAN_REVISED. (2011)
15. Bezzi, C.: La SWOT "dinamica" o "relazionale."
16. Albrechts, L.: Strategic (spatial) planning reexamined. Environ. Plann. B. Plann. Des. **31**, 743–758 (2004). https://doi.org/10.1068/b3065
17. Torrieri, F., Grigato, V., Oppio, A.: Un modello multi-metodologico a supporto dell'analisi di fattibilità economica per il ripristino della rete su ferro della Valsesia. TECHNE. **11**, 135–142 (2016). https://doi.org/10.13128/Techne-18413
18. Bottero, M., Caprioli, C., Datola, G., Oppio, A., Torrieri, F.: Regeneration of Rogoredo railway: a combined approach using multi-criteria and financial analysis
19. Bernasconi, M., Seri, R., Choirat, C.: The analytic hierarchy process and the theory of measurement. Manag. Sci. **56**, 699–711 (2010). https://doi.org/10.2307/27784145
20. Elena Fregonara*, Cristina Coscia** parole chiave: Multicriteria Decision Analysis, Analythic Hierarchy Process, Delphi Method, Life Cycle Costing e Life Cycle Assessment
21. Saaty, R.W.: THE ANALYTIC HIERARCHY PROCESS-WHAT IT IS AND HOW IT IS USED. (1987)
22. PROGETTO "RACCORDO" Connessioni ferroviarie tra il Porto di Livorno, interporto di Guasticce, linea Pisa-Collesalvetti-Vada e linea Firenze-Pisa Analisi multicriteria delle alternative

Development of a District Heating Resilience Index: A Multi-criteria Assessment Approach Based on Latvian Case Studies

Maksims Feofilovs(✉) 📵, Renate Lakste, and Francesco Romagnoli 📵

Institute of Energy Systems and Environment, Faculty of Electrical and Environmental Engineering, Riga Technical University, Riga, Latvia
{maksims.feofilovs,info.videszinatne}@rtu.lv

Abstract. The study proposes a new approach to evaluating the resilience of district heating (DH) infrastructure by developing a District Heating Resilience multicriteria analysis (MCA). In this context, resilience is defined as the ability of a DH system to absorb, adapt to, and recover from disruptions while maintaining essential heat supply services. The methodology incorporates 24 indicators spanning technical, economic, environmental, and social dimensions. The MCA approach developed is based on many indicators related to technical, economic, social, and environmental aspects of DH. A method known as TOPSIS was used to assess and compare resilience performance across three DH networks in Latvia. To establish the framework and indicators for resilience assessment, the work draws on a wide range of literature and interviews related to DH technologies, historical development, and energy system risks. The DH networks selected for cases studies were analyzed using the defined indicators, allowing the identification of factors that most strongly influence overall resilience. Among them, energy source dependency, aging infrastructure, and exposure to weather extremes stood out. The results of this study provide a structured way to assess the resilience of heat supply systems and can help guide future development of a standardized index development for DH resilience assessment, which can improve upgrades and planning strategies in line with sustainability and energy security goals.

Keywords: District heating · Resilience · Infrastructure · Multi-criteria analysis

1 Introduction

Energy security touches on many different concerns, all pointing toward the same goal: making sure that energy remains both dependable and within reach for those who need it. In this context, energy networks stand out as especially vital officially recognized as part of what's known as Critical Infrastructure [1]. According to national law, this refers to physical or functional systems that are considered essential for the of society, concerning public safety, health, the economy, or general wellbeing. This legal framing highlights just how deeply energy networks are tied to societal resilience.

Disruptions in supply, sharp spikes in cost, and environmental impacts even more concerning with the current especially pressing issues related to geopolitical tension due to the war in Ukraine, which sparked by Russia's invasion in 2021 and made it impossible to ignore how energy systems are effected by such conflicts. The problem isn't only about infrastructure under attack, but also the ripple effects across supply routes, availability of resources, and economic stability that leave entire regions exposed. Dependence on a narrow resource base is another major vulnerability. If a country relies too much on one energy source, especially if that source is imported, it can quickly find itself with few options when prices shift or supply is interrupted [2].

Climate-related risks also pose a growing threat, and they cut both ways. On one hand, extreme weather like flooding, windstorms, prolonged heat or freezing events can physically damage infrastructure across the energy chain, from generation to delivery. On the other, the continued use of fossil-based systems contributes to emissions, which in turn drive further climate instability. These feedback loops make the challenge even more urgent to tackle [3].

Within this context, DH networks form a crucial part of the broader energy infrastructure. These systems include a variety of technologies designed to deliver energy services efficiently to densely populated areas. For instance, electricity grids transfer power from generation sites to end users, gas and oil pipelines serve as the backbone for fuel distribution, while DH systems are specifically designed to provide thermal energy hot or chilled water (for cooling) via insulated pipes for space conditioning in buildings. When the focus is on heating, the system is referred to as DH; when cooling dominates, it is classified as district cooling (DC). [4] Despite technological advances, recent data about 2021 indicate that more than 50% of global energy is still produced from fossil sources [5].

Thermal energy represents a significant share of total energy demand. In Europe, the DH/DC sector accounts for roughly half of all final energy consumption, outpacing both transport and electricity. The majority of this is allocated to residential applications, with around 79% of energy going toward space heating, domestic hot water, and, increasingly, space cooling [6]. A DH system requires three core components: a cost-effective heat source, a clear and stable heat demand, and a distribution network that efficiently links the two. Distance between these components is critical, as shorter pipeline distances reduce both capital investment and heat losses.

Typical end users for DH include residential buildings, schools, hospitals, and commercial facilities. [7] Given the role of DH in ensuring reliable energy services to local communities, energy networks must remain robust in the face of external stressors. Their exposure to natural hazards such as flooding, storms, heatwaves, and sea-level rise means that even areas with temperate climates are not immune to disruption, thus long-term functionality of DH will depend not only on technical robustness but also on strategic adaptation measures that can minimize damage, service interruptions, and future repair costs [8].

This study sets out to explore the factors that influence the resilience of DH networks in Latvia. To achieve this, the research combines insights from a structured review of scientific publications with input gathered through interviews conducted with professionals working in the field. In addition, relevant technical and operational data are examined to supplement the findings. From this combined evidence base, a set of key indicators is developed—each reflecting an aspect of system resilience. These indicators are then applied in the evaluation of selected district heating networks, providing a grounded framework for assessing their capacity to withstand and adapt to various stresses.

2 Methodology

To achieve the aim of the study, following steps are performed in this study as indicated in Fig. 1. First, based on an in-depth review of academic literature and relevant studies, this work offers a contextualized understanding of what constitutes resilience in DH systems. In this research, DH resilience is understood as: *"the system's ability to absorb shocks and recover functionality following events that threaten the continuity of heat supply. A resilient network is one that can maintain service or restore it quickly, thereby minimizing disruption for residential and commercial consumers"*. This interpretation serves as the foundation for the development of a dedicated resilience indicators. The purpose of this indicators is to enable the evaluation and comparison of resilience across different DH networks by translating complex system characteristics into a structured set of measurable criteria.

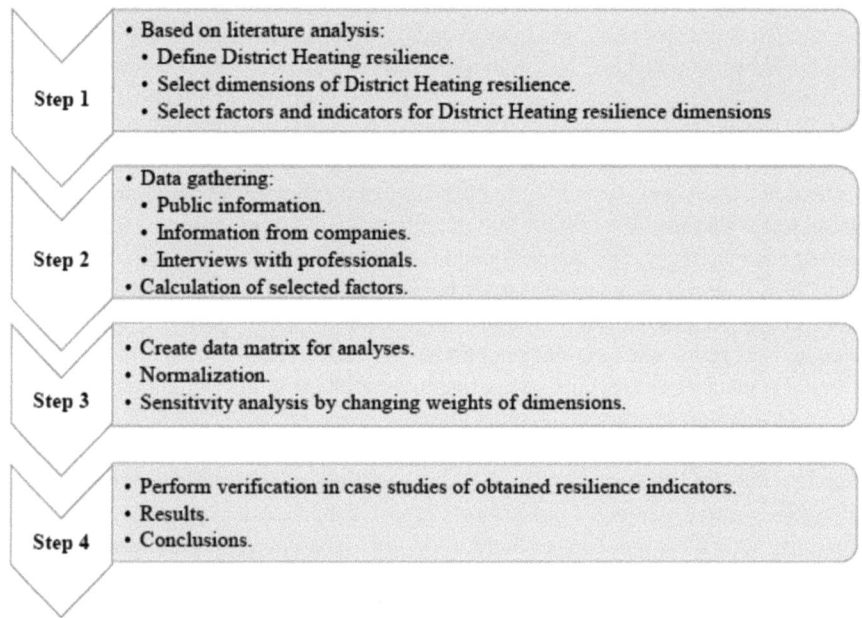

Fig. 1. Methodological steps of the study

2.1 Data Collection and Definition of DH Resilience Assessment Dimensions

In collaboration with professionals experienced in the field of district heating, this research identifies the most critical criteria influencing resilience across four main dimensions. Based on literature and expert judgment, four core dimensions were established as central to DH resilience evaluation. Expert interviews were conducted with professionals from the DH sector, including engineers and business representatives. Participants came from private companies specializes in DH solutions. Additional insights were gathered from Latvian DH companies selected for case studies. Interviews were carried out through a mix of in-person meetings, phone calls, and email correspondence.

As a result of this information gathering, the following dimensions are defined for DH resilience assessment:

- Technical Dimension: Captures the system's capacity to resist and adapt to mechanical faults, supply interruptions, or aging infrastructure while continuing to deliver heat to users.
- Economic Dimension: Addresses financial viability, investment capacity, and the affordability of heat supply; factors that determine whether the system can sustain resilience improvements over time.
- Climate and Environmental Dimension: Relates to how the system integrates renewable or low-emission sources and adapts to regulatory frameworks shaped by climate policy and environmental considerations.
- Social Dimension: Reflects the societal impact of resilience, including equitable access, public perception, and the ability to shield vulnerable groups from energy insecurity during disruptions.

Assessing resilience across multiple dimensions is essential because district heating systems are complex socio-technical infrastructures influenced by more than just technical reliability. A system may be technically sound yet economically unsustainable, environmentally incompatible, or socially inequitable. By evaluating resilience through technical, economic, environmental, and social lenses, it becomes possible to capture interdependencies and trade-offs that would be missed in a single-domain assessment. This comprehensive perspective allows for better-informed decisions that address not only system performance but also affordability, regulatory alignment, and societal acceptance. These dimensions, along with their respective indicators defined next step of methodology, form the analytical core of the DH Resilience Index.

2.2 Definition of DH Resilience Indicators

The process of indicator selection for defined DH resilience dimensions begins with a critical analysis of existing academic literature, where common themes and recurring elements in the definition of infrastructure resilience, particularly within energy systems, are identified. These findings are then tailored to a case of Latvia's energy landscape. The definition of indicators is based on the factors attributed to be important for describing DH resilience characteristics.

The selection of factors is guided by their relevance to reflect meaningful, system-level responses to various types of disturbance (e.g. technical failures, climate-related stresses, economic shocks, or social vulnerabilities). These factors are selected by summarizing the findings from academic studies, policy documents, and expert interviews conducted with engineers, utility operators, and specialists in DH system planning.

Once the key factors are defined, indicators are selected as measurable proxies that represent each factor in a quantifiable way. The selection process for indicators focuses on three main criteria:

- Relevance – The indicator must meaningfully represent a specific aspect of resilience within one of the four dimensions (economic, technical, environmental, or social).
- Data availability – Indicators are chosen based on the accessibility and reliability of underlying data, either from public sources or through direct cooperation with DH companies.
- Comparability – The selected indicators should be applicable across multiple case study locations to allow for comparative analysis.

Table 1. Presents a structured overview of the technical dimension of DH resilience, highlighting key factors, indicators, measurement units, and their impact on resilience. The technical resilience of a DH system is essential for ensuring stable and uninterrupted heat supply, especially in the face of infrastructure failures, supply disruptions, and external hazards. The table provides a structured overview of the technical indicators affecting DH resilience. Positive indicators (+) contribute to resilience, while negative indicators (−) indicate vulnerability within the system.

Table 1. Indicators of the Technical Dimension of DH Resilience

Factors of Technical Dimension	Indicator	Measure	Impact on Resilience
Heat production capacity	Excess production capacity	%	+
Diversification of production	Dependence on number of heat production plants	HHI	−
Diversification of resources	Dependence on one type of energy source	HHI	−
Heat losses	Heat losses in the DH network	MWh/km	−
Aging infrastructure	Industrially insulated pipes	%	+
Digitalization	Level of automation	Scale	+
Heat storage	Heat accumulation tank volume	L/MW	+
Low-temperature DH	DH technical parameters of supply and return temperature	Scale	+
Investments in infrastructure	Amount of investments in DH infrastructure over a 10-year period	EUR/MW	+

(*continued*)

Table 1. (*continued*)

Factors of Technical Dimension	Indicator	Measure	Impact on Resilience
Consumer energy efficiency	Average heat consumption per unit area	kWh/m^2	–
Natural hazards – Cold waves	Resilience to extreme cold conditions	Scale	–
Natural hazards – Floods	Resilience to flood risk	Scale	–

Table 2 presents economic indicators aligned with the key economic factors that influence the resilience of DH systems. Economic resilience ensures that DH operators can sustain operations, manage financial risks, and maintain affordable heating services despite fluctuations in energy markets and policy changes. A financially stable and cost-efficient DH system is better positioned to adapt to disruptions, invest in modernization, and maintain long-term service reliability.

Table 2. List of Indicators of the Economic Dimension of DH Resilience

Factors of Economic Dimension	Indicator	Measure	Impact on Resilience
Economic Stability of DH Production Company	Company profit	EUR/MWh	+
Prices of Energy Sources	Energy source price fluctuation	%	–
Heat Consumers	Average heat consumption by customers with individual substations	EUR/MWh	–
Efficiency of Heat Production	Cost of energy source	EUR/MWh	–
	Production cost	EUR/MWh	–
Workforce Productivity	Employees per unit of heat produced	Employees/MWh	–
Affordability of Heat Energy	Affordability of heat energy tariff	MWh	+
Subsidized Investments in Infrastructure	Subsidized investments in DH	%	+

Within this study, the climate and environmental aspects of DH resilience are captured through a set of specific factors and corresponding indicators, as outlined in Table 3.

In this context, the technologies and fuel sources used for heat generation are particularly influencing emissions, regulatory exposure, and adaptability to long-term climate goals.

Table 3. List of Indicators of the Climate and Environment Dimension of DH Resilience

Factors of Climate and Environment Dimension	Indicator	Measure	Impact on Resilience
Technologies and Innovation	Heat produced with renewable resources	%	+
GHG Emissions	Total greenhouse gas emissions	t/MWh	−
CO_2 Emissions	Carbon dioxide emissions	t/MWh	−
Air Quality	Particulate matter emissions	t/MWh	−

The social dimension of DH resilience focuses on how reliably and affordably heat is delivered to people, and how well systems are managed to prevent or respond to disruptions. Key factors include:

- Whether energy management and risk planning are in place at the municipal and company levels.
- The energy efficiency of buildings, which lowers demand and increases system stability.
- The impact of taxes on affordability, with higher taxes making heat less accessible.
- Consumer preference and trust, reflected in how many users stay connected to DH services.

Together, these factors determine how well DH systems support public well-being, especially during periods of stress or change (Table 4).

2.3 Creation of Model for Resilience Assessment

The defined indicators are integrated into multi-criteria decision analysis (MCDA) using the Technique for Order Preference by Similarity to Ideal Solution (TOPSIS) [9–11] for ranking of different district heating networks based on resilience performance. The TOPSIS allows to find best solution by defining closeness to the ideal solution (best-case scenario) and as far as possible from the worst-case scenario. This method helps understand which systems are most resilient and where improvements are needed. Steps in the TOPSIS Process:

1) Definition of indicators
   Each DH system is evaluated based on a set of resilience indicators, such as heat production capacity, energy source diversification, financial stability, emissions levels, and consumer affordability. These indicators represent both positive and negative factors affecting system resilience.

Table 4. List of Indicators of the Social Dimension of DH Resilience

Factors of Social Dimension	Indicator	Measure	Impact on Resilience
Municipal Energy Management System	DH as a separate focus in the municipality energy management system	Scale	+
DH Company Risk Management Plan	Existence and implementation of a risk management plan	Scale	+
Energy Efficiency Improvement of Consumers	Potential of heat consumption reduction at consumers	%	+
Tax on Fossil Fuels and Emissions	Excise tax on fossil fuel	EUR/MWh	−
	Tax on emissions	EUR/MWh	−
Customer Preference for DH	Proportion of DH consumers in the area	%	+

2) Standardization and Weighting of Indicators

Since indicators have different units and scales, they are standardized to ensure comparability across all DH systems. Each indicator is then assigned a weight, which reflects its importance in the overall resilience assessment. To ensure transparency and reduce the influence of subjective assumptions, the assignment of indicator weights was carried out using structured expert consultations. Specialists with experience in district heating operations, energy planning, and infrastructure risk analysis were invited to evaluate the relative importance of each resilience dimension and associated indicators.

3) Determining Ideal and Worst-Case Scenarios

The ideal solution represents the best possible performance across all indicators, such as high renewable energy integration, low emissions, and strong financial stability. The worst-case scenario represents poor performance, such as high reliance on fossil fuels, high emissions, and financial instability.

4) Comparison of DH Systems Against Ideal and Worst-Case Scenarios

Each DH system is then compared to both the ideal and worst-case scenarios. Systems that perform well across multiple indicators will be closer to the ideal solution, while less resilient systems will be closer to the worst-case scenario.

5) Final Ranking of District Heating Systems

A resilience score is calculated for each DH system based on its proximity to the ideal and worst-case scenarios. The systems are then ranked from most resilient to least resilient, providing a clear basis for decision-making and prioritizing improvements.

The TOPSIS method offers a comprehensive evaluation of DH resilience by considering multiple performance indicators simultaneously. Unlike single-metric assessments, which may overlook key resilience factors, TOPSIS ensures a holistic analysis that can incorporate technical, economic, environmental, and social dimension indicators. This approach allows for a fair comparison between different DH systems, even when they vary in size, technology, and energy sources, making it a valuable comparative tool.

Additionally, TOPSIS serves as a decision-support tool by providing a quantitative basis for policy and investment decisions. It enables energy planners to identify vulnerabilities, prioritize improvements, and allocate resources effectively, ensuring that resilience-enhancing measures are both strategic and impactful. Its flexibility and adaptability further strengthen its applicability, as the methodology can be extended beyond district heating to assess the resilience of other critical energy infrastructures.

2.4 Definition of Case Study

The methodology has been tested using three district heating case studies from Latvia. These three DH systems in Latvia were selected for the case study analysis, representing a range of infrastructure sizes, energy sources, and technological modernization levels as given Table 5.

Table 5. List of companies selected for research and description

Activities	Total Heat Capacity (MW)	Annual Heat Production (MWh)	Fuel Used	Heat Tariff (EUR, 2023)	Consumers	Ownership
Salaspils Siltums Ltd	37.71	65187	Woodchips, natural gas, solar	73.05	201	Municipality
Jūrmalas Siltums Ltd	78.57	137610	Woodchips, natural gas	120.77	324	Municipality
Ķekavas Nami Ltd	19.33	28083	Wood pellets, natural gas	141.78	135	Municipality

The selection of the case study systems is guided by the intention to capture a representative spectrum of district heating conditions in Latvia. These systems vary in terms of installed capacity, energy source diversity, infrastructure modernization level, and consumer base size. Together, they reflect common typologies found across Latvia's DH sector, ranging from small municipal operators to larger, more diversified systems.

3 Results

The results of the resilience evaluation using the TOPSIS method offer insight into how each DH company performs when assessed against ideal and non-ideal benchmarks (see Table 5). "Salaspils Siltums" Ltd came out on top, followed closely by "Jūrmalas Siltums" Ltd, while "Ķekavas Nami" Ltd ranked third (Table 6).

Table 6. Results of TOPSIS analysis for defined case study

DH Company	Ideal	Anti-Ideal	Pi Value	Final Valuation
"Salaspils Siltums" Ltd	0.0056	0.0163	0.7449	1
"Jūrmalas Siltums" Ltd	0.005	0.0133	0.7262	2
"Ķekavas Nami" Ltd	0.0233	0.004	0.1465	3

The Fig. 2. Shows normalized dimension scores with ranked weights, starting form Technical dimension with highest weight, followed by Economical dimensions, then Environmental, and Social with lowest weight. According to the results with ranked weights, Technical resilience plays the most decisive role in shaping final outcomes, but it also highlights the risks posed by weak economic performance, which can offset strengths in other areas. The relatively uniform distribution of values in the environmental and social dimensions across all three companies also suggests these may carry less discriminatory power in the current index weighting.

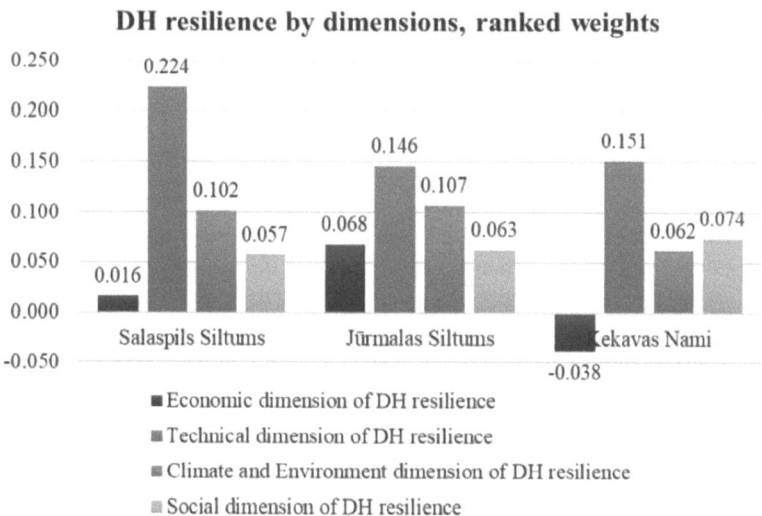

Fig. 2. DH resilience assessment: dimensions normalized and ranked weight values.

Certain indicators have a more significant impact on the final result simply because there is more variation in their values across the cases. Where companies differ greatly, for example, in emissions per MWh or network heat loss, those indicators tend to influence the distance to ideal more noticeably. Other indicators might show similar values across all companies, reducing their influence in the model regardless of their conceptual importance.

4 Conclusions

The results of the TOPSIS analysis for DH resilience assessment reflect a complex interplay of indicator values, dimension weights, and distances to benchmark performance levels. The high ranking of "Salaspils Siltums" suggests relatively strong performance across core dimensions, particularly technical and environmental. Conversely, "Ķekavas Nami" shows lower resilience due to weaker scores likely in technical and climate-related metrics. Improving the balance and transparency in weighting and indicator distribution would enhance the index's reliability, fairness, and applicability in future assessments.

Moreover, sensitivity testing can help clarify how much results change if weights are adjusted. This is especially useful for uncovering whether the model is overly dependent on one or two variables. Since real data can be hard to obtain and varies between companies, transparency in data availability and how it's treated is also key.

To improve the methodology and enhance fairness in future assessments of DH resilience with unitary index, a few considerations are worth noting. First, weights should be reviewed critically, not just assumed or assigned arbitrarily. Ideally, they should reflect expert input, stakeholder priorities, or observed impact, rather than being set equal by default. Second, the number of indicators in each dimension should either be balanced or the weighting structure should be correct for any imbalance. If one area dominates the data structure, it may overshadow other relevant aspects of resilience.

While the current version of the model provides a structured basis for comparing system resilience, further steps are planned to increase its practical value. This includes tailoring the framework to specific local conditions by introducing context-sensitive scoring criteria and exploring real-time data integration for adaptive updates. In the long term, the development of unitary DH resilience index could be strengthened by introducing more context-aware scoring. Not all DH systems operate under the same conditions—what's achievable in a large urban network may not be realistic in a smaller or more isolated system. Adapting benchmarks to reflect local conditions would make the tool more practical. Finally, as energy systems evolve, so should the indicators. The index should remain flexible to accommodate new risks, technologies, and policy developments over time. By integrating feedback from system operators and decision-makers, the approach can be further refined as a decision-support tool, guiding infrastructure investments and resilience planning in diverse settings.

Acknowledgments. The work has been supported by the following project: "Advanced Technologies for Physical ResIlience Of cRitical Infrastructures (APRIORI)", code: SPS G6140, funded by the NATO, Science for Peace and Security (SPS) Call for Proposals 2023-1.

References

1. Latvian Saeima, 'National Security Act of Latvia'. Accessed: Apr. 20, 2024. [Online]. Available: https://likumi.lv/ta/id/14011-nacionalas-drosibas-likums
2. Hartvig, Á.D., Kiss-Dobronyi, B., Kotek, P., Takácsné Tóth, B., Gutzianas, I., Zareczky, A.Z.: The economic and energy security implications of the Russian energy weapon. Energy **294**, 130972 (2024). https://doi.org/10.1016/J.ENERGY.2024.130972

3. Cherp, A., Jewell, J.: The concept of energy security: beyond the four as. Energy Policy **75**, 415–421 (2014). https://doi.org/10.1016/j.enpol.2014.09.005
4. Zajacs, A., Borodiņecs, A.: Assessment of development scenarios of district heating systems. Sustain. Cities Soc. **48**, 101540 (2019). https://doi.org/10.1016/J.SCS.2019.101540
5. Zhang, Y., Johansson, P., Sasic Kalagasidis, A.: Assessment of district heating and cooling systems transition with respect to future changes in demand profiles and renewable energy supplies. Energy Convers. Manag. (2022). https://doi.org/10.1016/j.enconman.2022.116038
6. Sandvall, A.F., Börjesson, M., Ekvall, T., Ahlgren, E.O.: Modelling environmental and energy system impacts of large-scale excess heat utilisation – a regional case study. Energy **79**(C), 68–79 (2015). https://doi.org/10.1016/J.ENERGY.2014.10.049
7. Werner, S.: District heating and cooling. Ref. Module Earth Syst. Environ. Sci. (2013). https://doi.org/10.1016/B978-0-12-409548-9.01094-0
8. Panteli, M., Pickering, C., Wilkinson, S., Dawson, R., Mancarella, P.: Power system resilience to extreme weather: fragility modeling, probabilistic impact assessment, and adaptation measures. IEEE Trans. Power Syst. **32**(5), 3747–3757 (2017). https://doi.org/10.1109/TPWRS.2016.2641463
9. Tzeng, G.-H., Huang, J.-J.: Multiple Attribute Decision Making: Methods and Applications (2011)
10. Susmaga, R., Szczęch, I., Brzezinski, D.: Towards explainable TOPSIS: visual insights into the effects of weights and aggregations on rankings. Appl. Soft Comput. **153**, 111279 (2024). https://doi.org/10.1016/J.ASOC.2024.111279
11. Kuo, T.: A modified TOPSIS with a different ranking index. Eur. J. Oper. Res. **260**(1), 152–160 (2017). https://doi.org/10.1016/J.EJOR.2016.11.052

Sustainable Event Management: A Comparative Analysis of Protocols and Music Festivals

Agnese Baldoni[1], Laura Calisi[2], Salvatore De Pascalis[2(✉)], Francesca Falconi[2], Matteo Napodano[2], and Giacomo Seratoni Gualdoni[2]

[1] Politecnico di Torino, Corso Duca degli Abruzzi, 24, 10129 Torino, Italy
s330655@studenti.polito.it
[2] Politecnico di Milano, Piazza Leonardo da Vinci, 32, 20133 Milano, Italy
{laura.calisi,salvatore.depascalis,francesca.falconi,
matteo.napodano,giacomo.seratoni}@mail.polimi.it

Abstract. The sustainability of music festivals has gained increasing attention, reflecting broader societal concerns about environmental responsibility. While several sustainability protocols exist to provide guidelines for reducing the environmental impact of events, their adoption remains inconsistent. This study examines the alignment between sustainability protocols and the actual practices implemented by music festivals, identifying key gaps and emerging best practices. The research employs a comparative qualitative analysis, using a structured framework to systematically assess both protocols and real-world festival implementations. A distinctive aspect of this study is its collaboration with MI AMI Festival 2025, allowing for direct validation of theoretical insights in a real-world setting. The findings highlight critical gaps in long-term strategic planning, social inclusivity, and transparency, alongside emerging best practices in waste management, energy efficiency, and sustainable mobility. A strong variation in the depth and scope of sustainability practices across European countries is revealed, with Northern and Western European festivals demonstrating higher levels of implementation and transparency. Additionally, the European Green Festival Roadmap 2030 and the Green Festivals and Events through Sustainable Tenders emerged as particularly comprehensive and applicable protocols, offering concrete tools and solutions that remain underutilized across the broader festival landscape. By bridging the gap between policy frameworks and practical applications, this research contributes to the development of a standardized sustainability model for the festival industry, with potential broader applicability.

Keywords: Sustainability Protocols · Music Festivals · Environmental Impact · Sustainable Event Management · Best Practices

1 Introduction

Over the last years, the sustainability of music festivals and live events has emerged as a critical concern, reflecting broader societal shifts toward environmental awareness. Recent studies highlight that participants increasingly prioritize sustainable practices at events, with the decision to attend being increasingly influenced by a widespread recognition of environmental issues [1]. Specifically, environmentally conscious individuals are more inclined to attend eco-friendly events rather than traditional ones, which tend to have higher negative environmental impacts [2]. According to a research study by A Greener Future (AGF) and Bucks University, 49.8% of audiences would be willing to pay an increased ticket price to reduce the festival's environmental impact. Moreover, of this sample, 56% think festivals have a negative carbon footprint and 90% think that this was the responsibility of the organisers [3].

Furthermore, Sisson and Alcorn [4], demonstrated that positive festival experiences can significantly influence participants' willingness to adopt sustainable behaviors, with attendees displaying measurable increases in sustainable behaviors after attending the event. Their findings align with the research survey conducted by AGF and Bucks University, as 43.1% of the audience involved said that they had changed their behaviour as a result of green initiatives or ideas they had discovered at festivals [3].

However, it is crucial for festivals to effectively convey their sustainability efforts. Indeed, as emphasized by Ramli et al. [5], there is a strong correlation between the perceived environmental commitment of an event and attendee satisfaction. Critical questions emerge at this point: how can attendees distinguish between festivals truly committed to sustainability and those making empty claims? For organizers, this poses a specular challenge: how can they avoid being perceived as greenwashers and instead authentically commit to sustainability?

The implementation of sustainable practices across festivals appears fragmented, with most festivals devising their own rules. The fragmented adoption of sustainable practices, combined with lack of transparency over sustainability data, has led to skepticism about the credibility of sustainability claims and accusations of greenwashing against music festivals by activists and scholars [6].

However, this does not imply that certifications and standards for sustainable event management are entirely absent. Existing frameworks such as the *Greener Festival Certification* and ISO 20121 standards provide templates for sustainable practices. Deespite that, their limited adoption resulting from the voluntary nature and low public awareness undermined their potential as universal benchmarks.

This chapter originates from a collaboration with BetterDays srl[1] - a creative agency specialized in the planning, production and distribution of events (festivals and concerts, exhibitions, in-store, corporate events) - and the sustainability assessments conducted during MI AMI Festival 2024. The study was developed within the Alta Scuola Politecnica (ASP)[2], an interdisciplinary honors program jointly organized by Politecnico di Milano and Politecnico di Torino, which provided the academic framework and support for this initiative. The collaboration was initiated with the specific goal of developing a sustainability protocol that BetterDays could implement to improve its environmental impact.

This research aims to analyze current sustainability management practices within music festivals, focusing on exemplary cases and established protocols. Specifically, the study examines ten festivals and four sustainability protocols, applying a structured

---

[1] https://betterdays.it
[2] https://www.asp-poli.it.

comparison framework with common assessment criteria. For festivals, the comparison is based on five macro-criteria: energy, materials and waste, food and beverage, water management and travel and transport. The combined analysis of sustainability protocols and the sustainability practices disclosed by festivals is essential to understanding how sustainable initiatives are effectively implemented and where critical challenges persist.

By bridging the gap between theoretical frameworks and practical applications, this study seeks to identify both best practices and areas for improvement. The ultimate goal is to propose actionable recommendations for the development of a universally recognized framework. The 2025 edition of MI AMI Festival will serve as the pilot case to validate the theoretical approach. The chapter proceeds by presenting the methodology and analytical framework, followed by a comparative discussion of protocols and festival practices, and concludes with key findings and open challenges that require special attention in future sustainability efforts.

2 Methodology

This study conducts a systematic examination of both sustainability protocols and the sustainability practices disclosed by festivals. Currently, festivals selectively incorporate certain practices while disregarding others. Conversely, there are innovative initiatives proposed by festivals that are not incorporated into any existing protocol yet.

The intended outcome of this study is twofold. Firstly, it aims to identify critical gaps between established frameworks and festivals' implementations. Secondly, it aims to develop a comprehensive set of best practices by integrating both widely adopted sustainability measures and emerging innovative approaches.

The research is designed as a qualitative comparative analysis (QCA), allowing for a detailed comparison of specific sustainability dimensions across a limited number of cases. This approach is suitable for identifying patterns of convergence and divergence between protocols and practices. The main tools used for the evaluation include checklists to verify whether each festival implemented the initiatives proposed by the protocols, and comparison grids designed to juxtapose, for each sustainability dimension, the measures outlined in the protocols with the actual practices observed in the selected festivals.

The research is based on data collected from publicly accessible sources, including official festival websites, sustainability reports and impact assessments, as well as documentation from organizations developing sustainability protocols.

The geographical focus of this study is Europe, with a particular emphasis on the Italian context. Figure 1 illustrates the locations of the ten European festivals examined in this study. To ensure that the insights gathered could be applied to our pilot case, the research was naturally oriented towards the Italian landscape. Indeed, the study takes into account the regulatory constraints posed by national and EU legislation, which influence the transposability of sustainability initiatives across countries. The long-term ambition of this research is to extend the study beyond the European context.

To provide a comprehensive analysis, the study includes festivals of various sizes. While large festivals often lead when it comes to innovative sustainability initiatives due to their greater financial capacity, exclusively focusing on them would risk overlooking issues of scalability and feasibility. By incorporating small and mid-sized festivals, the research considers how event scale influences sustainability adoption.

Fig. 1. Geographical distribution of the analyzed music festivals in Europe.

To ensure a consistent and comparable analysis, the study adopts two complementary sets of analytical dimensions: one for sustainability protocols and the other for music festivals. The analysis of sustainability protocols focuses on multiple key aspects. First, it considers the publication context, including the publication date and the issuing organization, which provides both a temporal and institutional frame of reference, helping to assess the relevance and credibility of each protocol. Another fundamental dimension is the main objectives that each protocol sets out to achieve, along with the key thematic areas it covers, such as energy, waste management, food systems, and mobility. Moreover, the analysis accounts for the presence of innovative approaches, including practical tools, certification schemes, or incentive-based strategies designed to support the implementation of sustainable measures.

The assessment of music festivals, on the other hand, shifts the focus toward their operational context. Factors such as location, duration, and the scale of participation provide an initial framework for situating each festival within the broader landscape of sustainable event management. Another key aspect is the transparency of sustainability-related data, which was evaluated not only in terms of how openly festivals communicate their environmental impact and the measures undertaken, but also with regard to the involvement of external evaluators or research institutions. Additionally, particular attention is given to the four core areas in which sustainability efforts are typically implemented: energy use, waste and recycling, food and water management, and mobility solutions.

By applying this dual framework, the study makes it possible to draw meaningful comparisons between the strategic intentions outlined in sustainability protocols and the real-world practices observed in festivals. This approach makes it possible to highlight points of alignment, identify existing gaps, and bring forward best practices that may serve as references for future improvements.

3 Comparative Findings

3.1 Protocols

This section explores four key protocols aimed at guiding the sustainability of festivals and cultural events in Europe. It covers strategies for reducing environmental impacts through comprehensive frameworks, providing tools and practices to enhance ecological and social responsibility in event organization.

3.1.1 European Green Festival Roadmap 2030

Publication Context. Published in 2023 by YOUROPE, in collaboration with A Greener Future and Greener Events Norway, this roadmap provides a comprehensive strategy for enhancing sustainability in European music festivals.

Objectives. The roadmap aims to support festivals in reducing their environmental impact through long-term planning, aligned with the philosophy of "cathedral thinking", a model that promotes vision, strategy, and shared responsibility.

Key Areas. This protocol adopts the GreenHouse Gas (GHG) Protocol classification, dividing emissions into three categories:

- 'Scope 1': direct emissions from on-site sources (e.g., generators, organizational vehicles, operational activities)
- 'Scope 2': indirect emissions from purchased electricity, heating, and cooling
- 'Scope 3': indirect emissions along the supply chain (e.g., logistics, audience transportation, waste, and material production)

Building on this structure, the action plan is organized around seven thematic areas:

- 'Energy': use of renewable sources and improvement of energy efficiency
- 'Materials and Waste': reuse, recycling, and responsible waste management
- 'Food and Beverage': sustainable sourcing, food waste reduction, and compostable packaging
- 'Water Management': responsible consumption and wastewater treatment
- 'Travel and Transport': promotion of low-emission transport options (e.g., public transit, cycling, walking)
- 'Strategy': development of sustainability roadmaps, allocation of resources, and team involvement
- 'Community and Biodiversity': ecological protection, community engagement, and biodiversity conservation

Innovations. To support festivals in the ecological transition, the protocol introduces innovative tools, including the Future Festival Tools, a set of free resources designed to support the sustainability of events. This toolkit includes a 'Self-Assessment Tool', which helps organizers identify gaps in their environmental knowledge and practices. Additionally, 21 exemplary case studies are provided, showcasing successful experiences in applying sustainability to festivals. To further enhance skill acquisition, an e-learning course is available, consisting of six modules, with the possibility of obtaining a completion certificate. Finally, the toolkit includes training materials and support packages for educators and event organizers.

3.1.2 GreenFEST – Green Festivals and Events Through Sustainable Tenders

Publication Context. Published in 2019 by the European Commission under the LIFE 2016 Environmental Governance and Information program.

Objectives. The protocol aims to contribute to the management and reduction of environmental impacts in the sector of cultural activities funded, promoted, or organized by public authorities. The document, published in 2019, has among its main objectives the introduction of Minimum Environmental Criteria (C.A.M.) in tender procedures to ensure that cultural activities are managed sustainably. Furthermore, the protocol seeks to facilitate the exchange of knowledge and best practices on Green Public Procurement (GPP) between public authorities and private operators, thus contributing to greater sustainability in cultural events.

Key Areas. This protocol identifies sustainability priorities across various stages of a cultural event's life cycle (organization, communication, implementation, and follow-up). The key areas include:

- 'Energy Consumption (pre-event and during the event)': efficient energy use before and during activities
- 'Transport of Materials': logistics and supply chain sustainability
- 'Waste Management': reduction, separation, and proper disposal of waste
- 'Setups and Furnishings': use of recycled/reused materials and sustainable furniture
- 'Catering': environmentally friendly food services
- 'Audience Transportation': promotion of sustainable travel options for attendees
- 'Communication Materials': reduction of paper use and use of eco-friendly printing
- 'Gadgets and Merchandise': selection of low environmental impact items
- 'Venue Selection': prioritization of biodiversity-conscious locations
- 'Accessibility and Equality': inclusive access for all participants
- 'Staff Training': capacity building on sustainability topics
- 'Public Information': awareness and transparency toward the audience

Innovations. GreenFEST introduces some innovative measures to promote the ecological transition in events, such as rewarding criteria for sustainability, with additional points for events that adopt advanced CO_2 reduction strategies, recovery of unsold food in collaboration with non-profit organizations, compensation of emissions through reforestation programs and carbon offsetting, and the use of certification systems such as ISO 20121 and EMAS to ensure compliance with sustainability goals.

3.1.3 Guidelines on Sustainable Event Organisation

Publication context. The 4th updated edition was published in August 2020 by the German Federal Ministry for the Environment, Nature Conservation and Nuclear Safety (BMU) and the German Environment Agency (UBA).

Objectives. The document provides a detailed framework for planning and managing sustainable events, with the goal of reducing environmental impact through practical measures and operational tools. The protocol aligns with Germany's Climate Action Plan 2050 and the European Green Deal, offering guidelines applicable to events of any size.

Key Areas. This protocol outlines thematic areas essential for planning environmentally and socially responsible events. Each area includes qualitative objectives and targets for emissions reduction:

- 'Energy and Climate': minimization of energy use, efficiency improvement, and offsetting unavoidable emissions
- 'Waste Management': strategies for reducing and properly handling waste
- 'Catering': sustainable food choices and waste reduction
- 'Water Management': efficient water use and treatment
- 'Mobility': sustainable transportation for participants and logistics
- 'Venue and Accommodation': selection based on sustainability criteria
- 'Procurement': environmentally conscious purchasing policies
- 'Guest Gifts': sustainable and meaningful gifting practices
- 'Communication': transparent and effective sustainability communication
- 'Social Aspects': equity, inclusiveness, and social responsibility

Innovations. The protocol enhances accessibility by implementing gender mainstreaming principles, ensuring the use of gender-neutral language, promoting balanced representation of experts across genders, and facilitating the participation of individuals with caregiving responsibilities through measures such as the provision of childcare services.

3.1.4 The Guide to Sustainable Events

Publication Context. The updated version was published in 2020 by the City of Stockholm.

Objectives. The document provides guidelines to reduce the environmental, economic, and social impact of events, aligning with the Sustainable Development Goals (SDGs) of the 2030 Agenda.

Key Areas. This protocol provides a comprehensive roadmap for event sustainability, covering all phases from planning to evaluation. The thematic areas are:

- 'Sustainability Management': organizational structures and responsibilities for sustainability
- 'Venue Selection': environmental impact, safety, and accessibility considerations
- 'Community Engagement': dialogue with local residents and businesses
- 'Sustainable Procurement': setting environmental criteria for suppliers and partners
- 'Food and Beverages': sustainable options and waste reduction strategies
- 'Health and Safety': ensuring well-being and protection of all stakeholders
- 'Sustainability Communication': informing stakeholders about sustainability efforts
- 'Event Evaluation': assessment and monitoring of sustainability outcomes

Innovations. The protocol introduces innovative tools to facilitate the adoption of sustainable measures, such as detailed checklists for each phase of the event, providing practical support for organizers, CO_2 emission offsetting, with suggestions to reduce and offset the carbon footprint of events, support for local businesses by encouraging local suppliers to reduce transport impacts and strengthen the local economy, and a guide to sustainable communication, with strategies to raise awareness among the public about the environmental impact of events (Fig. 2).

Protocol	Year	Focus	Approach	Tools/Innovations
Green Festival Roadmap 2030	2023	Music Festivals	Long-term strategy (Scope 1–2–3, 7 thematic areas)	Free toolkit, e-learning, case studies
GreenFEST	2019	Public Cultural Events	Environmental criteria in tenders (GPP)	Sustainability awards, certifications, CO_2 offsetting
German Guidelines	2020	General Events	Operational measures across 10 areas	Gender mainstreaming, accessibility, social inclusio
Stockholm Guide	2020	Urban Events	SDGs and local impact	Practical checklists, local economy support, communication

Fig. 2. Comparative overview of key sustainability protocols for cultural and festival events.

3.2 Sustainability Practices in European Music Festivals

This section offers a comparative overview of ten European music festivals that stand out for their commitment to sustainability. Each case is examined through a structured framework focused on transparency, energy, waste and materials, food and water, and mobility, with the aim of understanding how sustainability principles are applied across different contexts.

3.2.1 Boom Festival

Location, Duration, and Scale. Held in Idanha-a-Nova, Portugal, Boom Festival is a seven-day event that welcomes around 40,000 participants.

Transparency and Data Accessibility. Boom Festival regularly publishes detailed sustainability reports covering key impact areas such as energy, waste, and resource use. Data is made publicly available, supporting a culture of transparency and continuous improvement.

Key Areas. The festival's sustainability strategy is structured around targeted actions aimed at reducing environmental impact and fostering regenerative practices:

- 'Energy' relies entirely on renewable sources like solar panels and biofuel generators, enhanced by smart monitoring systems to optimize consumption.
- 'Materials and waste' is addressed through a zero-landfill policy, extensive composting, and initiatives that promote repair, reuse, and circularity.
- 'Food and beverage' focuses on organic, locally sourced vegetarian options, with a strong commitment to reducing packaging waste through compostable materials.
- 'Water management' includes free refill stations and a greywater recycling system used for irrigation.
- 'Travel and transport' is managed through car access restrictions, eco-shuttles from major cities, and a platform that facilitates carpooling.

3.2.2 Cambridge Folk Festival

Location, Duration, and Scale. The Cambridge Folk Festival takes place in Cambridge, United Kingdom. It spans four days and hosts approximately 14,000 participants.

Transparency and Data Accessibility. The festival outlines its sustainability commitments publicly on its website and conducts ongoing assessments of its carbon footprint and resource consumption, demonstrating a clear intent to monitor and improve its environmental impact.

Key Areas. Sustainability efforts at the Cambridge Folk Festival focus on practical interventions aimed at reducing the festival's ecological footprint:

- 'Energy' is managed through solar-powered stages and energy-efficient LED lighting, supported by hybrid generators to lower fuel consumption.
- 'Materials and waste' are addressed through a comprehensive recycling program, a ban on single-use plastics and disposable cutlery, and a returnable cup system to reduce waste.
- 'Food and beverage' initiatives include sourcing from local and sustainable suppliers and offering a growing range of plant-based options.
- 'Water management' is promoted through free refill stations to encourage the use of reusable bottles.
- 'Travel and transport' efforts include discounted train tickets, secure bicycle parking, and a shuttle service connecting key transport hubs to the venue.

3.2.3 Ciclope Festival

Location, Duration, and Scale. The event takes place in Berlin, Germany, spanning three days and welcoming approximately 5,000 participants.

Transparency and Data Accessibility. A dedicated sustainability section outlines the event's environmental policies, with annual reports detailing carbon offset initiatives to enhance transparency and accountability.

Key Areas. The event prioritizes sustainability through targeted initiatives across several key areas:

- 'Energy' is managed through renewable energy credits that offset all electricity usage, in collaboration with green energy suppliers.
- 'Materials and waste' policies include a strict ban on single-use plastics and the design of festival materials for reuse in future editions.
- 'Food and beverage' efforts focus on locally sourced vegetarian and vegan options to minimize.
- 'Water management' is supported by refill stations, eliminating the need for bottled water.
- 'Travel and transport' strategies encourage train and bus travel over flights, while a car-free festival area offers bike rental options to promote sustainable mobility.

3.2.4 DGTL Festival

Location, Duration, and Scale. The event takes place in Amsterdam, Netherlands, spanning three days and attracting approximately 50,000 participants.

Transparency and Data Accessibility. A detailed sustainability roadmap is published annually, supported by collaborations with circular economy experts to drive innovation. Publicly available data on energy consumption, waste management, and carbon footprint ensures transparency and accountability.

Key Areas. Sustainability initiatives are embedded throughout the event, addressing critical environmental aspects: several key areas:

- 'Energy' is fully renewable, with no diesel generators. Smart battery systems optimize usage, while partnerships with local energy cooperatives ensure clean power and grid stability.
- 'Materials and waste' are managed through a circular economy approach, achieving zero waste-to-landfill. Single-use plastics are eliminated in favor of biodegradable alternatives, and festival waste is repurposed into new production cycles. Compost toilets replace traditional chemical options, converting human waste into nutrient-rich compost.
- 'Food and beverage' offerings are entirely plant-based, with a focus on local and organic.
- 'Water management' includes refill stations to eliminate bottled water waste and clo-sed-loop systems to minimize overall consumption.
- 'Travel and transport' initiatives promote sustainable mobility, with electric shuttle buses connecting key transport hubs. No private car parking is available, encouraging public transportation, while attendee travel emissions are offset through carbon reduction programs.

3.2.5 Diluvio Festival

Location, Duration, and Scale. The festival takes place in Brescia, Italy, spanning two days and welcoming approximately 8,000 participants.

Transparency and Data Accessibility. Sustainability data is made available to attendees, with collaborations established with universities to study the festival's ecological footprint.

Key Areas. Sustainability initiatives focus on reducing environmental impact across multiple aspects:

- 'Energy' is managed through solar-powered installations and battery storage systems, with LED lighting minimizing overall consumption.
- 'Materials and waste' efforts emphasize composting organic waste and implemen-ting a reusable cup scheme across bars and vendors.
- 'Food and beverage' strategies prioritize local farmers and seasonal produce while eliminating plastic bottles in favor of refill stations.
- 'Travel and transport' initiatives include a bike-sharing program with docking stations near the venue and partnerships with train operators for discounted travel.

3.2.6 Festambiente

Location, Duration, and Scale. The event takes place in Grosseto, Italy, spanning ten days and hosting approximately 20,000 participants.

Transparency and Data Accessibility. An official sustainability report is published annually, complemented by workshops on ecological responsibility and activism.

Key Areas. The festival prioritizes long-term sustainability through targeted interventions:

- 'Energy' is supplied entirely by solar and wind power, with energy-efficient infrastructure reducing emissions.
- 'Materials and waste' are managed through a zero-waste strategy, high recycling targets, and a ban on non-biodegradable materials.
- 'Food and beverage' initiatives focus on locally sourced, organic food adhering to strict sustainability guidelines.
- 'Water management' includes conservation measures to reduce the festival's footprint.
- 'Travel and transport' efforts feature free shuttle services from nearby towns and discounted rates for attendees using public transportation.

3.2.7 Massive Attack Bristol

Location, Duration, and Scale. Held in Bristol, UK, the event lasts for one day and attracts approximately 34,000 participants.

Transparency and Data Accessibility. The festival partnered with the Tyndall Centre for Climate Change Research to analyze and publish live music event carbon footprints, with findings shared publicly as a resource for the industry.

Key Areas. Sustainability measures focus on minimizing environmental impact:

- 'Energy' is entirely battery-powered, charged with renewable energy. The largest battery, covered by a solar array, is displayed next to the stage, while electric trucks transport power units across the site.
- 'Materials and waste' initiatives enforce a no-landfill policy, dedicated bins for recycling vapes and batteries, compostable bathrooms, and a reusable cup scheme at all bars.
- 'Food and beverage' offerings are 100% plant-based, with multiple water refill stations promoting reusable bottles and accommodations for special dietary needs.
- 'Travel and transport' strategies include no general public parking, road closures, a partnership with Train Hugger to support UK reforestation, free e-bus transfers, an event shuttle within Bristol, and dedicated bike parking.

3.2.8 Paradise City Festival

Location, Duration, and Scale. The festival takes place in Steenokkerzeel, Belgium, spanning three days and welcoming approximately 43,000 participants.

Transparency and Data Accessibility. CO2 Logic provides extensive carbon footprint reporting, with a structured sustainability vision based on seven key pillars. A biodiversity assessment is planned to update the previous 2016 report.

Key Areas. The festival integrates sustainability into every operational aspect:

- 'Energy' management includes the Contrast Stage running on 99.22% solar power, algorithm-controlled generators to reduce surplus energy use, and 100% LED lighting.
- 'Materials and waste' initiatives feature reusable KioBox plates, off-site cleaned reusable cups, distributed pocket ashtrays, and recycled cardboard ashtrays. Production materials are reused whenever possible.
- 'Food and beverage' policies ensure a fully vegetarian menu, locally sourced and seasonal ingredients for food trucks, and non-alcoholic drinks served in large glass bottles to minimize single-use waste.
- 'Travel and transport' strategies promote night train schedules, electric shuttle buses between the venue and Vilvoorde train station, and high parking fees to discourage car use.

3.2.9 Terraforma

Location, Duration, and Scale. The event is held in Milan, Italy, spanning three days and attracting approximately 10,000 participants.

Transparency and Data Accessibility. While the festival has a sustainability section, it is somewhat hidden, and data is only approximate and aggregated. Visitor transportation choices are assessed through questionnaires, achieving a 98% participation rate.

Key Areas. Sustainability measures focus on low-impact solutions:

- 'Energy' is managed with a low-impact lighting system for the campsite, built with recycled materials and powered entirely by solar energy. LED and low-voltage lighting further reduce consumption, while electric cars and vans are used for staff and artist transportation.
- 'Materials and waste' initiatives enforce a plastic-free beverage policy, a no-straws policy, durable and reusable cups, biodegradable dinnerware, and waste sorting stations managed by 'Green Stewards.'
- 'Water management' strategies include self-closing valves on showers and sinks, alongside awareness campaigns promoting responsible water use.
- 'Travel and transport' solutions offer free shuttles from local train stations to Villa Arconati, along with car-sharing and carpooling promotions to minimize solo car trips.

3.2.10 We Love Green

Location, Duration, and Scale. The festival takes place in Bois de Vincennes, France, lasting three days and drawing approximately 80,000 participants.

Transparency and Data Accessibility. The festival features a dedicated "Green" sustainability section, conducting regular audits, measurements, and assessments to track progress. It also collaborates with associations and external partners to develop innovative eco-friendly solutions.

Key Areas. The event integrates circular economy principles across all operations:

- 'Energy' is supplied entirely by renewable sources through a partnership with Enercoop.
- 'Materials and waste' efforts enforce a ban on all single-use plastics, replacing them with reusable cups, plates, and cutlery. Waste collected through the EliSE program is reintegrated into new production cycles.
- 'Water management' features free refill stations to encourage reusable bottles and dry toilets to significantly reduce water consumption.
- 'Travel and transport' policies prohibit car parking near the festival, with strong incentives for public transportation as the preferred access mode.

3.3 Comparing Protocols and Festival Practices

The analysis of ten festivals and four sustainability protocols has revealed both critical gaps and emerging best practices in the implementation of sustainable event management. While festivals have made significant strides in adopting environmental measures, several aspects of the protocols remain underutilized or inconsistently applied.

A major gap lies in the long-term strategic planning recommended by frameworks such as the European Green Festival Roadmap 2030. Despite 9 out of 10 of the analyzed festivals publishing sustainability reports or commitments, many fail to develop a comprehensive, long-term strategy with measurable reduction targets for emissions, energy use, and resource consumption. Only 4 out of 10 of the festivals implement smart energy monitoring or optimized power management systems, indicating a disconnect between recommended strategies and actual execution. Furthermore, the lack of collaboration with external research institutions limits the ability of festivals to accurately assess their environmental impact, with only four out of ten festivals engaging in independent impact evaluations.

Another critical shortfall is the lack of focus on social sustainability and inclusivity, that is highlighted in the Guidelines on Sustainable Event Organisation. The prevailing focus remains on ecological responsibility, with limited recognition of how festivals can contribute to social well-being and community engagement. As a result, diversity, accessibility, and gender inclusivity are largely overlooked. Similarly, although some festivals engage in biodiversity conservation and land restoration, there is insufficient effort in ensuring that festivals positively impact local businesses, artisans, and communities. Despite their economic influence, most festivals fail to collaborate with local businesses or implement strategies that distribute economic benefits to surrounding areas. That said, early steps toward stronger community engagement are visible in food procurement: 6 out of 10 of the festivals analyzed prioritize local and seasonal food sourcing.

A further disconnect concerns communication and audience engagement. While festivals could serve as powerful platforms for environmental education and advocacy, few actively educate attendees on sustainability measures. The lack of transparent and structured sustainability communication limits the potential for festivals to influence long-term behavioral changes among participants.

In contrast to these gaps, several best practices have emerged as industry-leading sustainability initiatives that transcend festival size, duration, and location, positioning themselves as standardizable approaches for the sector.

Waste reduction strategies are at the forefront of sustainable festival management. Reusable cups, bans on single-use plastics, and comprehensive waste sorting systems are now widely implemented, with many festivals achieving zero-waste or circular economy approaches. Composting and waste reintegration programs are also gaining traction. Energy management has similarly become a cornerstone of sustainability efforts, with LED lighting and the integration of renewable energy sources appearing as standard features across most festivals. Some leading events have successfully deployed solar-powered stages, smart energy monitoring systems, and hybrid generators, significantly reducing their carbon footprint. Food sustainability initiatives are increasingly common, with a shift towards plant-based menus, local food sourcing, and food waste reduction programs. Nearly all festivals analyzed now offer vegetarian or fully plant-based catering, demonstrating a growing recognition of the environmental impact of food choices.

Mobility remains a complex challenge, yet strong alignment with sustainability protocols is evident. A significant 8 out of 10 of the festivals implement measures to reduce private car use, including shuttle buses, train partnerships, and public transport incentives. Additionally, 6 out of the 10 have eliminated or restricted parking, further encouraging low-carbon transportation methods.

Another key finding is the importance of transparency in driving sustainability improvements. Festivals that disclose their environmental impact through independent third-party assessments establish a higher standard of accountability and industry-wide progress. However, the lack of standardized sustainability reporting remains an obstacle, as many festivals still lack structured environmental impact assessments.

4 Conclusion

This study highlights the inconsistent implementation of sustainability protocols in music festivals, despite increasing environmental commitments. While waste reduction, renewable energy adoption, and low-carbon mobility solutions are becoming industry norms, long-term strategic planning, transparent reporting, and social sustainability remain critical weak points.

Looking ahead, enhancing data transparency, standardizing best practices, and fostering stronger industry-wide collaboration will be essential for ensuring that music festivals evolve into models of environmental and social responsibility. Furthermore, future research should focus on scaling such a framework across diverse festival sizes and regulatory contexts, ensuring greater standardization and long-term impact in the cultural events sector.

Acknowledgments. This research was carried out as part of the project MI AMI_BEATs (Better Equity Actions for Tomorrow sustainability), funded by Better Days and Alta Scuola Politecnica. It benefited from the collaboration of a multidisciplinary faculty group led by Marta Dell'Ovo, Silvia Ronchi, and Federico Dell'Anna, with contributions from Cristina Becchio, Eleonora Bruschi, Francesca Mattioli, Sara Monaci, Andrea Rebecchi, Louena Shtrepi, Sara Viazzo.

In addition, the research benefitted from the contribution of Carlo Pastore and Stefano Bottura, founders and directors of the MI AMI Festival.

Authors contribution. The present work is to be attributed in equal parts to the Authors.

References

1. Song, H.J., Lee, C.K., Kang, S.K., Boo, S.J.: The effect of environmentally friendly perceptions on festival visitors' decision-making process using an extended model of goal-directed behavior. Tour. Manag.Manag. **33**(6), 1417–1428 (2012)
2. Kim, N., Lee, K.: Environmental consciousness, purchase intention, and actual purchase behavior of eco-friendly products: the moderating impact of situational context. Int. J. Environ. Res. Public Health **20**(7), 5312 (2023)
3. Moore, T.: Audience Attitudes to the Environmental Impact of Live Events. A Greener Festival & Bucks New University (2013).
4. Sisson, A.D., Alcorn, M.R.: How was your music festival experience? Impacts on loyalty, word-of-mouth, and sustainability behaviors. Event Manag. **26**(4), 565–585 (2021). https://doi.org/10.3727/152599521X16288665119495
5. Ramli, N., Ghazali, A.R., Rashid, N.M., Nordin, A., Zamzuri, N.H.: The impact of eco-friendly perceptions on festival attendees' decision-making. Inf. Manag. Business Rev. **16**(3), 107–113 (2024)
6. Green Events.: Critics calling out music festivals for greenwashing. *Green Events*. https://www.greenevents.nl/news/critics-calling-out-music-festivals-for-greenwashing (2022, September 30)
7. European Green Festival Roadmap 2030.: YOUROPE. https://yourope.org/wp-content/uploads/2023/04/3f_european-green-festival-roadmap-2030_231018.pdf (2023).
8. GreenFEST – Green Festivals and Events through Sustainable Tenders.: https://www.greenfest.eu/download/20180226150205.pdf (2018).
9. Guidelines on Sustainable Event Organisation.: European Union. https://op.europa.eu/en/publication-detail/-/publication/4f8ccadf-2a03-11ef-9290-01aa75ed71a1/language-en (2020).
10. The Guide to Sustainable Events. (n.d.). Stockholm Business Region. https://foretagsservice.stockholm/globalassets/foretag-och-organisationer/foretagsservice/branscher/evenemangsrangor/guide-for-hallbara-evenemang/the-guide-to-sustainable-events.pdf
11. Boom Festival. Environment. https://www.boomfestival.org/environment
12. Cambridge Folk Festival. Environment. https://www.cambridgefolkfestival.co.uk/festival-information/environment
13. Ciclope Festival. Sustainability Protocol. https://www.ciclopefestival.com/sustainability/
14. DGTL. Sustainability. https://dgtl-festival.com/en/our-story/#sustainibility
15. Diluvio Festival. Sostenibilità. https://www.diluviofestival.it/sostenibilita
16. Festambiente. Ecofestival. https://www.festambiente.it/lecofestival/ecofestival/
17. BBC News. Climate change: Can music festivals be more eco-friendly? https://www.bbc.com/news/articles/ceqjlzd3w9no
18. Terraforma Festival. Archive. https://www.terraformafestival.com/archive/
19. We Love Green. Green. https://www.welovegreen.fr/green/?lang=en
20. Paradise City. Green. https://paradisecity.be/green

Investigating the Factors that Influence the Allocation of Nature-Based Solutions in Italy

Francesco Sica[1(✉)], Maria Rosaria Guarini[1], Francesco Tajani[1], and Pierluigi Morano[2]

[1] Department of Architecture and Design, Architecture Faculty, Sapienza University, Rome, Italy
francesco.sica@uniroma1.it
[2] Department of Civil, Environmental, Land, Building Engineering and Chemistry, Polytechnic University, Bari, Italy

Abstract. Nature-based Solutions (NbS), including artificial wetlands, raingardens, and reforestation, provide an effective strategy for enhancing living circumstances in rapidly expanding metropolitan areas. Nonetheless, empirical evidence suggests that the decision-making processes related to projects, especially in informal settlement improvement programs, are not favourable to the NbS incorporation. This study investigates the meta-functional relationships among the principal parameters influencing the concentration of Nature-based Solutions (NbS) in multidimensional regions. The methodology begin with a thorough examination of active NbS projects in Italy. The primary component starts to identify the key variables affecting NbS concentration. The principal driving forces are associated with the sustainable performance achievable through NbS implementation, alongside the luxury effect, which pertains to a city's productive prosperity. These factors can support a green transition plan for sustainable and equitable urban expansion by eco-system approach-design and programming public actions.

Keywords: NbS · Allocation study · Factorial analysis

1 Introduction

Nature-based solutions (NbS) including rain gardens, green roofs, and green pathways are increasingly preferred for bolstering urban resilience to climate change effects. These programs focus on the preservation, sustainable management, and restoration of modified or natural ecosystems. Cohen-Shacham et al. (2019) contend that they must adeptly and adaptively tackle societal challenges while concurrently improving public health and biodiversity [1]. These solutions improve living conditions in quickly growing cities because to their adaptability, offering a possible approach for advancing policy and ameliorating informal settlements [2].

Megacities globally accommodate significant proportions of their people in unregulated housing developments that pose a challenge for governments dedicated to enhancing the living conditions of residents in burgeoning cities [3]. Informal communities frequently emerge beyond planning regulations and provide restricted access to public services. The provision of inexpensive, climate-resilient, and sustainable choices is currently a critical priority for authorities at governmental level, especially in Africa and South Asia, where the majority of the global population living in informal settlements is located. This is particularly pertinent in light of the ongoing climate crisis.

To attain these aims, governments, international institutions, and scholars are increasingly advocating for the implementation of Nature-based Solutions (NbS) to support the lives of historically marginalized populations [4]. The implementation of these solutions is expected to enhance climate resilience and provide vital ecosystem services, including improved water quality, reduced flood risk, and mitigation of urban heat islands [5]. E.g., the restoration of mangroves, implementation of wetlands, and construction of interconnected gardens are framed as a promising strategy to deliver social, cultural, economic, and ecological benefits to historically marginalized communities [6].

European funding for NbS originates from various EU initiatives that promote sustainability, environmental preservation, and climate change adaptation. The Research and Innovation Programme (2021–2027) supports projects addressing climate change, biodiversity, and ecological resilience. The LIFE Programme advocates for nature conservation and climate action, particularly through Nature-Based Solutions for ecosystem preservation and climate adaptation. The EU Mission on Climate-Neutral and Smart Cities allocates resources for sustainable solutions in climate-neutral urban environments, including nature-based approaches for water management and urban renaturation. These offer extensive opportunities to finance nature-based initiatives focused on environmental sustainability and climate change adaptation. In 2015, the EU launched the Resilient Europe program, which selected 15 communities to test NbS measures like artificial wetlands, urban parks, and water front space to improve urban eco-environment [7].

Despite the increasing prevalence of Nature-based Solutions (NbS) in urban settings, substantial deficiencies persist in our understanding of their integration in a manner that aligns with existing policies [8]. This often results in pronounced disparities among the local population, fostering economic and social inequality within a singular territory. The allocation of NbS assets in a territory is influenced by essential multidimensional driving forces (economic, environmental, and social), which in turn dictate the significance of the NbS program relative to the territory's purpose. This poses a challenge of effective resource allocation for optimal territorial development, influenced by primary factors that affect territorial ecological transition [9].

The research seeks to examine the primary meta-forces that could affect the distribution of Nature-based Solutions (NbS) in urban areas addressing their ecological transition. The identification of the driving forces influencing investment allocation in natural projects anticipates equitable decision-making frameworks grounded in principles of environmental, social, and economic justice. This meta-analytical study focusses on Italian cities through the application of Principal Component Analysis (PCA), and the initial findings of this ongoing research are intended for dissemination.

The work is organised into the following sections: Sect. 2 (Materials and Method) presents a comprehensive review of the distribution principles for NbS according to pertinent literature, along with a description of the methodology employed for the meta-analytical analysis of the primary factors influencing the distribution of NbS in Italy; Sect. 3 delineates the case-study results accompanied by a succinct explanation, while Sect. 4 articulates the conclusions of the work.

2 Materials and Method

The World Bank originally proposed the idea of Nature-based Solutions (NbS) in its 2008 report titled "Biodiversity, Climate Change and Adaptation: Nature-based Solutions in World Bank Investments" [10]. As part of the framework for climate change and development strategies, NbS emphasizes how humans and nature can live in harmony through measures taken to preserve, manage, and restore ecosystems in a sustainable way [11]. Environmental restoration, ecological engineering, ecological infrastructure, and green infrastructure are all examples of NbS measures. However, these are not the only types of measures that should be considered. Ecological infrastructure is defined as the collection of conditions and the combination of actions that are required to preserve, improve, and increase the operation of ecosystem services [12].

From a pragmatic perspective, several Nature-based Solutions (NbS) can be strategically implemented to achieve similar objectives or anticipated outcomes [13]. NbS provide several functions, such as enhancing ecosystem services, creating habitable urban environments, and fostering social inclusion [14]. In urban ecology, NbS emphasises the ecological significance of urban green spaces. Its objective is to restore impaired urban ecosystems by establishing green infrastructure, hence facilitating enhanced solutions to ecological and environmental issues [15].

What socio-economic and environmental factors may affect the equitable distribution of nature-based investments? This question will be addressed by presenting a concise assessment of the primary functional correlations established from empirical evidence in sub-Sect. 2.2. The 2.3 provides an explanation of the principle component search algorithm.

2.1 Review of NbS Allocation Drivers

Aligning NbS with other policies for infrastructure provision and NbS development is key to ensuring that they are fair and connected with the needs and priorities of residents [16]. Little is known, however, about the decision-making processes and values that orient how key stakeholders perceive these systems within the realm of policy and practice of government-sponsored NbS projects [17]. The literature reveals that to ensure that greening projects are successful, cost-effective and fair, these solutions must be embedded in the local culture and decision-making processes [18]. For instance, proposing the use of these solutions within some of the largest megacities in the Global South requires the recognition that similar systems have been used for centuries for urban water management and agricultural irrigation systems in the Global South within specific governance models and aligned with traditional and knowledge systems [19].

Championing the use of NbS in urbanized, or not, settlements, several authors have delved into how nature is perceived and approached by residents and governmental officers in these contexts. Studies have shown that the relationships between residents and nature are site-specific and underpinned by social and economic factors [20]. Others have argued that accounting for the needs of local residents is key, since people value nature differently and their priorities may change over time depending on their life conditions [21]. The literature of values indicates that different perspectives of nature and preferences for specific types of NbS can lead to vastly different behaviors toward greening initiatives [22]. A prevalent observation is that prosperity and educational attainment are positively connected with increased abundance [23] and enhanced diversity of urban vegetation [24].

A range of complementing socio-technological theories has been suggested to clarify the robust correlation between socio-economic status and urban vegetation patterns. The relationship between urban landscapes and nature has been handled, anticipating various configurations of interactions like that shown in Fig. 1 below. It outlines the conflicts between the landscape environment and the socio-technical and innovative forces that can shape developmental pathways [25].

Considering this theoretical framework, the analytical procedure is formulated (Principal Component Analysis, PCA), as detailed in the subsequent Subsect. 2.3, for the identification of the primary factors influencing NbS allocation within the region.

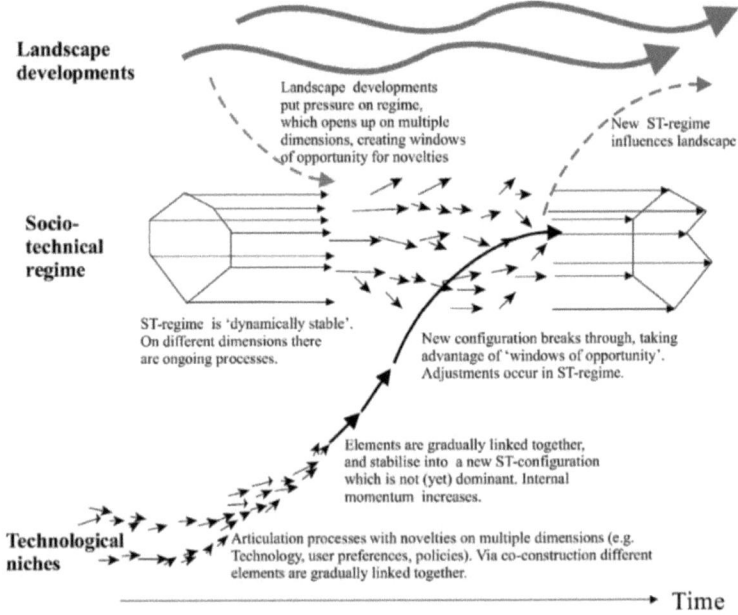

Fig. 1. Innovative system developments from a dynamic and multi-level perspective [25].

2.2 PCA for NbS Allocation

Principal Component Analysis (PCA) is a multivariate analysis technique that simplifies and synthesises a huge set of indicators into a smaller, more relevant subset, while minimising information loss.

According to Kendall's classification, these methods can be categorised into two groups: *a*) methods of dependency analysis; *b*) methods of interdependency analysis. The (a) encompasses variance and regression analysis; (b) encompasses various forms of correlation and contingency analysis. Kendall categorised PCA, which presupposes a linear relationship among n observed variables and k factors derivable a posteriori, as a multivariate analysis method.

The PCA model aims to synthesise n observed variables z_j (where $j = 1, 2,..., n$) using k a posteriori defined variables (*factors*), with the condition that $k \leq n$ results.

The primary attribute of a posteriori-defined variables is their linear independence, which enhances their structural clarity. The factors synthesising the n observed variables can be categorised into two groups: a) common, if they are present in all or only in some of the observed variables; b) unique, if they are present in only one observed variable.

If we then denote $F_1, F_2,..., F_m$ as the common factors and $U_1, U_2,..., U_n$ as the unique factors, each observed variable z_j can be expressed in the form (with $j = 1, 2, ..., n$):

$$z_j = a_{j1}F_1 + a_{j2}F_2 + \cdots + a_{jm}F_m + a_j U_j \tag{1}$$

Assuming the variable z_j can assume N values over N observations (with $i = 1, ..., n$), Eq. (1) can be articulated as:

$$z_{ji} = a_{j1}F_{1i} + a_{j2}F_{2i} + \cdots + a_{jm}F_{mi} + a_j U_{ji} \tag{2}$$

This is followed by the determination of the coefficients $a_{j1}, a_{j2}, \ldots, a_{jm}$ for each observed variable for the factors that were previously identified as common. Each coefficient denotes the relative significance of the individual analytical element.

To address (2), Thurstone's Centroid approach, that has been utilised in the proposed case study, can be employed to ascertain the matrix F, recognised as the matrix of factorial weights.

This is followed by Sect. 3 on the illustration of the case study analysed in order to rank the key parameters influencing the distribution of public investments in nature-based solutions in the Italian setting, specifically in a collection of cities where this type of project was discovered.

3 Case-Study

To identify the primary characteristics that, as of March 2025, have impacted the dispersion and subsequent concentration of Nature-based Solutions (NbS) in Italy, the quantity of NbS action programs executed in Italian cities was used as the dependent variable (z_i, where $i = 1,..., 14$). The NbS programs are derived from the census conducted by the EU Repository of Nature-Based Solutions *Oppla*, which facilitated the survey of 54 NbS throughout 14 Italian cities (1. Reggio Calabria, 2. Bari, 3. Rome, 4. Siena, 5. Lucca, 6. Genoa, 7. Bologna, 8. Piacenza, 9. Ferrara, 10. Padua, 11. Mantua, 12. Trento; 13. Milan, 14. Turin) resulting in the identification of 14 NbS action programs.

In this study, the 14 NbS action program were valuated with several related metrics (z_j, whit $j = 1,..., 7$), selected as control variables, including: Population Density (Pop-Den), URBanised area per-capita (URB), GDP, per-capita GDP (perGDP), per-capita

Green Area (GREEN), per-capita INCome (perINC), Sustainable Development Index (SDI). The SDI reflects the efficacy of the NbS program in attaining the SDG in relation to the development of the reference territory. The calculations were conducted based on the indicators gathered from the 14 cities where the NbS programs were evaluated, as provided by the OECD for review. The numbers for each indicator are determined for the period of time between 2022 and 2025, taking into account the most recent information that is available in OECD and *Il Sole24Ore* datasets.

Due to the absence of data on the relevant indicators for the 14 census cities on the *Oppla* website, the final collection of cities utilised in the principal component analysis comprises 7 cities: 1. Bari, 2. Roma, 3. Genoa, 4. Bologna, 5. Padua, 6. Milan, 7. Turin.

At follow, the Table 1 provides the matrix values of the variables z_j (PopDen, Urb, GDP, perGDP, GREEN, perINC, SDI) values and that of the dependent variable z_i (N° NbS). Table 2 presents NbS Italian initiatives that can be monitored within the *Oppla* case studies section. These are Nature-based Solutions (NbS) action programs mostly executed in urban settings and big metropolitan areas, focused chiefly on the defence against and mitigation of environmental hazards, including flood risk reduction.

Figure 2 depicts the geographical distribution of the interventions analysed by *Oppla* throughout the survey region of Italy.

Table 1. Values Matrix.

Cities	N° NbS [n.]	PopDen [ab/sqKm]	Urb [sqm/ab]	GDP [USD]	perGDP [USD/ab]	GREEN [sqm/ab]	perINC [€/ab]	SDI [n.]
1. Bari	2	643	155	19,604	29,993	63	22,419	44
2. Rome	6	697	162	196,135	57,107	90	27,206	52
3. Genoa	8	569	104	28,405	44,578	81	23,659	53
4. Bologna	1	387	139	39,193	53,599	98	27,626	56
5. Padua	2	872	258	22,105	45,379	127	27,936	44
6. Milan	10	1591	195	283,296	60,267	106	35,282	50
7. Turin	15	1005	153	67,728	45,367	58	25,224	46
Dev. St.	5	393	49	104,055	10,120	24	4,187	5
Max	15	1,591	258	283,296	60,267	127	35,282	56
Min	1	387	104	19,604	29,993	58	22,419	44
Avg	6	823	167	93,781	48,041	89	27,050	49

Table 2. NbS Italian projects.

Cities	NbS projects	Tot.
Bari	L. Braille Public Garden	2
	Lama Balice protected area	
Reggio Calabria	Bergamot production system	1
Rome	Let's Crop the Diversity (LCD)	6
	Greening Rome for human and ecosystem health	
	Transition Planning - Parco Agricolo	
	CES assessment through social media data in the urban parks of Rome (IT)	
	Participatory Reconversion Workshop	
	Reinventing the traditional use of rural commons through social and environmental innovation	
Siena	Co-Creation of an URBiNAT Healthy Corridor for Siena	1
Lucca	Improve hydraulic capacity of canal system	3
	Retention/sedimentation basin	
	Buffer strips along canals in the area of Lake Massaciuccoli	
Genoa	Green Façade Pilot Project, INPS	8
	Green Wall	
	Bioswale	
	Infiltration Basin	
	Rain Garden	
	Drought-resilient orchard	
	Slope afforestation	
	Tree groups and green areas	
Bologna	VEG-GAP Information Platform	1
Piacenza	Processed tomato supply chain	1
Ferrara	Green Infrastructure and Ecosystem Services for Urban Plan	2
	LIFE AGREE	
Padua	Biophysical analysis of public trees in Padova	2
	Uforest Case Study: WOWnature	
Mantua	Forest-habitat biodiversity payment scheme	1
Trento	Mapping and assessing ecosystem services to support urban planning in Trento	1

(*continued*)

Table 2. (*continued*)

Cities	NbS projects	Tot.
Milan	Environmental recovery of a quarry ATEg20	10
	Parco Nord Milan	
	NbS for urban regeneration	
	Greening Milan: Innovating Urban Spaces Through Nature-based Solutions	
	Environmental recovery of a quarry ATEg32 - Gaggiano, Trezzano sul Naviglio, Zibido San Giacomo	
	Environmental recovery of a quarry ATEg30 Pero	
	Environmental recovery of a quarry ATEg15 Paderno Dugnano	
	Flood Retention Basins of Lura River	
	Constructed wetlands	
	Integrated valuation of a nature-based solution for water pollution control	
Turin	Valdocco Vivibile: NbS for liveable and climate-proof neighbourhoods	15
	Farfalle in ToUr	
	Green indoor and outdoor walls	
	"OrtoMobile" - micro gardens in boxes	
	Didactic box gardens in schools	
	New green roof at WOW	
	Pollinator friendly garden	
	New soil production in Sangone Park	
	Butterfly gardens for schools and disadvantaged people	
	Mirafiori Castle's ruins recovery and new planting	
	Gardens integrated within housing	
	Green corridor and local natural heritage enhancement	
	Mirafiori Sud Living Lab	
	Gardens in Cascina Piemonte	
	Aquaponics test system	

3.1 PCA Implementation

The identification of the primary factors for the j-th variables is executed using Thurstone's centroid approach, which addresses PCA scenarios. The aforementioned algorithm is predicated on a sequence of following steps:

a) Creation of the normalised value matrix (X) for the analysis variables of dimensions [n × N] utilising the expression:

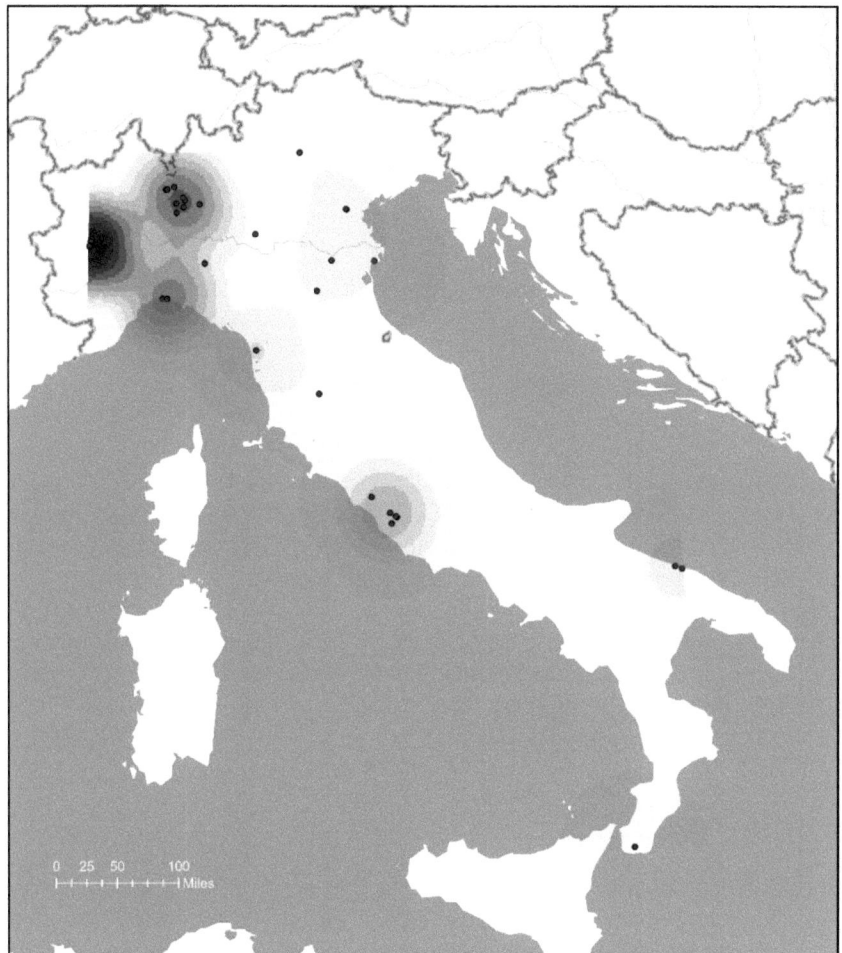

Fig. 2. Geographical-density distribution of NbS initiatives in Italy.

$$z_i = \frac{x_{ij} - \overline{x_j}}{\sigma_j} \qquad (3)$$

where:

z_i = i-th NbS programme in Italian study cities (with $i = 1, ..., 7$);

x_{ij} = value of the j-th variable for the i-th programme NbS (with $i = 1,..., 7$; $j = 1,..., 7$);

$\overline{x_j}$ = avg value of the numerical series of the j-th analysis variable;

σ_j = standard deviation of the numerical series of the j-th variable.

b) construction of the factorial weight matrix (F) of dimension $[1 \times 7]$.

Subsequently, the matrix (X) of dimension $[7 \times 7]$ containing the variables' values normalised according to (3). Conversely, Table 3 displays the weights (f_j) of the analytical variables organised in the matrix (F) of dimensions $[1 \times 7]$.

$$X = \begin{bmatrix} 0.4587 & \cdots & 1.2015 \\ \vdots & \ddots & \vdots \\ 0.4616 & \cdots & 0.6037 \end{bmatrix}$$

Table 3. PCA outputs.

	PopDen	Urb	GDP	perGDP	GREEN	perINC	SDI
f_j	0.78	0.76	0.86	0.82	0.83	0.72	0.89

The Sustainable Development Index (SDI) emerges as the most significant factor ($f_{SDI} = 0.89$) influencing the concentration of Nature-based Solutions (NbS) in Italian cities, followed closely by the economic wealth indicator, GDP ($f_{GDP} = 0.86$). The latter indicates a correlation between the feasibility of implementing NbS and the economic resources available, relative to the cities' productive capacity. The variable exerting the minimal impact on the concentration of NbS is per capita income (perINC), with a f_{SDI} of 0.72. This suggests that Nature-based Solutions (NbS) must be rendered as available as feasible to the populace, irrespective of wealth disparities, to uphold the tenets of environmental, social, and economic justice.

4 Conclusions

Urban planners and politicians are increasingly interested in Nature-based Solutions (NbS), acknowledging it as a crucial tool for rejuvenating urban ecosystems and bolstering urban resilience. Despite the growing acknowledgement of NbS, there exists a paucity of research clarifying their contribution measures to urban policy and planning, with the majority of studies predominantly featuring qualitative analyses and comparative evaluations of specific examples. Thus, a difficulty arises in thoroughly elucidating the effects of NbS measures on urban growth [26].

The research not only shows the efficacy of Nature-based Solutions (NbS) measures but also proposed an investigative methodology that considers the NbS perspective based on principal driving factors. The findings indicated that NbS are crucial for enhancing urban sustainability. In alignment with [26], it is imperative to customise NbS to the unique characteristics and conditions of a city's production system. The results corroborate this perspective and may serve as a source of inspiration for the strategic implementation of NbS measures. This strategy will promote the creation of new spaces that are both of high quality and contextually pertinent, aligned with current economic and productive characteristics that meet public and private requirements.

The conducted analysis signifies a preliminary stage of continuous effort, and the described technique necessitates additional clarification to enhance the outcomes, for instance, by integrating a sensitivity analysis [27]. The next phase will entail a comprehensive examination of NbS concentration across several analytical scales, particularly within specific cities, employing the detailed cases of Turin and/or Milan. This seeks to clarify the elements that may affect the distribution of particular Nature-based Solutions, notably the developmental green-trajectories of a region [28].

Acknowledgments. The current study is part of Sapienza University of Rome's minor research project, "ECO-think: Inte-grating the ECOsystem services by nature in urban environment" and the ongoing research P.R.I.N. Project 2022: "INSPIRE—Improving Nature-Smart Policies Through Innovative Resilient Evaluations" (Grant number: 2022J7RWNF). All authors contributed equally.

Disclosure of Interests. The authors have no competing interests to declare that are relevant to the content of this research.

References

1. Cohen-Shacham, E., et al.: Core principles for successfully implementing and upscaling nature-based solutions. Environ Sci Policy **98**, 20–29 (2019). https://doi.org/10.1016/j.envsci.2019.04.014
2. Wolff, E., Rauf, H.A., Hamel, P.: Nature-based solutions in informal settlements: a systematic review of projects in Southeast Asian and Pacific countries. Environ Sci Policy **145**, 275–285 (2023). https://doi.org/10.1016/j.envsci.2023.04.014
3. UN Habitat III. New urban agenda (A/RED/71/256. ed.). Quito: United Nations (2017)
4. Lechner, A.M., Gomes, R.L., Rodrigues, L., Ashfold, M.J., Selvam, S.B., Wong, E.P., Raymond, C.M., Zieritz, A., Sing, K.W., Moug, P., Billa, L., Sagala, S., Cheshmehzangi, A., Lourdes, K., Azhar, B., Sanusi, R., Ives, C.D., Tang, Y.-T., Tan, D.T., Gibbins, C.: Challenges and considerations of applying nature-based solutions in low- and middle-income countries in Southeast and East Asia. Blue-Green Syst. **2**, 331–351 (2020). https://doi.org/10.2166/bgs.2020.014
5. Sengupta, S.: Nature-based solutions for climate change. In: Cohen-Shacham, E., Walters, G., Janzen, C., Maginnis, S. (eds.), Nature-Based Solutions to Address Global Societal Challenges (p. 15). IUCN International Union for Conservation of Nature (2016)
6. Laeni, N., Ovink, H., Busscher, T., Handayani, W., van den Brink, M. A transformative process for urban climate resilience: The case of water as leverage resilient cities Asia in Semarang, Indonesia. In: de Graaf-van Dinther, R. (ed.) Climate resilient urban areas, Palgrave studies in climate resilient societies, pp. 155–173. Springer International Publishing, Cham (2021). https://doi.org/10.1007/978-3-030-57537-3_8
7. Frantzeskaki, N.: Seven lessons for planning nature-based solutions in cities. Environ Sci Policy **93**, 101–111 (2019)
8. O'Sullivan, F., Mell, I., Clement, S.: Novel solutions or rebranded approaches: evaluating the use of nature-based solutions (NBS) in Europe. Front. Sustain. Cities **2**, 572527 (2020). https://doi.org/10.3389/frsc.2020.572527
9. Pineda-Pinto, M., Frantzeskaki, N., Nygaard, C.A.: The potential of nature-based solutions to deliver ecologically just cities: Lessons for research and urban planning from a systematic literature review. Ambio (2021). https://doi.org/10.1007/s13280-021-01553-7

10. Randrup, T.B., Buijs, A., Konijnendijk, C.C., Wild, T.: Moving beyond the nature-based solutions discourse: Introducing nature-based thinking. Urban Ecosyst. **23**, 919–926 (2020). https://doi.org/10.1007/s11252-020-00964-w
11. Reguero, B.G., et al.: Nature-based solutions for natural hazards and climate change. Front. Environ. Sci. **10**, 1101919 (2022). https://doi.org/10.3389/fenvs.2022.1101919
12. Pan, H.Z., et al.: Contribution of prioritized urban nature-based solutions allocation to carbon neutrality. Nat. Clim. Chang. **13**, 862 (2023). https://doi.org/10.1038/s41558-023-01737-x
13. Cousins, J.J.: Just nature-based solutions and the pursuit of climate resilient urban development. Landsc. Urban Plann. **247**, 105054 (2024). https://doi.org/10.1016/j.landurbplan.2024.105054
14. Kabisch, N., Frantzeskaki, N., Pauleit, S., Naumann, S., Davis, M., Artmann, M., Haase, D., Knapp, S., Korn, H., Stadler, J., Zaunberger, K., Bonn, A.: Nature-based solutions to climate change mitigation and adaptation in urban areas: perspectives on indicators, knowledge gaps, barriers, and opportunities for action. Ecol. Soc. **21**, 39 (2016)
15. Bush, J., Doyon, A.: Building urban resilience with nature-based solutions: How can urban planning contribute? Cities **95**, 102483 (2019). https://doi.org/10.1016/j.cities.2019.102483
16. Diep, L.: Climate adaptation through housing: Examples of effective interventions for informal settlements (working paper). Habitat for Humanity (2023). https://www.habitat.org/sites/default/files/documents/climate-adaptation-through-housing-report.pdf
17. Torres, P.H.C., et al.: Just cities and nature-based solutions in the Global South: a diagnostic approach to move beyond panaceas in Brazil. Environ Sci Policy **143**, 24–34 (2023). https://doi.org/10.1016/j.envsci.2023.02.017
18. Boossabong, P.: Governing the policy network on urban agriculture in Bangkok: The role of social capital in handling cooperation and conflicts (PhD Thesis). University College London (2014)
19. Mashiyi, S., Weesakul, S., Vojinovic, Z., Sanchez Torres, A., Babel, M.S., Ditthabumrung, S., Ruangpan, L.: Designing and evaluating robust nature-based solutions for hydro-meteorological risk reduction. Int. J. Disaster Risk Reduct. **93**, 103787 (2023). https://doi.org/10.1016/j.ijdrr.2023.103787
20. Andal, A.G.: Greening in the margins: children's perception on the sustainability of urban gardening in informal settlements in San Jose del Monte City, Philippines. In: Ademović, N., Mujčić, E., Akšamija, Z., Kevrić, J., Avdaković, S., Volić, I. (eds.) Advanced Technologies, Systems, and Applications, vol. VI, pp. 721–734. Springer International Publishing, Cham (2021). https://doi.org/10.1007/978-3-030-90055-7_58
21. Balvanera, P., Pascual, U., Christie, M., Baptiste, B., Guibrunet, L., Lliso, B., David.: The role of the values of nature and valuation for addressing the biodiversity crisis and navigating towards more just and sustainable futures. Zenodo (2022). https://doi.org/10.5281/ZENODO.6418971
22. Pascual, U., Balvanera, P., Anderson, C. B., Chaplin-Kramer, R., Christie, M., González-Jiménez, D., Martin, A., Raymond, C. M., Termansen, M., Vatn, A., Athayde, S., Baptiste, B., Barton, D. N., Jacobs, S., Kelemen, E., Kumar, R., Lazos, E., Mwampamba, T. H., Nakangu, B., Zent, E.: Diverse values of nature for sustainability. Nature **620**, 813–823 (2023). https://doi.org/10.1038/s41586-023-06406-9
23. Drillet, Z., Fung, T.K., Leong, R.A.T., Sachidhanandam, U., Edwards, P., Richards, D.: Urban vegetation types are not perceived equally in providing ecosystem services and disservices. Sustainability **12**(5), 2076 (2020). https://doi.org/10.3390/su12052076
24. Nowak, D.J., Ellis, A., Greenfield, E.J.: The disparity in tree cover and ecosystem service values among redlining classes in the United States. Landsc. Urban Plan. **221**, 104370 (2022). https://doi.org/10.1016/j.landurbplan.2022.104370
25. Geels, F.W.: Understanding the dynamics of technological transitions. A co-evolutionary and socio-technical analysis (Thesis/Disertation). https://www.osti.gov/etdeweb/biblio/20330346

26. Marusic, B.G., Dremel, M., Ravnikar, Z.: A frame of understanding to better link nature-based solutions and urban planning. Environ Sci Policy Policy **147**, 47–56 (2023). https://doi.org/10.1016/j.envsci.2023.05.005
27. Sica, F., Tajani, F., Sáez-Pérez, M.P., Marín-Nicolás, J.: Taxonomy and indicators for ESG investments. Sustainability **15**(22), 15979 (2023). https://doi.org/10.3390/su152215979
28. Scorza, F., Pilogallo, A., Saganeiti, L., Murgante, B., Pontrandolfi, P.: Comparing the territorial performances of renewable energy sources' plants with an integrated ecosystem services loss assessment: A case study from the Basilicata region (Italy). Sustain. Cities Soc. **56**, 102082 (2020). https://doi.org/10.1016/j.scs.2020.102082

Introducing Indicators for Assessing the Readiness of Buildings for Greening Interventions

Lorenzo Diana(✉) , Federica Melotta , Francesca Pia Pondo , Roberto Castelluccio , and Francesco Polverino

DICEA, University of Naples Federico II, 80125 Napoli, Italy
lorenzo.diana@unina.it

Abstract. The adaptation of the built environment to climate change requires strategic interventions that enhance urban resilience against increasing environmental risks. Adaptation measures emphasize targeted solutions to minimize climate-related vulnerabilities. Among these, Nature-Based Solutions (NBS), such as green roofs and vegetated facades, play a crucial role in improving thermal regulation, storm water management, and urban biodiversity. However, their effectiveness depends on large-scale implementation guided by systematic evaluation criteria rather than isolated applications. This study presents a methodological framework for assessing buildings' suitability for green roof implementation, integrating technical feasibility, environmental impact, and economic viability. The approach consists of defining intervention areas, categorizing relevant parameters, and prioritizing buildings through a multi-criteria evaluation model. Advanced tools, including Geographic Information Systems (GIS) and environmental modeling, support data-driven decision-making. A structured weighting system, based on literature review, field observations, and expert consultations, ensures an objective evaluation of key feasibility indicators such as structural capacity, roof conditions, and accessibility. The methodology facilitates the identification of high-priority buildings where green roofs can be most effectively implemented, optimizing both environmental benefits and economic investments. By providing a scalable decision-support tool, this study contributes to advancing climate adaptation strategies and promoting sustainable urban transformations. The proposed methodology is applied on a case-study area in the city of Naples (Italy).

Keywords: Greening intervention · Transformability indicators · Technical Feasibility · Decision support system

1 Introduction

Adapting the built environment to climate change represents an increasingly urgent and complex challenge, requiring diversified strategies to address the multiple risks associated with the alteration of climatic balances. Unlike mitigation, which for many years has been linked to a model of sustainable development—widely promoted in global policies but with evident limitations in effectively slowing global warming—adaptation focuses on targeted interventions aimed at reducing the vulnerability of urban and built systems to climate impacts. However, the adaptation measures, to be truly effective, must address a broad range of risks that currently undermine urban resilience, extending beyond the management of heat waves and the improvement of building energy efficiency and system performances. A comprehensive, multi-risk urban perspective must also consider the increasing risks of flooding, the rise of vector-borne diseases favored by changing temperatures, declining air quality, and negative effects on public health. These interconnected challenges highlight the need for integrated, multi-sectoral solutions that can enhance the overall sustainability and resilience of urban environments.

In this context, the widespread application of Nature-Based Solutions (NBS) [1] emerges as a particularly effective approach to climate adaptation. Such an approach is not merely reactive but also proactive and multifunctional. Green infrastructure interventions, such as green roofs, vegetated walls, and the integration of urban green spaces, contribute not only to thermal regulation of buildings and the reduction of the urban heat island effect [2] but also to sustainable storm water management, reduction of air pollution, enhancement of urban biodiversity, and overall improvements in public health [3]. To ensure that these interventions generate a significant and systemic impact, however, it is essential that they be implemented on a large scale and guided by strategic selection criteria. A fragmented and uncoordinated approach, where these solutions are applied in isolated instances without urban planning considerations based on structured large-scale greening strategies, risks reducing them to virtuous but ultimately insignificant measures. The large-scale implementation of greening solutions in urban contexts must address multiple challenges, ranging from the need for adequate public space to accommodate interventions, to the integration of measures across both public and private buildings, and the securing of funding necessary to initiate such strategies.

A crucial aspect in guaranteeing the effectiveness and large-scale adoption of greening interventions is the development of tools that can assist decision-makers in the strategic selection of the most suitable areas and buildings for transformation, as well as support designers in the various phases of project definition.

Over the past decades, numerous support tools have been developed to assist decision-makers in assessing the effectiveness of retrofitting efforts affecting the existing built environment, particularly through multi-criteria evaluation approaches. One of the first notable tool is EPIQR [4, 5], which assesses retrofitting strategies, costs, and activities aimed at reducing energy consumption while improving indoor environmental quality. Similarly, the Design Quality Indicator (DQI) [6] employs user questionnaires to provide qualitative evaluations of building quality, drawing inspiration from Vitruvius' classical principles [7].

While widely recognized certification systems like LEED, BREEAM, GREEN GLOBES, and CASBEE [8–11] provide valuable frameworks for evaluating and accrediting building interventions, they primarily focus on assessing retrofitting measures rather than offering precise recommendations on optimal strategies and intervention timelines.

Future advancements of such kind of tools should integrate multiple variables, including climate vulnerability, available surface areas, potential for heat island reduction, water management capacity, and economic feasibility. Advanced technologies, such as

Geographic Information Systems (GIS), can play a fundamental role in storing and managing built environment data, facilitating informed decision-making processes. Furthermore, environmental simulation models and artificial intelligence-based optimization algorithms can provide valuable support in assessing intervention priorities and developing tailored design strategies for urban contexts. Additionally, the integration of climatic, morphological, and energy-related data through digital platforms enables a more dynamic and adaptive approach, enhancing the effectiveness of design choices and streamlining the implementation of impactful greening strategies.

This article aims to contribute to these objectives by implementing a methodological framework based on specific indicators designed to assess buildings' suitability for the adoption of greening strategies. The objective of this paper is to define indicators and their integration into an effective tool designed to support and guide the selection of buildings that should be considered for greening interventions, based on their technical feasibility and readiness for implementation. The interpretation of results obtained across large urban areas or extensive real estate assets allows for the prioritization of interventions, while the detailed analysis of individual cases provides valuable insights for practical, site-specific, architectural design applications. By adopting such an approach, urban adaptation strategies can be optimized to maximize resilience, sustainability, and overall environmental performance in the face of ongoing climate challenges.

2 Methodology

The methodology adopted to achieve the established objectives is structured into several phases (Fig. 1):

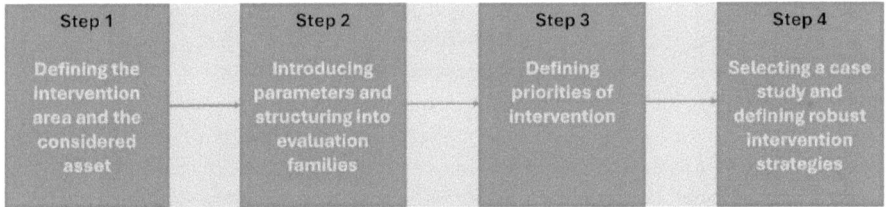

Fig. 1. Workflow of the various phases on which the methodology of the research is based.

2.1 Step 1: Defining the Intervention Area and the Considered Asset

The first methodological step involves identifying the intervention area. This area must possess specific urban, landownership, typological, and morphological characteristics that allow for the implementation of comprehensive strategies capable of generating an overall benefit for the selected site. The selection process must consider the broader urban context, ensuring that the proposed interventions align with the existing spatial and regulatory framework.

Depending on the characteristics of the context—whether urban or peri-urban—its primary function, and the ownership structure (public, private, or mixed), different strategies can be implemented to optimize the intervention's effectiveness. A well-defined intervention area enables a targeted approach that maximizes the potential impact of greening strategies while addressing the specific constraints and opportunities present in the built environment.

Once the area has been defined, an extensive data collection and documentation process must be initiated. This step involves storing key information regarding the urban environment that will be subject to greening interventions, whether open spaces or buildings. For instance, in cases where implementing greening strategies in open spaces is impractical—such as in dense urban fabrics with narrow streets and limited public spaces—attention may shift exclusively to buildings. In this scenario, the collected data should be referred to the case study buildings and include general information (year of construction, ownership, function), geometric attributes (building height, covered surface area, plot perimeter), construction characteristics (building materials, structural typology, percentage of openings in facades, overall state of maintenance), and environmental factors (local climatic conditions, surrounding urban morphology).

The collected data, recorded for each building through structured survey forms, can be systematically stored on a Geographic Information System (GIS) platform. This digital archive facilitates rapid visualization and analysis of the gathered information, supporting an informed decision-making process and enabling a more strategic and data-driven approach to the planning and implementation of greening interventions.

2.2 Step 2: Introduction of Parameters and Structuring into Evaluation Families

In the second methodological phase, a structured list of parameters is established, serving as a fundamental tool for comprehending the predisposition of buildings to undergo transformative interventions that consider the integration of green areas or vegetated portions. Subsequently, these parameters are rigorously determined for the analyzed buildings. When greening interventions are considered, the main possible interventions to be considered are the implementation of green roofs, the installation of vertical green facades, or the replacement of impermeable paving materials with permeable alternatives, thereby fostering a more ecologically attuned built environment. For the sake of brevity and analytical clarity, the present paper exclusively focuses on the realm of green roof applications.

From an operational point of view, the definition of these parameters, aimed at assessing the readiness of buildings to undergo greening interventions based on green roofs, originates from the theoretical framework introduced by Sommese and Diana [12]. This framework delineates the context, environmental, and urban parameters, as well as those directly referred to the architectural and technological characteristics of the buildings, that show the most profound influences on the definition of the design variables associated with green roof systems. The specificities of this framework, alongside the intricate ontologies between parameters and variables, are comprehensively illustrated in Figs. 2 and 3.

Starting from the assumptions established by [12], this paper explores a possible implementation of the framework. Building upon the established ontologies within this

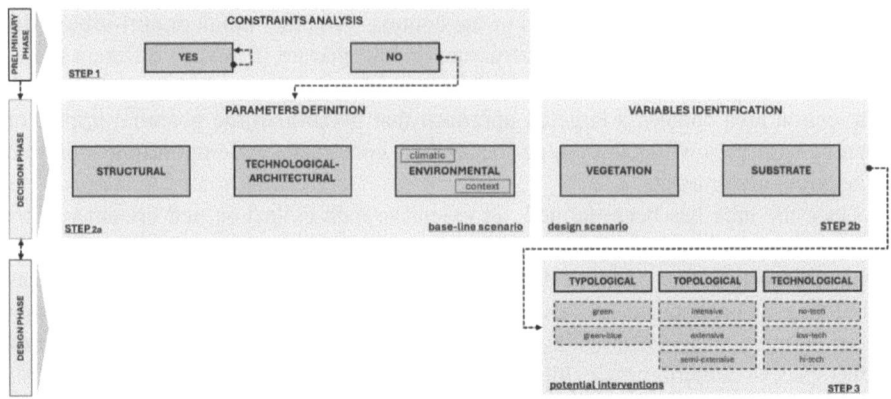

Fig. 2. Framework for green roofs (Picture taken from [12]).

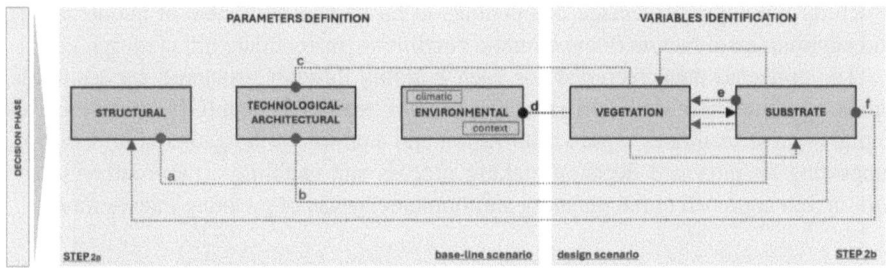

Fig. 3. Ontologies between parameters and variables (Picture taken from [12]).

conceptual structure connecting the dependencies between parameters and design variables, a diversified set of indicator families is formulated to delineate the readiness of buildings for green roof interventions. Parameters are measurable entities while indicators are synthetic measures derived from one or more parameters to represent or evaluate an aspect or phenomenon in a comparable way [13]. These categories encompass technical feasibility indicators, environmental feasibility indicators, economic feasibility indicators, as well as indicators assessing the environmental, economic, and social benefits derived from such interventions. While all these indicator families collectively contribute to the formulation of a synthetic index of transformability, the present study is limited solely to the aspects related to the technical feasibility (Table 1).

Concerning especially the indicators constituting the evaluation of technical feasibility, these are further categorized into two principal domains: structural and construction-related aspects on the one hand, and technological and architectural characteristics on the other. Within the structural and construction-related domain, particular attention is paid to indicators related to the year of construction (unit: year), the construction technology of the roof slab (Vaults without tie rods, Vaults with tie rods, Beams with a deformable slab, Beams with a semi-rigid slab, Beams with a rigid slab), and the load-bearing capacity of the roofing structure (unit: %). Meanwhile, within the technological and architectural domain, the main indicators include the slope of the roof surface (unit: °),

Table 1. Indicator families for the definition of an index of transformability for green roofs.

Technical Feasibility		Tot
Environmental Feasibility		Tot
Economic Feasibility		Tot
Environmental Benefits		Tot
Social Benefits		Tot
Economic Benefits		Tot
	Index of transformability	*TOT*

its state of maintenance (very poor, poor, sufficient, good, excellent/recently renovated), the overall height of the roof (unit: m), the incidence of usable roof area (unit: %), the incidence of accessible roof area (unit: %), the presence and the mean effective drainage area for a single downspout (unit: m^2), as well as the existence of a water supply system on the rooftop (yes/no). Some indicators are considered as costs, where a lower value is considered better, while some others are considered as benefits, where a higher value is considered better. The various indicators with the reference ID are listed in Table 2.

These parameters collectively delineate the potential and constraints inherent in the implementation of green roofing solutions, thereby fostering a more nuanced understanding of their applicability in existing buildings.

Table 2. Indicators' ID and Name for the technical Feasibility family

Indicator family	Indicator domain	Indicator code	Indicator Name	Weight
Tech. Feasibility	Structural and construction	In01	YEAR	0.08
Tech. Feasibility	Structural and construction	In02	CONST. TECH	0.11
Tech. Feasibility	Structural and construction	In03	LOAD CAPACITY	0.16
Tech. Feasibility	Technological and architect	In04	SLOPE	0.08
Tech. Feasibility	Technological and architect	In05	MAINTENANCE	0.12
Tech. Feasibility	Technological and architect	In06	HEIGHT	0.07
Tech. Feasibility	Technological and architect	In07	USABLE AREA	0.14
Tech. Feasibility	Technological and architect	In08	ACCESSIBILITY	0.13
Tech. Feasibility	Technological and architect	In09	DRAINAGE	0.07
Tech. Feasibility	Technological and architect	In10	WATER SUPPLY	0.04

2.3 Step 3: Defining Priorities of Intervention

Based on what was discussed above, the various technical feasibility indicators, briefly introduced in Sect. 2.2, can be employed—if calculated for the various buildings selected within the studied area—to establish a priority scale for interventions. This priority scale is based on an objective comparative evaluation of the various buildings analyzed. The evaluation method follows a analytic hierarchy process (AHP) multicriteria approach [14], which allows results expressed in different units of measurement to be converted into comparable numerical values, enabling assessments and comparisons.

This approach is particularly advantageous because it facilitates the comparison between purely quantitative indicators—expressed as numerical values with defined measurement units—and qualitative indicators, which do not inherently deliver numerical values. The ability to integrate these two types of data within the same assessment framework ensures a more comprehensive and structured decision-making process, allowing for a nuanced and multidimensional evaluation of feasibility.

The transformation of the various indicators' results follows a standardized normalization process. Quantitative indicators are adjusted to a scale ranging from 0 to 1, while qualitative indicators are aligned to the same scale through the definition of preference relationships. For instance, for the indicator "roof maintenance condition", a qualitative judgment of "very poor" corresponds to a score of 0, a "poor" condition corresponds to 0.25, a "sufficient" condition to 0.50, a "good" condition to 0.75, and an "excellent/recently renovated" condition to 1. The same approach is followed for the indicator "construction technology of the roof slab" and "existence of a water supply system on the rooftop". The assessment of the indicators relies on in-situ measurements as well as the retrieval of information from municipal technical departments and the heritage preservation authority.

Since the various indicators hold different levels of significance, a refined weighting system has been developed based on pairwise comparison matrix [15]. The assigned weights are derived from established literature in the field of large-scale rapid visual screening assessments, empirical field assessments, and expert deliberations and can be seen in Table 2, last column. The multicriteria method thus ensures that each building is assessed on a harmonized scale, enabling decision-makers to prioritize interventions in a rational and structured manner. This process is particularly beneficial in urban planning and architectural decision-making, where multiple conflicting factors—such as cost, technical feasibility, and long-term durability—must be considered simultaneously. On this basis, buildings that obtain higher overall scores will be those with a greater readiness for green roof installations, as they demonstrate higher values in terms of feasibility and benefits. Focusing solely on the study of technical feasibility, buildings with higher results indicate greater potential for green roof implementation, as these interventions would be easier to carry out and, intuitively, more cost-effective.

2.4 Step 4: Selecting a Case Study and Defining Robust Intervention Strategies

The application of the selected indicators to the various buildings within the study area allows, as established in Sect. 2.3, for the definition of a priority intervention scale. This procedure is essential for a strong and sustainable planning of greening interventions at the neighborhood scale, ensuring that resources are allocated effectively. However, beyond providing a broad framework for the definition of the priority of intervention based on technical feasibility, the interpretation of the specific results for each individual building offers designers valuable support in formulating precise, robust, and context-sensitive green roof intervention strategies.

For instance, a given value of "load-bearing capacity of the roofing structure" provides the designer with a clear indication of the most suitable type of green roof for that specific building—whether it should be an intensive green roof, an extensive one, or a combined green/blue roof system [16]. Additionally, factors such as the accessibility of the roof surfaces further influence the choice for a green roof typology that requires intensive maintenance interventions over time. In this way, the proposed methodology serves a dual purpose: on one hand, it aids decision-makers in establishing intervention priorities at a large scale, and on the other, it provides architects and engineers with a flexible, data-informed tool to optimize their design choices based on both structural, technological, and typological feasibility and long-term maintenance considerations.

3 Case Study

The area selected for the application of the methodology introduced in Sect. 2 is located in the historic center of the city of Naples. The historic center of Naples notably lacks ample, pedestrian-accessible green areas making it an ideal case study for implementing the proposed approach. The presence of many historic public buildings with large internal courtyards, cloisters, open spaces, and roof surfaces allows for considering potential integration of various greening strategies on horizontal building components or paved surfaces. The area is situated within the Forcella district (Fig. 4) and is enclosed by Piazza Garibaldi, Via D. Cirillo/Via Carbonara/Via A. Poerio, Via Foria, Via Duomo, and Corso Umberto. This area covers approximately 400,000 m^2 and has an estimated built coverage of approximately 60%, with a total constructed surface of 244,600 m^2. The buildings selected for the application of the methodology reach a total surface area of around 50,000 m^2, representing 12% of the overall study zone. These buildings are typically arranged around large, open courtyards or cloisters, which, on average, account for 25% of each lot's footprint. Many of the examined public buildings exhibit considerable wear and deterioration, with some possessing noteworthy historical and architectural value, officially recognized by the Ministry of Cultural Heritage. Due to these architectural and cultural constraints, interventions on vertical façades and monumental courtyards' paving for many buildings should be excluded. Within the studied area, the buildings considered for the assessment here presented are shown in Fig. 5.

The application of the indicators to the various buildings selected in the case study area are depicted in Table 3. The values in the second-last column represent the Technical Feasibility Index, obtained by averaging the results of the individual indicators weighted according to the values shown in Table 2. The Technical Feasibility Index for the analyzed case studies ranges from 0.38 for case study ID04 – Castel Capuano to 0.68 for case study ID08 – Ex Ospedale della Pace – Lazzaretto.

Based on the obtained results—although limited to the family of indicators related to technical feasibility—a priority scale for intervention can be established. This priority scale of intervention supports a generalized definition of measures across the entire study area, ensuring substantial results in terms of adaptation to climate change. Within this framework, buildings with a higher T.F. Index should be given higher priority for intervention (corresponding to lower values in the last column of Table 3). It is important to note that due to a lack of available data, some values for Indicator "In03 – load

Fig. 4. The case study area of the historical center of Napoli (Picture taken from [17]).

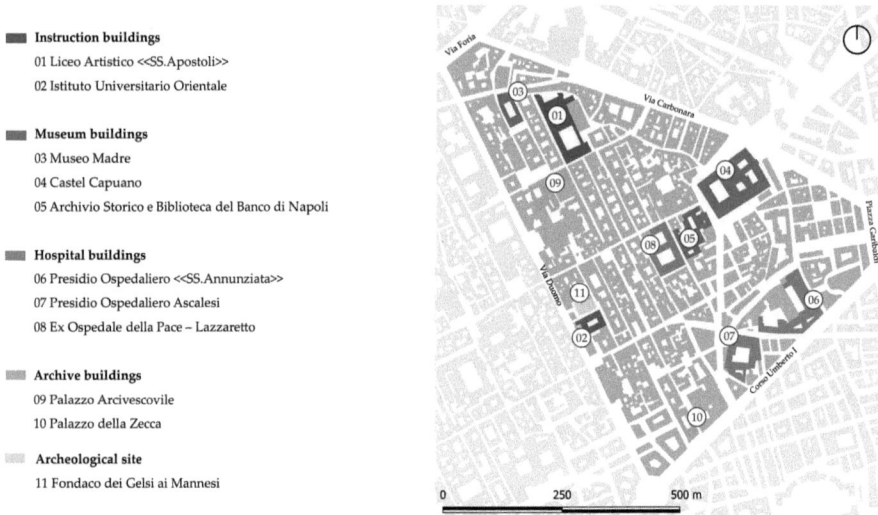

■ **Instruction buildings**
01 Liceo Artistico <<SS.Apostoli>>
02 Istituto Universitario Orientale

■ **Museum buildings**
03 Museo Madre
04 Castel Capuano
05 Archivio Storico e Biblioteca del Banco di Napoli

■ **Hospital buildings**
06 Presidio Ospedaliero <<SS.Annunziata>>
07 Presidio Ospedaliero Ascalesi
08 Ex Ospedale della Pace – Lazzaretto

▦ **Archive buildings**
09 Palazzo Arcivescovile
10 Palazzo della Zecca

▦ **Archeological site**
11 Fondaco dei Gelsi ai Mannesi

Fig. 5. List of the buildings studied in the area considered.

capacity" could not be determined. Consequently, a default value of 0 was assigned in these cases.

Among the various analyzed buildings, case study ID06 – Ospedale dell'Annunziata has been selected for a deeper analysis related to the design interventions, previously partially published in [12, 18, 19]. A site plan of the green roof intervention can be seen in Fig. 6. An intensive and walkable green roof has been designed on the portion of the building facing via A. Ranieri (east side). This choice is supported by the value of indicator "In08 – Accessibility" (0.67 points, resulting from an accessible surface area of the roof equal to 75%), indicator "In03 – Load Capacity" (0.85 points, based on the ratio between the design moment induced by a hypothetical intensive green roof and the resistant moment of the main current structural roof section, which is 65%),

Introducing Indicators for Assessing the Readiness 203

Table 3. Results of the various indicators for the calculation of the index of technical feasibility

Buil ID	In01	In02	In03	In04	In05	In06	In07	In08	In09	In10	T.F index	Priority
01	0.91	0.25	1	0	0.75	0.5	0	0.15	0.09	0	0.40	8
02	0.52	0.25	0*	1	1	0.67	0.33	1	0.59	1	0.58	2
03	1	0.50	0*	1	1	0.83	0.12	0.47	0.21	1	0.53	3
04	0.52	0.44	0*	0.42	0.25	0.58	1	0.11	0.40	0	0.38	10
05	0.39	0.25	0*	1	0.75	0.58	0.40	0	0.46	1	0.40	9
06	0.82	0.25	0.85	0.47	0.75	0	0.29	0.67	0	1	0.53	4
07	0.59	0.37	0*	1	0.75	0.25	0.39	0.71	0.40	1	0.49	6
08	0.91	0.25	1	0.75	0.25	0.75	0.93	1	0.32	0	0.68	1
09	0	0.50	0*	0.38	0.25	1	0.76	0.19	0.78	1	0.42	7
10	0.48	0.50	0*	1	0.25	0.75	0.48	1	1	0	0.52	5

and indicator "In10 – Water Supply" (YES). The last substantial intervention on the roof structure dates back to the post-World War II period ("In01 – Year" is equal to 0.87 point, derived from the year of last intervention 1950) when a system of steel beams and hollow brick blocks was implemented. On the other hand, the portion of the building facing via Egiziaca features an extensive and non-walkable green roof due to the presence of sloped roof, demonstrated by the value of the indicator "In04 – Slope" (0.47 points, resulting from a value of the slope of the roof of 11° 54′ 0″) and the indicator "In07 – Usable Area" (0.29 point, due to a low usable surface area of 29%).

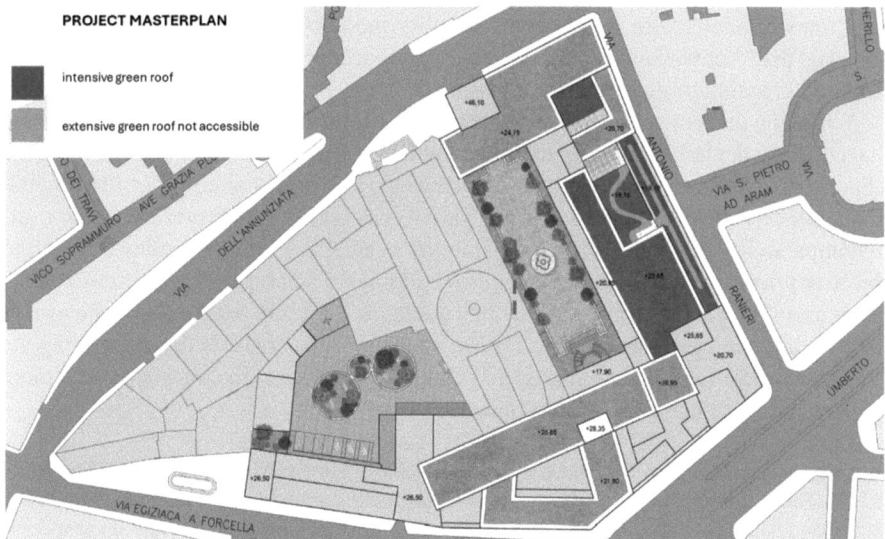

Fig. 6. Green roof intervention for Ospedale dell'Annunziata (Picture taken from [12]).

4 Conclusions

In conclusion, this paper presents a methodological approach for the evaluation of the technical feasibility of implementing green roofs on buildings located within dense central urban areas. The primary aim was to develop a decision-support tool that can assist stakeholders—such as urban planners, architects, and public administrators—in assessing the suitability and prioritization of green roof interventions. This tool is particularly relevant in highly dense urban areas, where the availability of open and green spaces is severely limited, and strategies for enhancing urban sustainability are urgent.

To reach this goal, a set of indicators, that have been derived from a framework of both urban and building-specific parameters and design-related variables, was defined to enable the assessment and comparison of the various case studies examined using a multicriteria method. The evaluation is grounded in technical feasibility of installing green roofs. The proposed methodology has been applied to a representative central area of Naples, characterized by the presence of numerous public buildings and properties managed by large institutions, such as the curia.

At a more detailed level, the interpretation of the results of the various indicators for the individual case study supports designers in defining the most suitable design intervention solutions at the building scale.

It is particularly significant that this approach addresses the potential of underutilized rooftop surfaces of historic buildings, where conventional greening strategies on monumental facades and open spaces may be infeasible, due to cultural and urban constraints. On the contrary, the roofs, often hidden behind large and tall parapets, tend to be poorly maintained or covered exclusively with dark rubber membranes. These surfaces still represent a preferred target for intervention, opening new avenues for the ecological enhancement of heritage-sensitive areas. Whitin the various buildings that have been analyzed, the "Ex Ospedale della Pace – Lazzaretto" (ID08) emerges as the most transformable, with a technical feasibility index of 0.68. A detailed analysis of Ospedale dell'Annunziata (ID06), ranked as the fourth priority building, along with the proposed greening project, has been presented.

While the current set of indicators provides a solid foundation, further refinement is needed, particularly regarding the improvement of normalization techniques and the refinement of the weighting system. Nonetheless, any potential errors in the normalization process are distributed across the various case studies, thus preserving the overall comparability of results. This comparability is essential for establishing a clear and objective priority scale among the examined buildings. The proposed prioritization scale serves as a strategic planning tool, enabling guidance for future interventions and a more effective and targeted deployment of green roofs in urban contexts. By identifying the most technically feasible and impactful solutions, this approach contributes to a more resilient and sustainable urban environment.

Funding. This research was founded by the European Union EU Next Generation Italian PRIN 2022 PNRR Programme under the "Greenwork—An interdisciplinary framework for urban health and urban resilience enhancement based on greening strategies on buildings and open spaces" project, CUP: E53D23019110001.

References

1. Frantzeskaki, N.: Seven lessons for planning nature-based solutions in cities. Environ Sci Policy **93**, 101–111 (2019). https://doi.org/10.1016/j.envsci.2018.12.033
2. Santamouris, M.: Cooling the cities - A review of reflective and green roof mitigation technologies to fight heat island and improve comfort in urban environments. Sol. Energy **103**, 682–703 (2014). https://doi.org/10.1016/j.solener.2012.07.003
3. Kosareo, L., Ries, R.: Comparative environmental life cycle assessment of green roofs. Build. Environ. **42**(7), 2606–2613 (2007). https://doi.org/10.1016/j.buildenv.2006.06.019
4. Bluyssen, P.M.: EPIQR and IEQ: Indoor environment quality in European apartment buildings. Energy Build. **31**(2), 103–110 (2000). https://doi.org/10.1016/S0378-7788(99)00024-9
5. Balaras, C., Dascalaki, E., Droutsa, P., Kontoyiannidis, S.: EPIQR – TOBUS – XENIOS – INVESTIMMO, European Methodologies & Software Tools for Building Refurbishment, Assessment of Energy Savings and IEQ. In: 33rd International HVAC Congress, Belgrade, Serbia, December 4–6, pp. 20–29 (2002). https://doi.org/10.13140/2.1.3759.4405
6. Whyte, J., Gann, D.: Design Quality Indicators: work in progress. Build. Res. Inf. **31**(5), 387–398 (2003). https://doi.org/10.1080/0961321032000107537
7. van der Voordt, T.: Quality of design and usability: a vitruvian twin. Ambient. Construido **9**(2), 17–29 (2009)
8. Lee, E.: Indoor environmental quality (IEQ) of LEED-certified home: Importance-performance analysis (IPA). Build. Environ. **149**, 571–581 (2019). https://doi.org/10.1016/j.buildenv.2018.12.038
9. Kubba, S.: Book Source type Book ISBN 978-012810433-0 Publisher Elsevier Inc. Original language English View less Handbook of Green Building Design and Construction: LEED, BREEAM, and Green Globes: Second Edition. 2016
10. Kumar, R., Aggarwal, V., Gupta, S.M.: Innovative sustainable design and techniques: a review of literature. Springer Nat. Singapore (2024). https://doi.org/10.1007/978-981-99-2676-3
11. Kujundžić, K., Stamatović Vučković, S.: Evolution of the concept of health and wellbeing through the international sustainability rating systems of buildings. Lect. Notes Networks Syst. **707** (LNNS), 360–367 (2023). https://doi.org/10.1007/978-3-031-34721-4_39
12. Sommese, F., Diana, L.: A holistic framework for the implementation of green roofs on existing buildings: a case study in the Mediterranean climate of Naples. Build. Environ. **274**, 112811 (2025). https://doi.org/10.1016/j.buildenv.2025.112811
13. Palumbo, M.: Definizioni, approcci e usi degli indicatori nella ricerca e nella valutazione. In: Bezzi, C., Cannavò, L., Palumbo, M. (eds.) Costruire e usare indicatori nella ricerca sociale e nella valutazione, FrancoAngeli, Milano (2010)
14. Keeney, R.L., Raiffa, H.: Decisions with Multiple Objectives: Preferences and Value Tradeoffs. New York: Wiley (1976). https://doi.org/10.1017/CBO9781139174084
15. Saaty, T.L.: The Analytic Hierarchy Process: Planning Setting Priorities, Resource Allocation. McGraw-Hill, New York (1980)
16. Sommese, F.: Nature-based solutions to enhance urban resilience in the climate change and post-pandemic era: a taxonomy for the built environment. Buildings (2024). https://doi.org/10.3390/buildings14072190
17. Diana, L., Sciuto, G., Colajanni, S.: Greening Intervention Strategies for the Enhancement of Urban Resilience of Public Buildings and Open Spaces.In: Corrao, R., Campisi, T., Colajanni, S., Saeli, M., Vinci, C. (eds.) Proceedings of the 11th International Conference of Ar.Tec. (Scientific Society of Architectural Engineering). Colloqui.AT.e 2024. Lecture Notes in Civil Engineering, vol. 611, pp. 283–299. Springer, Cham (2025). https://doi.org/10.1007/978-3-031-71863-2_18

18. Diana, L., Sommese, F., Ausiello, G., Polverino, F.: New green spaces for urban areas: a resilient opportunity for Urban Health. In: Cheshmehzangi, A., Sedrez, M., Zhao, H., Li, T., Heath, T., Dawodu, A. (eds.) Resilience vs Pandemics. Innovations in Public Places and Buildings, pp. 37–53. Springer Nature Singapore (2024). https://doi.org/10.1007/978-981-99-8672-9
19. Sommese, F., Diana, L.: Il ruolo degli ospedali monumentali nelle strategie di adattamento al cambiamento climatico. Urban. Inf. **306**(2), 132–134 (2022)

Towards a Methodological Framework for Evaluating Urban Resilience: Spatial Indicators for Addressing Complex Urban Systems

Ilaria Cazzola[✉], Benedetta Giudice, Manuela Rebaudengo, and Valeria Vitulano

Interuniversity Department of Regional and Urban Studies and Planning, Politecnico di Torino, Torino, Italy
{ilaria.cazzola,benedetta.giudice,manuela.rebaudengo, valeria.vitulano}@polito.it

Abstract. Resilience is a crucial factor in addressing contemporary challenges in urban development and planning, as cities increasingly face negative impacts of climate change, natural hazards, and rapid urbanization. Particularly, urban resilience is a complex, dynamic, and multilayered concept that refers to a city's ability to withstand and recover from both sudden shocks and long-term stresses. This study aims to develop a catalog of resilience indicators to support planning processes, and intends to test it in a real case study in future research. The methodological approach follows a structured process: (i) a literature review to identify and refine resilience indicators, (ii) the construction of an indicator catalog based on selected sources, and (iii) the application of selected indicators to a case study. The city of Turin (Italy) is proposed as a potential urban context for testing the catalog with a targeted set of indicators, with a focus on the northeastern districts of the city. The application process will involve mapping and analyzing resilience indicators to evaluate and monitor urban transformations resulting from plans and projects, including those linked to the Italian recovery fund (PNRR). This research contributes to the development of tools for evaluating urban resilience through a context-specific and planning oriented approach that seeks to balance natural and human capital.

Keywords: Urban Resilience · Resilience Indicators · Urban Planning

1 Introduction

Resilience plays a crucial role in urban development and planning, as cities face an increasing range of challenges, such as climate change, natural hazards, and rapid urbanization. Over time, various resilience concepts have emerged in various fields [1], resulting in no universally accepted definition. The increasing focus on resilience is also reflected in the expanding body of research on the topic. In urban context, "urban resilience" can be understood as a complex, dynamic and multi-layered concept that highlights a city's ability to endure and recover from both immediate shocks and long-term stresses. In particular, we adopt the definition given by Meerow et al. [2] which frames urban resilience as: «the ability of an urban system and all its constituent socio-ecological and socio-technical networks across temporal and spatial scales to maintain or rapidly return to desired functions in the face of a disturbance, to adapt, to change and to quickly transform systems that limit current or future adaptive capacity» [2]. This definition provides a thorough understanding of urban resilience by highlighting the interconnectedness of urban systems in their different dimensions. Furthermore, this perspective underscores the importance of considering all the components – social, ecological and technical – when applying resilience thinking [3] and resilience evaluation. However, many urban resilience frameworks often overlook these different dimensions, particularly in evaluation, even though, as initially stated, resilience is a complex issue and ideally, all aspects of an urban system should be considered in a resilience evaluation framework [4]. Additionally, the transformative character of resilience has the potential to reframe planning practices and interventions [5]. In this sense, the concept of transformative resilience helps to identify disturbances as drivers of positive change [6], allowing to incorporate in planning practices a more holistic and forward-looking approach to fostering resilient urban environments.

A comprehensive interpretation of resilience in urban systems allows for prioritizing radical and non-linear transformations within the urban fabric, fostering continuous adaptation. The dynamic nature of resilience can activate institutional, organizational and social change rather than simply acting as passive resistance. To achieve this, it is necessary to adopt an interdisciplinary approach that leverages diverse fields to promote systemic modification, with flexibility and responsiveness in governance being essential to effectively implement transformative resilience strategies over the medium to long term across multiple sectors and levels [7, 8].

These considerations have fostered the willingness to understand how these transformative statuses of urban systems could be measured to better support planning processes. In this context, the research aims to conceptualize urban and metropolitan territories as a social-ecological system, understood as dynamic and interdependent systems composed of both social (human) and ecological (natural) components, closely linked through feedback mechanisms. Cities, in view, are not isolated entities but open systems embedded in a complex web of relationships with their surroundings [9–11]. Urban environments, from this perspective, consist of a set of interconnected subsystems: people, communities, economies, societies and cultures [12]. To achieve this, a catalog of resilience indicators has been developed, with the aim of testing it in a real case study in future research. In particular, this paper outlines the methodological steps taken to create the catalog and introduces the city of Turin (Italy) as a potential site for application. The practical implementation of the indicator catalog – through the selection of a specific set of indicators based on a context-specific approach – could be a valuable tool for evaluating urban resilience. This evaluation can focus on the transformations resulting from plans and projects, including those associated with the Italian Recovery Fund (*Piano Nazionale di Ripresa e Resilienza* - PNRR).

The paper is structured as follows. Section 2 presents the research framework. The methodological approach adopted is outlined in Sect. 3, while Sect. 4 briefly introduces the case study proposed for the application. Section 5 details the organization of the catalog. Finally, Sect. 6 offers some conclusive remarks regarding possible implementation.

2 Research Framework: The RETURN Project

This study is part of the project RETURN - Multi-Risk sciEnce for resilienT commUnities undeR a changiNg climate, funded by the European Union Next-GenerationEU. The project aims to enhance the understanding of environmental, anthropogenic and natural risks, especially in the context of climate change. It seeks to develop improved tools and strategies for risk prevention and monitoring, as well as approaches for climate change adaptation and mitigation, improving the use of data and technology and strengthening the connection between research and practical applications.

The project involves collaboration among 26 different private and public entities and is organized into interlinked thematic areas known as "spokes", reflecting its multidisciplinary nature. There are four vertical spokes (VS) that concentrate on specific risks: water, ground instability, earthquakes and volcanoes, and environmental degradation. Three transversal spokes (TS) connect these VS to develop methods and tools for assessing and predicting impacts on urban and metropolitan settlements, critical infrastructure and communities. Additionally, a diagonal spoke (DS) is dedicated to creating innovative methods and models for predicting future climate conditions (Fig. 1).

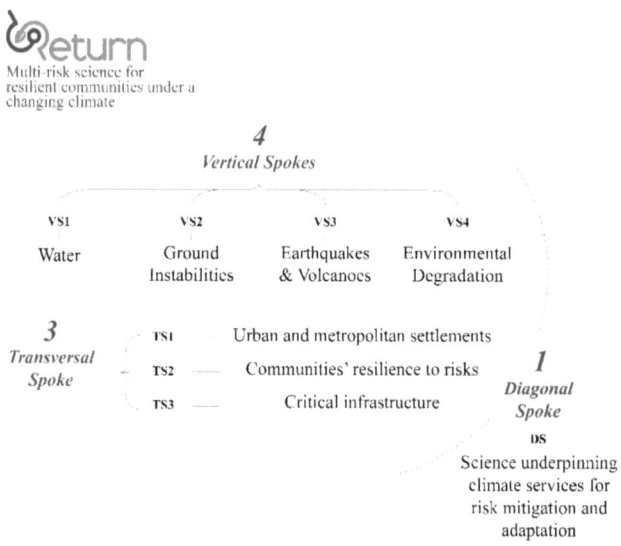

Fig. 1. Structure of the RETURN project articulated in thematic spokes.

More specifically, this research is part of TS1 - Urban and metropolitan settlements. The theme focuses on developing tools and approaches for effective adaptation through multi-risk analysis. It aims to reduce vulnerability and exposure while ensuring the continued functioning of buildings and urban systems during extreme events.

3 Methodological Approach

The goal of this study is to develop and test an effective tool for measuring urban resilience. The methodology is organized into three main phases, preceded by Phase 0 that focuses on defining the research objective and process. Each phase contains several sub-steps (Fig. 2).

Phase 0 involves formulating a precise research objective and question, delineating the study boundaries, developing a conceptual framework, identifying data sources, and defining relevant keywords and search queries. Conducting a preliminary exploration of keywords is essential to ensure that the queries align with the research objective.

Once the research process has been defined, the next step involves conducting the literature review (Phase 1). The purpose of this stage is twofold. First, it aims to explore the extent of existing scientific literature on approaches and methodologies for measuring urban resilience. This involves searching academic databases, applying filters, removing duplicate records, and selecting sources through a two-stage screening process: an initial review of titles and abstracts, followed by a comprehensive full-text reading and qualitative content analysis to ensure the inclusion of only relevant sources in the database. Initially, the search is limited to the Scopus database, a methodological choice shared by all participating research units. Scopus is selected for its capacity to support structured keyword searches and queries, which enhances the transparency and replicability of the process. Moreover, this approach ensures that the review is not limited to sources already familiar to the research components. The multidisciplinary coverage provided by Scopus further strengthens the review's comprehensiveness. In a subsequent phase, grey literature and institutional databases are consulted to address specific gaps observed during the initial review. The second objective of the review is to develop a catalog of indicators. This process involves structuring a table with key information fields. Indicators are then systematically extracted from the selected papers and grouped by thematic categories to help identify and eliminate redundant indicators. Similar indicators need to be standardized and harmonized in terms of terminology and units of measurement. The catalog is progressively updated, with missing information filled in from additional sources as needed. A pre-selection of indicators is made through group discussion to exclude those that are clearly irrelevant. This process also helps identify potential gaps and allow for the inclusion of indicators from non-scientific databases and grey literature, if necessary.

Once this initial extended version of the catalog is completed, a second selection is conducted through group discussion, during which clearly defined criteria are applied to evaluate the eligibility and relevance of each indicator. The outcome is a refined and more targeted catalog.

Based on the selection of case studies, a manageable number of significant indicators will be further chosen from the catalog for testing, taking into account contextual specificity, data availability, required processing methods, and data processability [13]. The catalog is intended to be a flexible tool and allows for the addition of other indicators if the conditions of the case study are not effectively represented. The case study of the city of Turin (Phase 2) allows for the practical validation of the proposed set of indicators and the assessment of their operational effectiveness in a real urban context. Once the final set of indicators is defined, each one is calculated and mapped using GIS software (QGIS ver. 3.40.6). This step will produce a series of thematic maps that visually interpret urban resilience patterns throughout the study area, that will be analyzed and critically read in Phase 3. Indicators will be organized into groups and will undergo an integrated reading to identify spatial correlations and patterns, areas of convergence, as well as zones with high potential or criticalities.

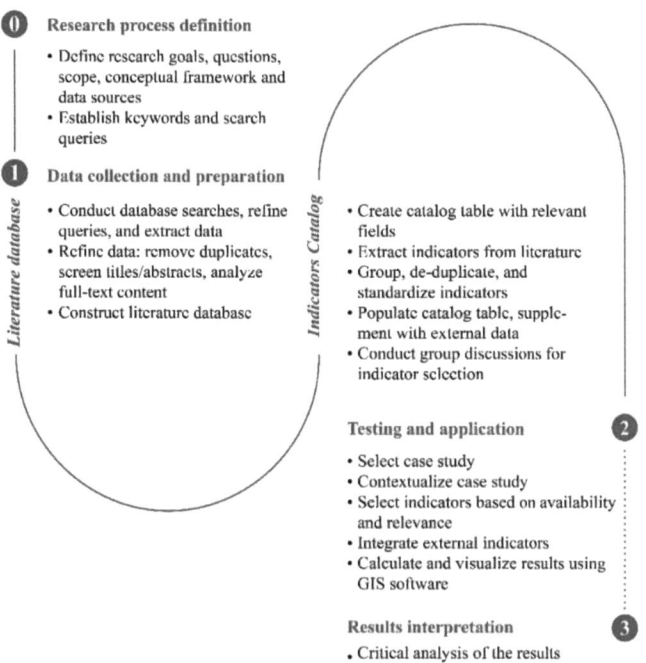

Fig. 2. Scheme of the methodological approach, illustrating its three main phases and corresponding sub-steps.

4 Case Study

The city of Turin is proposed as a potential urban context for applying a selected set of indicators derived from the catalog to evaluate its resilience, particularly concerning past and potential future urban transformations. Since each city differs in terms of disaster risks, demographic characteristics, data availability and collection capacity, and institutional frameworks, it is essential for each city to develop its own tailored set of indicators [14]. Located in the western part of the Po Valley in northern Italy, Turin boasts a complex landscape shaped by various natural, anthropogenic, and climate change-related risks. The eastern area features hilly terrain, while the core urban area is flat and densely built-up. A significant river system, comprising the Po River and its tributaries (Sangone, Dora, and Stura), supports a network of interconnected green spaces and protected areas that extend to the metropolitan and regional scale [15, 16].

The city faces hydrogeological risks due to the fact that over 65% of its surface is artificial [17]. This limits natural drainage and makes the city more susceptible to flooding, especially during extreme rainfall events. The high percentage of impervious surfaces also contributes to the urban heat island effect, intensifying the negative impacts of heat waves, particularly on vulnerable populations living in the most densely urbanized areas. Turin is also widely recognized as one of the most polluted cities in Italy and Europe, primarily due to its specific morphological position and a relatively slow shift toward sustainable mobility, along with high rates of car ownership [18]. Additionally, the city faces significant socio-economic challenges related to population decline caused by an increasingly aging demographic and a decreasing birth rate.

Over the past decades, urban planning in Turin has undergone significant changes to adapt to unexpected crises and align with international strategies. As a regional and metropolitan capital, the city has historically been shaped by structured planning, while also facing extensive deindustrialization that has prompted major urban transformation initiatives. Today, Turin requires targeted regeneration interventions to enhance resilience to both environmental hazards and socio-economic crises. These interventions should be guided by the framework of the municipal general land use plan, which is currently under revision. The revision process of Turin's municipal plan is time-consuming and influenced by changes within the municipal administration. Additionally, it must align with higher-level planning frameworks. These include regional plans such as the PTR and PPR, regional strategies for sustainable development and climate change adaptation, metropolitan plans such as PTC2 and PTGM, and nature park plans such as Piedmont Po Park Plan.

The application of resilience indicators will focus on the district level, specifically selecting an area within the city's riverine context. This area represents a multifaceted socio-ecological system, allowing for a comprehensive understanding of various dimensions, including environmental, ecological, natural, anthropogenic, and social. Specifically, three neighborhoods in the northeastern part of the city have been chosen: Vanchiglia, Regio Parco and Madonna del Pilone (Fig. 3). These districts provide an opportunity to examine diverse territorial and social conditions. Furthermore, this part of the city is expected to undergo significant transformation in the coming years. Several large-scale interventions are planned, including the construction of Metro Line 2, which is expected to facilitate urban transformations in previously overlooked areas. Another major project is the redevelopment of the former Manifattura Tabacchi industrial site, which will be converted into a new cultural hub and university campus. Additionally, the Meisino Sports and Environmental Education Centre, located near the Po River, will further contribute to the area's transformation. Alongside these major projects, numerous smaller-scale interventions are either planned or already completed, funded through the PNRR recovery program. These efforts primarily focus on redeveloping public green spaces and buildings, such as schools and libraries.[1]

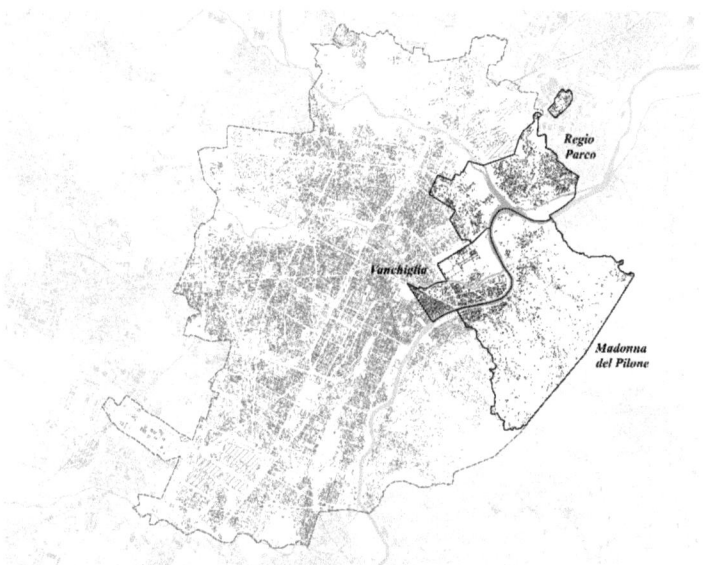

Fig. 3. The three neighbourhoods of Turin selected for the application and spatialization of the indicators.

5 Results

After establishing the research objective, we conducted preliminary research to identify the most appropriate keywords and databases for the literature review. This initial step also helped set two main limitations to better frame the research: the focus on urban settlements as the contextual framework, and the specific interest in spatial indicators as the object of analysis. Regarding the conceptual framework, we adopted a multidimensional and transformative perspective to capture the complexity and dynamic nature of urban resilience.

This preliminary study enabled the formulation of two queries through an iterative process, which progressively improved the relevance of the results. The first query focused on indicator-related terms, while the second included keywords associated with the assessment, evaluation and measurement of urban resilience.

5.1 Literature Database

Once the final queries were defined, the literature research was conducted on Scopus on April 4, 2024 (Fig. 4). The first query (Query 1) resulted in 477 records, while the

---

[1] The *Torino Cambia* website (https://www.torinocambia.it/) provides a list of all completed and ongoing projects, with approximately 60 located within the selected case study area.

second one (Query 2) produced 773 results. To refine these results, several filters were applied – publication year, subject area, language and the document type, as detailed in Tables 1 and 2. This filtering process reduced the number of results to 97 for Query 1 and 127 records for Query 2.

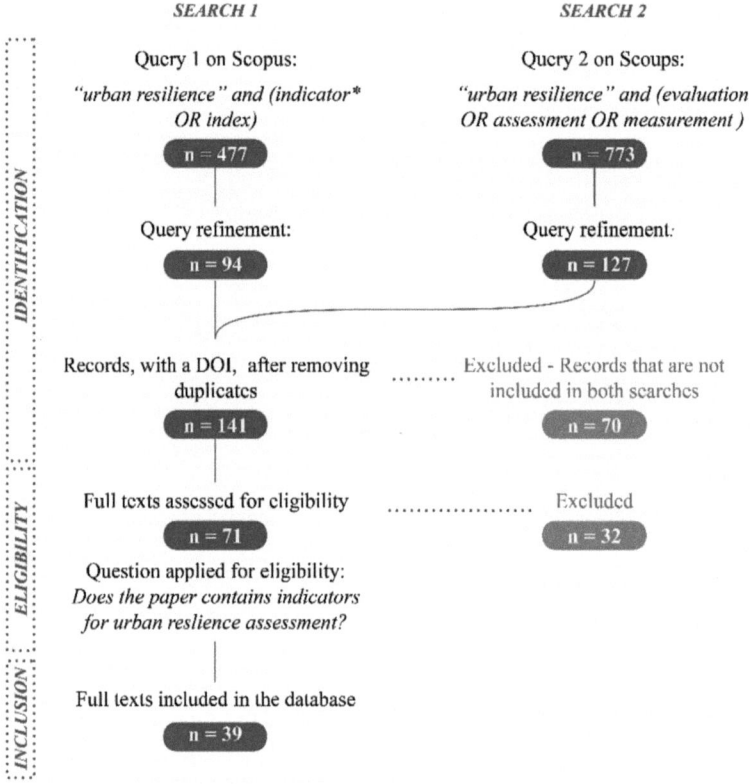

Fig. 4. Number of records at each stage of the literature review process. Accessed on 04/04/2024.

The first query identified studies that explicitly discussed measurement tools, while the assessment-focused string captured discussions of evaluation methodologies and approaches in a broader context.

Several records were found in both searches. After removing duplicates, 171 records with a DOI were left. To refine our selection further, we chose to include only the 71 papers that appeared in both searches.

This initial set of papers underwent a two-step selection process: first, we screened the papers based on their title and abstract, followed by a full-text review. The eligibility criterion applied was: Does this paper contain indicators for urban resilience assessment? The final selection consisted of 39 papers.

Table 1. Refinement process for Query 1: Number of records retrieved from Scopus after the application of each filter. Accessed on 04/04/2024.

Query 1	Records
TITLE-ABS-KEY ("urban resilience" AND (indicator* OR index)	477
AND AUTHKEY (evaluation OR assessment OR measurement OR indicator* OR index)	159
AND NOT KEY ("risk assessment" OR "hazard assessment" OR "vulnerability assessment")	142
AND PUBYEAR > 2013 AND PUBYEAR < 2025	135
AND (LIMIT-TO (SUBJAREA, "ENVI") OR LIMIT-TO (SUBJAREA, "SOCI") OR LIMIT-TO (SUBJAREA, "ENGI") OR LIMIT-TO (SUBJAREA, "ENER") OR LIMIT-TO (SUBJAREA, "EART") OR LIMIT-TO (SUBJAREA, "AGRI") OR LIMIT-TO (SUBJAREA, "MULT")	128
AND (LIMIT-TO (DOCTYPE, "ar") OR LIMIT-TO (DOCTYPE, "ch") OR LIMIT-TO (DOCTYPE, "bk"))	110
AND (LIMIT-TO (LANGUAGE, "English"))	94

Table 2. Refinement process for Query 2: Number of records retrieved from Scopus after the application of each filter. Accessed on 04/04/2024.

Query 2	Records
TITLE-ABS-KEY ("urban resilience" AND (evaluation OR assessment OR measurement)	773
AND AUTHKEY (evaluation OR assessment OR measurement OR indicator* OR index)	224
AND NOT KEY ("risk assessment" OR "hazard assessment" OR "vulnerability assessment")	185
AND PUBYEAR > 2013 AND PUBYEAR < 2025	179
AND (LIMIT-TO (SUBJAREA, "ENVI") OR LIMIT-TO (SUBJAREA, "SOCI") OR LIMIT-TO (SUBJAREA, "ENGI") OR LIMIT-TO (SUBJAREA, "ENER") OR LIMIT-TO (SUBJAREA, "EART") OR LIMIT-TO (SUBJAREA, "AGRI") OR LIMIT-TO (SUBJAREA, "MULT"))	171
AND (LIMIT-TO (DOCTYPE, "ar") OR LIMIT-TO (DOCTYPE, "ch") OR LIMIT-TO (DOCTYPE, "bk"))	144
AND (LIMIT-TO (LANGUAGE, "English"))	127

5.2 Indicators Catalog

Based on the 39 papers included in the literature database, a total of 970 indicators were systematically collected. For each indicator, the following information was gathered, when available: the indicator name, possible sub-indicators, the resilience dimension, direction (positive/negative), formula, unit of measurement, definition, and references. A selection process was essential to reduce the number of indicators, as illustrated in Fig. 5. Indicators with similar meanings were grouped to identify redundancies and eliminate duplicates. Although indicators can share similar concepts, they are often described using different wording, units or equations. Following this grouping, a structured process of group discussion and review was conducted. The various pieces of information were combined and harmonized to create a unified version of each indicator that best suits the final goal of measuring resilience. While the indicators derived from the literature formed the basis for this process, they have been extensively modified and refined. Additionally, indicators deemed irrelevant to the research objective were excluded.

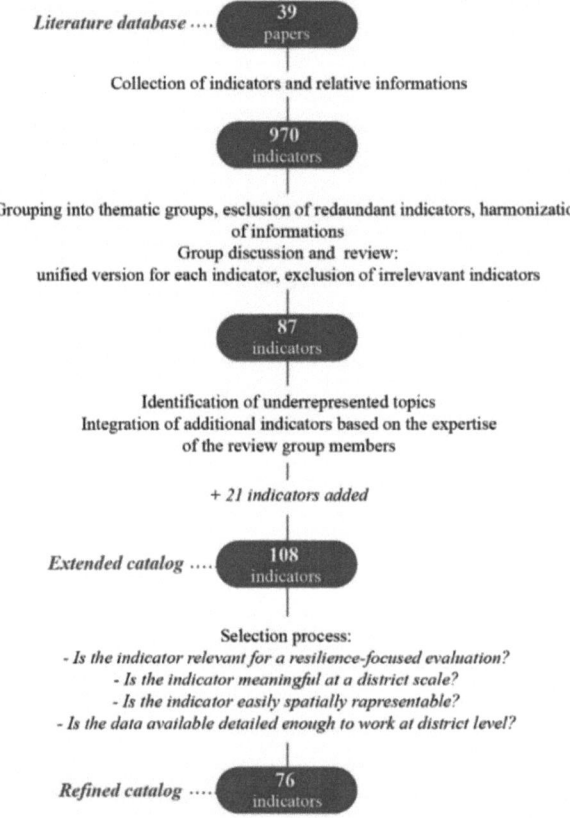

Fig. 5. Selection Process of Indicators and Resulting Numbers.

This process resulted in a refined set of 87 indicators. However, it became evident that certain topics were underrepresented or missing, indicating a need for further integration into the catalog. To address these gaps, 21 additional indicators were included, drawing upon grey literature and the expertise of the research group members, which is grounded in their knowledge and past and ongoing experience. This is particularly relevant since the field background of the research components relates to spatial planning and design and urban studies, and aligns with the phenomenon well described by Sharifi [19], which emphasizes the need for more integrated approaches to connect land use planning and green infrastructure in urban resilience assessment. This effort culminated in a comprehensive catalog of 108 indicators.

The following attributes describe each indicator:

- Resilience dimension: The dimensions of resilience addressed by the indicator. These include environmental, built environment, social, economic and institutional dimensions. A single indicator can cover one or more dimensions.
- Topic: Thematic categories including buildings, cooperation, demography, ecosystem services, emergency, heritage, income, infrastructure and networks, land use, landscape, natural/green spaces, planning and programming, pollution, resources/resource consumption, and services (Fig. 6).
- Definition: A short explanation of the indicator.
- Frequency: The occurrence of the indicator in the analyzed literature.
- Source ID: Identification number of the source from the literature database.
- Direction: Whether the indicator has a positive or negative effect on resilience.
- Formula: The mathematical representation, when possible.
- Unit of measurement: The unit in which the indicator is measured.
- Minimum Territorial Scale: The smallest geographical unit for which the indicator is meaningful.

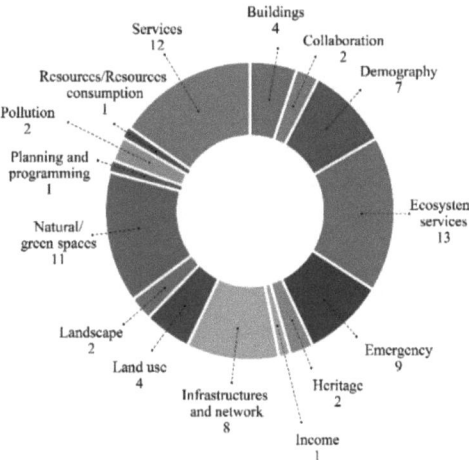

Fig. 6. Distribution of indicators by category in the refined catalog.

At this stage, a second selection was made based on the relevance, calculability, and spatial applicability of the indicators. The following exclusion criteria were applied:

1. *Not aligned with an urban resilience-focused evaluation*: Indicators related to risk, vulnerability assessment, or sustainability rather than resilience;
2. *Not relevant at the district scale*: Indicators not meaningful at the district level, but at smaller or bigger scales;

3. *Difficult to spatially represent*: Indicators that cannot be easily mapped (mainly with the use of GIS);
4. *Data not readily available at the district scale*: Indicators without consistent data sources for a district-level application.

The application of these selection criteria led to a refined version of catalog, consisting of 76 indicators. This includes 60 indicators sourced from the Scopus literature review and 16 additional indicators. While all indicators in the catalog are theoretically intended to be spatialized, the actual application to a specific case study inevitably confronts the issue of data availability. As a result, it is likely that not all indicators will be spatializable in practice, and further selection will be necessary. In this framework, the catalog will serve as the basis for deriving the indicators to be applied to the case study in northeastern Turin. The calculation process is currently underway, alongside the

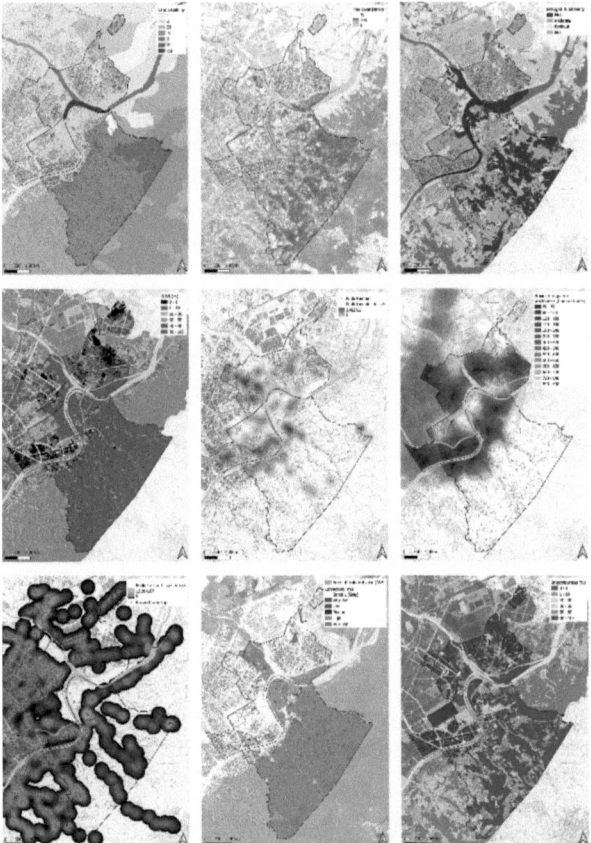

Fig. 7. First examples of the application of resilience indicators in the Turin case study: Land capability, Tree cover density, Ecological functionality, Normalized Difference Vegetation Index (NDVI), Concentration of public water fountains, Proximity to hospitals, Public transport stop density, Imperviousness, Elements of the Ecological Network (ordered from upper left to lower right)

development of visual outputs. These outputs consist of thematic maps that spatialize selected indicators. Figure 7 presents a selection of the outputs currently being developed, offering examples of the various dimensions and components of the urban system considered in this study—including for instance, indicators such as Land capability, Tree cover density, Ecological functionality, Normalized Difference Vegetation Index (NDVI), Concentration of public water fountains, Proximity to hospitals, Public transport stop density, Imperviousness, Elements of the Ecological Network (ordered from upper left to lower right). Once all the maps have been completed, they will contribute to an integrated spatial interpretation of the study area, enabling a critical reading of resilience conditions across the territory.

6 Conclusions

To develop effective methods for adapting to climate change, an integrated approach to urban planning is essential. Numerous studies on disaster risk reduction emphasize the need to combine proactive preventive measures with reactive "building back better" interventions to enhance resilience.

The measurement of urban resilience is a widely studied yet contentious topic. Indicators used in this field may not fully capture all aspects of the issues at hand, particularly when it comes to balancing human and natural capital amidst societal challenges. Much of the existing literature provides generic definitions and formulas designed for application across different territories, which risks inadequately representing the complexity of urban settlements. This research will have the added value of overcoming these gaps and critical issues by offering a more comprehensive and context-sensitive approach to measuring urban resilience. By addressing the limitations of generic indicators and incorporating localized factors, it will attempt to provide actionable insights that better reflect the complexities of different urban environments and facilitate targeted planning decisions.

To do this, this study aims to identify indicators capable of evaluating and monitoring urban resilience through spatial representation using GIS, with an approach oriented toward planning purposes. Therefore, it requires updated, comprehensive, and spatially applicable datasets—an aspect that significantly depends on and varies according to the application phase within a case study. Data availability plays a crucial role in selecting these indicators since, in many instances, the spatial information required for applying a set of indicators is not accessible from current open-source databases. In other cases, some indicators may only be effective for descriptive purposes related to the 'vulnerability status' rather than for directly measuring resilience response.

Recognizing these methodological limitations, the resilience catalog will be finalized in the next phases of the research, using the case study of Turin. Completed PNRR projects could be used, according to a scenario-based evaluation, to monitor potential progress in urban resilience, especially since the PNRR does not include a monitoring program for its interventions. The resilience indicators catalog could serve as a valuable tool in the drafting process of Turin's new municipal land use plan, particularly in relation to the Strategic Environmental Assessment procedures.

The catalog is designed to be a flexible and user-friendly tool, allowing for the inclusion of additional indicators if the conditions of the case study are not adequately represented.

Acknowledgments. This study was carried out within the RETURN Extended Partnership and received funding from the European Union Next-GenerationEU (National Recovery and Resilience Plan – NRRP, Mission 4, Component 2, In-vestment 1.3 – D.D. 1243 2/8/2022, PE0000005) – SPOKE TS 1 (2022–2025). POLITO Scientific Supervisor for Spoke TS1 Urban and metropolitan settlements: Angioletta Voghera, Coordinator: Benedetta Giudice, Research group: Grazia Brunetta, Manuela Rebaudengo, Ilaria Cazzola, Valeria Vitulano, Giosuè Pier Carlo Bronzino.

References

1. Davoudi, S., et al.: Resilience: A bridging concept or a dead end? Plan. Theory Pract.Pract. **13**(2), 299–333 (2012)
2. Meerow, S., Newell, J.P., Stults, M.: Defining urban resilience: a review. Landsc. Urban Plan.. Urban Plan. **147**, 38–49 (2016)
3. Berkes, F., Colding, J., Folke, C. (eds.): Navigating Social–Ecological Systems: Building Resilience for Complexity and Change. Cambridge University Press, Cambridge (2003)
4. Sharifi, A., Yamagata, Y.: Urban resilience assessment: multiple dimensions, criteria, and indicators. In: Yamagata, Y., Maruyama, H. (eds.), Urban Resilience. A Transformative Approach, pp. 259–276. Springer, Cham (2016)
5. Giovannini, E., Benczur, P., Campolongo, F., Cariboni, J., Manca, A.R.: Time for transformative resilience: the COVID-19 emergency. EUR 30179 EN. Publications Office of the European Union, Luxembourg (2020)
6. Asadzadeh, A., Khavarian-Garmsir, A.R., Sharifi, A., Salehi, P., Kötter, T.: Transformative resilience: an overview of its structure, evolution, and trends. Sustainability **14**(22), 15267 (2022)
7. Brunetta, G., et al.: Territorial resilience: toward a proactive meaning for spatial planning. Sustainability **11**(8), 2286 (2019)
8. Brunetta, G., Voghera, A.: Post-pandemic challenges. The role of local governance for territorial resilience. In Brunetta, G., Lombardi, P., Voghera, A. (eds.) Post Un-Lock. From Territorial Vulnerabilities to Local Resilience, pp. 3–9. Springer, Cham (2023)
9. Douglas, I.: The city as an ecosystem. Progress Phys. Geogr. Earth Environ. **5**(3), 315–367 (1981)
10. Odum, H.T., Sons, J.W.: Systems Ecology: An Introduction. Wiley, New York (1983)
11. Datola, G., Bottero, M., De Angelis, E., Romagnoli, F.: Operationalising resilience: a methodological framework for assessing urban resilience through system dynamics model. Ecol. Model. **465**, 109851 (2022)
12. Folke, C., Biggs, R., Norström, A.V., Reyers, B., Rockström, J.: Social-ecological resilience and biosphere-based sustainability science. Ecol. Soc. **21**(3), 41 (2016)
13. Gómez-Gil, M., Arbulu, M., Hernández-Minguillón, R.J., López-Mesa, B.: On the availability and quality of data in Spain for the development of indicators to measure building renovation policies effectiveness and the decarbonization of the building stock. In: López-Mesa, B., Oregi, X. (eds.), Assessing progress in decarbonizing Spain's building stock, pp. 291–316. Springer, Cham (2024)

14. Figueiredo, L., Honiden, T., Schumann, A.: Indicators for resilient cities. OECD Regional Development Working Papers 2018/02. OECD, Paris (2018)
15. Città di Torino.: Piano strategico dell'infrastruttura verde. http://www.comune.torino.it/verdepubblico/il-verde-a-torino/piano-infrastruttura-verde/ (2020)
16. Giudice, B., La Riccia, L., Negrini, G., Voghera, A.: Strategie per il verde e la collina di Torino. Storie e prospettive. In Giaimo, C. (ed.) Contenuti e strumenti della pianificazione urbana e territoriale. Dalla lezione di Giampiero Vigliano alle prospettive del Green New Deal. Urbanistica Dossier online vol. 27, pp. 79–82 (2022)
17. Munafò, M. (ed.): Consumo di suolo, dinamiche territoriali e servizi ecosistemici. Edizione 2024. Report SNPA 43/24. SNPA, Roma (2024)
18. European Environment Agency (EEA). Europe's Air Quality Status 2024. Briefing no. 06/2024 (2024). https://doi.org/10.2800/5970
19. Sharifi, A.: Urban resilience assessment: mapping knowledge structure and trends. Sustainability **12**(15), 5918 (2020)

Green Gentrification: A Literature Review of Trends, Challenges, and Research Opportunities

Marta Dell'Ovo[1,2](✉) , Giulia Datola[1] , Daniela Maiullari[3] ,
Alessandra Oppio[1] , and Martina Schretzenmayr[4]

[1] Department of Architecture and Urban Studies (DAStU), Politecnico di Milano, via Bonardi 3, 20133 Milan, (MI), Italy
marta.dellovo@polimi.it

[2] NBFC-National Biodiversity Future Center, 90133 Palermo, Italy

[3] Faculty of Architecture and the Built Environment, Delft University of Technology, Julianalaan 134, 2628 BL Delft, The Netherlands

[4] Institute for Spatial and Landscape Development, ETH Zurich, Stefano- Franscini-Platz 5, 8093 Zurich, Switzerland

Abstract. Green infrastructure projects, while enhancing environmental quality, often unintentionally exacerbate socioeconomic inequalities through "green gentrification." This phenomenon leads to rising property values, demographic shifts, and the displacement of vulnerable populations, raising critical concerns about social justice in urban greening. This study systematically reviews the literature to examine how the distribution of and access to green spaces contribute to green gentrification and explores strategies to mitigate its effects. Based on the analysis of peer-reviewed studies in urban planning, green infrastructure, and social dynamics, four key themes emerge: (i) the spatial and health outcomes of greening interventions, (ii) the socioeconomic impacts of green spaces on property values and resident demographics, (iii) the social justice challenges faced by marginalized communities, (iv) the role of urban policies in moderating gentrification.

The findings reveal that while urban greening initiatives provide significant environmental and health benefits, these are often inequitably distributed, disproportionately benefiting wealthier populations and displacing vulnerable groups. Studies highlight the importance of integrating affordable housing policies with green infrastructure projects. This approach aims to prevent the displacement of low-income residents while enhancing urban sustainability and inclusivity. Methodologies employed in the reviewed studies—such as spatial analysis, community surveys, and economic assessments—highlight the complex interactions between green infrastructure, housing markets, and social equity.

By outlining implications for policy and future research, this study provides a foundation for shaping urban greening strategies that balance environmental goals with social equity, ensuring sustainable and inclusive urban development.

Keywords: Green gentrification · Spatial analysis · Socioeconomic studies

---

Marta Dell'Ovo: The author belong to NBFC—National Biodiversity Future Center, 90133 Palermo, Italy

© The Author(s), under exclusive license to Springer Nature Switzerland AG 2026
O. Gervasi et al. (Eds.): ICCSA 2025 Workshops, LNCS 15893, pp. 222–233, 2026.
https://doi.org/10.1007/978-3-031-97645-2_15

1 Introduction

In contemporary urban studies, green gentrification is a critical phenomenon that highlights the intersection of environmental improvements and socioeconomic displacement [1, 2]. Investments in urban green spaces—such as parks, green roofs, and tree-lined streets—have become integral to urban planning as cities increasingly prioritize sustainability and climate resilience. Despite their beneficial environmental and public health impacts, these interventions often lead to unexpected consequences such as rising property values, exacerbating social inequalities, and the displacement of low-income residents [3].

Anguelovski et al. [4] provide an interesting overview about the conceptualization of "green gentrification", "ecological gentrification", and "environmental gentrification", explaining how the most relevant literature is situated in the US and Canada, and is defined as the output of the "restoration of an environmental amenity" [5]. Moreover, the concept of urban sustainability is central to promoting a holistic vision and approach.

Environmental Justice is central to understanding green gentrification [6, 7]. It emphasizes the fair distribution of environmental benefits across all social groups, particularly marginalized and disadvantaged communities [8]. Green gentrification could be considered a paradox since these initiatives aim to promote sustainability and livability but unintentionally contribute to social exclusion if not managed carefully [9]. Improving the attractiveness of a neighborhood could result in increasing property values, housing prices, and the consequent displacement of residents, especially the working class [9, 10]. SocioEconomic Equity is vital within green urbanism [3, 11], and to understand the leading factors that influence gentrification, it is important to look at the overall picture by analyzing positive and negative impacts as well as relationships among several variables.

The tangible and intangible values provided by the natural capital are well-known as Ecosystem Services (ESs) and are categorized with the support of the Millennium Ecosystem Assessment [12–14]. They improve air quality, reduce Urban Heat Island Effects (UHI), and enhance well-being, but since green areas are not equally distributed, wealthier populations can disproportionately benefit [15]. Disservice could be generated if not correctly designed and managed [16]. The rising demand for green neighborhoods often increases housing costs, making it difficult for lower-income residents to remain in their communities and access these environmental benefits. Moreover, the framework of Ecosystem Services is crucial in contemporary urban cities affected by climate change and non-communicable diseases [17–20]. Their provisions are related to Regulating Services such as climate regulation, Provisioning also related to medicinal resources, and Cultural, consisting of cultural, spiritual, and aesthetic values aimed to promote mental and physical health [14, 21, 22]. Integrating ESs and disservices in urban decision-making processes could raise awareness, communication, and support community participation, thus contributing to a more equitable greening planning decisions on the side of the process and of the outcome [23]. Urban policies would be strategic in this context in mitigating the negative impact of new green interventions and developing inclusive strategies that interplay climate adaptation, social need, and economic value [24]. The criticisms detected could underpin the request for an equity-based climate action and sustainable strategies while exploiting existing gaps and competing political values [9].

Given these premises, this paper examines the multidimensional impacts of green gentrification by comprehensively reviewing recent literature and comparing key findings on environmental justice and socioeconomic dimensions. After an introduction of the main topics related to the issue investigated by the paper (Sect. 1), the methodology developed to analyze the literature review is presented (Sect. 2), and contributions selected are compared and main findings and gaps discussed (Sects. 3 and 4). The conclusions (Sect. 5) aim to provide some possible new lines of research.

2 Research Methodology

An analysis of the literature review has been developed from September to October 2024 to understand how other studies have faced the concept of green gentrification, and from which perspective. Using the Scopus database, the search started by using the keywords "green gentrification" and "urban" to limit the context of the analysis. 165 papers were found initially, written between 2014 and 2024, and then, by filtering to European studies, the number decreased to 88 articles. It has been decided to limit the analysis to the European context because non-EU urban contexts, such as the US, have very different social dynamics that are not comparable with those under study in this research. As discussed by [4], most of the contributions on this topic come from American and Canadian scholars, who have primarily focused on experiences within their own national contexts. This paper, however, aims to explore whether the dynamics identified in those studies remain consistent or take on different forms when examined in a different geographical and socio-political setting.

The 88 papers have been further filtered considering the coherence of the title and the topics discussed within the abstract. At the end of these phases, 24 articles were analyzed (Fig. 1).

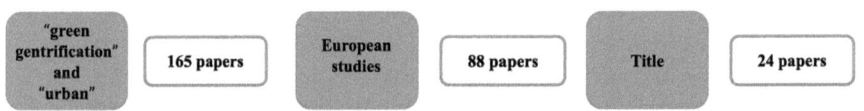

Fig. 1. Literature review's phases

Papers have been analyzed by considering the year, the country, the objectives, the primary methodologies applied, the results obtained from the case study, if present, how the concept of green gentrification has been discussed, if the research applies Geographic Information System (GIS) software to provide spatial analysis and which criteria have been defined how useful and with an impact for the topic. Table 1 shows an extract of the more extensive literature review developed for the 24 papers.

Table 1. Example of the structure of the literature review [1, 2, 8, 25–29].

Author(s)	Title	Year	Nation	Objective	Methodology	Results	Case Study	Green Gentrification	GIS Analysis	Criteria Analyzed
Cole et al.	Are green cities healthy and equitable? Unpacking the relationship between health, green space and gentrification	2017	Multiple (Global)	Analyze the relationship between urban health, green spaces, and gentrification	Comparative qualitative analysis of health and green space data across different global cities	Green spaces promote health but also increase the risk of displacement and inequality	Various cities	Green gentrification leads to better health outcomes for some while excluding or displacing lower-income residents.	No	Health outcomes, green spaces, equity, gentrification.
Ali et al.	Gentrification through green regeneration? Analyzing the interaction between inner-city green space development and neighborhood change	2020	Germany	Investigate the interaction between green regeneration and neighborhood change in Leipzig	Case study method using qualitative analysis of urban planning and demographic data	Green regeneration led to significant demographic shifts and increased property prices	Leipzig, Germany	Green regeneration attracted wealthier residents, resulting in gentrification and displacement of lower-income groups.	Yes	Neighborhood change, green regeneration, property prices, demographic shifts.
Goossens et al.	Livable streets? Green gentrification and the displacement of longtime residents in Ghent, Belgium	2020	Belgium	Investigate the impacts of street greening on displacement of long-time residents	Qualitative interviews, spatial analysis using GIS tools	Green street projects in Ghent led to displacement of vulnerable populations	Ghent, Belgium	Street greening projects were linked to gentrification and displacement of longtime residents.	Yes	Displacement, long-time residents, street greening projects.
Maia et al.	Hidden drivers of social injustice: uncovering unequal cultural ecosystems services behind green gentrification	2020	Multiple (Global)	Explore how cultural ecosystem services (CES) relate to social justice in green gentrification	Mixed methods: qualitative interviews, quantitative CES assessments	Unequal access to cultural ecosystem services drives social injustice in urban greening	Various cities	Hidden dynamics behind CES exacerbate green gentrification and social inequities.	Yes	Cultural ecosystem services, social justice, access inequality.
Bockarjova et al.	Property price effects of green interventions in cities: A meta-analysis and implications for gentrification	2020	Multiple (Global)	Analyze the effect of green interventions on property prices and potential for gentrification	Meta-analysis of previous studies examining property price effects	Green interventions systematically increase property prices, with high potential for gentrification	Multiple global cities	Green interventions drive up property prices, contributing to gentrification trends.	No	Property prices, green interventions, meta-analysis, gentrification risk.
Blok	Urban green gentrification in an unequal world of climate change	2020	Global	Examine how urban greening and climate change are interconnected with gentrification	Qualitative theoretical framework exploring climate change, urbanization, and green gentrification	Urban greening projects in the context of climate change exacerbate existing inequalities	Global	Urban green projects aimed at climate resilience often lead to gentrification, especially in unequal urban settings.	No	Climate change, urban greening, inequality.
Alexandrescu et al.	Green gentrification as strategic action: Exploring the emerging discursive and social support for the Green Tree Strategy in Porto Marghera, Italy	2021	Italy	Analyze the discursive strategies and social support for a green gentrification project in Porto	Discourse analysis, social network analysis	The Green Tree Strategy garnered strategic discursive support despite risks of gentrification	Porto Marghera, Italy	Social and discursive support for green gentrification emerged in the context of broader environmental strategies.	No	Discourse analysis, green gentrification strategies, social support.
Triguero-Mas et al.	Exploring green gentrification in 28 global North cities: the role of urban parks and other types of greenspaces	2022	Multiple (Global)	Explore the relationship between urban parks, other greenspaces, and green gentrification	Comparative analysis using GIS tools and demographic data	Urban parks and greenspaces were closely linked to gentrification trends across several cities	28 cities, Global North	Parks and other greenspaces are significant contributors to green gentrification, particularly in the Global North.	Yes	Urban parks, greenspaces, gentrification, demographic shifts.

3 Comparative Analysis

The selected studies approach green gentrification from multiple perspectives, focusing on the interplay between urban greening and socioeconomic dynamics. A key objective of many articles is to examine how the introduction or revitalization of green spaces contributes to gentrification. Research by [3, 26, 29] explores how green infrastructure projects drive up property values, often making neighborhoods unaffordable for long-term, lower-income residents. These studies analyze the tension between environmental benefits and rising living costs, highlighting the displacement risks marginalized populations face.

Another crucial focus is the social inequalities and environmental justice concerns tied to green gentrification. Studies such as those by [8, 30, 31] emphasize the uneven distribution of green spaces and how marginalized communities are often excluded from their benefits. Historically, it has been determined by zoning laws [32] and uneven distributions of public infrastructure funding [33]. It started to be recognized as a racial phenomenon, and the effect is contemporarily defined as racial residential segregation [34]. More recently, the concept that the new regeneration project brings to the mechanism of unaffordable living costs and higher rents has raised concerns. By investigating how green interventions reinforce these consolidated racial and economic inequalities, the studies underscore the importance of equitable access to natural capital through specific practices such as land recognition and more equitable access to housing.

Policy and governance are also central themes in the literature. Research by [35, 36] assesses the role of urban planning in shaping green development outcomes. These studies examine whether policies mitigate or exacerbate green gentrification, focusing on the effectiveness of affordable housing initiatives and collaborative governance models in ensuring that the advantages of urban greening are distributed more fairly.

Some studies take a socio-spatial and health-oriented approach, analyzing how green spaces reshape urban demographics and influence public health. Articles by [1, 37] employ spatial analysis to track neighborhood transformations following green interventions while also considering both the positive effects, such as improved air quality and well-being, and the negative consequences, particularly for displaced communities.

Finally, a few studies adopt a long-term and cross-city perspective to assess the broader impacts of urban greening. Research like [38] examines historical patterns of green infrastructure development, providing insights into how past urban planning decisions continue to shape contemporary gentrification dynamics. This longitudinal approach offers a deeper understanding of how cities evolve and how green gentrification unfolds over extended periods.

Figure 2 shows the central cluster of topics discussed within the literature analysis carried out with the support of the VOSviewer software tool.

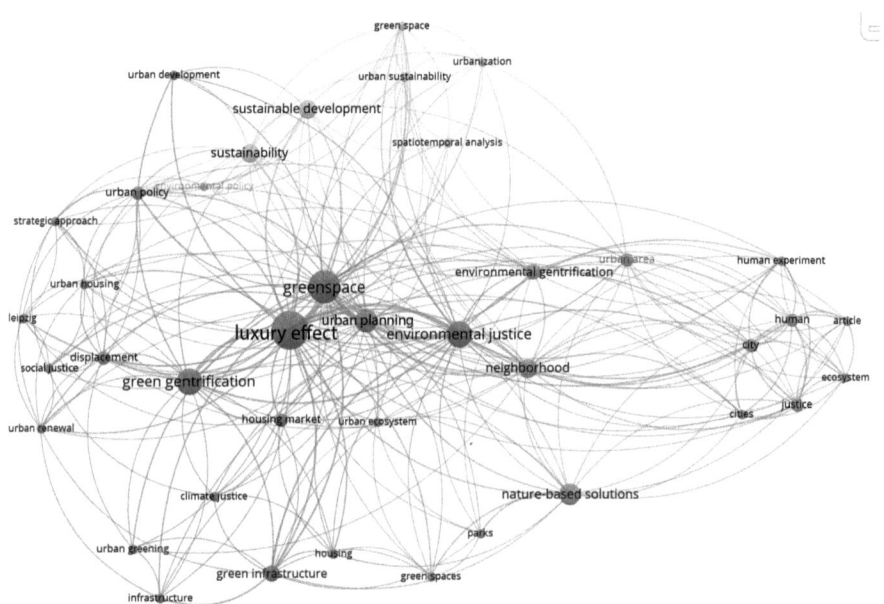

Fig. 2. Keywords analysis (VOSviewer software).

3.1 Methodologies Applied

The studies on green gentrification employ a range of methodologies to capture its complexities. Qualitative approaches, such as interviews and focus groups, are frequently used to explore residents' lived experiences affected by urban greening. Research by [25, 28] highlights displacement's social and emotional impacts, providing valuable insights into how communities perceive and respond to these changes. Qualitative analysis supports catching the perception of the community involved, its subjective experiences, and investigating the intangible values in play.

In contrast, quantitative methods and spatial analysis, mainly through Geographical Information Systems (GIS), offer a broader, data-driven perspective. Studies like those by [3, 37] examine shifts in property values and demographic patterns, illustrating how proximity to new green spaces often correlates with rising housing costs and the displacement of lower-income residents. These techniques enable researchers to visualize and statistically analyze the spatial dimensions of green gentrification. Distributing and visually representing the output of the analysis could support policymakers in urban decision-making processes and in engaging non-expert actors.

Meta-analysis also plays a crucial role in synthesizing findings across different contexts. For example, [8, 26] provide a comparative perspective on the economic impacts of urban greening, revealing overarching trends in housing market fluctuations following green infrastructure projects. Comparing previous analyses and case studies supports reading possible future dynamics.

Some studies adopt a mixed-methods approach, integrating qualitative and quantitative techniques to provide a more comprehensive analysis. Amorim Maia et al. [8] exemplify this strategy by combining resident interviews with statistical data, allowing for cross-validation of findings and a deeper understanding of the socioeconomic dynamics at play. By utilizing this diverse array of methodologies, researchers can capture green gentrification's structural and personal dimensions, offering a more holistic view of its impacts.

3.2 Analysis of the Results

The studies collectively highlight the environmental benefits, and the social inequalities associated with urban greening. Green infrastructure projects have been shown to contribute to healthier urban environments, e.g., improving air quality and mitigating urban heat islands [3, 29]. However, these benefits are not socio-spatially equitably distributed. Low-income residents, who could benefit most from such improvements, are often displaced before they can experience them. This phenomenon, known as green gentrification, underscores the unintended social consequences of urban greening when policies fail to protect vulnerable populations. Gentrification and displacement emerge as recurrent themes in the literature. Rising property values following the introduction of green spaces often lead to the relocation of long-term, lower-income residents. This process has been documented in cities such as Ghent [25], Lyon, Amsterdam, and Wien [30], where demographic shifts favor wealthier newcomers at the expense of pre-existing communities. These changes disrupt social cohesion and alter the socio-cultural fabric of neighborhoods, reinforcing socioeconomic divides. Green spaces are frequently introduced in previously underserved areas, yet their benefits often remain out of reach for the communities that once lived there [8, 30]. This reveals a deeper structural problem in urban planning, where environmental justice is not merely about creating green spaces but ensuring equitable access to them and protecting marginalized populations from displacement.

Governance and policy failures further complicate the issue, and research shows that urban greening can exacerbate socioeconomic disparities when affordable housing and inclusive planning are not prioritized [35, 36]. At the same time, some cases demonstrate that collaborative governance and community-led planning can help mitigate these effects by ensuring that environmental improvements do not come at the cost of social equity.

A key paradox in the discussion of green gentrification concerns public health. While green spaces are widely recognized for their positive impacts on mental and physical well-being, these benefits are often inaccessible to displaced communities [1]. As a result, marginalized and vulnerable communities that would most benefit from urban greening are frequently excluded from its advantages, highlighting the urgent need for policies that integrate environmental improvements with social protections.

This body of research collectively underscores the dual nature of urban greening. While it offers crucial environmental and health benefits, it also reinforces socioeconomic inequalities when implemented without safeguards for vulnerable populations. Addressing these challenges requires a more holistic approach to urban planning that balances ecological sustainability with social justice.

4 Critical Challenges and Research Opportunities

The studies propose various strategies to counteract green gentrification and promote more equitable urban development. A key approach is integrating affordable housing policies with green infrastructure projects to ensure that low-income residents are not displaced. Research by [36] emphasizes the need for proactive planning measures, such as mixed-income housing initiatives, rent control, and subsidies, to maintain affordability in neighborhoods undergoing greening efforts.

Fostering community participation and collaborative governance could be another strategy to understand the community's needs and avoid unexpected impacts. [35] highlight the importance of engaging residents in decision-making to ensure that green projects reflect the community's needs. Cities can create more inclusive planning models prioritizing social equity and environmental improvements by bringing residents, policymakers, and developers together to promote different ways of living for the various needs of the communities in the area.

Monitoring and regulation also play a crucial role in preventing displacement. Studies like [3] suggest that tracking property values, demographic trends, and green space accessibility through tools such as GIS mapping can help policymakers identify early signs of green gentrification. This data-driven approach allows for timely interventions to protect vulnerable populations from being priced out of their neighborhoods.

Finally, targeted investments in public housing and equity-focused green initiatives within the same neighborhood can help ensure marginalized communities benefit from urban greening. Research by [8] underscores the importance of designing green spaces for all. The paper highlights the importance of providing public amenities and infrastructures to offer the opportunity for social cohesion. Communities should appropriate and live in those spaces, moving from the aesthetic vision of a green space to a usable vision to improve livability, promoting their active involvement in the design phase.

By prioritizing inclusive development [8], cities can balance the environmental and social benefits of urban greening while mitigating its unintended consequences.

A step forward within the existing literature, to advance research on green gentrification and offer valuable insights for urban planning, future studies should focus on several key areas. First, conducting longitudinal research is crucial for tracking the long-term effects of green gentrification; by observing how property values, demographics, and health outcomes change, researchers can better understand its lasting impacts. Additionally, comparing different cities, as shown in the work of [29], can reveal how green gentrification manifests differently in various urban contexts.

A highly innovative and impactful approach involves integrating socioeconomic, spatial, and health data, paving the way for more comprehensive and equitable urban planning strategies. Combining data on socioeconomic factors, spatial analysis (such as GIS), and public health can help researchers understand how proximity to green spaces influences community health and social well-being. For example, correlating housing data with health metrics, such as asthma rates or mental health issues [39, 40], could provide a clearer picture of both the benefits and challenges of urban greening.

Understanding community perceptions and willingness to engage is also key. Future research should investigate how residents perceive and engage with green infrastructure projects. Studies like those by [8, 25] highlight the importance of exploring local perspectives on the changes brought by greening efforts.

Moreover, evaluating existing urban policies aimed at mitigating green gentrification is key. Researchers should examine case studies of cities successfully implementing inclusive green development policies. This can provide valuable empirical data to assess the effectiveness of these policies and help develop new solutions.

Finally, with climate resilience becoming a critical concern in urban planning, future research should explore how greening initiatives, such as flood defenses, green roofs, and sustainable infrastructure, might contribute to climate gentrification. Understanding the interplay between climate adaptation efforts and socioeconomic displacement, as noted in studies by [3, 27], is crucial for addressing the equity challenges in green urban development.

5 Conclusions

The literature analyzed shows that green gentrification can be understood as a complex process where environmental improvements in urban areas, such as creating or enhancing green spaces, unintentionally lead to the displacement of low-income residents and exacerbate social inequalities. The following elements characterize the process: i) environmental benefits and economic costs: greening projects bring tangible ecological benefits, such as reduced pollution, lower temperatures, and improved public health. However, these benefits often have economic impacts that disproportionately affect vulnerable populations, leading to increased property prices, rental fees, and demographic shifts. ii) social and racial inequities: green gentrification compounds existing inequalities, especially in marginalized communities. Wealthier residents benefit from the new amenities, while lower-income populations are either displaced or excluded from the benefits.

Based on the literature, different gaps emerge, which consist in the i) geographical distribution of these studies, mainly located in North American and Western European contexts; the ii) analysis of the effects of green infrastructure on socio-spatial transformations over time; the iii) lack of public health outcomes; iv) the tendency to have top-down assessment; the v) lack of evaluation framework for planning tools; vi) understanding how to replicate policies.

In conclusion, several key approaches should be considered to address the complex dynamics of green gentrification in future research. First, collecting socioeconomic and spatial data through GIS tools can offer valuable insights by mapping changes in neighborhood demographics, housing prices, and proximity to newly developed green spaces over time. This will help identify patterns of gentrification that may be linked to greening efforts, providing a clearer understanding of how these projects impact urban areas. Despite the importance of integrating and georeferencing information, data availability is a topic to consider while developing consistent methodologies.

Additionally, analyzing health and well-being indicators is crucial for assessing the broader effects of green gentrification on public health. Researchers can gain a more holistic view of green spaces' impacts on urban populations by collecting data on respiratory health, mental well-being, and other relevant outcomes alongside greening interventions.

Engaging directly with local communities through interviews, focus groups, and surveys is another vital aspect of the research process. This will allow a deeper understanding of residents' perceptions of green spaces, displacement, and accessibility. Including marginalized groups is significant, as their voices can shed light on the social justice implications of green gentrification, ensuring that all community members are considered in the process.

Finally, evaluating the effectiveness of existing urban policies to prevent green gentrification is essential. This combination of qualitative and quantitative analysis will offer valuable insights into what works and what needs improvement in policy development.

Incorporating these research methods will provide a comprehensive, multidimensional analysis of green gentrification, helping to develop actionable and replicable policy recommendations that can guide more equitable and inclusive urban greening efforts moving forward.

Acknowledgments. This paper is part of the results of the IDEA League Fellowships Program "Exploring the trade-off between Ecosystem Services, Social justice, and Economic evaluation.

Credit Author Statement. Conceptualization: M.D.O., D.M., M.S; Data curation: M.D.O., G.D.; Formal analysis: M.D.O.; Methodology: M.D.O.; D.M., M.S; Project administration: A.O.; Supervision: A.O.; Validation: M.D.O., D.M., M.S.; Visualization: M.D.O., G.D.; Writing – original draft: M.D.O; Writing - Review & Editing: M.D.O.

Funding. This research was funded by the Italian National Recovery and Resilience Plan (NRRP), Mission 4 Component 2 Investment 1.4—Call for tender No. 3138 of 16 December 2021, rectified by Decree n.3175 of 18 December 2021 of the Italian Ministry of University and Research funded by the European Union—NextGenerationEU. Award Number: Project code CN_00000033, Concession Decree No. 1034 of 17 June 2022 adopted by the Italian Ministry of University and Research, CUP,H43C22000530001 Project title "National Biodiversity Future Center—NBFC".

Disclosure of Interests. The authors have no competing interests to declare that are relevant to the content of this article.

References

1. Cole, H.V.S., Lamarca, M.G., Connolly, J.J.T., Anguelovski, I.: Are green cities healthy and equitable? Unpacking the relationship between health, green space and gentrification. J. Epidemiol. Commun. Health **71**, 1118–1121 (2017). https://doi.org/10.1136/JECH-2017-209201
2. Ali, L., Haase, A., Heiland, S.: Gentrification through green regeneration? Analyzing the interaction between inner-city green space development and neighborhood change in the context of regrowth: the case of Lene-Voigt-Park in Leipzig, Eastern Germany. Land **9**, 24 (2020). https://doi.org/10.3390/LAND9010024
3. Kim, J., Ewing, R., Rigolon, A.: Does green infrastructure affect housing prices via extreme heat and air pollution mitigation? A focus on green and climate gentrification in Los Angeles County, 2000–2021. Sustain. Cities Soc. **102**, 105225 (2024). https://doi.org/10.1016/J.SCS.2024.105225
4. Anguelovski, I., Connolly, J.J.T., Masip, L., Pearsall, H.: Assessing green gentrification in historically disenfranchised neighborhoods: a longitudinal and spatial analysis of Barcelona Assessing green gentrification in historically disenfranchised neighborhoods: a longitudinal and spatial analysis of Barcelona. Urban Geogr. (2017). https://doi.org/10.1080/02723638.2017.1349987
5. Gould, K.A., Lewis, T.L.: The Environmental Injustice of Green Gentrification The Case of Brooklyn's Prospect Park
6. Li, H., Parker, K.A., Kalcounis-Rueppell, M.C.: The luxury effect beyond cities: Bats respond to socioeconomic variation across landscapes. BMC Ecol. **19**, 1–13 (2019). https://doi.org/10.1186/S12898-019-0262-8/FIGURES/4
7. Leong, M., Dunn, R.R., Trautwein, M.D.: Biodiversity and socioeconomics in the city: a review of the luxury effect. Biol. Lett. (2018). https://doi.org/10.1098/RSBL.2018.0082
8. Amorim Maia, A.T., Calcagni, F., Connolly, J.J.T., Anguelovski, I., Langemeyer, J.: Hidden drivers of social injustice: uncovering unequal cultural ecosystem services behind green gentrification. Environ Sci Policy **112**, 254–263 (2020). https://doi.org/10.1016/J.ENVSCI.2020.05.021
9. Anguelovski, I., Connolly, J.J.T., Cole, H., Garcia-Lamarca, M., Triguero-Mas, M., Baró, F., Martin, N., Conesa, D., Shokry, G., del Pulgar, C.P., Ramos, L.A., Matheney, A., Gallez, E., Oscilowicz, E., Máñez, J.L., Sarzo, B., Beltrán, M.A., Minaya, J.M.: Green gentrification in European and North American cities. Nat. Commun. **13**, 1–13 (2022). https://doi.org/10.1038/s41467-022-31572-1
10. Anguelovski, I., Connolly, J.J., Garcia-Lamarca, M., Cole, H., Pearsall, H.: New scholarly pathways on green gentrification: What does the urban "green turn" mean and where is it going? Progress Hum. Geogr. (2018). https://doi.org/10.1177/0309132518803799
11. Rossitti, M., Oppio, A., Torrieri, F., Dell'Ovo, M.: Tactical urbanism interventions for the urban environment: Which Economic Impacts? Land (2023). https://doi.org/10.3390/land12071457

12. Caprioli, C., Bottero, M., Zanetta, E., Mondini, G.: Ecosystem services in land-use planning: an application for assessing transformation scenarios at the local scale. Smart Innov. Syst. Technol. **178**(SIST), 1332–1341 (2021). https://doi.org/10.1007/978-3-030-48279-4_124
13. Caprioli, C., Bottero, M., Zanetta, E., Mondini, G.: Ecosystem services in land-use planning: an application for assessing transformation scenarios at the local scale. In: Bevilacqua, C., Al., E. (eds.) NMP 2020, SIST 178. pp. 1–10. Springer Nature Switzerland AG (2021). https://doi.org/10.1007/978-3-030-48279-4_124
14. Assessment, M.E.: Living Beyond Our Means: Natural Assets and Human Well-being Statement from the Board. (2005)
15. TEEB: The Economics of Ecosystems and Biodiversity: Ecological and Economic Foundations. Routledge (2012)
16. Datola, G., Oppio, A.: NBS design and implementation in urban systems: dimensions, challenges and issues to construct a comprehensive evaluation framework. Lect. Notes Comput. Sci. (including subseries Lecture Notes in Artificial Intelligence and Lecture Notes in Bioinformatics). **14108**(LNCS), 444–454 (2023). https://doi.org/10.1007/978-3-031-37117-2_30/TABLES/1
17. Capolongo, S., Buffoli, M., Oppio, A.: How to assess the effects of urban plans on environment and health. Territorio (2015). https://doi.org/10.3280/tr2015-073021
18. D'Alessandro, D., Buffoli, M., Capasso, L., Fara, G.M., Rebecchi, A., Capolongo, S.: Green areas and public health: Improving wellbeing and physical activity in the urban context. Epidemiol. Prev. **39**, 8–13 (2015)
19. Capolongo, S., Buffoli, M., Mosca, E.I., Galeone, D., D'Elia, R., Rebecchi, A.: Public health aspects' assessment tool for urban projects, according to the urban health approach. Presented at the (2020). https://doi.org/10.1007/978-3-030-33256-3_30.
20. Alessandro, D.D.', Buffoli, M., Capasso, L., Fara, G.M., Rebecchi, A., Capolongo, S.: Green areas and public health: improving wellbeing and physical activity in the urban context Spazi verdi e salute pubblica: migliorare il benessere e l'attività fisica nei contesti urbani and the Hygiene on Built Environment Working Group on Healthy Buildings of the Italian Society of Hygiene, Preventive Medicine and Public Health (SItI) of the Hygiene on Built Environment WG
21. Oppio, A., Dell'Ovo, M., Caprioli, C., Bottero, M.: A proposal to assess the benefits of urban ecosystem services. Lect. Notes Netw. Syst. **482**(LNCS), 1947–1955 (2022). https://doi.org/10.1007/978-3-031-06825-6_187/COVER
22. Oppio, A., Caprioli, C., Dell'Ovo, M., Bottero, M.: Assessing ecosystem services through a multimethodological approach based on multicriteria analysis and cost-benefits analysis: a case study in Turin (Italy). J. Clean. Prod. **472**, 143472 (2024). https://doi.org/10.1016/J.JCLEPRO.2024.143472
23. Kathryn Rodgman, M., Anguelovski, I., Pérez-del-Pulgar, C., Shokry, G., Garcia-Lamarca, M., Connolly, J.J.T., Baró, F., Triguero-Mas, M.: Perceived urban ecosystem services and disservices in gentrifying neighborhoods: Contrasting views between community members and state informants. Ecosyst. Serv. **65**, 101571 (2024). https://doi.org/10.1016/J.ECOSER.2023.101571
24. Sugoni, G., Assumma, V., Bottero, M.C., Mondini, G.: Development of a decision-making model to support the strategic environmental assessment for the revision of the municipal plan of Turin (Italy). Land **12**, 609 (2023). https://doi.org/10.3390/LAND12030609
25. Goossens, C., Oosterlynck, S., Bradt, L.: Livable streets? Green gentrification and the displacement of longtime residents in Ghent, Belgium. Urban Geogr. **41**, 550–572 (2020). https://doi.org/10.1080/02723638.2019.1686307
26. Bockarjova, M., Botzen, W.J.W., van Schie, M.H., Koetse, M.J.: Property price effects of green interventions in cities: a meta-analysis and implications for gentrification. Environ Sci Policy **112**, 293–304 (2020). https://doi.org/10.1016/J.ENVSCI.2020.06.024

27. Blok, A.: Urban green gentrification in an unequal world of climate change. Urban Stud. **57**, 2803–2816 (2020). https://doi.org/10.1177/0042098019891050
28. Alexandrescu, F.M., Pizzol, L., Critto, A.: Green gentrification as strategic action: exploring the emerging discursive and social support for the Green Tree Strategy in Porto Marghera, Italy. Cities **118**, 103352 (2021). https://doi.org/10.1016/J.CITIES.2021.103352
29. Triguero-Mas, M., Anguelovski, I., Connolly, J.J.T., Martin, N., Matheney, A., Cole, H.V.S., Pérez-Del-Pulgar, C., García-Lamarca, M., Shokry, G., Argüelles, L., Conesa, D., Gallez, E., Sarzo, B., Beltrán, M.A., López Máñez, J., Martínez-Minaya, J., Oscilowicz, E., Arcaya, M.C., Baró, F.: Exploring green gentrification in 28 global North cities: the role of urban parks and other types of greenspaces. Environ. Res. Lett. **17**, 104035 (2022). https://doi.org/10.1088/1748-9326/AC9325
30. Lewartowska, E., et al.: Racial inequity in green infrastructure and gentrification: challenging compounded environmental racisms in the Green City. Int. J. Urban Reg. Res. **48**, 294–322 (2024). https://doi.org/10.1111/1468-2427.13232
31. Cucca, R., Friesenecker, M., Thaler, T.: Green gentrification, social justice, and climate change in the literature: conceptual origins and future directions. Urban Plan. **8**, 283–295 (2023). https://doi.org/10.17645/UP.V8I1.6129
32. Pulido, L.: Rethinking environmental racism: white privilege and urban development in Southern California. Ann. Assoc. Am. Geogr. **90**, 12–40 (2000). https://doi.org/10.1111/0004-5608.00182
33. Theodos, B., Hangen, E.: Tracking the Unequal Distribution of Community Development Funding in the US, https://www.urban.org/research/publication/tracking-unequal-distribution-community-development-funding-us, (2019)
34. Kirkland-Metropolitan, E., Church, I.: What's race got to do with it? Looking for the racial dimensions of gentrifícation. West J. Black Stud. **32**, (2008)
35. Casprini, D., Oppio, A., Rossi, G., Bengo, I.: Managing urban green areas: the benefits of collaborative governance for green spaces. Land **12**, 1872 (2023). https://doi.org/10.3390/LAND12101872
36. Friesenecker, M., Thaler, T., Clar, C.: Green gentrification and changing planning policies in Vienna? Urban Res. Pract. **17**, 393–415 (2024). https://doi.org/10.1080/17535069.2023.2228275
37. Liu, K., Du, J., Cheng, Y., Xia, Z., Liu, J.: Green gentrification and who will benefit from green infrastructure regeneration? A quasi-experimental study in China. Cities **153**, 105307 (2024). https://doi.org/10.1016/J.CITIES.2024.105307
38. Nygaard, C.A.: Green infrastructure and socioeconomic dynamics in London low-income neighbourhoods: a 120-year perspective. Cities **144**, 104616 (2024). https://doi.org/10.1016/J.CITIES.2023.104616
39. Riva, A., Rebecchi, A., Capolongo, S., Gola, M.: Can homes affect well-being? A scoping review among housing conditions, indoor environmental quality, and mental health outcomes. Int. J. Environ. Res. Public Health **19**, 15975 (2022). https://doi.org/10.3390/IJERPH192315975
40. Gianfredi, V., et al.: Association between urban greenspace and health: a systematic review of literature. Int. J. Environ. Res. Public Health **18**, 5137 (2021). https://doi.org/10.3390/IJERPH18105137/S1

Mapping Real Estate Values: A Semi-systematic Literature Review of Spatial Evaluation Methods and Approaches

Eugenio Muccio[1,2](✉) and Daniele Cannatella[3]

[1] Department of Architecture, University of Naples Federico II, Naples, Italy
eugenio.muccio@unina.it
[2] Department of Management in the Built Environment, Faculty of Architecture and the Built Environment, Delft University of Technology, Delft, The Netherlands
[3] Department of Urbanism, Faculty of Architecture and the Built Environment, Delft University of Technology, Delft, The Netherlands
d.cannatella@tudelft.nl

Abstract. As urban transformation processes grow more complex, traditional real estate valuation methods struggle in addressing rapid socio-economic, cultural, spatial, and environmental shifts. Although spatial data and analytics have advanced significantly, key challenges persist in terms of usability, transparency, and integration into practice. This study seeks to identify the most widely used and impactful spatial methods in real estate valuation, tracing their evolution over the past two decades. Employing a semi-systematic literature review grounded in the PRISMA protocol, the research analyzes peer-reviewed articles retrieved from Scopus to map the development of spatial valuation approaches. The findings highlight a growing reliance on Spatial Hedonic Approaches and Spatial Econometric techniques, which incorporate spatial dependencies and improve the accuracy of value estimates. Geographically Weighted Regression (GWR) emerges as the most commonly used GIS-based method for capturing geographic variations in property values. While traditional hedonic pricing models remain foundational, Automated Valuation Models (AVMs) are gaining momentum due to their scalability and ability to handle large datasets. The review also points to an increasing interest in spatial-temporal models, which support real-time monitoring and forecasting of property values. These trends suggest a shift toward more data-driven, spatially explicit valuation practices that bridge multiple disciplines. However, significant gaps remain, particularly in data accessibility, methodological clarity, and the incorporation of social and environmental values. Enhancing spatial intelligence in valuation frameworks could play a crucial role in shaping more sustainable urban development and informing evidence-based policy-making.

Keywords: Spatial real estate valuation · Semi-systematic literature review · Data-driven approaches

1 Introduction

The contemporary urban landscape is shaped by complex and interwoven transformative processes driven by socio-economic, cultural, technological, and environmental factors. These constant interplay deeply influences cities' spatial structure, altering their socio-economic characteristics and generating heterogeneous effects across neighbourhoods. Among the most critical dimensions affected by these transformations is the real estate market. As both a driver and an indicator of urban change, property values describe and consolidate urban growth, regeneration trends, and spatial conflict that arise in response to such processes [1, 2]. Understanding how and why real estate values change across space and time is therefore essential to informing more equitable, resilient, and sustainable urban development strategies.

Real estate valuation, traditionally grounded in economic fundamentals and market-based metrics, is now being revisited through a spatial and systemic lens [3, 4]. Classical approaches - based on comparable sales, income capitalization, or cost replacement - remain foundational, particularly for transactional purposes [5]. However, these methods often fall short in capturing the spatial heterogeneity and multi-dimensional drivers of property value dynamics in urban contexts. The evolution of real estate values is influenced not only by supply and demand but also by the spatial distribution and quality of amenities, services, land-use changes, accessibility, environmental conditions, and socio-cultural factors. As urban challenges such as gentrification, touristification, and residential displacement intensify, understanding these patterns has become critical for researchers, planners, and policymakers [6].

Real estate valuation frameworks are consequently evolving to address the complexity of urban transformations. In recent years, the growing availability of spatial data and the increasing computational capacity of analytical tools have enabled the emergence of more multi-dimensional, data-driven frameworks that account for the broad spectrum of factors underlined by urban phenomena [7]. These approaches strive for the integration of Geographic Information Science (GIScience), Multi-Criteria Decision Analysis (MCDA), and Machine Learning (ML) algorithms within Spatial Decision Support Systems (SDSSs), enabling the analysis of property values as spatially-embedded outcomes dependant on a range of different factors - from land use and environmental quality to accessibility, socio-demographic patterns, and cultural services [8–10].

This dramatic shift toward spatially-explicit and data-informed valuation frameworks reflects a wider trend in urban and real estate studies: the shift from static, transaction-based models to more dynamic tools that can better grasp the complexity of urban change. In this context, SDSSs represent a valuable methodological advancement in the field. SDSSs are "interactive, computer-based system(s) designed to support a user or group of users in achieving higher effectiveness in decision making" [11]. They provide decision-makers with the tools to synthesize large volumes of heterogeneous spatial data, address semi-structured problems, and structuring and assess scenarios, ultimately supporting planning and policy development processes that are both spatially aware and responsive to multiple objectives [12].

This study conducts a semi-systematic literature review to investigate how evolving spatial approaches to real estate valuation are represented in the academic literature landscape.

Unlike meta-analyses or narrowly defined Systematic Literature Reviews (SLRs) – which are designed to comprehensively identify, analyze, and synthesize the existing body of knowledge on a given topic – semi-systematic, or integrative, reviews combine elements of systematic protocols with the flexibility of narrative synthesis and expert judgment. This approach is particularly suited for mapping broad, interdisciplinary research landscapes, identifying convergences and gaps across different fields, and drawing interpretive conclusions across diverse methodologies. Rather than aiming for exhaustive coverage, this review focuses on the most relevant and impactful contributions that align with the evaluation criteria and research purpose [13]. It privileges significance over quantity, emphasizing the conceptual frameworks, analytical techniques, and spatial perspectives that emerge from the latest body of research on real estate valuation.

This research aims to: (i) identify the most widely adopted and impactful spatial methods and approaches in real estate valuation; (ii) map the scientific landscape emerging from the relevant body of literature; and (iii) critically reflect on the types of values these methods capture, the techniques they utilize, and the conceptual frameworks they advance. The central research question guiding this study is: Which values, evaluation methods, and approaches are most prevalent and influential in the spatial assessment of real estate dynamics?

Through the mapping of conceptual, methodological, and technological advances, the study aims to contribute to the ongoing debate on urban valuation practices by offering insights into the evolution, current state, and trajectories of spatially-explicit real estate assessment. Ultimately, this research seeks to support the development of more integrated, data-informed, and socially attuned valuation frameworks that are better suited to the complex challenges of contemporary urban and real estate management.

The remainder of the article is structured as follows: following the Introduction, Sect. 2 outlines the methodological workflow adopted for the semi-systematic literature review, drawing on the PRISMA protocol. Section 3 presents the findings that emerged from the critical analysis of the reviewed literature, while Sect. 4 offers a discussion on the effectiveness of the identified methods. Finally, Sect. 5 concludes the article by highlighting key research trends and future directions.

2 Methodology

The methodological framework of this semi-systematic literature review is grounded in the integration of systematic protocols with qualitative interpretation, aiming to synthesize emerging trends, dominant paradigms, and methodological innovations in the spatial assessment of real estate dynamics. In particular, this review adopts the Preferred Reporting Items for Systematic Reviews and Meta-Analyses (PRISMA) as its foundational structure, while extending its principles within a semi-systematic approach [14].

Originally developed to serve in evidence-based medical research, the PRISMA protocol [15] has since been adapted across multiple disciplines, including urban studies, real estate research, and data-driven policy analysis. PRISMA provides a structured four-phase flow diagram - identification, screening, eligibility, and inclusion -, complemented by a checklist to ensure methodological coherence and bias reduction in literature reviews.

By using PRISMA, this review adheres to a recognized and validated standard, which allows the mapping of a heterogeneous field while maintaining methodological accountability. However, rather than aiming for exhaustive coverage as in full systematic reviews, we adopted a semi-systematic approach incorporating interpretive judgment, trend identification, and conceptual synthesis. This enables a focus on highly cited, recent, and methodologically significant works that align with the review's aim and research question.

Following the PRISMA checklist, the first step involved designing a comprehensive and focused research query to identify relevant literature. The search string was applied to titles, abstracts, and keywords, and combined multiple conceptual domains:

("real estate valuation*" OR "real estate evaluation*" OR "real estate" OR "property appraisal" OR "residential real estate")

AND

("spatial analysis" OR "GIS" OR "spatial assessment" OR "geographic information system*")

AND

("value*" OR "evaluation method*" OR "valuation method*")

We chose the Scopus database as the primary information source due to its multidisciplinary coverage and the high quality of peer-reviewed journal publications it indexes. Several keyword combinations were tested before identifying the most suitable for the objectives of this review. For example, databases such as Scopus or Web of Science typically categorize real estate valuation literature using terms like "valuation" or "evaluation," rather than "assessment." Adopting these keywords ensures greater consistency with how authors and journals structure metadata, thereby improving the relevance and precision of search results. The review considered articles published from 2005 to 2025, covering two decades of research during which digital transformation and spatial intelligence have significantly reshaped urban studies and property evaluation practices.

We conducted a search for peer-reviewed journal articles written in English. Our focus was on empirical and methodological studies that emphasize the spatial dimension of real estate valuation. To capture the multidisciplinary nature of the topic, we included a broad range of subject areas. The inclusion and exclusion criteria are summarized in Table 1.

This selection protocol reflects the semi-systematic nature of the review: it prioritizes relevance and methodological clarity over exhaustive coverage, enabling the inclusion of highly cited, recent, and thematically aligned contributions. By combining PRISMA's structured rigour with expert-driven selection, this review provides both descriptive mapping and critical interpretation of the research landscape.

The methodological workflow follows the main steps outlined in the PRISMA 2020 flow diagram, as shown in Fig. 1. These are described below with reference to their role in shaping the final dataset of analyzed publications:

1. **Identification**: this phase involved the initial search using the designed query across the Scopus database. The result was a set of 333 potentially relevant studies addressing

Table 1. Inclusion and exclusion criteria.

Inclusion	Exclusion
Peer-reviewed journal articles;	Conference proceedings, book chapters, editorials, and other non-peer-reviewed formats;
Published between 2005 and 2025	Published before 2005;
Written in English;	Non-English publications;
Empirical or methodological studies focused on spatial aspects of real estate valuation;	Studies lacking a spatial dimension in their methodology or focus;
Belonging to one or more of the following subject areas: Social Sciences; Economics, Econometrics and Finance; Business, Management and Accounting; Computer Science; Decision Sciences	Publications centered primarily on "risk assessment" unrelated to valuation

   various aspects of spatial real estate valuation. Duplicates and irrelevant formats (e.g., conference proceedings) were excluded at this stage. Lastly, inclusion and exclusion criteria were applied. Output: 130 records identified.
2. **Screening**: it consisted of a more detailed inspection of titles and abstracts to determine thematic and methodological relevance. This step ensured the alignment of each study with the review's conceptual focus, discarding articles that lacked empirical grounding or spatial orientation. Output: 69 records retained after title/abstract screening.
3. **Selection** (Eligibility and Inclusion): in this final phase, full-text analysis was performed on the remaining publications to confirm their eligibility. Articles were assessed for methodological soundness, clarity of spatial valuation approach, and relevance to the research aim. Highly cited and recent works were prioritized in the qualitative synthesis. Output: 10 articles included in the review.

The selected body of literature provides the foundation for identifying dominant methods, assessing the evolution of spatial valuation practices, and highlighting conceptual and operational gaps in the field. This review process ultimately supports the formation of a trend-oriented narrative on how spatial intelligence, GIS technologies, and data-driven approaches are redefining the assessment of real estate dynamics in the context of contemporary urban transformation.

3 Results

The full-text analysis highlighted that, in recent years, the integration of GIS-based models and spatial econometrics techniques has become a cornerstone of innovation in real estate valuation.

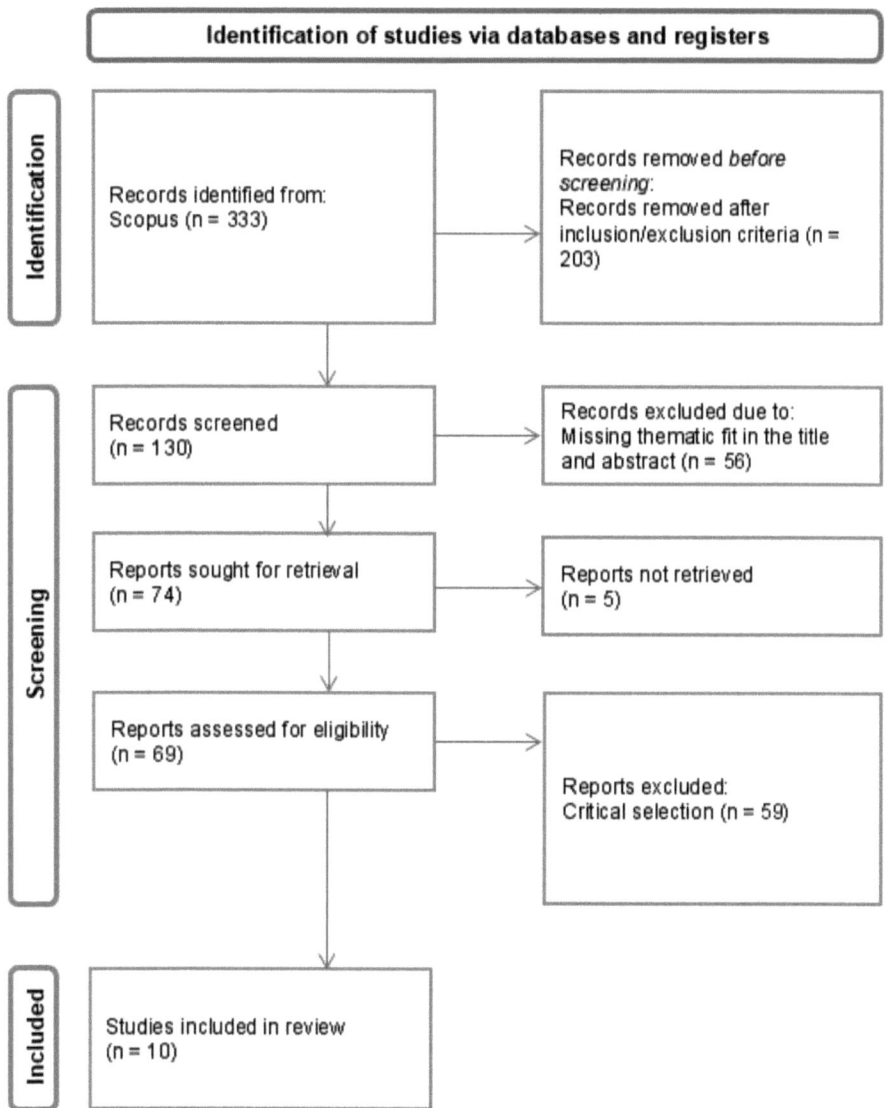

Fig. 1. PRISMA 2020 flow diagram of the selection process. Source: Authors' elaboration on Page et al., 2021.

This is evidenced by the development and refinement of a range of spatially explicit methodologies. Among these, the Spatial Hedonic Approach (SHA) has emerged as a prominent technique, combining the traditional hedonic approach with spatial econometric models [16, 17]. SHA allows analysts to account for spatial autocorrelation in property values and the geographic distribution of housing attributes. This approach has become popular in regional science, as it captures the interdependencies between properties and their surroundings, something that ordinary least squares (OLS) models often overlook [16].

Spatial econometrics as a broader field specifically addresses the spatial relationships between observations, recognizing that housing values are not randomly distributed but instead exhibit patterns of dependence shaped by location [16]. Applying spatial econometric principles to hedonic models has become standard in housing market analyses, as spatially explicit models in general are said to vastly outperform traditional OLS models [7]. Ignoring spatial effects can lead to flawed conclusions while spatial models provide more accurate estimations, especially when measuring the value of location itself.

Within this context, several spatial econometric models stand out. The Spatial Lag Model (SAR or SLM) accounts for the influence of nearby property prices on the valuation of a given unit, attempting to capture spatial dependence in the real estate market [2]. The Spatial Error Model (SEM), on the other hand, deals specifically with spatial autocorrelation in the error terms, in order to eliminate omitted variable bias from missing spatial variables. SEM has been shown to provide a better model fit in cases where disturbances are spatially structured and was notably preferred for integration into land-use transport models [18]. The Spatial Durbin Model (SDM) offers a more comprehensive framework, suitable when spatial dependence exists not only in the dependent variable but also in the explanatory variables. Among these, SAR and SEM are the most commonly applied in spatial econometrics, thanks to their robustness and interpretability [2].

In contrast to global approaches that produce more general regression models, Local Regression Approaches are particularly useful for examining geographic variation in housing price determinants [19]. Geographically Weighted Regression (GWR) is a local modeling technique and the most used GIS-based model, particularly relevant for its ability to model spatial heterogeneity [19, 20]. By allowing local regression analysis, GWR offers a more localized understanding of how housing prices respond to different factors in different areas [18, 21]. While it provides clearer analytical outcomes and higher accuracy levels compared to global OLS models, GWR can sometimes exhibit strong inter-correlation among parameter estimates [2, 7]. A recent evolution of this method is the Multiscale Geographically Weighted Regression (MGWR), which addresses one of GWR's limitations: the assumption that all variables operate at the same spatial scale [19]. MGWR acknowledges that some variables may have global effects while others have local effects, leading to models that are not only statistically sound but also more reflective of real-world housing market complexity [20]. MGWR models are increasingly used for both local and regional research, and it is advisable to use them to analyze housing prices and market activity.

The rise of machine learning and advanced computational techniques has further accelerated the evolution of spatial real estate valuation.

Automated Valuation Methods (AVMs) are relevant in spatial real estate assessment by utilizing GIS platforms to manage spatial data, analyze territorial characteristics, and implement market-based methods, especially in mass appraisal contexts [22]. The integration of Building Information Modeling (BIM) with GIS offers a dual advantage:

GIS facilitates the evaluation of extrinsic factors such as locational context, available services, environmental conditions, and land value, while BIM focuses on intrinsic property attributes and reconstruction costs. This combined approach enables a more objective and automated spatial valuation, even in cases where traditional market data is insufficient.

The challenges of valuing large numbers of properties simultaneously have led to the refinement of mass appraisal techniques, for which GIS technology became crucial, enabling more detailed and context-rich analyses of spatial attributes influencing property values [16, 18]. GIS-based models - such as GWR, SEM, SAR, and the Location Value Response Surface (LVRS) - proved particularly significant for evaluating the impact of environmental and spatial attributes on property values [23]. LVRS, in particular, supports appraisers in analysing the effect of location through GIS [18].

Altogether, the body of literature points to a paradigm shift in real estate valuation, moving from static, market-oriented approaches to dynamic, spatially-explicit, and data-driven frameworks. These methods not only offer improved predictive capabilities but also open new pathways for understanding the socio-spatial dimensions of urban property markets.

Based on the reviewed literature, Table 2 presents a comprehensive overview of the most relevant methods in the field. These approaches are predominantly grounded in spatial econometric models and GIS-based techniques, which are increasingly integrated into hybrid or mixed-method frameworks to enhance accuracy, spatial sensitivity, and analytical depth in real estate valuation.

The scientific landscape of spatial real estate assessment, visualized through VOSviewer software and presented in Fig. 2, reveals an interconnected network of research themes structured into four distinct clusters. These clusters - identified through co-occurrence analysis of terms from the reviewed literature - have been labelled as follows: Urban Planning (red), Econometrics (green), Spatial Decision-Making (blue), and Spatial Evaluations (yellow). The relative size and prominence of each cluster reflect the frequency and centrality of associated terms, illustrating their respective weight within the broader scientific discourse.

Strikingly, the term "real estate" emerges as a transversal element, intersecting and linking all four clusters, which underscores its role as a thematic pivot across disciplinary boundaries. At the heart of the entire network lies "spatial analysis," acting as the conceptual core of the landscape. Its central position highlights the growing importance of spatial thinking and geospatial methodologies in shaping contemporary approaches to real estate valuation. Figure 2 not only pinpoints the multidimensional nature of the field but also reveals the progressive convergence of apparently disconnected fields such as urban studies, economic modeling, GIScience, and decision sciences within the broader landscape of real estate research.

Table 2. Summary of reviewed literature.

Authors	Year	Methods employed	Objective	Application field	Mapping unit
Anselin and Lozano-Gracia [17]	2007	S2SLS; HAC	Assess impact of air quality on house prices using spatial econometrics	House sales price; Impact of environment and location	Property locations
Arcuri et al. [22]	2020	AVM	Combining GIS and BIM in automated valuation methods	Real estate valu-ation	Property location
Čeh et al. [23]	2018	OLS; RF	Prediction oh housing prices with random forest technique	Real estate valuation	Property locations
Cellmer et al. [20]	2020	GWR; MGWR; OLS	Analyse the effect of socio-demographic, economic, and environmental factors on average housing property prices	Real estate valuation	Local administrative units
Fotheringham et al. [21]	2015	GWR; GWR–TS	Explore spatiotemporal variations in the determinants of house prices	Real estate sales/house price prediction	Property locations
Ibeas et al. [2]	2012	Hedonic regression; SAR; SEM; SDM; GIS integration	Research influence of transport conditions on real estate prices	Real estate values/prices; Impact of transport	Property locations
L. Krause and Bitter [7]	2012	Spatial econometrics	Review and synthesis of academic literature to summarize major trends in real estate valuation research	Real estate valuation	Not applicable
Seya et al. [16]	2013	SLM/SAR; SDM	Develop automatic model selection algorithm for SLM and SDM	Boston housing dataset, Japanese real estate data	Property transactions

(*continued*)

Table 2. (*continued*)

Authors	Year	Methods employed	Objective	Application field	Mapping unit
Sisman and Aydinoglu [19]	2022	OLS; SLM/SAR; SEM; GWR; MGWR	Examine geographic variation of factors affecting housing price	Housing prices; Istanbul/Pendik District, Turkey	Property locations, Raster grids for geographic analysis
Wang and Li [18]	2019	GIS-Based and AI-Based Models	Systematic literature review of mass appraisal models and methods used for real estate assessment	Real estate mass appraisal	Property types

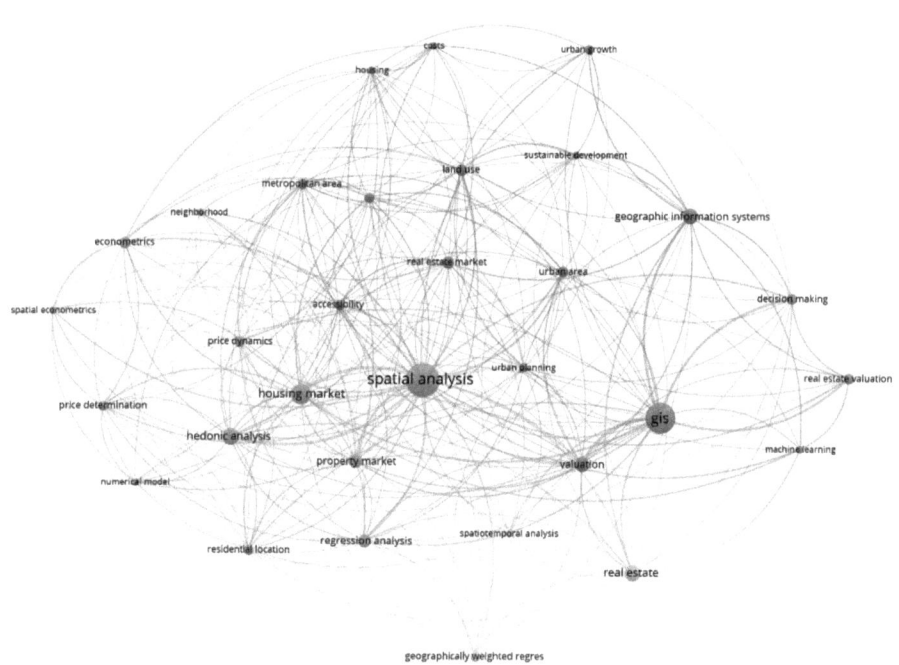

Fig. 2. The scientific landscape.

4 Discussion

Recent advancements in real estate valuation increasingly emphasize the integration of spatial analysis, GIS, and advanced data-driven techniques.

Spatially explicit models - particularly spatial econometric techniques such as SAR and SEM, and local regression models like GWR and MGWR - are increasingly recognized as valuable tools in real estate valuation [7]. Their ability to account for spatial dependence and heterogeneity enables them to outperform traditional non-spatial approaches, such as OLS, in both accuracy and explanatory power [19].

However, these models present certain challenges in practice. Their specification, estimation, and interpretation can be complex, and practitioners often face difficulties, especially regarding the construction of the spatial weight matrix, a critical component that significantly influences outcomes. Automated model selection algorithms can mitigate some of these challenges by guiding the specification process [16].

Local regression approaches like GWR and its multiscale extension, MGWR, offer valuable insights into spatially varying relationships, revealing how pricing determinants behave differently across locations. MGWR, in particular, enhances analytical precision by recognizing that not all variables exert influence at the same spatial scale [19, 20].

Despite their demonstrated effectiveness, advanced spatial methods remain underutilized in some emerging areas of valuation research - such as studies focusing on land values or sustainable urban development - pointing to untapped potential for future exploration. Neglecting spatial effects in such contexts risks introducing substantial bias into valuation outcomes [7].

Although the body of literature on spatial real estate valuation is constantly growing, several gaps and critical limitations persist. One of the main shortcomings is the scattered integration of spatial analysis techniques across different valuation models. While many studies highlight the potential of GIS and spatial econometric tools, their implementation often remains partial or detached from broader decision-making frameworks [24]. This fragmentation hampers the uptake of comprehensive SDSSs in practice.

Moreover, the application of data-driven methods is still limited by insufficient integration of spatial logic or consideration of the spatial relationships inherent in real estate markets. Many machine learning applications prioritize predictive performance over interpretability, leading to black-box models that fail to provide actionable, evidence-based insights for urban planners or policymakers. This raises concerns about the transparency, accountability, and replicability of such models, especially when used in regulatory or public-sector contexts.

The literature also tends to focus primarily on economic and market-related values, often sidelining social, environmental, and cultural dimensions of property valuation. Non-economic values are rarely incorporated into spatial valuation models, despite their increasing relevance in sustainable urban development agendas. This narrow valuation scope can lead to biased assessments that overlook important components of urban well-being and resilience.

Lastly, although methodological advancements are evident, there is a lack of consistent frameworks for evaluating the comparative effectiveness of different spatial valuation approaches. Studies rarely provide robust criteria for assessing model performance beyond accuracy metrics, and few engage in cross-model comparisons that consider data requirements, scalability, and contextual adaptability. As a result, decision-makers are often left without clear guidance on which methodologies are best suited to particular urban challenges or planning needs.

5 Conclusions

In the evolving field of real estate valuation, the integration of spatial analysis and GIS technologies is progressively shaping the landscape of future methodologies. As urban environments become increasingly complex and data-rich [25], the capacity to process, model, and visualize data to generate spatial knowledge has become not only a technical advantage but a fundamental requirement for meaningful property appraisal. Drawing on methodological approaches ranging from spatial econometrics and geostatistics to machine learning and local regression approaches, the reviewed literature demonstrates a shift towards integrated, data-driven strategies for understanding and modeling property values in complex urban contexts.

This body of work has shown how spatial analysis enables the transition from static, location-independent assessments to dynamic, spatially explicit evaluations, capable of capturing local heterogeneity, urban dynamics, and the influence of externalities such as tourism or land use change. The integration of temporal dimensions, and the increasing relevance of open and crowdsourced data sources marks an important evolution in how urban phenomena are analyzed and visualized.

Despite the maturity of some areas, such as hedonic modeling and the use of GIS for data integration, significant gaps remain. In particular, there is a need for stronger theoretical foundations that bridge urban theory, valuation principles, and socio-spatial dynamics. The limited attention to causal inference and the underutilization of advanced spatial-temporal models suggest opportunities for further methodological innovation. Moreover, the challenge of capturing the intangible, immaterial, or latent dimensions that shape real estate markets, such as the perception of place, heritage value, or cultural capital, remains largely unresolved.

While the literature demonstrates considerable innovation in the use of spatial and data-driven approaches for real estate valuation, it remains fragmented, unevenly distributed, and often methodologically opaque. Bridging these gaps requires greater interdisciplinary collaboration, broader geographic coverage, more transparent modeling practices, and a deliberate effort to incorporate non-market values into spatial valuation frameworks.

The review concludes that while the integration of GIS-based models and spatial econometrics in property valuation has made remarkable strides, it remains an evolving domain that must continue to adapt to the complexity of urban systems, the fluidity of markets, and the growing demand for equitable and sustainable development outcomes.

Several emerging trends are expected to define the trajectory of spatial-explicit real estate valuation, with machine learning and automation playing a central role. Among the most significant developments is the expanding use of machine learning algorithms in property valuation. Techniques such as artificial neural networks, ensemble learning, and hybrid models are demonstrating notable potential in exceeding the predictive accuracy of traditional econometric approaches [26]. By drawing on large, often heterogeneous datasets, these models are capable of capturing complex, non-linear relationships and interaction effects that typically elude conventional regression-based methods. When combined with spatial data, machine learning models evolve into highly adaptive tools for mass appraisal, responsive to local market variations and regional characteristics. The integration of GIS further enhances their capabilities, enabling real-time valuation updates and scenario-based forecasting [27]. An increasingly prominent trend is the integration of spatial methods, particularly GIS-based models, with Artificial Intelligence and other hybrid techniques, fostering the development of more robust and adaptive mass appraisal systems—a direction often referred to as the "3I-trend."

At the same time, spatial analysis continues to offer critical perspectives on housing markets. Spatial econometric techniques and GWR models remain essential for capturing the influence of location-specific factors on property values [28]. As concerns over environmental sustainability and urban livability become more prominent in planning and policy, spatial methods are increasingly valued for their ability to assess the geographic distribution of these influences.

Another key development is the growing adoption of AVMs. As observed, AVMs are especially effective in large-scale or resource-constrained contexts, where traditional methods may fall short [29]. Embedded within GIS platforms, they enable dynamic integration of diverse data layers and spatial cross-analysis. As data infrastructures expand and computational tools become more widely available, AVMs are set to become essential instruments for stakeholders across the real estate sector.

Looking forward, the combination of data science, geospatial intelligence, and urban analytics is expected to lead to a new generation of valuation tools that are both automated and context-sensitive. These tools will likely evolve from descriptive to predictive - and eventually to prescriptive - systems capable of simulating the impacts of urban policies, infrastructure developments, and environmental changes on property values. Furthermore, the integration of participatory GIS, crowdsourced data, and qualitative dimensions may contribute to more holistic evaluations that incorporate user perceptions, cultural assets, and non-market values into the appraisal process.

In sum, the future of real estate valuation is defined by convergence: the convergence of spatial data, artificial intelligence, and multi-scalar analysis. These advancements not only enhance the accuracy and efficiency of appraisals but also empower decision-makers with actionable insights that reflect the nuanced and dynamic nature of urban real estate markets. As technological capabilities expand, the field must also ensure ethical data use, transparency in modeling processes, and responsiveness to social and environmental concerns, maintaining a critical balance between innovation and public interest.

Authors Contributions. E.M.: Writing – original draft, Writing – review & editing, Validation, Methodology, Conceptualization, Data curation, Visualization. D.C.: Writing – review & editing, Validation, Methodology, Conceptualization.

Disclosure of Interests. The authors have no competing interests to declare that are relevant to the content of this article.

References

1. Fragoso Januário, J., Costa, Á., Oliveira Cruz, C., Miranda Sarmento, J., Faria e Sousa, V.: Transport infrastructure, accessibility, and spillover effects: an empirical analysis of the Portuguese real estate market from 2000 to 2018. Res. Transp. Econ. **90**, 101130 (2021). https://doi.org/10.1016/j.retrec.2021.101130
2. Ibeas, Á., Cordera, R., dell'Olio, L., Coppola, P., Dominguez, A.: Modelling transport and real-estate values interactions in urban systems. J. Transp. Geogr. **24**, 370–382 (2012). https://doi.org/10.1016/j.jtrangeo.2012.04.012
3. Cellmer, R.: The possibilities and limitations of geostatistical methods in real estate market analyses. Real Estate Manag. Valuation **22**, 54–62 (2014). https://doi.org/10.2478/remav-2014-0027
4. Pagourtzi, E., Assimakopoulos, V., Hatzichristos, T., French, N.: Real estate appraisal: a review of valuation methods. J. Property Investment Finance **21**, 383–401 (2003). https://doi.org/10.1108/14635780310483656
5. Herath, S., Maier, G.: The Hedonic Price Method in Real Estate and Housing Market Research: A Review of the Literature https://doi.org/10.57938/e55da0fe-d130-415d-9a5d-7bbc07c329a1
6. Cocola-Gant, A.: Place-based displacement: touristification and neighborhood change. Geoforum **138**, 103665 (2023). https://doi.org/10.1016/j.geoforum.2022.103665
7. L. Krause, A., Bitter, C.: Spatial econometrics, land values and sustainability: trends in real estate valuation research. Cities **29**, S19–S25 (2012). https://doi.org/10.1016/j.cities.2012.06.006
8. Cerreta, M., Panaro, S., Poli, G.: A spatial decision support system for multifunctional landscape assessment: a transformative resilience perspective for vulnerable inland areas. Sustainability **13**, 2748 (2021). https://doi.org/10.3390/su13052748
9. Sugumaran, R., Degroote, J.: Spatial decision support systems: Principles and practices. CRC Press (2010)
10. Campagna, M.: GIS for sustainable development. In: GIS for Sustainable Development, pp. 2–20. CRC Press (2005)
11. Malczewski, J.: GIS and multicriteria decision analysis. John Wiley & Sons (1999)
12. Keenan, P.B., Jankowski, P.: Spatial decision support systems: three decades on. Decis. Support. Syst. **116**, 64–76 (2019). https://doi.org/10.1016/j.dss.2018.10.010
13. Snyder, H.: Literature review as a research methodology: an overview and guidelines. J. Bus. Res. **104**, 333–339 (2019). https://doi.org/10.1016/j.jbusres.2019.07.039
14. Liberati, A., et al.: The PRISMA statement for reporting systematic reviews and meta-analyses of studies that evaluate health care interventions: explanation and elaboration. Ital. J. Public Health **6** (2009). https://doi.org/10.2427/5768
15. Page, M.J., et al.: The PRISMA 2020 statement: an updated guideline for reporting systematic reviews. BMJ. n71 (2021). https://doi.org/10.1136/bmj.n71
16. Seya, H., Yamagata, Y., Tsutsumi, M.: Automatic selection of a spatial weight matrix in spatial econometrics: application to a spatial hedonic approach. Reg. Sci. Urban Econ. **43**, 429–444 (2013). https://doi.org/10.1016/j.regsciurbeco.2013.02.002
17. Anselin, L., Lozano-Gracia, N.: Errors in variables and spatial effects in hedonic house price models of ambient air quality. Empirical Econ. **34**, 5–34 (2007). https://doi.org/10.1007/s00181-007-0152-3
18. Wang, D., Li, V.J.: Mass appraisal models of real estate in the 21st century: a systematic literature review. Sustainability **11**, 7006 (2019). https://doi.org/10.3390/su11247006
19. Sisman, S., Aydinoglu, A.C.: A modelling approach with geographically weighted regression methods for determining geographic variation and influencing factors in housing price: a case

in Istanbul. Land Use Policy **119**, 106183 (2022). https://doi.org/10.1016/j.landusepol.2022.106183
20. Cellmer, R., Cichulska, A., Bełej, M.: Spatial analysis of housing prices and market activity with the geographically weighted regression. ISPRS Int. J. Geo Inf. **9**, 380 (2020). https://doi.org/10.3390/ijgi9060380
21. Fotheringham, A.S., Crespo, R., Yao, J.: Exploring, modelling and predicting spatiotemporal variations in house prices. Ann. Reg. Sci. **54**, 417–436 (2015). https://doi.org/10.1007/s00168-015-0660-6
22. Arcuri, N., De Ruggiero, M., Salvo, F., Zinno, R.: Automated valuation methods through the cost approach in a BIM and GIS integration framework for smart city appraisals. Sustainability **12**, 7546 (2020). https://doi.org/10.3390/su12187546
23. Čeh, M., Kilibarda, M., Lisec, A., Bajat, B.: Estimating the performance of random forest versus multiple regression for predicting prices of the apartments. ISPRS Int. J. Geo Inf. **7**, 168 (2018). https://doi.org/10.3390/ijgi7050168
24. Kobylińska, K.: The application of spatial autoregressive models for analyzing the influence of spatial factors on real estate prices and values. Real Estate Manag. Valuation **29**, 23–35 (2021). https://doi.org/10.2478/remav-2021-0027
25. Kitchin, R., Lauriault, T.P., McArdle, G.: Knowing and governing cities through urban indicators, city benchmarking and real-time dashboards. Reg. Stud. Reg. Sci. **2**, 6–28 (2015). https://doi.org/10.1080/21681376.2014.983149
26. Lin, R.F.-Y., Ou, C., Tseng, K.-K., Bowen, D., Yung, K.L., Ip, W.H.: The Spatial neural network model with disruptive technology for property appraisal in real estate industry. Technol. Forecast. Soc. Chang. **173**, 121067 (2021). https://doi.org/10.1016/j.techfore.2021.121067
27. Calainho, F.D., van de Minne, A.M., Francke, M.K.: A machine learning approach to price indices: applications in commercial real estate. J. Real Estate Finance Econ. **68**, 624–653 (2022). https://doi.org/10.1007/s11146-022-09893-1
28. Dimopoulos, T., Yiorkas, C.: Implementing GIS in real estate price prediction and mass valuation: The case study of Nicosia District. In: Fifth International Conference on Remote Sensing and Geoinformation of the Environment (RSCy2017), p. 72. SPIE (2017)
29. Krämer, B., Stang, M., Doskoč, V., Schäfers, W., Friedrich, T.: Automated valuation models: improving model performance by choosing the optimal spatial training level. SSRN Electron. J. (2022). https://doi.org/10.2139/ssrn.4272379

Measuring Settlement Efficiency. Application to an Urban Regeneration

Federica Cicalese(✉) , Michele Grimaldi , and Isidoro Fasolino

University of Salerno, Via Giovanni Paolo II, 132 Fisciano, (SA), Italy
fcicalese@unisa.it

Abstract. Urban regeneration is defined as a set of comprehensive actions aimed at providing solutions and leading to the recovery of physical conditions, and economic activity, the socio-cultural integration of community members and the restoration of environmental quality in places where these aspects have declined. In this context, there is a need to incorporate sustainable development goals into the decision-making process. In fact, there is currently no concrete and applicable tool that planners can use to obtain empirical and measurable results on how to achieve these goals.

This paper proposes a methodology to assess the urban settlements efficiency. The focus is on the settlement, which can be identified as a neighbourhood or an urban area that is the subject of a neighbourhood plan, in an attempt to lead the debate to an operational scale and to reflect on the contents of the plan on a detailed scale. The model uses a system of indicators specifically built from a broad survey of scientific articles and international experience. More than twenty quantitative and qualitative criteria are proposed as the basis for evaluation. This methodology led us to define and calculate the composite settlement efficiency index (EI). Identifying indicators for the urban environment is essential for monitoring urban trends. Their use makes it possible to control both the measurement and evaluation of each system's component's contribution to the overall efficiency of the settlement.

The methodology was applied to an urban regeneration case study, located in Nocera Inferiore (Southern-Italy). The evaluation permits performance comparisons to be made between different project scenarios, and variations on an indicator set basis. The overall goal is to provide the urban planning process with tools for designing livable and inclusive settlements, in line with sustainable development goals.

Keywords: Urban regeneration · Settlement efficiency · Neighbourhood plan

1 Introduction

Nowadays, cities face numerous environmental problems such as pollution, the effects of climate change, and depletion of natural resources that affect the quality of life of people living in urban environments [1]. The ongoing process of global warming, driven by the escalating concentration of greenhouse gases generated by human activities, especially in urban areas, significantly impacts public health.

Urban policies aim at climate neutrality by 2050 (Net Zero), managing the energy crisis and improving cities' capacity to absorb CO_2 through targeted climate change mitigation and adaptation strategies [2].

In this context, urban planners have a key role to play in creating and maintaining attractive and liveable cities [3] and the most comprehensive and effective tool that governments can adopt is urban regeneration [4, 5]. It can be defined as an integrated and inclusive process that combines physical, environmental, and socio-economic measures [4]. With the potential to advance almost all Sustainable Development Goals (SDGs) of the 2030 Agenda, urban regeneration serves as a multifaceted solution addressing challenges such as social equity, human health, carbon emissions, infrastructure improvement, livability, and housing [6]. It acts as a comprehensive driver for the localization of the SDGs, employing data-driven insights, participatory planning, and targeted interventions to create sustainable urban transformations.

Today, more than ever, it is necessary to address the question of how efficient our settlements are, considering the environmental, social and economic challenges we face every day. The increasing complexity of urban problems calls for a methodological approach that allows for an objective assessment of the efficiency of the adopted strategies. For this reason, it becomes essential to identify suitable measurement tools, through clear and measurable indicators, capable of returning a precise evaluation of the actions adopted.

The use of the term "efficiency" rather than "effectiveness" highlights the critical role that resources play. "Efficiency" refers to the ability to achieve a system of objectives with the minimum expenditure of resources, thereby maximizing the instrumental value of the approach, its productive capacity, and its overall performance [7]. In a setting marked by structural scarcity of resources of all kinds, the relationship between available resources and the objectives to be achieved takes on exceptional importance. Indeed, general settlement inefficiency reflects the outcome of a complex interplay between weaknesses in urban planning, social dynamics, the often unintended consequences of sectoral policies, and the market forces that often intersect with these factors [7].

This article aims to fill the gap in the assessment of measures that exists at the planning and design level. Therefore, a methodology is proposed as a tool to support planners in assessing the efficiency of different design choices in the context of urban regeneration. Through a holistic approach, an attempt is made to offer an overview to guide urban planning towards more sustainable and efficient solutions. Measuring the efficiency of interventions makes it possible not only to monitor the achievement of set objectives, but also to adapt strategies according to specific local needs. An approach based on quantitative and qualitative indicators makes it possible to optimise the use of resources, maximise the benefits for the community and ensure truly sustainable interventions in the long term.

In particular, a definition of the settlement efficiency index (EI) is carried out (Sect. 2), to formulate a synthetic judgement on the overall performance of a portion of an urban area; a comparison of different scenarios of an urban regeneration project is envisaged (Sect. 3). The main results (Sect. 4) of this research concern the possibility of numerically measuring the aspects that influence urban quality at the urban scale, considered the most suitable as a self-sufficient spatial unit to show the results of regeneration.

2 Methodology

In the face of an established awareness dictated by the agenda and the resources planned to achieve the objectives of sustainable development, the need emerges to introduce decision support mechanisms that effectively allow the urban transformation to be evaluated on an urban scale starting from the elements of the project that can effectively contribute to the achievement of sustainability, hereinafter referred to as "urban devices". The methodology relies on three main stages:

- Urban devices measurement
- Construction of different project scenarios
- Construction of a composite index

2.1 Phase 1: Urban Devices Measurement

The methodology consists of 22 urban devices that make up the settlement efficiency model. Then, concerning the nature of the different criteria, 3 homogeneous areas were identified into which the selected indicators could be grouped: Artificial Capital – AC, Natural Capital – NC and Social Capital – SC (Table 1). More precisely, the Artificial Capital is understood as the set of artefacts created by man to raise the quality of life. About Natural and Social Capital, reference is made to concepts already present in the literature [8–10] that refer to the role of nature in urban areas and to the heritage of knowledge and awareness of settled communities.

Qualitative and quantitative indicators have been identified for their measurement [11]. Identifying indicators for the urban environment is crucial to monitor urban trends and manage the measurement and evaluation of the contribution of each component to the overall functioning of the settlement, in a controlled manner. They were specifically developed through an extensive review of scientific literature and international experiences. They have also been selected taking into account that the sustainable design of spaces must: adapt to climate change; ensure an adequate level of soil permeability; allow the collection of rainwater as a result of massive storms; generate spaces to manage emergencies, suitable for gathering a huge number of people in safe conditions.

Many existing approaches focus on single aspects of sustainability, tending to privilege only one of the capitals or to consider them separately. Instead, the proposed methodology systematically integrates the three components - artificial, natural and social capital - allowing for a holistic assessment of the quality and efficiency of a settlement. Moreover, the methodology only includes indicators that can be monitored and modified by implementing urban planning tools (e.g. permeable surface, functional mix, etc.). This ensures consistency between assessment and intervention possibilities, filling an operational gap that many theories leave open.

To obtain a comprehensive evaluation of the performance of each urban device and to assess the success and efficiency of specific design choices, performance bands were assigned. An equal number of performance bands were established, with threshold values derived from existing literature when available. For qualitative criteria, efforts were made to translate them into corresponding quantitative ranges. The four performance bands are scored from 0 to 3, where a score of 0 shows that the calculated value is zero or insufficient relative to the efficiency objectives, while a score of 3 reflects performance

Table 1. The 22 urban devices categorised by capital

Artificial capital		Natural Capital		Social Capital	
1	Cycle paths	13	Permeable surfaces	18	Multifunctional square
2	Pedestrian spaces	14	Ecological habitat	19	Urban center
3	Intermodal nodes	15	Urban gardens	20	Functional mixité
4	Recycling and composting infrastructure	16	Ecological micro-corridors	21	Social mixité
5	Building geometry	17	Tree density	22	Water square
6	Urban compactness				
7	Photovoltaic roof				
8	District heating				
9	Water mirrors				
10	Green roof				
11	Sustainable urban drainage system				
12	Water collection and reuse system				

most aligned with the efficiency goals. For qualitative indicators, the score remains consistent: a score of 0 indicates the absence of the evaluated indicator, while a score of 3 indicates a high presence.

Artificial Capital

The *artificial* capital derives from the transformation of natural capital (e.g., houses, roads, bridges). In this category is possible to identify four main themes: energy, mobility, water and waste management. Each consists of one or more urban devices, representing particular features of an efficient neighbourhood, in order to ensure the realisation of the overall principles and objectives [12].

The "energy" sub-category encompasses the use of passive design strategies, district heating and cooling systems and the use of photovoltaic roofs. Appropriate passive design considerations account for key building parameters such as building structure and orientation, district heating and cooling system. The methodology also considers elements such as urban compactness by promoting solutions that reduce land consumption and settlement dispersion [13].

The "waste management" encompasses the implementation of recycling and composting infrastructures while the "water" sub-category takes into account different aspect of sustainable water management, that's an integral aspect of the overall drive toward sustainable development [12]. Water management includes implementing water conservation strategies and the use of water-efficient devices, through sustainable urbane drainage system, water collection and reuse system, mirror of waters and green roofs.

Then, the "mobility" sub-category takes into account pedestrian spaces, cycle paths and internodal modes. These are an essential factor in a community's transportation infrastructure and are vital components to promote physical and mental health [12]. They reduce traffic congestion by providing an alternate mode of travel, which accordingly reduces the associated atmospheric pollution and provides a healthier living environment with more clean, fresh air to breathe in.

Natural and Social Capital
Natural capital, includes ecosystems, biodiversity, and environmental matrices essential for preserving natural resources [14, 15]. Tree-lined streets provide an attractive and shaded walking environment. They provide a visual wall and clear edges to sidewalks which helps motorists control their speed, hence creating safer walking environments. In addition, the trees close proximity to moving vehicles allows them to absorb harmful pollutants released from their tailpipe emissions. Trees are also highly effective at obscuring unappealing vertical street features such as lighting and utility poles [12].

The *social* capital, encompasses the wealth of knowledge and interactions within settled communities [9, 16, 17]. Here are taken into account the presence of water square, multifunctional square, urban center, and the functional and social mixite.

2.2 Phase 2: Construction of Different Project Scenarios

In the context of urban regeneration, scenarios are used to predict the effects of different design configurations and interventions on urban areas. This method is an essential tool, as it allows us to model hypothetical scenarios by evaluating the effects produced by different strategies on urban settlement. Through this process, we can identify which urban devices have a more or less significant impact on achieving settlement sustainability.

Scenarios allow for exploring preferences between alternative strategies in the context of a range of future worlds: some representing how they would like their political and social environment to evolve, others less desirable futures [18]. They can be used to help the decision maker develop a better understanding of the complex relationships among uncertainties, objectives and strategic options [19]. By having alternative policies, the decision makers can better understand the range of possibilities and the diverse interests of the stakeholders [20]. When combined with option planning and a clear, structured view of what is desirable, scenarios provide a coherent framework for evaluating strategic options [19].

The methodology relies on three project scenarios:

- *Scenario 0 - Trend* represents the design choices in the study area relative to the planivolumetric distribution of buildings on the territory according to the sizing and proportioning calculations, as established by the Technical Implementation Regulations (NTA).
- *Scenario 1 - Intermediate*, proposes to improve the efficiency index calculated in the previous scenario, imagining to design interventions to be carried out in the "short term".

– *Scenario 2 - Final*, the last scenario developed, is proposed as an evolution of the previous scenarios, implementing actions aimed at the progressive improvement of the district's energy and environmental performance, imagining the design of interventions to be implemented in the "long term". The objective is thus to realise a scenario of maximising settlement efficiency, making the most of certain solutions and urban devices.

2.3 Phase 3: Construction of a Composite Index

The last phase of the model construction concerns the definition of the Settlement Efficiency Index (EI), a key parameter to evaluate the overall performance of the scenarios developed in the previous stage.

This index plays a key role in urban planning, as it provides a numerical framework that summarises how well each scenario meets the objectives of sustainability, quality of public space and efficiency of infrastructure. Using a summary parameter makes it possible to compare the various urban configurations objectively and to identify which design solutions have the greatest positive impact on the context under consideration.

Since the indicators considered come from different thematic areas and have different units of measurement, it is essential to adopt an aggregation method that allows the various dimensions of urban sustainability to be compared. This is necessary to harmonise data on distinct urban phenomena, such as energy efficiency, biodiversity and social inclusion, which cannot be directly compared due to their different nature.

The aggregation of the data is done through normalisation techniques that make the different values homogenous, thus allowing a comparative analysis and the creation of an overall index that accurately represents the quality of the urban scenario as a whole.

The normalised total efficiency index ($EI_{t,n}$) can be evaluated through the weighted sum of three indices:

$$EI_{t,n} = \sum w_k EI_{k,n} = w_{CA} EI_{CA,n} + w_{CN} EI_{CN,n} + w_{CS} EI_{CS,n} \quad (1)$$

where:

k = identified thematic areas (Artificial Capital - CA, Natural Capital - CN and Social Capital - CS);
w = weights assigned to the three capitals;
$EI_{k,n}$ = normalised efficiency index referring to the k-th capital.

The normalised index $EI_{k,n}$ related to each capital k (k = CA, CN, CS) is calculated by dividing the total score obtained in the analysed scenario ($p_{m,k}$) for the total score of the maximised scenario ($p_{m,k_{max}}$):

$$EI_{k,n} = \frac{\sum_{m=1}^{24} p_{m,k}}{\sum_{m=1}^{24} p_{m,k_{max}}} \quad (2)$$

3 Application

The case study concerned an urban regeneration hypothesis of an area located in the municipality of Nocera Inferiore, in southern Italy (see Fig. 1a). Following an analysis of the structural framework of the Municipal Urban Plan (PUC), it emerges that the area examined is class D7 'Reused disused industrial areas'. In particular, they include disused industrial complexes variously subdivided and destined for tertiary activities, with occasional arrangements of the covered surfaces, almost entirely paved and used as pertaining parking and manoeuvring spaces.

The intervention area (see Fig. 1b) consists of 2 compartments: the first, with an area of 40,687 square metres, and the second, further south, covers an area of 31,296 square metres, for a total of 71,983 square metres. Currently, the area is marked by the presence of disused or underused production lots, which are located within a consolidated urban fabric.

3.1 Scenario 0

The first scenario (see Fig. 2) was drawn up on the basis of the Technical Implementation Regulations (NTA) of the Municipal Urban Plan (PUC) of the Municipality of Nocera Inferiore.

The planned interventions, therefore, follow the regulatory prescriptions without introducing significant innovations. A percentage of permeable surfaces equal to 35% is guaranteed, and the tree planting index (0.005 trees/sqm) is respected, ensuring the insertion of trees in the subdivision. Although at this early stage, the presence of greenery is still limited compared to future scenarios, the inclusion of green spaces is crucial for improving air quality and creating more liveable environments. Increased tree cover provides natural shade, lowering temperatures in public areas during the summer and making open spaces more usable.

From a functional and social point of view, Scenario 0 manages to maintain a good balance between different uses. Fifty per cent of the gross usable surface (Slp) is dedicated to the residential function, with 15% reserved for social housing (Ers). This is crucial to ensure greater housing accessibility, promoting social inclusion and offering residential opportunities also to those who have difficulty accessing the housing market. The remaining 50% of the Slp is intended for non-residential functions, such as relational offices, commercial activities and public establishments. This distribution makes it possible to create a balanced mix between residential and services, avoiding the formation of monofunctional quarters and ensuring a constant animation of the area, contributing to a more dynamic and attractive urban fabric.

An adequate road system has been planned to facilitate the connection with the surrounding urban context and support the new functional layout. Sub-area 2 is provided with a cycle track, given the presence of a pre-existing cycle network outside the area, which is thus implemented to improve the connection with the rest of the city and ensure greater continuity in the cycle routes. At the same time, larger and well-organised pedestrian spaces are created, making the area more accessible for pedestrians and increasing their safety and comfort.

3.2 Scenario 1

This scenario (see Fig. 3) represents an evolution of Scenario 0 in that urban devices are introduced that improve efficiency through the conversion of various impermeable, extensive and flat roofs into green roofs, and in photovoltaic roofs for public buildings.

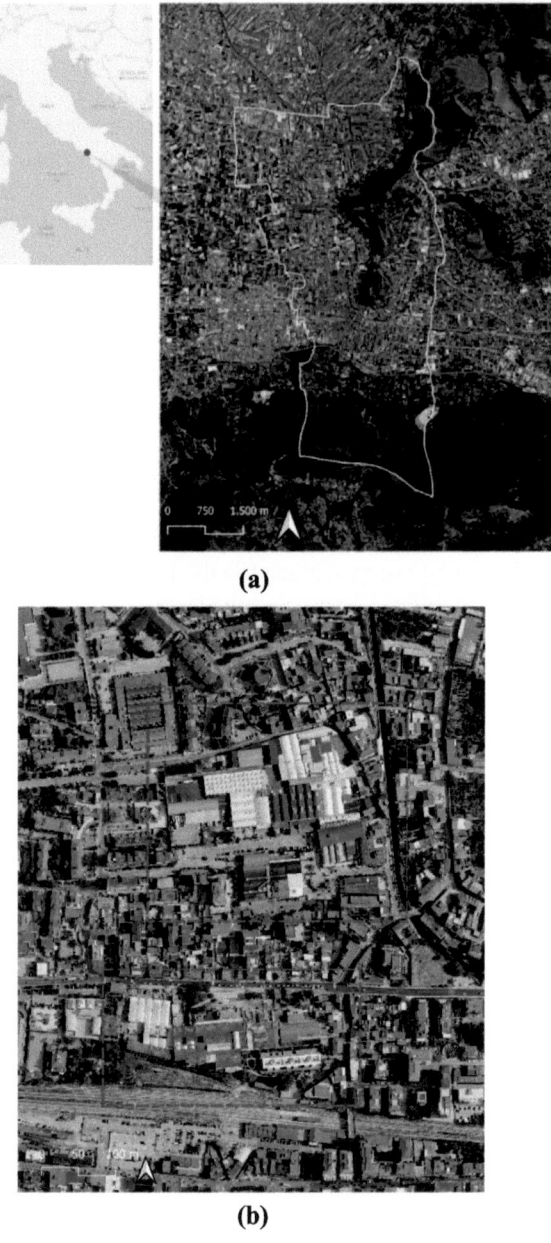

Fig. 1. (a) Territorial framework. Identification of the location of the intervention area in the municipality of Nocera Inferiore (outline in white); (b) Intervention area: sub-area 1 (top – outline red) and sub-area 2 (bottom – outline red) (Color figure online).

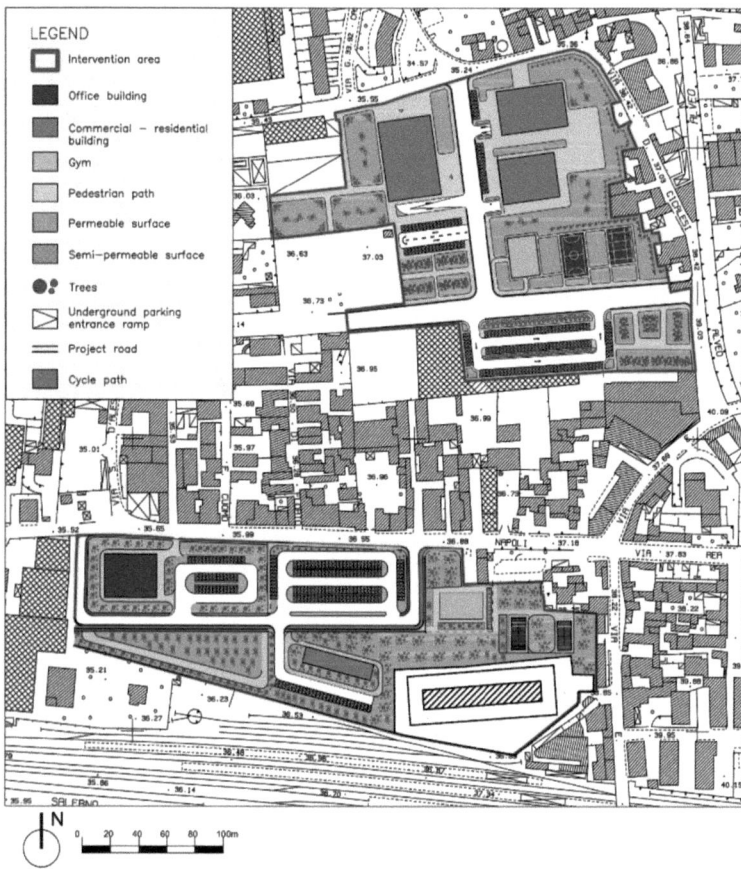

Fig. 2. Project plan of Scenario 0 (source: Author's elaboration)

Water mirrors and collection tanks have been provided. An urban garden is planned to promote inclusion and well-being, as well as to promote a short food chain and sustainable, ecological agriculture.

An intermodal node is also planned. These places ensure the integration of public and private transport by overcoming the purely transport-related aspect of interchanges, which are useful not only for the fluidification of travel and the improvement of the use of public transport, but also for the quality of life, health and safety of citizens.

The presence of an intermodal node shelter favors integrated mobility and implies the presence of an interconnection between at least two or more different services and transport systems, in this case between pedestrian mobility, mobility using public transport and cycle mobility. The shelter is designed in such a way as to have the following requirements: stopping bay; pavement; connection with cycle path; waiting area protected by shelter, with photovoltaic covering, partially closed to protect against wind and rain, equipped with seating and illuminated; presence of bicycle racks and parking

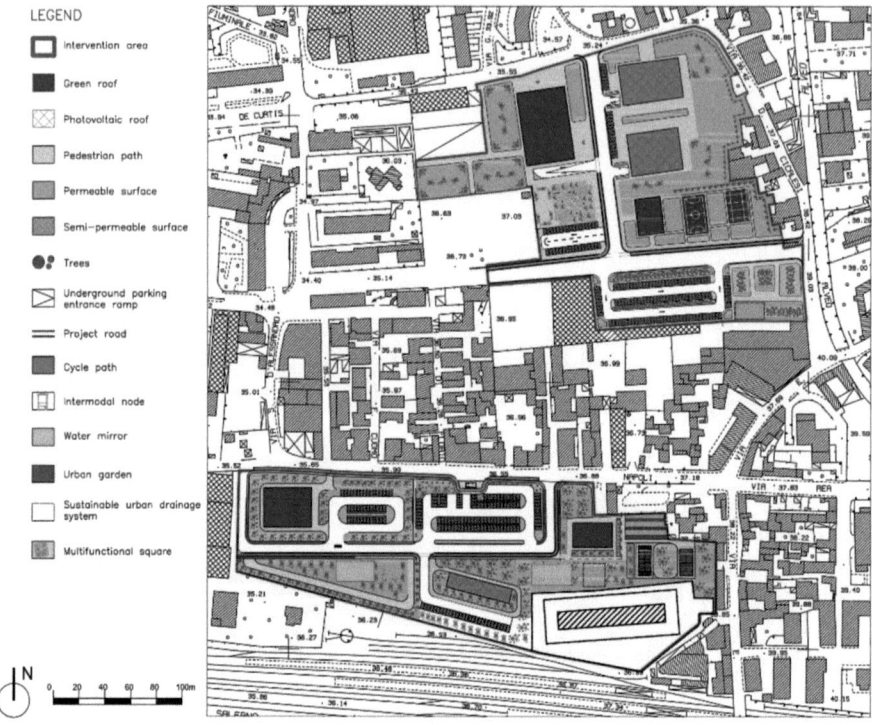

Fig. 3. Project plan of Scenario 1 (source: Author's elaboration)

spaces, also connected to a possible bike sharing service; or electric vehicle charging station.

3.3 Scenario 2

Finally, the third scenario (see Fig. 4) represents the culmination of the design evolution, improving the connections between the different urban functions, enhancing the bicycle network with more efficient connections between the subdivisions, and introducing an Urban Center as a strategic point for governance and active participation of the municipality.

4 Results and Discussions

To exemplify the proposed procedure, different planning scenarios were formulated. The scenarios are differentiated by design choices involving surfaces, volumes, roofs and urban devices. For clarity, a summary table (Table 2) of the urban devices implemented in the three scenarios is given below.

It should be emphasised that the application of the methodology at the neighbourhood scale is a methodological choice closely linked to the operational and implementation

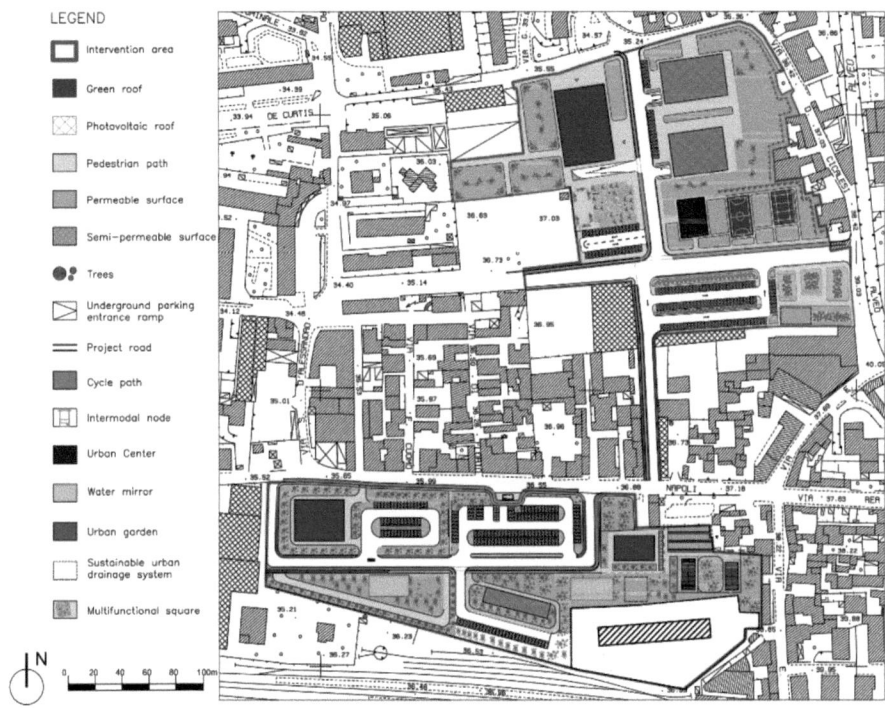

Fig. 4. Project plan of Scenario 2 (source: Author's elaboration)

nature of urban planning and to the need for direct controllability of the indicators used. The neighbourhood is the territorial context in which the implementation tools envisaged by urban planning are concretely applied, it is the scale at which it is possible to concretely intervene in order to modify urban structures, without losing the readability and governability of the context. It is only at the neighbourhood scale that the indicators used in the methodology can be measured and controlled through rules and regulations. On larger scales, these indicators would become too aggregated or inconsistent with direct urban planning action: for example, the percentage of permeable surface area of an entire municipality does not provide useful operational indications for intervening on a specific urban area. In this way, the object of study would change, no longer having the same level of detail nor the same capacity to affect punctual settlement patterns, and the methodology would have to be completely rethought to reflect the dynamics of the new scale.

The analysis of the three scenarios offered the opportunity to assess how efficient the different urban configurations are. Looking at the overall results, we can verify the increasing trend in the values of the normalised total efficiency index $EI_{t,n}$ (Table 3) (Fig. 5).

Scenario 0, derived from the simple application of the NTAs, presents a low level of efficiency, due to a lack of infrastructure, scarcity of public spaces and poor integration

Table 2. Urban devices implemented in different scenarios.

N.	URBAN DEVICE	SCENARIO 0	SCENARIO 1	SCENARIO 2
1	Cycle paths	X	X	X
2	Pedestrian spaces	X	X	X
3	Intermodal nodes	–	X	X
4	Recycling and composting infrastructure	–	–	–
5	Building geometry	X	X	X
6	Urban compactness	X	X	X
7	Photovoltaic roof	–	X	X
8	District heating	–	–	–
9	Water mirrors	–	X	X
10	Green roof	–	X	X
11	Sustainable urban drainage system	–	X	X
12	Water collection and reuse system	–	–	–
13	Permeable surfaces	X	X	X
14	Ecological habitat	–	–	–
15	Urban gardens	–	X	X
16	Ecological micro-corridors	–	–	–
17	Tree density	X	X	X
18	Multifunctional square	–	X	X
19	Urban center	–	–	X
20	Functional mixité	X	X	X
21	Social mixité	X	X	X
22	Water square	–	–	–

Table 3. Comparison of results between the three scenarios analysed.

	Scenario 0	Scenario 1	Scenario 2
	EI_k	EI_k	EI_k
Artificial Capital	0,18	0,36	0,39
Natural Capital	0,17	0,50	0,50
Social Capital	0,13	0,27	0,47
$EI_{t,n}$	**0,48**	**1,13**	**1,36**

of natural elements into the urban environment to highlight the fact that considerations of settlement efficiency are neglected within the regulation.

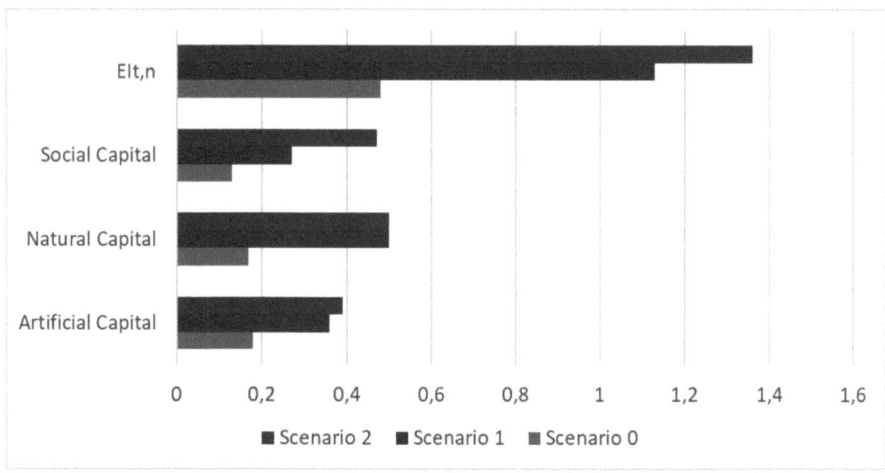

Fig. 5. Comparison of the 3 scenarios (source: Author's elaboration)

As far as Scenario 1 and Scenario 2 are concerned, it can be seen, by reading the values obtained, that certain choices can guarantee a certain degree of success in terms of improving energy and environmental efficiency performance, towards a path ever closer to sustainability.

The introduction of new urban devices, infrastructures and services (bicycle lanes, water squares, green roofs, efficient intermodal nodes, urban centres, etc.) and the correct management and possible implementation of existing devices lead to a systematic improvement of settlement efficiency.

This result demonstrates how a strategic and integrated approach can truly maximise urban performance, ensuring a more sustainable, accessible and resilient environment.

5 Final Remarks

In this contribution, a methodology has been proposed that allows for quantifying the added value resulting from the gradual introduction of urban devices, providing a clear view of the efficiency of the strategies adopted and creating a basis for future planning and design decisions. The integration of mixed-use developments, green infrastructure, and sustainable mobility solutions plays a fundamental role in shaping urban areas that are more liveable, accessible, and environmentally friendly.

In particular, the article concerned the application of the model to a case of urban regeneration. Urban transformation resulting from the reutilization of urban areas, formerly occupied by industrial complexes, represents a great opportunity for regeneration and urban renewal, to balance the physical and functional structure of the existing city. Mostly these areas are real voids to be returned to the city, assigning new functions, catalysts of different activities and generators of a substantial housing income, and defining new spaces, both for public and private use, aimed at combining social and collective urban interaction.

The model development perspectives are embedded in the potential of the methodology and in the way it is structured. Hence, the proposed model is configured as a controlling tool, in quantitative terms, of the effects induced by town planning choices on the degree of settlement efficiency. In this way, it is possible to make the necessary changes to increase the quality of the solutions identified in the municipal urban plan. In this sense, it is emphasised that this model is designed to be applied exclusively on an implementation level for two reasons. Firstly, the difficulty of managing this approach to the whole city, as its application to a neighbourhood or settlement implies fewer variables to be controlled.

Secondly, from the perspective of "think globally, act locally", it is considered necessary, in order to increase the resilience of the city as a whole, to act first of all on individual neighbourhoods and settlements.

On the basis of the model, the domain of intervention is defined by the possibility of affecting the physical and functional organisation of the settlement. The contents, that is, are all those that can credibly be found in the technical rules of a plan and, consequently, define the settlement in all its parts in an urban planning controllable way.

The full implementation within a settlement of the urban devices imagined in the model presupposes upstream conditions that consist of far-sighted policies and regulations that substantiate them. It also presupposes that interventions are allowed or foreseen in the superordinate planning tools so that they can be effectively implemented through urban implementation plans or urban projects.

Through a comparative analysis of the elaborated scenarios, it was possible to observe how different design choices influence the ability of the intervention to meet the needs of liveability, environmental resilience and social inclusion.

While the results obtained are not intended to represent absolute values, the proposed model serves as a valuable tool to systematically monitor all design aspects contributing to the efficiency of an urban settlement. The practical application of this model provides decision-makers with a more precise understanding of the effects of urban transformations.

This study, in fact, is limited to checking the contents of the urban plan, putting forward proposals in support of the project, with respect to the three themes considered relevant. Specifically, the usefulness of the presented model will lie in the possibility of its use both for evaluations and to support decision-making. In the first case, it can provide a tool to integrate strategic environmental assessment to the areas for which the municipal urban plan refers to detailed forecasts or make up for its absence on a municipal level by allowing for the evaluation of urban implementation plans. In the second case, it can provide quantitative information on the effects induced by the urban choices on the environment. These allow for the appropriate changes to be made in order to raise the quality level of the settlement. Therefore, in order to make these assessments comparable, it is necessary to base the construction of indicators on an ontology of urban structure. Finally, they can be used to stimulate participation as an indispensable element to support decision-making processes in the allocation of priorities and in the selection of possible alternatives.

Acknowledgments. Thanks to Carmela Giliberti for drawing up the calculations and design plans.

Disclosure of Interests. The authors have no competing interests to declare that are relevant to the content of this article.

References

1. Oliverio, M., Conticelli, E.: Steering net zero land take urban growth. a decision support method applied to the city of Castelfranco Emilia, Italy. In: Marucci, A., Zullo, F., Fiorini, L., and Saganeiti, L. (eds.) Innovation in Urban and Regional Planning. pp. 171–182. Springer Nature Switzerland, Cham (2024). https://doi.org/10.1007/978-3-031-54096-7_16
2. Nuvolari-Duodo, I., et al.: Integrated climate change mitigation and public health protection strategies: the case of the City of Bologna, Italy. IJERPH **21**, 1457 (2024). https://doi.org/10.3390/ijerph21111457
3. Carter, J.G., Cavan, G., Connelly, A., Guy, S., Handley, J., Kazmierczak, A.: Climate change and the city: building capacity for urban adaptation. Prog. Plan. **95**, 1–66 (2015). https://doi.org/10.1016/j.progress.2013.08.001
4. UN-Habitat: Urban regeneration as a tool for inclusive and sustainable recovery. https://unhabitat.org/urban-regeneration-as-a-tool-for-inclusive-and-sustainable-recovery, (2021)
5. Roberts, P., Sykes, H.: Urban Regeneration: A Handbook. SAGE Publications Ltd, 1 Oliver's Yard, 55 City Road, London EC1Y 1SP United Kingdom (2008). https://doi.org/10.4135/9781446219980
6. UN-Habitat: Urban Regeneration for Localizing the Sustainable Development Goals (2024)
7. Fasolino, I., Grimaldi, M.: The urban planning efficiency of settlements. Techniques and actions. ARCHIVIO DI STUDI URBANI E REGIONALI, 5–10 (2020). https://doi.org/10.3280/ASUR2020-127-S1001
8. Fasolino, I., Coppola, F., Grimaldi, M.: A model for urban planning control of the settlement efficiency. A case study. In: Archivio di studi urbani e regionali, pp. 181–210. FrancoAngeli, Milano, Italy (2020)
9. Schetke, S., Haase, D., Kötter, T.: Towards sustainable settlement growth: a new multi-criteria assessment for implementing environmental targets into strategic urban planning. Environ. Impact Assess. Rev. **32**, 195–210 (2012). https://doi.org/10.1016/j.eiar.2011.08.008
10. Singh, R.K., Murty, H.R., Gupta, S.K., Dikshit, A.K.: An overview of sustainability assessment methodologies. Ecol. Ind. **15**, 281–299 (2012). https://doi.org/10.1016/j.ecolind.2011.01.007
11. Cicalese, F., Fasolino, I.: A multidimensional assessment model of settlement efficiency at the urban scale. In: Marucci, A., Zullo, F., Fiorini, L., and Saganeiti, L. (eds.) Innovation in Urban and Regional Planning, pp. 251–262. Springer Nature Switzerland, Cham (2024). https://doi.org/10.1007/978-3-031-54118-6_24
12. El-Haggar, S., Samaha, A.: sustainable urban community development guidelines. In: Roadmap for Global Sustainability — Rise of the Green Communities. pp. 75–102. Springer International Publishing, Cham (2019). https://doi.org/10.1007/978-3-030-14584-2_6
13. Seto, K.C., Güneralp, B., Hutyra, L.R.: Global forecasts of urban expansion to 2030 and direct impacts on biodiversity and carbon pools. Proc. Natl. Acad. Sci. U.S.A. **109**, 16083–16088 (2012). https://doi.org/10.1073/pnas.1211658109
14. Fang, K., Zhang, Q., Yu, H., Wang, Y., Dong, L., Shi, L.: Sustainability of the use of natural capital in a city: Measuring the size and depth of urban ecological and water footprints. Sci. Total. Environ. **631–632**, 476–484 (2018). https://doi.org/10.1016/j.scitotenv.2018.02.299
15. Olewiler, N.: Environmental sustainability for urban areas: the role of natural capital indicators. Cities **23**, 184–195 (2006). https://doi.org/10.1016/j.cities.2006.03.006

16. Bott, L.-M., Ankel, L., Braun, B.: Adaptive neighborhoods: the interrelation of urban form, social capital, and responses to coastal hazards in Jakarta. Geoforum **106**, 202–213 (2019). https://doi.org/10.1016/j.geoforum.2019.08.016
17. Wentink, C., Vaandrager, L., Van Dam, R., Hassink, J., Salverda, I.: Exploring the role of social capital in urban citizens' initiatives in the Netherlands. Gac. Sanit. **32**, 539–546 (2018). https://doi.org/10.1016/j.gaceta.2017.05.011
18. Stewart, T.J., French, S., Rios, J.: Integrating multicriteria decision analysis and scenario planning—Review and extension. Omega **41**, 679–688 (2013). https://doi.org/10.1016/j.omega.2012.09.003
19. Ram, C., Montibeller, G., Morton, A.: Extending the use of scenario planning and MCDA for the evaluation of strategic options. J. Oper. Res. Soc. **62**, 817–829 (2011). https://doi.org/10.1057/jors.2010.90
20. Hämäläinen, R.P., Lahtinen, T.J., Virtanen, K.: Generating policy alternatives for decision making: a process model, behavioural issues, and an experiment. EURO J. Deci. Processes. **12**, 100050 (2024). https://doi.org/10.1016/j.ejdp.2024.100050

5th Workshop on Privacy in the Cloud/Edge/IoT World (PCEIoT 2025)

Invisible Threats: Rethinking Privacy in Digital Healthcare

Parinaz Tabari[(✉)], Mattia De Rosa, Gennaro Costagliola, and Vittorio Fuccella

Department of Informatics, University of Salerno, Fisciano, Italy
{ptabari,matderosa,gencos,vfuccella}@unisa.it

Abstract. The concept of privacy is essential, as it simultaneously considers other core values such as respect, individuality, dignity, and personal autonomy. Safeguarding data in health research is also crucial since the process generally involves gathering, storing, and utilizing a vast amount of Personally Identifiable Information (PII) or Protected Health Information (PHI), which can be sensitive. This study aims to examine privacy measures in healthcare, providing a comparative analysis of privacy problems and technical solutions. To extract articles, we searched the PubMed database. Manual searches were also conducted in Google Scholar and the reference lists of relevant papers to ensure comprehensiveness. The results show, among others, that the pseudonymization of healthcare data is a widely valued approach as it addresses the challenges posed by other methods. Users and patients can also be actively involved in this process. In some cases, AI models are not only vulnerable to breaches but can also be exploited to amplify privacy attacks. Additionally, while standards like FHIR provide guidance on privacy and security, full compliance with regulations such as HIPAA or GDPR may not always be feasible. Therefore, implementers must carefully consider relevant legal requirements to mitigate privacy risks.

Keywords: Privacy · user concerns · healthcare · telehealth · mHealth · EHR

1 Introduction

Over the past decades, a large number of healthcare applications have been created to enhance medical practices [1]. Digital health systems such as Electronic Health Records (EHRs) significantly improve information and healthcare delivery and can vastly transform patient treatment and disease diagnosis [2]. Clinical Decision Support Systems (CDSSs) are beneficial systems that can be embedded in EHRs to assist clinicians in the decision-making processes. These systems can provide disease-specific and personalized recommendations based on patient data in multiple forms, such as expert systems and diagnostic tools [3,4]. Digital health has introduced several possibilities, such as enhanced information retrieval, telemedicine, and Machine Learning (ML)-based applications.

However, due to the nature of e-health, a wide range of individuals and users can access health-related data, raising privacy concerns. This issue becomes even more critical when these applications involve AI, as they require access to larger amounts of data [5]. Privacy and security of patient data are critical issues in healthcare systems. Privacy considerations may be even more critical when dealing with information about drug use or certain special diseases, as information leakage could potentially cause psychological distress to patients [6]. The system designers and developers need to ensure the confidentiality and security of this information to ultimately maintain trust between patients and healthcare providers. To mitigate these concerns, some solutions have been proposed, such as utilizing advanced encryption methods, enforcing stringent access control measures, and trying to comply with applicable legal privacy standards and frameworks, including the Health Insurance Portability and Accountability Act (HIPAA) [4]. The concept of privacy is essential, as it simultaneously considers other core values such as respect, individuality, dignity, and personal autonomy. Safeguarding data in health research is also crucial since the process generally involves gathering, storing, and utilizing a vast amount of Personally Identifiable Information (PII) or Protected Health Information (PHI), which can be sensitive [7]. Security breaches expose individuals whose healthcare information was improperly accessed to various risks and harms. This revelation of personal details may result in inherent harm since private and identifiable information has now been disclosed to others. Apart from these harms, one might be affected economically or psychologically by private information disclosure [7,8]. Therefore, privacy remains a critical concern when managing and evaluating online trust [9]. To address this, it is essential to protect this information by implementing privacy and security measures from the data origin [10]. Accordingly, these considerations will make consumers—*specifically, patients in this context*—more comfortable sharing their health-related information once comprehensive privacy regulations are established [11]. Additionally, these protective measures, such as *strict authorized access*, positively influence public trust in healthcare systems and the willingness to utilize data stored in EHRs and other electronic systems for various purposes, *such as medical research and big data analysis*. These possibilities will ultimately benefit a wide range of patients in the future with more personalized care [12].

1.1 Research Questions and Objectives

This study aims to review privacy measures, concerns, and solutions in healthcare settings, providing a basis for future researchers and implementers of electronic medical systems. Additionally, we provide a comparative analysis of privacy concerns and technical solutions. While previous reviews have examined the privacy and security aspects of healthcare systems [2,13], our study seeks to provide a more comprehensive analysis. We focus on core concepts, technical approaches, risks, and regulations related to privacy, incorporating recent publications to offer an up-to-date perspective. The research questions are as follows:

- **RQ1:** How do privacy, security, confidentiality, other core concepts, and related approaches for their protection emerge in digital health systems?
- **RQ2:** What are the privacy risks and challenges in healthcare systems and platforms?
- **RQ3:** What mechanisms *(from the methodological point of view)* ensure secure data sharing between healthcare providers while preserving patient privacy?
- **RQ4:** Which privacy regulations must be considered when implementing digital health applications?

1.2 Paper Structure

In Sect. 2, we present the survey methodology. Then, in Sect. 3, we give the results about core privacy concepts (Sect. 3.1 -> RQ1), privacy-preserving concepts in healthcare (Sect. 3.2 -> RQ1), privacy risks and challenges in electronic health (Sect. 3.3 -> RQ2), more technical privacy approaches (Sect. 3.4 -> RQ3), and privacy regulations for e-health (Sect. 3.5 -> RQ4). Section 4 provides the conclusion of the research.

2 Methods

To extract articles, we searched PubMed using related keywords, Medical Subject Headings (MeSH) terms, and Boolean operators. The full search strategy is presented in the following text box. *For the PubMed search*, we restricted the results to the papers published within the last 10 years restricting to original studies. Additionally, manual searches in Google Scholar and paper reference lists were conducted to also include extra aspects needed to be declared. We excluded the papers that did not address the privacy considerations in health-related systems or platforms.

((((((((((((((((telemedicine[MeSH Terms]) OR (data processing, electronic[MeSH Terms])) OR (electronic health record[MeSH Terms])) OR (clinical decision support systems[MeSH Terms])) OR (clinical decision support systems[MeSH Terms])) OR (health information technologies[MeSH Terms])) OR (telemedicine[Title/Abstract])) OR (telehealth[Title/Abstract])) OR (tele-health[Title/Abstract])) OR ("electronic health"[Title/Abstract])) OR (ehealth[Title/Abstract])) OR (e-health[Title/Abstract])) OR (m-health[Title/Abstract])) OR (mhealth[Title/Abstract])) OR ("mobile health"[Title/Abstract])) AND ((((((privacy[Title/Abstract]) OR ("trust"[Title/Abstract])) OR ("user privacy"[Title/Abstract])) OR (data privacy, patient[MeSH Terms])) OR (patient data privacy[MeSH Terms])) OR (privacy[MeSH Terms]))

This research focused on papers that discuss privacy or security concepts, technical methodologies, or privacy standards and regulations within the healthcare sector. Consequently, studies that did not address these aspects were excluded from this research. In the first phase of article screening, the title and abstract of each paper were assessed, and the papers not conforming to the inclusion criteria were discarded. In the second step, the same approach was performed for the full texts of the remaining articles. *Zotero* web library was used for data collection and organization of papers.

3 Results

Based on the initial search on PubMed, 88 papers were retrieved. Of those, 23 papers were selected for the initial round by reading titles/abstracts and full texts. Subsequently, a manual search on Google Scholar and papers' reference lists was performed, retrieving an additional 36 papers. In total, 59 papers plus nine webpages were analyzed to structure the content of the results section. First, concepts and techniques related to privacy are discussed. Next, privacy challenges and risks in healthcare applications are examined. This is followed by a section focusing on technical methodologies for privacy preservation in electronic health systems. Finally, relevant regulations and standards concerning e-health privacy and security are presented.

3.1 Core Privacy Concepts in Healthcare

With the rapid expansion of health-related data and the subsequent need for data sharing among individuals, patient privacy is a critical aspect that should be protected. Patient attitudes towards data and information privacy should be understood correctly to design privacy protection strategies and methods. As health data becomes more accessible through multiple heterogeneous sources, health informaticians should consider and balance data sharing along with privacy safeguards [14].

Privacy and Security. The concepts of privacy and security are closely related in the field of software engineering and design. However, there are subtle differences in these concepts. While privacy addresses personal data protection, security considers the processes and methods to safeguard assets essential for a system. Sensitive data inherent in electronic health apps demands stringent privacy and information security considerations. Privacy attacks and breaches incur financial and health-related costs that endanger patients' lives due to decisions based on faulty information. Therefore, it is important to consider protecting this information in designing and implementing e-health apps [15]. Security concerns and challenges to accessing EHR data include data ownership, confidentiality and integrity, access control, and user authentication [16]. Various access control models have been implemented in EHR, including Role-Based Access Control (RBAC), Attribute-Based Access Control (ABAC), Mandatory Access Control (MAC), and Discretionary Access Control (DAC), each employing unique authorization mechanisms to manage data access [17].

Confidentiality. As described before, privacy refers to patients' right to control access to their health data. The concept of confidentiality, however, extends the privacy domain, focusing on the protection of sensitive clinical information. It emphasizes the agreement between patients and healthcare providers (or settings) regarding confidential data handling and preservation. Health professionals with access to healthcare data (specifically sensitive information) are ethically and legally obliged to maintain the confidentiality of this information. Security measures within health information systems are fundamental to protecting the privacy and confidentiality of health data [18]. Additionally, in some critical areas such as adolescent care, preserving the privacy and confidentiality of EHR data may pose several challenges. One issue is the parents' or guardians' access to sensitive health information, such as sexual health or mental health records, through billing systems or patient portals. One solution is developing adolescent-specific modules inherent in EHRs with a customized confidentiality consideration. Healthcare providers should ultimately address the balance between patient privacy, legal requirements, and the accessibility of medical records in an evolving digital domain [19].

Informed Consent. The rise of health information exchange for secondary purposes (such as research, policy development, or public health programs) has brought about various discussions among health professionals, patient advocacy groups, and privacy organizations. The most critical issue is whether patients (*and in some cases the general public*) are appropriately informed of these uses and whether proper consent procedures are in place to ensure responsible, secure, and informed data exchange [20]. The idea of informed consent is a critical field in medicine. This concept entails patients "voluntarily" making decisions regarding associated risks, research procedures, protective measures, and possible benefits. This information should be based on accurate and relevant information delivered to patients. Therefore, patients' participation in research should stem from their trust in healthcare settings and clinicians. Providing clear and fact-based information about privacy protections in research can help improve participants' long-term trust, satisfaction, and voluntariness in research processes. Essentially, when researchers and institutions emphasize *privacy measures and ethical protections*, participants may feel more secure and informed, which leads to a greater willingness to participate in research, as they trust the institutions conducting it [21]. Additionally, the process of obtaining consent from individuals should include systems that make it easy for them to access their data. When users can request the correction or removal of improperly stored or inaccurate data, they have a sense of control over their data. These rights are currently protected under the General Data Protection Regulation (GDPR), which ensures that individuals can manage and safeguard their personal information [22]. Research on consumer willingness to share electronic data showed that a significant number of users were unwilling to share their data for health-related purposes. This reluctance suggests that current privacy-preserving measures may not be sufficient, and introducing stronger and stricter regulations could help build consumer trust to consent to data sharing [23].

Ethical Approval. Obtaining research ethics approval is a critical and necessary step that should be performed before clinical research, even for low-risk studies. Most academic journals mandate that each research, including human participants, should report and confirm the acquisition of ethical approval by the Human Research Ethics Committee (HREC) in the manuscript body. This confirmation guarantees the compliance of the research with relevant ethical standards and strengthens the credibility of health promotion research processes [24]. Without appropriate informed consent and ethical approval, participants' information may be at risk of privacy and confidentiality violations [25].

Audit Trails and Access Control. The "audit" method focuses on the assessment of e-health software security and is defined by usability, agility, objectivity, repeatability, and systematicity [15]. Access control measures can be used for credentials identification and patient registration when using EHRs or patient portals. A **shared** or proxy access control can also be implemented in special cases, such as in elderly profiles. This is a usable approach, however, it is important to recognize its technical, workflow, and informational barriers [26].

3.2 Privacy-Preserving Concepts in Healthcare

Anonymization. This method involves an irreversible de-identification process (*removing identifiable data elements*) designed to transform personal data into anonymous data before sharing. Anonymizing personal data reduces the risk of identifying an individual [27]. For data to be truly *anonymous* under the General Data Protection Regulation (GDPR), it must be processed in a way that re-identification is impossible by reasonable means. While GDPR provides overarching principles for anonymization, its practical application is not quite straightforward, considering the technological constraints and evolving data processing abilities. Anonymization can be performed using noise addition, micro-aggregation, and rank swapping. Different organizations may, however, interpret the requirements differently, making the anonymization method selection subject to factors like data type, scope, and intended use [28]. In the healthcare domain, data anonymization preserves patient privacy and anonymity during the secondary use of health data maintained in EHR. One suggested approach to overcome the limitations and challenges of dealing with heterogeneous data sources is converting source data to Common Data Model (CDM) standards to obtain suitable metadata for sharing and research purposes. Anonymization of this converted data guarantees secure and private sharing of harmonized data. Privacy models include l-diversity, t-closeness, differential privacy, and k-anonymization. These approaches can be performed on CDM databases such as PCORnet, Clinical Data Interchange Standards Consortium (CDISC), Informatics for Integrating Biology & the Bedside (i2b2), Observational Medical Outcomes Partnership (OMOP), or Fast Healthcare Interoperability Resources (FHIR)-formatted data [29].

De-identification. Some measures to preserve patient confidentiality include data *de-identification* that can follow the Health Insurance Portability and Accountability Act of 1996 (HIPAA) Privacy Rule guidelines. HIPAA suggests the *safe harbor* method or *expert determination* to ensure the correct de-identification. The former involves removing PHI elements, while the latter relies on statistical analysis conducted by experts to ensure the minimal risk of re-identification [30]. In some cases, both methods can be used together to ensure privacy. In one study, to ensure the compliance of the de-identified clinical notes with HIPAA rules, the "safe harbor" criterion was applied to all PHI, except for dates. The expert determination was then used for de-identifying date-type fields [31]. The de-identification process can sometimes be rather insufficient, as the de-identified data has the potential to be re-identified, allowing the participants to be traced back. However, some data types, such as genomics, are not always classified as "identifiable data," which can make privacy protection even more complicated [32]. Unlike anonymization, the de-identification of healthcare data can be reversible, re-linking the data to external datasets to re-identify patients. Therefore, the decision to select each privacy approach depends on the scope and purpose of data usage [33]. De-identification technologies based on "*encryption*" may become susceptible to future computing advancements. To mitigate the massive leakage of de-identified healthcare data, data protection practices should be implemented among healthcare providers. Additionally, regulatory and legal safeguards should be enhanced [34]. Patient privacy and safety precautions become even more critical when applying ML and Artificial Intelligence (AI) methods, as these approaches often require extensive data access and transfer. The de-identification process of patient notes was previously performed using Artificial Neural Networks (ANN) with high precision and recall, without the need for manual feature engineering (i.e., a human-performed process for PHI removal) [35]. However, de-identification is not always an optimal technique for maintaining privacy since it may be susceptible to a Membership Inference Attack (MIA) (*i.e., revealing the inclusion of a data point in a dataset or a training set of an ML model*) when ML methods are utilized. Therefore, using the Large Language Model (LLM)-generated *"synthetic"* data has been considered an alternative technique for preserving patient privacy [36].

Pseudonymization. While both anonymization and encryption of medical data offer privacy protection, they each encompass limitations:

- *Anonymization:*
  - *Irreversible* - limiting the ability of healthcare providers to use this data for primary care purposes when the corresponding patient should be known.
  - *Identity removal* - patients cannot be informed about new findings from clinical studies [37]. This poses a bigger challenge in research when the data relates to rare diseases, as clinicians need to identify participants/patients [38].

- *Encryption:*
  - *Access restriction* - prevents clinical research progress without explicit patient permission (as decryption reveals the patient's identity).
  - *Time-consuming* - encryption of large medical records [37].

Therefore, the *"pseudonymization"* approach, *a specific type of anonymization*, is presented to overcome these challenges. EHR extracts can be pseudonymized either partially or totally; the former retains some demographic data (such as date of birth, sex, and place of birth) at a user-defined precision level, while the latter removes all references to demographic data [39]. In this method, the identifiable information is modified and substituted with a unique identifier (i.e., pseudonym) that remains unconnected with the original data without access to a "secret" key. Pseudonymization (also called linked-anonymization or pseudo-anonymization) enables the link between data and the corresponding patient only under controlled and specified conditions. This process requires two tables: one to store personal data and another to encompass pseudonyms and pseudonymized data. The process of isolating personal information from other data is known as *"depersonalization"*. In some cases, re-identification is also possible. PIPE *(Pseudonymization of Information for Privacy in e-Health)* is a protocol for health data pseudonymization that can securely integrate both the primary and secondary use of healthcare data. It offers *"traceable anonymity"* to safeguard the confidentiality of health records [37]. In the pseudonymization process, certain issues need to be identified and resolved, including the generation of pseudonyms *without the possibility of being traced back* to a patient's real identity, ensuring *verifiability of multiple different pseudonyms* generated for one patient, ensuring verification of the *genuineness of the pseudonyms* at patient registration and administration settings, and *enabling authorized access* to all the encrypted EHRs associated with a patient's different pseudonyms and IDs to enhance update or secondary use (*in the patient's absence*) [40]. There are several pseudonymization tools for biomedical research, including but not limited to OpenPseudonymiser, SPIDER, and Mainzelliste, each with different specifications and contexts of use. Other tools like the *"FHIR Pseudonymizer"* are also available to maintain clinical data in various interoperability formats [41]. Some approaches are also presented in order to enable patients to be involved in the pseudonymization process. EHR systems can ensure privacy by pseudonymizing healthcare records before storage. Identifiers and QIs can be removed to prevent patient data (identity) disclosure. Each patient generates a unique and locally-created pseudonym (a long and random number) without any information exchange with the system. These pseudonyms are encrypted and then appended to the healthcare records, requiring subsequent decryption by the same patient at the time of new data addition [16]. Another suggestion is using different/separate information centers to manage EHR metadata in hospitals. Clinicians can submit diagnoses and request medical records from these centers without being necessarily involved in the processes of EHR sharing, searching, encryption, and decryption. Patients use different pseudonyms for each visit and control the encryption and decryption keys of their EHRs. This approach is mainly useful when dealing with the medical information of *Very Important Patients (VIPs)* like political leaders [40]. Multicentric pseudonymization was also considered in another study. It was suggested to use an identical pseudonym regardless of the data collection center/setting. In this approach, two steps were recommended to link data across different institutions; first, the study center pseudonymizes the patient's identity locally. Then, a trusted service takes the pseudonymized data from the previous step and generates a consistent and unique pseudonym that can be shared across different settings without exposing the patient's identity [42]. Although pseudonymization has several merits, it is crucial to perform this procedure without compromising data quality for research.

3.3 Privacy Risks and Challenges in Healthcare Platforms

PII leak is a serious threat to patient privacy. However, *with recent advancements in AI (such as supervised learning paradigms), online repositories, and analytics methods*, sensitive patient data can be learned without access to PII. Advanced data analytics and ML techniques can be used to link seemingly anonymous data back to specific individuals [43,44]. Even in the absence of PII, privacy can be compromised either through identity disclosure or attribute/membership disclosure. Patient data privacy can be at risk by AI inference, linkage attack, attribute disclosure, differential attack, and Membership inference attack. *Training data extraction* attacks and *model invasion* attacks pose privacy risks to AI models. Therefore, these models are not only vulnerable to breaches but can also be used to amplify privacy attacks [43]. These privacy issues can be exacerbated when EHR data (*even de-identified*) is used and shared for AI research projects. There have been cases where PHI was sold to companies "*without written authorization*" from patients, constituting a HIPAA violation. Nonetheless, in these cases, the *data use agreement (DUA)* may explicitly hinder AI companies from EHR data re-identification [45]. Due to these concerns and the lack of strict legal and ethical considerations for privacy preservation, a limited number of AI-based apps are utilized in real healthcare settings. In this respect, *federated learning* and some *hybrid approaches* can be utilized to enhance privacy [46]. Digital radiologic images can also be vulnerable to threats such as data breaches, hacking, and ransomware (*where hospital data is held hostage*), which can lead to fraud and identity theft [47]. Telemedicine can introduce some privacy challenges as well, during online meetings and videoconferencing, which may include intruder participation and eavesdropping due to weak encryption techniques [48]. Furthermore, in some areas, such as **genomics**, there are specific privacy threats like phenotype inference and identification, each with relevant attack techniques (*e.g., inference from markers, data linkage, genotype imputation, or DNA phenotyping*) [49]. In the field of big data, guidelines and recommendations are needed to enhance ethics and collaboration between partners. There are some challenges in big data and AI, including data source and collection (*gathering and storing data while ensuring ethics and privacy*), interpreting complex data models (*understanding and interpreting the results from advanced data analyses*), and clinical implications (*determining how to translate big data insights into practical applications for healthcare decision making*) [50].

3.4 More Technical Aspects of Privacy Preservation

Privacy-enhancing technologies (PET) can be generally categorized into *architectural*, *algorithmic*, and *augmentation* categories. Federated Learning (FL) and multi-party computation are among the techniques considered as architectural PETS; homomorphic encryption, Differential Privacy (DP), and zero-knowledge proofs are categorized as algorithmic PETS; and synthetic data and digital twining are categorized as augmentation PETS [51]. According to the definition provided by NIST, DP is described as "a mathematical definition of what it means to have privacy" [52]. In other words, the inability to differentiate between two distributions of output probability is considered DP. Figure 1 illustrates this concept, where $\mathcal{M}$ represents the *mechanism*, which is the differentially private analysis. As the Large Language Models (LLMs) are now very popular in every field, such as medicine, DP can be used to mitigate privacy concerns before utilizing the EHR data as LLM input. In addition to DP, other strategies - such as de-identification, FL, surrogate generation, and synthetic data generation - are recommended as context-aware approaches to preserving healthcare data privacy when using LLMs [53].

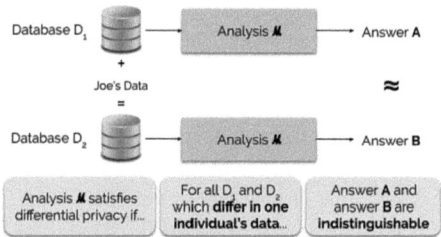

Fig. 1. Definition of Differential Privacy (DP). Credit: Nist.gov [52]

Healthcare data interoperability specifications, like OpenEHR, can be tested for their conformance with broader privacy regulations like the GDPR. Souza et al. [54] declared that it is challenging to fulfill some of GDPR's organizational requirements with any EHR specification standards like OpenEHR. In a study, the researchers identified 50 General Data Protection Regulation (GDPR) requirements and mapped them against 8 openEHR design principles. Each openEHR principle was compatible with GDPR; however, as a set, they addressed only 30% of the GDPR requirements (15 out of 50). This implies that openEHR is principally "privacy by design" but its intrinsic mechanisms are not sufficient to achieve **complete** GDPR compliance [55]. Like OpenEHR, the full conformance of the FHIR standard to HIPAA or GDPR may not be possible. Therefore, implementers should take the relevant requirements and regulations into consideration. FHIR offers some guidance to preserve privacy and security according to the specific risks and nature of each data type. Most resources need access control measures to *Create, Update, or Delete*. However, for READ and QUERY access, some general guidance is needed based on the resource specifications such as **anonymous READ access resources** (not containing sensitive data, privacy approach: *server authenticated https (TLS)*), **business sensitive resources** (contain business or service-sensitive data, authentication approaches: *"mutual-authenticated-TLS, APIKey, App signed JWT or App OAuth client-id JWT"*), **individual sensitive** (not contain patient data but other participants', access control: *role-specific Role specific methods such as ABAC or RBAC*), **patient sensitive** (with very sensitive health information, access control: *privacy consent, security labels, and declared purpose of use*), **no dominant category** (a broad domain containing non-sensitive to very sensitive, privacy measures: *various above-mentioned approaches*) [56]. As mentioned earlier, anonymization is defined as removing PHI using the HIPAA safe harbor guideline. Nevertheless, before all else, it is important to correctly distinguish this data before eliminating it. The most common method for assessing detection quality is by comparing it to a human expert-curated model solution. One such solution is CensorCheck, designed to assess PHI detection in text specifically for anonymization and to define what qualifies as a match [57]. Considering security, the **audit** approach can utilize the combination of several methodologies, such as *manual evaluation*, *SAST* (Static Application Security Testing), and *DAST* (Dynamic Application Security Testing) to assess the security quality of an application. The security requirements of mHealth applications can be evaluated using a **continuous audit** method, which aligns with DevSecOps (Development, Security, and Operations). In this ongoing approach, the list of security requirements, referred to as the *catalog*, is implemented to ensure that measures are in place. Furthermore, it is continuously monitored and tested to verify that these measures function as intended. It is also verified for compliance with relevant security regulations and standards [15]. For multi-centric medical data protection, cryptographic methodologies have been recommended, such as public key and symmetric key encryption systems. The symmetric key approach uses an identical key for the encryption and decryption processes, while the public key method utilizes a pair of keys for encryption and decryption separately. Cryptographic approaches can be utilized in CDM-based research within multi-centric healthcare settings simultaneously enables coherent analysis while ensuring data protection throughout the process [58]. The multi-institutional or collaborative studies (*such as clinical trials*) can also be performed using privacy-preserving approaches to ensure compliance with strict data protection regulations, such as GDPR, by not sharing patient data. These ideas include local analysis at a single center and sharing only summary statistics. Further, meta-analyses can be performed at a multi-center level to synthesize results from different centers or studies. This method prevents privacy breaches and complies with GDPR by safeguarding individual patient data within each local center [59]. Anonymization techniques can be used to anonymize personal records by clustering similar Quasi-Identifier (QI) attributes (*such as sex, weight, and age of the patients*), ensuring they become indistinguishable from other record sets within the same table. In the absence of direct identifiers (*e.g., Social Security*

Number (SSN) or name), QI can be considered an identifier, too. Therefore, the disclosure of identity is a major privacy breach in EHRs that arises internally (within the organization) or externally (between the data collector and the owner). In this respect, multiple data owners can anonymize their records separately in a collaborative approach. Then, *with k-anonymity*, the identity disclosure is prevented while allowing dynamic participation of data owners using a greedy heuristic technique. The researchers acknowledged the trade-off between privacy and data utility in the anonymization procedure. However, they did not quantitatively measure the impact of anonymization on data utility or report information loss metrics [60]. Generally, the core challenge in sharing EHR sensitive data for AI- and ML-based studies is performing valuable and meaningful research while ensuring patient confidentiality and data privacy. Additionally, there are limitations and risks in traditional privacy-preserving methods (*such as de-identifications*) and a lack of clear recommendations and guidance on proper anonymization of PII [61]. For k-anonymity, the challenge lies in identifying the best approach for data suppression and generalization that preserves as much data utility as possible while satisfying the requirements of k-anonymity and ensuring the lowest information loss. The anonymized dataset's utility is evaluated by the degree to which it can still represent the statistical characteristics of the original data, while ensuring privacy [62]. It has been reported that using the ARX de-identification tool to preserve data privacy also compromised dataset utility since certain records were eliminated and predictor variables were concealed [63]. To overcome these challenges, an approach called the Anonymization through Data Synthesis using Generative Adversarial Networks (ADS-GAN) was proposed by Yoon et al. [61]. This framework generates synthetic EHR data that preserves patient confidentiality. By defining and minimizing the "identifiability" of private and identifiable data (*using the generation of de-identified synthetic versions*), ADS-GAN ensures secure and legally compliant anonymized data sharing to enhance the development of ML tools. Therefore, this approach models a stronger privacy-utility tradeoff compared to other methods. Other researchers proposed ML approaches to automatically de-identify healthcare narratives. The *two-pass tagging, priority sorting, and multi-class models* method was proposed and validated in the study by Dehghan et al. [64] to enhance entity recognition in psychiatric evaluation notes. They proved that this approach could successfully identify HIPAA-defined PHI. However, some identities, such as "organization and profession", were challenging due to expression variability in these classes. In the cases of digital health images, it is advisable to maintain only the minimum required information for experiments and de-identified data. The de-identification of medical images can be performed by either using *"Digital Imaging and Communications in Medicine (DICOM) header de-identification"* or *"file conversion de-identification"*. Before the de-identification process, data should be stored in a secure and isolated location with no internet connection (*"air-gapped"*) and protected through data encryption and obfuscation. This minimizes the risk of unauthorized access to personal data and data tampering [65]. Additionally, the de-identification process of medical images was performed previously, involving the anonymization of metadata and pixel data while allowing authorized access and search of the original data. This method was integrated into an open-source *Picture Archiving and Communication System* (PACS) archive and validated in a collaborative setting [66]. Mobile health (mHealth) apps can be evaluated for their compliance with user privacy policies. In a study, researchers employed supervised ML techniques to analyze these policies and predict whether personal data disclosures were included in the policy text. A dataset of 350 expert-annotated privacy policies (APP-350) from popular mHealth apps was used to train the ML-based system. The results showed that about 94.4% of the most popular mHealth apps available on Google Play included a privacy policy [67].

3.5 E-health Data Privacy Standards and Regulations

Despite various privacy regulations, the dynamic nature of healthcare technologies like cloud storage, AI, and telemedicine introduces new challenges in maintaining EHR-based data privacy [5,68]. The understanding and application of

Table 1. Electronic health data communication standards

Privacy regulation/standard	Description
ISO 25237:2017(en) [69]	*"Health informatics - Pseudonymization"*, facilities the clinical information exchange for secondary use [39]
ISO 27799:2016 [70]	*"Health informatics—Information security management in health using ISO/IEC 27002"*, provides further guidance to address some specific requirements of health information security [71]
ISO 22857:2013(en) [72]	*"Health informatics—Guidelines on data protection to facilitate trans-border flows of personal health data"*, the training and predictions should remain consistent with the intended purposes and permissions granted at the time of data collection [73]
ISO 81001-1:2021(en) [74]	*"Health software and health IT systems safety, effectiveness and security"*, it states that adopting health IT systems affects clinical and business workflows; therefore, these changes should be carefully managed [75]
ISO/TR 21332:2021 [76]	*"Health informatics—Cloud computing considerations for the security and privacy of health information systems"* and EHRs [77]
ISO/TS 14441:2013 [78]	*"Health informatics—Security and privacy requirements of EHR systems for use in conformity assessment"*

these privacy standards are critical to preserving confidentiality, integrity, and trust in EHR systems in an increasingly interconnected healthcare environment. Table 1 summarizes some of these standards and regulations related to electronic healthcare data.

The Health Information Technology for Economic and Clinical Health - (HITECH) Act aims to promote patient engagement in their care and coordinated healthcare and considers information safety, privacy, and security. This act strengthened HIPAA privacy and security rules [79]. More specifically, the National Institute of Standards and Technology (NIST) SP 800-53 rev. 5 introduces a broader guideline for "Security and Privacy Controls for Information Systems and Organizations" [80]. It is worth noting that NIST has also introduced a more specialized practice guide on *"Securing Electronic Health Records on Mobile Devices"*. Best practices and related standards in the NIST cybersecurity framework and the HIPAA security rule can be implemented using this guide [81]. Other concerns *namely confidentiality and personal data integrity* can be addressed with audit trail, versioning, and access control [54].

4 Conclusion

This study aimed to provide a comprehensive overview of the privacy concepts, techniques, regulations, and challenges in the healthcare domain. We categorized and assessed the papers dealing with these items in developing healthcare systems and applications such as EHRs. The privacy-preserving techniques in healthcare contain approaches such as automatic de-identification, pseudonymization, and anonymization. Some approaches utilized AI and ML methodologies to ensure privacy in healthcare. However, these approaches themselves may pose some extra privacy threats. Therefore, the developers of healthcare systems need to consider compliance with privacy regulations and standards from the beginning of the development phase to prevent data leakage and other privacy hazards.

References

1. Ali, T.E., Ali, F.I., Dakić, P., Zoltan, A.D.: Trends, prospects, challenges, and security in the healthcare internet of things. Computing **107**(1), 28 (2025)
2. Gariépy-Saper, K., Decarie, N.: Privacy of electronic health records: a review of the literature. J. Can. Health Libr. Assoc. **42**(1), 74 (2021)
3. Spini, G., et al.: New approach to privacy-preserving clinical decision support systems for HIV treatment. J. Med. Syst. **46**(12), 84 (2022)
4. Chen, Z., et al.: Harnessing the power of clinical decision support systems: challenges and opportunities. Open Heart. **10**(2), e002432 (2023)
5. Yadav, N., Pandey, S., Gupta, A., Dudani, P., Gupta, S., Rangarajan, K.: Data privacy in healthcare: in the era of artificial intelligence. Indian Dermatol. Online J. **14**(6), 788–92 (2023)
6. Gong, M., et al.: Privacy protection of sexually transmitted infections information from Chinese electronic medical records. Sci. Rep. **15**(1), 1296 (2025)

7. Nass, S.J., Levit, L.A., Gostin, L.O., et al.: The value and importance of health information privacy. In: Beyond the HIPAA Privacy Rule: Enhancing Privacy, Improving Health Through Research. National Academies Press (US) (2009)
8. Nowrozy, R., Ahmed, K., Kayes, A., Wang, H., McIntosh, T.R.: Privacy preservation of electronic health records in the modern era: a systematic survey. ACM Comput. Surv. **56**(8), 1–37 (2024)
9. Costagliola, G., Fuccella, V., Pascuccio, F.A.: Towards a trust, reputation and recommendation meta model. J. Vis. Lang. Comput. **25**(6), 850–7 (2014)
10. Filkins, B.L., et al.: Privacy and security in the era of digital health: what should translational researchers know and do about it? Am. J. Transl. Res. **8**(3), 1560 (2016)
11. Gupta, R., et al.: Consumer views on privacy protections and sharing of personal digital health information. JAMA Netw. Open **6**(3), e231305-5 (2023)
12. Belfrage, S., Helgesson, G., Lynøe, N.: Trust and digital privacy in healthcare: a cross-sectional descriptive study of trust and attitudes towards uses of electronic health data among the general public in Sweden. BMC Med. Ethics **23**(1), 19 (2022)
13. Basil, N.N., Ambe, S., Ekhator, C., Fonkem, E., Nduma, B.N.: Health records database and inherent security concerns: a review of the literature. Cureus **14**(10) (2022)
14. Holmes, J.H., Soualmia, L.F., Séroussi, B.: A 21st century embarrassment of riches: the balance between health data access, usage, and sharing. Yearb. Med. Inform. **27**(01), 005–006 (2018)
15. Mejía-Granda, C.M., Fernández-Alemán, J.L., de Gea, J., García-Berná, J.A.: A method and validation for auditing e-Health applications based on reusable software security requirements specifications. Int. J. Med. Inform. **194**, 105699 (2025)
16. Rai, B.K.: Patient-controlled mechanism using pseudonymization technique for ensuring the security and privacy of electronic health records. Int. J. Reliable Qual. E-Healthcare (IJRQEH) **11**(1), 1–15 (2022)
17. Al-Zubaidie, M., Zhang, Z., Zhang, J.: PAX: using pseudonymization and anonymization to protect patients' identities and data in the healthcare system. Int. J. Environ. Res. Public Health **16**(9), 1490 (2019)
18. Bani Issa, W., et al.: Privacy, confidentiality, security and patient safety concerns about electronic health records. Int. Nurs. Rev. **67**(2), 218–30 (2020)
19. ACOG-Committee, et al.: Confidentiality in adolescent health care: ACOG committee opinion, number 803. Obstet Gynecol. **135**(4), e171-7 (2020)
20. Riordan, F., Papoutsi, C., Reed, J.E., Marston, C., Bell, D., Majeed, A.: Patient and public attitudes towards informed consent models and levels of awareness of electronic health records in the UK. Int. J. Med. Inform. **84**(4), 237–47 (2015)
21. Golembiewski, E.H., et al.: An electronic tool to support patient-centered broad consent: a multi-arm randomized clinical trial in family medicine. Ann. Fam. Med. **19**(1), 16–23 (2021)
22. Heslop, P.A., Davies, K., Sayer, A., Witham, M.: Making consent for electronic health and social care data research fit for purpose in the 21st century. BMJ Health Care Inform. **27**(1), e100128 (2020)
23. Grande, D., et al.: Consumer willingness to share personal digital information for health-related uses. JAMA Netw. Open **5**(1), e2144787-7 (2022)
24. Newson, A.J., Lipworth, W.: Why should ethics approval be required prior to publication of health promotion research? Health Promot. J. Austr. **26**(3), 170–5 (2015)

25. Harnett, J.D.: Research ethics for clinical researchers. In: Clinical Epidemiology: Practice and Methods, pp. 53–64 (2021)
26. Gleason, K.T., et al.: A multisite demonstration of shared access to older adults' patient portals. JAMA Netw. Open **8**(2), e2461803-3 (2025)
27. Saporito, A., Tabari, P., De Rosa, M., Fuccella, V., Costagliola, G.: Exploring the privacy horizons: a survey on HCI & HRI. In: International Conference on Computational Science and Its Applications, pp. 113–125. Springer (2024)
28. Mehtälä, J., et al.: Utilization of anonymization techniques to create an external control arm for clinical trial data. BMC Med. Res. Methodol. **23**(1), 258 (2023)
29. Wabo, G.K., Prasser, F., Gierend, K., Siegel, F., Ganslandt, T., et al.: Data quality- and utility-compliant anonymization of common data model-harmonized electronic health record data: protocol for a scoping review. JMIR Res. Protoc. **12**(1), e46471 (2023)
30. Appelbaum, L., et al.: Development and experience with cancer risk prediction models using federated databases and electronic health records. Exon Publ., 17–31 (2022)
31. Radhakrishnan, L., et al.: A certified de-identification system for all clinical text documents for information extraction at scale. JAMIA Open. **6**(3), ooad045 (2023)
32. Goodman, D., Johnson, C.O., Bowen, D., Smith, M., Wenzel, L., Edwards, K.L.: A comparison of views regarding the use of de-identified data. Transl. Behav. Med. **8**(1), 113–8 (2018)
33. Differences Between De-Identification And Anonymization. https://www.protecto.ai/blog/differences-between-de-identification-and-anonymization/. Accessed 14 Mar 2025
34. Mandl, K.D., Perakslis, E.D.: HIPAA and the leak of "deidentified" EHR data. N. Engl. J. Med. **384**(23), 2171–2173 (2021)
35. Dernoncourt, F., Lee, J.Y., Uzuner, O., Szolovits, P.: De-identification of patient notes with recurrent neural networks. J. Am. Med. Inform. Assoc. **24**(3), 596–606 (2017)
36. Sarkar, A.R., Chuang, Y.S., Mohammed, N., Jiang, X.: De-identification is not enough: a comparison between de-identified and synthetic clinical notes. Sci. Rep. **14**(1), 29669 (2024)
37. Neubauer, T., Heurix, J.: A methodology for the pseudonymization of medical data. Int. J. Med. Inform. **80**(3), 190–204 (2011)
38. Shin, S.Y., Kim, H.S.: Data pseudonymization in a range that does not affect data quality: correlation with the degree of participation of clinicians. J. Korean Med. Sci. **36**(44) (2021)
39. Somolinos, R., et al.: Service for the pseudonymization of electronic healthcare records based on ISO/EN 13606 for the secondary use of information. IEEE J. Biomed. Health Inform. **19**(6), 1937–44 (2014)
40. Zhu, H., Keong, N.W.: Transitive pseudonyms mediated EHRs sharing for very important patients. In: Web Services–ICWS 2019: 26th International Conference, Held as Part of the Services Conference Federation, SCF 2019, San Diego, CA, USA, 25–30 June 2019, Proceedings, vol. 26, . pp. 80–94. Springer (2019)
41. Abu Attieh, H., Müller, A., Wirth, F.N., Prasser, F.: Pseudonymization tools for medical research: a systematic review. BMC Med. Inform. Decis. Mak. **25**(1), 1–10 (2025)
42. Iacono, L.L.: Multi-centric universal pseudonymisation for secondary use of the EHR. Stud. Health Technol. Inf. **126**, 239 (2007)

43. Narayan, S.M., Kohli, N., Martin, M.M.: Addressing contemporary threats in anonymised healthcare data using privacy engineering. npj Digit. Med. **8**(1), 145 (2025)
44. Murdoch, B.: Privacy and artificial intelligence: challenges for protecting health information in a new era. BMC Med. Ethics **22**, 1–5 (2021)
45. Duffourc, M.N., Gerke, S.: Health care AI and patient privacy–Dinerstein v Google. JAMA **331**(11), 909–10 (2024)
46. Khalid, N., Qayyum, A., Bilal, M., Al-Fuqaha, A., Qadir, J.: Privacy-preserving artificial intelligence in healthcare: techniques and applications. Comput. Biol. Med. **158**, 106848 (2023)
47. Desjardins, B., et al.: DICOM images have been hacked! Now what? Am. J. Roentgenol. **214**(4), 727–35 (2020)
48. Jalali, M.S., Landman, A., Gordon, W.J.: Telemedicine, privacy, and information security in the age of COVID-19. J. Am. Med. Inform. Assoc. **28**(3), 671–672 (2021)
49. Bonomi, L., Huang, Y., Ohno-Machado, L.: Privacy challenges and research opportunities for genomic data sharing. Nat. Genet. **52**(7), 646–654 (2020)
50. Gossec, L., et al.: EULAR points to consider for the use of big data in rheumatic and musculoskeletal diseases. Ann. Rheum. Dis. **79**(1), 69–76 (2020)
51. Jordan, S., Fontaine, C., Hendricks-Sturrup, R.: Selecting privacy-enhancing technologies for managing health data use. Front. Public Health **10**, 814163 (2022)
52. Differential Privacy for Privacy-Preserving Data Analysis: An Introduction to our Blog Series. https://www.nist.gov/blogs/cybersecurity-insights/differential-privacy-privacy-preserving-data-analysis-introduction-our. Accessed 24 Mar 2025
53. Jonnagaddala, J., Wong, Z.S.Y.: Privacy preserving strategies for electronic health records in the era of large language models. npj Digit. Med. **8**(1), 34 (2025)
54. Sousa, M., et al.: openEHR based systems and the general data protection regulation (GDPR). In: Building Continents of Knowledge in Oceans of Data: The Future of Co-Created eHealth, pp. 91–95. IOS Press (2018)
55. Gonçalves-Ferreira, D., et al.: OpenEHR and general data protection regulation: evaluation of principles and requirements. JMIR Med. Inform. **7**(1), e9845 (2019)
56. FHIR security. https://build.fhir.org/security.html. Accessed 24 Mar 2025
57. Klapaukh, R., Boyle, D.: CensorCheck: a tool for evaluating protected health information detection systems. In: Health Innovation Community: It Starts With US, pp. 174–175. IOS Press (2024)
58. Jeon, S., Shin, C., Ko, E., Moon, J.: A security scheme for distributing analysis codes supporting CDM-based research in a multi-center environment. Comput. Methods Programs Biomed. **226**, 107159 (2022)
59. Duraku, L.S., et al.: Collaborative hand surgery clinical research without sharing individual patient data; proof of principle study. J. Plast. Reconstr. Aesthetic Surgery **75**(7), 2242–50 (2022)
60. Andrew, J., Eunice, R.J., Karthikeyan, J.: An anonymization-based privacy-preserving data collection protocol for digital health data. Front. Public Health **11**, 1125011 (2023)
61. Yoon, J., Drumright, L.N., Van Der Schaar, M.: Anonymization through data synthesis using generative adversarial networks (ADS-GAN). IEEE J. Biomed. Health Inform. **24**(8), 2378–88 (2020)
62. Karagiannis, S., Ntantogian, C., Magkos, E., Tsohou, A., Ribeiro, L.L.: Mastering data privacy: leveraging K-anonymity for robust health data sharing. Int. J. Inf. Secur. **23**(3), 2189–201 (2024)

63. Im, E., Kim, H., Lee, H., Jiang, X., Kim, J.H.: Exploring the tradeoff between data privacy and utility with a clinical data analysis use case. BMC Med. Inform. Decis. Mak. **24**(1), 147 (2024)
64. Dehghan, A., Kovacevic, A., Karystianis, G., Keane, J.A., Nenadic, G.: Learning to identify protected health information by integrating knowledge-and data-driven algorithms: a case study on psychiatric evaluation notes. J. Biomed. Inform. **75**, S28-33 (2017)
65. Parker, W., et al.: Canadian association of radiologists white paper on de-identification of medical imaging: Part 2, practical considerations. Can. Assoc. Radiol. J. **72**(1), 25–34 (2021)
66. Silva, J.M., Pinho, E., Monteiro, E., Silva, J.F., Costa, C.: Controlled searching in reversibly de-identified medical imaging archives. J. Biomed. Inform. **77**, 81–90 (2018)
67. Tangari, G., Ikram, M., Ijaz, K., Kaafar, M.A., Berkovsky, S.: Mobile health and privacy: cross sectional study. BMJ, 373 (2021)
68. Sharma, S., Rawal, R., Shah, D.: Addressing the challenges of AI-based telemedicine: best practices and lessons learned. J. Educ. Health Promot. **1**, 338 (2023)
69. ISO 25237:2017 Health informatics—Pseudonymization. https://www.iso.org/standard/63553.html. Accessed 21 Mar 2025
70. ISO 27799:2016 - Health informatics—Information security management in health using ISO/IEC 27002. https://www.iso.org/standard/62777.html. Accessed 21 Mar 2025
71. Box, D., Pottas, D.: Trust–Can it be controlled? In: MEDINFO 2010, pp. 651–655. IOS Press (2010)
72. ISO 22857:2013-Health informatics—Guidelines on data protection to facilitate trans-border flows of personal health data. https://www.iso.org/standard/52955.html. Accessed 21 Mar 2025
73. Dai, L., Zhou, M., Liu, H.: Recent applications of convolutional neural networks in medical data analysis. In: Federated Learning and AI for Healthcare 5.0, pp. 119–131. IGI Global Scientific Publishing (2024)
74. ISO 81001-1:2021 Health software and health IT systems safety, effectiveness and security. https://www.iso.org/standard/52955.html. Accessed 21 Mar 2025
75. MacMahon, S.T., Richardson, I.: Pathways, technology and the patient–connected health through the lifecycle. Front. Digit. Health **5**, 1057518 (2023)
76. ISO/TR 21332:2021 Health informatics—Cloud computing considerations for the security and privacy of health information systems. https://www.iso.org/standard/70568.html. Accessed 21 Mar 2025
77. Carello, M.P., Spaccamela, A.M., Querzoni, L., Angelini, M.: A systematization of cybersecurity regulations, standards and guidelines for the healthcare sector (2023). arXiv preprint arXiv:2304.14955
78. ISO/TS 14441:2013 Health informatics—Security and privacy requirements of EHR systems for use in conformity assessment. https://www.iso.org/standard/61347.html. Accessed 21 Mar 2025
79. Rosenbloom, S.T., Smith, J.R., Bowen, R., Burns, J., Riplinger, L., Payne, T.H.: Updating HIPAA for the electronic medical record era. J. Am. Med. Inform. Assoc. **26**(10), 1115–9 (2019)
80. Force, J.T.: Security and privacy controls for information systems and organizations. NIST Spec. Publ. **1**(5), 465 (2020)
81. O'Brien, G., et al.: Securing electronic health records on mobile devices, 1b. NIST Special Publication (2018)

Privacy Risks in Connected Vehicles: Profiling Threats and Mitigation Strategies

Marco De Santis[1](), Christian Esposito[1](), and Michele Mastroianni[2]()

[1] University of Salerno, Fisciano, Italy
{mdesantis,esposito}@unisa.it
[2] University of Foggia, Foggia, Italy
michele.mastroianni@unifg.it

Abstract. The increasing connectivity of modern vehicles enables advanced services but also raises serious privacy concerns. Continuous data collection from sensors and V2X communications can lead to detailed user profiling and potential misuse, such as tracking, discrimination, or identity theft. This work presents a preliminary methodology for analyzing and mitigating privacy risks in connected vehicles. It combines a Privacy Impact Assessment (PIA) with misuse-case-based threat modeling to identify critical scenarios involving unauthorized access, data tampering, and data loss. We propose targeted technical and organizational mitigation strategies, taking into account the real-time and resource constraints of automotive systems. A re-evaluation of the PIA demonstrates a notable reduction in the likelihood and impact of these risks. Our results highlight the value of structured risk assessments and practical safeguards in protecting user privacy. Beyond enhancing privacy posture, the proposed approach supports alignment with increasingly strict European regulations such as the GDPR and the AI Act, promoting the compliant and responsible deployment of connected vehicle technologies.

Keywords: Cybersecurity · Threat Modelling · Privacy · Connected Vehicles · Data Protection · Profiling Risks · Privacy Impact Assessment (PIA)

1 Introduction

Connectivity is profoundly transforming the automotive sector, redefining not only the driving experience, but also the interaction between vehicles, infrastructure, and users. Connected vehicles equipped with Vehicle-to-Everything (V2X) systems continuously communicate with other vehicles, road infrastructure, pedestrians, and smart devices through advanced wireless technologies such as DSRC, LTE, and emerging 5G/6G networks. This connectivity is supported by a wide range of sensors: GPS, radar, LiDAR, cameras, and microphones that continuously gather data from the surrounding environment [1,12], making these vehicles key components in the development of Intelligent Transportation Systems (ITS) [3]. The connected vehicle ecosystem is the result of joint efforts by automakers, technology providers, standardization bodies, public authorities, and research institutions [1]. Recent deployments in smart cities and Advanced Driver-Assistance Systems (ADAS) have shown tangible benefits, including reduced traffic congestion and improved road safety, thus increasing public interest in these technologies [9,19]. Beyond mobility, connected vehicles enable advanced services such as high-quality infotainment, remote diagnostics, and emerging applications like health monitoring. Real-time integration of sensor data allows dynamic responses to road conditions, improving comfort and contributing to traffic management and environmental sustainability [8,14]. However, these technological capabilities also introduce critical privacy challenges. Connected vehicles collect sensitive data such as location, driving behaviour and user preferences which, when aggregated, can create detailed profiles of individuals' habits [8,10,12]. For instance, GPS and telematics data can track frequent routes, while audio and video recordings may capture private conversations. Without proper safeguards, such data may be exposed to unauthorized entities. One of the most pressing concerns is user profiling. While personalization can improve driving experience, correlating diverse data streams may inadvertently reveal sensitive information. Malicious actors could exploit these profiles for identity theft, phishing attacks, or manipulative advertising [6]. The risk of re-identification from anonymized datasets becomes especially relevant when multiple sources are combined, potentially leading to discrimination in services or insurance pricing [13]. This study presents a Privacy Impact Assessment (PIA) tailored to the connected vehicle context, enriched by an approach based on misuse case modeling. Our contribution lies in the systematic identification of profiling risks arising from the interconnection of multiple vehicular data streams. Unlike generic approaches, our methodology models realistic threats and enables quantitative evaluation of proposed mitigations. The approach combines a literature review with practical misuse case modeling. By simulating realistic attack scenarios, we analyze current system vulnerabilities and assess technical countermeasures, such as encryption, anonymization, and differential privacy, alongside organizational measures such as data minimization, user consent management, and regulatory compliance. This work provides a dual contribution: It improve understanding of privacy risks in connected vehicles and offers practical guidance for developing more secure systems. The proposed framework aims to build trust and promote the responsible deployment of connected technologies. Finally, this preliminary study lays the groundwork for future research toward automated tools supporting PIA in compliance with current regulations, helping bridge the gap between innovation and privacy protection in the automotive domain.

2 Related Work

The increasing connectivity of modern vehicles has raised significant privacy concerns for both users and manufacturers. Connected vehicles continuously collect and process sensitive data such as location, driving habits, and user preferences. This section reviews existing approaches to privacy risk assessment and mitigation, highlighting key gaps that motivate our preliminary work.

The evolution of PIA frameworks in the automotive domain shows a growing move toward specialized and tailored methodologies. General standards like ISO 27005 have been adapted for vehicular systems but often lack the required specificity. Bella et al. [4] combined ISO 27005 with STRIDE threat modeling, while Panda et al. [15] extended NIST PRAM with cybersecurity considerations for autonomous vehicles. Stingelová et al. [17] and Wu et al. [18] propose integrated methods combining STRIDE and LINDDUN, although these often address isolated phases of the analysis process. Another approach may be found in Di Martino et al. [7], in which data processing activities (i.e. business processes involving personal data) have been represented in BPMN notation and the DPIA has been carried out using ontologies. Attack modeling research identifies recurring threats, such as spoofing, tampering, and disclosure [4,15]. Carlton and Malik [5] focus on persistent user profiles in infotainment systems. However, these works often lack a direct link between threats and measurable privacy impacts. Data profiling risks have been discussed in relation to vehicle telemetry [2,11,16], especially regarding the potential for re-identification when combining multiple data sources. While these contributions provide detailed threat characterization, they generally do not include structured tools for assessing the effectiveness of mitigation measures. Mitigation strategies include technical controls like encryption, multi-factor authentication, and Privacy Enhancing Technologies (PETs) such as anonymization and differential privacy [15,18]. Some solutions, like the VIPR system [5], focus on specific components. However, many approaches remain conceptual and do not fully consider the implementation challenges in constrained automotive environments.

To address these limitations, our work presents a preliminary solution aimed at analyzing privacy risks in connected vehicles through a structured and systematic approach. The proposed methodology combines privacy impact assessment with realistic attack modeling, incorporating both technical and organizational considerations. Particular emphasis is placed on understanding the operational context, identifying profiling-related risks, and evaluating the effectiveness of mitigation strategies. This study serves as an initial step toward developing practical tools for privacy-aware system design, aligned with the constraints of automotive environments and recent regulatory developments.

This study provides a foundational step toward developing practical tools for privacy assessment in connected vehicles, offering initial insights that align with current regulatory trends and operational constraints.

3 Methodology

Our methodology consists of seven sequential phases, designed to assess privacy risks in connected vehicles in a structured and iterative manner, from data analysis to risk mitigation and validation.

1. Context: Overview, Data, Processes & Supporting Assets. We first define the operational scope of connected vehicles, mapping key data sources (e.g., GPS, telematics, cameras, radars, LiDAR, biometric sensors, V2X systems), associated processes, and supporting assets (software, hardware, protocols).

2. Fundamental Principles: Proportionality, Necessity & Controls. We assess whether collected data is proportionate and necessary for system functionality. This includes evaluating compliance with privacy principles and regulations (e.g., GDPR, ISO/SAE 21434) and documenting existing safeguards such as data minimization, encryption, and pseudonymization.

3. Risks: Identification & Assessment. We identify privacy threats in four categories: unauthorized access, data tampering (unwanted modification), data loss (disappearance), and a consolidated risk overview. Each threat is evaluated based on its likelihood and potential impact.

4. Attack Modeling: Misuse Cases. We simulate realistic attack scenarios—such as man-in-the-middle, injection, or insider threats—to understand how vulnerabilities could be exploited and validate the relevance of identified risks.

5. Mitigation Strategies: Technical & Organizational Measures. To address the risks, we define targeted countermeasures including end-to-end encryption, differential privacy, and RBAC at the technical level, and data minimization policies, consent frameworks, and audits at the organizational level.

6. PIA Update: Risk Reduction. We re-assess the risks by updating the Privacy Impact Assessment. This step quantifies the effectiveness of the mitigations, ensuring that residual risks are acceptable and compliant with legal thresholds.

7. Results & Discussion: Visualization & Evaluation. We evaluate pre- and post-mitigation outcomes, using visual comparisons and analysis to validate the overall effectiveness and adaptability of the methodology.

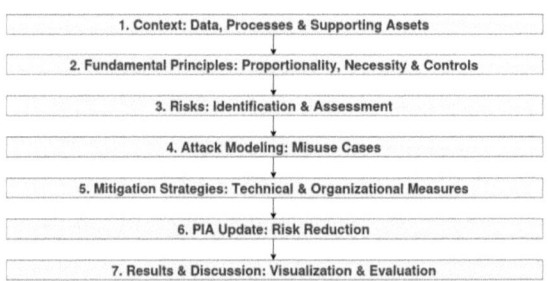

Fig. 1. Workflow overview of the proposed methodology.

This structured process provides a practical foundation for privacy-aware design in connected vehicles. Its iterative nature, especially the feedback loop between mitigation and reassessment, makes it adaptable to evolving threats and technologies.

4 Privacy Risks Analysis in Connected Cars

The increasing interconnectivity of vehicles has opened a new frontier in transportation, where large amounts of data are continuously generated and processed. While these data streams enable significant advancements, such as enhanced road safety, improved traffic management, and personalized user services, they also introduce critical privacy challenges. In particular, the risk of profiling, where personal data is aggregated to infer sensitive information about drivers, is of growing concern.

4.1 Data Sources for Profiling

Connected vehicles are equipped with multiple subsystems that generate various types of data. The table below maps key data sources, describes the nature of the information collected, indicates whether the data can be used for profiling, and qualitatively assesses the associated privacy risk.

Table 1. Mapping of Data Sources in Connected Vehicles and Their Profiling Risk

Data Source	Description	Profiling	Privacy Risk
GPS	Provides precise location data, route history, and travel times	Yes	High
Telematics	Records driving behavior such as speed, acceleration, braking, and engine performance	Yes	High
Cameras	Capture images of the environment, driver, and in-cabin activities	Yes	High
Radar	Measures distances and detects obstacles in real time	No	Limited
LiDAR	Generates 3D maps of the surrounding environment	No	Limited
Infotainment Systems	Logs user interactions, app usage, and multimedia preferences	Yes	High
Biometric Sensors	Collects data for authentication	Yes	High
V2X Communications	Exchanges information with other vehicles and infrastructure	Yes	High

As shown in Table 1, certain data sources, such as GPS, telematics, cameras, infotainment systems, and biometric sensors, are directly linked to user profiling and pose a high privacy risk. These data streams provide detailed and continuous insights into individuals' habits, routines, and behaviors. Other sources, like radar and LiDAR, are less directly linked to personal identification but may still contribute to privacy risks when combined with other data. V2X communications, although valuable for real-time coordination and safety, can also expose sensitive behavioral patterns if not properly secured. Their associated risk is considered limited only if strong access control and encryption mechanisms are implemented. In the absence of such protections, even data originally designed for cooperative driving can be exploited for profiling purposes. In this context, data protection strategies are not optional safeguards, but essential components in determining the actual level of privacy risk. Without technical countermeasures, such as end-to-end encryption, pseudonymization, and strict role-based access policies, even seemingly innocuous data can contribute to invasive profiling. Furthermore, when advanced AI techniques such as clustering, classification, or behavioral prediction are applied to these datasets, the privacy implications are significantly amplified. These models can reveal commuting patterns, frequent destinations, or even personal preferences, transforming raw data into detailed and sensitive user profiles. The combination of high-resolution data and predictive analytics underscores the need for rigorous risk assessment and proactive mitigation.

4.2 Data Protection Impact Assessment (DPIA)

A Data Protection Impact Assessment (DPIA) is a crucial tool for systematically identifying and mitigating privacy risks associated with the processing of personal data in connected vehicles. Under GDPR and related standards, the DPIA process ensures that the design and operation of data processing systems adhere to privacy by design and by default principles.

Our DPIA framework evaluates privacy risks based on two key dimensions: the likelihood of a risk occurring and the severity of its impact. For example, the probability of an attacker intercepting unencrypted V2X communications is assessed alongside the potential consequences, such as unauthorized tracking or data manipulation. Risk levels are classified using a scale from Negligible to Maximum. Table 2 provides a summary of the risk classification criteria used in this study.

Table 2. Risk Classification Scale for DPIA

Risk Level	Description
Negligible	Minimal risk with little or no impact on privacy; effective technical and organizational controls are in place
Limited	Risk exists but with low impact; mitigations reduce the likelihood or severity of a breach
Significant	Noticeable risk where data exposure could lead to moderate privacy violations; requires prompt mitigation actions
Maximum	High risk with potential for severe impact on individuals' privacy, possibly leading to significant legal and reputational consequences

Within our DPIA, we systematically identify and assess several critical categories of privacy risk. These include the risk of illegitimate access, where unauthorized interception or breaches of data may occur; the possibility of unwanted modification, which refers to tampering or alteration of data that could result in inaccurate or even fraudulent profiling; and the threat of data disappearance, involving the loss of information due to system failures, malicious deletion, or ransomware attacks. In addition to these specific risks, we also construct an overall risk overview that provides a comprehensive picture of all potential privacy threats across the connected vehicle ecosystem. This broader perspective enables us to analyze how different vulnerabilities may interact and compound one another, ultimately offering a more complete foundation for mitigation strategies.

Figure 2 illustrates the comprehensive risk overview derived from our DPIA. In this figure, you can observe the distribution of potential impacts, threats, and sources. For example, under the *Illegitimate Access* category, the diagram highlights the risk of unauthorized surveillance and data theft through vulnerabilities such as weak API authentication and insufficient encryption. Similarly, the *Unwanted Modification* category underscores risks associated with data tampering that can distort user profiles, while the *Data Disappearance* segment indicates the impact of losing critical data due to ransomware or insider actions.

The comprehensive mapping of data sources (Table 1) and the DPIA risk classification (Table 2) together provide a robust framework to assess, quantify, and ultimately mitigate privacy risks in connected vehicles. This integrated approach enables stakeholders to identify vulnerable areas, implement effective countermeasures, and continuously monitor the performance of the system against evolving threats.

5 Attack Modeling with Misuse Cases

Based on our risk assessment, we identified several critical attack scenarios that pose significant threats to the privacy of connected vehicles, particularly with respect to user profiling. Drawing from a comprehensive overview of the risks (see Fig. 2), we focused on modeling attacks that present high severity and a high probability of occurrence. Our analysis is driven by the need to understand how an attacker can exploit vulnerabilities in the system and the resultant damage that such attacks can cause. These attacks, which allow the profiling of both the vehicle and the driver, represent some of the most pressing privacy risks in connected vehicles.

The three key scenarios we have modeled are Behavioral Profiling via Telemetry, Unauthorized Access to Sensitive Infotainment System Data, and Surveillance via Internal and External Cameras. These scenarios were chosen because they represent attacks that allow an attacker to exploit critical components of a connected vehicle, enabling them to profile both the vehicle and the driver. In each of these cases, the attacker can gather and misuse sensitive data, leading to severe privacy breaches.

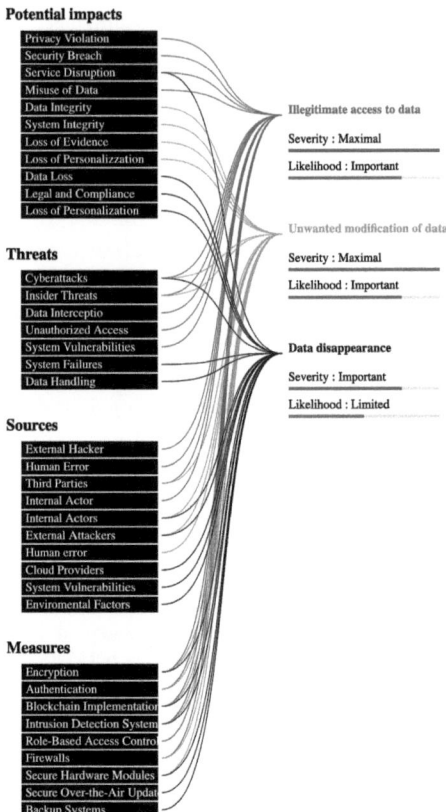

Fig. 2. Risk Overview from the DPIA. This diagram maps potential impacts, threats, and sources in connected vehicle systems.

In the first scenario, an attacker intercepts data from the GPS and the Telematics Control Unit (TCU) of the vehicle, exploiting vulnerabilities in the communication with the Cloud API. This allows the attacker to reconstruct a detailed profile of the driver, including frequently visited routes, driving times, and habits. By gaining access to this data, the attacker can track the driver in real time, exposing their private movements and daily routines. The impact on privacy is significant, as this data could be used for unauthorized tracking, targeted advertising, or even discriminatory practices, such as manipulation of insurance premiums or advertising targeting. This type of attack is particularly concerning because it allows continuous surveillance of the driver without their consent, making it a critical risk in terms of privacy and data security. Figure 3 illustrates the Behavioral Profiling via Telemetry misuse case, showing how an attacker can exploit vehicle communication systems to collect detailed profiling data.

The second scenario focuses on unauthorized access to sensitive infotainment system data. In this case, the attacker exploits vulnerabilities in the infotain-

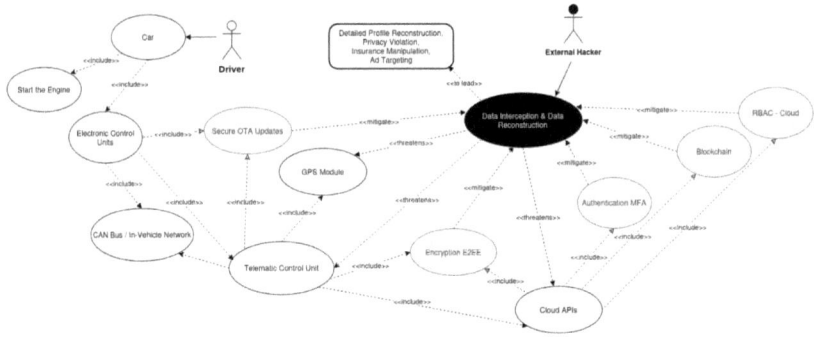

Fig. 3. Behavioral Profiling via Telemetry misuse case

ment system or in the Bluetooth/Smartphone Sync connections to gain access to sensitive information such as contacts, call logs, multimedia preferences, and even audio recordings through the vehicle's microphone. The attacker may monitor and intercept these data streams, allowing them to eavesdrop on private conversations and gain access to the vehicle user's personal information. This unauthorized access can lead to severe privacy violations, as the attacker can listen to private conversations and gather personal data without the driver's knowledge. The risks associated with this type of attack include identity theft, invasive profiling, and phishing attacks. Given the widespread use of Bluetooth and mobile device connections, this type of vulnerability is particularly concerning in the context of connected vehicles, as it opens the door to significant privacy breaches and potential exploitation of sensitive information. Figure 4 provides a UML diagram that models this scenario, illustrating the methods through which an attacker can access the infotainment system.

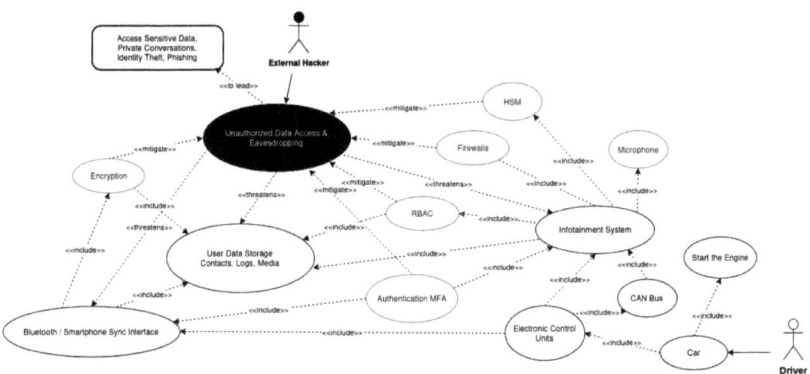

Fig. 4. Unauthorized access to sensitive infotainment system data misuse case

The third scenario involves surveillance via internal and external cameras. In this scenario, the attacker gains remote access to the vehicle's cameras, either internal or external, by exploiting vulnerabilities in the camera management systems or wireless connections. The internal cameras can be used to monitor the driver's behavior and emotional state, while the external cameras can track the vehicle's movements. This type of surveillance allows the attacker to continuously monitor the vehicle and its occupants without consent, potentially gathering intimate details about the driver's emotional responses and daily interactions. The external cameras also provide the attacker with the ability to track the vehicle's location and movement patterns, which could be used for malicious purposes. The impact of this attack is profound, as it compromises the privacy of the driver and passengers, making it a significant security concern. Figure 5 visually represents this misuse case, showing how surveillance via both internal and external cameras can be exploited by an attacker.

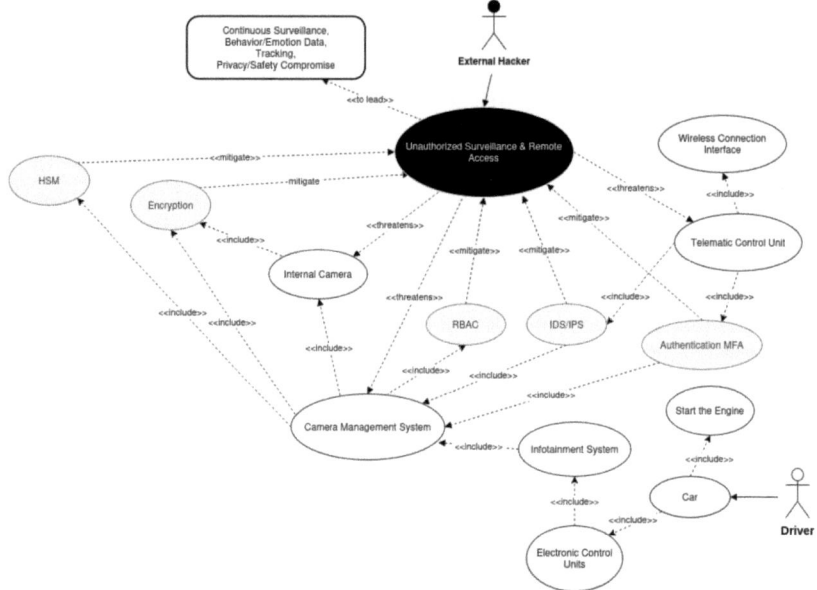

Fig. 5. Surveillance via internal and external cameras misuse case

These three scenarios: Behavioral Profiling via Telemetry, Unauthorized Access to Sensitive Infotainment System Data, and Surveillance via Internal and External Cameras, have been selected because they capture the most critical and relevant privacy risks in connected vehicle systems. Each of these attacks involves exploiting vulnerabilities in key vehicle systems, allowing attackers to gather and misuse personal data. By modeling these attacks, we highlight the severe consequences of privacy breaches that can occur when an attacker successfully exploits these vulnerabilities.

In addition to the three primary misuse cases described, there are several other potential threats that could further compromise the privacy of connected vehicle users. Unauthorized profiling data access is one such threat, where an attacker gains unauthorized access to profiling data through weak access controls or vulnerabilities in the data storage systems. This could allow the attacker to gather and misuse detailed personal data about the driver's habits and preferences. Another potential threat involves tampering with driver profiling data, where an attacker deliberately alters the data associated with the driver's profile, such as falsifying driving behavior or modifying driving logs. This could be achieved through methods such as data injection or exploiting cloud database vulnerabilities. The goal of such attacks could be to manipulate insurance premiums or obscure risky driving behavior.

Profiling data erasure attacks represent another critical risk, where an attacker deletes or makes critical profiling data inaccessible, either through ransomware or by exploiting weaknesses in backup and recovery systems. The loss of this data could impair personalized services, disrupt data retention compliance, or even expose the vehicle owner to legal consequences. Finally, the extraction of geolocation data for surveillance is a growing concern. In this case, an attacker exploits vulnerabilities in cloud APIs or intercepts unsecured V2X/GPS communications to continuously harvest location data. This data could be used to reconstruct detailed movement patterns, providing the attacker with sensitive information about the user's whereabouts and daily habits.

These additional potential threats reinforce the diverse ways in which an attacker can compromise the privacy of connected vehicle users. Together with the three primary misuse cases, they highlight the need for robust security measures to protect user data and prevent unauthorized access, manipulation, or loss of sensitive information. By thoroughly modeling these attack scenarios, we provide a clearer understanding of the critical risks and the need for strong countermeasures to safeguard the privacy of connected vehicle users.

6 Mitigation Strategies and PIA Update

Following the identification of privacy risks and the modeling of potential attack scenarios through misuse cases, our study has analyzed and proposed a set of mitigation strategies aimed at addressing the specific vulnerabilities highlighted in our analysis. The goal of this section is to assess how these strategies, if implemented, could significantly reduce the likelihood and impact of privacy violations related to user profiling in connected vehicles. These strategies include both technical countermeasures that could be integrated into the system architecture and organizational measures that focus on governing data management practices. It is important to note that while we are not directly implementing these solutions, our focus is on evaluating their potential effectiveness in improving security and reducing the privacy risks identified in our analysis. The selection and implementation of these strategies must also consider the specific constraints of the automotive environment, such as real-time processing requirements and limited computational resources available on the vehicle. Subsequently, we conducted an analytical reassessment of the PIA to quantify the potential effectiveness of these proposed mitigations in reducing the overall risk landscape.

6.1 Technical Countermeasures

To counter the identified threats, such as unauthorized data access, tampering, and potential re-identification from aggregated datasets, we analyzed several advanced technical controls that could be applied in the specific context of connected vehicles. These measures are aligned with the strategies defined in our PIA, including those related to encryption, authentication, and blockchain. While we are not implementing these solutions directly, our analysis shows how they could help mitigate the risks identified.

We recommended the mandatory use of robust End-to-End Encryption protocols, such as TLS, for all data transmissions between the vehicle, backend servers, and any third-party services. The implementation of cryptographic algorithms must balance security with the performance demands of the real-time environment, favoring computationally efficient solutions or leveraging hardware acceleration where available. Our analysis highlights that this measure directly addresses the risk of data interception during transit, as shown in the misuse cases involving V2X communication sniffing or interactions with cloud APIs. Furthermore, we discussed the need for encryption for data at rest, ensuring that stored profiling information (e.g., location history, driving behavior logs) is protected in the event of a storage system compromise, while adhering to performance constraints.

In line with the Anonymization of Data strategy outlined in the PIA, we analyzed the application of robust Pseudonymization and Anonymization techniques throughout the data lifecycle. Where feasible, particularly for large-scale analysis or research purposes, we evaluated techniques such as k-anonymity, l-diversity, or t-closeness, taking into account the computational overhead these may introduce. Our analysis demonstrated that these techniques are effective in preventing re-identification when datasets are combined or released, thereby mitigating the risks associated with correlating behavioral and infotainment data.

For scenarios requiring aggregated user data analysis (e.g., traffic pattern analysis, service enhancement), we assessed the use of Differential Privacy mechanisms. By adding carefully calibrated noise to query results, differential privacy allows valuable insights to be extracted from collective data without disclosing sensitive information about individual users. Our evaluation indicated that differential privacy can effectively protect against inference attacks, while maintaining the utility of the data for analysis.

To counter threats such as unauthorized access to profiling data by insiders or external attackers (Fig. 3), we analyzed the implementation of strict Role-Based Access Control (RBAC) policies, as part of the PIA's Role-Based Access Control mitigation strategy. These policies ensure that access to sensitive profiling data is granted according to the principle of least privilege, reducing exposure and limiting the attack surface. We also evaluated the integration of multi-factor authentication for privileged access, selecting methods that are feasible in the vehicular environment.

Finally, to address the misuse case of tampering with driver profiling data (Fig. 4), we analyzed the use of cryptographic techniques such as digital signatures or Hash-based Message Authentication Codes to guarantee the Integrity and Authenticity of collected data. For critical logs, we explored the feasibility of using blockchain or distributed ledger technologies to create immutable records. While blockchain solutions are resource-intensive, our analysis suggests that they could be feasible in specific cases, such as ensuring the integrity of critical vehicle logs.

These technical measures, though not directly implemented in our study, were assessed for their potential integration into the connected vehicle's architecture and associated backend systems, forming the first line of defense against privacy threats, while considering specific operational constraints.

6.2 Organizational and Legal Measures

Technical solutions alone are insufficient without solid organizational policies and adherence to legal frameworks. Therefore, we analyzed the integration of these technical countermeasures with organizational and legal measures, which are in line with the PIA's Privacy by Design and Privacy by Default strategy. We established guidelines promoting a Data Minimization Policy, supporting the collection of only the data strictly necessary for the intended purpose. This involved reviewing every data point identified in Table 1 and evaluating its necessity, thereby reducing the total volume of sensitive data processed and stored. We also proposed the creation of a transparent and user-friendly Consent Management Framework, in line with the Explicit Consent for Data Collection mentioned in the PIA. This framework provides users with granular control over what data is collected, how it is used, and with whom it may be shared. Our analysis confirmed that such a framework would ensure compliance with GDPR requirements by providing clear explanations of the privacy implications for each data category, while also offering mechanisms for easy consent withdrawal. To ensure ongoing Compliance and Governance with relevant regulations such as GDPR, and industry standards like ISO/SAE 21434 (Cybersecurity Engineering for Road Vehicles), we recommended regular internal and external audits, staff training programs, and protocols for data breach notification and response. Furthermore, we emphasized the importance of integrating privacy and security considerations throughout the vehicle and system development lifecycle (Secure Development Lifecycle - SDL), incorporating the principles of "Privacy by Design" and "Security by Design" from the early requirement stages through to deployment and maintenance.

These organizational measures, when paired with technical countermeasures, aim to create a culture of privacy awareness and responsibility, ensuring that data management practices align with legal requirements and user expectations.

6.3 PIA Reassessment

Following the implementation of the technical and organizational mitigation strategies, we conducted a reassessment of the PIA to evaluate the extent to which these interventions reduced the previously identified privacy risks. The objective was to quantify how the measures influenced both the likelihood and the severity of each risk scenario.

Our focus remained on the three core threats identified earlier: unauthorized data access, unwanted modification of data, and data disappearance. Each of these risks was re-evaluated by re-estimating its probability of occurrence and its potential impact on user privacy. For example, the adoption of End-to-End Encryption and RBAC significantly lowered the likelihood of unauthorized access, while techniques such as pseudonymization and data minimization effectively reduced the severity of the resulting impact.

This reassessment was carried out using the same qualitative risk classification scale as the initial PIA (Negligible, Limited, Significant, Maximum). The comparison between pre- and post-mitigation assessments revealed a noticeable shift in risk levels. In particular, risks initially considered significant, such as persistent access to sensitive data or the silent loss of information—were downgraded to more acceptable levels.

To visually illustrate this reduction in risk, we performed a comparative analysis represented in Fig. 6. The figure shows how many of the assessed risks have moved from higher-risk zones (typically characterized by high likelihood

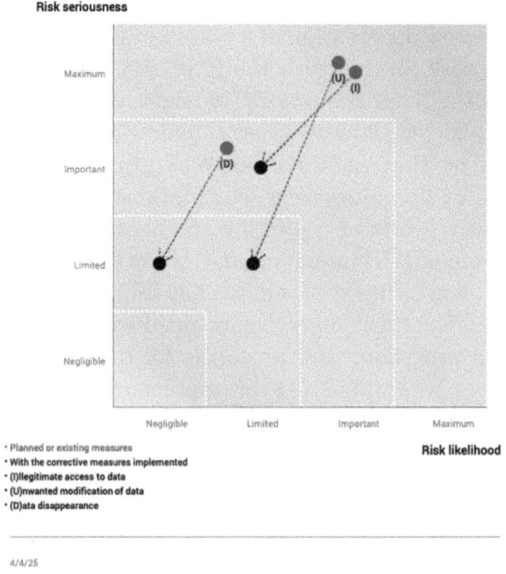

Fig. 6. Graphical representation of risk severity and likelihood estimation pre- and post-mitigation for privacy threats in connected vehicle profiling.

and high impact) to lower-risk quadrants, confirming the overall effectiveness of the proposed mitigation strategies.

In addition to these improvements, we analyzed the relative contribution of different mitigation categories. Technical measures proved especially effective in reducing both unauthorized access and unwanted data modification. Organizational controls played a key role in minimizing risks related to data disappearance—particularly through data retention policies and access audits. When combined, these technical and organizational safeguards resulted in a comprehensive risk reduction across all categories.

Finally, we identified the residual risks, those that remain despite the application of mitigation strategies. These were reviewed in light of organizational policy thresholds and relevant regulatory standards, confirming that the remaining risks fall within acceptable bounds.

This PIA reassessment provides a critical validation of our preliminary framework. It demonstrates, through a structured and comparative analysis, that the applied combination of technical and organizational measures meaningfully reduces privacy risks in connected vehicle ecosystems, particularly those associated with user profiling and misuse of vehicular data.

7 Results and Discussion

The application of our integrated methodology, which combines data source analysis, misuse case modeling, and an iterative PIA, has yielded significant results regarding the privacy risks associated with profiling in connected vehicles and the effectiveness of the proposed mitigation strategies.

The main result emerging from our analysis is the quantification of risk reduction achieved through the combined application of the technical and organizational countermeasures proposed in Sect. 6. As illustrated in the comparative analysis (Fig. 6), the most critical risks identified in the initial phase, specifically illegitimate access, unwanted modification, and disappearance of personal data related to profiling, show a notable decrease in both the likelihood of occurrence and the severity of potential impact. The combined effectiveness of End-to-End Encryption techniques (optimized for real-time contexts), pseudonymization, access control (RBAC), integrity verification, together with data minimization policies and transparent consent management, proved fundamental in reducing the overall exposure to profiling risks.

These findings fully support our initial hypotheses: a systematic and multi-layered approach, based on the PIA methodology and enriched by threat modeling through misuse cases, is effective not only in identifying critical vulnerabilities but also in validating the impact of countermeasures. The PIA reassessment confirmed that the proposed strategies bring the residual risk within potentially acceptable thresholds, demonstrating the practical validity of the adopted methodological framework.

The implications of these results for the automotive industry and future regulations are manifold. Firstly, they underscore the urgency for vehicle manufacturers (OEMs) and technology providers to proactively adopt "Privacy by Design" and "Privacy by Default" principles in the development of connected systems. Our study provides an operational framework that can guide this process in a structured manner. Secondly, the results suggest that future regulations (such as updates to GDPR or specific standards like ISO/SAE 21434) should not only require the execution of PIAs but potentially also the quantifiable demonstration of risk reduction achieved through implemented mitigations, before launching new services based on vehicular data.

To adapt to these growing privacy requirements, automotive companies can adopt several strategies. They can use methodologies similar to ours to conduct thorough internal assessments of their current and future systems, identifying and prioritizing mitigation interventions based on quantified risk analysis. It is crucial, as highlighted in Sect. 6, to select and implement technical countermeasures that balance security and privacy robustness with the computational and latency constraints typical of the automotive environment. Furthermore, investing in more transparent and granular consent mechanisms and clearly communicating the adopted protection measures can help strengthen user trust, an increasingly decisive factor for market acceptance. Collaboration within the industry for sharing best practices and adhering to recognized standards (like ISO/SAE 21434) represents another fundamental step.

8 Conclusion

This work introduced a preliminary methodology for identifying and mitigating privacy risks arising from user profiling in connected vehicles. The proposed approach integrates a structured Privacy Impact Assessment (PIA) with threat modeling through realistic misuse cases, enabling the identification of critical vulnerabilities related to the collection, processing, and potential misuse of personal data generated within vehicular systems. The results confirm that profiling risks are particularly acute when data from multiple subsystems—positioning, telemetry, infotainment, or biometric modules—are aggregated without adequate safeguards. Our methodology demonstrates that a coordinated application of technical mechanisms, including encryption, pseudonymization, and access control, together with organizational policies focused on data minimization, consent management, and regulatory adherence, can substantially reduce both the likelihood and the impact of these risks. The structured and iterative nature of the process allows for continuous refinement and validation of privacy protection strategies. Effectively, the execution of the PIA in this study constitutes a complete Data Protection Impact Assessment (DPIA) under the GDPR framework. However, the proposed methodology extends beyond typical compliance exercises by incorporating concrete threat modeling through misuse cases and simulating realistic attack scenarios. This allows not only for early identification of vulnerabilities but also for the quantitative estimation of risk and the evaluation of mitigation effectiveness, thus offering a more operational and risk-driven approach to privacy management. Beyond risk mitigation, this work contributes to aligning system design with the requirements of evolving European regulations, particularly the General Data Protection Regulation (GDPR) and the Artificial Intelligence Act (AI Act). These frameworks impose strict obligations to ensure data protection and prohibit high-risk practices such as manipulation or exploitation through AI, but often lack prescriptive technical standards. In this context, our methodology offers a structured, adaptable, and replicable baseline that anticipates regulatory expectations while enhancing the trustworthiness of connected vehicle systems. The methodology is especially relevant for embedded and AI-based automotive functions, where the combination of real-time constraints and sensitive data flows creates complex privacy challenges. Early-stage privacy assessments become essential to detect vulnerabilities, reduce attack surfaces, and ensure that user rights are protected by design. This study lays the groundwork for future developments aimed at transforming the proposed methodology into a practical, regulation-ready tool. Key directions for future research include empirical validation through prototyping and real-world deployment, assessment of system performance impacts, and adaptation of the framework to emerging technologies such as cooperative V2X communication, onboard AI inference, and IoT integration. In this perspective, the methodology we propose aligns with and complements regulatory instruments like the DPIA under the GDPR and the Fundamental Rights Impact Assessment (FRIA) introduced in the AI Act. These tools are not only legal requirements but also essential for systematically identifying, evaluating, and minimizing risks associated with data processing and AI deployment. By extending and operationalizing these assessments, our work contributes to the development of automotive systems that are not only compliant but also resilient, transparent, and accountable by design.

Acknowledgements. This work has been partially supported by the Secure Federated Learning for Mobility (SEM) project, funded by the Agreements for innovation in the automotive sector supply chain of the Ministry of Business and Made in Italy and has been partially supported by project PRODIGI (PROcessi decisionali DIGitalizzati per una propulsione ad Idrogeno efficiente ed efficace), CNMS – Centro Nazionale Mobilità Sostenibile – Codice Identificativo CN00000023, SPOKE 12 – SUSTAINABLE PROPULSION – CUP B43C22000440001.

References

1. Abdo, A., Chen, H., Zhao, X., Wu, G., Feng, Y.: Cybersecurity on connected and automated transportation systems: a survey. IEEE Trans. Intell. Veh. **9**(1), 1382–1401 (2023)
2. Aljzaere, H.S.J., Kaladi, R.K., Hardt, W.: Analysis of privacy risks of vehicle telematics. In: 2024 International Conference on Computing, Internet of Things and Microwave Systems (ICCIMS), pp. 1–3. IEEE (2024)
3. Alnasser, A., Sun, H., Jiang, J.: Cyber security challenges and solutions for V2X communications: a survey. Comput. Netw. **151**, 52–67 (2019)
4. Bella, G., Biondi, P., Tudisco, G.: A double assessment of privacy risks aboard top-selling cars. Automot. Innov. **1**, 1–18 (2023)

5. Carlton, J., Malik, H.: Safeguarding personal identifiable information (PII) after smartphone pairing with a connected vehicle. J. Sens. Actuator Netw. **13**(5), 63 (2024)
6. De Vincenzi, M., Moore, J., Smith, B., Sarma, S.E., Matteucci, I.: Security risks and designs in the connected vehicle ecosystem: in-vehicle and edge platforms. IEEE Open J. Veh. Technol. (2024)
7. Di Martino, B., Mastroianni, M., Campaiola, M., Morelli, G., Sparaco, E.: Semantic techniques for validation of GDPR compliance of business processes. In: Barolli, L., Hussain, F.K., Ikeda, M. (eds.) CISIS 2019. AISC, vol. 993, pp. 847–855. Springer, Cham (2020). https://doi.org/10.1007/978-3-030-22354-0_78
8. Ghosh, S., Zaboli, A., Hong, J., Kwon, J.: An integrated approach of threat analysis for autonomous vehicles perception system. IEEE Access **11**, 14752–14777 (2023)
9. He, Q., Meng, X., Qu, R.: Towards a severity assessment method for potential cyber attacks to connected and autonomous vehicles. J. Adv. Transp. **2020**(1), 6873273 (2020)
10. Hossain, S., Senouci, S.M., Brik, B., Boualouache, A.: A privacy-preserving self-supervised learning-based intrusion detection system for 5G–V2X networks. Ad Hoc Netw. **166**, 103674 (2025)
11. Li, H., Ma, D., Medjahed, B., Kim, Y.S., Mitra, P.: Analyzing and preventing data privacy leakage in connected vehicle services. SAE Int. J. Adv. Current Pract. Mob. **1**(2019-01-0478), 1035–1045 (2019)
12. Limbasiya, T., Teng, K.Z., Chattopadhyay, S., Zhou, J.: A systematic survey of attack detection and prevention in connected and autonomous vehicles. Veh. Commun. **37**, 100515 (2022)
13. Mastroianni, M., Palmieri, F., Ficco, M., Kozik, R., Choraś, M.: Privacy risk analysis and metrics in capturing and storing network traffic. In: 2023 24th International Conference on Control Systems and Computer Science (CSCS), pp. 580–585 (2023). https://doi.org/10.1109/CSCS59211.2023.00097
14. Panda, J., Jain, R.D.: Cyber security challenges in V2C and in vehicle network. Technical report, SAE Technical Paper (2024)
15. Panda, S., Panaousis, E., Loukas, G., Kentrotis, K.: Privacy impact assessment of cyber attacks on connected and autonomous vehicles. In: Proceedings of the 18th International Conference on Availability, Reliability and Security, pp. 1–9 (2023)
16. Pesé, M.D., Shin, K.G.: Survey of automotive privacy regulations and privacy-related attacks. SAE Technical Paper (2019)
17. Stingelová, B., Thrakl, C.T., Wrońska, L., Jedrej-Szymankiewicz, S., Khan, S., Svetinovic, D.: User-centric security and privacy threats in connected vehicles: a threat modeling analysis using stride and LINDDUN. In: 2023 IEEE International Conference on Dependable, Autonomic and Secure Computing, International Conference on Pervasive Intelligence and Computing, International Conference on Cloud and Big Data Computing, International Conference on Cyber Science and Technology Congress (DASC/PiCom/CBDCom/CyberSciTech), pp. 0690–0697. IEEE (2023)
18. Wu, X., Xu, X., Bilal, M.: Toward privacy protection composition framework on internet of vehicles. IEEE Consum. Electron. Mag. **11**(6), 32–38 (2021)
19. Yoshizawa, T., et al.: A survey of security and privacy issues in V2X communication systems. ACM Comput. Surv. **55**(9), 1–36 (2023)

A TOPSIS-Based Approach to Evaluate Alternative Solutions for GDPR-Compliant Smart-City Services Implementation

Lelio Campanile[1], Mauro Iacono[1], Michele Mastroianni[2(✉)], Christian Riccio[1], and Bruna Viscardi[3]

[1] DMF, Università degli Studi della Campania "L. Vanvitelli", viale Lincoln 5, 81100 Caserta, Italy
{lelio.campanile,mauro.iacono,christian.riccio}@unicampania.it
[2] DAFNE, Università degli Studi di Foggia, Via A. Gramsci 89/91, 71122 Foggia, Italy
michele.mastroianni@unifg.it
[3] Caserta, Italy

Abstract. Adapting or designing a system which operates on personal data in EU is impacted by the privacy-by-design and privacy-by-default principles because of the prescriptions of the GDPR.

In this paper we propose an approach to decision making which is based on TOPSIS (Technique for Order Preference by Similarity to Ideal Solution). The approach is applied to a GDPR system compliance design process, based on a case study about system performance evaluation by means of queuing networks, but is absolutely general with respect to analogous problems, in which cost issues should be balanced with technical performances and risk exposure.

Keywords: Privacy · GDPR · Decision support · Performance evaluation · Queuing networks · Data management · Risk Analysis · Risk Assessment · Information systems

1 Introduction

Adapting or designing a system which operates on personal data in EU is impacted by the privacy-by-design and privacy-by-default principles because of the prescriptions of the GDPR. The GDPR imposes that privacy should be involved into the design process since the earliest stages, introducing mandatory non-functional specifications [5], and that non-compliant systems must be adapted in order to continue operations.

Anyway, in coherence with the praxes of European regulations[1], the GDPR does not specify how privacy-by-default or privacy-by-design principles can be

---

B. Viscardi—Independent Expert.

[1] Differently from this case, for example, technical regulations issued according to the Italian legal tradition do explicitly specify how to be technically compliant with technical regulations when posing limitations.

satisfied in a design, nor there is any technical regulation or standard describing a compliance procedure. This implies that specific investments should be put on the compliance and related implementation issues in a new design, and that this is anyway not granting that, in case of incidents, the system will be considered compliant notwithstanding the efforts, exposing the owner of the system to significant risk of liability depending exclusively on the opinion of experts delegated by the court, with little possibility for opposing unquestionable arguments or exhibiting universally accepted proofs of compliance. In the case of existing systems, moreover, each deployed copy should be properly updated and related maintenance procedures should be consistently changed, implying a fixed evolutionary update cost per deployed item, which may involve unplanned hardware costs and introduce potential bugs and security vulnerabilities, and possibly a different cost for periodic maintenance and different maintaining procedure and personnel, still with the same risk in case of incidents; or replacement may be needed, falling back in the previous case, before the end of the planned operational life of the system, before the amortization of the asset, if no fix is possible or viable.

These costs should be careful taken into consideration for a business. Depending of their amount and the nature of the system, on one hand the manufacturer of the system may continue selling it without any actual privacy-related action claiming for compliance, estimating a low risk of involvement in case the user may incur into an incident with a third party, hypothesizing a sloppy behavior of the user running the system with reference to the obligation to report privacy breaches, so a direct responsibility of the user; on the other hand, the user owning an already installed system may decide not to take any action to make it compliant, aiming at reaching the end of its operational life without incidents and replacing it with a compliant one afterward, or fixing the system at the first major update, estimating a low risk of incidents before.

Such decisions are not necessarily originated by malicious intentions. They may just be needed because the manufacturer or the user could not take the extra costs and related burden without suffering significant consequences, jeopardizing their survival in their field, or because decisions are taken on the basis of partial information, erroneous self confidence or naive decision processes. This is more likely in the case of subjects which operate in the small scale of their sector. Anyway, the related decision process is not to be inscribed in the sphere of strategy, as in the long term new products or new versions are generally taking the place of the problematic one, so the horizon is the mid term, and the decision level is on the tactical level; nevertheless, the mid term is still exposing to non negligible risk, which should be considered.

In this paper we propose an approach to decision making which is based on TOPSIS (Technique for Order Preference by Similarity to Ideal Solution) [26]. The approach is applied to a GDPR system compliance design process, based on a case study about system performance evaluation by means of queuing networks [6], but is absolutely general with respect to analogous problems, in which cost issues should be balanced with technical performances and risk exposure.

This paper is organized as follows: next Section provides backgound and related work, followed by a section in which TOPSIS computation has been detailed. In the following in Sect. 4 the used approach is described, while in Sect. 5 the case study is detailed, and Sect. 6 presents the results of the analysis and the last Section is devoted to conclusions and future work.

2 Background

2.1 TOPSIS and Evaluation of Alternatives

The *Technique for Order Preference by Similarity to Ideal Solution* (TOPSIS), introduced in 1981 by Hwang and Yoon [13], is a consolidated method in the family of multicriteria decision analysis techniques that provides support to complex decisions, characterized by multiple contrasting criteria, in a wide range of application scenarios [26,28]. Methodologically, TOPSIS is grounded on the identification and comparison of one ideal positive solution (i.e. the best one, composed of the most advantageous criteria under consideration) and an ideal negative solution (the worst one, composed of the less desirable values a criteria might take) [3]. The decision process starts from the construction of a decision matrix, in which rows identify alternatives and columns the criteria under evaluation. The rationale is to identify the best choice in a series of alternatives applying the principles of compromise solutions. The compromise solution can be viewed as selecting the option having the minimal Euclidean distance from the ideal solution and the maximal Euclidean distance from the negative ideal solution.

In the context of Information and Communication Technology (ICT), TOPSIS has found a vast amount of applications thanks to its efficacy in the evaluation of various aspects, such as technical performances, reliability of systems, data security, and associated operation costs [11,15,23]. Moreover, TOPSIS is employed in many scholarly and applied research projects to compare hardware and software configurations, cybersecurity approaches, and network protocols [1,17,23].

In the last years, there has been an increasing interest in TOPSIS to simultaneously analyze operational performance criteria while preserving privacy, especially in advanced technological contexts such as 5G networks, storage systems such as both Cloud and distributed ledgers (i.e., Blockchain-based systems [7]), as well as Cloud computing and Internet of Things (IoT) [20,21,30]. In [4] the relevance is emphasized of having a systematic approach, which includes specific risk criteria due to the exposure of sensitive data, to correctly balance the trade-off between operation efficiency and security.

2.2 Privacy and GDPR

The growing importance of data protection to individuals has seriously reshaped the European regulatory agenda, and, to this end, the General Data Protection

Regulation (GDPR)[2] came into force [19,22]. The GDPR has its foundations built on a host of underlying concepts, including privacy-by-design and privacy-by-default, which are outlined in Article 25. This principle asserts that security and data protection safeguards must be ingrained in systems seamlessly right at the outset of their design. Hence, all such data systems dealing with personal information shall provide negligible (or nil) chances of unlawful treatments, more so keeping the potential contraventions at bay [12].

The GDPR is under rigorous rules as regards data privacy with strict monetary penalties, which may constutute a major risk exposure to all organizations operating in EU or handling European residents' personal data, irrespective of their size. Notably, in 2023, Ireland Data Protection Commission imposed a massive penalty of €1.2 billions on Meta Platforms Limited for the transfer of EU citizens' personal data to the United States without implementing adequate protection measures. This fine constitutes the largest fine ever imposed under the GDPR to date[3].

The regulation establishes roles and responsibilities for well-defined key figures, such as the data controller and data processor (presented in Article 4, paragraphs 7 and 8). These figures are compelled to implement all feasible technical and organizational measures to ensure compliance with the regulation[4]. Although international organizations like the European Data Protection Board (EDPB) and the International Organization for Standardization (ISO) have published guidelines and best practices to help organizations implement the privacy-by-design and privacy-by-default principles in practice, the GDPR does not provide detailed operational guidelines. This leaves room for interpretation, particularly when it comes to precisely identifying the organizational and technical measures that are required, managing the responsibilities between controller and processor, and defining audit and compliance verification procedures. Different recent studies, among them the one in [4], suggest how this gap can be filled through the adoption of structured methods, such as the multicriteria TOPSIS technique, capable of systematically addressing the decision-making complexity arising from the need to balance technical performance, security, and privacy [1,14,16]. By enabling thorough and reliable comparisons between various design choices, the application of structured methodological approaches—like TOPSIS makes it easier to choose the best solutions and lowers the possibility of facing fines for regulatory infractions. Through proactive and strategic management of data security issues, this approach encourages more thoughtful management of technical and operational resources, such as IT infrastructures, security software, specialized personnel, and internal regulatory compliance procedures, which can be successfully integrated among the evaluation criteria adopted in the TOPSIS methodology for a more informed and methodical decision-making process [2].

---

[2] https://gdpr-info.eu.
[3] https://www.dataprotection.ie/en/news-media/press-releases/Data-Protection-Commission-announces-conclusion-of-inquiry-into-Meta-Ireland.
[4] Their obligations and responsibilities are explored in depth respectively in Article 24 and 28.

3 The TOPSIS Method

The formalism adopted in *Technique for Order Preference by Similarity to Ideal Solution (TOPSIS)* is described in the following subsections [3].

3.1 Step 1: Construct the Decision Matrix

Given m alternatives and n criteria, the decision matrix X is:

$$X = \begin{bmatrix} x_{11} & x_{12} & \cdots & x_{1n} \\ x_{21} & x_{22} & \cdots & x_{2n} \\ \vdots & \vdots & \ddots & \vdots \\ x_{m1} & x_{m2} & \cdots & x_{mn} \end{bmatrix} \quad (1)$$

where x_{ij} represents the performance of alternative i on criterion j.

3.2 Step 2: Normalize the Decision Matrix

The normalized decision matrix R is calculated using:

$$r_{ij} = \frac{x_{ij}}{\sqrt{\sum_{i=1}^{m} x_{ij}^2}} \quad \text{for } i = 1, \ldots, m; j = 1, \ldots, n \quad (2)$$

3.3 Step 3: Calculate (or Set) the Weights of the Criteria

In the scientific literature, scholars have tested many different techniques to determine weight values [31]. In this work, we choose to use the Entropy method [18] due to the vast adoption. The advantages of Entropy method to compute weights value are:

- the value of weights are based on data dispersion, avoiding subjective bias from decision-makers;
- uses the dataset variability to assign weights, making it statistically robust: higher entropy (more dispersion) in a criterion leads to a higher weight, indicating greater importance;
- widely applicable and simple to compute.

The disadvantages are that this kind of computation is purely data-based, so it may overlook expert knowledge or policy requirements, and it is sensitive to data quality. Due to the choice done, the following steps are devoted to present the details on Entropy weight computation.

Calculate the Entropy Measure
For each criterion j, compute the entropy measure e_j:

$$e_j = -k \sum_{i=1}^{m} f_{ij} \ln f_{ij} \quad (3)$$

where:

$$f_{ij} = \frac{r_{ij}}{\sum_{i=1}^{m} r_{ij}}$$

$$k = \frac{1}{\ln m} \quad \text{(normalization factor)}$$

Calculate the Degree of Diversion

$$d_j = 1 - e_j \tag{4}$$

Calculate the Entropy Weights

$$w_j = \frac{d_j}{\sum_{j=1}^{n} d_j} \tag{5}$$

3.4 Step 4: Construct the Weighted Normalized Decision Matrix

Multiply the normalized decision matrix by the entropy weights:

$$V = [v_{ij}]_{m \times n} = [w_j \cdot r_{ij}]_{m \times n} \tag{6}$$

3.5 Step 5: Determine the Ideal and Negative-Ideal Solutions

$$A^+ = \{v_1^+, v_2^+, \ldots, v_n^+\} = \left\{ \left(\max_i v_{ij} \mid j \in J \right), \left(\min_i v_{ij} \mid j \in J' \right) \right\} \tag{7}$$

$$A^- = \{v_1^-, v_2^-, \ldots, v_n^-\} = \left\{ \left(\min_i v_{ij} \mid j \in J \right), \left(\max_i v_{ij} \mid j \in J' \right) \right\} \tag{8}$$

where:

- J is the set of benefit criteria (larger is better)
- J' is the set of cost criteria (smaller is better)

3.6 Step 6: Calculate the Separation Measures

$$S_i^+ = \sqrt{\sum_{j=1}^{n} (v_{ij} - v_j^+)^2} \quad \text{(Distance to ideal solution)} \tag{9}$$

$$S_i^- = \sqrt{\sum_{j=1}^{n} (v_{ij} - v_j^-)^2} \quad \text{(Distance to negative-ideal solution)} \tag{10}$$

3.7 Step 7: Calculate the Relative Closeness to the Ideal Solution

$$C_i = \frac{S_i^-}{S_i^+ + S_i^-}, \quad 0 \leq C_i \leq 1 \tag{11}$$

3.8 Step 8: Rank the Alternatives

Rank the alternatives in descending order of C_i values. The alternative with the highest C_i value is the best choice.

4 Approach

Our approach is based on a decision process considering system performances, risk and costs in an as-is and a to-be implementations of the same system. In order to apply TOPSIS, three quantitative metrics must be identified, one per decision parameter: the metrics will be evaluated in the same regime conditions for the as-is and the to-be implementation, to allow a comparison.

The metric for system performances should consider the same operational conditions with respect to the actual application for which the system is supposed to be used, evaluated in the two implementations. As the implementations may have different architecture, a possibility is offered by the workload: as the workload must be invariant with respect to the implementation and is defined by the environment in which the system operates, the common reference can be properly provided by the workload. The behavior of the two implementations may be modeled by means of an analytical [8] or a simulative approach [10], which do not rely on actual implementation details, as functional specifications and basic dimensioning of non functional performance parameters suffice: evaluating a suitable performance index (e.g., the throughput of a relevant component or the time needed to perform a relevant processing operation) on models under the same workload provides the first metric.

The metric for risk may be obtained by means of common risk analysis techniques; in the chosen domain, the risk parameter should combine the privacy risk level estimated by an expert per exposure, the number of potential exposure events in a reference period and the duration of the use of the system until its end of life. A good reference may be obtained by exploiting the throughput of the component processing risk related items and the duration of each processing operation as provided by the performance model.

The metric for costs should consider the cost of being fined considering the estimated probability of being fined until the end of life of the system, the processing cost per item in the two implementations and the fixed cost of the substitution of the as-is with the to-be implementation.

5 A Case Study

To assess the feasibility of the TOPSIS approach, the same case study presented in [6] was adopted. This is a smart city information system in which data is affected by privacy and security issues. In fact, images, videos, and other information from the various IoT sensors on the road are the type of data captured. The system collects information from the urban environment (moving vehicles, plate numbers, images of people on board, and even people walking on the pavement or crossing the street), and there is a privacy-sensitive data process that should be handled with extreme caution. The most obvious solution to the problem would be to invoke the law by turning all persons involved into data controllers (GDPR, Art. 28). This would put one in a defensive position from a legal point of view. Leaving out the regulatory path, a solution can be found at the level of planning the data management cycle by adding an initial unplanned protection phase [6]. In Fig. 1 a life cycle model indicated with the name *as-is* is shown, while in Fig. 3 a similar model called *to-be*, presents the addition of a protection phase. The diagrams were designed following the UML state machine method. In these data workflows, there are five common phases: collection, preparation, analysis, storage, and sharing. Below, common phases in the as-is and the to-be models:

- *Collection phase*: aggregation of a heterogeneous volume of data. The input of this phase is a 'job' performed as described in the subsystem designed in Fig. 2;
- *Preparation phase*: raw data are processed automatically without human intervention;
- *Analysis phase*: transition from data to information;
- *Storage phase*: the cleaned data and their metadata are generated in the desired form and made available;
- *Sharing phase*: data are delivered to users following a request; since the use of the data is subject to acceptance by the client.

The actors involved in the process are the *Data Collectors* who collect data from road cameras and IoT sensors and send them to the *Data Broker* who is the second actor and has the role of managing and processing the acquired data that must be sent to the last of the actors in this system, the *Data consumers* or final recipients of the data. Since there is a risk of privacy violation, a protection phase was added to the original model to improve it. The proposed solution is fully automatic, and the process consists of anonymization and pseudo-anonymization of data through encryption and automatic handling of the extreme case of spurious data acquisition through deletion. This new phase is inserted without complications as in the to-be model. One can see that the analysis phase, which is the first to operate on semantically valid information, can be extended by including a further sub-phase in charge of an automatic privacy risk assessment. At this point, artificial intelligence could be used to distinguish and select nonsensitive cases from sensitive cases, as studied in [25], in which authors demonstrate how machine learning models automate sensitivity classification through pattern recognition in unstructured data. Finally, it must be added that there could also be cases that must be handled by human inspection.

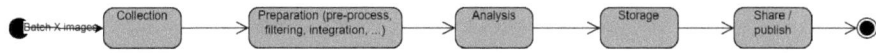

Fig. 1. As-is data workflow

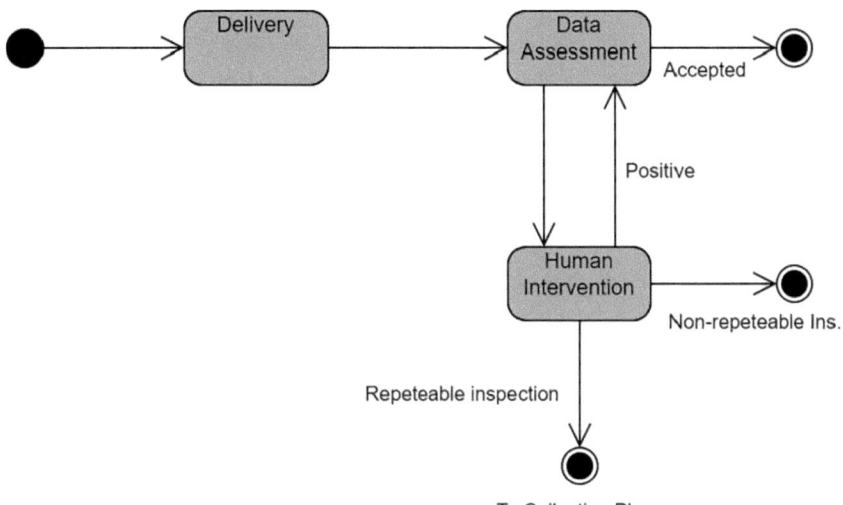

Fig. 2. As-is subsystem diagram

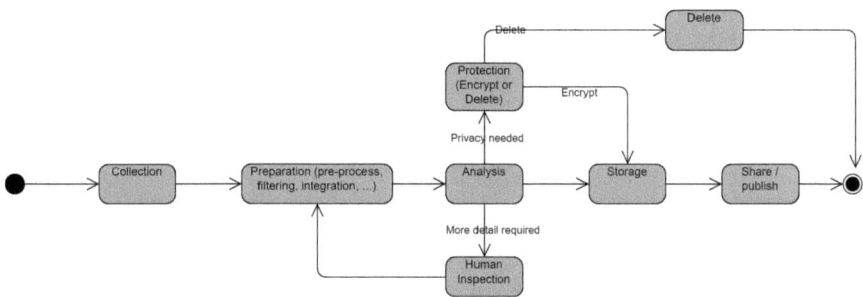

Fig. 3. To-be data workflow

In [6], a performance model for this system, in the two alternate implementations, has been proposed: this allowed the authors to state that the to-be model is proved to be valid. The comparison of the simulation results of the two models carried out in the cited work yielded positive results: the average response time of the as-is model is 43.86 [s] while that of the to-be model is 66.82 [s], the system throughput presents an average value of more than 0.5 [s] for both models, and finally, the results of the what-if analysis suggest that by increasing the service capacity of the privacy protection station the average response time of the system throughput improves. Therefore, the trade-off between lower performance and low risk compliance is beneficial and quantifiable, and the proposed approach is feasible. The results obtained therefore proved the validity of the solution. This result was effective, which is also the reason why this case study was chosen.

In this paper, instead, the issue we want to address is to compare, on the basis of a cost-benefit comparison, the two different implementations using a quantitative method based on TOPSIS.

6 Comparison of Alternatives and Results

The first step of the evaluation process is to define the alternatives for the as-is implementation, described in Fig. 1, and the to-be system, described in Fig. 3. Taking into account the impact of possible administrative fines on the costs of the system, we choose to include in the TOPSIS comparison a third alternative, which is the as-is alternative in which costs are increased due to a penalty imposed by national data protection authority.

The three alternatives are the following:

1. **AS-IS-1**: the original system, designed without concern about GDPR;
2. **AS-IS-2**: the original system with costs increased due to a fine (other criteria have the same value of the previous);
3. **TO-BE**: the system designed to be GDPR-compliant.

Afterwards, it is necessary to define the criteria, i.e., a series of parameters related to different characteristics of the alternative solutions and to apply TOPSIS to evaluate which of those alternative is the best suited.

To do so, we define three different criteria:

1. **COST** of the alternative solution;
2. **ART** Average Response time in seconds;
3. **IMG**, the rate of images standing in "non-safe" zone (unencrypted).

Regarding the cost for the alternatives, at this time the real implementation of architecture to evaluate is not yet estimated, but there are several studies to estimate the ratio of a GDPR compliant modification of an existing architecture in a smart city environment [9,24,27,29]. So a 4/1 ratio was chosen between the cost of AS-IS-1 and TO-DO solutions; taking into account the possibility of fines by Personal Data Authorities, we estimate that the amount of the fine due to GDPR violation can double the cost of the whole system (so, Cost = 2 for AS-IS-2).

Regarding the average response time for the alternatives, we use the values of simulated systems as shown in [6]. So, for AS-IS-1 and AS-IS-2 the value is 43.86 s and for TO-DO is 66.82 s.

Using the simulator values as in the previous sentence, we obtain a value of 240 img/s for AS-IS-1 and AS-IS-2 and 10 img/s in TO-DO.

For the computation, we used the TOPSIS online tool implemented by OnlineOutput[5]. Given that the tool do not implement the computation of weight using entropy technique, the weight have been manually computed using Formula 5.

The Decision matrix (Formula 1) is the following (Table 1):

Table 1. The decision matrix for the system alternatives

	COST	ART	IMG
AS-IS-1	1.00	43,86	240.00
AS-IS-2	2.00	43,86	240.00
TO-DO	4.00	66,82	77.00

After the computation of the formula 2, the normalized decision matrix is (Table 2):

Table 2. The Normalized decision matrix and the weights computed using the Entropy method

	COST	ART	IMG
AS-IS-1	0,218	0,481	0,69
AS-IS-2	0,436	0,481	0,69
TO-DO	0,873	0,733	0,221
Weights	0.200	0.154	0.646

The results of the final comparison, shown also in Fig. 4, are:

1. **TO-BE**, score $= 0.687$;
2. **AS-IS-1**, score $= 0.313$;
3. **AS-IS-2**, score $= 0.239$.

From the final comparison results, it is clear that the system implemented in the "TO-BE" mode is the better alternative, and the distance between the two AS-IS solutions is even more evident when it is taken into account costs eventually due to fines from Authorities. It should be noted that, in the case the weights have been set at the same value $= 0,33$ (Equal weights), the rank is different, as highlighted in Fig. 4. In this case, the first two values are very similar, with a slight advantage to the "AS-IS-1"; this means that both solutions

---
[5] https://onlineoutput.com/topsis-software/.

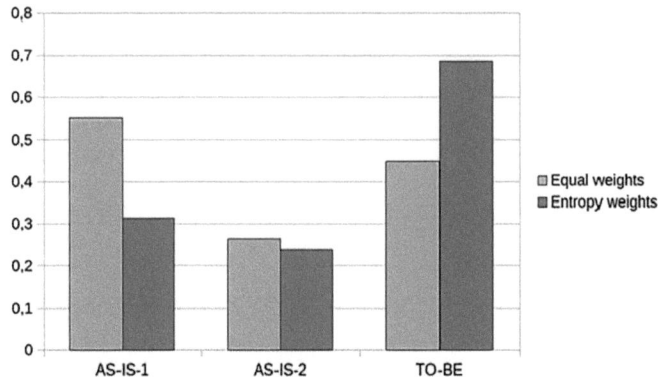

Fig. 4. TOPSIS ranking of all presented alternatives using Entropy-computed weight (red bars) vs. ranking of the same alternatives computed using equal weights = 0.33 (light blue bars). (Color figure online)

have similar efficiency (the greater cost of the second solution is compensated by the better privacy performance), but in the case of fines by authority (AS-IS-2) the increase of cost due to the high amount of penalty results in a much higher efficiency of the "TO-BE" solution. An in-depth analysis of the impact of the weights in the evaluation of alternatives is out of the scope of this work, and will be faced in future work.

7 Conclusion and Future Work

In this paper a TOPSIS-based approach to select the best design alternatives in privacy-aware environment has been proposed. In the case study presented, a massive image storage system for smart roads, the method used highlight that the privacy compliant system could be the best alternative.

Future work will split in two main directions: i) redact a more precise design of the alternatives with the aim of better compute costs and other values; and ii) define other quantitative metrics for privacy purposes to test a more comprehensive analysis using TOPSIS.

Acknowledgements. This research was partially funded by MUR PRIN PNRR 2022 grant number P20227W8ZC.

References

1. Adebiyi, S.O., Olayemi, G.A.: Predicting the consequences of perceived data privacy risks on consumer behaviour: an entropy-TOPSIS approach. Studia Humana **11**(2) (2022)

2. Ali, Z., et al.: A generic internet of things (IoT) middleware for smart city applications. Sustainability (2022). https://api.semanticscholar.org/CorpusID:255737292
3. Behzadian, M., Khanmohammadi Otaghsara, S., Yazdani, M., Ignatius, J.: A state-of the-art survey of TOPSIS applications. Expert Syst. Appl. **39**(17), 13051–13069 (2012). https://doi.org/10.1016/j.eswa.2012.05.056
4. Campanile, L., Iacono, M., Levis, A.H., Marulli, F., Mastroianni, M.: Privacy regulations, smart roads, blockchain, and liability insurance: putting technologies to work. IEEE Secur. Priv. **19**(1), 34–43 (2021). https://doi.org/10.1109/MSEC.2020.3012059
5. Campanile, L., Iacono, M., Mastroianni, M.: Towards privacy-aware software design in small and medium enterprises (2022). https://doi.org/10.1109/DASC/PiCom/CBDCom/Cy55231.2022.9927958
6. Campanile, L., Iacono, M., Mastroianni, M., Viscardi, B.: Estimating performance costs of enabling privacy-awareness in data lifecycles. In: Proceedings of the The 1st International Conference on Modeling, Simulation and Computer Technology. Springer (2024)
7. Feng, Q., He, D., Zeadally, S., Khan, M.K., Kumar, N.: A survey on privacy protection in blockchain system. J. Netw. Comput. Appl. **126**, 45–58 (2019)
8. Franceschinis, G., Gribaudo, M., Iacono, M., Mazzocca, N., Vittorini, V.: DrawNET++: model objects to support performance analysis and simulation of systems. LNCS (LNAILNB), vol. 2324, pp. 233–238 (2002). https://doi.org/10.1007/3-540-46029-2_18
9. Frey, C.B., Presidente, G.: Privacy regulation and firm performance: estimating the GDPR effect globally. Econ. Inq. **62**(3), 1074–1089 (2024). https://doi.org/10.1111/ecin.13213
10. Gribaudo, M., Iacono, M., Manini, D.: Improving reliability and performances in large scale distributed applications with erasure codes and replication. Futur. Gener. Comput. Syst. **56**, 773–782 (2016). https://doi.org/10.1016/j.future.2015.07.006
11. Hoe, L.W., Siew, L.W., Fai, L.K.: Performance analysis on telecommunication companies in Malaysia with TOPSIS model. Indonesian J. Electric. Eng. Comput. Sci. **13**(2), 744–751 (2019)
12. Hong, P., Ahn, N.Y., Jung, E.: Linkage role of ICT and big data in covid-19: a case of Korea's digital and social communication practices. J. Inf. Commun. Ethics Soc. **21**(2), 161–180 (2023)
13. Hwang, C.L., Yoon, K.: Methods for multiple attribute decision making, pp. 58–191. Springer, Heidelberg (1981). https://doi.org/10.1007/978-3-642-48318-9_3
14. Jiang, H., Pei, J., Yu, D., Yu, J., Gong, B., Cheng, X.: Applications of differential privacy in social network analysis: a survey. IEEE Trans. Knowl. Data Eng. **35**, 108–127 (2023). https://api.semanticscholar.org/CorpusID:235083200
15. Khan, A.W., Khan, M.U., Khan, J.A., Khan, J., Gul, W.: Identification and prioritization of security challenges of big data on cloud computing based on SLR: a fuzzy-TOPSIS analysis approach. J. Softw. Evol. Process **33**(12), e2387 (2021)
16. Khumalo, Z.P.: Privacy and security for applications and services in future generation smart grids. https://api.semanticscholar.org/CorpusID:252019773
17. Koss, R., Champagne, S., Battles, J.: Toward an optimal patient safety information system (TOPSIS)
18. Le Roux, D., Olivès, R., Neveu, P.: Combining entropy weight and TOPSIS method for selection of tank geometry and filler material of a packed-bed thermal energy storage system. J. Clean. Prod. **414**, 137588 (2023). https://doi.org/10.1016/j.jclepro.2023.137588

19. Lokare, D.A., Pathan, S.M., Dhotre, P.S.: Exploring privacy challenges: a survey of issues, research gaps, and strategies for protection. In: 2025 1st International Conference on AIML-Applications for Engineering & Technology (ICAET), pp. 1–6. IEEE (2025)
20. Maček, D., Magdalenić, I., Reep, N.B.: A systematic literature review on the application of multicriteria decision making methods for information security risk assessment. Int. J. Saf. Secur. Eng. **10**(2), 161–174 (2020)
21. Ogonji, M.M., Okeyo, G., Wafula, J.M.: A survey on privacy and security of internet of things. Comput. Sci. Rev. **38**, 100312 (2020)
22. Oyewole, A.T., Oguejiofor, B.B., Eneh, N.E., Akpuokwe, C.U., Bakare, S.S.: Data privacy laws and their impact on financial technology companies: a review. Comput. Sci. IT Res. J. **5**(3), 628–650 (2024)
23. Park, J.H., Younas, M., Arabnia, H.R., Chilamkurti, N.: Emerging ICT applications and services—big data, IoT, and cloud computing (2021)
24. Rimba, P., Tran, A.B., Weber, I., Staples, M., Ponomarev, A., Xu, X.: Comparing blockchain and cloud services for business process execution. In: 2017 IEEE International Conference on Software Architecture (ICSA), pp. 257–260 (2017). https://doi.org/10.1109/ICSA.2017.44
25. Sebastian, G.: Privacy and data protection in ChatGPT and other AI chatbots: strategies for securing user information. Int. J. Secur. Priv. Pervasive Comput. (IJSPPC) **15**(1), 1–14 (2023)
26. Setiawan, H., Istiyanto, J.E., Wardoyo, R., Santoso, P.: The group decision support system to evaluate the ICT project performance using the hybrid method of AHP, TOPSIS and Copeland score. Int. J. Adv. Comput. Sci. Appl. **7**(4) (2016)
27. Stefanouli, M., Economou, C.: Data protection in smart cities: application of the EU GDPR. In: Nathanail, E.G., Karakikes, I.D. (eds.) Data Analytics: Paving the Way to Sustainable Urban Mobility, pp. 748–755. Springer International Publishing, Cham (2019)
28. Tohidi, M., Homayoun, S., RezaHoseini, A., Ehsani, R., Bagherpour, M.: Sustainability-driven supplier selection: insights from supplier life value and Z-numbers. Sustainability **16**(5), 2046 (2024)
29. Vandercruysse, L., Buts, C., Dooms, M.: A typology of smart city services: the case of data protection impact assessment. Cities **104**, 102731 (2020). https://doi.org/10.1016/j.cities.2020.102731
30. Yang, Y., Wu, L., Yin, G., Li, L., Zhao, H.: A survey on security and privacy issues in internet-of-things. IEEE Internet Things J. **4**(5), 1250–1258 (2017)
31. Çelikbilek, Y., Tüysüz, F.: An in-depth review of theory of the TOPSIS method: an experimental analysis. J. Manag. Anal. **7**(2), 281–300 (2020). https://doi.org/10.1080/23270012.2020.1748528

Toward Privacy-Aware Environmental Monitoring of CO_2 and Air Pollutants in Southern Italy

Lelio Campanile[✉][iD], Luigi Piero Di Bonito[iD], Fiammetta Marulli[iD], Antonio Balzanella, and Rosanna Verde

Department of Mathematics and Physics, Università degli Studi della Campania "L. Vanvitelli", Caserta, Italy
lelio.campanile@unicampania.it

Abstract. The increasing levels of CO_2 and air pollutants represent a major challenge to environmental sustainability and public health, particularly in regions characterized by complex geographic and socio-economic dynamics. This work proposes a study focused on the Southern Italy regions, where environmental vulnerabilities are displayed, along with a limited availability of high-granularity data. The main aim of this work is to build and provide a comprehensive and detailed dataset tailored to the region's unique needs, by leveraging datasets from EDGAR for greenhouse gases and air pollutants, integrated with demographic and territorial morphology data from ISTAT. The creation of composite indicators to monitor trends in emissions and pollution on a fine spatial scale is supported by the data set. These indicators enable initial insight into spatial disparities in pollutant concentrations, offering valuable data to inform targeted policy interventions. The work provided a foundation for next analytical studies, integrating different datasets and highlighting the potential for complex spatiotemporal analysis. The study provides a robust dataset and preliminary insights, enhancing the understanding of environmental dynamics in Southern Italy. Subsequent efforts will focus on extending this methodology to more extensive geographic contexts and incorporating real-time data for adaptive monitoring. The proposed framework also lays the groundwork for privacy-aware environmental monitoring solutions, enabling future integration with edge and IoT-based architectures while addressing privacy and data protection concerns.

Keywords: Greenhouses gas · Data aggregation · Air quality Monitoring · Data Analysis · IoT · Privacy-aware analytics

1 Introduction

The increasing concentration of CO_2 and air pollutants represents one of the most pressing challenges to environmental sustainability and public health worldwide. Anthropogenic activities, such as industrial production, urbanization, and vehicular emissions, have significantly accelerated the accumulation of greenhouse gases and other pollutants in the atmosphere, resulting in accelerated climate change and negative impacts on ecosystems. Beyond global concerns, the localized effects of pollution are profound, especially in regions with unique geographic and socio-economic characteristics. Southern Italy exemplifies such a region, where environmental vulnerabilities intersect with limited access to detailed and usable data. Although significant advancements in environmental monitoring have been made, the granularity of available datasets remains a critical bottleneck. Existing data on CO_2 emissions and air pollutants often lacks the spatial and temporal resolution needed to capture variations at municipal or regional levels. This limitation hinders the development of targeted interventions and complicates efforts to evaluate the effectiveness of mitigation strategies. Furthermore, the interplay between demographic factors, territorial morphology, and pollution intensities is inadequately represented in many studies, leaving critical gaps in understanding the socio-environmental dynamics of vulnerable areas like Southern Italy. To address these challenges, this study focuses on constructing a high-quality, comprehensive dataset tailored to the unique needs of the specific analysis target, as Southern Italy. The integration of greenhouse gas and air pollutant data from the EDGAR database with demographic and territorial morphology data from ISTAT (National Institute of Statitics for Italy) is intended to address the data deficit, thereby establishing a foundation for advanced environmental analyses. The dataset has been designed to facilitate the development of composite and evolutionary indicators that reflect pollution trends over time and space. These indicators are considered to be crucial for identifying spatial disparities in pollutant concentrations and their potential health impacts, thereby supporting informed decision-making for policymakers and stakeholders.

In addition to addressing environmental concerns, the increasing reliance on high-resolution and real-time environmental data collected through distributed IoT infrastructures raises important privacy considerations. Although the datasets employed in this study are collected from publicly available sources and do not include directly identifiable information, the integration of granular spatial, demographic, and temporal data may still pose risks related to re-identification and location-based profiling. As environmental monitoring systems evolve toward edge and cloud-based architectures with real-time data acquisition, the adoption of privacy-aware data processing methods becomes essential. This study anticipates these challenges and proposes a methodological foundation that can be extended with privacy-preserving techniques in future implementations.

A distinctive feature of this work is represented by the emphasis on the process adopted for integrating diverse and heterogeneous datasets to capture the multifaceted nature of environmental and demographic phenomena. Furthermore, this integration provides a unique opportunity to construct fine-grained indicators that account for spatial dependencies and temporal variations, offering deeper insights into the dynamics of pollution in Southern Italy. Preliminary analysis of the integrated dataset reveals significant heterogeneity in pollution levels across the region, underscoring the importance of localized interventions. For instance, coastal areas near industrial hubs and urban centers exhibit higher concentrations of pollutants. These findings underscore the value of high-resolution data in identifying critical areas for intervention and in shaping region-specific policies to mitigate environmental and health impacts. In addition to addressing immediate challenges, this study establishes the foundation for future research that explores advanced methodologies for spatiotemporal analysis. By providing a robust data set and demonstrating its potential through preliminary findings, our objective is to inspire further investigations that incorporate real-time data streams and adaptive monitoring systems. Such advancements would enhance the granularity of environmental monitoring and enable dynamic responses to emerging threats, contributing to the long-term sustainability of vulnerable regions such as Southern Italy. The remainder of this paper is organized as follows. Section 2 provides an overview of related work, highlighting existing approaches to environmental monitoring and identifying gaps addressed by this study. Section 3 details the integrated methodology and data sources, describing the processes of data acquisition, pre-processing, and indicator development. The results of the preliminary dataset analysis are presented in Sect. 4. Section 5 discusses the results and evaluates the proposed indicators. Section 6 explores the implications of the findings and the limitations of the study. Finally, Sect. 7 concludes the paper by summarizing the main contributions and outlining potential applications of this research and describing the future works.

2 Related Works

Monitoring CO_2 emissions and air pollutants is a cornerstone of environmental research and policy development. Janssens-Maenhout et al. [12] propose an integrated system that combines satellite and in situ measurements to provide near-real-time updates on anthropogenic CO_2 emissions, facilitating global monitoring efforts. Similarly, Liu et al. [16] demonstrate the impact of near-real-time monitoring during the COVID-19 pandemic, revealing significant reductions in global CO_2 emissions, in [5] a security aspect is analyzed. The interplay between greenhouse gases and air pollutants is further explored by Lin et al. [15], who provide insights into their correlated emissions and implications for synergistic mitigation strategies. Cromar et al. [7] emphasize the importance of accurate air pollution monitoring networks, particularly for health research and patient care, where in [6] a specific southern Italy Campania region was investigated. Furthermore, Manisaldis et al. [17] offer a comprehensive review of the environmental and health impacts of air pollution, underscoring the critical need for robust monitoring systems.

In recent years, the integration of data and predictive models has emerged as a pivotal approach to addressing environmental challenges. High-granularity datasets, when coupled with advanced modeling techniques, offer unprecedented insights into pollutant dynamics and their impacts on ecosystems and human health. Govea et al. [9] discuss the integration of air quality and noise data in urban environments, demonstrating the potential of sensor networks for localized monitoring. Similarly, Superfund Research Program [10] highlights the importance of interoperability and data reuse to tackle complex environmental challenges effectively. These advancements are further complemented by efforts to estimate air pollution concentrations at a continental scale, as presented by Thomas et al. [19], who utilized data integration techniques to enhance resolution and accuracy.

The application of semantic middleware architectures for heterogeneous environmental data sources, explored by Akanbi and Masinde [1], underscores the necessity of integrating diverse datasets to achieve comprehensive environmental assessments. In the same vein, [8] propose leveraging grid computing frameworks to process and analyze large-scale environmental data, emphasizing the scalability of such approaches for global applications.

Indicators and predictive models play a crucial role in monitoring and forecasting environmental changes. In [2] the authors delve into artificial intelligence applications for environmental monitoring, showcasing the use of predictive models to evaluate air and water quality. Hybrid models combining empirical decomposition and neural networks, as discussed in [20], have been employed to improve the accuracy of water quality predictions. The integration of environmental data into models for vector-borne disease prediction, as demonstrated by [14], highlights the versatility of these methods across different domains.

Machine learning-based approaches have gained traction in advancing sustainability efforts. Mazumder et al. [18] propose a novel machine learning model for holistic environmental health monitoring, emphasizing the role of composite indicators in understanding complex interactions. These innovations pave the way for robust analytical frameworks capable of addressing multifaceted environmental issues.

The spatiotemporal analysis of environmental phenomena is integral to understanding pollutant behaviors over time and space. The utility of wireless sensor networks in conducting spatiotemporal analyses is evident in the work of [21], which highlights their role in monitoring air quality dynamics. A novel framework for spatiotemporal prediction using deep learning, introduced by [3], underscores the potential of advanced algorithms to forecast environmental data with high precision. Reviews on spatiotemporal event detection, such as [22], provide a comprehensive understanding of methodologies and applications in environmental monitoring.

Finally, the development of spatiotemporal LSTM models, as explored in [11], showcases the adaptability of these techniques to predict across multiple scales, addressing both temporal and spatial complexities.

These studies collectively underscore the advancements and challenges in integrating data, indicators, and spatiotemporal methodologies for environmental monitoring. By leveraging these approaches, researchers can develop comprehensive frameworks to inform policy interventions and foster sustainable development. Despite these advances, few existing works integrate high-resolution environmental data with socio-demographic variables in a privacy-aware manner. This study proposes to fill this gap.

3 Data Integration and Methodology

3.1 Data Sources

This analysis utilizes two principal data sources: the EDGAR database, which supplies comprehensive emissions data for greenhouse gases and air pollutants, and ISTAT datasets, which present demographic and territorial morphology information. The amalgamation of these information facilitates a more thorough environmental evaluation, permitting elevated geographical resolution with a specific emphasis on Southern Italy.

The Emissions Database for Global Atmospheric Research (EDGAR) is extensively utilized for tracking human emissions. This study employs the data retrieved from EDGAR v8.1 and 2024 GHG datasets, encompassing CO_2 emissions from 1970 to 2023, alongside the EDGAR v8.1_AP dataset, which offers comprehensive data on air pollutants including carbon monoxide (CO), ammonia (NH_3), nitrogen oxides (NO_x), particulate matter (PM_10, $PM_2.5$), and sulfur dioxide (SO_2) from 1970 to 2022. The emissions data is presented as annual gridmaps, providing significant insights into long-term trends and facilitating spatial disaggregation for localized research.

The ISTAT databases, in addition to emissions statistics, offer insights into population density, urbanization rates, land utilization, and socio-economic variables for all Italian municipalities.

This research concentrates on Southern Italy, in accordance with the project's aim to tackle environmental risks unique to this area. The region is marked by substantial pollution sources, elevated population density in metropolitan areas, and reliance on industrial and agricultural practices that affect CO_2 and air pollutant emissions. The scarcity of high-granularity data in this setting necessitates the utilization of sophisticated approaches for spatial disaggregation and data augmentation.

3.2 Data Processing and Integration

Integrating datasets from several sources necessitates a comprehensive preparation pipeline to guarantee consistency, correctness, and compatibility across varied spatial and temporal scales. The preliminary phase of data processing entails meticulous data cleansing and standardization, encompassing the resolution of inconsistencies in variable nomenclature, the imputation or elimination of absent values, and the synchronization of datasets to a unified temporal framework. Due to the extensive temporal range of the EDGAR datasets, meticulous alignment with ISTAT data is essential for preserving comparability and facilitating significant cross-referencing between emissions and demographic factors. This harmonization step improves data coherence and supports subsequent analytical procedures by maintaining temporal integrity across various sources.

A significant obstacle in integrating emissions data with demographic databases is the alignment of varying spatial resolutions. Emissions data are initially presented in a grid format, whereas demographic data adhere to administrative borders. Emissions values are correlated with ISTAT-defined territorial units by GIS-based interpolation techniques, facilitating a cohesive integration of pollution and population data. This procedure guarantees that the dataset maintains a high degree of specificity while facilitating comparison analysis across various environmental indicators.

To improve spatial granularity, we utilized statistical downscaling methods that incorporate auxiliary factors such road network density, industrial activity levels, and weather data. These characteristics are associated with emissions and function as proxies to enhance spatial allocation. Furthermore, temporal interpolation techniques were utilized to address data deficiencies and provide uninterrupted time series, so enabling trend analysis across several decades. This method guarantees that data integration preserves historical consistency and geographic precision, facilitating comprehensive environmental evaluations.

In addition to integration, the processed datasets underwent validation methods to evaluate their compatibility with current environmental reports and official statistics. Statistical analyses of aggregated emissions data and national inventories were performed to confirm consistency with overarching trends. This validation process is essential for verifying the dependability of the produced indicators and ensuring their relevance in environmental policy discourse.

3.3 Methodological Framework for Environmental Indicators

This study employs a methodological framework to develop spatiotemporal environmental indicators, including the diversity of emission sources and the intricacies of demographic dynamics. These indicators function as analytical instruments to track pollution trends, evaluate environmental concerns, and furnish data-driven insights for policymakers. High-granularity indicators are essential for recognizing localized pollution patterns and their temporal changes, enabling a more focused approach to mitigation activities.

The development of environmental indicators adheres to a systematic technique. Composite indicators are established by amalgamating many factors, such as emissions statistics, population density, and land use patterns, to provide synthetic metrics that signify pollution exposure levels. Moreover, evolutionary indicators are intended to identify temporal trends, facilitating the detection of rising or falling pollution levels over time. Advanced interpolation techniques are utilized to estimate emissions at a more refined spatial resolution than the original records offer, hence improving the dataset's applicability for environmental monitoring.

This paper introduces multi-source data fusion techniques, which improve the granularity and interpretability of pollution indicators. By integrating emissions data with supplementary datasets—such as land cover information, traffic flow statistics, and meteorological observations—we develop enhanced indicators that yield more insights into pollution dynamics. These indicators are classified into absolute and relative measurements, facilitating comparison evaluations across geographies and various timeframes.

A crucial component of the methodological framework is the application of geostatistical modeling to enhance spatial estimations. The different spatial interpolation techniques were utilized to predict pollution levels in regions with limited observational data. These models enhance the precision of emissions estimates and improve the resolution of exposure assessment by utilizing spatial dependencies. Furthermore, Bayesian hierarchical modeling was utilized to integrate uncertainty estimation in the generated indicators, yielding confidence intervals that inform decision-making processes.

This work primarily emphasizes dataset construction and indicator formulation; future research will investigate the deployment of machine learning models to improve prediction capabilities. Possible avenues encompass the identification of emission hotspots through historical trends, the examination of significant environmental and socio-economic factors affecting pollution levels, and the creation of adaptive monitoring systems for real-time policy guidance. These developments would enhance the methodological framework and facilitate data-driven decision-making in environmental management.

This study's methodology establishes a basis for future progress in environmental monitoring. This research enhances the understanding of pollution dynamics in Southern Italy by integrating several data sources, utilizing new spatial approaches, and creating enhanced indicators. The findings establish a solid foundation for focused interventions and policy formulation, guaranteeing that environmental sustainability is prioritized in regional planning initiatives.

In addiction, this framework could evolve toward real-time monitoring using edge ad IoT-based systems, where data privacy and security becomes crucial. In future implementation, some privacy preserving and security improving techniques, such as differential privacy and spacial generalization, could be integrated

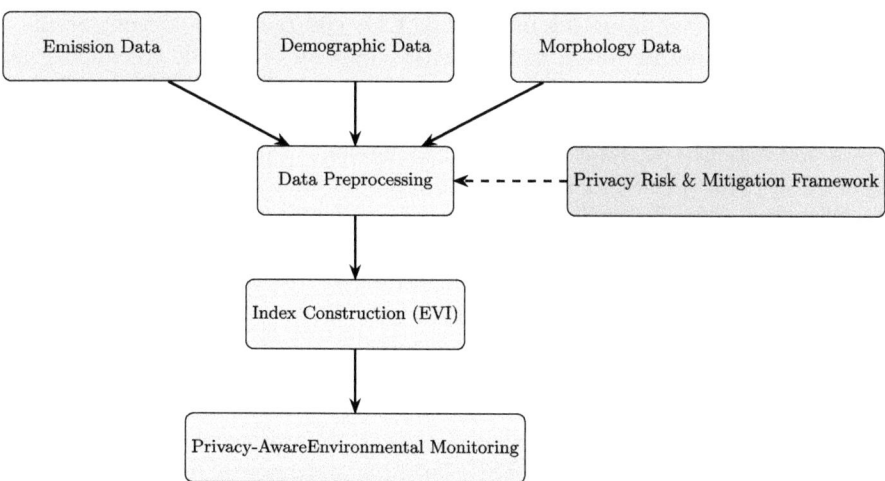

Fig. 1. Methodological workflow: from data acquisition to privacy-aware indicator computation.

to protect sensitive demographic and geographic patterns. These enhancements would mitigate risks of misuse of environmental data in sensitive areas. Figure 1 illustrates the methodological pipeline adopted for dataset integration, indicator construction, and analysis.

4 Preliminary Analysis

This initial analysis examines the integrated dataset, verifies its consistency, and derives essential information regarding the spatial distribution of air pollutants and greenhouse gas emissions in Southern Italy. The research amalgamates many data sources, encompassing emissions data from the EDGAR database, demographic and geographic information from ISTAT, and land cover attributes. This method facilitates a detailed environmental evaluation customized to the region's own geographical and socio-economic characteristics.

Southern Italy exhibits a diverse distribution of urbanized regions, rural areas, industrial hubs, and natural landscapes. The ISTAT dataset offers critical demographic and territorial morphology information, encompassing population density, urbanization rates, and land use attributes for each municipality. This dataset comprises essential properties such administrative codes, surface area, population statistics from 2021 and 2022, elevation data, and geographic coordinates. These criteria provide a thorough examination of socio-economic impacts on environmental conditions.

The land cover collection also includes essential information on surface classifications within Italian municipalities. It delineates manmade surfaces, wooded regions, shrublands, herbaceous flora, and aquatic bodies. These factors are essential for assessing environmental quality, as they affect the dispersion and absorption of air pollutants. Comprehending the spread of plant cover facilitates the evaluation of its mitigating impacts on CO_2 and pollution concentrations.

The EDGAR dataset offers comprehensive data on worldwide greenhouse gas and air pollutant emissions, provided at a high-resolution grid. It encompasses emissions of CO_2, NO_x, SO_2, CO, NH_3, and particulate matter, classified by sector and region. The dataset documents emissions in tons annually each coordinate grid point, providing insights into temporal and spatial trends. Through the filtration and extraction of pertinent data for Southern Italy, we rebuilt region-specific emission patterns.

We utilized GIS-based visualization techniques to study the spatial distribution of contaminants, creating maps to identify emission hotspots and spatial trends. The initial results reveal considerable discrepancies among various regions. Elevated levels of NO_x and CO are detected in urban and industrial areas, especially in Naples, Palermo, and Bari. In contrast, rural and poorly populated areas, such as inland Calabria and certain sections of Sardinia, demonstrate reduced pollution levels. This variation indicates a robust correlation among population density, economic activities, and emission levels.

To enhance comprehension of the relationship between socio-economic characteristics and air pollution, we conducted correlation studies. The findings demonstrate a robust positive association between population density and NO_x and CO emissions, validating the anticipated influence of urbanization on pollution levels. The proportion of artificial surfaces in a specific location correlates with elevated SO_2 and PM concentrations, underscoring the impact of industrial and transportation infrastructure on pollution levels. In contrast, regions with increased vegetation density generally have reduced concentrations of CO_2 and NO_x, indicating a possible ameliorative impact of green spaces on air quality.

The temporal examination of emissions, utilizing historical data from EDGAR, indicates significant trends. A significant fall in CO and SO_2 emissions was noted in 2020, corresponding with the decrease in industrial and transportation operations due to the COVID-19 pandemic. Nevertheless, emissions have subsequently increased, with CO_2 concentrations persisting in high-traffic areas, indicative of continued urban development and economic resurgence. Moreover, anomaly detection techniques revealed isolated emission surges in industrial areas, necessitating further examination to evaluate their environmental consequences.

The amalgamation of these datasets establishes a solid basis for environmental evaluation in Southern Italy. Linking emission levels with socio-economic and land cover data enables the construction of targeted environmental indicators and the identification of important places for intervention. The variations in pollution levels among several geographical regions highlight the necessity of tailored policy interventions. Subsequent study will concentrate on enhancing geographical models, integrating real-time monitoring systems, and utilizing machine learning methodologies for predictive environmental evaluations. These initiatives will augment the potential to formulate adaptive solutions for reducing pollution and enhancing sustainability in the region. The subsequent part will provide a comprehensive quantitative assessment of these initial findings utilizing sophisticated statistical methods and predictive modeling.

5 Results and Evaluation

This part provides a thorough study of the updated dataset, including methodological enhancements and significant findings regarding emissions distribution, socio-environmental correlations, carbon balance, and environmental fragility. By consolidating municipal-level data to align with emissions grid cells, we assured that demographic, land cover, and economic activity indicators could be effectively compared with emissions data. This enabled us to enhance our comprehension of the spatial and statistical correlations between CO_2 emissions and the wider environmental context of Southern Italy.

5.1 Dataset Refinement

The initial dataset posed a challenge: CO_2 emissions were reported at a grid resolution rounded to one decimal place, whereas municipal demographic and territorial data maintained exact geographic coordinates. Municipal data were consolidated inside their respective emissions grid cells to reconcile these datasets. This entailed aggregating the total population across all municipalities within a specified emissions coordinate.

- Calculating the total land area to precisely depict the magnitude of each emissions grid cell.
- Calculating population density by dividing the total population by the entire land area.
- Compiling land cover variables (tree cover, shrublands, herbaceous plants, artificial surfaces) to yield a significant depiction of the environmental composition of each grid cell.
- Computing carbon balance as the difference between total CO_2 emissions and the estimated carbon absorption capacity of vegetation within each grid cell.
- Classifying regions as either 'carbon deficit' or 'carbon surplus' based on whether their emissions exceeded or were offset by their natural absorption potential.

An extract of this dataset is shown in the following Table 1:

Table 1. Sample of Environmental Metrics per Grid Cell

Grid Cell	CO_2 Emissions (tons)	Carbon Balance	Carbon Status
36.7N, 14.8E	211047.42	−19685.82	Surplus
36.8N, 14.5E	13213.86	36928.49	Deficit
36.8N, 14.9E	13577.91	−5672.14	Surplus
37.0N, 15.2E	59084.27	43972.58	Deficit

This approach enables direct analysis of emissions data in conjunction with socio-economic and land use factors, hence assuring more trustworthy statistical interpretations.

5.2 Spatial Distribution of Emissions and Statistical Correlations

Our spatial study indicates that CO_2 emissions are primarily concentrated in urban and industrial regions, with Naples, Palermo, and Bari identified as major hotspots. This pattern conforms to expectations due to the elevated population density, industrial operations, and extensive transportation networks typical of these areas. In contrast, rural regions in Calabria and inland Sardinia demonstrate much reduced emissions, underscoring the idea that economic and infrastructure activity, rather than mere population density, are the principal contributors to greenhouse gas output.

To investigate these associations further, we conducted correlation studies and regression modeling. The correlation heatmap in Fig. 2 demonstrates that CO_2 emissions exhibit weak correlations with population size, land area, population density, and land cover attributes.

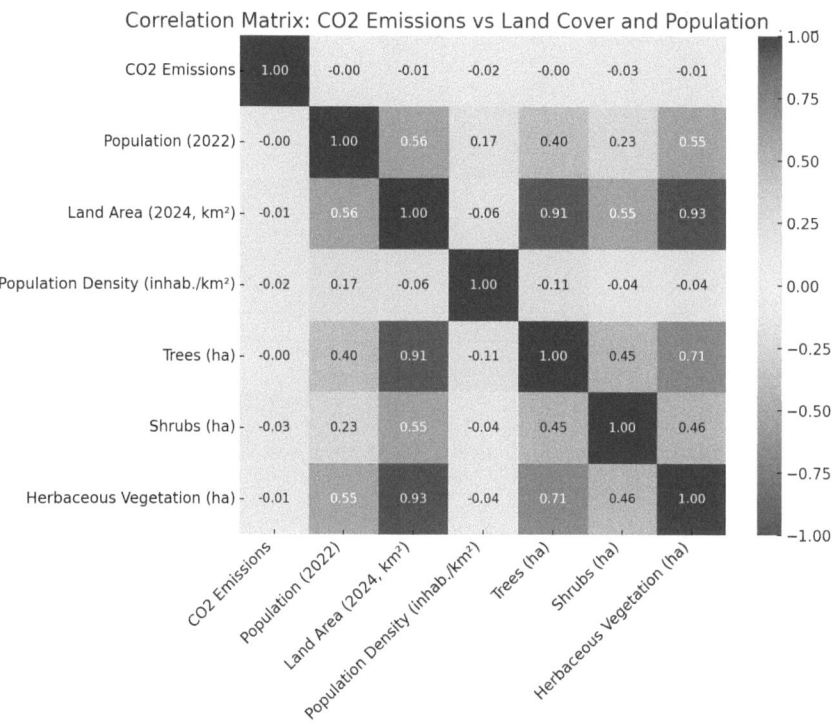

Fig. 2. CO_2 Emissions vs Land Cover and Population

A regression analysis of CO_2 emissions and tree cover, depicted in Fig. 3, produced a R^2 value of 0.000003 (p-value = 0.96), signifying an absence of significant association between forest coverage and emissions. The correlation between CO_2 emissions and population density, shown in Fig. 4, yielded a R^2 of 0.00022 (p-value = 0.66), indicating that urbanization alone does not directly influence emission levels. Ultimately, land area demonstrated an unreliable correlation, yielding a R^2 of 0.000094 (p-value = 0.78). These findings underscore that industrial infrastructure, transportation systems, and energy generation are the principal sources of emissions, rather than mere settlement patterns or vegetation cover.

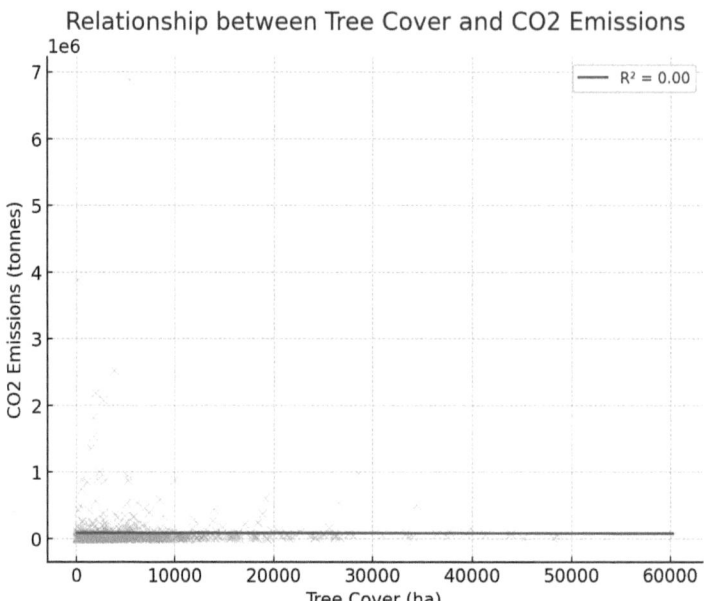

Fig. 3. Relationship between Tree Cover and CO_2 Emissions

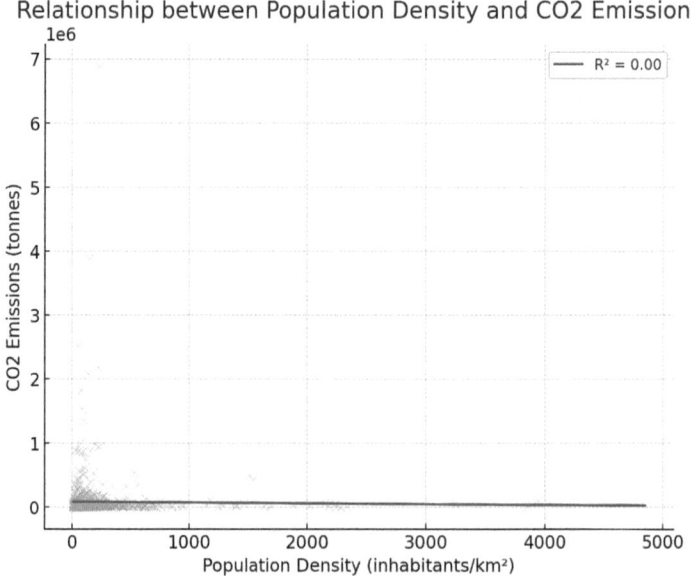

Fig. 4. Relationship between Population Density and CO_2 Emissions

5.3 Ecological Susceptibility Index

To assess sustainability, we calculated a carbon balance metric by evaluating the potential CO_2 sequestration of area flora. Using conventional estimates per hectare of carbon sequestration [4,13]:

- Forests sequester roughly 10 tons of CO_2 per hectare annually.
- Shrublands sequester approximately 3 tons per hectare annually.
- Grasslands sequester approximately 1 ton per hectare annually.

By aggregating the absorption capacity within each emission grid cell and juxtaposing them with documented emissions, we discerned areas that function under a carbon deficit (where emissions significantly surpass the natural sequestration potential) and carbon surplus zones where vegetation can mitigate emissions. The majority of regions have a shortfall highlighting the necessity for enhanced carbon management measures.

Furthermore, we developed an Environmental Vulnerability Index (EVI) to quantify the environmental stress levels experienced by each region. The EVI was calculated by integrating three primary factors: CO_2 emissions intensity, urbanization levels, and population density. All variables were normalized on a 0–1 scale to facilitate comparability, and the index was calculated as the weighted mean of these indicators. An elevated EVI score signifies increased exposure to environmental stressors, characterized by high emissions levels, dense urbanization, and significant population concentrations. This index facilitates an objective assessment of environmental vulnerability, identifying regions in need of immediate intervention. Significant EVI values were recorded in major metropolitan hubs and industrial centers, highlighting the unequal burden these regions experience regarding air pollution and climate effects.

The Carbon Balance metric represents the net difference between CO_2 emissions and the estimated carbon absorption capacity of vegetation in a given emissions grid cell. A positive carbon balance indicates that emissions exceed the sequestration potential, placing the region in a carbon deficit status. Conversely, a negative carbon balance suggests that local vegetation absorbs more CO_2 than is emitted, classifying the area as a carbon surplus region.

The Carbon Status classification provides a clear distinction between areas that contribute significantly to net CO_2 increases (deficit regions) and those that may act as potential carbon sinks (surplus regions). This classification enables targeted environmental policies by identifying areas where emissions reduction or reforestation efforts would be most effective.

These findings underscore the immediate need for specific initiatives to reduce emissions, especially in industrial areas and on transportation routes. Conventional strategies such as replanting may yield minimal advantages due to the tenuous correlation between vegetation cover and emission levels. More effective strategies may encompass limits on industrial emissions, sustainable urban mobility initiatives, and incentives for the adoption of renewable energy.

The subsequent study should focus on amalgamating real-time air quality surveillance with these results, utilizing machine learning algorithms to construct prediction models for adaptive environmental policy modifications. This study establishes a foundation for evidence-based climate action and sustainable urban planning in Southern Italy by enhancing our comprehension of emissions patterns and their socio-environmental causes.

6 Discussion

The results of this study provide important insights into the spatial distribution and determinants of CO_2 emissions in southern Italy. The results show that emissions are mainly concentrated in industrialized and urban areas, with minimal correlation with population density and land cover characteristics. This suggests that industrial activities and transport infrastructure are the main sources of CO_2 emissions, rather than human settlement patterns or vegetation distribution.

The Environmental Vulnerability Index (EVI) highlights the disparities between emission sources and population exposure. The high-risk areas identified by the EVI align with metropolitan areas and industrial corridors, highlighting the need for targeted policies that focus on emission control, urban air quality improvement, and regulation of industrial activities. Policymakers should prioritize interventions targeting sectors with significant impact, including improvements in industrial energy efficiency, development of low-carbon transport networks, and rigorous monitoring of emissions in urban areas.

While the dataset integration and aggregation methods are robust, it is important to recognize their limitations. The application of grid-approximated emissions data introduces spatial uncertainty due to the aggregation of community-level data to fit the emissions grid framework. Future research should investigate higher resolution emissions data to improve spatial analyses and increase the accuracy of observed relationships. Another limitation is the omission of real-time emission variations due to seasonal and daily variations in industrial activity and traffic emissions. The integration of real-time monitoring data from IoT sensors with satellite-based remote sensing can improve the understanding of emission patterns in a dynamic and responsive manner.

Simply increasing forest cover is an insufficient countermeasure to offset high-emitting activities, especially in areas of high population density and industrialization. Interventions such as carbon pricing mechanisms, regulatory frameworks for industrial pollution, and investments in renewable energy should be implemented to achieve significant reductions in CO_2 emissions. Urban areas identified as high-risk zones in the EVI should be prioritized for initiatives to improve air quality, including the expansion of public transportation, the creation of pedestrian zones, and the development of green infrastructure. Policymakers should use these findings to set emission reduction targets that are spatially optimized to address the most pressing areas of concern.

This discussion highlights the importance of data-driven policy interventions in mitigating CO_2 emissions and enhancing environmental resilience. Thus, this study provides a basis for formulating targeted sustainability strategies by identifying high-risk areas and key emission drivers. Future research should prioritize the integration of real-time emissions tracking, sophisticated machine learning models, and policy impact assessments to enhance mitigation strategies. Advancing these methods enhances our ability to develop resilient, low-carbon urban environments that are better prepared to meet the climate challenges of the coming decades.

7 Conclusions and Future Works

This study highlights the importance of implementing data-driven environmental policies that focus on reducing emissions at the source, offering a comprehensive evaluation of CO_2 emissions in Southern Italy, combining high-resolution emissions data alongside demographic, land use, and environmental indicators.

The spatial accuracy of emissions assessments and their correlation with socio-economic factors has been enhanced by structuring and refining the dataset to align municipal data with emissions grid cells. Preliminary findings indicate that emissions are predominantly affected by industrial activities and transportation networks, rather than by population density or vegetation cover.

The analysis revealed weak correlations between CO_2 emissions and tree cover, supporting the conclusion that source reduction of emissions is more effective than exclusive reliance on sequestration strategies. The Environmental Vulnerability Index (EVI) underscores the discrepancies between emission intensity and population exposure.

While the data integration methodology is robust, it is important to recognize its limitations. The spatial aggregation of emissions creates uncertainty, especially in areas characterized by significant spatial heterogeneity. Future research should investigate higher-resolution emissions datasets to improve the precision of spatial modeling. The study fails to include real-time emissions variations, which are crucial for comprehending seasonal and diurnal fluctuations. The incorporation of IoT-based monitoring systems alongside remote sensing data facilitates a more dynamic and responsive evaluation of emissions trends.

Finally, future developments of this framework will integrate privacy-enhancing technologies to ensure compliance with ethical and regulatory standards when deploying IoT-based environmental monitoring systems. It will also consider the use of formal privacy accounting techniques and the incorporation of DPIA evaluations for any new data source or processing module. The adoption of edge computing and real-time data collection pipelines must be balanced with robust privacy safeguards, enabling sustainable innovation that is both socially responsible and aligned with data protection principles.

Acknowledgements. This study was funded by the European Union - NextGenerationEU, in the framework of the GRINS - Growing Resilient, INclusive and Sustainable project (GRINS PE00000018 – CUP C93C22005270001). The views and opinions expressed are solely those of the authors and do not necessarily reflect those of the European Union, nor can the European Union be held responsible for them.

References

1. Akanbi, A.K., Masinde, M.: Semantic interoperability middleware architecture for heterogeneous environmental data sources. In: 2018 IST-Africa Week Conference (IST-Africa), p. 1. IEEE (2018)
2. Alotaibi, E., Nassif, N.: Artificial intelligence in environmental monitoring: in-depth analysis. Discov. Artif. Intell. **4**(1), 84 (2024)
3. Amato, F., Guignard, F., Robert, S., Kanevski, M.: A novel framework for spatio-temporal prediction of environmental data using deep learning. Sci. Rep. **10**(1), 22243 (2020). https://www.nature.com/articles/s41598-020-79148-7
4. Bai, Y., Cotrufo, M.F.: Grassland soil carbon sequestration: current understanding, challenges, and solutions. Science **377**(6606), 603–608 (2022)
5. Bobbio, A., Campanile, L., Gribaudo, M., Iacono, M., Marulli, F., Mastroianni, M.: A cyber warfare perspective on risks related to health IoT devices and contact tracing (2023). https://doi.org/10.1007/s00521-021-06720-1
6. Campanile, L., Cantiello, P., Iacono, M., Lotito, R., Marulli, F., Mastroianni, M.: Applying machine learning to weather and pollution data analysis for a better management of local areas: the case of Napoli, Italy (2021). https://www.scopus.com/inward/record.uri?eid=2-s2.0-85135227609&partnerID=40&md5=5a7c117fa01d0ba8d779b0e092bc0f63
7. Cromar, K.R., et al.: Air pollution monitoring for health research and patient care. An official American thoracic society workshop report. Ann. Am. Thorac. Soc. **16**(10), 1207–1214 (2019)
8. Fascista, A.: Toward integrated large-scale environmental monitoring using WSN/UAV/Crowdsensing: a review of applications, signal processing, and future perspectives. Sensors **22**(5) (2022). https://doi.org/10.3390/s22051824
9. Govea, J., Gaibor-Naranjo, W., Sanchez-Viteri, S., Villegas-Ch, W.: Integration of data and predictive models for the evaluation of air quality and noise in urban environments. Sensors (2024). https://www.mdpi.com/1424-8220/24/2/311
10. Heacock, M.L., et al.: Enhancing data integration, interoperability, and reuse to address complex and emerging environmental health problems. Environ. Sci. Technol. **56**(12), 7544–7552 (2022). https://doi.org/10.1021/acs.est.1c08383. pMID: 35549252
11. Hu, Y., O'Donncha, F., Palmes, P., Burke, M., Filgueira, R., Grant, J.: A spatio-temporal LSTM model to forecast across multiple temporal and spatial scales (2021). https://arxiv.org/abs/2108.11875
12. Janssens-Maenhout, G., et al.: Toward an operational anthropogenic CO_2 emissions monitoring and verification support capacity. Bull. Am. Meteor. Soc. **101**(8), E1439–E1451 (2020)
13. Jones, M., Donnelly, A.: Carbon sequestration in temperate grassland ecosystems and the influence of management, climate and elevated CO_2. New Phytol. **164**(3), 423–439 (2004)
14. Kiryluk, H.D., Beard, C.B., Holcomb, K.M.: The use of environmental data in descriptive and predictive models of vector-borne disease in North America. J. Med. Entomol. **61**(3), 595–602 (2024). https://doi.org/10.1093/jme/tjae031
15. Lin, X., et al.: An integrated view of correlated emissions of greenhouse gases and air pollutants in China. Carbon Balance Manage. **18**(1), 9 (2023)
16. Liu, Z., et al.: Near-real-time monitoring of global CO_2 emissions reveals the effects of the covid-19 pandemic. Nat. Commun. **11**(1), 5172 (2020)

17. Manisalidis, I., Stavropoulou, E., Stavropoulos, A., Bezirtzoglou, E.: Environmental and health impacts of air pollution: a review. Front. Public Health **8**, 14 (2020)
18. Mazumder, A., Engala, S.R., Nallapuraju, A.: Towards sustainable development: a novel integrated machine learning model for holistic environmental health monitoring. In: 2023 IEEE MIT Undergraduate Research Technology Conference (URTC), pp. 1–5. IEEE, October 2023. https://doi.org/10.1109/urtc60662.2023.10534927
19. Thomas, M.L., Shaddick, G., Simpson, D., de Hoogh, K., Zidek, J.V.: Data integration for high-resolution, continental-scale estimation of air pollution concentrations. arXiv preprint arXiv:1907.00093 (2019)
20. Wang, Z., Duan, L., Shuai, D., Qiu, T.: Research on water environmental indicators prediction method based on EEMD decomposition with CNN-BiLSTM. Sci. Rep. **14**(1), 1676 (2024)
21. Yasutani, R., Kitazumi, K., Narieda, S., Fujii, T., Umebayashi, K., Naruse, H.: Spatio-temporal analyses of environmental monitoring based on wireless sensor networks. In: 2021 IEEE Sensors. pp. 1–4 (2021). https://doi.org/10.1109/SENSORS47087.2021.9639557
22. Yu, M., et al.: Spatiotemporal event detection: a review. Int. J. Digit. Earth **13**(12), 1339–1365 (2020). https://www.tandfonline.com/doi/full/10.1080/17538947.2020.1738569

Multidimensional Evolutionary Evaluations for Transformative Approaches (MEETA 2025)

Exploring Spatial Distribution and Interactions Toward SDG 11 Indicators at the Neighborhood Level: An Experimental Analysis

Francesco Piras(✉) and Valeria Saiu

DICAAR, Università degli Studi di Cagliari, via Marengo 2, Cagliari, Italy
francesco.piras@unica.it

Abstract. The current study analyzes the spatial distribution of SDG 11 targets across neighborhoods in Cagliari, Italy. Using aggregated indicators at the different SDG 11 targets and spatial autocorrelation techniques, the research identifies clusters and outliers across key dimensions such as housing, transport, disaster resilience, and green space access. Results reveal strong spatial structuring for targets like SDG 11.1 and SDG 11.4, while others show weaker patterns. Correlation analysis uncovers both synergies and trade-offs, notably between SDG 11.4, SDG 11.5 and SDG 11.6. The proposed methodology emphasizes the importance of neighborhood-scale analysis for targeted interventions and offers a replicable methodology for localizing SDG monitoring in urban contexts and identifying spatial correlations.

Keywords: Urban Sustainability Assessment Tools · 2030 Agenda · SDG 11 · Multicriteria Evaluation Framework

1 Introduction

Urbanization is one of the defining forces of the 21st century, profoundly reshaping economies, societies and ecosystems worldwide. According to the United Nations, by 2050, the global urban population is projected to surpass 6.6 billion, with near 68% of people living in cities [1]. While cities serve as engines of innovation and economic growth, they also present intricate challenges, functioning as interconnected systems where economic, social, and environmental factors continuously interact [2]. Consequently, urban planning and governance must evolve to address these complexities in a strategic and adaptive manner.

In response to these pressing challenges, the United Nations' 2030 Agenda has become increasingly pivotal. The 17 Sustainable Development Goals (SDGs) outlined in this framework provide a roadmap for fostering social, economic, and environmental progress. Among them, SDG 11, "Sustainable Cities and Communities", underscores the importance of interrelated actions, including several targets related to key issues such as housing, transportation, cultural heritage, disaster resilience, environmental sustainability, green and public spaces.

A growing body of research has examined the implementation of SDG 11, with various studies proposing urban indices and analytical frameworks to measure progress [2–4]. However, significant gaps persist in the assessment and quantification of SDG 11 targets. Most evaluations have been conducted at national or regional levels, with relatively few studies focusing on the neighborhood scale [1, 3]. However, evaluating sustainability at the neighborhood level is essential, as urban phenomena are highly localized and context dependent. Without a localized understanding of sustainability performance, policymakers risk implementing broad-stroke policies that fail to address the unique needs of different urban districts.

A neighborhood-scale assessment enables a finer resolution for identifying disparities in sustainability performance within a city, allowing for targeted interventions that maximize impact. This localized approach not only improves decision-making but also facilitates the identification of spatial patterns that shape urban sustainability. By mapping SDG 11 performance at finer resolutions, planners can uncover synergies and tensions among different urban sectors, leading to more strategic resource allocation and policy design. Previous studies have investigated cross-boundary interactions in relation to one or several aspects of sustainable development, such as climate change, economic development, or health [5–8]. However, only a few have addressed these interactions specifically for the SDGs, and SDG 11 targets in particular, and mostly at the regional level. Feng *et al.* [9] computed an integrated index for SDG 11 at the prefecture level in Chinese cities and assessed spatial correlations across areas. They found that most cities with a higher integrated index also had neighbors with similarly high index values, and vice versa. Xiao *et al.* [10] used spatial econometric models to examine transboundary impacts on SDG progress across Chinese cities, concluding that the SDG performance of adjacent cities positively influences the performance of focal cities.

Moreover, understanding the interrelationships among SDG 11 targets is critical. Cities operate as dynamic, interconnected ecosystems where improvements in one domain can either enhance or undermine progress in another [9, 11]. Some targets exhibit strong synergies, where progress in one target promotes progress in another, or trade-offs, when progress in one target hinders another. For instance, advancements in public transportation or green spaces contribute to improved air quality and social inclusion. Conversely, trade-offs may arise, such as when rapid housing development leads to the loss of green infrastructure. Ignoring these interconnections can result in counterproductive policies. Thus, a systemic approach that anticipates these dynamics is essential for achieving balanced and sustainable urban development.

Within this context, the present study aims to compute integrated indices of SDG 11 targets at the neighborhood level and assess their spatial distribution. The context of the study is the municipality of Cagliari, a middle-size city in Italy. Cagliari's urban landscape is highly diverse, encompassing densely built historic districts alongside more fragmented suburban developments. This variability makes it an ideal testbed for evaluating sustainability performance across different urban typologies. By advancing granular sustainability evaluations, this research contributes to more informed, context-sensitive urban policies, ultimately fostering cities that are both more equitable and resilient in the face of contemporary urbanization challenges.

The structure of the paper is as follows: in Sect. 2 we outline the methodology used in the study, while in Sect. 3 we introduce the contextual background of the research. In Sect. 4 we present the main results of the analysis, and in Sect. 5 we provide some of the key findings of the study.

2 Methodology

The methodology employed in the current work included different steps:

1. Indicator identification and selection.
2. Computation of indicator values.
3. Standardization of indicator values.
4. Calculation of composite SDG 11 targets.
5. Comparison of SDG scores, autocorrelation spatial analysis, correlation analysis.

2.1 Indicator Identification and Selection

We selected indicators based on a combination of past research studies, national and international sustainability protocols, and national and regional sustainable development strategies. For each SDG target, we included as many indicators as feasible, considering data availability at the neighborhood level, complexity, and relevance. This approach aligns with previous studies [3, 12]. Our final list consists of 19 indicators, as reported in Table 1.

2.2 Computation of Composite SDG 11 Targets

Once we computed all the indicators listed in Table 1 for each neighborhood, we standardized them to a scale from 0 to 1 to facilitate comparison. We distinguish between negative indicators, which hinder the achievement of SDG 11 targets, and positive indicators, which contribute to their achievement. The following formulas were used for standardization:

$$\text{For negative indicators}: Ind' = \frac{Max(Ind) - Ind}{Max(Ind) - Min(Ind)} \tag{1}$$

$$\text{For positive indicators}: Ind' = \frac{Ind - Min(Ind)}{Max(Ind) - Min(Ind)} \tag{2}$$

Here, Ind' represents the standardized value of an indicator at the neighborhood level, while Ind denotes its original (non-standardized) value. After standardization, we constructed a composite index for each SDG 11 target by calculating the arithmetic mean of all standardized indicators associated with the specific SDG 11 target, as expressed in the following formula:

$$SDG_k = \frac{1}{M} \sum_{m=1}^{M} Ind'_m \tag{3}$$

where M represents the total number of indicators linked to the specific SDG.

Table 1. Description of SG11 indicators

Target	Indicator	Unit measure
11.1	Accommodation space per inhabitant	[m^2/inhabitant]
11.1	Diversity of building types	[N]
11.1	Percentage of buildings equipped with photovoltaic systems	[%]
11.1	Number of energy communities	[N]
11.1	Percentage of residential buildings with 5G internet connection	[%]
11.2	Percentage of road surface dedicated to pedestrian areas	[%]
11.2	Number of pedestrian crossings per 100 m	[N/100 m]
11.2	Percentage of streets with bike lanes	[%]
11.2	Percentage of streets with the presence of public transport	[%]
11.2	Percentage of population that can reach a bus stop within 150 m	[%]
11.3	Percentage of unused buildings	[%]
11.4	Number of historical-cultural heritage sites and landscape assets	[N]
11.4	Number of cultural associations per inhabitant	[N/inhabitant]
11.5	Percentage of the population exposed to flood risk	[%]
11.5	Percentage of the population exposed to landslide risk	[%]
11.6	Percentage of high-traffic roads	[%]
11.7	Public green space per inhabitant	[m^2/inhabitant]
11.7	Percentage of neighborhood area covered by green spaces	[%]
11.7	Percentage of population that can reach a green area within 300 m	[%]

2.3 Spatial Autocorrelation Analysis

To investigate the presence of spatial clustering of similar SDG 11 target values at the neighborhood level, where high target values might be concentrated in specific neighborhoods of a city, we conduct a spatial autocorrelation analysis. One of the most commonly used methods for this is the computation of Moran's Index, which is defined as:

$$I_k = \frac{N \sum_{i=1}^{N} \sum_{j=1}^{N} w_{i,j} z_{i,j} z_{j,k}}{\sum_{i=1}^{N} \sum_{j=1}^{N} w_{i,j} \sum_{i=1}^{N} z_{i,k}^2} \quad (4)$$

where I_k is the Global Moran's index for SDG 11 target k, $z_{i,k}$ and $z_{j,k}$ represent the deviations of the integrated SDG 11 target k for the neighborhoods i and j from its means, N is the number of neighborhoods, $w_{i,j}$ is the spatial weight between neighborhood i and j. In this study, the weight matrix used is the Queen Contiguity Matrix.

The Global Moran's Index provides an overall measure of spatial autocorrelation for the entire city, assuming homogeneity among neighborhoods. However, to identify local spatial clusters, where certain neighborhoods exhibit high or low values of SDG

11 targets, we compute Local Moran's I, expressed as:

$$I_{i,k} = z_{i,k} \sum_{i=N, j \neq i}^{N} w_{i,j} z_{j,k} \quad (5)$$

When the local Moran's value is positive, the area under study has similarly high or low values as its neighbors, resulting in High-High or Low-Low clusters. Conversely, when the local Moran's I is negative, the area in question may be a potential outlier, as its value differs from that of its neighbors. In this case, we observe either a High-Low cluster (an outlier with a higher value) or a Low-High cluster (an outlier with a lower value).

2.4 Correlation Analysis

To measure the correlation between SDG 11 targets, Pearson's and Spearman's correlation coefficients are the most commonly used in literature. Pearson's coefficient is employed when the variables are continuous and normally distributed, while Spearman's coefficient is used when the analyzed variables do not meet these criteria. In the specific case of our study, where not all variables are normally distributed, we apply Spearman's correlation coefficient. Following the work of Liu *et al.* [13], we considered a correlation coefficient greater than 0.5 as indicative of synergy between SDG 11 targets, while a coefficient smaller than −0.5 was considered a trade-off.Case study

3 Study Area

The study area chosen for our case study is the city of Cagliari. Cagliari is the capital and largest city of the Sardinia region, with a population of about 155,000 inhabitants and an area of 85.45 km2. Geographically, the city is located in the southern part of Sardinia, on the Gulf of Cagliari, which overlooks the Mediterranean Sea.

Cagliari has 31 neighborhoods (Fig. 1), four of which constitute the historic city center. Beginning in the first half of the 20th century, other neighborhoods developed around this core. The city's current urban configuration is the result of transformations from 1943 to 1980, driven by war damage and rapid urbanization [14]. Three main trends shaped its growth: the development of social housing districts, the depopulation and decline of historic areas like Marina and Castello, and the consolidation of Via Roma and surrounding streets as the city's economic and political hub. Since 1994, various urban regeneration interventions have revitalized the historic districts and seafront.

3.1 Data Acquisition

To compute the indicators reported in Table 1 and conduct spatial and correlation analysis, we developed a GIS database. For its construction, we utilized various sources:

- Open data provided by national, regional, and municipal administrations (ISTAT census dataset, RUNTS Registry of Associations, Regional Geotopographic Database, Regional Landscape Plan, Regional Hydrogeological Management Plan, GTFS transit service data, Revenue Agency data, Ministry of Education data).

Fig. 1. Neighborhoods in Cagliari

- Open data from services such as OpenStreetMap and Google Maps.
- Manually digitalized data.

4 Results

4.1 Spatial Distribution of SDG 11 Targets

The first analysis examined the performance of Cagliari's various neighborhoods across the seven SDG 11 targets. Table 2 presents a statistical overview of the SDG 11 targets, including averages, variances, and value distributions, while Fig. 2 illustrates their spatial distribution across the different areas of the city.

Regarding SDG 11.1 (safe and affordable housing), the average score is 0.362, with most neighborhoods in the city scoring below 0.5. From a spatial standpoint, there are limited variations among different areas. The generally low score for this SDG target can be attributed to poor performance in terms of sustainable energy efficiency, as only a small percentage of buildings are equipped with photovoltaic systems or are part of an energy community. In some areas, such as the southern and northern parts of the city, the low score may also be due to a lack of diverse building types, which limits housing options for different population groups, or to limited living space per inhabitant.

We now turn our attention to SDG 11.2 (affordable and sustainable transport systems). The average score is 0.440, indicating a moderate level of achievement toward this target. Approximately 67.7% of neighborhoods have a score between 0.25 and 0.50, while 29.0% score above 0.5. From the map in Fig. 2, it is possible to identify the areas that emerge as high performers. These are mainly concentrated in the central part of

Cagliari, due to the presence of high-quality public transport services, and in the eastern areas, thanks to well-developed walkability infrastructure.

SDG 11.3 (inclusive and sustainable urbanization) shows a relatively high average score of 0.651, with 80% of areas scoring above 0.50. From the analysis of the maps, the two lowest-scoring neighborhoods are the peripheral area of Monreale and the historic district of Castello, located in the city center. In the Monreale neighborhood, several buildings are under construction but remain unfinished. In Castello, by contrast, many historic buildings are abandoned and in poor condition.

As for SDG 11.4 (Protect the World's Cultural and Natural Heritage), this target records the lowest average score (0.241) among all the SDG 11 indicators, with over 60% of areas falling into the lowest bracket (0–0.25), and an additional 16% scoring zero. Nevertheless, disparities between areas are evident. Neighborhoods located in the city center of Cagliari tend to feature cultural assets and active cultural associations, whereas neighborhoods, particularly those in the city's periphery, lack heritage resources and community-driven cultural initiatives.

In contrast, SDG 11.5 (Reduce the Adverse Effects of Natural Disasters) emerges as the best-performing target, with a high average score of 0.860 and a low variance (0.038), indicating consistent progress in reducing the exposure of urban populations to flood and landslide risks. More than three-quarters (77.4%) of observations fall within the top performance bracket (0.75–1.00). The main problem areas are in the northern part of the city, particularly the neighborhood of Terramaini, which has historically been prone to flooding, and in the southern neighborhoods of Stampace and Tuvixeddu, where landslides represent the primary risk.

SDG 11.6 (Reduce the Environmental Impact of Cities) has an average score of 0.559, with a variance of 0.05, indicating a moderate degree of inequality in this target. In some parts of the city, the presence of high-traffic roads leads to poorer air quality compared to other areas.

Finally, we analyze SDG 11.7 (Provide Access to Safe and Inclusive Green and Public Spaces). On average, this target scores 0.378, indicating that access to public green and open spaces remains limited. Most observations (61.3%) fall within the 0.25–0.50 range. From this perspective, the least-performing areas in Cagliari are the historical neighborhoods, which, due to their urban development and layout, were not designed to include green spaces and are often located far from accessible parks or open areas within walking distance.

4.2 Spatial Autocorrelation Analysis

To assess the presence of spatial autocorrelation among different neighborhoods, we computed the global Moran's I. The results are presented in Table 2, where we report on the Moran's I value and corresponding p-value for each SDG 11 target.

We found statistically significant Moran's I values for nearly all SDG 11 targets, except for SDG 11.3, SDG 11.6, and SDG 11.7. For SDG 11.1, we observed a Moran's I of 0.444, indicating a high degree of positive spatial clustering for this target. This can be attributed to the low variability in the target across neighborhoods, as discussed in Sect. 4.1. Another target with a relatively high global Moran's I is SDG 11.4, with a value of 0.462. This is likely to reflect historical urban development patterns, where

Table 2. Values of SDG 11 Targets

	SDG 11.1	SDG 11.2	SDG 11.3	SDG 11.4	SDG 11.5	SDG 11.6	SDG 11.7
Average	0.362	0.440	0.651	0.241	0.860	0.559	0.378
Variance	0.010	0.019	0.054	0.051	0.038	0.050	0.027
0	0.0%	0.0%	3.2%	3.2%	0.0%	3.2%	3.2%
0 – 0.25	9.7%	3.2%	3.2%	61.3%	0.0%	3.2%	16.1%
0.25 – 0.50	83.9%	67.7%	12.9%	16.1%	9.7%	19.4%	61.3%
0.50 – 0.75	6.5%	25.8%	41.9%	16.1%	12.9%	58.1%	16.1%
0.75 – 1.00	0.0%	3.2%	38.7%	3.2%	77.4%	16.1%	3.2%

Table 3. Global Moran I values for different SDG 11 targets

	SDG 11.1	SDG 11.2	SDG 11.3	SDG 11.4	SDG 11.5	SDG 11.6	SDG 11.7
Global Moran I	0.444	0.179	0.039	0.462	0.309	0.047	0.127
P value	0.001	0.041	0.230	0.001	0.003	0.237	0.086

Fig. 2. Spatial distribution of SDG 11 targets across neighborhoods in Cagliari

cultural sites are concentrated in the city's most ancient neighborhoods. Other SDG 11 targets, while statistically significant, show only moderate levels of spatial clustering.

As discussed in the methodology section, global Moran's I only provides a metrics of spatial autocorrelation at the city level. To assess the presence of spatial cluster at the neighborhood level, we compute for each neighborhood local Moran's I. Results are reported in Fig. 3, from which emerged that different neighborhoods display statistically significant spatial clusters.

In terms of SDG 11.1, we observe the presence of low-low clusters in the southern peripheral areas of the city, specifically in neighborhoods like Borgo Sant'Elia and Nuovo Borgo Sant'Elia, which are currently considered slums. Within this context, Quartiere del Sole and Monte Mixi emerge as high-low clusters, meaning they stand out as outliers with significantly higher SDG 11.1 values compared to the surrounding areas. This is consistent with their status as affluent residential neighborhoods. In the northern part of the city, we see the presence of high-high clusters, although there are also low-high outliers within this zone, specifically the neighborhoods of Monreale (previously discussed) and Terramaini. To the west, Sant'Avendrace forms part of a low-low cluster, sharing similar challenges related to SDG 11.1 with the neighboring districts of San Michele, Is Mirrionis, and Mulinu Becciu.

Regarding sustainable mobility (SDG 11.2), a high-high cluster is observed in the central area of Cagliari, specifically the neighborhoods of La Vega, Villanova, and Sant'Alenixedda. Within this cluster, the neighborhood of Genneruxi stands out as a low-high outlier due to its relatively limited public transport connectivity compared to the other neighborhoods in the same cluster. The map also reveals a high-low cluster in the northern periphery, represented by the neighborhood of San Michele, which distinguishes itself from nearby areas through better public transport coverage and more pedestrian-friendly infrastructure. In contrast, other northern peripheral neighborhoods form a low-low cluster. These areas generally lack sidewalks and are served by a limited number of public transport lines, which contributes to their poor performance in sustainable mobility.

For SDG 11.3, it is interesting to observe that neighborhoods such as Cep, Fonsarda, and Sant'Alenixedda form High-High clusters, suggesting a commonly low share of unused buildings in these areas. In the north, the neighborhoods of Is Mirrionis and Mulinu Becciu form a High-Low cluster, likely due to their proximity to the Monreale neighborhood, which has a high level of unused buildings.

SDG 11.4 and SDG 11.5 also exhibit noteworthy spatial dynamics. Stampace and Castello are clear High-High clusters for SDG 11.4 indicators, consistent with their historical significance and central location, which makes them attractive locations for cultural associations. Disaster resilience (SDG 11.5) shows fewer clusters overall, though the northern neighborhoods of the city once again emerge as High-High clusters.

As for SDG 11.6, some spatial patterns can also be detected. High-High clusters appear in the peripheral northern neighborhoods of the city, due to the lack of dense road infrastructure. On the other hand, Mirrionis and Villanova are identified as High-Low outliers, as their share of high-intensity traffic roads is lower compared to that of adjacent neighborhoods.

Finally, SDG 11.7 highlights the presence of Low-Low clusters in the historical neighborhoods of Marina, Castello, and Villanova, located in the southern part of the city. This is due to limited accessibility to green and open spaces, as explained in the

Fig. 3. Spatial clusters of SDG 11 targets in Cagliari

previous section, which is a result of their urban development history. Another Low-Low cluster can also be observed in the northern periphery of the city.

4.3 Correlation Analysis

Finally, we analyze the correlations among the different SDG 11 targets, as shown in Table 4. A negative correlation is observed between SDG 11.5 (disaster resilience) and SDG 11.4 (cultural heritage), suggesting that areas with a higher concentration of cultural heritage sites are also more exposed to disaster risk. This inverse relationship may be attributed to the presence of older infrastructure in these neighborhoods, which increases their vulnerability to natural disasters. A negative correlation is also found between SDG 11.6 (urban environmental quality) and SDG 11.4. This may be explained by the absence of major high-traffic road infrastructure in central neighborhoods, which also serve as the city's cultural hubs.

Interestingly, a positive correlation ($r = 0.578$) emerges between SDG 11.5 and SDG 11.6. This result may indicate that high-traffic road infrastructure tends to be located outside areas with high hydrogeological risk, thereby contributing to greater disaster resilience.

As for the correlations among the other SDG 11 targets, they generally show only weak or modest relationships. This suggests that interventions targeting a specific dimension of sustainability are unlikely to produce unintended consequences, positive or negative, on others.

Table 4. Correlation analysis

	SDG 11.1	SDG 11.2	SDG 11.3	SDG 11.4	SDG 11.5	SDG 11.6	SDG 11.7
SDG 11.1	1						
SDG 11.2	−0.179	1					
SDG 11.3	−0.062	0.393	1				
SDG 11.4	−0.162	0.127	−0.241	1			
SDG 11.5	−0.052	0.039	0.258	−0.609	1		
SDG 11.6	0.282	−0.405	0.086	−0.512	0.578	1	
SDG 11.7	−0.342	0.105	0.204	−0.135	−0.011	−0.132	1

5 Conclusions

The pursuit of SDG 11 in a city requires a detailed understanding of the current status and progress of sustainable development at the neighborhood level. Neighborhoods often experience varying levels of progress toward SDG 11 targets, which can lead to spatial disparities in access to essential services and overall quality of life. Nevertheless, although identifying spatial clusters and correlations among different SDG 11 targets is critical for effective urban planning and policy interventions, only a few studies have attempted such analyses at the neighborhood scale.

To address this gap, the present study proposes a methodology to investigate the spatial distribution of SDG 11 targets at the neighborhood level. The methodology involves identifying the indicators underpinning each SDG 11 target, computing target values through indicator aggregation, spatially characterizing the aggregated SDG 11 targets, and analyzing spatial autocorrelation and cross-target correlations.

The construction of neighborhood-level maps for each SDG 11 target enabled a clearer understanding of the city's progress at the local scale. While some neighborhoods perform well across multiple SDG 11 dimensions, others reveal localized challenges or fragmented sustainability outcomes in key areas such as housing, public transport, green spaces, and disaster resilience.

The results of the spatial autocorrelation analysis revealed that spatial relationships are a relevant dimension for understanding how sustainable development outcomes vary within urban areas. Global Moran's I analysis showed statistically significant spatial clustering for most SDG 11 targets, with particularly high values for SDG 11.1 and SDG 11.4, suggesting strong spatial structuring influenced by urban form and historical development. In contrast, targets such as SDG 11.3, 11.6, and 11.7 exhibited weak or non-significant spatial autocorrelation at the city level.

Local Moran's I analysis further highlighted the presence of distinct spatial clusters and outliers across neighborhoods. For example, low-low clusters for SDG 11.1 were observed in the southern peripheral neighborhoods, aligning with the presence of informal settlements, while high-low outliers represented affluent areas that stand out from their surroundings. Similar spatial dynamics were observed across other SDG 11 targets, including sustainable mobility (SDG 11.2), disaster resilience (SDG 11.5), and access to green spaces (SDG 11.7), revealing the uneven distribution of urban sustainability indicators.

As for the correlations among different SDG 11 targets, no significant relationships were detected for most of them. The only identified synergy was between SDG 11.5 and SDG 11.6, while trade-offs were observed between SDG 11.4 and SDG 11.5, as well as between SDG 11.4 and SDG 11.6.

From a policy standpoint, the findings of the current study emphasize the importance of neighborhood-scale analysis for monitoring progress toward SDG 11. Understanding where spatial clusters and disparities occur allows for more targeted and effective urban policy interventions, promoting equitable and sustainable urban development. At the same time, the presence of trade-offs and synergies among certain SDG 11 targets enables the identification and implementation of interventions that can positively impact multiple aspects of SDG 11, or draw attention to those that may have detrimental effects on other aspects of SDG 11. The proposed methodology offers a replicable approach for other cities seeking to localize SDG assessments and address spatial inequalities in urban sustainability.

Nevertheless, this study is not without limitations. First, the selection of indicators was constrained by data availability. Although additional indicators relevant to the SDG 11 targets could have been used, we excluded them due to insufficient data for reliable computation. Since both the spatial autocorrelation analysis and the cross-target correlation analysis are influenced by the specific indicators selected, the results could be biased by the choice of indicators. Second, our analysis was conducted at the neighborhood level. However, in some cases, neighborhoods may be too large or heterogeneous, suggesting that a more granular scale, such as the census tract level, would yield more detailed insights. This is a direction future studies could explore. Despite these limitations, our study emphasizes the importance of spatially localizing SDG 11 targets at the neighborhood level. Further research is encouraged to deepen the understanding of spatial dynamics and interconnections between sustainable development goals in urban contexts.

Acknowledgments. This study was conducted within the framework of the project "A GLOcal Knowledge System for Sustainability Assessment of Urban Projects (GLOSSA)", a Research Project of National Relevance (PRIN) supported by the Ministry of Education, University, and Research (MIUR) (CUP: F53D23005650001). The project received financial support under the National Recovery and Resilience Plan (NRRP), Mission 4, Component 2, Investment 1.1, through Call for Tender No. 104, published on February 2, 2022, by the Italian Ministry of University and Research (MUR), with funding from the European Union – NextGenerationEU.

Disclosure of Interests. The authors have no competing interests to declare that are relevant to the content of this article.

References

1. Ma, D., et al.: Research on the spatiotemporal evolution and influencing factors of urbanization and carbon emission efficiency coupling coordination: From the perspective of global countries. J. Environ. Manage. **360**, 121153 (2024)
2. Feng, X., Wang, S., Li, Y., Yang, J., Lei, K., Yuan, W.: Spatial heterogeneity and driving mechanisms of carbon emissions in urban expansion areas: a research framework coupled with patterns and functions. Land Use Policy **143**, 107209 (2024)
3. Thomas, R., Hsu, A., Weinfurter, A.: Sustainable and inclusive–Evaluating urban sustainability indicators suitability for measuring progress towards SDG-11. Environ. Plann. B: Urban Anal. City Sci. **48**(8), 2346–2362 (2021)
4. Berisha, E., Caprioli, C., Cotella, G.: Unpacking SDG target 11. a: What is it about and how to measure its progress?. City Environ. Interact. **14**, 100080 (2022)
5. Liu, G., Yang, Z., Tang, Y., Ulgiati, S.: Spatial correlation model of economy-energy-pollution interactions: the role of river water as a link between production sites and urban areas. Renew. Sustain. Energy Rev. **69**, 1018–1028 (2017)
6. Zhang, J., Zhang, K., Zhao, F.: Research on the regional spatial effects of green development and environmental governance in China based on a spatial autocorrelation model. Struct. Chang. Econ. Dyn. **55**, 1–11 (2020)
7. Mahato, R.K., Htike, K.M., Sornlorm, K., Koro, A.B., Kafle, A., Sharma, V.: A spatial autocorrelation analysis of road traffic accidents by severity using Moran's I spatial statistics: a study from Nepal 2019–2022. BMC Public Health **24**(1), 3086 (2024)
8. dos Santos, D.D.A., Lopes, T.R., Damaceno, F.M., Duarte, S.N.: Evaluation of deforestation, climate change and CO2 emissions in the Amazon biome using the Moran Index. J. S. Am. Earth Sci. **143**, 105010 (2024)
9. Feng, Y., Huang, C., Song, X., Gu, J.: Assessing progress and interactions toward SDG 11 indicators based on geospatial big data at prefecture-level cities in the yellow river basin between 2015 and 2020. Remote Sens. **15**(6), 1668 (2023)
10. Xiao, H., Bao, S., Ren, J., Xu, Z.: Transboundary impacts on SDG progress across Chinese cities: a spatial econometric analysis. Sustain. Cities Soc. **92**, 104496 (2023)
11. Lusseau, D., Mancini, F.: Income-based variation in sustainable development goal interaction networks. Nat. Sustain. **2**(3), 242–247 (2019)
12. Abastante, F., Lami, I.M., Gaballo, M.: Pursuing the SDG 11 targets: the role of the sustainability protocols. Sustainability **13**(7), 3858 (2021)
13. Liu, X., Yuan, M.: Assessing progress towards achieving the transport dimension of the SDGs in China. Sci. Total. Environ. **858**, 159752 (2023)
14. Murgante, B., Patimisco, L., Annunziata, A.: Developing a 15-minute city: a comparative study of four Italian Cities-Cagliari, Perugia, Pisa, and Trieste. Cities **146**, 104765 (2024)

Energy Performance Certificates and Housing Transaction Prices: Empirical Evidence from Market Data Analysis

Alice Barreca(✉)[iD], Elena Fregonara[iD], Giorgia Malavasi[iD], and Diana Rolando[iD]

Department of Architecture and Design, Politecnico di Torino,
Viale Pier Andrea Mattioli 39, 10125 Turin, Italy
`alice.barreca@polito.it`

Abstract. In recent years, the intersection between real estate market dynamics and environmental sustainability has gained increasing attention, particularly in light of the European Union's regulatory efforts to decarbonize the building sector. Energy Performance Certificates (EPCs), initially conceived as informational tools, are now emerging as significant drivers of housing prices and investment decisions. This study investigates the impact of EPCs on real estate transaction prices within the urban context of Turin, Italy, with a specific focus on spatial effects often neglected in traditional analyses. Using a dataset of over 5,000 property listings from 2022–2023, a Spatial Error Model (SEM) is implemented to capture spatial autocorrelation and improve model accuracy. The results reveal a statistically and economically significant "green premium" for high-efficiency dwellings (EPC A and B–C) and a corresponding "brown discount" for inefficient properties (EPC F–G). These findings not only validate the role of EPCs in price formation but also align with the broader objectives of the EU Green Deal and the Green Asset Ratio (GAR), which increasingly integrates energy performance into financial valuation. The study offers novel insights into the spatial valuation of sustainability and suggests that market forces, coupled with regulatory instruments, are reshaping investment patterns in the built environment.

Keywords: Energy Performance Certificates · Housing Prices · Spatial Econometric Models

1 Introduction

In the last decades, the influence of energy-building performance on pricing processes has been deeply explored in European and international contexts due to the growing relevance of environmental policies and their related norms and regulations. The role of Energy Performance Certificates (EPCs) – a measure of the building performance adopted by several governments - in the real estate market has evolved significantly over the years, shaping both property valuation methodologies and financial decision-making processes. More precisely, in the Italian context, from their introduction EPCs have been increasingly recognized as a key factor influencing market value [1, 5, 26,

31], rental prices, and investment attractiveness [10, 27]. Recent regulatory and updates at the European level, particularly EU Directive 2024/1275 on the energy performance of buildings, have further reinforced the importance of environmental sustainability in the building construction sector and, consequently, in the real estate market sector, introducing new challenges for property owners, investors, and financial institutions.

Besides, the growing emphasis on environmental, social, and governance (ESG) factors in real estate finance has led to the development of key performance indicators (KPIs) such as the Green Asset Ratio (GAR), which financial institutions must disclose as of January 1, 2024 [24]. The GAR measures the proportion of credit assets financing activities aligned with the EU Taxonomy for sustainable finance, highlighting the need for more detailed data on the energy performance of buildings. Real estate assets that meet the environmental standards introduced by GAR taxonomy (such as energy-efficient buildings or those undergoing substantial renovations to improve sustainability) are more likely to attract green financing and institutional investments. As a result, market participants are increasingly incentivized to develop, retrofit, or acquire properties that comply with green criteria, potentially reshaping investment strategies and driving broader changes in the built environment. In particular, the residential real estate sector plays a crucial role in this framework, as real estate-backed loans (Fig. 1) represent 93.6% of eligible assets within financial institutions [23].

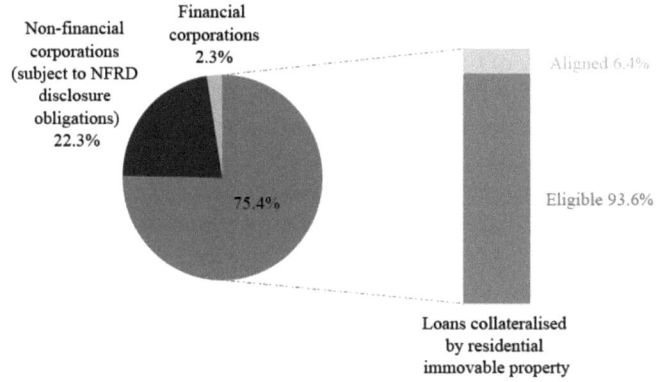

Fig. 1. Breakdown of eligible and aligned shares of the stock by macro-components as of December 31, 2023, Elaboration from European Banking Authority, 2022

The EPC is a crucial tool in assessing the eligibility of real estate assets under the EU Taxonomy, and thus their inclusion in the GAR. The EPC provides standardized information on a building's energy efficiency, a core criterion for determining whether a property qualifies as environmentally sustainable. Consequently, the EPC functions as a key data source for financial institutions calculating their GAR, reinforcing the role of energy performance as a central pillar of sustainable finance in the real estate market sector.

Despite the growing importance of EPCs in the financial and regulatory landscape, the availability and granularity of EPC data remain key challenges [22].

The share of "aligned" residential properties—those meeting the highest energy efficiency standards—remains relatively low due to factors such as:

- The absence of EPC data in real estate transactions and mortgage assessments [28];
- The lack of systematic digitalization in energy certification records [36];
- The exposure of the European housing stock to older, less efficient buildings that do not fall within the top 15% in terms of energy performance [25].

To address these issues, recent initiatives in real estate digitalization and data analytics have focused on improving EPC-based property valuation models. Real estate platforms such as Immobiliare.it are now integrating Automated Valuation Models (AVMs) to refine price predictions based on energy efficiency levels [40]. Similarly, financial institutions increasingly adopt data-driven approaches to assess EPC-related risks and opportunities within their portfolios [38].

In this context, this paper aims to explore the impact of EPCs on real estate transaction prices, analysing how the market perception of energy certification has changed over time and how advancements in database structures and analytical models are influencing real estate valuation. Unlike previous studies that focused on case-specific results, this research emphasizes the broader methodological evolution in EPC data integration and its implications for both real estate markets and financial compliance with EU sustainability directives.

Understanding the influence of EPCs in real estate transaction prices is essential for multiple reasons, particularly in the current European regulatory and financial landscape. The increasing stringency of EU sustainability policies is pushing both property buyers and investors to reconsider the weight of energy efficiency in their decision-making processes [37]. Several studies have demonstrated that properties with higher EPC ratings tend to command higher sales prices and shorter time on the market, as energy-efficient properties offer lower operational costs and increased comfort [27, 30]. By analysing transaction prices, it is possible to quantify the premium associated with EPCs, and understand how market segments react to regulatory and economic changes [14–16, 35]. As banks and financial institutions are now required to disclose their Green Asset Ratio (GAR), the role of EPCs extends beyond the real estate market sector into the financial market. Mortgage-backed loans and real estate assets constitute a huge portion of banks' portfolios, meaning that the energy efficiency of collateralized properties directly impacts a financial institution's GAR score and, consequently, its attractiveness to investors focused on ESG compliance [23].

Analysing the impact of EPC data on real estate transaction prices helps anticipate how regulatory changes shape lending policies, credit risk assessments, and mortgage pricing. Cities and municipalities also leverage EPC data to shape urban planning and building retrofitting policies. Understanding how EPCs influence real estate market trends can support policymakers in designing incentives for energy-efficient renovations, green mortgages, and subsidies to accelerate the transition toward a more sustainable housing stock [33]. The availability and quality of EPC data remain key limitations in many European markets, affecting the accuracy of property valuation models and real estate investment risk assessments [17]. Analysing how new data-driven methodologies, such as machine learning algorithms for price prediction and blockchain-based

EPC registries, are reshaping the market can provide valuable insights into future trends and policy effectiveness [31].

Given the rapid evolution of regulations, financial mechanisms, and digital tools surrounding EPCs, it is crucial to analyse their impact on real estate transaction prices. This study will contribute to the existing literature by exploring how EPC-driven market perceptions have changed over time and evaluating the potential of emerging data integration methodologies. Doing so will offer valuable insights for policymakers, investors, and real estate professionals navigating the evolving landscape of sustainable property markets.

2 Materials

In past studies, the impact of Energy Performance Certificate (EPC) labels on real estate prices in the Turin housing market using different datasets and methodologies was investigated (Table 1.). These previous studies were conducted availing the data set implemented during decades by the Turin Real Estate Market Observatory - TREMO (https://oict.polito.it/). Established in 2000 through a partnership between the Politecnico di Torino and the Municipality of Turin, and subsequently also by the Turin Chamber of Commerce, for decades the Observatory has continuously monitored and analyzed housing prices along with their intrinsic and extrinsic characteristics across different territorial segments of the city, which correspond to distinct real estate submarkets. Recently, TREMO evolved in the "Turin Real Estate Market Observatory – Research" (TREMO-R), a Research Center in the Architecture and Design Department of the Politecnico di Torino.

In a first study [28] a dataset of 577 property listings from 2012 was analyzed, focusing on the effect of EPC labels on listing prices through a hedonic regression model (Ordinary Least Squares), incorporating additional property characteristics such as location, housing attributes, and apartment features.

Then, a second study [27] examined a sample of 1,131 transactions from 2011 to 2014, assessing EPC labels' influence on listing and transaction prices. This study employed a hedonic pricing model that included variables such as construction period, EPC ratings, and apartment-specific features. A third study [10] analysed a more extensive dataset of 2,092 housing properties listed in Turin between 2015 and 2018, applying spatial econometric models (Spatial Error Model) to assess the joint effects of EPC labels, architectural and typological attributes, and location on property prices [2]. Furthermore, the research subdivided the dataset into territorial clusters, as well as a subset of energy-inefficient buildings constructed between 1946 and 1990, to analyse spatial price variations.

Figure 2 illustrates the evolution of EPC levels from 2014 to 2025 in the considered datasets, highlighting significant shifts in energy performance distribution considering the abovementioned past studies. The most notable trend concerns EPC Level G and Level F. In 2014, Level G accounted for 41.4% of properties, but it dropped significantly to 17.9% in 2017. However, the share of Level G properties increased again to 21.4% in 2021 and 25.9% in 2025. Similarly, Level F increased from 13.3% in 2014 to 20.5% in 2017, declined to 17.5% in 2021, then rose again to 24.2% in 2025. This pattern in the

Table 1. Past and current studies on EPC labels on the real estate market of Turin. (Source: Authors' elaboration)

ID	Authors	Title	Pub Year	Ads Years	Ads Type	N. of records
01	Fregonara, E., Rolando, D., Semeraro, P., & Vella, M	The impact of Energy Performance Certificate level on house listing prices. First evidence from Italian real estate	2014	2012	Listing	577
02	Fregonara, E., Rolando, D., & Semeraro, P	Energy performance certificates in the Turin real estate market	2017	2011–2014	Listing + Transaction	1,131
03	Barreca, A., Fregonara, E., & Rolando, D	Epc labels and building features: Spatial implications over housing prices	2021	2015–2018	Listing	2,092
04	Present research		2025	2022–2023	Transaction	5,118

lowest classes suggests that while initial progress was made in reducing low-performing properties, the improvements were not sustained over time, partly because the EPC classification criteria were revised in 2015 [41], raising the performance thresholds. Level E followed a similar pattern, rising from 14.6% in 2014 to 22.3% in 2017, with fluctuations leading to 24.6% in 2025. Considering the middle-range classes, Level D initially increased from 18.4% in 2014 to 26.1% in 2017 but gradually decreased to 15.5% in 2025. The share of properties rated with a class equal to A and over remained almost negligible until 2021, when it rose to 0.6%, reaching 3.0% by 2025. This steady increase, though modest, suggests progress in adopting higher efficiency standards, highlighting a positive but still limited shift towards top-tier energy performance. It is noteworthy to mention that in 2021 and 2025, all the A classes (A4, A3, A2, A1, and A) were considered as unique classes for the analysis.

Following the previous research, the analysis presented in this paper is based on a dataset of existing housing units transacted between 2022 and 2023 in Turin (Northern Italy), using data from the TREMO-R GIS. The dataset included 5,118 real estate transaction prices sourced from Immobiliare.it, which one of Italy's leading real estate advertisement websites. Real estate transaction prices in Italy are not publicly available,

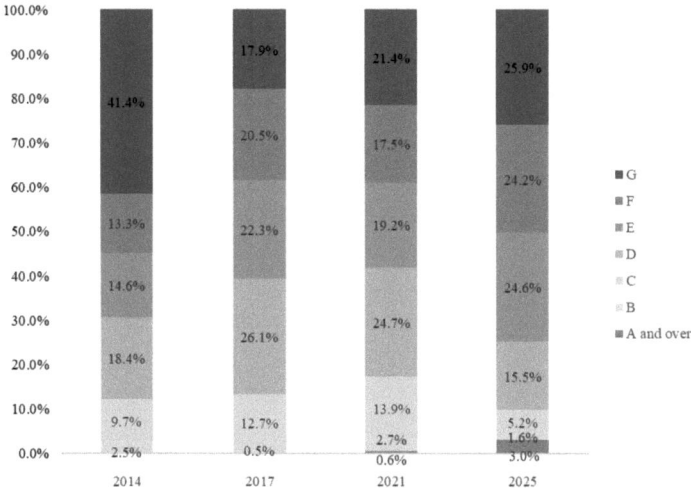

Fig. 2. EPC levels distribution during the years (Source: Authors' elaboration on TREMO and TREMO-R data, 2022–2023)

making them difficult to observe. Consequently, researchers, appraisers, and real estate companies frequently rely on listing prices for market analysis and property valuation [19]. As demonstrated in previous academic studies, listing prices play a crucial role in shaping asset value [19], influencing both sales processes and price predictions.

The data sample underwent a cleaning process and outlier removal using the Interquartile Range (IQR) method [21, 44] for each considered timeframe (year 2022 and 2023) by measuring the spread of the middle 50% of the data. The authors applied the IQR method by calculating the difference between the third quartile (Q3) and the first quartile (Q1) to obtain the interquartile range (IQR). Outliers were defined as values falling below Q1 − 1.5 * IQR or above Q3 + 1.5 * IQR. This process is suitable for real estate data cleaning process because it effectively removes extreme values without being influenced by skewed distributions.

Table 2. illustrates the final data sample's summary statistics, including 5,118 total records. The average TLP (Total Transaction Price) in the dataset is €150,093, with a standard deviation of €91,346, indicating a high variability in property prices. The minimum price is €21,000, and the maximum is €870,000. Similarly, the average PVMQ (Transaction Price per Square Meter) is €1,733, with a standard deviation of €567.

The EPC feature is analysed and categorized into three different variables:

- EPC, which examines the EPC labels of the properties individually, ranging from the least efficient class (G = 1) to the most efficient A1-A4 = 7);
- EPC_2021 categorises properties into 3 different levels based on their EPC class: 1 = Lowest efficiency (E-F-G), 2 = Medium-low efficiency (D-C), 3 = Medium-high efficiency (B-A);
- EPC_2025 refines the previous classification by further dividing properties into 4 different levels: 1 = Lowest efficiency (F-G), 2 = Medium-low efficiency (D-E), 3 = Medium-high efficiency (B-C), 4 = Highest efficiency (A1-A4);.

Table 2. Data sample summary statistics (Source: Authors' elaboration on TREMO-R data, 2022–2023)

Variables	Description	Unit	Freq	Average	St. Dev	Min	Median	Max
Dependent variables								
TTP	Total Transaction Price	Euro	5,118	150,093	91,346	21,000	128,000	870,000
PVMQ	Transaction Price per square meter	Euro/m^2	5,118	1,733	567	575	1,635	3,469
Independent variables								
EPC	EPC label (Levels, G = 1, F = 2, E = 3, D = 4, C = 5, B = 6, A4-A3-A2-A1 = 7)	dummy	1,779	2.97	1.30	1	3	7
EPC_2021	EPC label group (Levels, E,F,G = 1, Levels D-C = 2, Levels B-A4 = 3)	dummy	1,779	1.34	0.56	1	1	3
EPC_2025	EPC label group (Levels F-G = 1, Levels D-E = 2, Levels B-C = 3, Levels A4-A3-A2-A1 = 4)	dummy	1,779	1.75	0.76	1	2	5
GS	Gross Surface	m^2	5,118	84.13	33.13	30	79	300
BOX	Number of garages	dummy	5,118	0.13	0.35	0	0	2
ALL	Allocation level	numeric	5,118	6.14	2.4	0	6	16

(*continued*)

Table 2. (*continued*)

Variables	Description	Unit	Freq	Average	St. Dev	Min	Median	Max
MTL	Maintenance status level (Levels, 0 = NA; 1 = to renovate, 2 = partially to renovate; 3 = good; 4 = renovated)	dummy	1,780	1.57	0.63	1	1	3
CPT	Cadastral Property Type (Levels, Ultra-popular housing = 1, Popular housing = 2, Economic housing = 3, Standard housing = 4, Luxury housing = 5, Villa-style housing = 6)	dummy	5,118	3.13	0.58	1	3	7
PT	Property Type (Levels, Economic housing = 1, Apartment = 2, Luxury apartment = 3, Terraced house = 4)	dummy	5,118	1.22	0.43	1	1	4
D_YEAR	Deed year	dummy	5,118	-	-	-	-	-

It is important to mention that the EPC class is available for only 1,779 out of 5,118 records, highlighting a 35% completion rate by real estate agents.

3 Methods

This study employs two well-established methodologies: Moran's Index[6] and the Spatial Error Model (SEM) [4]. Moran's Index is employed to detect spatial autocorrelation, a phenomenon commonly observed in real estate markets [6, 13, 34]. To complement the statistical results, a LISA (Local Indicators of Spatial Association) Cluster Map is generated, providing a visual representation of Local Moran's I values across all spatial units. The study assumes that when property prices and their features are examined across spatial units, it is crucial to identify both global and local spatial associations between each unit and its neighboring [18, 32, 39, 43].

3.1 Local Moran's I and Lisa Cluster Map

Moran's Index [2] is employed to quantify spatial autocorrelation, a widely used measure for detecting spatial dependence. Moran's I is formulated as follows:

$$I = \frac{N}{W} \cdot \frac{\sum_i \sum_j w_{ij}(z_i)(z_j)}{\sum_i z_i^2}$$

where N is the total number of spatial units, w_{ij} are elements of the spatial weight matrix W, which defines the neighborhood structure (with $w_{ii} = 0$ by convention), and z_i and z_j are the standardized values of the variable of interest for spatial units i and j, typically computed as deviations from the mean. The term $W = \sum_i \sum_j w_{ij}$ represents the sum of all spatial weights.

Moran's I values range from -1 to 1 as follows:

- A positive value (close to 1) indicates positive spatial autocorrelation, meaning that similar values cluster together (high values with high values, low values with low values);
- A negative value (close to -1) suggests negative spatial autocorrelation, where high values are surrounded by low values and vice versa;
- A value near 0 indicates a random spatial distribution, implying no significant spatial dependency.

Building on the results of the Local Moran's I statistic, the LISA Cluster Map serves as a spatial visualization tool that translates statistical outputs into interpretable geographic patterns. While Local Moran's I quantifies the strength and direction of spatial autocorrelation at the local level, the LISA Cluster Map leverages these values—along with their statistical significance—to classify each spatial unit into categories such as high-high, low-low, high-low, or low-high clusters. In this way, Local Moran's I provides the analytical foundation, and the LISA Cluster Map offers an intuitive representation of spatial clusters and outliers, facilitating deeper insights into the spatial structure of the data [3].

3.2 Spatial Error Model (SEM)

The linear formulation assumes that observations are independent and identically distributed. However, if significant spatial autocorrelation is detected in residuals, standard

OLS regression may yield biased and inefficient results. To correct this, spatial regression models must be employed. Two primary spatial models are considered: the Spatial Lag Model (SLM) and the Spatial Error Model (SEM). The most appropriate model is selected based on the comparative results of Moran's I and the LM (Lagrange Multiplier) tests.

In this study, price variability exhibits a nonlinear relationship with explanatory variables, and residuals show spatial dependence, necessitating the application of the SEM. The SEM is estimated using the Maximum Likelihood Estimation (MLE) algorithm, which assumes normality in the error term. This model is particularly suitable when measurement errors in locational characteristics exist or when omitted variables are spatially correlated.

Given these conditions, the SEM—also referred to as the Spatial Error Correction Model—is specified as follows:

$$Pi = \beta_0 + \sum_{k=1}^{K} \beta_k X_{ik} + u_i \text{ with } u_i = \lambda \sum_{j=1}^{N} w_{ij} u_j + \xi_i$$

where u_i is the spatially correlated error term, λ is the spatial autoregressive coefficient (to be estimated), and w_{ij} are elements of the spatial weight matrix W indicating the spatial relationship between units i and j. The term ξ is a white noise error term with standard properties, namely ($E[\xi_i] = 0$, $Var[\xi_i] = \sigma^2$)

4 Results

The TREMO-R research group has been analysing the impact of Energy Performance Certificates (EPCs) on real estate pricing for nearly a decade. Through various econometric models, the researchers have tracked how energy efficiency influences housing market prices, identifying key trends in the city of Turin [7–9, 11, 12, 29]. This extensive research allows a deeper understanding of how sustainability factors integrate into market dynamics over time.

4.1 EPC Levels Over Time

Table 3. presents the evolution of the sample size and the presence of EPCs in real estate listings (ADVs) over time. It allows for three levels of interpretation: the type of data used, the statistical representativeness of the sample, and the significance and method of EPC presence analysis.

The data type used has remained consistent over time: real estate listings from the leading online platform. However, while the data from 2011 to 2018 were collected using a stratified random sampling method, in 2025 it was possible to work with the entire set of listings available in 2022–2023 within the municipal area. These 2022–2023 listings were used solely to verify the presence of EPC information in real estate advertisements, while all subsequent analyses in the results section are performed on transaction prices.

Moreover, the shift from listing-based to transaction-based values in 2022–2023 is particularly relevant for understanding whether market expectations regarding energy efficiency align with current buyer behavior.

Table 3. Evolution of the presence of EPC labels in ADVs (Source: Authors' elaboration)

ID	Publishing Year	Ads Years	Ads Type	Total number of ads	Records with EPC label (n)	Records with EPC label on the total 2024 (%)
01	2014	2012	Listing	577	473	4%
02	2017	2011–2014	Listing + Transaction	1,131	879	8%
03	2021	2015–2018	Listing	2,092	1,691	15%
04	2025	2022–2023	Listing	11,493	8,114	71%
			Transaction	5,118	1,779	15%

In 2014 study, 4% of the sample was analyzed, focusing only on listings that included EPC information. Over time, this number has increased and now serves as a proxy for the overall presence of EPCs in real estate advertisements. This growth has been steady, with a relevant increase in the last years.

Finally, an analysis of the average listing prices by EPC cluster in 2022–2023 reveals a price gap of approximately €300/m² between the "B–C" and the "D–E" clusters, and around €200/m² between the "D–E" and the "F–G" clusters. A comparison with 2022–2023 data (as shown in Table 4.) indicates that price differentiation by EPC label has become more pronounced over time: while in 2015, the average price of properties in the F–G classes was about 20% lower than those in B–C, by 2023 this gap had increased to 42%. Interestingly, prices for A-class properties appear slightly lower than those for B–C, indicating a trend reversal at the top of the energy rating scale, as shown in Table 4..

Table 4. Listing prices (2015–2018), Listing and Transaction prices (2022–2023) for different EPC labels (Authors' elaboration).

2015 – 2018 - LP	Frequency	Mean	St. Dev	Min	Max
A-A4	0.004	3,295.49	1,404.28	677.42	5,535.71
B-C	0.1	2,997.34	1,032.36	1,362.73	5,588.23
D-E	0.27	2,699.09	1,267.38	947.37	8695.65
F-G	0.45	2,491.28	1,088.82	916.67	7,000.00
2022–2023 - LP	Frequency	Mean	St. Dev	Min	Max
A-A4	0.03	3,164.46	1,256.93	583.33	7,853.11
B-C	0.08	2,247.34	942.46	568.63	7,710.28
D-E	0.37	1,863.35	766.26	527.78	6,300.81
F-G	0.52	1,712.77	835.15	503.60	7,361.11

(continued)

Table 4. (*continued*)

2022–2023 TP	Frequency	Mean	St. Dev	Min	Max
A-A4	0.01	2,019.25	434.87	1,865.50	2,173.00
B-C	0.05	2,096.04	736.92	1,370.50	2,916.50
D-E	0.54	1,836.00	539.28	878.50	3,174.00
F-G	0.40	1,478.73	492.36	633.00	2,545.50

Over the years, how we've analyzed real estate data to understand whether—and how much— EPCs impact housing prices has also changed. In 2014 and 2017 studies, the analyses primarily relied on standard OLS regression models [42]. Starting in 2021, spatial information was incorporated, restricting the dataset to listings with available geographic data. This methodological shift naturally affected the estimation of the marginal price effect of energy efficiency. Still, even with the more complex spatial models, EPC ratings have continued to play a significant role in shaping listing and transaction prices, as shown in Table 5..

Table 5. Marginal prices of EPC labels derived from different regression models and datasets (Authors' elaboration).

	OLS	OLS		SEM	SEM
	2012	2011–2014		2015–2018	2022–2023
	LOGLP (Listing Price)	LOGLP (Listing Price)	LOGTP (Transaction Price)	LOGLP (Listing Price)	LOGTP (Transaction Price)
	Adjusted R^2 = 0,76	Adjusted R^2 = 0,63	Adjusted R^2 = 0,68	$R^2 = 0,54$	$R^2 = 0,44$
A (A1-A4)	NP	not significant	not significant	0,025	0,13
B	(omitted)				0,1
C				(omitted)	
D	−0,06	(omitted)	(omitted)		(omitted)
E		not significant	not significant	−0,033	
F	−0,09				−0,06
G			−0,056		

Table 5. presents the marginal price variations associated with different EPC levels over time, derived from regression models applied to different datasets.

A direct comparison across periods is not feasible, as the regression models employed were inconsistent. Notably, the two final models (Spatial Errors Models - SEM) introduced a strong spatial component, capturing localized market dynamics that are not directly comparable to previous specifications.

Despite this methodological shift, some trends are apparent. Analyzing the results derived from the first SEM (2015–2018 dataset of listing prices), EPC categories 'A' and 'B–C' consistently show positive marginal price effects, suggesting that higher energy efficiency has only recently become associated with price premiums. In contrast, the marginal effects for the 'D–E' and 'F–G' categories tend to be negative or close to zero, reinforcing the idea that lower-efficiency dwellings generally have weaker market positioning, even if the magnitude of this effect varies over time.

The results derived from the second SEM (2022–2023 dataset of transaction prices) show a clearer ordering of marginal price values by EPC class, along with an overall increase in the premiums for efficient properties. However, the model's explanatory power ($R^2 = 0.44$) remains modest, indicating that while EPC level plays a role, its impact on price formation may be mediated by other factors in the transaction data.

4.2 Local Moran's Index, LISA Map and Spatial Error Model (SEM) results (2022 and 2023 Data)

The Local Indicators of Spatial Association (LISA) clustering analyzes Turin's 2022–2023 real estate transaction prices [2]. This approach helps understand how real estate prices are geographically distributed and whether high or low values tend to concentrate in specific zones (Fig. 3).

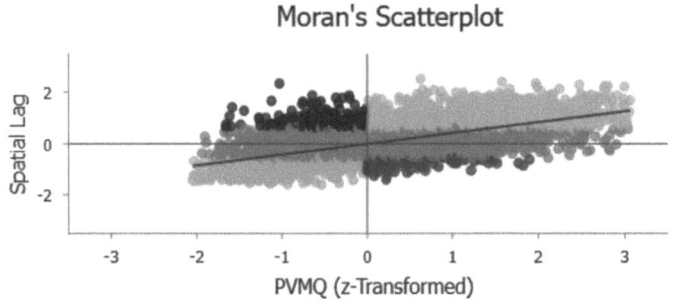

Fig. 3. Moran's Index Scatterplot (Source: Authors' elaboration)

Moran's Scatterplot visually represents the global spatial autocorrelation of standardized housing prices (PVMQ, z-transformed). Each dot corresponds to a real estate listing, plotted according to its standardized price (x-axis) and the average standardized price of its spatial neighbors (y-axis). The slope of the regression line is positive, indicating positive spatial autocorrelation: similar price values tend to cluster together. The Moran's I statistic was calculated using a Queen contiguity spatial weights matrix, which accounts for both edge- and corner-sharing neighbors. The analysis was performed in

ArcGIS Pro 3.4 (Esri, 2023) using the *Spatial Autocorrelation (Global Moran's I)* tool, ensuring an accurate assessment of the spatial structure of standardized housing prices.

The R2 value of 0.44 suggests a moderate level of explanatory power—spatial proximity accounts for a significant share of price variability. The four quadrants classify observations:

- Top-right (High-High): high prices in high-price neighborhoods (pink dots);
- Bottom-left (Low-Low): low prices in low-price areas (light blue dots);
- Top-left / Bottom-right: potential outliers or transitional zones.

This result justifies using spatial regression models (e.g., Spatial Lag or Error Models), as the traditional OLS assumption of independence between observations is violated (Fig. 4).

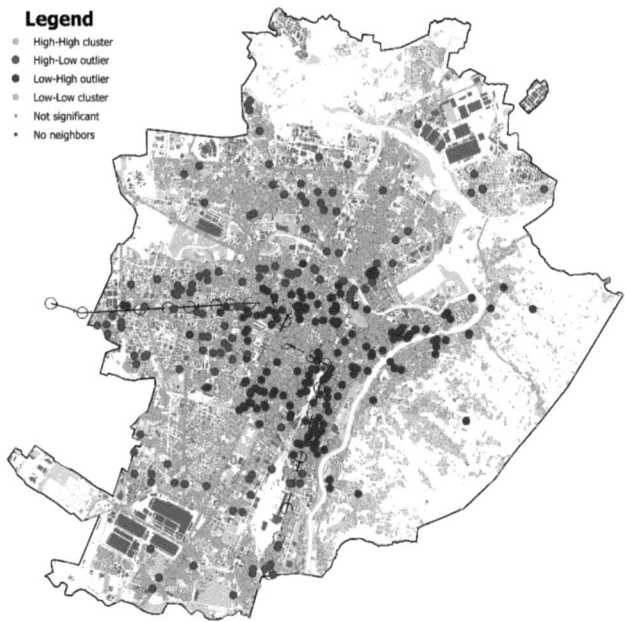

Fig. 4. LISA Map (Source: Authors' elaboration)

The accompanying map spatializes the local clusters of standardized property prices based on LISA. The colored dots correspond to the same classification in Moran's Scatterplot, geographically located across the urban territory.

- High-High clusters (pink dots) are concentrated in the central and semi-central areas, confirming the persistence of strong value zones in the urban core;
- Low-Low clusters (light blue dots) are more frequent in peripheral or industrial areas, often aligned with socio-economic disadvantage or lower market attractiveness.

The hexagonal base layer seems to represent a grid or neighborhood aggregation, visually supporting spatial density and trend analysis. Some Low-High (blue) and High-Low (red) points appear along transition corridors—areas where market values are less stable or undergoing transformation. This map adds local granularity to the global insight from the scatterplot, allowing urban planners or housing market analysts to identify areas of interest for intervention, investment, or further investigation.

Table 6. SEM model on 2022–2023 TP data (Source: Authors' elaboration)

SPATIAL ERROR MODEL - MAXIMUM LIKELIHOOD ESTIMATION				
Dependent Variable: log_PVMQ	**Number of Observations**: 5118			
Mean dependent var: 7.405149	**Number of Variables**: 7			
S.D. dependent var: 0.326569	**Degrees of Freedom**: 5111			
Lag coeff. (Lambda): 0.699809				
R-squared: 0.444168	**R-squared (BUSE)**: -			
Sq. Correlation: -	**Log likelihood**: -235.027825			
Sigma-square: 0.0592781	**Akaike info criterion**: 484.056			
S.E of regression: 0.243471	**Schwarz criterion**: 529.839			
Variable	Coefficient	Std. Error	z-value	Probability
CONSTANT	6,775	0,024	277,383	0,000
EPC_1	-0,0618	0,010	-6,309	0,000
EPC_3	0,103	0,020	5,024	0,000
EPC_4	0,130	0,039	3,329	0,00087
building_f	0,0107	0,0024	6,001	0,000
cadastra_1	0,000	0,000	4,789	0,000
cadast_pro	0,173	0,007	25,081	0,000
LAMBDA	0,700	0,015	47,846	0,000
DIAGNOSTICS FOR HETEROSKEDASTICITY RANDOM COEFFICIENTS				
TEST D VALUE PROB				
Breusch-Pagan test 6 166.7584 0.00000				
DIAGNOSTICS FOR SPATIAL DEPENDENCE				
SPATIAL ERROR DEPENDENCE FOR WEIGHT MATRIX: vendita_22_23_log				
TEST DF VALUE PROB				
Likelihood Ratio Test 1 1893.0527 0.00000				

The SEM model (Table 6.), estimated via Maximum Likelihood on a dataset of over 5,000 observations (log-transformed price per square meter, 2022–2023 data), reports a highly significant spatial error term ($\lambda = 0.6998$, $p < 0.001$). This confirms the presence of spatial autocorrelation in error terms, reinforcing the need to account for unobserved spatial heterogeneity. The EPC variables reveal a statistically robust and economically meaningful impact on housing prices, even after accounting for spatial effects and other structural and cadastral controls. EPC_1 (reference category likely representing the lowest energy classes, F–G) has a negative and significant coefficient: $\beta = -0.0618$. This indicates that properties in this group are associated with lower log prices, all else being equal. The price penalty can be interpreted as roughly –6.2% in marginal price, signaling an evident market devaluation for energy-inefficient dwellings. EPC_3 (presumably intermediate classes, e.g., C–D) has a positive and significant effect: $\beta = +0.1034$, a strong positive premium of about +10.3%, suggesting that these dwellings are increasingly perceived as market-competitive regarding energy efficiency. EPC_4 (likely high-efficiency classes, e.g., A–B) shows the highest premium $\beta = +0.1309$, A price increase of +13.1%, confirming that high-efficiency homes are rewarded in the marketplace, consistent with growing environmental awareness and regulatory emphasis. These results align with broader empirical evidence indicating a "green premium" for more energy-efficient dwellings and reinforce the idea that energy labels are now a significant component of price formation—especially in urban markets like the one analyzed.

The R2 (0.44) indicates a good level of explanatory power for a cross-sectional housing model, especially considering the inclusion of spatial error terms. Breusch-Pagan test for heteroskedasticity is significant ($p < 0.001$), suggesting the presence of heteroskedasticity—but the SEM still provides consistent estimators under ML. The Likelihood Ratio test for spatial dependence is highly significant ($p < 0.001$), justifying the spatial specification.

This regression provides compelling evidence that EPCs are now embedded into the real estate value system—not just symbolically but with quantifiable effects on listing prices. Even after controlling for spatial dependencies and property characteristics, the strong statistical significance of EPC classes suggests that energy efficiency is not a marginal feature but a central component in how housing markets evolve. This has critical implications for: urban policy (e.g., retrofitting incentives), real estate valuation, and behavioral economics (buyers now react to EPC labels in measurable ways). It also suggests that future models should continue to incorporate both spatial and energy-related variables, especially in cities facing regulatory and environmental transformation.

5 Conclusion and Future Insight

The TREMO-R research group has been analysing the impact of EPCs on real estate values since years to contribute to the growing body of research on the relationship between energy performance and housing prices through a spatial econometric lens [10, 19, 20, 27–29]. Leveraging a dataset of over 5,000 property listings in the urban context of Turin during 2022–2023, a Spatial Error Model (SEM) was implemented to account for spatial dependencies that traditional OLS models cannot capture.

The results highlight that EPCs are statistically significant and economically relevant in explaining transaction price variability. Higher energy efficiency ratings (EPC A and B–C) are associated with positive marginal price premiums, whereas lower ratings (EPC F–G) correspond to a negative price impact. These findings confirm the emergence of a "green premium" and a "brown discount" in the housing market, aligning with broader European evidence.

The spatial diagnostics validate the presence of spatial autocorrelation in both the data and model residuals, justifying the use of spatial error correction. Notably, the spatial structure explains a considerable share of price variation, with the spatial coefficient ($\lambda \approx 0.70$) and R^2 values demonstrating a solid model fit. These patterns are further visualized through Moran's scatterplot and local cluster mapping, illustrating how high- and low-efficiency properties are geographically concentrated in specific urban zones. The significance of the spatial error term in the SEM indicates that unobserved spatially structured factors—such as neighborhood amenities, accessibility, or local policies—affect housing prices. This underlines the importance of accounting for spatial autocorrelation to avoid biased coefficient estimates and improve model fit. The spatial correlation also reflects that the housing market is not composed of independent transactions but operates within spatially interconnected sub-markets.

From a policy perspective, the findings suggest that market mechanisms are increasingly internalizing energy efficiency considerations, supporting the role of EPCs not only as informational tools but also as signals of value. This implies that market trends already in motion may reinforce public incentives and regulatory frameworks aiming at building retrofits. Moreover, the significant spatial dependence captured by the SEM implies that interventions in one area may have spillover effects on neighboring zones. For instance, improvements in infrastructure or zoning changes in a specific district could influence property values beyond its administrative boundaries. Policymakers should therefore adopt spatially informed strategies when designing housing or urban development policies, recognizing the interconnectivity across urban space.

Future research could build upon this foundation by incorporating transaction price data, controlling for mortgage conditions, or exploring longitudinal dynamics to assess how EPC premiums evolve over time. Expanding the analysis to other urban contexts may provide comparative insights into how energy efficiency is valued across diverse real estate markets.

In conclusion, this study provides robust evidence that energy performance is currently a salient component in property valuation and that spatially aware econometric models are essential to capture the structure and drivers of urban housing markets accurately. Importantly, these findings have direct implications for the application of the GAR as the EPC serves as a critical instrument in determining the taxonomy-alignment of real estate assets. The observed price premiums for high-efficiency buildings indicate a growing market recognition of sustainability attributes, suggesting that the GAR may further reinforce this dynamic by channeling investment toward greener assets. As financial institutions increasingly integrate GAR considerations into their lending and portfolio decisions, the interplay between regulatory metrics and market valuation is likely to become a powerful driver of transformation within the built environment.

Acknowledgments. The authors would like to thank the TREMO-R research group (https://oict.polito.it/) for providing access to the data used in this study.

References

1. Andaloro, A.P.F., et al.: Energy certification of buildings: a comparative analysis of progress towards implementation in European countries. Energy Policy **38**(10), 5840–5866 (2010)
2. Anselin, L.: Contiguity-Based Spatial Weights. https://geodacenter.github.io/workbook/4a_contig_weights/lab4a.html. Accessed 7 Apr 2025
3. Anselin, L.: Local indicators of spatial association—LISA. Geogr. Anal. **27**(2), 93–115 (1995). https://doi.org/10.1111/J.1538-4632.1995.TB00338.X
4. Anselin, L., Griffith, D.A.: Do spatial effecfs really matter in regression analysis? Pap. Reg. Sci. **65**(1), 11–34 (1988). https://doi.org/10.1111/J.1435-5597.1988.TB01155.X
5. Aune, M.: Energy comes home. Energy Policy **35**(11), 5457–5465 (2007). https://doi.org/10.1016/J.ENPOL.2007.05.007
6. Baltagi, B.H., et al.: Testing for serial correlation, spatial autocorrelation and random effects using panel data. J. Econom. **140**(1), 5–51 (2007). https://doi.org/10.1016/J.JECONOM.2006.09.001
7. Barreca, A.: Architectural quality and the housing market: values of the late twentieth century built heritage. Sustainability **14**(5), 2565 (2022). https://doi.org/10.3390/SU14052565
8. Barreca, A. et al.: Assessing social and territorial vulnerability on real estate submarkets. Buildings **7**(4), 94 (2017). https://doi.org/10.3390/BUILDINGS7040094
9. Barreca, A. et al.: Energy retrofitting for the modern heritage enhancement in weak real estate markets: the Olivetti housing stock in Ivrea. Sustainability **14**(6), 3507 (2022). https://doi.org/10.3390/SU14063507
10. Barreca, A. et al.: EPC labels and building features: spatial implications over housing prices. Sustainability **13**(5), 2838 (2021). https://doi.org/10.3390/SU13052838
11. Barreca, A. et al.: Is the real estate market of new housing stock influenced by urban vibrancy? Complexity (2020). https://doi.org/10.1155/2020/1908698
12. Barreca, A. et al.: Urban vibrancy: an emerging factor that spatially influences the real estate market. Sustainability **12**(1), 346 (2020). https://doi.org/10.3390/SU12010346
13. Basu, S., Thibodeau, T.G.: Analysis of spatial autocorrelation in house prices. J. Real Estate Financ. Econ. **17**(1), 61–85 (1998). https://doi.org/10.1023/A:1007703229507/METRICS
14. Bourassa, S.C., et al.: Do housing submarkets really matter? J. Hous. Econ. **12**(1), 12–28 (2003). https://doi.org/10.1016/S1051-1377(03)00003-2
15. Bourassa, S.C., et al.: Predicting house prices with spatial dependence: a comparison of alternative methods. J. Real Estate Res. **32**(2), 139–159 (2010). https://doi.org/10.1080/10835547.2010.12091276
16. Bourassa, S.C., et al.: Spatial dependence, housing submarkets, and house price prediction. J. Real Estate Financ. Econ. **35**(2), 143–160 (2007). https://doi.org/10.1007/S11146-007-9036-8/FIGURES/3
17. Brounen, D., Kok, N.: On the economics of energy labels in the housing market. J. Environ. Econ. Manage. **62**(2), 166–179 (2011). https://doi.org/10.1016/J.JEEM.2010.11.006
18. Cajias, M., Ertl, S.: Spatial effects and non-linearity in hedonic modeling: will large data sets change our assumptions? J. Property Invest. Finan. **36**(1), 32–49 (2018). https://doi.org/10.1108/JPIF-10-2016-0080/FULL/PDF
19. Curto, R. et al.: Prezzi di offerta vs prezzi di mercato: un'analisi empirica. Asking Prices vs Market Prices: An Empirical Analysis. Territorio Italia, pp. 53–72 (2012)
20. Curto, R., Fregonara, E.: Monitoring and analysis of the real estate market in a social perspective: results from the Turin's (Italy) Experience. Sustainability **11**, 3150 (2019). https://doi.org/10.3390/SU11113150
21. Dekking, F.M. et al.: A Modern Introduction to Probability and Statistics (2005). https://doi.org/10.1007/1-84628-168-7.

22. Deng, Y., et al.: Economic returns to energy-efficient investments in the housing market: evidence from Singapore. Reg. Sci. Urban Econ. **42**(3), 506–515 (2012). https://doi.org/10.1016/J.REGSCIURBECO.2011.04.004
23. European banking authority: On Management and Supervision of Esg Risks for Credit Institutions and Investment Firms (2022)
24. European banking authority: Pillar 3 disclosure framework finalising the implementation of the Base. https://www.eba.europa.eu/publications-and-media/press-releases/eba-updates-pillar-3-disclosure-framework-finalising-implementation-basel-iii-pillar-3-framework. Accessed 7 Apr 2025
25. European Commission: Directive (EU) 2024/1275 Of The European Parliament and of The Council of 24 April 2024 on The Energy Performance of Buildings (Recast). https://eur-lex.europa.eu/legal-content/EN/TXT/HTML/?uri=OJ:L_202401275. Accessed 7 Apr 2025
26. Fabbri, K. et al.: Real estate market, energy rating and cost. Reflections about an Italian case study. Procedia Eng. **21**, 303–310 (2011). https://doi.org/10.1016/J.PROENG.2011.11.2019
27. Fregonara, E., et al.: Energy performance certificates in the Turin real estate market. J. Eur. Real Estate Res. **10**(2), 149–169 (2017). https://doi.org/10.1108/JERER-05-2016-0022
28. Fregonara, E. et al.: The impact of energy performance certificate level on house listing prices. First evidence from Italian real estate. Aestimum. **65**, 143–163 (2014). https://doi.org/10.13128/AESTIMUM-15459
29. Fregonara, E., Barreca, A.: Economics for sustainability: impacts on the real estate appraisal and economic evaluation of projects
30. Fuerst, F., et al.: Does energy efficiency matter to home-buyers? An investigation of EPC ratings and transaction prices in England. Energy Econ. **48**, 145–156 (2015). https://doi.org/10.1016/J.ENECO.2014.12.012
31. Fuerst, F., Warren-Myers, G.: Does voluntary disclosure create a green lemon problem? Energy-efficiency ratings and house prices. Energy Econ. **74**, 1–12 (2018). https://doi.org/10.1016/J.ENECO.2018.04.041
32. Getis, A.: A history of the concept of spatial autocorrelation: a geographer's perspective. Geogr. Anal. **40**(3), 297–309 (2008). https://doi.org/10.1111/J.1538-4632.2008.00727.X
33. Giraudet, L.-G., Houde, S.: Double moral hazard and the energy efficiency gap. Working Papers (2014)
34. Goodchild, M.F..: Spatial autocorrelation (1987)
35. Goodman, A.C., Thibodeau, T.G.: Housing Market Segmentation. J. Hous. Econ. **7**(2), 121–143 (1998)
36. Guerra-Santin, O., Itard, L.: The effect of energy performance regulations on energy consumption. Energy Effic. **5**(3), 269–282 (2012). https://doi.org/10.1007/S12053-012-9147-9/TABLES/6
37. Hyland, M., et al.: The value of domestic building energy efficiency—Evidence from Ireland. Energy Econ. **40**, 943–952 (2013). https://doi.org/10.1016/J.ENECO.2013.07.020
38. Kaza, N., et al.: Home energy efficiency and mortgage risks. Cityscape **1**, 279–298 (2014)
39. LeSage, J. et al.: An Introduction to Spatial Econometrics. Revue d'économie industrielle, no 123, 3, pp. 19–44 (2008)
40. McCord, M., et al.: A spatial analysis of EPCs in the Belfast metropolitan area housing market. J. Prop. Res. **37**(1), 25–61 (2020). https://doi.org/10.1080/09599916.2019.1697345
41. Ministro dello Sviluppo Economico: Applicazione delle metodologie di calcolo delle prestazioni energetiche e definizione delle prescrizioni e dei requisiti minimi degli edifici (2015)

42. Rosen, S.: Hedonic prices and implicit markets: product differentiation in pure competition. J. Polit. Econ. **82**(1), 34–55 (1974)
43. Seymour, L. et al.: Spatial data analysis: theory and practice. Robert Haining. J. Am. Stat. Assoc. **100**, 353–354 (2005)
44. Upton, Graham.: Understanding statistics (1997)

Contextualising Indicators for SDG 11: The GLOSSA Approach to Impact Assessment of Local Plans

Marco Ederle, Giuliano Poli[✉], and Stefano Cuntò

Department of Architecture, University of Naples Federico II, via Toledo 402, Naples, Italy
marco.ederle@studenti.unina.it, {giuliano.poli, stefano.cunto}@unina.it

1 Introduction

The United Nations' 2030 Agenda emphasises the need to make cities and human settlements inclusive, safe, resilient and sustainable – an objective enshrined within Sustainable Development Goal (SDG) 11. At the urban scale, assessing the impacts of planning and territorial transformations and measuring progress towards sustainability are critical factors to support decision-makers in evaluating the effectiveness of adopted solutions [1, 2], providing the opportunity to redefine strategies. In this context, Neighbourhood Sustainability Assessment Tools (N-SATs) have gained increasing prominence as impact assessment and monitoring systems, enabling a systematic evaluation of multidimensional aspects of sustainability, ranging from environmental performance to social inclusion [3, 4]. In particular, the urban decision-making context needs more data-driven approaches based on evidence to support transition processes through Integrated Impact Assessment [5–7]. In this perspective, N-SATs can be conceived as multi-criteria methodologies that integrate qualitative and quantitative indicators to measure and compare ex-ante and ex-post neighbourhoods sustainability levels. The assessment protocols, indeed, can provide DMs with powerful indicators to measure the impacts of urban policy and design strategies at a local scale when implemented by spatial Geographic Information Systems (GIS) analysis [8]. This contribution tries to foster the thesis that a crucial element for the success of N-SATs is the localisation of indicators with respect to specific context, as demonstrated by some recent developments of these tools, which prove that the selection of indicators has to reflect local priorities and urban landscape features [9, 10].

Identifying Key Performance Indicators (KPIs) capable of capturing the valued components from regional to local scale enables tackling complex assessments even in contexts where data availability is not guaranteed. Two illustrative examples of this approach can be found in the work of Sutherland (2016) and de Castro-Pardo (2023). The first study proposes an approach that begins with the definition of *values*, fundamental, shared principles that reflect what matters most to a community or system. These values are then linked to *valued components*: concrete, observable, or tangible attributes that represent the chosen values. Indicators are subsequently selected to monitor these components, following a process that emphasises transparency, traceability, and stakeholder participation [11]. The second study adopts a very similar framework, though it employs a more technical and operational terminology. It starts by identifying the dimensions of sustainability, which serve as the guiding "values" of the assessment process, along with their related sub-dimensions, specific aspects contributing to the definition of each dimension. These are then translated into KPIs, which represent the measurable elements [12]. The authors thus construct a *tree-structured indicator system*, where the KPIs are logically and functionally connected to the selected dimensions.

In this way, not only is the measurement of SDG 11 made more effective, but the adoption of measures that are both practically feasible and beneficial to the affected communities is also encouraged [3, 13]. The approach of localisation, often referred to as *contextualisation*, thus becomes essential for providing tailored responses to challenges such as reducing land consumption, improving sustainable mobility, promoting social inclusion, and safeguarding cultural heritage [14]. The scientific literature fosters the continuous development of new indicators, assessment methodologies, and classification systems that reflect urban and social changes [15]. On the other hand, NSATs can be essential for identifying KPIs capable of capturing the territorial values and valued components suitable for assessing urban-scale sustainability. However, although they are based on assessment protocols that illustrate specific indicator calculation processes, it is not always possible to adapt these processes to different territories [16]. In such contexts, the GIS environment allows for the definition of "proxy" variables that can be used as ancillary data to measure or estimate other variables that are more difficult to calculate directly due to practical limitations or unsustainable costs, by utilising heterogeneous data from various sources [17].

Moreover, the application of geospatial technologies - particularly those based on GIS – has been increasingly opening up advanced prospects for assessing urban planning actions, integrating the N-SATs into Spatial Decision Support Systems (SDSSs) for impact assessment in urban settings. Indeed, spatial data enable decision-makers to better understand the social and economic dynamics of cities, supporting the design of more effective urban policies which can improve the multidimensional impacts of urban infrastructures [18], allow to highlight critical areas of environmental protection [19], and improve the involvement and understanding of decision-making choices by stakeholders and local community [20]. Currently, the most established methodologies tend to prioritise the environmental aspect, yet SDG 11 demands that factors such as safety, resilience, and inclusivity have also to be included in the evaluation [21, 22].

This contribution is part of the National Interest Project (PRIN) GLOSSA - GLOcal knowledge System for Sustainability Assessment of urban projects - funded in 2022 by the Italian Ministry of Education and coordinated by the Politecnico di Torino (POLITO) in collaboration with the *Università di Napoli Federico II* (UNINA) and *Università di Cagliari* (UNICA). The fundamental aim of GLOSSA is to define a knowledge system based on SDG11 indicators that supports PAs in decision-making processes focused on territory monitoring, the selection of sustainable urban transformation projects, and the assessment of the impact of plans and policy. The principal tool developed by the GLOSSA research team is the Indicators-Based Tool (IBTool), a decision support system (DSS) capable of integrating NSATs at both the neighbourhood and building scales into multi-criteria decision-making processes to support PAs during the key phases of project evaluation and territory monitoring.

The work presented here aims to contribute to the debate on a consistent methodology for assessing the sustainability impacts of individual plan actions portfolios at both municipal and neighbourhood levels, by proposing an operational framework for indicators measurement that, based on a set of 27 SDG11 indicators selected within the GLOSSA project and stored within the IBTool software, aims to produce spatial mapping of impact indicators linked to the *valued components* of the urban context of Bacoli, a municipality within the Metropolitan City of Naples. The research seeks to address: i) the need to contextualize sustainability indicators derived from the scientific literature within real urban contexts; ii) the possibility of defining an operational workflow for measuring proxy variables for these indicators within a GIS framework; and iii) the future implementation of a SDSS through the definition of a structured decision-making process.

2 Case Study: The City of Bacoli

The case study presented in this contribution aims to build a spatial mapping of impact indicators to support the GLOSSA project in terms of making operational the application of the IBTool in the city of Bacoli. The goal is to assess the impacts of the projects planned by PAs through the proposal of an evaluation framework able to highlight areas of concerns and potentials for the management of the territory (Fig. 1).

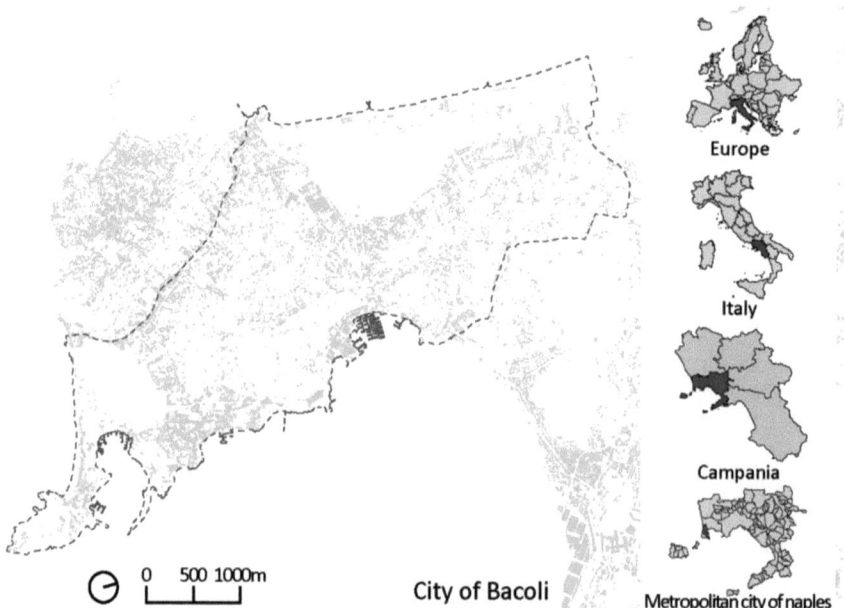

Fig. 1. The city of Bacoli in its territorial framework

The city of Bacoli is part of the Metropolitan city of Naples (Italy). Located to the west of Naples, it is part of the geological complex of the "Campi Flegrei", characterized by a volcanic field which has been active for more than 80.000 years. According to the census data provided by the Italian National Statistics Institute (Istat, 2021), the city is inhabited by 25.410 people, distributed on a surface of 13,47 Km^2, subdivided into 10 municipalities. The first findings suggest that the city of Bacoli saw its first development with the Romans, following the Greek city of Cuma. The thermal area of Baia attracted even the Roman Empire, who built their villas in this area, suggesting an environmental value which has been remaining relevant during the time. The urban layout was not subject to heavy transformation up until the end of the Second World War and during the 1980s, when heavy expansion concerned the city. This expansion was partially regulated by the general urban development plan of 1972, which was focused on the preservation of the ancient centre and the development of areas of new urbanization, as well as the expansion of the road layout. Constraints to further constructions were applied in 1976, with the variant to the general urban development plan, and in 1999 with the landscape plan of the "Campi Flegrei". In spite of them, abusive expansions determined the formation of new and informal agglomerations. To this day, unregulated building stands as a pressing issue: more than 5000 building amnesty applications have been received by the local administration. The main problems the city faces today are related to the seasonal tourism flow. During the summer months, congestion of the road network causes a real issue for the inhabitants of the city. Furthermore, this poses risks regarding air quality, heavily impacted by gases released by thermal motors. The state of the public transport, which is not sufficient to answer the demand, poses as one of the issues that need to be faced by the PAs, also with regards to the need for immediate evacuation of the city in case of seismic or volcanic events. With regards to public services, the main registered deficits regard the lack of green areas for leisure and parking spaces for private vehicles.

3 Materials and Methods

The methodological process was addressed to lay the foundations of a SDSS based upon the three decision-making phases which Simon has identified as: Intelligence, Design, and Choice [23].

As shown in Fig. 2, the proposed methodological framework has focused on the Intelligence phase, in which the problem to be faced was structured to identify *valued components* and linked impact indicators for the case study of Bacoli.

The Design phase was oriented to data gathering and selection to build spatial indicators contextualised to the focus area.

The Choice phase - whether not discussed in this contribution - relates to future developments of the SDSS for developing impact assessment of project portfolios using GIS-MCDA scenarios maps.

Starting from the selection and validation of the 27 indicators proposed by GLOSSA, the proposed methodological framework was addressed to operationalize and contextualize impact indicators linked to 6 valued components for the testing phase of the IBTool in the case study of Bacoli. The following sections explore the tools and methods used to structure the SDSS for Bacoli.

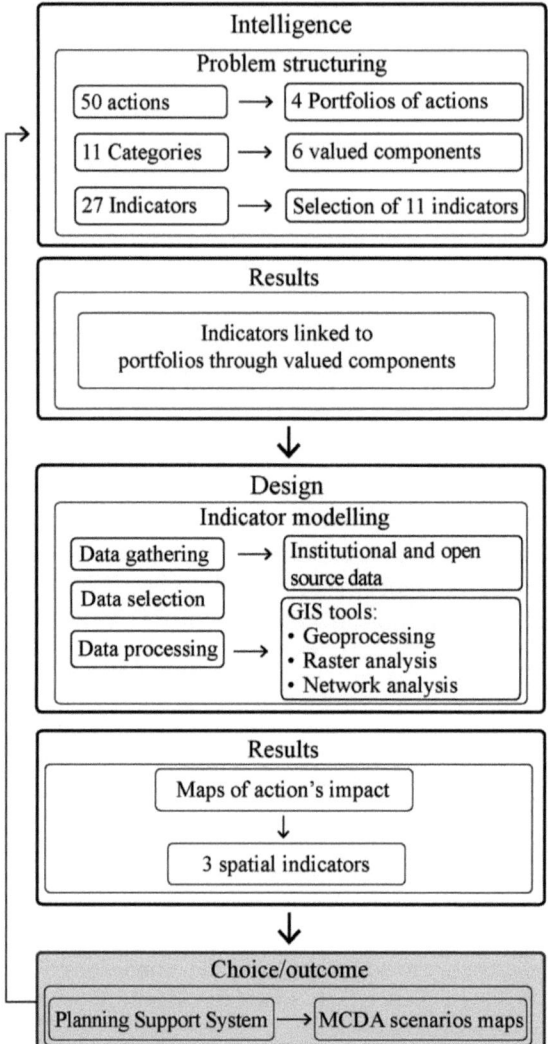

Fig. 2. The methodological workflow

3.1 Intelligence: Identification of Portfolios, Valued Components, and Linked Indicators

The intelligence phase, fundamental to the structuring of the decision-making problem, was divided into three main steps:

- the analysis of all the plan actions provided by local authorities and their classification into four portfolios;
- the clustering of indicator categories - derived from Glossa - into six groups, associated to each valued component;

- the identification of existing relationships among indicators and plan actions.

This phase made it possible to structure the decision-making problem of the impact assessment by integrating the processes of selecting and validating the SDG 11 indicators identified within the GLOSSA project by contextualising and linking those indicators to the primary features of the study area. This process has allowed to foster a strong coherence between the valued components identified and the effects of the plan actions on the territory.

3.1.1 Structuring Portfolios of Actions

Firstly, a qualitative content analysis was performed to organise the actions into four portfolios [24]. The aim was to group into the following 4 portfolios the 50 actions planned by the local authorities, based on their similar scope.

- *Environmental and cultural redevelopment and enhancement interventions*, which includes 8 actions aimed at improving the quality and accessibility of natural and cultural assets. These actions are: 1A_Redevelopment and completion of the east-side cycle-pedestrian path (from Vanvitellian Park to Quarantine Park); 1E_Redevelopment of the Quarantine Natural Park, with pedestrian connections to the dune system and the sea, and the creation of a research center on the biodiversity of the lake-dune system; C1_Equipped sports park in Cuma, enhancement of the columbarium on Via Virgilio; C2_Enhancement of the columbarium on Via Scamardella and the route leading to the Tomb of Agrippina, pedestrian connection between Villa Ferretti, Baia Castle up to Via Ortenzio, and redevelopment of the road section; C3_Redevelopment of the cycle-pedestrian connection between the Theater, the Sacellum of the Augustals, the Dragonara Cave and pedestrian square of San Sossio; E2_Redevelopment of pedestrian paths between the Tomb of Agrippina (Odeion) and the Piscina Mirabilis; F2_Enhancement of the Baths of Baia and creation of a new entrance route from Piazza De Gasperi; F4_Enhancement of the system of archaeological sites in Bacoli (Odeion, Centum Cellae, and Piscina Mirabilis) and in Miseno (Theater, Sacellum of the Augustals, and Dragonara Cave).
- *Restoration and safety interventions for the historical and infrastructure Heritage*, which contains 9 actions focused on the conservation, structural rehabilitation, and safety upgrading of historical buildings and existing infrastructure. These actions are: D_Completion of the park around Lake Miseno with the redevelopment of the cycle-pedestrian path; 1B_Restoration of the thermal archaeological sites known as 'Grotte dell'acqua'; A1_Safety measures and usability improvements for Villa Ferretti.A2_Safety measures for the seafront of Villa Ferretti; A3_Safety measures for 101 housing units; A4_Safety measures for the 'Marconi' school complex; C1_Consolidation and repair of the bridge of Casina Vanvitelliana; E1_Reuse of the decommissioned tunnel of the Cumana railway line from Piazza De Gasperi to Sella di Baia and its enhancement as an exhibition-informative space; F1_Completion of the Baia Castle Museum, including the restoration of the Cavaliere bastion and the creation of an urban park around the castle.
- *Infrastructure interventions for mobility and road networks,* which regards 32 actions encompassing projects to improve urban mobility and accessibility through

the upgrading of road infrastructure, the enhancement of public transport facilities, and the development of sustainable mobility solutions, these actions are: A_Redevelopment and enhancement of the Vanvitellian Historical Park, the Casina, and other 18th-century buildings (Ostrichina, Casone, fishermen's buildings, mussel farmers' buildings); 1A_Redevelopment and completion of the east-side cycle-pedestrian path (from Vanvitellian Park to Quarantine Park); B1_Cycle-pedestrian path on the west side of Lake Fusaro and F4b interchange parking; B2_Restructuring of the square on Via Bellavista (Church) for bus interchange; B3_Expansion of Via Risorgimento between the Via De Curtis intersection and the Municipal Villa, including a roundabout at the intersection with Via De Curtis; B4_Roundabout at Miseno; B5_Roundabout at Miliscola; B6_Roundabout at Fusaro; C3_Redevelopment of the cycle-pedestrian connection between the Theater, the Sacellum of the Augustals, and the Dragonara Cave; pedestrian square of San Sossio; E2_Redevelopment of pedestrian paths between the Tomb of Agrippina (Odeion) and the Piscina Mirabilis; G1_New connection between Via di Cuma and Via Spiaggia Romana with the East-West Naples Ring Road, including a bypass of the Old Felice Arch and the creation of interchange parking lots; G2_Redevelopment and expansion of Via Spiaggia Romana, level crossing, and roundabout on Via Giulio Cesare; G3_Relocation of the Cumana Station at Torregaveta and connection between Via Papinio Stazio and Via Servilio Vatia (Gavitello); B_Redevelopment and completion of the west-side cycle-pedestrian path of Lake Fusaro (from Quarantine Park to the Cuma Amphitheater) and construction of the F4b interchange parking lot; C_Redevelopment of the connection between the Baths of Baia and the Vanvitellian Park with a cycle-pedestrian path; E_Construction of an internal service road in the area between Lake Miseno and the beach, and enhancement of the existing road into a cycle-pedestrian avenue with connections to the path around the lake; T1_Completion of the 'Cumana' Baia railway station; T2_Extension of the Cumana Line from Torregaveta to Bacoli center; F4a_Construction of Scalandrone interchange parking; F4b_Construction of Cuma interchange parking; F4c_Construction of Torregaveta interchange parking; F4d_Construction of Cappella interchange parking; F4e_Construction of Via Bellavista interchange parking; F4f_Construction of Baia - Castle interchange parking; At-P_Creation of a waiting/parking area as per the municipal civil protection plan – 2016_ Pi1_Construction of Sella di Baia interchange parking; Pi2_Construction of Fusaro interchange parking; Pi3_Construction of Baia - Cantieri interchange parking; Pi4_Construction of Torregaveta Station interchange parking; Pi5_Construction of Center interchange parking; Pi6_Construction of Lido Fusaro interchange parking; 1C_Expansion of the Pi7 service parking.
- *Creation and enhancement of sports and urban spaces*, which includes 5 actions for the development, renovation, or expansion of sports facilities and urban recreational areas, these actions are: C1_Equipped sports park in Cuma; C2_Construction of an equipped sports park; C3_Pedestrian square of San Sossio; F3_Enhancement of the lower city of Cuma; F_Recovery of the 'Cinque Lenze' complex on Lake Miseno and connected areas for tourism, hospitality, and leisure activities.

The classification has highlighted the strategic dimensions on which the city of Bacoli relies for sustainable urban planning and transformation. From this classification, it is possible to understand that the issues of mobility, accessibility, and local public transport represent the dominant issues dealt with by the local administration.

3.1.2 Identification of Valued Components

The next step involved the reframing of the thematic categories proposed by GLOSSA according to the identification of specific *valued components* common to the selected indicators. As shown in Table 1, six different components were thus identified, referred to as: Housing, Infrastructure and mobility, Environment, Culture and heritage, Risk, and Waste. In addition, the corresponding NSAT - from which the computation method and the indicator meaning has been derived - is specified for each indicator. The Housing component expresses values linked to the quality of the living environment and access to affordable and sustainable housing solutions. It is articulated into 2 categories: Housing Liveability and Housing Affordability. Within these categories, 5 distinct themes were found: overcrowding, outdoor spaces, costs, energy efficiency, and network, which are explored through overall 7 indicators. These indicators range from the percentage of people living in overcrowded homes, to aspects such as housing cost overload, energy efficiency, and the availability of common spaces.

The Infrastructure and mobility component highlights the value of accessibility and sustainable transport, both at the individual and collective level. It was structured into 3 categories: Accessibility and connection presence, Type of vehicles used, and Quality of public transport. The themes related to this component are the following: connections, parking areas, and sustainable organisation, supported by 6 indicators. These include, as an example, the level of bicycle and public mobility, presence of interchange points, incentives to use bicycles, and the maximum parking capacity available.

The Environment component captures the values placed on land preservation, ecological quality, and the condition of public spaces. It encompasses three categories: Land Consumption, Presence and Quality of Green or Public Areas, and Decay. These categories are further developed into 4 themes: land preservation, building renovation, green, and decay, through 7 related indicators. These cover issues such as soil sealing, environmental remediation, green space distribution, and dissatisfaction with the landscape of the living space. The Culture and Heritage component reflects the value of community participation, cultural accessibility, and heritage protection. It is divided into 3 categories: Participation in urban Planning and management, Presence and quantity of cultural goods or services, and Quality of cultural goods. There are four themes: participation, heritage, inclusion, and building accessibility, represented by 5 indicators. These indicators explore both the level of citizen involvement and the presence of cultural and landscape heritage, as well as universal accessibility. The Risk component refers to the vulnerability of the population to natural hazards. It includes only 1 category, Population at Risk, and 1 theme, Natural Disasters, which is detailed through 2 indicators: population exposed to flood risk and population exposed to landslide risk. Finally, the Waste component addresses the value associated with recycling and sustainable resource management. It is represented by a single category, Quantity and recycling of waste, and 1 theme, Waste, described by 1 indicator: level of recycled or recovered materials. Table 1 represents the database of the indicators which were clustered. While the first column are the valued components identified in this paper, the remaining columns are based on the structure of GLOSSA indicators dataset.

Table 1. Valued components and indicators dataset

VALUED COMPONENT	CATEGORY	THEME	INDICATOR	NSAT
Housing	Housing Liveability	H1 - Overcrowding	H1.1 - Percentage of people living in overcrowded homes	ISTAT 2023
		H2 - Outdoor spaces	H2.1 - Common areas: relationship and common spaces	GBC 2016
	Housing Affordability	H3 - Costs	H3.1 - Housing cost overload	GBC 2016
			H3.2 - Housing typologies and social housing	GBC 2015
		H4 - Energy efficiency	H4.1 - Energy sustainability	PINQUA 2022
			H4.2 - Energy efficiency	PINQUA 2022
		H5 - Network	H5.1 - Utility	BREEAM 2012
Infrastructure and mobility	Accessibility/Connections presence	I1 - Connections	I1.1 - Bycicle mobility	PINQUA 2022
			I1.2 - Public mobility	PINQUA 2022
			I1.3 - Families declaring difficulties connecting to public transport in their neighborhood	ISTAT 2023
			I1.4 - Accessibility to public transport	ISTAT 2019

(*continued*)

Table 1. (*continued*)

VALUED COMPONENT	CATEGORY	THEME	INDICATOR	NSAT
	Type of **V**eichles used	**I2** - Parking areas	**I2.1** - Incentive to use bycicles	ITACA 2019
			I2.2 - Maximum parking capacity	BREEAM 2021
	Quality of **P**ublic **T**ransport	**I3** - Sustainable organization	**I3.1** - Interchange points	GBC 2015
Environment	**L**and **C**onsumption	**E1** - Land preservation	**E1.1** - Soil waterproofing from artificial cover	SNSvS 2022
			E1.2 - Buildings not used by state of use	ISTAT 2011
		E2 - Building renovation	**E2.1** - Environmental remedation	PINQUA 2022
	Presence and **Q**uality of **G**reen or **P**ublic **A**reas	**E3** - Green	**E3.1** - Green areas distribution	GBC 2015
			E3.2 - Green areas	SNSvS 2022
		E4 - Decay	**E4.1** - Dissatisfaction with the landscape of the living place	PINQUA 2022
Culture and heritage	**P**artecipation in **U**rban **P**lanning and **M**anagement	**C1** - Partecipation	**C1.1** - Involvement and opening towards communities	MIM 2021; SNSvS 2022
	Presence/**Q**uantity of **C**ultural **G**oods or services	**C2** - Heritage	**C2.1** - Safety towards inclusion	ISTAT 2023
		C3 - Inclusion	**C3.1** - Historical-cultural goods and landscape goods	ISTAT 2023

(*continued*)

Table 1. (*continued*)

VALUED COMPONENT	CATEGORY	THEME	INDICATOR	NSAT
	Quality of Cultural Goods	C4 - Building accessibility	C4.1 - Buildings equipped with specific measures to overcome architectural barriers	ITACA 2019
Risk	Popolation at Risk	R1 - Natural distasters	R1.1 - Population exposed to flood risk	Chao, 2022
			R1.2 - Population exposed to landslide risk	PINQUA 2022
Waste	Quantity and Recycling of Waste	W1 - Waste	W1.1 - Recycled/recovered materials	Battisti, 2023; ISTAT 2023

3.1.3 Selection of 11 Indicators Based on the Valued Components

The last step of the Intelligence phase was aimed to identify the relationships among GLOSSA indicators and the actions planned by local authorities of Bacoli, specifically to understand which of the 27 indicators should be used to monitor the impact of actions against SDGs 11 targets. This goal was achieved by consulting the sources of the indicators and calculation methods stored within the IBTool, to understand the methods of calculations, and comparing them with the actions planned by the PAs. As a result, 11 cross-cutting indicators were selected which can be associated with the four identified portfolios. This made it possible to define a basic set of indicators through which the impact has been evaluated in a spatial GIS environment.

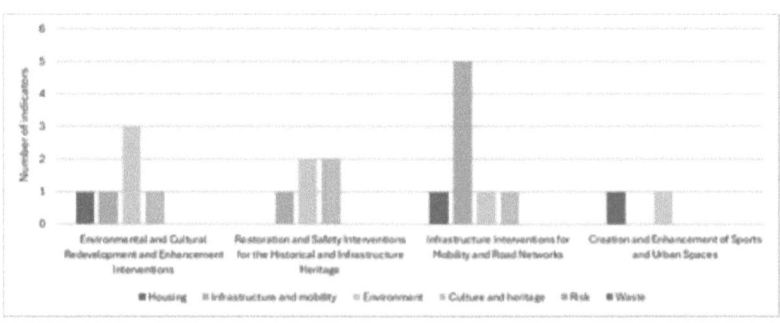

Fig. 3. Indicators linked to portfolios through valued components

As shown in Fig. 3, out of the four portfolios of actions identified, the one that can be monitored by the most number of indicators is "Infrastructure interventions for mobility and road network", it is also worth noting that the indicators of the valued components Risk and Waste are not found among the 11 indicators selected, highlighting a lack of actions impacting these domains.

3.2 Design: Proxy-Indicators Modeling

The second phase of the methodological process is the design phase, in which the focus is emphasized on the modeling of the indicators previously identified. This phase is subdivided into three steps: 1. Data gathering, in which data regarding the indicators was structured in a database to be further analysed; 2. Data selection, in which data regarding the four proxy indicators was filtered and refined; 3. Data processing, in which the data was processed through GIS to spatialize it and obtain the values of the proxy indicators.

3.2.1 Data Gathering

The first step of the design phase was to gather raw data to construct the indicators. The research of data ranged from institutional data to crowd-sourced data, because of a lack of availability. The research was based on the calculation methods of the indicators, which were found consulting the initial sources stored within the IBTool. As an example, indicator I 1.1 *Bicycle mobility* expresses the overall linear metres of the new project of cycle paths and was derived by Urban development plan. Given the spatial nature of the proposed DSS, the research focused on spatial data to be processed through GIS software, but also on statistics data available to the general public via institutional database. The main institutional sources consulted were: the Urban development plan (Piano Urbanistico Comunale), which contained information regarding the actions planned by local authorities, the Italian National Statistics Institute (Istat), which allowed for specific data on the population of the case study through the census of 2011 and 2021; the Military Geographic Institute (IGM), and crowd-sourced data from OpenStreetMap (OSM), which was used for the base map. The information collected from the identified sources and related to the indicators proposed by GLOSSA and previously selected were collected in Table 2.

Table 2. Data gathered

ID	NAME	UM	SOURCE	VALUE	YEAR
H1.1	Pop 2021	n	ISTAT	25410	2021
H1.1	Residing families - 6 and more components	n	ISTAT	156	2021
H3.1	Annual expenses of families for energy consumption	€	ISTAT	1242	2021

(continued)

Table 2. (*continued*)

ID	NAME	UM	SOURCE	VALUE	YEAR
I1.1	Length of bike lanes	km	Bacoli urban plan	4,4	2020
I1.2	Railway length	km	IGM	7	2020
I1.2	Number of commuters	n	ISTAT	5120	2011
I2.2	veichle fleet - all veichles	n	ISTAT	21318	2023
I1.2	veichle fleet - cars	n	ISTAT	15791	2023
I2.2	Public parking	m^2	OSM	77215	2023
I3.1	Interchange nodes - existing	n	Bacoli urban plan	2	2020
I3.1	Interchange nodes - projects	n	Bacoli urban plan	1	2020
W1.1	recycling rate	%	ORGR	66,46	2023
R1.1	Popolation exposed to medium hydraulic risk	n	Regional River Basin plan	7674	2019
R1.1	Popolation exposed to maximum hydraulic risk	n	Regional River Basin plan	3788	2019
R1.2	Popolazione esposta a rischio da frana medio	n	Regional River Basin plan	1164	2019
R1.2	Popolation exposed to high landslide risk	n	Regional River Basin plan	9833	2019
R1.2	Popolation exposed to very high landslide risk	n	Regional River Basin plan	5985	2019

3.2.2 Data Selection

In this step of the design phase, the objective was to select some indicators to be modeled into GIS environment to produce impact assessment maps. In this meaning, 3 indicators were selected and produced: bicycle mobility (I1.1), Accessibility to public transport (I1.4) and maximum parking capacity (I 2.2). The indicators are linked to the portfolio referred to as: "infrastructure interventions for mobility and road networks", which is the one that encompasses the most amount of actions planned, which in return are also the ones with the most amount of indicators that can monitor them. The selection phase was then focused on the dataset by specifically filtering and retaining the information directly relevant to the selected proxy indicators. This step involved removing redundant, inconsistent, or incomplete data points to enhance accuracy and relevance (Table 3).

3.2.3 Data Processing

All of the data collected and selected has then been processed with the use of GIS, to obtain KPI related to the actions planned. Three main processing tools were used, based on the extension of the data and the indicator needed to be calculated.

Proxy indicator 1 relates to the length of bike lanes. To obtain this indicator geoprocessing tools for data analysis were utilized for deriving the segment length. Raster

Table 3. Data selected

ID	NAME	U.M	SOURCE	VALUE	SCALE	YEAR
I1.1	Length of bike lanes	km	PUC Bacoli	4,4	City	2020
I1.1	Length of informal bike lanes	km	PisteCiclabili.com	11,8	City	2024
I1.2	Railway length	km	IGM	7	City	2020
I1.2	Number of commuters	n	ISTAT	5120	City	2011
I2.2	Public parking	m^2	OSM	77215	City	2023

analysis was used to overlap the documents from the urban development plan in order to calculate the dimensions of project cycle paths. Proxy indicators 2 and 3 required more advanced spatial analysis tools. Specifically, proxy indicator 2, Maximum parking capacity, has required raster analysis to overlap the areas of future parking expected by the urban development plan. Consequently, each attribute table of each census tract of the city of Bacoli has been remodeled to gather information of the total sqm falling within each section. This value has then been divided by the area of each section to obtain a normalized index of sqm of parking area on sqm of census tract. For proxy indicator 3: accessibility index to railway service several steps were needed. First, service areas were constructed starting from existing stations and project stations, with timings of 10, 20 and 30 min at walking speed (considered to be 5 km/h). Subsequently, the attribute table of the 2011 census tract (as it is the last census available that contains the values regarding commuters) was updated to contain the information regarding the number of stations reachable at each time interval considered. These values were then weighed and summed, following formula (1),

$$I = (\alpha_{T3} * N_{T3}) + (\alpha_{T2} * N_{T2}) + (\alpha_{T1} * N_{T1}) \tag{1}$$

where α is the weight assigned to each time (1 for 10 min, 0,66 for 20 min and 0,33 for 30 min); N is the number of stations reachable from each section; and the subscripts (t1, t2, t3) are respectively equal to 10, 20, 30 min. The results of all these processes were action's impact maps, which allowed the visualization of impact derived from the actions planned by local authorities, which will be discussed in the next paragraph.

3.3 Choice: Towards a MCDA Scenario Maps for Impact Assessment

The last phase of the structuring process of the SDSS is the choice phase. Further development of the indicators modelled in the previous steps will enable the realization of MCDA scenarios maps, showing the different impact derived from different actions planned on the territory, with the aim of guiding local authorities towards structured decision making processes.

4 Results and Discussion

The three proxy indicators which represent the KPIs for Bacoli derived from GIS spatial analysis are presented as follows.

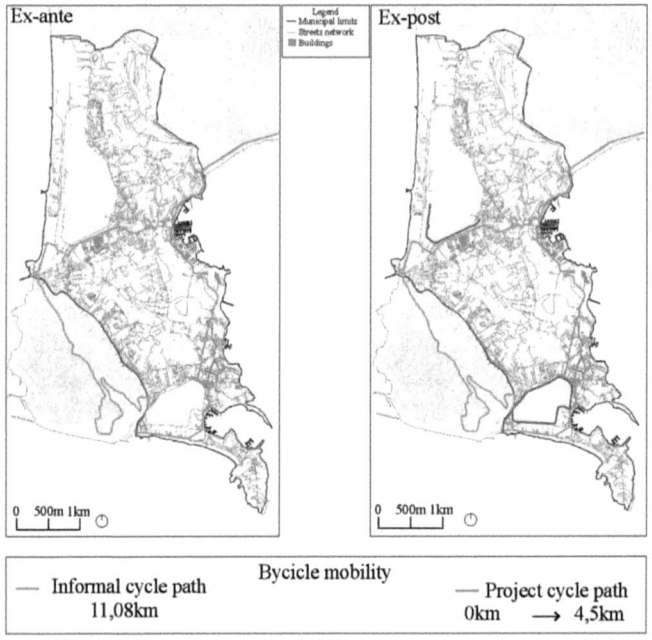

Fig. 4. Bicycle mobility

As shown in Fig. 4, *Proxy indicator 1 - bicycle mobility* highlights the length of bike lanes available in the city of Bacoli. This indicator was derived from the *PINQuA 2022* NSAT [25], in which it is defined as the "*expansion or new construction of cycle paths*", expressed in Kilometres. In current state, no bike lanes are present in the territory, thus, the indicator is expected to grow up to 4,5 km. In the indicator map, informal bike paths were highlighted, since these paths are generally followed by cycle-tourists. In this perspective, the urban development plan has integrated these paths into the city design project in which they were conceived as tourist paths crossing localities of lakes Miseno and Fusaro. Actually, these paths do not provide strategic connections for alternative transport modalities, but they facilitate the tourism activities.

Proxy indicator 2 – maximum parking capacity provides a normalized index of the parking availability value related to the size of each Census tract. The source for this indicator is the *BREEAM 2022* [26] technical manual, in which the indicator is produced with a scenario measure unit, relating the parking's number to the number of users of the building. As shown in Fig. 5, it is possible to notice that a significant increase in parking spaces availability from the expected state will take place after planned actions, especially in the western side of the city of Bacoli, as well as in the southern area close to the city centre.

Proxy indicator 3 - accessibility to railway services contextualses the indicator I1.4, which refers to the accessibility to public transport. The source for this indicator is the 2019 ISTAT report [25]. The index discussed shows the level of accessibility to railway stations through the above-mentioned normalized index. The changes related to the projects expected are significant, as at the current state of the southern side of the city of Bacoli presents a zero value, indicating a serious inaccessibility to the railway services. The plan of Bacoli has expected to change this value presenting a project with an acceptable level of accessibility to the stations (Fig. 6).

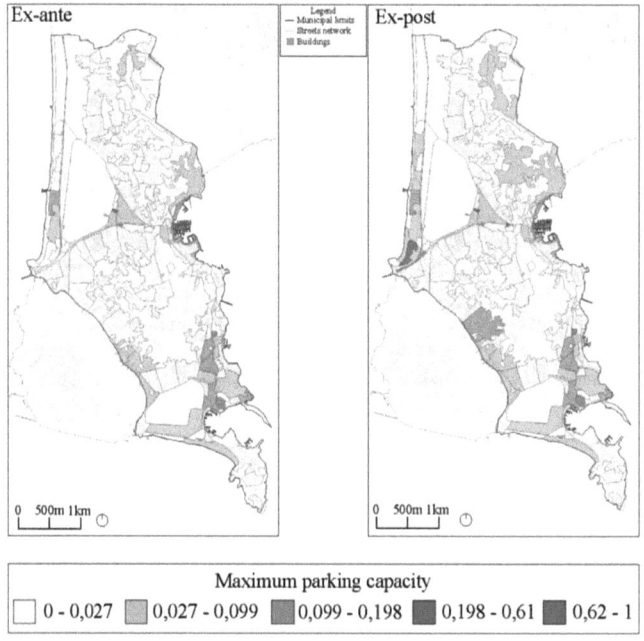

Fig. 5. Maximum parking capacity

5 Conclusions and Further Developments

This research has presented an operational framework aimed at contextualising sustainability indicators within the urban context of Bacoli, by applying a structured methodological approach grounded in the three phases of DSS: Intelligence, Design, and Choice. In the Intelligence phase, the valued components were identified and matched with corresponding SDG 11 indicators, enabling a coherent classification of local planning actions into thematic portfolios. The Design phase provided the selection and modelling of proxy indicators using geospatial data and GIS tools, demonstrating the practical feasibility of assessing urban impacts in a spatially explicit way. Although the Choice phase remains in development, the groundwork laid by the current research allows for future integration of MCDA to support scenario-based decision-making processes.

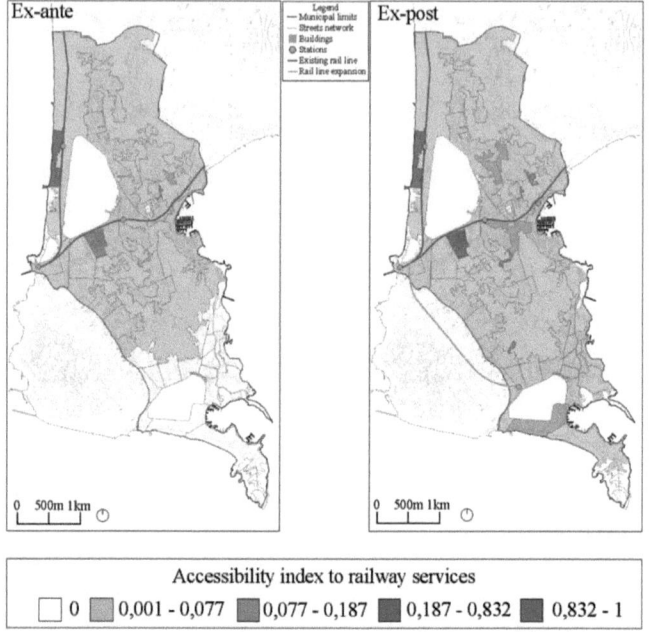

Fig. 6. Accessibility index to railway services

Despite the robustness of the approach, some limitations emerged during its application. Firstly, the availability and quality of data—especially at the local scale—posed challenges for the calculation of certain indicators. Moreover, while proxy indicators offer a pragmatic solution where direct measurement is difficult, they inevitably introduce a level of approximation that should be critically considered when interpreting results. Additionally, the lack of integration of spatial-temporal data restricts the ability to monitor changes over time, thereby limiting dynamic assessments.

Further developments of this research will be focused on the full implementation of the Choice phase through MCDA scenario mapping, allowing for the simulation of different planning alternatives and their relative impacts. Future work should also involve expanding the range of indicators to better capture social and cultural dimensions, integrating real-time data streams, and enhancing the participatory dimension of the tool. These steps would contribute to the construction of a fully operational SDSS capable of guiding municipalities in the evaluation and optimisation of their planning actions towards sustainable and inclusive urban development.

References

1. Sturiale, L., Scuderi, A., Timpanaro, G., Foti, V.T., Stella, G.: Social and inclusive "value" generation in metropolitan area with the "urban gardens" planning. In: Mondini, G., Oppio, A., Stanghellini, S., Bottero, M., Abastante, F. (eds.) Values and Functions for Future Cities. GET, pp. 285–302. Springer, Cham (2020). https://doi.org/10.1007/978-3-030-23786-8_16

2. Huang, L., Wu, J., Yan, L.: Defining and measuring urban sustainability: a review of indicators. Landsc. Ecol. **30**, 1175–1193 (2015)
3. Khatibi, M., Khaidzir, K.A.M., Syed Mahdzar, S.S.: Measuring the sustainability of neighborhoods: a systematic literature review. iScience **26**, 105951 (2023)
4. Cuntò, S., Muccio, E., Sacco, S., Zizzania, P.: A collaborative spatial decision support system for assessing transformative potential of minimum ecological units (MEUs) in a circular regeneration perspective. In: Gervasi, O., et al. (eds.) ICCSA 2023. LNCS, vol. 14112, pp. 235–252. Springer, Cham (2023). https://doi.org/10.1007/978-3-031-37129-5_20
5. Hugé, J., Waas, T.: Converging impact assessment discourses for sustainable development: the case of Flanders, Belgium. Environ. Dev. Sustain. **13**, 607–626 (2011)
6. Poli, G., Cuntò, S., Muccio, E.: A data-driven approach to monitor sustainable development transition in Italian regions through SDG 11 indicators. In: Gervasi, O., Murgante, B., Garau, C., Taniar, D., Rocha, A.M.A.C., Faginas Lago, M.N. (eds.) ICCSA 2024. LNCS, vol. 14820, pp. 337–355. Springer, Cham (2024). https://doi.org/10.1007/978-3-031-65285-1_22
7. Peltonen, L., Sairinen, R.: Integrating impact assessment and conflict management in urban planning: experiences from Finland. Environ. Impact Assess. Rev. **30**, 328–337 (2010)
8. Miyazaki, G., Kawakubo, S., Murakami, S., Ikaga, T.: How can CASBEE contribute as a sustainability assessment tool to achieve the SDGs? In: IOP Conference Series: Earth and Environmental Science, vol. 294, p. 012007 (2019)
9. Cheshmehzangi, A., Dawodu, A., Song, W., Shi, Y., Wang, Y.: An introduction to neighborhood sustainability assessment tool (NSAT) study for China from comprehensive analysis of eight Asian tools. Sustainability **12**, 2462 (2020)
10. Saiu, V., Blečić, I., Meloni, I., Piras, F.: SDGs localization: a new tool for a comprehensive assessment of neighbourhood sustainability. In: Gervasi, O., Murgante, B., Garau, C., Taniar, D., Rocha, A.M.A.C., Faginas Lago, M.N. (eds.) ICCSA 2024. LNCS, vol. 14818, pp. 101–112. Springer, Cham (2024). https://doi.org/10.1007/978-3-031-65273-8_7
11. Sutherland, G.D., Waterhouse, F.L., Smith, J., Saunders, S.C., Paige, K., Malt, J.: Developing a systematic simulation-based approach for selecting indicators in strategic cumulative effects assessments with multiple environmental valued components. Ecol. Ind. **61**, 512–525 (2016)
12. De Castro-Pardo, M., Cabello, J.M., Martín, J.M., Ruiz, F.: A multi reference point based index to assess and monitor European water policies from a sustainability approach. Socioecon. Plan. Sci. **89**, 101433 (2023)
13. Abastante, F., Gaballo, M.: Assessing the SDG11 on a neighborhood scale through the integrated use of GIS tools. an Italian case study. In: Calabrò, F., Della Spina, L., Piñeira Mantiñán, M.J. (eds.) NMP 2022. LNNS, vol. 482, pp. 957–967. Springer, Cham (2022). https://doi.org/10.1007/978-3-031-06825-6_91
14. Cerreta, M., Mura, F.D., Muccio, E.: Digital platforms, imaginaries and values creation: opportunities for new urban dynamics. In: Calabrò, F., Della Spina, L., Piñeira Mantiñán, M.J. (eds.) NMP 2022. LNNS, vol. 482, pp. 1505–1515. Springer, Cham (2022). https://doi.org/10.1007/978-3-031-06825-6_145
15. Kumar, D., Shandilya, A.K., Varghese, S.G.: Mapping sustainable cities and communities (SDG 11) research: a bibliometric review. In: RAiSE-2023, Basel, Switzerland, p. 125. MDPI (2023)
16. Abastante, F.: Limits and perspectives of neighbourhood sustainable assessment tools (NSATS) in sustainable urban design. Valori e Valutazioni **32**, 31–43 (2023)
17. Jiménez-Espada, M., Martínez García, F.M., González-Escobar, R.: Sustainability indicators and GIS as land-use planning instrument tools for urban model assessment. ISPRS Int. J. Geo Inf. **12**, 42 (2023)
18. Ferretti, V., Pomarico, S.: Ecological land suitability analysis through spatial indicators: an application of the analytic network process technique and ordered weighted average approach. Ecol. Ind. **34**, 507–519 (2013)

19. Banai, R.: Land resource sustainability for urban development: spatial decision support system prototype. Environ. Manag. **36**, 282–296 (2005)
20. Balaras, C.A.: Building energy audits—diagnosis and retrofitting towards decarbonization and sustainable cities. Energies **15**, 2039 (2022)
21. Diaz-Sarachaga, J.M., Jato-Espino, D.: Development and application of a new resilient, sustainable, safe and inclusive community rating system (RESSICOM). J. Clean. Prod. **207**, 971–979 (2019)
22. Ren, S., Li, Y., Peng, Z., Yin, M., Liu, X.: Developing an urban environment examination system by incorporating construction, economic, environmental, cultural and development dimensions. Sustainability **16**, 3065 (2024)
23. Simon, H.A.: The New Science of Management Decision. Prentice Hall, Hoboken (1977)
24. Schreier, M.: What is qualitative about qualitative content analysis? In: Qualitative Content Analysis in Practice, pp. 20–36. SAGE Publications Ltd., Thousand Oaks (2012)
25. https://www.istat.it/storage/rapporto-annuale/2019/Rapportoannuale2019.pdf. Accessed 07 May 2025
26. BREEAM. https://breeam.com/. Accessed 07 May 2025

EURECA: Exploring Urban touRist Environment Through Child-Based Activities

Laura Di Tommaso[1]("✉") ⓘ, Caterina Loffredo[1] ⓘ, Ludovica La Rocca[1] ⓘ, Simona Panaro[2] ⓘ, and Maria Cerreta[1] ⓘ

[1] Department of Architecture, University of Naples Federico II, via Toledo 402, Naples, Italy
{laura.ditommaso,caterina.loffredo,ludovica.larocca, cerreta}@unina.it

[2] Department of Architecture and Industrial Design, University of Naples Luigi Vanvitelli, Via San Lorenzo, Abbey of San Lorenzo, 81031 Aversa, Italy
simona.panaro@unicampania.it

Abstract. The touristification is affecting specific urban contexts on an international scale, highlighting how economic interests drive decision-making dynamics regarding public space. Specific stakeholders - such as children - are often excluded from decision-making processes aimed at enhancing public spaces. Starting from previous research, the article presents some results that emerged from the implementation of a replicable hybrid methodology aimed at including child-inhabitants in the analysis of urban contexts under tourist pressure. This is a first step to activate a territorial process capable of placing under-represented stakeholders at the center, reinterpreting the co-city model, to co-evaluate – in an evolutionary approach - shared strategies for mitigating over-tourism, aiming at the transition towards sustainable tourism's development. This was possible by involving the children-inhabitants co-exploring an exemplary place - Capri Island - through the school collaboration - as an institution capable of accelerating urban and social regeneration. Therefore, starting from an action-research participatory approach, the kids' involvement has required an in-depth study of ethical issues that limit their inclusion in the research, orienting for slower research that collects qualitative data, building a process of continuous exchange between adult and child researcher, in a logic of mutual learning. This approach is implemented by recognizing the children's skills, by developing a three-day creative workshop called "EURECA" as an enabling context aimed at stimulating them in co-exploring the socio-urban context, using photography, drawing, collaborative mapping and situational interviews, to intercept issues of children's interest, focusing on the reclaimed public space, to collectively develop a non-touristic children-based imaginary.

Keywords: Children's engagement · Public space values · Tourism co-governance

1 Introduction

The reflection surrounding the sustainable conversion of cities presupposes a specific focus on the necessity that such transformations be measurable [1] and guided by equity and justice [2, 3] promoting new forms of citizen participation in the collaborative and horizontal governance of the city [4]. This growing interest can be explained by observing the evident distance that persists between public policies and the concrete needs of the contexts and the communities that inhabit them [5] given that the formulation processes of these policies often do not include ex-ante participatory evaluation methods capable of effectively guiding decisions [6]. In addition, even when experiments are developed including the contribution of communities for the sustainability of inhabited contexts, it is necessary to investigate whether and how these processes may be considered truly inclusive, genuinely fostering a holistic socio-cultural representation.

All of this is interesting when applied to public space, where the development of inclusive decision-making processes, which enable everyone to offer their perspective in the formulation of decisions about public space, fosters the regeneration of neighbourhoods through the aggregation of new communities, centralizing the under-represented in the co-creation of new shared values [7]. Numerous innovative experiments are underway [8], involving the community in decision-making that aim to validate hybrid methodologies as well as new inclusive tools for more sustainable cities.

Even in the field of tourism, the debate on sustainability is particularly lively [9], and some emerging models are developing in this regard [10–12]. In the art cities and coastal areas of Southern Italy, the tourism sector has experienced exponential growth in recent years which, following the partial slowdown during the pandemic, is now undergoing renewed growth [13, 14], generating multidimensional impacts on the communities that inhabit these pressured locations [15]. Today, a deeper reflection urgently emerges, both from politics and research [16], on the opportunities for conversion to more sustainable models, approaches, and practices in tourism promotion and management. It is hoped that in the coming years urban planning, evaluation, and tourism management will activate synergistic collaborations, aimed at building joint reflections on overtourism. This would favour - on the one hand - the promotion and innovation of under-touristed areas such as the Inland Areas or other fragile territorial contexts, which today constitute a cluster with strong tourism potential [17, 18], and - on the other hand - the protection and regeneration of the values of hyper-touristed places such as art cities and coastal areas. Also in the tourism sector, it is urgent to envision greater inclusion of all community segments in the decision-making processes aimed at converting pressured destinations into more balanced places. Indeed, literature shows that among the least represented community segments in this field are children and young people [19]. There is a tendency in the tourism literature to consider the opinions of minors only to the extent that they can influence the choice of family holidays, and therefore from the perspective of the guest rather than the resident. Scientific research in recent years is developing interesting lines of inquiry, such as the role of the "child resident" of places under tourist pressure and the need to integrate tourism management into the general framework of urban planning, in order to equip itself with tools for measuring the impact of tourism on inhabited contexts. Evaluation, particularly when interpreted as co-evaluation [20] through the direct involvement of the various segments of the resident community, can and must assume a significant role, as it can bridge the gap related to a deeper understanding of the territory. Therefore, the key questions emerge that constitute the core of this contribution: 1) what elements, aspects, and challenges contribute to building the ethical framework of reference, with respect to which the children-researchers relationship may be defined? 2) what models, approaches, and tools can be adopted to promote the fair and ethical participation of child-inhabitants in the decision-making processes aimed at the sustainable urban conversion of hyper-touristed places - and how can they be combined to develop an effective methodology? 3) more specifically, how is it possible to explore and explicate the multiple values of tourist places with children, and therefore, how is it possible to generate new shared values with them?

This contribution develops a methodological process aimed at the construction of a Permanent Urban Laboratory that places child at the centre of shared strategies for the sustainable conversion of contexts with strong tourism pressure. Furthermore, the research aims to develop the "Exploring Urban touRist Environment through Child-based Activities" (EURECA) replicable workshop, as a useful tool to investigate a tourist territory with the contribution of children. The contribution also describes a first test of the workshop in a typical territorial context, presenting the concrete application and the main results. The following paragraphs are structured as follows: Sect. 2 provides an in-depth review of the literature related to the relevant ethical issues in the interaction with children; Sect. 3 describes the methodology and the main materials; Sect. 4 describes the study cluster and the spatial context in which the experimentation was carried out; Sect. 5 describes the results of the test and, Sect. 6 concludes with final reflections and discussions.

2 Ethical Issues for Involving Children into Co-Research

Within the scope of participatory action research (PAR), there has recently been a strong interest in the numerous ethical issues to consider when including specific community segments in research. Certainly, children and their participation in research imply a reflection on the part of researchers regarding the necessity that their engagement be respectful, integrating ethical precepts with participatory methodologies aimed – on a case-by-case basis - at producing shared knowledge with children. In tourism literature, some authors [21] explicitly state the need to delve deeper into the ethical questions pertaining to children's participation, emphasizing that the absence of guidelines represents one of the main difficulties in their inclusion in research concerning tourist destinations. This paragraph summarizes an in-depth analysis of the ethical challenges linked to children's participation. Firstly, the key ethical issues are summarized, among which the topic of informed consent emerges, encompassing various aspects. Then, the link between ethical issues and methodology is explored. Subsequently, the role of the child and the aspect of the adult researcher's reflexivity are examined. Finally, some critical aspects are highlighted as starting points for further investigation.

Many contributions aim to frame the ethical issues related to children's participation in research. According to Lewis & Porter [22], the issues to consider when including minors in research are six: 1) modes of access – by researchers – to interaction with children and their protection; 2) children's consent/assent; 3) confidentiality, privacy, and data processing; 4) feedback/sharing of results with children; 5) respect for data ownership; and 6) social responsibility. A second study [23] adopts these six principles within the context of a workshop conducted with children, during which qualitative data were produced. Starting from the 9 principles of ethical participation of minors related to the UN Convention on the Rights of the Child (UNCRC) for the meaningful inclusion of children [24] – which include transparent, voluntary, respectful, relevant, child-friendly, inclusive, training-supported, safe and risk-sensitive, and accountable research – Angelow & Psouni [25], instead, propose a 21-point ethical framework. Another contribution highlights how, out of 58 studies conducted with children, 30 explicitly stated the source of ethical approval, while the privacy and consent of guardians were considered in 42 articles. It is emphasized that in 33 research studies, children's consent was explicitly requested. Furthermore, in 5 studies, the request for consent from children was not treated as a single step, but rather as an evolving process. Health et al. [26] – in this sense – speak of "process consent", indicating consent that must be constantly "reaffirmed" [27], in addition, highlight three aspects in the process of requesting consent from minors: the explanation of research objectives (with language and an approach suitable for minors), the explicit statement of the right to withdraw, and the observation of any non-verbal dissent. The study explicates a new perspective on written informed consent. Regarding the latter, some studies propose "child-friendly" informed consent forms. This issue is already highlighted by Flewitt [28], who focuses on the processes of negotiating ongoing consent, problematizing the concept of "informed" consent in research with children, addressing anonymity in data collection and reporting. Dockett et al. [29] explore children's non-verbal interactions and the ways in which they express dissent to participate in research, fostering a growing debate on the techniques for interpreting informed consent/assent, stating that it is necessary to consider the ways in which children might express their desire not to participate. Subsequently, informed consent becomes a prevalent aspect in many contributions. In this regard, Jenkin et al. [30] highlight the need to obtain "double" informed consent, where the child's consent represents an indispensable aspect for the success of the research. Larsson et al. [31], then identify some relevant aspects: 1) offering genuine opportunities to withdraw from the research; 2) recognizing children as participants with valid voices; and 3) acknowledging children's curiosity towards the researcher and the research process. The contribution highlights how the minor's position as a person whose responsibilities are entrusted to others does not legally oblige the researcher to satisfy the minors' desires.

Schweiger [32] frames the ethical challenges of minors' participation in research, highlighting how an interpretation of the child as a co-researcher is now fundamental. Three issues to consider are identified: 1) the minor's autonomy; 2) the child's participation; and 3) the child's best interests. Regarding the first, it is highlighted that the minor's autonomy of thought is a complex aspect that includes potential conflicts with parental consent and the right to withdraw. Secondly, participation is linked to the need not to alter children's "voices". Finally, the theme of the child's best interests prevails over the others, requiring that the research not only does not harm the minor but can bring them benefits. From an ethical point of view, the research included obtaining informed consent from parents and the children's acceptance to participate in the research. The Ethical Research Involving Children project [33], through which an ethical framework is developed that promotes reflexivity, rights, and relationships (the "3 Rs") as essential elements of an ethical research process. Reflexivity is defined as the "ability of researchers to critically reflect on the impact of their research on participants and their communities, on the researchers themselves, and on the body of knowledge under investigation" [34].

3 Method, Approach, and Tools

The methodological framework is constructed within an experimental context strongly influenced by the phenomenon of overtourism. In this context, locals' perception of public space, particularly children, acquires special significance. Furthermore, the framework is defined based on several assumptions.

The first assumption is that the investigation is part of a broader research path that experiments with applying an Evolutionary Evaluation (EE) process [35] within a participatory urban transformation. Specifically, EE is understood as an adaptive and iterative assessment, designed to accompany the evolution of complex interventions. EE does not start with a fixed set of objectives or indicators to be applied in the real context. Instead, it develops in parallel with the process, co-evolving with it [36]. It is based on a non-linear logic, where the evaluation does not follow a predetermined scheme, but constantly adapts to the context, emerging feedback, and changes in program goals and strategies. In particular, EE is characterized by several distinctive dimensions, including: continuous adaptivity of the evaluation process; iteration and cyclicality in data collection and feedback processes, pursuing a fluid temporality; systemic co-learning as an objective, in which reflexivity becomes a methodological practice of mutual learning [37] volving citizens, researchers, and policy-makers; and the co-production of knowledge, through the direct involvement of different actors and stakeholders in the evaluation, enabling not only accountability, but also the generation of new hypotheses, relationships, and design directions. Although the structure may vary depending on the context, it is possible to identify some typical phases that characterize the methodological framework: 1) *shared contextual framing*: this begins with a co-design phase of the evaluation process, in which evaluators and involved actors (policymakers, implementers, beneficiaries) jointly define the mandate, evaluation priorities, and initial boundaries [36]; 2) *flexible definition of the theory of change* continuously reviewed and refined through learning cycles [38]. The program logic is therefore a working hypothesis, not a definitive model; 3) *iterative and multi-level data collection:* evidence gathering is based on rapid, repeated cycles, using qualitative and quantitative tools; 4) *participatory sense-making and continuous feedback* to transform evidence into strategic learning, fostering targeted adaptations and incremental improvements; 5) *adaptation of the program and evaluation*: the cycle ends (and restarts) with integrating evaluation insights into the decision-making process.

The second assumption is that the experience represents the initial phase of a broader process of urban transformation of public space. This part of the research focuses on the first phase of the territory co-exploration. The objective is to determine an exploratory method - the "EURECA" workshop - aimed at collaboratively defining a new, emerging set of criteria to guide policymakers' decisions by reinterpreting the priorities of inhabitants. In this sense, the co-evaluation has the specific goal of providing a mutually agreed-upon assessment [20] with the stakeholders involved in the process, to create a democratic evaluation system - from the construction of indicators to assessment, to discussion of results - that promotes participation and decision-making [39]. From this perspective, the EURECA workshop does not start from a fixed set of objectives or indicators to be applied but follows an adaptive development that evolves with the context and the participants' contributions. Through progressive cycles of exploration, observation, and shared reflection, the workshop becomes a space for mutual learning and transformation, where tools and actions are defined throughout the experience, in response to emerging needs gathered during the process. The research objectives are not all predefined; some are co-created by the children themselves during the process, and the methodology develops gradually, depending on the outcomes of the activities and the acquisition of the skills needed to achieve the desired goal.

The third assumption is that this part of the research focuses on engaging a specific target group - children aged between 7 and 10. For this reason, the process expands and contracts in its phases to better respond to the cognitive capacities of the age group considered, allowing space for a broad reflection on possible ethical frameworks to consider when involving minors.

By combining the principles of evolutionary evaluation with those of mutual learning in the involvement of children within urban transformation processes - particularly in urban contexts heavily affected by overtourism - the key pillars that guide the research's methodological framework clearly emerge (Fig. 1).

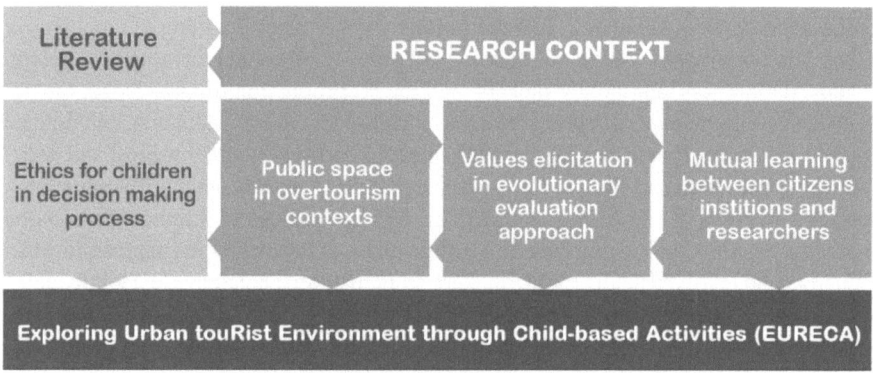

Fig. 1. Main pillars of the theoretical framework

In summary, the operational context in which the research takes place is that of public space transformations in areas affected by overtourism. Within this, mutual learning between citizens, policymakers, cultural institutions, and researchers is a foundational pillar of the collaborative and adaptive nature through which the process of involving children in decision-making is interpreted, with specific attention to ethics. Finally, the entire transformation process - as well as the defined workshop - aims at the elicitation of shared values through evolutionary evaluation approaches.

Building on the described methodological framework, the approaches, methods, and tools used to develop the EURECA workshop (Fig. 2) are analysed.

The workshop is structured into six phases: 1) Objective Sharing; 2) Knowledge Sharing; 3) Individual Values Explicitation; 4) Collective Values Explicitation; 5) Topic Prioritization; 6) Sharing of Results and Reflection.

The first phase, *Objective Sharing*, defines the specific objectives of the territory co-exploration. In this phase, contextual conditions and goals are collaboratively identified in an Action Plan to map and engage the most relevant stakeholders to achieve

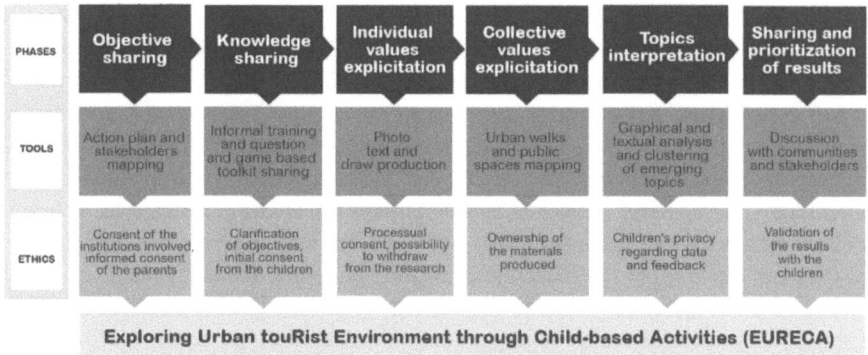

Fig. 2. EURECA Workshop's phases scheme

these objectives, using network maps co-developed with the participants. Following the quintuple helix innovation model [40], in which collective decision-making is developed by at least five distinct actors, the most significant include: private entities, civil society organizations, creative and social innovators, public institutions, and knowledge institutions. To develop the research, engaging in children's environments is strategic. The school is interpreted as a device capable of triggering territorial enhancement through collaboration with local communities and the engine of participatory, evaluative, and cultural processes, with direct impacts on how places are inhabited, perceived, and imagined. Schools involve all new generations that form the community, capturing their expectations for the future [41].

The second phase, *Knowledge Sharing*, exchanges skills and knowledge among those involved in the participatory process, through informal training sessions and question and game-based toolkit sharing with kids. Evaluators share content and educational approaches with teaching staff, parents, and subsequently with students. Based on the analysis of the European Union Recommendations [42], some aspects emerge to structure this knowledge-sharing process. The first is *Lifelong Learning*, which places school learning within the broader framework of lifelong education; the second is *informal learning*, which can occur outside the classroom and may not always be intentional; the third concerns the *cognitive differences* among students, as everyone's cognitive domain shapes their participation in learning processes. Finally, crucial are the *didactic methodologies* that encourage students to take active roles, such as problem solving, to stimulate curiosity and problem-oriented thinking, as well as *inquiry-based learning* and *cooperative learning*, supported by the works of Dewey [43] and Piaget [44] along with all *hands-on* approaches rooted in lab-based education.

The third phase, identified as *Individual Values Explicitation*, involves participants revealing individual values closely tied to their surrounding environment, through photo, text and draw production. In this phase, children bring out material and immaterial elements of the territory to which they attribute specific environmental, historical, cultural, or emotional significance. This is done through various visual and graphic-narrative techniques, customized for the target group. Another tool used is *photography*, which helps identify the key features of the explored spaces. The output of this phase could be a rich photographic archive made up of individual narratives, making visible the plurality of children's emotional and cognitive connections with their context, and serving as the operational foundation for subsequent collective sharing.

Next, during the *Collective Values Explicitation* phase, individual values are re-contextualized within a collective dimension, mapping out the individual preferences that emerged and identifying new spaces and characteristics of the territory deemed particularly significant by the group, through urban walks and public spaces mapping. Additional tools include the *exploratory walk* and *situated interviews*, along with photography and drawing, to spatialize the emergent values and identify places considered important by the co-researchers and the material and immaterial characteristics of the territory. This enables a deeper investigation of the relationships between communities and their context on a broader territorial scale.

The fifth phase of the workshop, *Topics Interpretation*, responds to the reflective dynamics of a dynamic and iterative approach. The interpretation of results, especially when shared with all co-researching participants, is a sense-making process that offers a deep understanding of what has emerged and leads to prioritising key issues, translating shared values into design criteria, through graphical and textual analysis and clustering of emerging topics.

Finally, the sixth phase *Sharing and Prioritization* aims to return: to the community the exploration process carried out, through events and assemblies; to the children, the visions developed based on their involvement; to educational institutions, the visions that emerged as traces on which to continue working in school and out-of-school contexts; and to policymakers, the most relevant criteria with which children have expressed themselves about public space, as valuable pointers for structuring an inclusive child-based spatial transformation process.

4 Case-Study: Anacapri (Capri Island) as an Example of *Under Pressure* Places

Places subject to strong tourism pressure are a territorial cluster that requires urgent responses from research. In these places, over-tourism triggers closely interconnected phenomena that contribute to generating high impacts on communities. These impacts produce the falsification of identity values and the *disneyfication* of contexts [45].

In some cases, they lead to the disintegration of resident communities and their removal. Over-tourism favours the introduction of multinational corporations into the local market which - while improving the competitiveness of the "destinations" [46] - also alters economic dynamics. The hotel chains undermine the sustainability of family-run businesses [47], as the influx of external economic resources leads to an increase in labour costs, a rise in the quality standards, and the consequent inability of local businesses to be competitive. This causes the failure of family-run structures and their sale or lease to these corporations. This also generates impacts on the spatial context, starting with the alteration of the real estate market, which is further stressed by the increase in second homes [48] and the proliferation of non-hotel accommodation in the short-term market. This undermines the ability of residents to find housing and activates housing resistance practices. Regarding public space, recent studies reveal how tourist flows are transforming it, for example by domesticating squares, adapting them to the commercial interests related to satisfying tourist demand. In some cases, the public space design is influenced by private tourism interests. This generates spatial injustice - particularly concerning vulnerable community segments - which consists of a progressive erosion or privatization of public space, carried out by the Ho.Re.Ca. sector. These functions not only overflow into public space but also multiply, generating what has been defined as the *foodification* of historic centres [49]. All these aspects contribute to defining a new way of inhabiting touristed areas, temporary and seasonal, and to outlining the ever-increasing urgency of addressing the touristification instrumentally and through the involvement of resident communities.

The experimentation was activated within an illustrative study context. Capri is in the province of Naples and is part of the minor Italian islands. Since 2021, Capri has fallen within the *SNAI* (National Strategy for Inner Areas) demarcation, although it constitutes an anomalous case. Its peculiarity is intricately linked to a temporary habitation that is punctuated by the alternation of "tourist seasons" and "non-tourist seasons". One of the most affected areas is the port district, where a careful evaluation of tourist dynamics would be necessary [50]. Recently, the issue has become particularly urgent as the island has witnessed the growth of its tourist flows and - with the advent of the sharing economy - the proliferation of bed spaces caused by the emergence of B&Bs. This and numerous other causes are strongly undermining the island's identity values, generating significant impacts on the local community. The causes of the island's overtourism can be found in its peculiarities and historical-cultural heritage, which even today generate excessive tourist demand compared to it carrying capacity. In the last thirty years, the interest in these specificities has transformed into an undisciplined *invasion*, encouraged by the development of some private monopolies related to both maritime transport in the Gulf of Naples and island tourist road transport enterprises. The local institutions are adopting new tools. Since 2024, the management of museums and archaeological parks on the Island of Capri has been entrusted to a single body. A procedural process for the island's Marine Protected Area is underway. The City of Capri is proceeding with a new Land Use Plan (PUC) [51], for which the authors themselves emphasize that "territorial planning certainly cannot manage the entire tourism machine". Legambiente's latest Report [52] calculates the Sustainability Index in minor islands and describes Capri as an island with a virtuous trend (62% sustainable). It should be noted that the report refers only to the condition of strict environmental sustainability, not considering other dimensions in the assessment. Other research contributions offer interesting perspectives. Mousavi et al. [53] interpret the regeneration of the "Oro di Capri" trees as a practice aimed at the sustainable conversion of the territory, also from a tourism perspective. A recent contribution has been carried out regarding the reactivation of a cultural heritage in Anacapri in relation to the implementation of a new collaborative idea of sustainable tourism, more related to the necessities of youth community and the opportunities of the underused cultural heritage [54].

5 EURECA Implementation and Main Results

The EURECA workshop was launched in Anacapri during February 2025 (winter season) and involved 22 children (aged 7–10) of an Anacapri Primary School, with the participation of two teachers (Fig. 3). To make the children the protagonists of the research experience, they were given the role of "explorers", and their support was requested in discovering the public space of Anacapri. The documentation of the activities is detailed, as it does not exclusively represent the manifestation of an output, but rather narrates the entire process, witnessing the implementation of the process in all its phases, with drawings, writings, images, interviews, photographs, on which researchers, co-researchers, and all involved parties reflect.

Fig. 3. Workshop EURECA activities implementation in Anacapri

The *Objective Sharing* phase represented the initial moment of the co-exploration process and allowed the emergence of the youngest participants' needs, desires, and visions, which were collected and interpreted during the exploratory journey, paying particular attention to the territorial context in which the experimentation takes place. In this first phase, which also saw the identification of stakeholders to involve, the designed activities enabled their participation in support of the research objectives, building a reciprocal exchange. Among the stakeholders included in the research is the Municipality of Anacapri, which recognized the value of the research activity and is working to support the researchers in the implementation of the Laboratory; equally important is the direct dialogue built with the Anacapri Youth Forum (FGA), which acts as a facilitator thanks to already established relationships of trust in the territory. The main stakeholder is the school, interpreted as the driving force of a transformation process as well as an enabling device, as it can weave relationships and becoming a child-led "construction site". The first contact was initiated by FGA, which connected with the school management, illustrating the proposal and forming the first link with the research team. A key point of this phase was the development of a relationship of trust with the first school that joined the initiative: the "Padre Ludovico da Casoria" Private Primary School. In this regard, teachers and families received in advance the program of the

"Space Adventures" activity, as well as a *vademecum* of the materials needed for the children to participate ("Explorer's Kit"). The main output of this phase consists of an initial map of the actors interested in the research, which visually and collaboratively gathers the relevant stakeholders for understanding and acting in the context. The map is configured as dynamic and open output. Before starting the activities, during the first meeting with the children, they were repeatedly asked if they wanted to take part in the research, using the word "adventure". The children's assent to participate and the explicit expression of their interest and enjoyment were essential elements of the workshop.

The *Knowledge Sharing* phase, therefore, involved the transfer of some key concepts with which to observe the territory. Through the medium of images, a reflection on the concept of space was initiated, during which the children were invited to consider how this abstract concept could instead describe a real and tangible context. To make this element more explicit, supporting illustrative materials were prepared, which helped the children visualize the differences between solids and voids, between closed and open spaces, built and natural spaces, public and private spaces. To the question "What is space for you?" the children replied: "For me it's where we can do many things"; "for me it's something beautiful, you can't feel it or see it"; "for me it's a place where you can plant, run, play, and walk"; "for me it's spending time in an open place"; "for me it's where I can play and read"; "it's a place where we have fun"; "it's everything that surrounds us and occupies a space". The workshop activity focused on public space, also defined as "community space". To stimulate the imagination, some tactical urban planning projects carried out for school communities near some Italian schools were shown. Therefore, starting from the concept of space as "empty", some representative images of urban contexts were distributed, on which the children redesigned the void. The resulting drawings represent a confirmation of the concept learning, as well as their visual interpretation, aimed at illustrating how an "empty" space can be occupied through imagination. Another important activity was the observation of early 20th-century photographs of Capri, depicting moments of children's daily life. One image on which the children particularly focused portrayed some peers playing soccer in the port village of Marina Grande. The image sparked some considerations about how the public space of Marina Grande has transformed and the current impossibility of playing in those places due to the high number of commercial activities and the large number of tourists.

During the *Individual Values Explicitation* phase, the main objective was to foster a subjective exploration of the proposed theme, encouraging children to reflect on their emotional connections in relation to space, with the aim of making explicit and valuing individual perceptions, which risk being marginalized in collective design processes. Stimulating the emergence of personal values allows for the construction of a richer and more articulated repertoire of meanings, going beyond shared stereotypes or iconographic images. To start the activity, the theme of the island was introduced, providing the co-researchers with some information about islands in Italy.

Among the items listed in the *vademecum*, participants were asked to find some postcards of the island. The collective observation of these images highlighted the systematic repetition of certain emblematic places: the Blue Grotto, the Piazzetta of Capri. This allowed the children to recognize how there is a standardized image of the island.

The children were invited to identify an island place to which they felt connected, even if less known or absent from the classic representations of the island. They were asked to describe this place on a prepared sheet and to depict it on a blank postcard. The aim of the activity was to give value to the affective and everyday dimension of the experience of places. At the end, each child shared the description of their place and the postcard they created with the group. In the next phase, these postcards were spatialized: each participant placed their representation on a Anacapri's map, posted in the classroom. From the non-tourist postcards drawn by the children, it emerged that an alternative reading of the island's context is possible, more linked to the intimate dimension, which focuses on the identity values specific to the socio-cultural context of the territory. This activity made it possible to construct a new geography of the island, generated by the children's lived experiences, which contrasts with the stereotypical images that initially emerged.

The *Collective Values Explicitation* phase allowed for the emergence and negotiation of shared values related to public spaces through a dual approach of on-site exploration and participatory mapping. During an exploratory walk, the group of researchers traversed the historic centre of Anacapri, using essential tools such as notebooks to jot down observations and suggestions aimed at improving the quality of the spaces they inhabit: "I would like a playground in an enclosed space because you can't play anywhere"; "they could remove the appliance store that has been closed for a while and turn it into a museum or an association that does charity or a house since they are not easily found on the island"; "the closed store can become a toy library"; "the fountains could be improved and the rule of not blocking them applied"; "add a fountain for animals". During this activity, the children pointed out several characteristic elements of the public space. Among the issues relevant from their point of view, it emerged that in some Anacapri public spaces "ball playing is prohibited". Another prohibition that was pointed out concerns the use of bicycles. Furthermore, the co-researchers noted the presence of many closed commercial activities (also noting that they only open during the summer) and that "a lot of space will be occupied by bar tables". During the walk, the group of explorers, at a square, sat in a circle to have a snack. The circular arrangement in the open air encouraged the sharing of new considerations; the children highlighted the lack of shade, a closed gate concealing an underutilized area, and pointed out the closure of a shop once very popular with locals. Subsequently, as if representing a small symbolic "conquest"; the children spontaneously began to play with pinecones from a pine tree near a sign reminding them of the prohibition against playing ball. At the end of the exploratory walk, back at school, guided by the researchers, they populated the map of Anacapri previously affixed to a classroom wall. Each child indicated their home with a marker, then together they traced the route and stops of the walk, highlighted critical issues such as the lack of sufficiently large play spaces and "of trees and plants" with sticky notes, and reported their final considerations starting from the statement "I liked this experience because"; "we discovered more things about the territory"; "we went out and understood how much space we have on this island"; "because it makes us become explorers"; "we understood how - space - we can occupy it".

The *Prioritization of Topics* phase aimed to transparently synthesize the results that emerged during the workshop, valuing the children's contribution and transforming their experiences into an operational method of urban analysis and interpretation, reproducible in different contexts. The subsequent experimentation is expected to reveal shared values such as active participation, transparency of choices, and the critical capacity to imagine spaces, in addition to ensuring the reproducibility of the methodological path.

6 Conclusions and Discussion

The process has developed and concretely tested a methodology aimed at eliciting shared values with children in touristic places and identified some relevant issues around which the next phases of the research will allow for inquiry, to co-evaluate transformative shared strategies. This was possible by activating the engagement of a new community, whose contribution will continue to be included in the next phases, involving a quintuple helix including child-inhabitants, the school, the third sector, the local authority, and the university. The test highlighted some aspects of particular importance, as well as the potential and limitations of the implemented methodology.

With regard to the indispensable tools, the following are mentioned: 1) the involvement of the school institution as a necessary bridge between researchers, families, and children; 2) the presence of a local association (and young people) as a facilitator and generator of trust in the other parties involved at the local level; 3) the use of images, drawings, and photographs as a privileged tool for shared reflection on the tourist and non-tourist imaginary of the territory; 4) the spatial element and its direct observation as catalysts for reflections, and in this sense, the exploratory walk as a tool suitable for observation and innovative reinterpretation of the living spaces of the community; 5) the adoption of language appropriate to the age of the co-researchers, which, however, facilitates deep understanding (and acceptance to participate) in the process in which they are involved; 6) the activation of the process within a broader framework of EE, which favoured the initiation of a reflection that will continue with further practical experiments in a logic of reiteration of the different phases, encouraging the improvement of the methodology; 7) the integration of appropriate strategies, techniques, and tools aimed at addressing the ethical difficulty of including children in research and their interpretation as co-researchers in a context of mutual learning as particularly successful in PAR contexts. Furthermore, the implementation of the EURECA workshop made it possible to focus on some aspects that can be further explored in subsequent experiments and that are highlighted below: 1) the need to carry out the activities with a limited number of co-researchers, currently identified as 15, as a higher number risks limiting the capacity for equitable listening on the part of adult researchers; 2) the need for a large environment that encourages children's expression, within which to carry out the activities; 3) the adoption of a longer timeframe to effectively conduct the research and collect systematic results. In this regard, it is important that researchers consider the needs of the various parties involved, agreeing with them on the schedule of activities to be conducted. Regarding the results related to the context of the Island of Capri, EURECA made it possible to map some issues relevant to children in their interaction with living spaces, which can be summarized in three essential clusters: 1) the "play" space denied or absent; 2) "home" as an asset at risk, as it is rare and precious; 3) the right to the sea (perceived as a luxury good) and to nature as essential issues for children's well-being; 4) the urban public space "eroded" by tourism. The identification of these clusters will allow for the initiation of a deeper shared reflection, calibrated to the needs identified with the co-researchers, aimed at guiding the future choices of policymakers, as well as offering different points of view to be adopted in urban transformations.

Acknowledgments. The contribution is part of the research activity developed in the "GRINS - Growing Resilient, Inclusive and Sustainable" project, financed by the National Recovery and Resilience Plan (NRP), Mission 4 (Infrastructure and Research), Component 2 (From Research to Enterprise), Investment 1.3 (Extended Partnerships), Theme 9 (Economic and Financial Sustainability of Systems and Territories) (https://www.grins.it/progetto).

Contributions. The authors jointly conceived and developed the approach and decided on the overall objective and structure of the paper. Conceptualization, L.D.T., L.L.R., C.L.; methodology, L.D.T., L.L.R., C.L.; validation, M.C., S.P.; formal analysis, L.D.T, C.L.; case-study investigation, L.D.T, C.L., S.P.; data curation, L.D.T, C.L., L.L.R.; writing - original draft preparation, L.D.T, C.L., L.L.R.; writing - review and editing, M.C., L.D.T., L.L.R., C.L., S.P.; visualization, L.D.T., C.L., L.L.R.; supervision, M.C., S.P. All authors have read and agreed to the published version of the manuscript.

References

1. Poli, G., Cuntò, S., Muccio, E.: A data-driven approach to monitor sustainable development transition in Italian regions through SDG 11 indicators. In: Gervasi, O., Murgante, B., Garau, C., Taniar, D., Rocha, A.M.A.C., Faginas Lago, M.N. (eds.) ICCSA 2024. LNCS, vol. 14820, pp. 337–355. Springer, Cham (2024). https://doi.org/10.1007/978-3-031-65285-1_22
2. CEDEFOP: Cities in transition: how vocational education and training can help cities become smarter and greener, pp. 1–23 (2022)
3. ASviS: Coltivare ora il nostro futuro: L'Italia e gli Obiettivi di Sviluppo Sostenibile, pp. 149–150 (2024)
4. Iaione, C.: The CO-City: sharing, collaborating, cooperating, and commoning in the city. Am. J. Econ. Sociol. **75**(2), 415–455 (2016). https://doi.org/10.1111/ajes.12145
5. REAL DEAL: Gap assessment of the European green deal, pp. 1–15 (2018)
6. Zizzania, P., Muccio, E., Sacco, S., Cerreta, M.: Prediction and uncertainty in social impact evaluation: a classification framework. In: Calabrò, F., Madureira, L., Morabito, F.C., Piñeira Mantiñán, M.J. (eds.) NMP 2024. LNNS, vol. 1186, pp. 49–58. Springer, Cham (2024). https://doi.org/10.1007/978-3-031-74679-6_5
7. Somma, M., La Rocca, L., Loffredo, C.: A methodological approach for activate a community-based archive as a decision-support system in urban regeneration processes. In: Gervasi, O., Murgante, B., Garau, C., Taniar, D., Rocha, A.M.A.C., Faginas Lago, M.N. (eds.) ICCSA 2024. LNCS, vol. 14820, pp. 421–435. Springer, Cham (2024). https://doi.org/10.1007/978-3-031-65285-1_27
8. Daldanise, G., Giovene di Girasole, E., Stella, S., Clemente, M.: Cultural and touristic valorization processes: towards a collaborative governance for development in Southern Italy. In: Bevilacqua, C., Calabrò, F., Della Spina, L. (eds.) NMP 2020. SIST, vol. 178, pp. 167–176. Springer, Cham (2021). https://doi.org/10.1007/978-3-030-48279-4_16
9. TEHA Group: Rapporto strategico sul turismo sostenibile e i patrimoni dell'umanità. Dalle radici alle nuove tendenze: l'evoluzione del Turismo Sostenibile nei territori italiani, pp. 1–71 (2024)

10. Mohamadi, S., Abbasi, A., Ranaei Kordshouli, H.A., Askarifar, K.: Conceptualizing sustainable–responsible tourism indicators: an interpretive structural modeling approach. Environ. Dev. Sustain. **24**, 399–425 (2022). https://doi.org/10.1007/S10668-021-01442-9
11. Balaban, E., Keller, K.: A systematic literature review of slow tourism. Hung. Geogr. Bull. **73**, 303–323 (2024). https://doi.org/10.15201/HUNGEOBULL.73.3.6
12. Mihalic, T., Mohamadi, S., Abbasi, A., Dávid, L.D.: Mapping a sustainable and responsible tourism paradigm: a bibliometric and citation network analysis. Sustainability **13**, 853 (2021). https://doi.org/10.3390/SU13020853
13. SRM: Turismo & Territorio: tendenze, impatti e dinamiche d'impresa. Focus Mezzogiorno. https://www.sr-m.it/index.php. Accessed 07 May 2025
14. ISTAT: Presenze turistiche in aumento nel quarto trimestre, 2024 nuovo anno record (2025)
15. Dilshan, N.W.T., Nakabasami, C.: Overtourism: a systematic review of global issues and management strategies. Int. J. Tour. Policy **15**, 50–66 (2025). https://doi.org/10.1504/IJTP.2025.144178
16. WTA: Tourism. A Driver for Shared Prosperity, pp. 1–120 (2025). https://doi.org/10.18111/9789284425822
17. Grieco, B., Somma, M., Raiola, M.L., Sacco, S., Zizzania, P., Cerreta, M.: A decision support system for cultural and territorial infrastructures: a place-based and community-driven strategy in inner Italy. In: Gervasi, O., Murgante, B., Garau, C., Taniar, D., Rocha, A.M.A.C., Faginas Lago, M.N. (eds.) ICCSA 2024. LNCS, vol. 14820, pp. 373–387. Springer, Cham (2024). https://doi.org/10.1007/978-3-031-65285-1_24
18. Barač-Miftarević, S.: Undertourism vs. overtourism: a systematic literature review. Tour. Int. Interdiscip. J. **71**, 178–192 (2023). https://doi.org/10.37741/T.71.1.11
19. Yang, M.J.H., Khoo, C., Yang, E.C.L.: Exploring host-children's engagement in tourism: transcending the dichotomy of universalism and cultural relativism. Tour. Manag. **100** (2024). https://doi.org/10.1016/j.tourman.2023.104838
20. Dochy, F., Segers, M., Sluijsmans, D.: The use of self-, peer and co-assessment in higher education: a review. Stud. High. Educ. **24**, 331–350 (1999). https://doi.org/10.1080/03075079912331379935
21. Canosa, A., Graham, A., Wilson, E.: Reflexivity and ethical mindfulness in participatory research with children: what does it really look like? Childhood **25**, 400–415 (2018). https://doi.org/10.1177/0907568218769342
22. Lewis, A., Porter, J.: Interviewing children and young people with learning disabilities*: guidelines for researchers and multi-professional practice. Br. J. Learn. Disabil. **32**, 191–197 (2004). https://doi.org/10.1111/j.1468-3156.2004.00313.x
23. Macdonald, A.: Researching with young children: considering issues of ethics and engagement. Contemp. Issues Early Child. **14**, 255–269 (2013). https://doi.org/10.2304/CIEC.2013.14.3.255
24. UN: General comment no. 12: The right of the child to be heard, pp. 1–31 (2009)
25. Angelöw, A., Psouni, E.: Participatory research with children: from child-rights based principles to practical guidelines for meaningful and ethical participation. Int. J. Qual. Methods **24** (2025). https://doi.org/10.1177/16094069251315391
26. Heath, S., Charles, V., Crow, G., Wiles, R.: Informed consent, gatekeepers and go-betweens: negotiating consent in child and youth-orientated institutions. Br. Edu. Res. J. **33**, 403–417 (2007). https://doi.org/10.1080/01411920701243651
27. Sun, Y., Blewitt, C., Edwards, S., Fraser, A., Newman, S., Cornelius, J., Skouteris, H.: Methods and ethics in qualitative research exploring young children's voice: a systematic review. Int. J. Qual. Methods **22** (2023). https://doi.org/10.1177/16094069231152449
28. Flewitt, R.: Conducting research with young children: some ethical considerations. Early Child Dev. Care **175**, 553–565 (2005). https://doi.org/10.1080/03004430500131338

29. Dockett, S., Einarsdóttir, J., Perry, B.: Young children's decisions about research participation: opting out. Int. J. Early Years Educ. **20**, 244–256 (2012). https://doi.org/10.1080/09669760.2012.715405
30. Jenkin, E., Wilson, E., Campain, R., Clarke, M.: The principles and ethics of including children with disability in child research. Child. Soc. **34**, 1–16 (2020). https://doi.org/10.1111/CHSO.12356
31. Larsson, J., Williams, P., Zetterqvist, A.: The challenge of conducting ethical research in preschool. Early Child Dev. Care **191**, 511–519 (2021). https://doi.org/10.1080/03004430.2019.1625897
32. Schweiger, G.: Children as co-researchers. Epistemological, methodological and ethical challenges. Cogent Soc. Sci. **10**(1), 2422550 (2024). https://doi.org/10.1080/23311886.2024.2422550
33. Graham, A., Powell, M.A., Truscott, J.: Exploring the nexus between participatory methods and ethics in early childhood research. Australas. J. Early Child. **41**, 82–89 (2016). https://doi.org/10.1177/183693911604100111
34. Graham, A., Powell, M., Taylor, N., Anderson, D., Fitzgerald, R.: Ethical Research Involving Children. UNICEF Office of Research - Innocenti, Florence (2013)
35. Urban, J.B., Hargraves, M., Trochim, W.M.: Evolutionary evaluation: implications for evaluators, researchers, practitioners, funders and the evidence-based program mandate. Eval. Program Plan. **45**, 127–139 (2014). https://doi.org/10.1016/j.evalprogplan.2014.03.011
36. Patton, M.Q.: Developmental Evaluation: Applying Complexity Concepts to Enhance Innovation and Use. Guilford Press, New York (2011)
37. Scholz, R.W.: The mutual learning sessions. In: Klein, J.T., Häberli, R., Scholz, R.W., Grossenbacher-Mansuy, W., Bill, A., Welti, M. (eds.) Transdisciplinarity: Joint Problem Solving among Science, Technology, and Society. Schwerpunktprogramm Umwelt/Programme Prioritaire Environnement/Priority Programme Environment. Birkhäuser, Basel, pp. 117–129 (2001). https://doi.org/10.1007/978-3-0348-8419-8_11
38. Rogers, P.J., Funnell, S.C.: Purposeful program theory: effective use of theories of change and logic models (2013)
39. Gómez-Ruiz, M.A., Quesada Serra, V.: Análisis de las calificaciones compartidas en la modalidad participativa de la evaluación colaborativa entre docente y estudiantes. RELIEVE **26** (2020). https://doi.org/10.7203/relieve.26.1.16567
40. Iaione, C., de Nictolis, E.: La quintupla elica come approccio alla governance dell'innovazione sociale. In: Montanari, F., Mizzau, L. (eds.) I luoghi dell'innovazione aperta. Modelli di sviluppo territoriale e inclusione sociale, pp. 75–89. Fondazione Giacomo Brodolini, Roma (2016)
41. MIUR: Indicazioni nazionali per il curricolo della scuola dell'infanzia e del primo ciclo dell'istruzione. Ministero dell'Istruzione dell'Università e della Ricerca, Rome (2012)
42. European Council: Raccomandazione del Consiglio del 22 maggio 2018 relativa alle competenze chiave per l'apprendimento permanente (2018/C 189/01), Bruxelles (2018)
43. Dewey, J.: Experience and Education. Touchstone, New York (1997)
44. Piaget, J.: The Psychology of the Child. Basic Books Publisher (1969)
45. Matusitz, J., Palermo, L.: The disneyfication of the world: a grobalisation perspective. J. Organ. Transform. Soc. Change **11**, 91–107 (2014). https://doi.org/10.1179/1477963313Z.00000000014
46. Ivanov, S., Ivanova, M.: Do hotel chains improve destination's competitiveness? Tour. Manag. Perspect. **19**, 74–79 (2016). https://doi.org/10.1016/J.TMP.2016.04.007
47. Lowe, A.: Small hotel survival-an inductive approach. Int. J. Hosp. Manag. **7**, 197–223 (1988). https://doi.org/10.1016/0278-4319(88)90021-7
48. Opačič, V., Mikačic, V.: Second home phenomenon and tourism in the Croatian littoral - two pretenders for the same space? Tourism **57** (2009)

49. Freire Varela, A.: Eating the city: socio-spatial analysis of the foodification process in the city of Naples (Italy). Int. J. Gastron. Food Sci. **39**, 101130 (2025). https://doi.org/10.1016/J.IJGFS.2025.101130
50. Ciciriello, G., Sacco, S., Torre, C.M., Cerreta, M.: Port cities and evaluation: a literature review to explore their interplay in planning. In: Gervasi, O., Murgante, B., Garau, C., Taniar, D., Rocha, A.M.A.C., Faginas Lago, M.N. (eds.) ICCSA 2024. LNCS, vol. 14818, pp. 192–209. Springer, Cham (2024). https://doi.org/10.1007/978-3-031-65273-8_13
51. Acierno, A., Pistone, I.: Sustainable planning and overtourism in the island of Capri. In: Calabrò, F., Madureira, L., Morabito, F.C., Piñeira Mantiñán, M.J. (eds) NMP 2024. LNNS, vol. 1184, pp. 93–106. Springer, Cham (2024). https://doi.org/10.1007/978-3-031-74608-6_9
52. Battistelli, F., Minutolo, A., Nanni, G., Laurenti, M., Lugli, D., Tomassetti, L., Petracchini, F.: La transizione ecologica nelle isole minori, Roma (2024)
53. Mousavi, S., Pandolfi, S., Lo Conte, A., Lelj Garolla, C.A., Mariotti, R.: The ancient olive trees of Capri Island renaissance of an abandoned treasure. Scientia Horticulturae **328** (2024). https://doi.org/10.1016/j.scienta.2024.112930
54. Di Tommaso, L., Daldanise, G., La Rocca, L., Panaro, S., Cerreta, M.: A co-governance process for the adaptive reuse of cultural heritage: the experience of St. Michael Cloister in Anacapri. In: Gervasi, O., Murgante, B., Garau, C., Taniar, D., Rocha, A.M.A.C., Faginas Lago, M.N. (eds.). ICCSA 2024. LNCS, vol. 14824, pp. 236–252. Springer, Cham (2024). https://doi.org/10.1007/978-3-031-65332-2_16

Ex-Post Evaluation Framework for Intersectional Bottom-Up Regeneration Process of Public Spaces: Learning from a Youth Empowerment Experience

Renata Boeri[✉], Piero Zizzania, and Maria Cerreta

Department of Architecture, University of Naples Federico II, via Toledo 402, Naples, Italy
renat.boeri@gmail.com, {piero.zizzania,cerreta}@unina.it

Abstract. This contribution presents an ex-post evaluation of the Girls Make the City! project, an initiative launched in Brussels to explore the potential of young women's empowerment in inclusive urban regeneration. Situated at the intersection of feminist practices, participatory spatial transformation, and critical pedagogy, the project aimed to amplify the voice and agency of adolescent girls in a structurally marginalised neighborhood. The analysis employed an evolutionary evaluation approach grounded in theoretical principles of intersectionality, Theory of Change, and realistic evaluation. A qualitative framework was reconstructed ex-post by analysing the case study. Six key evaluative criteria emerged: active engagement of diverse groups, collective re-signification of public space, transferability of acquired competences, emergence of cross-group dialogues and alliances, durability of spatial transformation, and urban care practices. These dimensions reflect transformative mechanisms relevant for equity-oriented urban policies. The project demonstrates how feminist and participatory practices can serve as effective levers for urban regeneration, advancing spatial justice and inclusion. The adoption of adaptive and context-sensitive evaluation frameworks is essential to make visible the social and cultural impacts of such initiatives and to inform future urban strategies.

Keywords: Evolutionary Evaluation (EE) · Theory-Based Evaluation (TBE) · Spatial Justice · Intersectionality approach · Urban Inequalities

1 Introduction

Public spaces are not static backdrops, but dynamic arenas shaped by economic dynamics, policy interventions and lived experiences [1, 2]. As cities undergo rapid transformation, inequalities are increasing, and sustainability challenges are becoming increasingly complex. Urban planning faces the task of creating spaces that are not only safe and accessible but also genuinely inclusive, to respond to the diverse needs of inhabitants, while reducing exclusion through a lens of spatial justice [3, 4]. In this complex context, innovative evaluation frameworks are essential for capturing the intersecting factors that shape urban experiences, including gender, age, ethnicity, socio-economic status (and more) and which cause a systemic invisibility of certain groups in urban spaces [5–7]. Integrating the evolutionary evaluation approach within an intersectional framework [8, 9] becomes crucial in understanding, defining and addressing this phenomenon.

This paper addresses a key gap in urban studies and the evaluation tools for sustainability: the lack of systematic evaluation frameworks that meaningfully incorporate youth experiences, especially from a gendered and intersectional lens [9]. While feminist urbanism and intersectionality have enriched critical discussions on urban inequality [8, 10–13], few studies explore how young people can shape urban regeneration through participatory, evaluative processes. By exploring these themes, the research contributes to a broader reflection on the specific tools and methods that can foster greater youth engagement in decision-making processes through an empowerment approach [14]. The overall reflection aims to understand how urban public spaces can be designed, managed, and transformed in a more inclusive and pluralistic way [15].

The theoretical foundation for this research is anchored in four interrelated frameworks: feminist urbanism, participatory design, intersectionality and spatial justice. Feminist urbanism critiques traditional urban planning paradigms that marginalise women's experiences and advocates for inclusive, equitable urban spaces [11, 13]. Participatory design, meanwhile, emphasises the democratisation of urban planning through the active involvement of community members, ensuring that those directly affected by urban policies have a meaningful role in shaping their environments [16, 17]. The intersectional approach, as defined by Crenshaw [9], allows for the examination of overlapping identities, such as gender, age, ethnicity and socio-economic status, compound experiences of marginalisation: an essential perspective to understanding the challenges faced by young women in urban contexts. Finally, the concept of spatial justice frames the discussion by focusing on how the equitable distribution of urban resources and a different way of imagining decision-making processes can either reinforce or mitigate social inequalities [4, 7].

Each of these four fields is widely recognised by the scientific community as crucial for understanding and addressing urban inequalities [10]. However, the relationships among these concepts remain complex and are the subject of ongoing debate, with no clear or commonly agreed-upon framework. Integrating these perspectives to make decision-making processes affecting urban spaces more inclusive from an intersectional standpoint is still an open challenge. The systemic nature of these interconnections is difficult to translate into effective practices, especially in the context of public policies or regeneration processes that aim to meaningfully engage marginalised social groups, especially young people [18]. To date, there is still a notable lack of evaluation frameworks specifically dedicated to these issues, capable of assessing their impact and guiding urban transformation toward greater equity.

The research centres on two key-questions: (kq1) why is it essential to address intersectionality and youth empowerment in urban regeneration? (kq2) how can evaluation practices support more inclusive transformation processes?

To investigate this, the paper examines "Girls Make the City!" (GMtC!) [19], a participatory urbanism initiative in Brussels developed in response to a municipal call to reduce gender disparities in planning. The project offers a valuable case study for exploring how young women can become central actors in shaping public space through co-creation and empowerment strategies. In doing so, it disrupts top-down urbanism and reframes inclusion as a tool for both equity and innovation [20]. The goal of GMtC! is to cultivate environments where young women not only feel safe but also become key actors in shaping the future of specific public spaces in the city. This emphasis on inclusion and empowerment challenges traditional approaches in urban planning, opening a discourse that focuses on equity and sustainable transformation [21].

Adopting an Impact Evaluation as a learning process approach [22, 23], this research proposes an ex-post impact evaluation grounded in a concrete case study and developed in dialogue with the creators of the GMtC! project. The evaluation framework is theory-based [24, 25], focusing on reconstructing the mechanisms of change activated by the project to achieve long-term positive outcomes. Additionally, the overall methodology draws on Evolutionary Evaluation (EE) [26], which is particularly well-suited to capturing the dynamic, non-linear, and multi-actor nature of urban change.

Through this process of mutual learning [27], it was possible not only to recognise the value of GMtC! within the broader landscape of intersectionality and youth empowerment policies, but also identify the generative mechanisms that were activated and can be replicated in other contexts, and to hypothesise the potential dimensions of social and cultural impact. The framework developed aims to reflect the complexity of lived urban experiences and to highlight the transformative potential of the intersectional bottom-up regeneration process.

The paper is articulated in the following sections: Sect. 2 is dedicated to materials and methods, describing the methodology and the case study; Sect. 3 presents the results, considering the analysis of the case study, constructing an evaluative lens and mechanism, criteria and upscaling; Sect. 4 describes the conclusions and final reflections.

2 Materials and Methods

Rather than applying a predefined evaluation model to assess the program's performance, a case-based framework [28, 29] was constructed that could co-evolve alongside the analysis itself, in alignment with the principles of Evolutionary Evaluation (EE).

EE is a methodological paradigm developed to accompany the ongoing development of programs [26]. Unlike traditional evaluation models that are linear and static, EE is based on a dynamic approach of continuous learning, deeply rooted in complexity theory [30, 31]. This approach is aligned with the theoretical contributions of Funnell and Rogers [32], who integrated EE with tools from Program Theory [33] and Theory of Change [25], emphasising the need for a flexible yet specific and situated structure that still maintains internal logical coherence. By adopting a mixed-methods approach [34] to impact evaluation that integrates Theory-Based and Realistic approaches [31], it becomes possible to prioritise the identification of the impact dimensions generated by an urban process, with particular attention to CMO configurations. This involves clarifying the causal links and synergistic relationships between the operational context (C), the mechanisms (M) of change that have been activated, and the outcomes (O) observed or expected [33].

The methodology adopted proved to be particularly well-suited for evaluating interventions that are emergent, non-linear, and embedded within real-time learning cycles.

Specifically, the GMtC! case study represents a bottom-up regeneration initiative that engaged young women in a process characterised by clearly defined initial goals, but high uncertainty regarding effective outcomes. In this field-based research context, evaluation became a reflective and formative act [34, 35], more closely aligned with practices of social inquiry than with tools of accountability or metrics-based impact measurement. Given that the research focused on inclusivity and spatial justice, it was deemed essential to build a methodological process open to reflection and direct engagement with both the case context and the actors involved. This approach provided crucial insights into the complexity of the processes, allowed for a more accurate identification of the subjectivities involved, and helped avoid reproducing patterns of exclusion and power asymmetries, often embedded within evaluation practices themselves [36].

The recursive and incremental evaluation methodology made it possible to "attribute value" [37] to unexpected social and cultural dynamics - no longer interpreted as programmatic failures to be corrected, but as meaningful elements of the broader system [38]. Evaluation, when applied to complex processes that integrate goals of spatial transformation with objectives of positive social change [39, 40], can contribute to the elicitation of collective and shared values [41, 42] and the emergence of subjectivities that were previously excluded or marginalised [43]. From this perspective, the goal is not merely to determine whether a project "worked," but to understand "what works and how" [44]: the values generated through the process, the changes it initiated, and the capacities it developed within a broader ecology of transformation.

2.1 The Case Study

This research was initially developed to evaluate the outcomes and impacts generated by the GMtC! initiative as part of a thesis for the U-RISE Second-Level Master's Program (IUAV University of Venice). The project was initially launched in response to a public call by the Ville de Bruxelles, aimed at supporting youth participation in public space design. Several local associations working with young people, situated in the Marolles neighbourhood, responded to the call. The initiative brought together a diverse group of young women, aged between 14 and 18, to co-design and activate public space interventions. Their involvement reflected both a response to the structural exclusion of youth and gender-diverse bodies from urban space and an opportunity to build new narratives of belonging, visibility, and empowerment.

The ex-post impact evaluation was designed to critically reflect on a complex and evolving participatory urban process, seeking to understand how young women's presence and agency were mobilised in the public space of Brussels through this initiative. The *GMtC!* project was selected as a case study because its objectives, methods, and context aligned closely with our research questions, which explore the intersection of youth empowerment, gender, and urban transformation. The initiative stood out for its explicit focus on feminist urbanism and its attempt to challenge structural exclusions in public space through participatory design. Its open and adaptive nature made it suitable for testing an evaluative approach rooted in complexity and intersectionality. The engagement with the case began after the project had formally concluded, which shaped both the scope and structure of our evaluation process. We approached it retrospectively, analysing its trajectory and outcomes to construct a critical and contextualised understanding of its impacts.

The case study reconstruction served as a foundational moment: by chronologically and thematically mapping the phases of the initiative, from its inception and partnership-building to the selection and engagement of participants, and finally to the public restitution of their spatial interventions, we could identify its key components and underlying goals. To reconstruct the development of the initiative and its broader context, we undertook a process of qualitative data collection and systematisation. This included an in-depth analysis of project documentation, namely official reports, public communications and visual material, as well as informal interviews with the project initiators. These materials offered insight into both the organisational dimension and the lived experiences of the young participants, allowing us to trace the project's trajectory and unpack the socio-political dynamics it engaged with.

2.2 The Methodological Workflow

The evaluative approach has been elaborated not to offer a fixed model or to extract replicable indicators. Rather, it sought to accompany the complexity of the initiative, acknowledging that its value lies as much in the process as in the results. By adopting an evolutionary perspective, we embrace the project's open nature while offering a structured yet flexible methodology to interrogate its outcomes (Fig. 1).

Starting from the above premise, the analysis proceeded through three interconnected phases:

1) *Analysis of the Case Study*: reconstructed the initiative's development through interviews and document analysis, which allowed us to situate the project within its institutional and socio-spatial context and to foreground the voices of its young protagonists.
2) *Constructing an Evaluative Lens*: articulated the theoretical framework underpinning our evaluation, drawing on four interrelated lenses: feminist urbanism, participatory design, intersectionality, and spatial justice. These perspectives enabled us to make sense of the project not only in terms of its procedural innovation but also through the power relations it sought to shift and the spatial imaginaries it activated.
3) *Mechanism, Criteria and Upscaling*: applied the evaluative framework to assess the project's capacity for transformation. Importantly, the criteria used were not drawn from pre-established models but were instead developed in response to the specific trajectory and character of GMtC! project.

As we reconstructed the project's evolution and defined its theoretical framing, key areas of analysis emerged organically, such as intersectionality, the depth of youth participation, and the spatial dimensions of transformation. These criteria were shaped through an iterative dialogue between the material collected and the conceptual lenses we adopted, allowing us to situate the project within broader discussions of feminist urban practices and intersectional empowerment.

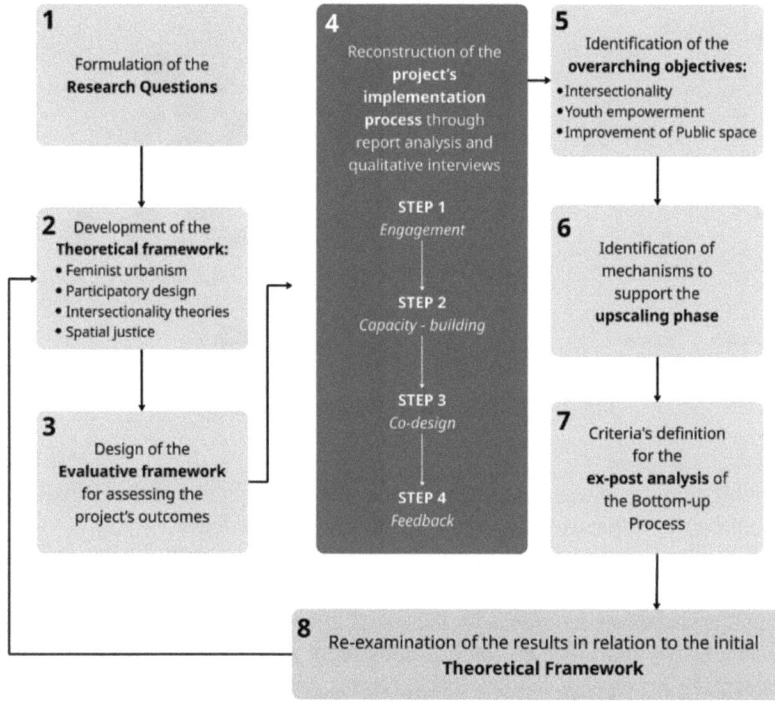

Fig. 1. The evaluation problem setting.

3 Results

3.1 Analysis of the Case Study

The evaluation started with the reconstruction of the entire project's process, both in chronological terms and its activities, starting from the municipal call to the analysis carried out by the associations at the end of the event.

The "Girls Make the City!" (https://girlsmakethecity.com/) project was conceived in response to a call for proposals launched by the Municipality of Brussels in 2021, within the framework of the "Equal Brussels" program (Fig. 2).

The call aimed to support local initiatives promoting gender equality and social inclusion through innovative approaches to urban transformation. The project, developed by the two associations of ZIJkant and Wetopia, focused on adolescent girls as both subjects and agents of urban change, intending to create a participatory pathway that linked everyday urban experiences with feminist and spatial practices. The initial design of the project reflected a deep awareness of the barriers young women face in accessing and appropriating public space. As outlined in the project proposal and reiterated in several interviews with organisers, the approach was intentionally process-oriented and grounded in feminist pedagogical principles. Rather than focusing on fixed outputs, the project prioritised relationships, collective learning, and the empowerment of participants through creative and critical engagement with their urban environment.

Fig. 2. The "Girls Make the City!" manifesto.

From this analysis, it was possible to identify four main phases of the GMtC! Project: 1) Engagement; 2) Capacity-building; 3) Co-design; 4) Feedback.

The first step involved outreach and recruitment, conducted in collaboration with local partners already active in the Marolles neighborhood. These included youth centers, schools and associations familiar with the social dynamics of the area. The goal was to create an inclusive and diverse group of adolescent girls between the ages of 14 and 18, representing a range of cultural backgrounds and life experiences. According to the facilitators, this initial phase was crucial for building trust and ensuring that the workshops would be perceived as a safe and welcoming space. The decision to work within familiar environments and to build existing relationships was seen as essential for reaching participants who might not otherwise engage in urban or civic initiatives. Once the group was formed, the project unfolded over several months through a series of weekly workshops and intensive sessions organized during school holidays.

The second part of the project sees the direct involvement of participants through different moments of activities. These workshops combined creative methods, urban analysis, and feminist consciousness-raising. Activities included collective mapping, photography, storytelling, and urban walks, through which the girls explored their everyday routes and spatial routines, identifying places where they felt safe, excluded, visible, or invisible. The practices served as a way of surfacing effective and embodied geographies, which often challenged dominant representations of public space. One facilitator described this phase as one of "mutual listening and emergence", where the adult team learned as much from the participants as the participants learned from the tools and methods provided. The data collected during this phase, including hand-drawn maps, annotated photographs, and recorded conversations, formed the basis for identifying spatial issues that mattered to the girls. These ranged from feelings of vulnerability in certain streets or squares to the lack of seating, lighting, or welcoming signs in spaces they frequented.

The third phase of the project focused on translating these observations into design proposals. Here, the co-design process was activated through workshops involving architects, designers, and artists. Participants were introduced to basic design tools and encouraged to envision how their ideas could take physical form. Instead of providing predefined solutions, facilitators supported the girls' own processes of ideation and experimentation. The co-design sessions emphasised collaboration, iteration, and play, allowing participants to explore various materials, forms, and messages. What emerged were diverse temporary and symbolic interventions, each shaped by the participants' priorities. Some proposals addressed spatial comfort, such as colourful benches or shade structures; others were more explicitly political, like signage that challenged gender norms or encouraged bystanders to reflect on the right to occupy space (Fig. 3). Throughout this phase, the girls retained a central role in decision-making. As one participant noted in a recorded reflection: "It was the first time someone asked me what I wanted in my neighbourhood and then helped me make it happen".

Fig. 3. Some photos from the event, taken during the workshop activities. Credits ZIJkant vzw (2022), "Girls Make The City!".

The final phase of the project involved realising and publicly presenting the co-designed interventions. With logistical and material support from the association and its partners, several proposals were implemented on-site in the Marolles neighbourhood. These interventions, though temporary, changed the spatial narrative of the locations where they were installed. Their visibility also sparked conversations among passersby, residents, and municipal stakeholders.

The project culminated in a public event organised as both a celebration and an advocacy platform. During this event, the girls showcased their work through exhibitions, guided walks, and performances. City officials, community members, and representatives from other organisations were invited to witness the outcomes and hear directly from the participants. For many girls, this moment represented a powerful affirmation of their ability to contribute to urban life. As reflected in multiple interviews, the event was a symbolic closure and a political act of reclaiming visibility and recognition in spaces from which they often felt excluded.

3.2 Constructing an Evaluative Lens

The second phase of the evaluation process was dedicated to understanding how the theoretical framework, grounded as mentioned before in intersectionality, youth empowerment and spatial transformation, could be translated into project-specific criteria that could lead us in building an evaluative framework. This required a reflexive effort to bridge the analytical framework previously outlined with the lived, situated experience of the initiative. Rather than applying a pre-established evaluative grip, we engaged in a synoptic process, constructing our evaluative lens by closely reading the workshop dynamics, participants' outputs and our role in shaping the project's direction. Unlike traditional evaluation processes where indicators are defined ex-ante, the objective was to construct an evaluative framework ex-post, aligning the analysis with previously elaborated theoretical dimensions.

This process did not involve measuring pre-defined standard outcomes, but rather interpreting the project's goal implicitly pursued and identifying the mechanisms through which they were articulated and enacted. The work focused on critically reading the project's materials and reconstructing a coherent evaluative structure that could serve both as a tool for analysing this specific case and as a possible contribution to a broader, feminist-informed methodology for evaluating youth-centred urban projects.

The reconstruction of the actions implemented within the GMtC! project made it possible to identify three primary objectives, through which the main expected impact dimensions will be determined: Intersectionality; Youth Empowerment; Public Space Improvement.

Intersectionality emerged first and foremost in the project's attention to inclusion. The decision to work with a group of adolescent girls from diverse social and cultural backgrounds in a neighbourhood marked by structural marginality positioned the project within a logic of addressing urban inequality. While the project did not explicitly articulate an intersectional agenda, we observed how participatory mapping, photo exploration and storytelling created multiple entry points for expression. These approaches offered participants a variety of modes through which to voice their experiences and perspectives, which we interpreted as a meaningful engagement with difference.

Youth empowerment, as a second axis, was inferred through the structure and evolution of the activities. The project transitioned from moments of facilitation to more open-ended creative processes in which the girls defined themes, made collective decisions and expressed critical views on their environment. This process suggested a shift in agency from adult-led guidance to youth-led exploration.

The third dimension, Public Space Improvement, was reconstructed through an analysis of how the girls reinterpreted and reimagined the spaces of their neighbourhood. The materials reveal a shift from conventional spatial representations to personal, affective and political readings of space. These readings made visible areas of exclusion or discomfort. The use of alternative mapping techniques, creative renaming of places and public displays of critique and hope contributed to a re-signification of urban space. Our evaluative lens included a criterion related to symbolic and experiential transformation of space, as expressed through these situated practices.

In this evaluation framework, the project became a fertile site for testing the applicability of our theoretical framework. Through this ex-post reconstruction, we propose a

Ex-Post Evaluation Framework for Intersectional Bottom-Up Regeneration Process 415

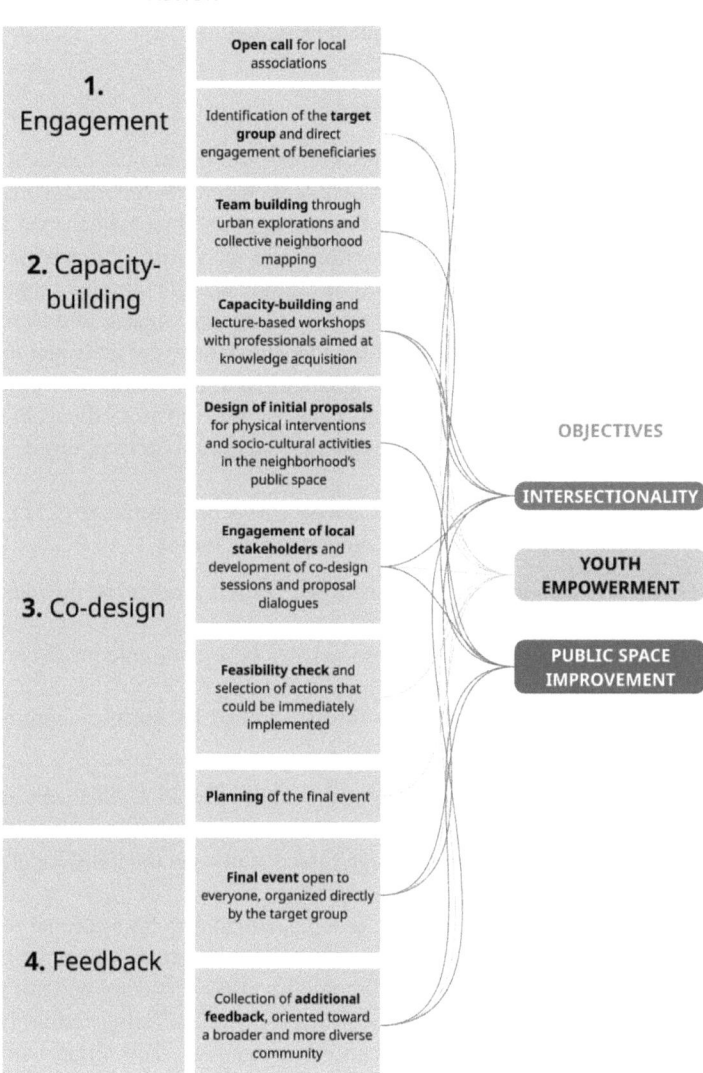

Fig. 4. Descriptive diagram of the relationship between the actions implemented in the GMtC! project and the objectives pursued.

model of evaluation that centres process, values plurality, and recognises the importance of contextual and relational dynamics in assessing urban co-creation projects involving young people. This retrospective construction of evaluative criteria required a delicate balance between remaining faithful to the specificity of the project and interpreting it through a broader theoretical lens. Our role was not to judge the project's success based on external standards, but to highlight how it enacted, consciously or not, principles aligned with feminist urban and youth-centred frameworks. By doing so, we aimed to not only assess the project's impact but also contribute to the development of an evaluative methodology that is both critical and situated.

3.3 Mechanism, Criteria and Upscaling

Building upon the reconstruction of the project and the theoretical-practical dialogue established through our evaluative lens, this final section outlines the criteria that emerged through the analysis and reflects on their broader applicability. Rather than a discrete list detached from the lived process, these criteria are the results of a continuous interplay between the mechanism observed in the case study and the principles underpinning our theoretical framework. Their formulation is inherently situated and retrospective, constructed to illuminate how certain values and dynamics were activated throughout the project. The processual nature of our evaluation led to the identification of six interconnected criteria. Each encapsulates a mechanism observed from the analysis of the project while also pointing toward such dynamics that could be recognized, supported and scaled in future initiatives.

With reference to the previously introduced CMO configuration (CIT), the constructed framework reveals three primary dimensions of inquiry:

- Context (C): corresponds to the analysis of the GMtC! project and the identification of its key actions.
- Mechanisms (M): are deduced from the interplay between implemented actions and the identified operational contexts.
- Outcomes (O): represent the impacts directly linked to specific combinations of mechanisms and contexts.

Figure 3 depicts the relationship between the eight inferred mechanisms and the six criteria used to describe and evaluate the generated outcomes. For each criterion, the associated mechanism combinations are highlighted, and potential indicators for ex-post measurement of the GMtC! project are proposed.

Active engagement of a diverse target group emerged as a foundational dimension. The project's deliberate outreach to adolescent girls from different cultural, linguistic and socio-economic backgrounds in the Marolles neighbourhood exemplified this principle. Here, inclusivity was not only demographic but experiential, offering various modalities of expression to accommodate diverse forms of engagement. This aligns with feminist calls for plural forms of participation that recognise embodied and affective experiences [18]. The proposed indicator is a composite one: it considers not only the number and background of participants but also their active involvement across phases. From a policy perspective, this invites institutions to design programs that go beyond representation and actively cultivate conditions for differentiated participation to flourish.

Collective Re-signification of Public Space captures how symbolic and material urban transformation can be enacted through collaborative reflection and situated creativity. The project facilitated a shift in how participants perceived and narrated their neighbourhood, culminating in temporary interventions that redefined shared spaces. Indicators such as the number of micro-interventions and events can help trace the material footprint of these changes, but the deeper value lies in how participants re-imagined the urban landscape in ways that resonated with their needs and desires. This echoes feminist urban scholarship that frames space as both a physical and political construct, constantly redefined through practices of occupation and making [1, 4]. Scaling this criterion requires supporting the use of creative, feminist and youth-driven tools that emphasise spatial narrative and agency.

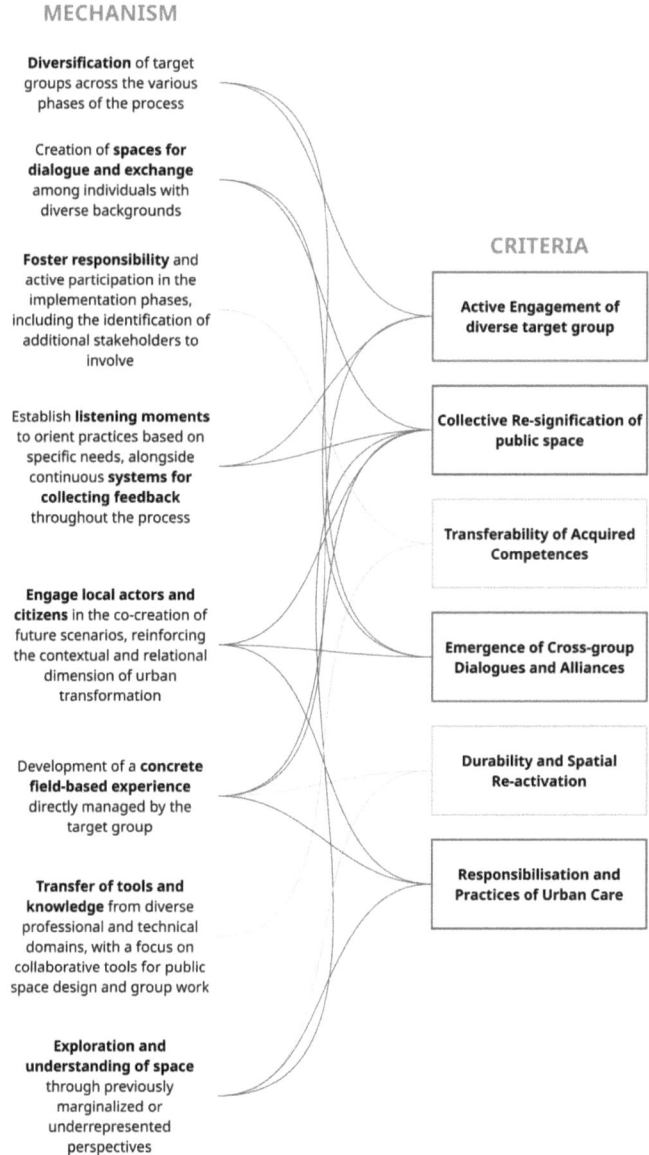

Fig. 5. Descriptive diagram of the relationship between the interpreted mechanisms of change and the six criteria identified for the ex-post impact evaluation.

Transferability of Acquired Competences points to how the project generated skills and forms of confidence that extended beyond its own timeline. Through interviews with participants, we could trace how some of the girls reactivated their learning in other contexts, be it school, civic engagement, or new creative expressions. While not all outcomes are immediately visible or quantifiable, this speaks to the potential of such projects to build longer-term capacities [18]. Institutions might consider incorporating follow-up moments into similar initiatives to track and support this diffusion over time.

"Emergence of Cross-group Dialogues and Alliances" is less a stated objective and could be more an unexpected outcome. Through shared activities and public presentation, the project fostered interactions between adolescents, community members, and professionals, some of which could led to the formation of informal networks or ongoing collaborations. This criterion emphasises the importance of relational infrastructure and the potential of temporary projects to seed more durable coalitions. Feminist and community planning literatures underline the importance of these alliances as forms of mutual learning and collective action [4]. In an upscaling perspective, municipalities could explore ways to support these emergent networks beyond the funding cycle.

"Durability and Spatial Re-activation" reflect on the legacy of the project in spatial terms: whether and how the spaces involved remain animated after the intervention. While the project's interventions were temporary by design, some sites continued to be used for informal gatherings or inspired further events. This suggests that even ephemeral acts of re-appropriation can generate longer-term resonance. Indicators might include continued activity in project spaces or new uses emerging in their wake. For future programs, this underscores the value of lightweight yet visible interventions capable of leaving an imprint on spatial practices [4].

"Responsabilisation and Practices of Urban Care" refers to the way participants engaged in direct actions of care toward their environment, from cleaning and decorating spaces to initiating conversations about their maintenance and meaning. These acts, while small, repositioned the girls not just as users but as co-stewards of public space. In terms of policy, embedding such practices in participatory urbanism can reshape the roles young people are allowed to play within governance frameworks, moving from passive recipients to active city makers [18].

While these criteria were constructed ex-post, their clarity and relevance highlight the potential of employing such a framework from the beginning. An ex-ante application, co-developed with participants, would allow future projects to align intentions, adapt methods, and reflect more systematically throughout their development. This would not only support more responsive evaluation but also deepen participants' agency in shaping the project itself [18]. In terms of generalisation, these criteria are not presented as universal metrics, but as generative heuristic tools to support reflection and adaptation across diverse contexts. Their strength lies in their openness and rootedness in situated practices. As such, they are particularly suited to contexts where urban interventions are shaped by complex social dynamics and where participatory processes aim to foreground the voices of marginalised youth.

4 Conclusions

This work has explored the "Girls Make the City!" project through the lens of an ex-post evaluation, highlighting its capacity to foster inclusive urban regeneration by centring intersectionality, youth empowerment, and participatory spatial transformation. Although the absence of an ex-ante evaluative framework presents limitations, the criteria constructed during the analysis, derived from the project documentation and participants' narratives, enabled critical reflection on the outcomes achieved. The Brussels iteration of the initiative demonstrates how targeted, community-driven actions can stimulate both symbolic and material change in the urban landscape, empowering young women to co-create futures. The project affirms that investing in the voices and agency of youth, particularly young women, is not only a matter of inclusion but also a strategic entry point to rethinking the city as a space of equity, identity, and collective belonging. In this sense, it directly answers our first research question (kq1): addressing intersectionality and youth empowerment is essential in urban regeneration because it fosters more grounded, transformative, and socially just spatial practices.

This research also offers actionable insights for policymakers and urban practitioners by critically reviewing and reconstructing evaluative criteria. It reinforces the idea that gender-sensitive urban regeneration is most effective when developed as a situated process, responsive to the unique socio-spatial dynamics of each place. The evaluation does not attempt to universalise its model but instead illustrates how feminist and intersectional approaches can be locally rooted while maintaining a transferable methodology. The cautious optimism around generalizability stems not from assumptions of scalability but from the replicability of its core values and tools, particularly the participatory methods that encourage deep engagement between youth, institutions, and urban space.

Furthermore, the research highlights the importance of establishing an adaptive evaluation framework from the outset. Participatory design is already widely recognised and applied in urban practice, and its inclusion here further supports its validity. However, our findings emphasise that the ability to assess the effectiveness, especially the transformative potential, of such interventions depends on the early definition of evaluative criteria. This directly addresses our second research question (kq2): evaluation practices can support more inclusive transformation processes when they are co-constructed, iterative, and sensitive to context. Ex-ante evaluation frameworks would enhance the ability to track impact over time and provide clearer indicators for replication and upscaling in future projects.

"Girls Make the City!" thus serves as a compelling case for how inclusive, feminist practices can act as a lever for urban regeneration. While further testing and adaptation are necessary to explore its broader applicability, the project exemplifies how youth empowerment can be meaningfully integrated into urban strategies. The small scale of the intervention and reliance on self-reported data constitute limitations, but the results already indicate a hopeful trajectory, one in which inclusive design and evolutionary evaluation frameworks become foundational to urban transformation. As cities continue to evolve, the lessons drawn from this initiative underscore the potential for participatory evaluation not only to measure change but to actively shape it.

Acknowledgements and Contributions. This research is an advancement of the master's thesis developed by Renata Boeri within the Urban Regeneration and Social Innovation (U.RISE) program at IUAV University of Venice, in collaboration with the independent research collective "Sex and The City. The research was subsequently further developed in collaboration with the Department of Architecture at the University of Naples Federico II.

The research was jointly framed and developed by the authors: Conceptualisation, R.B., P.Z., and M.C.; Methodology, P.Z. and M.C.; Fieldwork and Data Collection, R.B.; Formal Analysis, R.B.; Original Draft Preparation, R.B. and P.Z.; Review and Editing, R.B., P.Z. and M.C.; Supervision and Final Review, M.C. All authors have read and agreed to the published version of the manuscript.

References

1. Lefebvre, H.: Writings on Cities. Blackwell, Oxford (1996)
2. Brenner, N., Schmid, C.: Planetary urbanization. In: Gandy, M. (ed.) Urban Constellations, pp. 10–13. Jovis Verlag, Berlin (2012)
3. Secchi, B.: La città dei ricchi e la città dei poveri. Laterza, Roma, Bari (2017)
4. Soja, E.W.: Seeking Spatial Justice. University of Minnesota Press, Minneapolis (2010)
5. UN-Habitat: Global Public Space Toolkit: From Global Principles to Local Policies and Practice. UN-Habitat (2015)
6. Jagori, UN-Habitat, UN-Women: Building Safe and Inclusive Cities for Women: A Practical Guide. Jagori, New Delhi (2011)
7. Bailey, A., Otsuki, K.: Inclusive Cities and Global Urban Transformation: Infrastructures. Intersectionalities, and Sustainable Development. Springer, Singapore (2023). https://doi.org/10.1007/978-981-97-7521-7
8. Oberhauser, A.M., Johnston-Anumonwo, I. (eds.): Global Perspectives on Gender and Space: Engaging Feminism and Development. Routledge, London (2014)
9. Crenshaw, K.: Mapping the margins: intersectionality, identity politics, and violence against women of color. Stanf. Law Rev. **43**(6), 1241–1299 (1991). https://doi.org/10.2307/1229039
10. Sutton, S.E.: The Paradox of Urban Space: Inequality and Transformation in Marginalized Communities. Palgrave Macmillan, London (2011)
11. Kern, L.: Feminist City: Claiming Space in a Man-Made World. Verso, London (2020)
12. Franck, K.A., Paxson, L.: Women and the Everyday City: Public Space in San Francisco, 1890–1915. SUNY Press, Albany (2007)
13. Sánchez de Madariaga, I., Roberts, M. (eds.): Fair Shared Cities: The Impact of Gender Planning in Europe. Ashgate, Farnham (2013)
14. Cornwall, A., Edwards, J.: Introduction: negotiating empowerment. IDS Bull. **47**(1), 1–9 (2016). https://doi.org/10.19088/1968-2016.100
15. Fenster, T.: The right to the gendered city: different formations of belonging in everyday life. J. Gend. Stud. **14**(3), 217–231 (2005). https://doi.org/10.1080/09589230500264109
16. Sanders, E.B.N., Stappers, P.J.: Co-creation and the new landscapes of design. CoDesign **4**(1), 5–18 (2008). https://doi.org/10.1080/15710880701875068
17. Cerreta, M., Daldanise, G., La Rocca, L., Panaro, S.: Triggering active communities for cultural creative cities: the "Hack the City" play ReCH mission in the Salerno historic centre (Italy). Sustainability **13**(21), 11877 (2021). https://doi.org/10.3390/su132111877
18. Cerreta, M., La Rocca, L.: Urban regeneration processes and social impact: a literature review to explore the role of evaluation. In: Gervasi, O., et al. (eds.) ICCSA 2021. LNCS, vol. 12954, pp. 167–182. Springer, Cham (2021). https://doi.org/10.1007/978-3-030-86979-3_13

19. ZIJkant & Wetopia: Girls Make the City! Final Project Report, Brussels (2022)
20. Nesti, G.: Co-production for innovation: the urban living lab experience. Policy Soc. **37**(3), 310–325 (2018). https://doi.org/10.1080/14494035.2017.1374695
21. Sala, S., Ciuffo, B., Nijkamp, P.: A systemic framework for sustainability assessment. Ecol. Econ. **119**, 314–325 (2015)
22. Sánchez, L.E., Mitchell, R.: Conceptualizing impact assessment as a learning process. Environ. Impact Assess. Rev. **62**, 195–204 (2017). https://doi.org/10.1016/j.eiar.2016.06.001
23. Zizzania, P., Muccio, E., Sacco, S., Cerreta, M.: Prediction and uncertainty in social impact evaluation: a classification framework. In: Calabrò, F., Madureira, L., Morabito, F.C., Piñeira Mantiñán, M.J. (eds.) NMP 2024. LNNS, vol. 1186, pp. 49–58. Springer, Cham (2024). https://doi.org/10.1007/978-3-031-74679-6_5
24. Belcher, B., Rasmussen, K., Kemshaw, M.E., Zornes, D.: A refined method for theory-based evaluation of the societal impacts of research. Res. Eval. (2020)
25. Hivos: Hivos Theory of Change Guidelines: Theory of Change Thinking in Practice. Hivos (2015). https://hivos.org/document/hivos-theory-of-change/
26. Patton, M.Q.: Developmental Evaluation: Applying Complexity Concepts to Enhance Innovation and Use. Guilford Press, New York (2011)
27. Ellerani, P., Barca, D.: Valutazione narrativa e trasformativa: co-costruzione di comunità e di apprendimento. Educ. Sci. Soc. **2**, 17–32 (2021). https://doi.org/10.3280/ess2-2021oa12395
28. Stern, E., Stame, N., Mayne, J., Forss, K., Davies, R., Befani, B.: Broadening the range of designs and methods for impact evaluations: report of a study commissioned by the department for international development (DFID). Working Paper 38, DFID, London (2012)
29. Grieco, B., Somma, M., Raiola, M.L., Sacco, S., Zizzania, P., Cerreta, M.: A decision support system for cultural and territorial infrastructures: a place-based and community-driven strategy in inner Italy. In: Gervasi, O., Murgante, B., Garau, C., Taniar, D., Rocha, A.M.A.C., Faginas Lago, M.N. (eds.) ICCSA 2024. LNCS, vol. 14820, pp. 373–387. Springer, Cham (2024). https://doi.org/10.1007/978-3-031-65285-1_24
30. Rogers, P.J.: Using programme theory to evaluate complicated and complex aspects of interventions. Evaluation **14**(1), 29–48 (2008). https://doi.org/10.1177/1356389007084674
31. Preskill, H., Parkhurst, M., Splansky Juster, J.: Learning and evaluation in the collective impact context. Collect. Impact Forum (2014)
32. Funnell, S.C., Rogers, P.J.: Purposeful Program Theory: Effective Use of Theories of Change and Logic Models. Wiley, San Francisco (2011)
33. Pawson, R.: The Science of Evaluation: A Realist Manifesto. Sage Publications Ltd., London (2013). https://doi.org/10.4135/9781473913820
34. Stern, E.: Philosophies and types of evaluation research. In: The Foundations of Evaluation and Impact Research. Third Report on Vocational Training Research in Europe: Background Report. Cedefop, Luxembourg (2004)
35. Stame, N.: Valutazione Pluralista. Franco Angeli, Milano (2016)
36. Del Rey, A.: La Tirannia della Valutazione. Elèuthera, Milano (2018)
37. Zamagni, S., Venturi, P., Rago, S.: Valutare l'impatto sociale: la questione della misurazione nelle imprese sociali. Impresa Sociale **6**, 77–97 (2015)
38. Stame, N.: Tra Possibilismo e Valutazione: Judith Tendler e Albert Hirschman. Rubbettino, Soveria Mannelli (2022)
39. Santos, F.M.: A positive theory of social entrepreneurship. J. Bus. Ethics **111**, 335–351 (2012). https://doi.org/10.1007/s10551-012-1413-4
40. Vicari Haddock, S., Moulaert, F. (eds.): Rigenerare la Città. Pratiche di Innovazione Sociale nelle Città Europee. Il Mulino, Bologna (2009). ISBN 978-88-15-11550-8
41. Cerreta, M., Panaro, S., Poli, G.: A spatial decision support system for multifunctional landscape assessment: a transformative resilience perspective for vulnerable inland areas. Sustainability **13**, 2748 (2021). https://doi.org/10.3390/su13052748

42. Cerreta, M., Panaro, S., Cannatella, D.: Multidimensional spatial decision-making process: local shared values in action. In: Murgante, B., et al. (eds.) ICCSA 2012, Part II. LNCS, vol. 7334, pp. 54–70. Springer, Heidelberg (2012). https://doi.org/10.1007/978-3-642-31075-1_5
43. Venturi, P.: La Valutazione d'impatto sociale come pratica 'trasformativa'. Short Paper 19/2019, AICCON (2019)
44. Davies, H.T.O., Nutley, S.M., Smith, P.C. (eds.): What Works? The Policy Press, Bristol (2000)

Music Meets Sustainability: First Steps Toward a Framework for Greener Festivals

Agnese Baldoni[1], Laura Calisi[2], Salvatore De Pascalis[2](✉), Francesca Falconi[2], Matteo Napodano[2], and Giacomo Seratoni Gualdoni[2]

[1] Politecnico di Torino, Corso Duca degli Abruzzi 24, 10129 Torino, Italy
s330655@studenti.polito.it
[2] Politecnico di Milano, Piazza Leonardo da Vinci 32, 20133 Milano, Italy
{laura.calisi,salvatore.depascalis,francesca.falconi,
matteo.napodano,giacomo.seratoni}@mail.polimi.it

Abstract. Given their significant environmental impact, the increasing emphasis on sustainability has become a crucial factor in the organization of music festivals. These large-scale events consume substantial energy, generate waste, and contribute to carbon emissions, necessitating the adoption of sustainable practices. While some festivals have implemented sustainability measures, there is a lack of standardized, publicly accessible frameworks that provide quantitative metrics to evaluate and enhance sustainability performance. This study addresses this gap by developing guidelines for a comprehensive sustainability framework tailored to music festivals.

The proposed framework is based on existing sustainability initiatives and case study findings from the 2024 MI AMI Festival in Milan (Italy). It employs a data-driven methodology that defines impact categories, including resource consumption, waste management, food and beverage, transportation, and community engagement. The research methodology includes a literature review, structured interviews with festival staff and artists, audience surveys, and expert consultations to grasp real insights and tangible data to build the framework. Preliminary findings reveal a strong demand for sustainable festival practices among stakeholders, emphasizing the need for clear evaluation criteria. The guidelines are designed to facilitate transparency, benchmarking, and continuous improvement in sustainability performance. By providing festival organizers with a practical tool to monitor sustainability performance, this framework will reduce the environmental footprint and promote the broader goal of integrating sustainability practices within the live music industry. Practices within the live music industry.

Keywords: Sustainability Framework · Music Festival Sustainability · Sustainability Metrics · Environmental Impact Assessment

1 Introduction

1.1 Sustainability in Music Festivals

Sustainability has become a global policy priority, reflected in initiatives like the United Nations' Sustainable Development Goals (SDGs), the European Green Deal, and national climate action plans. These frameworks emphasize sustainability as essential for addressing climate change, resource scarcity, and social inequality through coordinated, long-term governance and systemic transformation. Consequently, this topic has become a critical focus in the event and entertainment industry, driven by increasing awareness of environmental degradation, resource depletion, and large-scale gatherings' social and economic impacts [15]. Events such as concerts, exhibitions, and music festivals consume vast resources. The events industry is now being called upon to implement sustainability strategies that reduce negative environmental impacts and contribute positively to the communities and economies they engage with [15]. According to Getz [9], events serve as both a source of cultural and economic value and a challenge in terms of sustainability, requiring organizers to balance economic viability with environmental and social responsibility.

Music festivals present significant sustainability challenges. Large-scale festivals require temporary infrastructure, extensive transportation networks, and high energy consumption to power lighting, sound systems, and digital technologies [6]. Additionally, they generate substantial waste, including single-use plastics, food waste, and discarded promotional materials. Studies have highlighted that music festivals can contribute to carbon emissions through attendee travel, energy use, and waste generation, making sustainability an essential consideration for their long-term viability [13].

The growing emphasis on sustainability across industries responds to global environmental concerns and the need for more responsible resource management [4].

The positive impact that these kinds of events can generate by improving social awareness and expanding sustainability culture among attendees is immense and increasingly recognized [1]. Nevertheless, festival organizers often encounter significant barriers in implementing sustainability measures. Financial constraints, lack of clear guidelines, and difficulties securing sustainable suppliers are among the most cited challenges [8]. Smaller or independent festivals, in particular, struggle to invest in green technologies and infrastructure, limiting their ability to adopt sustainability initiatives effectively. Moreover, festival attendees' behavior plays a critical role in achieving sustainability goals, yet research indicates that many festivalgoers prioritize convenience over environmental responsibility, making behavioral interventions essential [1]. Festivals can be platforms for engaging audiences in sustainability initiatives, from waste reduction programs to renewable energy usage and carbon offset schemes. Major festivals such as Glastonbury in the UK and Roskilde Festival in Denmark have pioneered sustainability efforts by banning single-use plastics, promoting eco-friendly transport options, and integrating renewable energy solutions [6].

Moreover, sustainability frameworks such as ISO 20121, a global standard for sustainable event management, provide guidelines that help festivals implement structured and accountable sustainability measures [16]. Such initiatives ensure that sustainability becomes an integral part of the festival industry rather than an after-thought. Integrating green technologies, circular economy models, and sustainable event design will be crucial for future developments in the music festival sector.

1.2 MI AMI BEATs Project

The MI AMI BEATs Project was developed within the Alta Scuola Politecnica (ASP), an interdisciplinary honors program jointly organized by Politecnico di Milano and Politecnico di Torino. As part of ASP's 20th cycle, the BEATs Project (Better Equity Actions for Tomorrow's Sustainability) focuses on enhancing sustainability practices within the music festival industry, using the MI AMI Festival in Milan as a case study. The project aims to identify key sustainability challenges in festival operations, including waste management, energy efficiency, and audience engagement. By collaborating with festival organizers and stakeholders such as staff members, artists, and event managers, the project seeks to develop practical solutions that can be implemented at MI AMI and serve as a model for other festivals in Italy and internationally. The practical value of the MI AMI BEATs Project lies in its potential to influence the broader music festival landscape by providing actionable insights and tools to promote sustainable practices. This aligns with ASP's commitment to addressing real-world problems through multidisciplinary collaboration and innovation.

1.3 Paper Structure

The paper is structured in 4 Sections. After an introduction focused on discussing the strengths and criticalities of music festivals under the sustainability perspective, Sect. 2 reviews existing literature on sustainability in music festivals, highlighting key challenges and gaps. Section 3 details the research methodology, including data collection, stakeholder engagement, and framework development. The study presents findings from the MI AMI Festival case study, analyzing sustainability indicators and industry best practices. Based on these insights, a comprehensive sustainability framework is proposed in Sect. 3.2, outlining evaluation criteria and practical implementation steps. Section 4 presents a conclusion discussing the framework's potential applications, validation process, and future developments, emphasizing its role in promoting sustainable practices within the music festival industry.

2 Research Gap and Objectives

2.1 Research Gap

Sustainability has become a crucial consideration in the organization and operation of music festivals, with various private and public entities proposing frameworks to enhance environmental, social, and economic responsibility [6, 14]. However, a significant gap remains in the availability of a quantitative, publicly accessible sustainability framework that can be replicated and used in different contexts. While existing initiatives offer guidelines and principles, they often lack clear, objective, and measurable methodologies that allow festivals to independently assess their sustainability performance [7, 18, 19]. These frameworks tend to be qualitative or require proprietary assessments, limiting their applicability for festivals seeking a transparent and standardized approach. For example, the DGTL festival (one of the most important music festivals held in the Netherlands) does not provide an actual framework but presents all the initiatives and practices they are pursuing; although it is a great example of sustainability, it is hard to replicate. Furthermore Legambiente, the most important Italian environmentalist association, sponsored a sustainability focused festival named Festambiente that unfortunately lacks measurable indexes and figures that can be applied and calculated by other event organizers. The absence of a publicly available framework that provides an autonomous, data-driven scoring system creates a big challenge for festival organizers who wish to benchmark their sustainability efforts objectively and systematically.

2.2 Objectives

This study aims to develop guidelines for a comprehensive sustainability framework for music festivals that provide quantitative and standardized metrics. The framework will be built using insights from sustainability reports by A Greener Future, one of the biggest non-profit companies aimed at helping venue and event organizers to reduce environmental impacts, as well as on-field research conducted at the 2024 MI AMI Festival in Milan combined with expert opinions and articles closely related to the topic. This mixed-method approach will ensure that the framework is grounded in industry best practices and real-world festival operations. By establishing a data-driven and replicable scoring method, this study will provide festival organizers with a practical and transparent tool to autonomously assess and improve their sustainability performance, thereby promoting accountability and driving continuous improvement across the industry.

3 Methodology

The development of a methodology for evaluating the sustainability of a music event necessitates a multifaceted and systematic evaluation of the event itself, as well as a comprehension of the underlying processes and mechanisms.

The proposed framework has been designed to provide a comprehensive evaluation tool that each festival must independently apply to its own event if it chooses to adopt. This tool assesses the festival's overall sustainability, assigning it an aggregate sustainability score. Based on this score, the event will be classified into one performance tier, with lower tiers indicating poorer sustainability performance. The framework is thus multicriteria, based on Multi-Attribute Value Theory (MAVT) [3], as the sustainability field demands, given the numerous and frequently conflictual factors to be considered.

The final score is derived from aggregating distinct sub-scores attributed to various impact categories. These categories include Energy, Materials and Waste, Food and Beverage, Travel and Transport, Water, Community and Biodiversity. Each category is evaluated using specific indicators, which are standardized with value functions, and they are assigned weights based on their relative importance and impact on overall sustainability. In particular, specific weights will be given according to the latest report of A Greener Future of 2024, in which the relative contribution of each impact category on the overall emissions is defined, resulting from the analysis of 40 different festivals in 11 different countries. For instance, it emerges that the transport category has the biggest share of emissions, accounting for 41.4% of the total, followed by food & beverage

(31.9%) [2]. Lastly, the final score is determined by applying the Weighted Linear Sum (WLS).

In this Section, the sequence of steps that were followed to design the framework will be discussed. Figure 1 provides a graphical representation of these steps, to be considered sequential, where continuous arrows are for those steps already executed, while dotted arrows indicate a step that has yet to be achieved.

The methodology employed is articulated as follows:

1. Data collection.
2. Framework development.
3. Validation and Diffusion.

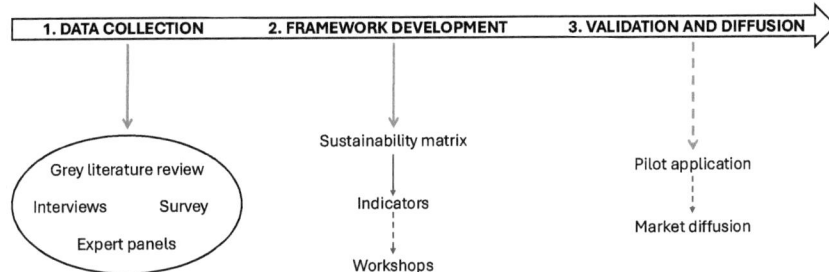

Fig. 1. Framework development process.

It is evident then that the interaction with the festival selected for the case study, MIAMI, was instrumental in catalyzing the progression and facilitation of the work.

The MI AMI Festival,[1] Musica Importante A Milano, organized by Better Days s.r.l which has been held annually since 2005 during the last weekend of May in Milan, exclusively features Italian artists from the independent and alternative musical sphere, irrespective of musical genre, with a meticulous selection process encompassing both musical and cultural dimensions. The 2024 edition featured approximately 100 artists across 5 different stages, attracting 25,000 attendees. Based on the presented evidence, the festival has been evaluated as in a state of "health", demonstrating consistent growth and ongoing development. This finding positions the festival as the most suitable case study for analysis within the context of the Milan metropolitan area.

The festival's commitment to sustainability, as reflected in its organizers' dedication to delve deeply into the subject, has been pivotal. This commitment has enhanced direct interaction and the exchange of information with individuals involved in the operational processes of a music event. Consequently, the process of collecting relevant and valuable data has undergone a considerable acceleration, along with the easing of access to the festival sites before, during, and following the event for site surveys.

The following approach entailed integrating and complementing practical and field observations with theoretical and literary findings.

---

[1] https://www.miamifestival.it/2025/index.php.

3.1 Data Collection

The data collection process was initiated with a review of grey literature on existing frameworks and best practices in music festivals. A comprehensive overview of the acquired information is provided in a companion paper.

The following interviews and surveys were submitted to festival stakeholders. The MI AMI 2024 provided an opportunity to carry out on-field research to collect information about the event's sustainability, with this goal being approached from multiple perspectives. Specifically, three viewpoints were of particular interest: those of the staff, the artists, and the attendees. During the three days of the events, interviews were conducted with artists and staff, while a survey was administered to the audience. The decision to differentiate the data collection approach was influenced by two primary factors: the distinct nature of the interview questions and the varying time availability of the participants. These factors will be discussed in the following sections.

Additionally, a series of meetings were held with sustainability experts, including those with a primary focus on environmental issues and those with a specialized understanding of music events. These sessions aimed to delve into specific areas of interest. For instance, an ornithologist was consulted to assess the potential acoustic impact of the event on local birdlife. Two separate meetings were conducted with green certification managers from Triadi [20] and Ecoevents [7] to gain insight into their methodologies, strengths, and challenges. Triadi assisted in understanding the importance of involving local actors in the decision and the design process, from the citizens to the supply chain, as they are directly affected by the implemented measures. Ecoevents offered insights into various potential solutions that a festival could adopt to enhance its sustainability, along with an overview of their framework and the process which led to its development.

Interviews

During the festival weekend of 24–26 May 2024, interviews were conducted with all those who expressed interest and availability. Specifically, 30 individuals were interviewed, including 13 artists and 17 staff members.

The prompt focused on four primary categories, for a total number of questions posed of approximately 15:

1. General information: Here, the aim was to gather background information on the interviewees, their role in the festival, and their professional experience to better understand their perspective.
2. The MI AMI festival: This category explores the interviewee's experience with the festival, their level of involvement, and their impressions of the event. Additionally, it explores feedback on how the festival compares to others.
3. Sustainability: Here, the interviewee's awareness of the festival's sustainability efforts is assessed. Their opinion on existing initiatives is investigated, as well as potential areas of improvement. Moreover, environmental challenges related to their profession are identified, if any.
4. Suggestions: Lastly, the intention is to gather recommendations on how the festival can enhance its social and environmental sustainability. Best practices from other festivals are sought.

The responses provided were instrumental in identifying significant critical issues, exploring potential solutions, and gathering suggestions. For instance, 62.7% of the interviewees requested an increase in recycling points, while 57.7% suggested exclusive use of biodegradable materials. Artists, conversely, noted the absence of waste sorting in the dressing rooms. Other salient points included green mobility in terms of agreements with local transport authorities and car-sharing companies and a preference for more sustainable food and beverages.

Survey
The survey was submitted in two ways: initially, at the festival, and subsequently, via the internet, due to its dissemination on the festival's social media platforms and the project's Instagram profile. The total number of responses collected was 718, corresponding to 3% of the total number of attendees. It was challenging to capture the public's attention, and they were often reluctant to fill in a form.

The survey was structured into five distinct sections, enumerated below, comprising 25 questions, some of which permitted open responses and others closed-ended responses.

1. Socio-Demographics: A range of demographic and socio-economic information about the attendee is collected, including age, gender, occupation, and place of residence. This helps define the audience profile.
2. Behavioral habits: This section explores the attendees' knowledge about environmental issues, willingness to pay more for sustainable products, participation in sustainability-related events, eco-friendly habits, and dietary choices.
3. Festival participation: The aim here is to understand the reasons for attending the festival, how attendees discovered it, their level of participation, and their feedback on potential improvements. Additionally, the social impact of the event on the city of Milan is investigated.
4. Perception of the Sustainability of the Festival: The objective is to evaluate attendees' perceptions of the festival's sustainability efforts, their awareness of existing green initiatives, and their satisfaction with them. Also, they're asked about other festivals that are considered more sustainable and what their best practices are.
5. Mobility: An assessment of the transportation habits of attendees is conducted. The data collected includes how they arrived at the festival and their propensity to use sustainable mobility options such as carpooling.

The findings revealed a notable interest among the audience in topics related to sustainability, as evidenced by their responses. For instance, more than 63% of the participants were willing to pay a premium for tickets in exchange for a more sustainable festival. Suggestions proposed by the participants included enhancing recycling amenities, incorporating biodegradable materials, and promoting sustainable merchandise.

Generally, the staff members, artists, and attendees appeared to share a congruent vision of the festival's sustainability, with their comments and contributions reflecting a shift toward this common perspective.

3.2 Framework Development

The development of the framework followed the second phase illustrated in Fig. 1. The initial step involved creating a sustainability matrix to identify the most common criteria and parameters used to assess sustainability in music festivals, as well as in existing frameworks and protocols. Once these criteria are established, it becomes more straightforward and more systematic to determine which can be transformed into robust and objective indicators for the framework.

This indicator definition phase will also be supported by on-field research conducted during the MI AMI 2024 festival, allowing for alignment between the theoretical matrix and the practical realities observed on-site.

Finally, once the set of indicators is defined, they will undergo a validation phase through dedicated workshops involving experts and key stakeholders from the festival sector, ensuring their relevance, reliability, and applicability.

Matrix

Given the analysis previously performed the six dimensions of sustainability mentioned in Sect. 3 (i.e. Energy, Materials and Waste, Food and Beverage, Travel and Transport, Water, Community and Biodiversity) can be considered as the main drivers to better investigate relevant protocols, frameworks, reports, and case studies of recognized sustainable festivals to explore how these topics have been measured. By analyzing the intersections between these dimensions and the selected references, we can determine which best practices or criteria each report, framework, and festival adopts for each specific sustainability dimension.

The six sustainability dimensions were selected and defined based on the European Green Festival Roadmap, developed by Yourope [21] and supported by the European Union. Table 1 shows the different dimensions.

Regarding the selection of the different references, although the focus was initially on existing protocols and reports, many are either not publicly available or difficult to access. To address this limitation, the matrix also includes festivals recognized as sustainable, either through official certifications or their demonstrated commitment to sustainability.

The selected protocols include the *European Green Festival Roadmap* developed by Yourope [21], the *Music Innovation Hub* by Triadi [17]—a spin-off of POLIMI, RP Legal & Tax, and MIH—the *GreenFEST* framework [10], and the *Super-Low Carbon Live Music* initiative led by the Tyndall Centre [11]. Additionally, guidelines such as the *Guidelines on Sustainable Event Organization* issued by the German government [12] and *The Guide to Sustainable Events* published by the Stockholm municipality [5] provide essential frameworks for sustainable event management.

Regarding sustainable festival case studies, the matrix includes notable examples such as the *DGTL Festival* in Amsterdam, Netherlands, and *Massive Attack's* sustainability-focused initiatives in Bristol, UK.

Not directly included in the matrix but part of the preliminary analysis, the following festivals were also selected: Boom (Idanha-a-Nova, PR), Cambridge Folk (Cambridge, UK), Paradise City (Perk, BE), We Love Green (Paris, FR), Terraforma (Milan, IT), Diluvio Festival (Brescia, IT).

Table 1. Sustainable dimension descriptions.

Dimension	Description
Energy	Measures the festival's energy consumption and its reliance on renewable or low-impact energy sources
Materials & Waste	Evaluates the use of sustainable materials and waste management strategies, including reduction, recycling, and reuse
Food & Beverage	Assesses the sourcing, sustainability, and environmental impact of food and drinks offered at the festival
Travel & Transport	Examines the carbon footprint of attendee and staff transportation, promoting sustainable mobility options
Water	Focuses on water consumption, conservation, and wastewater management to minimize environmental impact
Community & Biodiversity	Considers the festival's impact on local communities and ecosystems, ensuring social responsibility and ecological preservation

Once the matrix was completed, it became evident that all the selected protocols and frameworks address the dimensions of Energy, Travel, & Transport. Nearly all of them cover Waste & Materials, Food & Beverage, and Community & Biodiversity. However, the Water dimension is included in only 5 of the 8 protocols and frameworks analyzed.

Then, further analysis identified the most common and relevant criteria or best practices for each sustainability dimension, as shown in Table 2.

Based on these shared best practices, the sustainability indicators for the festival framework will be defined.

Sustainable Indicators Framework
Combining the sustainability matrix with on-field research conducted through the MI AMI 2024 case study made it possible to define festival sustainability indicators with greater accuracy and precision. The matrix helped identify the most common best practices found in sustainable protocols, frameworks, and festivals. At the same time, the case study highlighted which indicators were most suitable for the proposed framework, for instance, which metrics were most straightforward to measure and most relevant to real-world application.

Below, in Table 3, is a list of the indicators, each briefly described and grouped according to the various dimensions of sustainability. In addition to the six sustainability dimensions outlined in Sect. 3.1 of the Matrix, an additional section, Emissions Monitoring and Communication, has been introduced. Unlike the other dimensions, this section does not focus on a single aspect of sustainability but encompasses broader indicators spanning multiple sustainability dimensions.

This list is still a draft of the final set of indicators that will form the complete framework. However, it serves as a strong foundation, covering the key indicator categories necessary for a comprehensive assessment and analysis of a festival's impact.

Table 2. List of the standard criteria in festivals divided by sustainable dimensions

Category	Criteria	Description
Energy	Energy monitoring and measurement	Baselines and automated systems
	Energy efficiency	Low-energy technologies and strategies
	Renewable energy sources	Replacing diesel and onsite generation
	Green contracts and offsetting	Certified electricity and carbon compensation
	Stakeholder and user engagement	Awareness and responsibility
	Innovation	R&D for sustainable solutions
Materials & Waste	Recycling systems	Ensure clear signage, sufficient collection points, and composting options
	Sustainable materials	Prioritize eco-label products, durable designs, and modularity
	Circularity	Track materials, promote reuse, and engage with recycling markets
	Engagement	Educated stakeholders and incentivize sustainable practices
	Monitoring and compliance	Implement waste quantification and continuous improvement strategies
Food & Beverage	Plant-based menus and local sourcing	Promote vegetarian/vegan food options and using locally grown, seasonal ingredients to minimize environmental impact)
	Reusable and compostable serve ware	Use environmentally friendly, reusable or compostable plates, cups, and utensils instead of single-use plastic items
	Food waste management and donation	Minimize food waste by carefully planning portions and donating leftover food to local charities or shelters

(*continued*)

Table 2. (*continued*)

Category	Criteria	Description
	Special dietary options	Offer a variety of food choices to cater to different dietary needs such as gluten-free, vegan, or allergen-free
	Collaboration with sustainable suppliers	Work with food and beverage vendors who prioritize sustainability in their practices, including sourcing, packaging, and transport
Travel & Transport	Sustainable Mobility	Promote walking, cycling, and public transport
	Parking reduction	Eliminate parking spaces to encourage greener alternatives
	Accessible location	Choose venues accessible by eco-friendly transport
	Travel Surveys	Gather data to improve sustainable practices
	Emission Tracking	Monitor CO_2 from stakeholder travel
Water	Water Points	Provide free drinking water facilities
	Tap Access	Ensure free tap water availability in public spaces
	Water Conservation	Educate and promote efficient water use
	Efficient Appliances	Use water-saving equipment
	Reduce Consumption	Minimize overall water use
Community & Biodiversity	Stakeholder Involvement	Include locals in planning for better outcomes
	Local Partnerships	Collaborate with community organizations
	Biodiversity-safe Locations	Select venues with minimal ecological impact
	Accessible Guidance	Provide systems for individuals with impairments
	Waste Management	Minimize overall waste use

Table 3. List of sustainable indicators.

Category	Indicator	Description
Emissions monitoring & Communication	*GHG emissions intensity*	Total GHG emissions (measured in CO2e) divided by the number of festival participants
	Sustainability communication	Measures the frequency of sustainability-related communications during different phases of the festival: pre-event, during the event, and post-event
Energy	*Energy intensity*	Total energy consumption divided by the number of festival participants
	Share of renewable energy	Percentage of total energy sourced from renewable sources (solar, wind, hydro, etc.) and/or biodiesel
Materials & Waste	*Recycling rate*	Percentage of total waste directed to recycling. Waste volume is estimated using bin capacity and collection frequency, with an average weight per waste type measured
	Waste generation intensity	Average waste generated per participant per festival day
Food & Beverage	*Vegetarian and vegan option*	Percentage of vegetarian or vegan options in the total menu offerings
	Compostable cutlery and reusable cups	Availability of both compostable cutlery and reusable cups to minimize festival waste
Travel & Transport	*GHG emissions intensity from audience transport*	Total transport related GHG emissions (measured in CO2e) divided by the number of festival participants

(continued)

Table 3. (*continued*)

Category	Indicator	Description
	Sustainable transport initiatives	Presence of initiatives promoting sustainable transport, such as no-parking policies, bicycle parking, shuttle services, partnerships with public transport, and car-sharing options
Water	*Free water access for participants*	Number of free water access points proportionate to the number of participants per day
	Water consumption intensity	Total water consumption divided by the number of festival participants
Community & Biodiversity	*Accessibility for people with disabilities*	Full accessibility across festival grounds for wheelchair users and individuals with mobility impairments
	Biodiversity initiatives	Presence of projects focused on preserving, monitoring, and enhancing local flora and fauna

Certainly, one of the most fundamental but also most complex steps is the definition of the scoring system and threshold values for each individual indicator. In fact, where possible, efforts are made to gather data from reliable online sources. However, when indicators are being defined for the first time and no trustworthy data is available, it becomes necessary to rely on expert opinions to ensure accuracy and relevance. A possible example of a threshold can be found in the indicator *Sustainability Communication*: to achieve the maximum score, a festival could be expected to actively communicate its sustainability initiatives through its social media channels both before and during the event, and to publicly disclose its environmental impact after the event.

At the same time, it will also be crucial to specify the types of festivals to which these indicators can be applied. Possible variables to consider are certainly the size of the venue, the number of participants, and the location of the festival.

3.3 Future Steps

The list of indicators presented in Sect. 3.2, as previously mentioned, is still under revision to ensure maximum accuracy; these indicators must first be validated through dedicated workshops involving experts and key stakeholders from the festival industry. This process is essential to establish precise value scales for each indicator, ultimately enabling the calculation of a final sustainability score. The validation of the indicators is essential, as it must ensure their scientific validity and significance. The validation process will therefore be carried out with particular care. Experts will be selected from industry professionals and faculty members from technical universities in order to provide a clear and informed perspective. Furthermore, the indicators will be supported by industry-wide research and academic literature to substantiate their validity as thoroughly as possible.

Once the framework is finalized, the next step will be its practical application. A trial implementation will occur at the MI AMI Festival in Milan in May 2025.

Finally, as the last phase, the framework will be introduced to the market and promoted for adoption by other festivals, encouraging widespread implementation within the industry.

4 Conclusions and Limitations

The growing focus on sustainability in the music festivals reflects a broader global movement toward environmental responsibility. While festivals have the potential to contribute positively to social and economic sustainability, they also present significant environmental challenges, including energy consumption, waste generation, and carbon emissions. Developing a comprehensive sustainability framework is therefore necessary to minimize negative impacts and promote industry best practices.

This study outlined creating a publicly accessible sustainability framework for music festivals, offering an easy-to-use and replicable assessment tool. Integrating insights from existing literature, sustainability reports, and field research conducted at MI AMI Festival 2024, the framework identifies key dimensions of sustainability, divided into the following categories: Emissions monitoring & Communication, Energy, Materials & Waste, Food & Beverage, Travel & Transportation, Water, and Community & Biodiversity. Each category includes specific, measurable indicators designed to assess a festival's sustainability performance.

However, this work is still ongoing, as the list of indicators has not yet been finalized. Indeed, to ensure accuracy and effectiveness, the framework requires further validation through dedicated workshops with industry experts and festival organizers. These sessions will help refine the indicators and establish standardized evaluation scales, ultimately ensuring that the framework is practical and widely applicable across different festival contexts.

Finally, once the workshops evaluate and finalize the indicators, the developed framework will be implemented and tested at the MI AMI 2025 Festival. Following this initial application, it will be further refined if necessary and eventually made available for adoption by other festivals, promoting broader industry-wide sustainability practices.

There are also some limitations of this project that should be noted. First, our framework requires active involvement from the festival organizer in adapting to the framework and measuring the various indicators. This could create friction and hinder the widespread adoption of the solution. Moreover, the default language of the project is English, which could also represent a limitation for its expansion into regions such as Asia. Additionally, the standardization of measurement units for the indicators is another constraint that could lead to friction in countries where different systems are used, such as the U.S. or parts of Asia.

Acknowledgements. This research was carried out as part of the project MI AMI_BEATs (Better Equity Actions for Tomorrow sustainability), funded by Better Days and Alta Scuola Politecnica. It benefited from the collaboration of a multidisciplinary faculty group led by Marta Dell'Ovo, Silvia Ronchi, and Federico Dell'Anna, with contributions from Cristina Becchio, Eleonora Bruschi, Francesca Mattioli, Sara Monaci, Andrea Rebecchi, Louena Shtrepi, Sara Viazzo.

In addition, the research benefitted from the contribution of Carlo Pastore and Stefano Bottura, founders and directors of the MI AMI Festival.

Authors Contribution. The present work is to be attributed in equal parts to the Authors.

References

1. Abdulredha, M., Al Khaddar, R., Jordan, D., Kot, P., Abdulridha, A., Hashim, K.: Estimating solid waste generation by hospitality industry during major festivals: a quantification model based on multiple regression. Waste Manag. **77**, 388–400 (2018). https://doi.org/10.1016/j.wasman.2018.04.025
2. A Greener Future: AGF Annual Festival Sustainability Report 2023. A Greener Future (2024). https://static1.squarespace.com/static/633313551ca2e94aca4f545a/t/661cf546c6b84a6fce4585b6/1713173837980/AGF-Annual+Festival+Sustainability+Report+2023.pdf
3. Belton, V.: Multi-criteria problem structuring and analysis in a value theory framework. In: Gal, T., Stewart, T.J., Hanne, T. (eds.) Multicriteria Decision Making. ISORMS, vol. 21, pp. 335–366. Springer, Boston (1999). https://doi.org/10.1007/978-1-4615-5025-9_12
4. Calvano, G.: Greening European music festivals: environmental sustainability strategies, practices, and. Dissertation, University of Barcelona (2024)
5. City of Stockholm: The Guide to Sustainable Events (2020). https://foretagsservice.stockholm/globalassets/foretag-och-organisationer/foretagsservice/branscher/evenemangsarrangor/guide-for-hallbara-evenemang/the-guide-to-sustainable-events.pdf
6. Collins, A., Cooper, C.: Measuring and managing the environmental impact of festivals: the contribution of the ecological footprint. J. Sustain. Tour. **25**(1), 148–162 (2016). https://doi.org/10.1080/09669582.2016.1189922
7. Ecoevents: Ecoevents | Riduciamo l'impatto ambientale dei tuoi eventi (2024). https://www.ecoevents.it/
8. Frost, W.J.: How green was my festival: exploring challenges and opportunities associated with staging green events. Int. J. Hosp. Manag. **29**, 261–267 (2010). https://doi.org/10.1016/j.ijhm.2009.10.009
9. Getz, D.: Policy for sustainable and responsible festivals and events: institutionalization of a new paradigm. J. Policy Res. Tour. Leis. Events **1**(1), 61–78 (2009). https://doi.org/10.1080/19407960802703524
10. GreenFest Project: Guidelines for the Implementation of GPP in the Field of Cultural Events (Festivals and Cultural Events - Musical Events) (2020). https://www.greenfest.eu/download/20201109155154.pdf
11. Jones, C., McLachlan, C., Mander, S.: Super-Low Carbon Live Music: a roadmap for the UK live music sector to play its part in tackling the climate crisis. The University of Manchester (2021). https://documents.manchester.ac.uk/display.aspx?DocID=56701

12. Mager, A., et al.: Guidelines on Sustainable Event Organisation. German Federal Ministry for the Environment, Nature Conservation and Nuclear Safety (BMU) (2020). https://www.bmuv.de/fileadmin/Daten_BMU/Pools/Broschueren/veranstaltungsleitfaden_en_bf.pdf
13. Mair, J., Jago, L.: The development of a conceptual model of greening in the business events tourism sector. J. Sustain. Tour. **18**(1), 77–94 (2009). https://doi.org/10.1080/09669580903291007
14. Mair, J., Laing, J.: The greening of music festivals: motivations, barriers and outcomes. Applying the Mair and Jago model. J. Sustain. Tour. **20**(5), 683–700 (2012). https://doi.org/10.1080/09669582.2011.636819
15. Mair, J. (ed.): The Routledge Handbook of Festivals. Routledge, London (2019). https://doi.org/10.4324/9781315186320
16. Mair, J., Smith, A.: Events and sustainability: considering the implications for policy and research. J. Sustain. Tour. **29**(11–12), 1841–1854 (2021). https://doi.org/10.1080/09669582.2021.1942480
17. Music Innovation Hub: Protocollo per gli eventi sostenibili (2023). https://musicinnovationhub.org/wp-content/uploads/2023/05/PROTOCOLLO-EVENTI-SOSTENIBILI2.pdf
18. Our story: DGTL (2025). https://dgtl-festival.com/en/our-story/#sustainibility
19. Sustainability Diagnosis — A Greener Future (2024). https://www.agreenerfuture.com/sustainability-diagnosis
20. Triadi: Consulenza strategica sulla sostenibilità. https://www.triadi.it
21. YOUROPE e.V., A Greener Future, Greener Events Norway (2023). European Green Festival Roadmap 2030. YOUROPE – The European Festival Association. https://static1.squarespace.com/static/633313551ca2e94aca4f545a/t/64f9b88a2584d43bbddbe879/1694087310837/yourope-european-green-festival-roadmap-2030.pdf

Author Index

A
Antonia, Gravagnuolo 102
Assumma, Vanessa 73

B
Baldoni, Agnese 166, 423
Balzanella, Antonio 317
Barbieri, Sebastiano 38
Baronetto, Barbara 38
Barreca, Alice 350
Boeri, Renata 406
Bonini, Sofia 3
Bottero, Marta 38
Buongiovanni, Giulia 137

C
Calisi, Laura 166, 423
Camerota, Marianna 137
Campanile, Lelio 303, 317
Canesi, Rubina 55
Cannatella, Daniele 234
Caprioli, Caterina 38, 120
Castelluccio, Roberto 194
Cavalaglio, Gianluca 102
Cazzola, Ilaria 207
Cerreta, Maria 389, 406
Cicalese, Federica 249
Cosentino, Francesco 21
Costagliola, Gennaro 267
Cozzi, Alberto 3
Crisopulli, Alessia 89
Cuntò, Stefano 370

D
D'Alpaos, Chiara 55
Datola, Giulia 222
De Luca, Marco 3
De Pascalis, Salvatore 166, 423
De Rosa, Mattia 267
De Santis, Marco 285
Dell'Anna, Federico 21, 120

Dell'Ovo, Marta 21, 222
Di Bonito, Luigi Piero 317
Di Tommaso, Laura 389
Diana, Lorenzo 194

E
Ederle, Marco 370
Esposito, Christian 285

F
Fabbrocino, Francesco 102
Falconi, Francesca 166, 423
Fasolino, Isidoro 249
Feofilovs, Maksims 154
Fiermonte, Francesco 120
Fregonara, Elena 350
Fuccella, Vittorio 267

G
Giudice, Benedetta 207
Giustinelli, Valentina 137
Grimaldi, Michele 249
Guarini, Maria Rosaria 181

I
Iacono, Mauro 303

L
La Rocca, Ludovica 389
Lakste, Renate 154
Lamanna, Marta 3
Liljenfeldt, Johanna 73
Loffredo, Caterina 389

M
Maiullari, Daniela 222
Malavasi, Giorgia 350
Marella, Giuliano 55
Mariarosaria, Angrisano 102
Marulli, Fiammetta 317

© The Editor(s) (if applicable) and The Author(s), under exclusive license
to Springer Nature Switzerland AG 2026
O. Gervasi et al. (Eds.): ICCSA 2025 Workshops, LNCS 15893, pp. 439–440, 2026.
https://doi.org/10.1007/978-3-031-97645-2

Mastroianni, Michele 285, 303
Melotta, Federica 194
Morano, Pierluigi 181
Muccio, Eugenio 234

N
Napodano, Matteo 166, 423
Neglia, Grazia 102

O
Oppio, Alessandra 222

P
Panaro, Simona 389
Petronio, Lucia 73
Piras, Francesco 337
Pittau, Francesco 137
Poli, Giuliano 370
Polverino, Francesco 194
Pondo, Francesca Pia 194

R
Rebaudengo, Manuela 207
Riccio, Christian 303
Rolando, Diana 350
Romagnoli, Francesco 154

Romagnolo, Diletta 55

S
Saiu, Valeria 337
Santangelo, Angela 73
Sasaki, Shizuka 3
Schretzenmayr, Martina 222
Seratoni Gualdoni, Giacomo 166, 423
Sica, Francesco 181
Sugoni, Giorgia 137

T
Tabari, Parinaz 267
Tajani, Francesco 181
Torrieri, Francesca 89
Turrini, Umberto 55

V
Valle, Marco 38
Verde, Rosanna 317
Viscardi, Bruna 303
Vitulano, Valeria 207

Z
Zizzania, Piero 406
Zorzan, Alice 3

MIX
Papier aus verantwortungsvollen Quellen
Paper from responsible sources
FSC® C105338

If you have any concerns about our products,
you can contact us on
ProductSafety@springernature.com

In case Publisher is established outside the EU,
the EU authorized representative is:
**Springer Nature Customer Service Center GmbH
Europaplatz 3, 69115 Heidelberg, Germany**

Printed by Libri Plureos GmbH
in Hamburg, Germany

MIX
Papier aus verantwortungsvollen Quellen
Paper from responsible sources
FSC® C105338

If you have any concerns about our products,
you can contact us on
ProductSafety@springernature.com

In case Publisher is established outside the EU,
the EU authorized representative is:
**Springer Nature Customer Service Center GmbH
Europaplatz 3, 69115 Heidelberg, Germany**

Printed by Libri Plureos GmbH
in Hamburg, Germany